BUSINESS LAW

BUSINESS LAW

SECOND EDITION

D. CHANDRA BOSE

Professor Emeritus of Commerce
Formerly Principal
Sree Narayana College
University of Kerala
Chengannur
Kerala

PHI Learning Private Limited

Delhi-110092
2019

₹ 650.00

BUSINESS LAW, Second Edition
D. Chandra Bose

ISBN-978-93-87472-23-5 (Print Book)
ISBN-978-93-87472-24-2 (e-Book)

The export rights of this book are vested solely with the publisher.

Sixth Printing (Second Edition)   ...   ...   **July, 2019**

Published by Asoke K. Ghosh, PHI Learning Private Limited, Rimjhim House, 111, Patparganj Industrial Estate, Delhi-110092 and Printed by Rajkamal Electric Press, Plot No. 2, Phase IV, HSIDC, Kundli-131028, Sonepat, Haryana.

To
My beloved wife
G.R. Ajita
(Kuttamangalam, Valathungal, Kollam, Kerala)

Contents

Part One   MERCANTILE LAW

SECTION 1   *Law of Contracts*

SECTION 2   *Special Contracts*

SECTION 3 *Other Laws*

Part Two   LAW OF INSURANCE

Part Three   COMPANY LAW

Part Four INDUSTRIAL LAW

Part Five GENERAL LAW

Preface

I take a great pleasure in bringing out the second edition of the book entitled *Business Law* for B.Com (Pass and Hons.) students of all universities in India. This book has also been designed to serve the needs of the students of MBA, The Institute of Chartered Accountants, The Institute of Company Secretaries and other professional courses. The aim of the book is to present the legal aspects of Mercantile, Insurance, Industrial and Company Law in the most concise, lucid and illustrative manner, for easy grasping of various provisions of different Acts.

In the **Second Edition,** the company's law is written in accordance with the New Companies Act, 2013.

The book is further enriched with the inclusion of *four new chapters*, namely, *Corporate Governance, Intellectual Property Rights, Right to Information Act* and *Telecom Regulatory Authority of India.*

The book has been divided into five parts. Part One dealing with Mercantile Law consists of three sections. Section 1 deals with the general principle of the Law of Contracts. Section 2 is concerned with Special Contracts, while Section 3 describes a few other mercantile laws. Part Two, Three, Four and Five consist of the Insurance Law, the Company Law, the Industrial Law and the General Law, respectively.

I have taken due pain to study case laws/data and information from various reports, journals, and authoritative books. I am indebted to all those authors whose publications on the subject of 'Business Law' have benefited me in the course of my perusal of interest in this subject matter.

I am confident that my present book will meet the growing needs of the students preparing themselves for various examinations on the subject. Suggestions from teachers and students are solicited with a view to improving this work in the future.

The publishers deserve credit for the timely publication of this book. I am deeply indebted to them for their encouragement and cooperation.

D. Chandra Bose

Table of Cases

Part One   MERCANTILE LAW

Part Two   LAW OF INSURANCE

Part Three   COMPANY LAW

Part Four   INDUSTRIAL LAW

Part Five   GENERAL LAW

PART ONE

MERCANTILE LAW

0

Introduction

Law is "that portion of the established habit and thought of mankind which has gained distinct and formal recognition in the shape of uniform rules backed by the authority and power of the Government".

—Woodrow Wilson

NEED FOR LAW

No society can exist without law. It is essential for the upkeeping of peace in the society. As a social being, man comes into contact with people in various capacities. He comes into contact, for example, with landlords as a tenant, with Government as a taxpayer, with customers as a seller and with suppliers as a buyer. In all these associations he is expected to follow a set of rules.

Without law, life and business would become a matter of survival, not only of the fittest but also of the most ruthless. Law is a potential tool of social change. In fact, law and society are complementary.

WHAT IS LAW?

Law in its widest sense means those rules and principles which regulate our relations with other individuals, as well as the state. A well recognised definition of law however, is the one put forward by Blackstone in his commentaries on the law of England. Law is there defined as, "a rule of Civil Conduct, prescribed by the supreme power of a state, commanding what is right and prohibiting what is wrong". In the words of Salmond, "Law is the body of principles recognised and applied by the state in the administration of justice". It represents a code of conduct for securing order in the community.

Law is not rigid. Social conditions vary. So also are laws. They have to suit to the requirements of the society. Law is a living phenomenon with a separate entity in relation to the human affairs.

BRANCHES OF LAW

Law as a faculty has several branches. They are Constitutional Law,

3

Administrative Law, Criminal Law, Civil Law, Commercial Law, etc. Constitutional Law means the rule which regulates the structure of the principal organs of the Government and their relationship to one another, and determines their principal functions. The rules consist both of legal rules and of usages, commonly called conventions, which, without being enacted are accepted as binding by all concerned with Government.

Administrative Law is the law that governs the executive branch of the Government. It is as old as the executive.

Criminal Laws are those laws with which wrong doers are punished. At the same time, civil laws are those laws with which the private rights of an individual are enforced.

Commercial or Mercantile Law deals with the rights and obligations of commercial persons emerging from commercial transactions in respect of commercial property. The term commercial person means an individual or a partnership or a company, carrying on a business.

SOURCES OF MERCANTILE LAW OR COMMERCIAL LAW

Commercial Law is that branch of law which is related to trade and commerce. The bulk of the Indian Commercial Law, is to a large extent an adaptation of the English Law. In order to trace the sources of Indian Commercial Law, we have to trace the sources of English Commercial Law. The sources of the English Commercial Law are: (a) the Common Law, (b) Equity, (c) the Law Merchant and (d) the Statute Law.

(a) **The Common Law:** The Common Law refers to a system of law based on judicial precedents handed down from generation to generation. It is an unwritten law as it is not written in any Statute or Act of Parliament. The Common Law had existed in England even before the Parliament came into being.

(b) **Equity:** Equity is based on the concepts of justice developed by the judges whose decisions subsequently became precedents. These precedents are now considered Equity Law.

Equity saw an unprecedented growth when compared to that of Common Law. It is also unwritten. Both Equity and Common Law are case laws. Equity Law is more flexible. But when there is a conflict between the rules of Common Law and the rules of Equity, the latter prevails. The distinction between them was, however, eliminated by the Judicature Acts of 1873 and 1875. Consequently, the Common Law and Equity are now applied to all cases.

(c) **The Law Merchant:** The term 'Law Merchant' or 'Lex Mercatoria' signifies a body of legal principles founded on the custom of merchants in their dealings with one another. It developed through the 14th and 15th centuries and was gradually recognised by the Common Law Courts.

The early Common Law Courts had not known anything about the rules and practices of trade and commerce. The traders, therefore, organised guilds and established Merchants Courts which were in operation for a short period every year. The rules pronounced in these courts came to be known as the 'Law Merchant'. This law was in due course accepted by the Common Law Courts. The Law Merchant is the Principal source of the law relating to negotiable instruments, trade marks, partnerships, insurance, sales, etc.

(d) **The Statute Law:** The Statute Law means the Act of parliament. It is the written law and it overrides any rules of Common Law or Equity.

Besides, the following are the additional sources of the Indian Commercial Law:

(i) *Precedents:* Precedents are the past judicial decisions of the Courts. They are generally followed by the court in deciding similar cases before them. In India, the Supreme Court is the highest court and its decisions have binding force on all the courts subordinate to it. But among the courts of the same stature, (e.g., Two High Courts) the decisions of one court have only a guiding and persuasive value for the other.

(ii) *Customs among Local Merchants:* The customs and usages established by long use are an important source of Indian Commercial Law. A custom to be binding on the parties must be reasonable, certain, definite, consistent with other customs, and uniformly accepted in the ordinary course of business. A custom becomes a legally recognised one, when it is accepted by a Court and is incorporated in a judicial decision.

(iii) *Statutes of the Legislatures:* The Acts passed by the Indian legislature are the chief sources of the Indian Commercial Law. In India the bulk of Commercial Law is Statute Law based largely on the English Law. The law making power in India is vested in the parliament and the state legislatures. The Contract Act, 1872, the Partnership Act, 1932, the Companies Act, 1956 are the instances of the important Acts passed by the Indian Legislature.

REVIEW QUESTIONS

1. What is 'Law'? Explain the need for the knowledge of law.

2. Explain the different branches of Law.

3. Define 'Commercial Law'. What are the sources of Indian Commercial Law?

4. Write short notes on:

   (a) Equity

   (b) Lex Mercatoria

   (c) Precedents

1

Nature of Contracts

Contract is an agreement creating and defining obligations between parties.

—Salmond

INTRODUCTION

The law of contract constitutes the most important branch of the commercial law. It is the very foundation of the modern civilised world. Everyone of us normally enters into a number of contracts everyday. The law of contract is defined as the branch of law that determines the circumstances in which a promise or an agreement shall be legally binding on the person making it.

The law of contract forms part of the private law which deals with the rights of individuals inter se. The rights of individuals are classified into rights in personam and rights in rem. A right in personam is a right for which the corresponding duty is towards an individual or a definite number of body of individuals. For instance, if X has a right to recover a sum of money from Y that right can be exercised only by X but not by others, because the right which X has against Y is a right in personam. If right in rem is a right against the public at large, there is a negative duty not to interfere with the right, e.g., right of ownership, right of freedom, right to reputation, etc.

LAW RELATING TO CONTRACTS

Law of contract under English law is common law whereas in India it is statutory. The Indian law on the subject is contained in the Contract Act, 1872, which came into force on the 1st day of September, 1872. Sections 1 to 75 of the Contract Act deal with the general principles. Sections 76 to 123 related to the law of Sale of Goods, were repealed by the Sale of Goods Act, 1930. Sections 124 to 147 deal with the law relating to contract of Indemnity and Contract of Guarantee. Sections 148 to 181 deal with law relating to Bailment. Sections 182 to 238 deal with the law of Agency.

DEFINITION OF CONTRACT

The word contract owes its origin to the Latin term *contractum* which means drawn together.

Contract is an agreement creating and defining obligations between parties (Salmond).

A contract is defined in the Contract Act, [Sec. 2(h)] as "an agreement enforceable by law".

Anson defines a contract as a "legally binding agreement made between two or more persons by which rights are acquired by one more to act or forbearance on the part of the other or others".

The juristic concept of a contract consists of two elements, viz., obligation and agreement. Obligation is understood "as a legal tie, which imposes upon a person or persons, the necessity of doing or abstaining from doing a definite act or acts". In Roman law, it is defined as a *"Vinculum juris"* or the bond of legal necessity which binds together two or more determinate individuals. When two or more parties reach in identity of minds regarding a particular subject-matter and express to each other that identity of minds in some understandable manner, we call it an agreement.

Agreement = Offer + Acceptance

The requirements of an obligation are:

   (a) There must be two persons;

   (b) The obligation must relate to definite act or acts;

   (c) The obligation must relate to legal matters and not social or domestic affairs;

      Example: D, who had come to England on leave, finding his wife's health did not permit her to accompany him to Ceylon where D was employed, promised to send her £ 30 a month so long as she had to remain separate. D did not send any money to her. The wife sued for the allowance but failed because no legal obligation was created on D by the promise. (*Balfour* v. *Balfour* (1919) 2 K.B. 571).

   (d) Consensus ad idem or Identity of minds

   (e) An agreement is necessarily the outcome of consenting minds. This means parties to the agreement must have agreed about the subject matter of the agreement in the same sense and at the same time.

   (f) Mutual Communication

      There should be communication of their respective intentions. (*Felthouse* v. *Bindley* (1862) 142 E.R. 1037).

Sir John Salmond says "The law of contract is not the whole law of agreement nor is it the whole law of obligations; it is the law of those agreements which create obligations and of those obligations which have their source in agreements". According to Salmond agreements affecting obligations may be:

(a) agreements which destroy rights or obligations, e.g., surrender, release, etc.

(b) agreements creating a trust.

(c) agreements which create rights or obligations.

(d) agreements which transfer rights from one person to another, e.g., conveyances, assignments, etc.

The law of contract falls under the head (c) above. To conclude,

Contract = Agreement + Enforceability at law

ESSENTIALS OF A VALID CONTRACT

Contracts arise under various circumstances. They may arise from face-to-face conversations or from conversations over telephone or by any other means of communication. All contracts are agreements, but all agreements are not contracts.

Section 10 of the Contract Act reads:

"All agreements are contracts if they are made by the free consent of parties competent to contract, for lawful consideration and with a lawful object, and are not hereby expressly declared to be void".

An analysis of the above provisions would reveal that for a valid contract the following elements should be present.

1. **Consensus ad idem:** There must be identity or meeting of minds. Parties are said to consent when they agree upon the same thing in the same sense.

   For instance, if X who owns two estates, one at Bombay and another at Delhi, offers to sell Y one estate, X intending it to be the one at Bombay and Y accepts the offer, thinking that it is the estate at Delhi, there is no consensus, and hence no contract. Such a contract is void.

ELEMENTS OF CONTRACT

- Consensus ad idem
- There should be no flaw in the consent of the parties
- Competency of parties
- Lawful consideration
- Lawful object
- Agreement not declared to be void

2. **There should be no flaw in the Consent of the Parties:**
   Consent is said to be free when it is not caused by coercion,
   undue influence, fraud, misrepresentation or mistake. The
   existence of any of these vitiating elements would make the
   contract a voidable one.

3. **Competency of Parties:** The parties of the agreement
   must have the capacity to contract. Sections. 11 and 12 of the
   Act deal with this aspect. Every person of full age and sound
   mind is competent to contract. Flaw in capacity to contract
   may arise from minority, lunacy, idiocy, drunkenness, etc.,
   and status. If either party has suffered incapacity to contract,
   the contract is rendered void.

4. **Lawful Consideration:** An agreement without consideration is void. Consideration means an advantage or benefit
   moving from one person to the other. In other words, it is
   something in return.

5. **Lawful Object:** The object of the agreement must not be
   illegal, immoral or opposed to public policy. The rule is that,
   an agreement the object of which is unlawful is void.

6. **Agreement not Declared to be Void:** The agreement
   should not have been expressly declared void by any law in
   force of the land. Thus, the agreements in restraint of trade,
   in restraint of marriage are all void.

Apart from the above, the English law would insist for a
further element, viz., "the intention to create a legal relationship".
Agreements of a social or domestic nature do not contemplate legal
relations, and hence it would not constitute a contract. This principle
is also accepted in India.

Above all, an agreement must conform to the particular
requirement of any other laws which require them to be attested,
stamped or registered for its validity.

KINDS OF CONTRACTS

Contracts may be classified according to their (1) Legal effects,
(2) Formation, (3) Performances, and (4) Form.

1. **Classification according to Legal Effects:** Contracts
   brought in accordance with legal effects may be valid, void,
   voidable, illegal and unenforceable.

   (a) *Valid Contract:* Valid contracts are those contracts which
       satisfy all the essential elements of a contract as laid
       down by Sec. 10.

Example: A offers to sell his horse for ₹50,000. B agrees to buy for this price. It is a valid contract.

(b) *Void Contract:* A contract may be enforceable at the time when it was made but later on it may become void and unenforceable due to some reasons. Such a contract is called void contract.

Examples of void contracts are:

(i) A contract becomes void by supervening impossibility or illegality (Sec. 56).

Example: A promises to marry B. Later on B died. In this case, the contract becomes void on the death of B.

(ii) A contingent contract to do or not to do something on the happening of an event becomes void when the event becomes impossible (Sec. 32).

Example: A agrees to sell 500 tonnes of rice to B at ₹1,000 per tonne in case his ship reaches the port safely by 10th January. The ship fails to reach by the stipulated date. The contract between A and B is void.

Void Agreement: An agreement not enforceable by law is said to be void agreement. It is devoid of legal effect. It is a nullity.

All illegal or immoral agreements are void. Bilateral mistake of a material fact also makes an agreement void.

Example: A agrees with B in consideration of ₹500 to draw two parallel lines in such a way as to cross each other. The agreement is impossible to perform and therefore, void.

Void agreement and void contract: A void agreement is void from the very beginning, i.e., void ab initio. On the other hand, a void contract was valid at the time when it was made but becomes void later. They will have the following effects.

(i) The agreement shall be unenforceable.
(ii) Money paid or property transferred by one party to another is recoverable.
(iii) Collateral transactions shall not become void unless the agreement has also been illegal.

Example: A test match is going on between India and Australia. X agrees to pay a sum of ₹200 to Y, if India wins the match. India wins and in order to pay off Y, X borrows a sum of ₹200 from Z. Z knows the purpose.

The agreement between X and Z is a collateral transaction. Since a wagering agreement (between X and Y) is void and not illegal, the collateral agreement between X and Z is perfectly valid.

(iv)   All lawful promises which are severable shall remain valid and can be enforced.

(c)   *Voidable Contract:* A contract which can be put to an end at the option of one party to the contract is called a voidable contract. A voidable contract continues to be valid and binding till it is avoided by the aggrieved party. He has the option either to affirm it and elect to carry out the contract in spite of the defect or to reject it. Third parties can validly acquire a title from a person claiming title under such a contract.

An agreement which is enforceable by law at the option of one or more of the parties thereon, but not at the option of the other or others, is a voidable contract [Sec. 2(i)].

Agreements induced by coercion, undue influence, fraud or misrepresentation are examples of voidable contracts.

Example: X agreed to sell his horse to Y for ₹1,000. The consent of X was obtained by use of force. The contract is voidable at the option of X. And he (X) may put an end to this contract if he decides so. The party rescinding the contract is entitled to get damages for any loss that he might have suffered from the other party on account of making that contract. But if the aggrieved party has received some benefit under the contract he must restore such benefit to the person from whom it was received.

Distinction between void agreements and voidable contracts

Void Agreements	*Voidable Contracts*
1. Void agreement is unenforceable from the very beginning. It is void ab initio.	It becomes unenforceable only when the aggrieved party chooses to rescind it. It continues to be valid till it is repudiated.
2. Restitution is always allowed except where illegality or void nature of the agreement was known or expected to be known to both the parties from the very beginning.	Benefits will be restored as far as may be possible when a voidable contract is rescinded.
3. There arises no question of compensation on account of the non-performance of the agreement.	Aggrieved party is entitled to compensation for loss or damages on account of the recission of the contract.

4. It does not affect the collateral agreements. But where the agreement is void on account of the illegality of the object and consideration, the collateral agreements will also become void.	It does not affect the collateral agreements.

(d) *Illegal Contracts (Illegal Agreements):* A contract is said to be illegal where consideration or object of it is illegal. An illegal contract is void and avoids connected contracts also. Money paid under an illegal contract cannot be recovered.

Example: X promises to pay a sum of ₹1,000 to Y if he (Y) gives a good beating to Z and X in order to pay Y, borrows from M a sum of ₹1,000. M knows the purpose for which money has been borrowed from him. The agreement between X and Y being illegal, the collateral transaction between X and M will also be illegal.

Distinction between void and illegal agreements

Void Agreements	*Illegal Agreements*
1. Sometimes valid contracts may subsequently become void.	Illegal agreements are void from the very beginning.
2. Agreements collateral to void agreements are valid.	Agreements collateral to illegal agreements are void ab initio.
3. Parties to a void agreement shall not be punishable.	Parties to an illegal agreement shall be punishable.
4. All void agreements are not illegal.	All illegal agreements are void.

(e) *Unenforceable Contract:* An unenforceable contract is one which cannot be enforced in a court of law on account of some technical defects, like want of a written form or stamp.

Some of the unenforceable contract can be enforced if the technical defect is removed. For example, if a document embodying a contract is under stamped, the contract is unenforceable, but if the requisite stamp is affixed (if allowed) the contract becomes enforceable.

2. **Classification according to Formation:** Contracts may be classified in accordance with the mode of their formation as follows:

(a) *Express Contract:* A promise made in words is called an express contract. In other words, an express contract is one which is made in writing or by the word of mouth.

Example: A wrote a letter to B, "I am prepared to sell my car for ₹1,00,000". B also accepted the offer by a letter. This is an express contract.

(c) *Implied Contract*: A contract which is not made in words is known as implied contract. Such contracts come into existence on account of an act or conduct of the parties.

Example: X went to a restaurant, and took a cup of tea. Here, there is an implied contract that he will pay for the cup of tea.

(c) *Quasi Contract:* It is a contract in which there is no intention on either side to make a contract, but the law imposes a contract. In reality, it is not a contract at all, e.g., Finder of lost goods.

Example: X, a merchant left certain goods at Y's house by mistake. Y treated the goods as his own. In this case, Y is bound to pay for the goods.

3. Classification according to Performance

(a) *Executed Contract:* A contract is said to be executed if both the parties to the contract have fulfilled their respective obligations. In other words, an executed contract is one that has been completely performed, e.g., Cash Sales.

Example: X sells a car to Y for ₹50,000. Y pays the price. Both the parties have performed their respective obligations, and, therefore, it is an executed contract.

(b) *Executory Contract:* A contract is said to be an executory if under the terms of a contract something remains to be done by the parties. In other words, where one or both the parties to the contract have still to perform their obligations in future, the contract is termed as an executory contract. For example, delivery of goods has been given but price has not been paid or both the delivery of goods and payment of price have to be made at a future date.

Example: A agrees to paint a picture for B and B in consideration promises to pay A a sum of ₹200. The contract is executory.

Where one party has performed his promise but the other party has still to perform his part, the contract will be treated as partly executed and partly executory.

Example: A agrees to paint a picture for B and B in consideration pays a sum of ₹200 to A. The contract is executed as regards B, but executory as regards A.

(c) *Unilateral Contract:* A unilateral contract is one in which only one party to the contract has performed his part and the obligation against the other is outstanding. For example, an offer of a reward for bringing back a lost article.

Example: X, a coolie puts Y's luggage in the carriage. The contract comes into existence immediately the luggage is put in. It is now for Y to perform his obligation by paying the charges to the coolie.

(d) *Bilateral Contract:* In a bilateral contract a promise on one side is exchanged for a promise on the other. It is a contract in which there is an obligation on the part of both the parties. For example, offer to sell for a price to be paid.

Example: X promises to sell his horse to Y after 10 days. Y promises to pay the price on the delivery of the horse. The contract is bilateral as obligation of both the parties are outstanding at the time of the formation of the contract.

4. Classification according to Form

(a) *Formal Contract:* A contract which is required to satisfy certain legal formalities in order to be valid and binding is known as formal contract. No consideration is necessary in such a contract and its validity depends on its form alone.

Formal contracts may be either contracts under seal or contracts of record.

Contracts, the terms of which have been written upon paper or parchment and are signed, sealed and delivered, are termed as *contracts under seal or speciality contracts.* Certain contracts should be made under seal, otherwise they will not be valid. They are: (i) contracts made without consideration, (ii) lease contracts relating to land for more than three years, (iii) contracts entered into by corporations, and (iv) contracts relating to transfer of a British ship or any share therein.

Contracts of record include judgement of courts and recognisances. The obligations imposed on a party by the judgement or recognisance are entered into the courts records. They are, therefore, known as contracts of record.

Recognisance implies a written acknowledgement of a debt due to the State.

Example: X has been arrested under a bailable offence. He has been released on bail with a promise to the court that he will be produced before the court as and when required by the court. In the case of failure, his surety shall be liable to a sum of ₹10,000 as fine. This obligation imposed on the surety is called *recognisance*.

(b) *Simple Contracts:* All contracts other than formal contracts are known as simple or parol contracts. A parol contract is valid only when it is supported by consideration. It is made by words spoken or written.

The Indian Law recognises only simple contracts and does not recognise formal contracts.

REVIEW QUESTIONS

1. "The law of contract is not the whole law of agreement nor is it the whole law of obligations" (Salmond). Comment.

2. "All contracts are agreements, but all agreements are not contracts". Comment.

3. Distinguish between (i) executed and executory contracts (ii) formal and simple contracts.

4. Define the term contract. What are the essentials of a valid contract?

5. Write short notes on:

   (a) Illegal contract

   (b) Unenforceable contract

   (c) Obligation

   (d) Consensus ad idem

6. How do you distinguish between void, voidable, unenforceable and illegal contracts?

PRACTICAL PROBLEMS

Attempt the following problems, giving reasons.

1. A invites B to dinner at his house on 1st January. B reaches the house of A at the specified time, but A fails to carry out his promise. Can B recover any damages from A?

   Hint: No. (*Balfour* v. *Balfour*)

2. X forced Y to enter into a contract at the point of a pistol. What remedy is available to Y?

   Hint: Y can repudiate the contract as there is a flaw in the consent.

3. A borrows ₹2,000 from B and makes a promissory note and a 10 paise stamp is pasted on the pronote. Is this agreement enforceable?

   Hint: No. Because of the technical defect, i.e., promissory note being under stamped.

4. A who owns two estates, one at Bombay and another at Delhi offers to sell B one estate. A intends the one at Bombay while B accepts the offer, thinking, that it is the estate at Delhi. Is this contract valid?

   Hint: No. Such a contract is void as there is no consensus.

5. State whether there is any contract in the following cases:

   (a) X and Y agree to marry each other.

   (b) X takes a seat in a local bus.

   (c) X and Y agree to go for hunting.

   (d) X agrees to sell some goods to Y at a price to be fixed by Z.

   Hint: In (a), (b) and (d) there is no contract (c) there is a contract.

2

Offer or Proposal

Proposal is the signification by one of his assent to do or abstain from doing something with a view to obtaining the assent of another to such an act or abstinence.

—Sec. 2(a)

INTRODUCTION

The process of making an agreement commences with offer. Offer is a proposal by one party to another to enter into a legally binding agreement with him. A proposal is an expression of will or intention. A person is said to have made a proposal, when he signifies to another his willingness to do or abstain from doing something in order to obtain the assent of another to such act or abstinence. The word proposal is synonymous with the English word 'offer'. The person who makes the offer is called the offeror, proposer or promisor and the person to whom it is made is known as the offeree or promisee.

ESSENTIALS OF A VALID OFFER

1. **Express and Implied Offer:** An express offer is one which is made by words, spoken or written.
   Example: A offers to sell his pen to B for ₹ 20.
   An implied offer is one which is gathered from the conduct of the parties or the circumstances of the case.
   Example: When a transport company runs a bus on a particular route, there is an implied offer by the transport company to carry passengers for a certain fare.

2. **Specific and General Offer:** An offer is said to be specific when it is addressed to a definite person or body of persons. A general offer is one which is addressed to the world at large even though it may be accepted by a definite person. General offers are also termed as offers at large or offers to the public, and specific offers as offers to the individual.

18

An offer of a reward for finding out a lost dog is a general offer and the finding out the dog by an individual amounts to acceptance. The leading case on general offer is *Carlill. v. Carbolic Smoke Ball Co.* (1893) I.Q.B. 256.

In this case, the defendants who were the proprietors of a medical preparation called the Carbolic Smoke Ball issued an advertisement in which they offered to pay £ 100 to any person who succumbed to influenza after using their Smoke Ball for a fortnight as per printed directions. It was also added in the advertisement that they had deposited £ 1,000 in the Alliance Bank showing their sincerity in the matter. The plaintiff, Mrs. Carlill trusting the advertisement, bought a Smoke Ball and used it as directed, but was attacked by influenza. She sued for £ 100. Held, she could recover the amount as by using the smoke ball she had accepted the offer. In this case, acceptance and performance go together and no communication of acceptance is necessary.

3. **Offer and Standing Offer or Tender:** An offer for the continuous supply of certain goods at a certain rate over a definite period is called a standing offer. Such offers though accepted do not give rise to a contract unless an actual order is placed. The offeror can withdraw his offer at any time, before an order is placed with him. But when a particular order is placed for goods the person who made the tender cannot refuse to supply those goods [*Great Northern Rly. v. Witham* (1873)].

> **ESSENTIALS OF VALID OFFER**
>
> • Express and implied offer
> • Specific and general offer
> • Offer and standing offer or tender
> • Offer and invitation to treat
> • Offer must be capable of creating legal relations
> • Offer must be definite
> • Conditional offer
> • Offer must be communicated to the offeree
> • Communication of special conditions
> • Cross offers

4. **Offer and Invitation to Treat:** An invitation to treat is sometimes called an invitation to offer. Every expression of willingness to enter into a contract may not amount to an offer. It is only an initial step in the formation of a contract. So, quotations, catalogues, advertisement in a newspaper for sale of an article or goods displayed by the shopkeeper in a shop window or on shelves do not constitute an offer. They are instead an invitation to the public to make an offer.

In *Harvey* v. *Facey* (1893) A.C. 552, *Harvey* telegraphed to Facey "Will you sell us Bumber Hall Pen? Telegraph lowest price. Answer paid". Facey replied—Lowest price for Bumber Hall Pen £ 900 and Harvey telegraphed—We agree to buy Bumber Hall Pen for £ 900 asked by you. Facey did not reply and Harvey sued for specific performance. It was observed by the Judicial Committee of the Privy Council that there was no concluded contract between the parties.

In *Fisher* v. *Bell* (1960), the respondent exhibited among other things in his shop a flick knife with a marked price. The question was whether the exhibition of that knife constituted 'an offer for sale'. Lord Parker C.J. held that it is quite impossible to say that an exhibition of goods in a shop is itself an offer for sale.

In 'Auction Sales' the question frequently arises whether an auctioneer can retract an article from sale. An auction sale is a sale by public auction to the highest bidder. It may be either 'with reserve' or 'without reserve'. It is 'with reserve' when upset price is fixed below which the auctioneer objects to complete the sale. It is 'without reserve' when the article is to be sold to the highest bidder whether the sum bid be equivalent to the original value or not.

In *Harris* v. *Nickerson* (1873) L.R. 28.B 286, the plaintiff sued for the expenses incurred in attending an auction of certain furniture advertised by the defendant, which was withdrawn from sale. Held that the plaintiff must fail because mere advertisement to sell was no offer which can ripen into contract by the intending purchaser accepting the same by attending the auction.

In 'Railway Cases', the question has arisen whether the time table published by a Railway Company amounts to an offer or only an invitation to offer. This question was decided in *Denton* v. *G.N. Rly*. Co. (1856) 5 E&B 860.

A timetable issued by the defendant had advertised a certain train from Peterborough to Hull. After the timetable had been printed but before its publication the train was cancelled. On relying on the timetable the plaintiff demanded a ticket to Hull and was then told that there was no such train. The Court decreed the claim for damages on the ground that there was a concluded contract. Therefore, a misleading announcement of timings of trains by railway companies in their timetables will be actionable only if that statement stemmed from fraud or deceit, and not on the basis of contract.

5. **Offer must be Capable of Creating Legal Relations:** To constitute an offer, the offeror must intend to create a legal obligation. Social invitation, even though it is accepted, does not create legal relations. To offer a friend a dinner, does not involve a legal action.[*Balfour* v. *Balfour* (1919) 2 K.B. 571].

6. **Offer must be Definite:** Section 29 states "Agreement, the meaning of which is not certain, or capable of being made certain, are void". So no contract can come into existence if the terms of the offer are vague and uncertain.

   In *Taylor* v. *Portington* (1855) E.R. 128 a contract for the lease of a house for three years at £ 85 per annum if the house was put into thorough repairs and the drawing rooms handsomely decorated according to the present style. The Court refused specific performance on the ground that the terms were indefinite.

7. **Conditional Offer:** A conditional offer can be accepted only subject to that condition. It lapses when the condition is not accepted.

8. **Offer must be Communicated to the Offeree:** An offer is effective only when it is communicated to the offeree. Since a contract requires identity of minds, and if the offeree is not aware of the offer it cannot be considered as acceptance.

   Example: Snedaker, the defendant offered a reward to anyone who returned his lost dog. Fitch, the plaintiff brought the dog to Snedaker without knowing that a reward was offered for it. Fitch claimed the amount of the reward subsequently. Held, there was no contract. [*Fitch* v. *Snedaker* (1868) 38. N.Y. 288]

9. **Communication of Special Conditions:** When an offer has several terms, the question arises whether every term should be communicated to the offeree. When special conditions are to be included in a contract, they should not only be particularly mentioned but communicated to the offeree as well. Otherwise, such terms will not be binding to the acceptor. This question has been decided in several cases knows as 'Ticket Cases'.

   In *Henderson* v. *Stevenson* (1875) 32 LT 709: The plaintiff bought a steamer ticket on the face of which it was printed 'From Dublin to White Heaven'. On account of the negligent navigation on the part of the servants of the defendant the ship struck a rock and the plaintiff lost his luggage and he sued for damages. The contention of the defendant was that a condition which was printed on the back of the ticket absolved the defendant from liability. It was held that the plaintiff was entitled to recover his loss on the ground that the defendant had not taken reasonable steps to communicate the terms to the plaintiff. The same view was laid down in *Parker* v. *South Eastern Railway Company* (1877) 2 C.P.D. 416.

The result would have been different if words like "for conditions, see back", had been printed on the face of the ticket. Then the person concerned is as a matter of law held to be bound by the conditions subject to which the ticket is issued whether he takes care to read them or not.

10. **Cross Offers:**   When two parties make identical offers to each other, in ignorance of each other's offer, the offers are cross offers. No contract arises from cross offers.

LAPSE OF OFFER

Section 6 of the Act states that a proposal is said to be lapsed on account of the following causes:

(a) If the offeror communicates a notice of revocation to the offeree.

(b) If the offeree does not accept the offer within the prescribed time. If no time is fixed, the offer lapses after a reasonable time.

(c) If the acceptor fails to fulfil conditions in the offer.

(d) If the offeror or the offeree dies before the acceptance of the offer. Under the Indian law an acceptance in ignorance of the death or insanity of the offeror, gives rise to a contract. But under the English Law if a person accepts the offer in ignorance of the offeror's death, there could be no contract.

REJECTION OF OFFER

An offer is said to be rejected:

(a) If the offeree makes a counter offer.

(b) If the offeree communicates his rejection to the proposer.

(c) If the offeree puts forward conditions after the proposal is accepted.

REVOCATION OF OFFER

An offer also ceases to exist by revocation. The term revocation may be defined as the 'taking back' or 'withdrawal'. An offer is revoked:

(a) By communication to the offeree at any time before the offer is accepted. [*Byrne* v. *Van Tienhoven* (1880) 42 LT 371].

(b) Even if the offer is made for a specified period, the offeror is free to withdraw the offer before the expiration of the period specified provided it has not been accepted till then.

Communication of Revocation

Under Indian Law, Sec. 6(1) states that the communication of revocation should be by the offeror himself. In English Law a communication of revocation should proceed from the offeror and must be made either by himself or by his duly authorised agent.

The notice of revocation is complete as against the person making it when it is in transit. As against the person to whom the revocation is made, it is complete when it comes to his knowledge.

> **Example:** X offers, by letter, to sell a plot of land to Y for ₹ 10,000. X revokes his offer by telegram. The revocation is complete as against X when the telegram is despatched. It is complete as against Y when Y receives it.

REVIEW QUESTIONS

1. Define the term 'offer'. State the rules of a valid offer.

2. "The communication of an offer is complete when it comes into the knowledge of the person to whom it is made". Elucidate.

3. Distinguish between the following:
   (a) Specific and General Offer
   (b) Offer and Tender
   (c) Offer and Invitation to Treat

4. Write short notes on:
   (a) Cross offers
   (b) Lapse of offer
   (c) *Carlill* v. *Carbolic Smoke Ball Co.*

5. How and on what grounds does a proposal stand revoked? When is the communication of revocation of an offer deemed to be complete?

PRACTICAL PROBLEMS

Attempt the following problems, giving reasons.

1. Are the following offers valid?

   (a) X advertises in the Hindu that he would pay ₹50 to anyone who finds and returns his lost dog.

   (b) A says to B. "I will sell you a car". A owns three different types of cars of various prices.

   (c) An auctioneer displays a TV set before the gathering in an auction shop.

   Hint: (a) This is a valid offer. Any person can accept it by performing the acts with the knowledge of the reward. (*Fitch* v. *Snedaker*). In (b) and (c) there is no offer.

2. P sees a camera displayed in a shop. It is labelled "Japan made, ₹100". P enters the shop and puts ₹100 on the counter and asks for the camera. The owner of the shop does not agree to sell saying that the real price of the camera is ₹1,000 and that it had been marked as ₹100 by mistake. Is the owner of the shop bound to sell the camera for ₹100?

   Hint: No.

3. X intends to make an offer to Y and tells Z about it. Z in turn conveys it to Y but X himself does not communicate the offer to Y. Y accepts the offer and conveys to X the acceptance. Is there a contract between X and Y?

   Hint: No.

4. X an auctioneer advertised in The Statesman that a sale of office furniture would be held at Bombay. Y, a businessman of Madras, reached Bombay on the specified time and date. But the auctioneer X withdrew all the furniture from the auction sale. The businessman, Y sues X for his loss of time and expenses. Will he succeed?

   Hint: No. (*Harris* v. *Nickerson*)

3

Acceptance

*Acceptance is the manifestation by the offeree of his assent
to the terms of the offer.*

INTRODUCTION

The assent given to a proposal may be understood as acceptance. A
proposal when accepted becomes a promise. In other words, offer +
acceptance = contract. An application for the shares in a company
is in the nature of offer while the allotment of the shares by the
company is an acceptance resulting in a contract. An acceptance
once completed cannot be revoked. Sir William Anson very aptly
compares the offer to a train of gun powder and the acceptance to
a lighted match. It produces something which cannot be recalled,
or undone. This means when the offeree signifies his assent to the
offeror, the offer is said to be accepted.

An acceptance may be express or implied. It is express when it is
communicated by words spoken or written or by doing some required
act. It is implied when it is to be gathered from the surrounding
circumstances or the conduct of the parties.

ESSENTIALS OF VALID ACCEPTANCE

For a valid acceptance, the following are essential.

1. Acceptance must be by the offeree.
2. Acceptance must be absolute and unconditional.
3. Acceptance should be before an offer lapses.
4. Acceptance should be communicated.

1. **Acceptance must be by the Offeree:** When an offer is
   made to a specified person it can be accepted by him alone.
   No person can give himself a contractual right by inter-
   posing in an offer which was not intended for him.

25

In *Boulton* v. *Jones* (1857) 157 E.R. 232, the defendant sent an order to a firm with whom he had past dealings and right of set off. The plaintiff who had purchased the firm obtained a letter addressed to the firm and he accepted the order and sent the goods without informing that he was the purchaser of the firm. In a suit for the price it was held that he could not recover the price, as there was no contract.

General offer can be accepted by any person who has the knowledge of the existence of such an offer [*Carlill* v. *Carbolic Smoke Ball Co.*].

2. **Acceptance must be Absolute and Unconditional:** The acceptance of the offer should correspond to the terms of the offer, and the acceptor should not impose any condition while accepting the offer. Acceptance must be in toto and without any condition.

In *Hyde* v. *Wrench* the defendant, H offered to sell an estate to the Plaintiff, W for £ 1,000. Plaintiff in reply made an offer of £ 950 which was refused by the defendant. Later, plaintiff wrote that he was prepared to pay £ 1,000. It was held that no contract had been made between them because plaintiff had rejected the original offer. If an offer is destroyed, it cannot be revived to form a contract by acceptance.

3. **Acceptance should be before the Offer Lapses:** An offer in order to ripen into a contract by acceptance should continue to exist at the time of acceptance. Until an offer is accepted, it creates no legal obligations, and it may be terminated at any time.

4. **Acceptance should be Communicated:** Just as the communication of the offer, acceptance also should be communicated. The communication need not be of a particular kind, but silence can never be prescribed as a mode of communication.

The communication must be to the offeror himself. However, this requirement may be waived by the offeror Such a waiver may be inferred from the offeror recommending or authorising a mode of acceptance which does not involve communication to him. For instance, if the offeror says "If you mean to accept my offer inform W or wave a flag or fire a gun". In all these cases if the offeree acts accordingly, it is a valid acceptance.

In *Felthouse* v. *Bindley* (1862) 6 LT 157, acceptance communicated to a stranger was held to be not sufficient.

In that case it was also held that the offeror cannot prescribe silence as a mode of acceptance.

Communication of acceptance is not necessary in the case of unilateral contract [*Carlill* v. *Carbolic Smoke Ball Co.*].

ACCEPTANCE BY POST OR TELEGRAM

An offer sent through post may be accepted by post, if the offeror does not indicate some other mode of communication. An offer sent by post is communicated only when it reaches the offeree and not when it would, in the ordinary course of post, reach him [*Adams* v. *Lindsell* (1818) IBT. Ald. 681].

An acceptance is complete, the moment the letter of acceptance is posted, provided the letter is correctly addressed to the offeror and put into the post and it is no longer within the power of the acceptor to recall it. The posting of acceptance concludes the contract, even if the letter of acceptance is delayed or lost in the post. What applies to the post applies equally to an acceptance by telegram.

The communication of an acceptance is complete as against the offeror, when it is put in a course of transmission to him, as against the acceptor, when it comes to the knowledge of the power of the proposer (Sec. 4).

In *Bhagwandas* v. *Giridharilal* (AIR 1966 S.C. 543) the Supreme Court of India considered the validity of a contract entered over a telephone and held that such a type of contract becomes complete when "the acceptance was received by the offering party". As against the acceptor the communication of an acceptance is complete when it comes to the knowledge of the offeror.

REVOCATION OF ACCEPTANCE

An acceptance, in English Law, cannot be revoked [*Household Fire Insurance Co.* v. *Grant* (1879) L.R.4 Ex. D.26]. In India Sec. 5 of the Act reads:

An acceptance may be revoked at any time before the communication of the acceptance is complete as against the acceptor, but not afterwards.

REVIEW QUESTIONS

1. Define the term acceptance. Give legal rules regarding acceptance with suitable examples.

2. "Acceptance is to offer what a lighted match is to a train of gun powder". Comment.

3. Write short notes on:

   (a) Communication of Acceptance

   (b) Revocation of Acceptance

   (c) Contracts by Post

   (d) Contracts over Telephone

PRACTICAL PROBLEMS

Attempt the following problems, giving reasons.

1. P offered to sell his house to Q for 20,000. Q said, "I accept your offer. Here is ₹10,000 in cash and a 90 days' promissory note for the balance. Did a contract result?

   Hint: No, as the acceptance is conditional.

2. X made an offer to Y by post. Y died before the letter reached him. The son of Y accepted the offer. Is X bound by the acceptance?

   Hint No, as an offer is made to Y, it can be accepted by him alone.

4

Consideration

Consideration is the price for which the promise of the other is bought.

—*Pollock on Contracts,* 13th ed., p. 113

INTRODUCTION

Consideration is a technical term in the sense of quid pro quo, i.e., something in return.

> **Example:** A agrees to sell his car to B for ₹50,000. In this case, the promise of B to pay a sum of ₹50,000 is the consideration for the promise of A to sell the car. And the promise of A to sell the car is the consideration for the promise of B to pay a sum of ₹50,000.

An agreement to be enforceable, it must be supported by consideration which is the foundation of every contract.

Consideration, offer and acceptance are an indivisible trinity of a valid contract. Mutual assent takes place by offer and acceptance, but to have mutual assent, there must be something to be assented and agreed to on each side. This something is known as consideration. The legal maxim being EX NUDO PACTO NON ORITUR ACTIO (out of a bare agreement no action arises.).

> **Example:** A mere promise to make a gift is not enforceable at law as the person to whom the promise of a gift does not give anything in return.

In England consideration is not essential for contract under seal (Contract by Speciality). Such a contract depends for its validity on its form alone. In the case of simple contracts (Parole) consideration is essential.

EXCEPTIONS TO THE RULE 'NO CONSIDERATION NO CONTRACT'

The general rule is that an agreement made without consideration is void and unenforceable. But Sec. 25 of the Act enumerates certain exceptions to that rule.

1. **Love and Affections:** Where an agreement is in writing and registered and made out of natural love and affection between parties standing in near relationship to each other.

> **NO CONSIDERATION NO CONTRACT—EXCEPTIONS**
>
> - Love and affections
> - Promise to pay a time barred debt
> - Compensation for voluntary service
> - Agency
> - Completed gift

2. **Promise to Pay a Time Barred Debt:** Where a promise is made in writing and signed by the debtor to discharge a time barred debt.

3. **Compensation for Voluntary Service:** A promise to compensate wholly or in part, a person who voluntarily rendered some services in the past.

4. **Agency:** No consideration is essential to create an agency.

5. **Completed Gift:** The rule "No consideration, no contract" does not apply to a completed gift.

DEFINITION OF CONSIDERATION

In *Currie* v. *Misa* (1875) 10 Ex.153, Lush J., defined "A valuable consideration in the sense of the law may consist either in some right, interest, profit or benefit accruing to one party or some forbearance, detriment, loss, responsibility, given, suffered or undertaken by the other. The shortest definition of consideration is "It is the price of a promise".

Consideration is defined in Sec. 2(d) of the Contract Act thus "when at the desire of the promisor, the promisee or any other person has done or abstained from doing or does or abstains from doing or promises to do or to abstain from doing, something, such act or abstinence or promise is called a consideration for the promise". It is clear from the above definition that consideration consists of either some benefit to the promisor or some detriment to the promisee. Moreover, consideration is:

(a) An act, i.e., doing of something. In this sense consideration is an affirmative form.

Example: X promises Y to guarantee payment of price of the goods which Y sells on credit to Z. Here sales by Y to Z is a consideration for the promise of X.

(b) An abstinence or forbearance, i.e., abstaining or refraining from doing something. In this sense, consideration is in a negative form.

Example: X promises Y not to file a suit against him if he pays him ₹1,000. The abstinence of X is the consideration for the payment of Y.

(c) A return promise.

ESSENTIALS OF VALID CONSIDERATION

1. **Consideration is Essential:** Consideration in the sense of detriment is quite indispensable to support a simple promise.

   In *Lee* v. *White Combe*, it was held that promise to spend two years for learning tailoring was unenforceable due to the lack of consideration.

2. **Consideration must Move at the Desire of the Promisor:** The act or forbearance must be at the desire of the promisor. The act done at the desire of the third party cannot be a consideration. A promise which is gratuitous is void.

   A promise to give a donation is not enforceable as there is no benefit to the promisor. But if the promisee has incurred liability relying upon the promise, it is enforceable.

> **ESSENTIALS OF VALID CONSIDERATION**
>
> • Consideration is Essential
> • Consideration must move at the desire of the promisor
> • Consideration may move from the promisee or any other person
> • Consideration may be the past, present or future
> • "Something", consideration need not be adequate
> • Consideration must be competent
> • Consideration must be lawful

In *Abdul Aziz* v. *Mazum Ali* (1914) 36 All. 268, a person promised to the secretary of the Mosque committee to subscribe a sum of ₹500 for the rebuilding of a Mosque, but failed to pay the amount. It was held that the promise was not enforceable and the contract was void because there was no consideration either in the sense of benefit to the promisor or detriment to the promise.

In *Kedarnath* v. *Gori Mohammed* (1886) 14 Cal. 64, the defendant made a promise to give a donation of ₹100 for the construction of a Town Hall in Howrah Municipality. Plaintiff, the Secretary of the Committee, on the faith of the promise, called for plans and entrusted the work to contractors and undertook liability to pay for them. In a suit upon the promise, it was held that though consideration in the sense of benefit to the promisor was not present, still consideration in the sense of detriment to the promisee was present, because the secretary undertook a liability on the faith of the promise made by the defendant.

3. **Consideration may Move from the Promisee or any other Person:** In Indian Law, a stranger to consideration may maintain a suit if he is a party to the contract. But under the English Law, consideration must move from the promisee. [*Tweddle* v. *Atkinson* (1861) IB&S. 392].

In *Chinnya* v. *Ramayya* (1881) 4 Mad 137, an old lady, by a deed of gift, made over certain property to her daughter with a direction to pay a certain sum of money to the maternal uncle by way of annuity. On the same day, the daughter executed a writing in favour of the brother agreeing to pay the annuity. The daughter did not, however, pay the annuity and the uncle sued to recover it. It was held that there was sufficient consideration for the uncle to recover the money from the daughter.

4. **Consideration may be Past, Present or Future:** Under the English Law, past consideration is no consideration. In other words, consideration must be either executed or executory, but can never be past.

In Indian Law, the words used in Sec. 2(d) shows that consideration, may be past, present or future.

Past Consideration: A past consideration is one where the consideration by a party for a present promise was given in the past.

Example: A lawyer abandoned his practice and served as manager of a landlord at the latter's request of which the landlord subsequently promised a pension, it was held that there was good past consideration. [*Shiv Saran* v. *Kesho Prasad* 42, 1. C.122].

Present or Executed Consideration: It is a present act or forbearance. In a cash sale, the consideration is present or executed.

Future or Executory Consideration: It is a promise to do or forbear in return for a like promise.

Example: X promises to deliver certain goods to Y after a fortnight.

5. **"Something", Consideration Need not be Adequate:** Consideration for a promise need not be adequate to the promise, but it must be of some value in the eye of law. Adequacy of consideration banks upon the appetite of the parties. Inadequacy is not at all a ground for refusing the performance of promise, unless it is an evidence of fraud.

In *Thomas* v. *Thomas* (1842) 2 Q.B. 851, a ground rent of £ 1 was held to be sufficient consideration for the promise. In that case, it was also held that the motive was not a good consideration.

6. **Consideration must be Competent:** Although consideration need not be adequate, it must be real, competent and not illusory.

In *Collins* v. *Godfrey* (1831) I.B & A.0.950, A promised to pay money to a police officer to investigate into a crime. It was held that the agreement was invalid because, the officer was already under duty to do so by law.

7. **Consideration must be Lawful:** If the consideration is unlawful, the contract is unenforceable and void.

DOCTRINE OF PRIVITY OF CONTRACT

Privity of contract means the relationship subsisting between
the parties who have entered into contractual obligations.

Under the English Law, consideration for a contract must move from the promisee. In other words, a stranger to a consideration cannot sue. Whereas under the Indian Law the consideration may move either from the promisee or from any other person. In other words, a stranger to a consideration can sue.

Both under the Indian Law and English Law, a stranger to a contract cannot sue. This is known as doctrine of privity of contract. Privity of contract is said to exist between two persons when there is a valid contract which can be enforced between them. A person who cannot show such a privity of contract is a stranger to the contract.

A stranger to a contract cannot sue as laid down by the House of Lords in the leading case *Dunlop* v. *Selfridge* (1915) A.C. 847.

In the above case one Dew & Co., who were the manufacturing agents of the Dunlop Company agreed with Dunlop Company not to sell the tubes and tyres below a certain listed price and insisted on similar terms when dealing with retailers. In an agreement between the Dew & Co., and the Selfridge, the retailer Selfridge agreed with Dew & Co., not to sell the tyres and tubes below the listed price and for every sale below the price, he shall pay £ 5 to Dunlop & Co. The Selfridge & Co., (defendants) sold 2 tyres below the listed price and committed a breach of contract. Dunlop Company (plaintiffs) who were strangers to the contract, sued for an injunction to restrain its breach and for recovering £ 10 as damages.

It was held by the House of Lords that the plaintiffs could not succeed in the action as they were strangers to the contract. It may be noted that the plaintiffs were strangers to the consideration too and would fail on that account also.

EXCEPTIONS TO THE RULE THAT A STRANGER TO A CONTRACT CANNOT SUE

1. **Trusts:** In a contract creating a trust, the beneficiary who is a stranger to the contract can enforce the trust.

2. **Acknowledgement or Estoppel:** Where a promisor by his conduct, acknowledges or otherwise constitutes himself as an agent of a third party, a binding obligation is thereby incurred towards him.

   Example: If X admits to Z that he had received some money from Y for payment to Z, he constitutes himself as an agent of Z, who can successfully recover the amount from X.

3. **Statutory:** Under the Road Traffic Act in England and Motor Vehicles Act in India, the third party who suffers an injury in an accident can enforce the contract of insurance.

   In addition to the above three exceptions, Indian Law recognises two more exceptions:

1. *Charge Created over Property:* A person in whose favour a charge over immovable property is created may enforce it even though he is not a party to the contract.

   In *Khwaja Muhamad* v. *Hussaini Begum* (1910) 32 All, 410 (PC), A, a Muhammadan entered into a contract with B on the occasion of the marriage of A's son with B's daughter, the plaintiff. Under that contract, A agreed to pay ₹500 per month to the plaintiff as 'Betel Leaf' expenses from the date of her marriage. The amount thus payable was made a charge over certain immovable property. It was held that he must succeed.

2. *Family Arrangement:* A provision for marriage expenses of a female member of a Hindu Joint Family can be enforced by the female beneficiary when such a provision is part of a family arrangement.

   In *Sundaryya* v. *Lakshmi Ammal* (1915) 38 Mad. 788, a sister sued successfully for marriage expenses provided in a partition between brothers.

REVIEW QUESTIONS

1. Define 'consideration'. Point out the salient features of the term 'consideration' as defined in the Indian Contract Act.

2. "A contract without consideration is void". Discuss.

3. Explain the term consideration as an element of a valid contract, and discuss the effects of:
   (a) total absence of consideration
   (b) inadequacy of consideration
   (c) past consideration

4. "Consideration is something in return". Comment.

5. "Consideration may be past, present or future". Explain with examples.

6. "A stranger to a contract cannot sue, but a stranger to a consideration can sue". Discuss.

7. Explain the doctrine of privacy of contract and give an account of the exceptions to the doctrine.

PRACTICAL PROBLEMS

Attempt the following problems, giving reasons.

1. P agrees with Q to sell his house worth ₹10,000 for ₹100 only. Is this agreement valid?

   Hint: Yes, as the consideration for a promise need not be adequate.

2. P finds the purse of Q and gives it to him. Q promises P to give him ₹50. Can P claim the money?

   Hint: Yes, P can recover the amount from Q.

3. A promises a subscription of ₹ 20,000 to the National Defence Fund. He does not pay. Is there any remedy against him?

   Hint: No. [*Abdul Aziz* v. *Mazum Ali*].

4. X promises to make a gift of ₹100 for the construction of a Town Hall. The Secretary of the committee on the faith of his promise incurs liabilities. X does not pay. Can the Secretary recover the amount from X? Give reasons.

   Hint: Yes. Consideration in the sense of detriment to the promisee was present because the Secretary undertook liability on the faith of the promise. [*Kedarnath* v. *Gori Mohammed*].

5. A Muhammadan lady sued her father-in-law to recover arrears of allowance payable to her by him under an agreemnt between him and her own father in consideration of her marriage. Will she succeed?

   Hint: Yes. [*Khwaja Muhamad* v. *Hussaini Begum*]

5

Capacity of Parties

Capacity means competence of the parties to enter into a valid contract.

INTRODUCTION

Section 11 of the Contract Act deals with the competency of parties. It states that every person is competent to enter into a contract if he has attained the age of majority and is of sound mind provided he is not disqualified from contracting by any law to which he is subject. Thus, incompetency to contract must be either by infancy or insanity, or through the provisions of personal law.

MINOR

A minor or an infant is a person who is not a major. A person domiciled in India is deemed to have attained majority on his completing eighteen years of age (Sec. 3 of the Indian Majority Act, 1875). In the case, where the minor is under the Guardianship of the Courts of Wards or a guardian has been appointed under the Guardian and Wards Act, he attains majority only when he completes 21 years. But in England, a person's minority ceases only on the attainment of 21 years of age.

CONTRACT BY A MINOR

Sec. 11 of the Contract Act has not provided whether a minor's contract is void or voidable. Previous to the decision of the Privy Council in *Mohori Bibi* v. *Dharmodas Ghose* (1903) 30 Cal. 539 PC., there was no unanimity on this point among the Indian High Courts. The more prevalent view was that the contract was only voidable at the option of the minor. This difference was set at rest by the authoritative pronouncement of the Privy Council in this case.

In this case, Dharmodas Ghose who was a minor representing himself to be a major executed a mortgage deed of his property for ₹20,000 and received ₹ 8,000 in cash. He became a major a few months later and filed a suit for the declaration that the mortgage executed by him during his minority was void and should be cancelled. It was held that mortgage by a minor was void and Mohori Bibi was not entitled to the repayment of money.

The present positions of the law in India regarding minor's capacity to contract are as follows:

1. **Contract with a Minor is Absolutely Void:** A minor is incompetent to contract and a contract by a minor is void 'ab initio'. All those contracts to which a person incompetent to contract is a party are void, as against him, but he can derive benefit under them.

2. **No Ratification:** Ratification means the act of confirming or approving.

   An agreement by a minor cannot be ratified by him on attaining the age of majority. Thus consideration given during minority is no consideration.

   Example: X, a minor borrows ₹4,000 from Y and executes a promissory note. After attaining majority, he executes another promissory note in the settlement of the first note. The second promissory note is void for want of consideration.

3. **Minor can be a Promisee or a Beneficiary:** Incapacity of a minor to enter into a contract means incapacity to bind himself by a contract. There is nothing which debars him from becoming a beneficiary.

4. **No Estoppel against a Minor:** Estoppel is a rule of evidence by which a person is not allowed to go back upon his earlier representations.

   A minor is not estopped from pleading his infancy for avoiding a contract. This, however, does not mean that a minor can cheat men with impunity. If a minor has obtained any property by cheating, he can be forced to return it.

> **RULES REGARDING MINOR'S AGREEMENT**
> - Contract with minor is absolutely void
> - No ratifications
> - Minor can be a promisee or a beneficiary
> - No estoppel against a minor
> - Specific performance
> - Liability for necessaries
> - Position of minor's parents
> - Partnership
> - Liability for torts
> - Minor as agents

In *Stocks* v. *Wilson*, a minor who overstated his age and took delivery of a motor car after executing a promissory note in favour of the trader, was not estopped from pleading minority, but the Court ordered restitution on equitable ground. A minor can be forced to return a car he had bought on credit by overstating his age if it can be traced. But if the car cannot be traced, can the trader request the Court to pass a decree against the minor for the price of the car? The answer is not positive. The dictum is "restitution stops when repayment begins".

5. **Specific Performance:** A minor's contract being absolutely void, there can be no question of the specific performance of such a contract.

6. **Liability for Necessaries:** A minor is liable for necessaries supplied or necessary services rendered to him or his minor dependents. Necessaries are defined in Sec. 2 of the Sale of Goods Act, 1893 (English Act) as.

"Goods suitable to the condition in life of such an infant or minor or other person and to the actual requirements at the time of sale and delivery". Expenses on minor's educations, on funeral ceremonies of the wife, husband, children of the minor come within the scope of the word necessaries.

In *Martin* v. *Gale* (1876) 4ch. D.428, a loan taken by a minor to obtain necessaries also binds him and is recoverable by the lender as if he himself had supplied the necessities. But he is not personally liable.

7. **Position of Minor's Parents:** A contract with a minor does not give the creditor any rights against the minor's parents, even though the contract is for the supply of necessaries to the minor.

8. **Partnership:** A minor cannot be a partner in a partnership firm, but he can be admitted to the benefits of partnership as per Sec. 30 of the Indian Partnership Act.

9. **Liability for Torts:** Tort means a kind of Civil wrong. A minor is liable in torts. But a minor cannot be made liable for a breach of contract by framing the action on tort.

10. **Minor as Agent:** A minor can act as an agent. He binds the principal by his acts without incurring any personal liability.

PERSONS OF UNSOUND MIND

As per Sec. 12 lunatics cannot enter into a contract. Similarly, a drunken person, or congenital idiots not possessing even a ray of thinking power cannot enter into a contract. As per the Indian Law, all these persons stand on the same footing as minors, and their contracts are void. According to the English Law a contract entered into by a lunatic or a drunken person is only voidable. But, both in England and in India a lunatic may enter into valid contract during a lucid interval. In a lucid interval, the mentally deranged person regains his sanity.

INCAPACITY ARISING FROM STATUS

(a) *Foreign Sovereigns, Ambassadors, etc.:* Foreign Sovereigns and Accredited Representatives of a foreign state or Ambassadors are immune from the jurisdiction of Local Courts, unless they voluntarily submit to its jurisdiction. These persons have a right to contract but can claim the privilege of not being sued. In India Sec. 86 of the Civil Procedure Code, lays down that a prior sanction of the Central Government should be obtained in order to sue the Rulers of foreign states, Ambassadors and Envoys.

(b) *Alien Enemies:* A person who is not an Indian is an alien. An alien living in India is competent to contract with Indian citizens during peace time. But if a war is declared, an alien enemy is not able to enter into any contract with citizens of India. Contracts entered into before the declaration of war are either stayed or terminated, but contracts entered into during the war are not enforceable.

(c) *Insolvents:* When a debtor is adjudged insolvent, his property vests in the Official Receiver or Official Assignee and thereby he cannot enter into a contract.

(d) *Convicts:* A convict while undergoing imprisonment is incapacitated to enter into a contract. But this disability comes to an end when the period of sentence expires or when he is pardoned.

(e) *Corporations:* A corporation is an artificial being created by law. It is competent to enter into contracts only through its agents and in accordance with the powers conferred by the Memorandum of Association.

REVIEW QUESTIONS

1. Define the term 'capacity to contract'. What is the effect of agreements made by person not qualified to contract?
2. Discuss the provision of law relating to minor's contracts.
3. Discuss the contractual capacity of:

   (a) Aliens
   (b) Insolvents
   (c) Lunatics
   (d) Drunken persons
   (e) Corporation and Companies

4. Explain the legal effect of a minor's misrepresentation of his age while entering into a contract.

PRACTICAL PROBLEMS

Attempt the following problems, giving reasons.

1. P, an infant obtains a loan from Q by falsely representing his age. Q seeks to recover the loan from P. Will he succeed?

   Hint: No. (*Mohori Bibi* v. *Dharmodas Ghose*)

2. X, a minor borrows ₹10,000 from Y and executes a pronote for the amount in favour of Y. The pronote was renewed by X in favour of Y when he attained the age of majority. Y sues X on the second pronote. Will he succeed?

   Hint: No, as the second pronote is void for want of consideration.

3. X, a trader supplies Y, a minor with the necessaries of life. He makes out a pronote in favour of the trader. Is the trader entitled to claim payment under the pronote (a) from minor personally, (b) against his estate?

   Hint: (a) No. (b) Yes.

6

Free Consent

Free consent is the consent which is secured by the free will of the parties out of their own accord.

—Sec. 14

INTRODUCTION

A contract implies consensus ad idem. It means that the parties to a contract should have the identity of mind. A contract which is regular in all other respects may still fail because there is an absence of real consent to it by one or both of the parties.

Section 10 states that all agreements are contracts if they are made by the free consent of the parties. "Two or more persons are said to consent when they agree upon the same thing in the same sense" (Sec. 13). Consent is said to be free and voluntary if it is not caused by:

    (a) Coercion as defined in Sec. 15, or

    (b) Undue influence as defined in Sec. 16, or

    (c) Fraud as defined in Sec. 17, or

    (d) Misrepresentation as defined in Sec. 18, or

    (e) Mistake subject to Secs. 20–22.

In other words, free consent is the consent which is secured by the free will of the parties. When consent is not free the contract is not binding to the parties and the same can be avoided at the option of the party whose consent is not free. Thus, the Indian Law, makes it obvious that if any one of the above invalidating elements is present, there is a flaw in consent.

COERCION (SEC. 15)

When a person is compelled to enter into a contract by the use of force by the other party, 'coercion' is said to be employed. A contract entered into under coercion is voidable at the option of the coerced. A person to whom money had been paid or anything delivered under coercion must repay or return it.

> **Example:** A railway company refuses to deliver certain goods to the consignee, except upon the payment of illegal charge for carriage. The consignee pays the sum charged for obtaining the goods. He is entitled to recover as much of the charges as was illegally excessive.

Coercion is defined in Sec. 15 as "the committing, or threatening to commit, any act forbidden by the Indian Penal Code or the unlawful detaining, or threatening to detain, any property, to the prejudice of any person whatever, with the intention of causing any person to enter into an agreement".

In the English Law, the near equivalent of the term coercion is 'duress' or 'menace'. Duress is defined "as the causing or threatening to cause, bodily violence or imprisonment, in order to obtain the consent of the other party to the contract". The definition of duress is narrower than coercion under Sec. 15. The differences between duress and coercion are:

(a) Duress is confined to bodily violence and imprisonment, while coercion is the commission or threat to commit any act forbidden by the Indian Penal Code.

(b) Duress must proceed from a party to the contract or his agent whereas coercion may proceed from any person.

(c) In duress, the act must be such as to affect a man of ordinary firmness of mind whereas it is not necessary to constitute coercion under Sec. 15.

(d) In the Indian Law, unlawful detention of goods is coercion, but this will not amount to duress in the English Law.

UNDUE INFLUENCE (SEC. 16)

Undue influence is the improper exercise of authority over the mind of one of the contracting parties by the other.

Section 16 of the Indian Contract Act lays down that a contract is induced by 'undue influence' where the relations subsisting between the parties are such that one of the parties is in a position to dominate the will of the other and uses that position to obtain an unfair advantage over the other. Examples of the relationship where one is in a position to dominate the will of the other are:

(a) Parent and Child;

(b) Guardian and Ward;

(c) Trustee and Beneficiary;

(d) Religious Superior and Disciple;

(e) Legal Adviser and Client; and

(f) Doctor and Patient.

The leading English case on the subject is *Allcard* v. *Skinner* (1887).

The plaintiff, a rich young woman joined a Nunnery, after taking certain vows. While she was a member of the convent, she executed so many gift deeds in respect of the properties in favour of the Mother Superior. Later on she left the Nunnery and immediately revoked the will. She moved the Court after six years to rescind the gift deed on the ground of undue influence. The court held that there was undue influence. But the suit was dismissed on the ground of unreasonable delay in bringing the suit.

A contract entered into undue influence is voidable at the option of the party thus influenced,

> **Example:** X, a money lender, advanced ₹200 to Y an agriculturist and by undue influence induces Y to execute a bond for ₹400 with interest at 6 per cent per month. The Court may set the bond aside ordering Y to repay ₹200 with such interest as may seem just.

MISREPRESENTATION (SEC. 18)

A misrepresentation is a representation that is falsely made. Representation always means a statement of fact made by one party to the other before or at the time the contract is made with regard to some existing fact or some past event which materially induces the formation of the agreement.

A representation when wrongly made either innocently or wilfully is a misrepresentation. Thus, misrepresentation may be innocent or wilful. The former is called 'misrepresentation' and the latter 'fraud'.

INNOCENT MISREPRESENTATION

In innocent misrepresentation, however, the person making it honestly believes it to be true or does not know it to be false.

According to Sec. 18 of the Act, misrepresentation means and includes:

1. The positive assertion, in a manner not warranted by the information of the person making it, of that which is not true, though he believes it to be true.

2. Any breach of duty by a person which brings an advantage to the person committing it by misleading another to his prejudice.

3. Causing, however innocently, a party to an agreement, to make a mistake as to the substance of the thing which is the subject of the agreement.

A representation may be true when made. But if it becomes untrue to the knowledge of the person making the representation, before the contract is entered into, it becomes misrepresentation and renders the contract voidable.

The effect of innocent misrepresentation of fact is that the party misled by it may repudiate the contract and:

(a) raise the misrepresentation as a defence to any action the other party may bring against him, or

(b) sue for rescission of the contract and restitution has transferred to the misrepresenter.

When the consent is obtained by misrepresentation, and the person who misled has the means of finding the veracity with the ordinary diligence, the contract cannot be rescinded.

> **Example:** X, by misrepresentation leads Y to believe that 1000 maunds of indigo are made annually at the factory of X. Y examines the accounts of the factory, which show that only 800 maunds of indigo have been made. After this Y buys the factory. The contract is not voidable on account of the misrepresentation of X because Y, had the means of discovering the truth with ordinary diligence.

WILFUL MISREPRESENTATION OR FRAUD (SEC. 17)

Fraud is the wilful misrepresentation made by one party of the contract to the other with an intention to deceive.

The essential elements of fraud are:

(a) The suggestion by a person that a fact is true when it is not true.

(b) The active concealment of fact by a person who believes it to be true (i.e., all efforts are made to conceal fact).

(c) A promise made without any intention of performing it.

(d) Any such act or omission as the law specifically declares to be fraudulent.

(e) Any other act intended to deceive.

There is no fraud without damages. Therefore, to constitute fraud it is necessary that the plaintiff must have suffered some loss or damages.

Mere silence on the part of a person without any legal duty to speak will not amount to fraud. This rule has two exceptions:

(i) the circumstances of the case are such that it is the duty of the person keeping silence to speak, and

(ii) the silence in itself is equivalent to speech.

When consent to any agreement is caused by fraud it makes a contract voidable at the option of the party defrauded; the aggrieved party has, however, the following remedies:

1. He may rescind the contract.

2. He can insist on the performance of the contract on the condition that he shall be put in the position in which he would have been if the representation made had been true:

   Example: X fraudulently informs Y that the estate of X is free from encumbrance. Y thereupon buys the estate. The estate is subject to a mortgage. Y may avoid the contract or may insist on its being carried out and the mortgage debt repaid by X.

3. He can sue for damages.

Difference between misrepresentation and fraud

Misrepresentation	*Fraud*
1. There is no intention to deceive the party.	There is clear intention to deceive the party.
2. Misrepresentation is an innocent wrong. The person making the suggestion believes it to be true.	Fraud is intentional or wilful wrong. The person making the suggestion does not believe it to be true.
3. In misrepresentation, the aggrieved party can rescind the contract. There can be no suit for damages.	In fraud, the aggrieved party can claim damages in addition to his right to rescind the contract.
4. Misrepresentation does not amount to tort.	Fraud amounts to tort.

MISTAKE

The next vitiating element of consent is mistake. The term mistake may be defined as an erroneous belief about something.

> **Example:** A and B enter into a contract on the erroneous belief that a particular debt is barred by the Indian Law of Limitation.

Mistake does not vitiate a contract in all cases. If the mistake prevents the formation of consensus then the contract is void. This is called operative mistake. Mistake may be either of law or of fact.

Mistake of Law

Mistake of law may be of the law of land or foreign law. Mistake of law does not vitiate a contract as expressed in the maxim "Ignorantia juris non excusat", i.e., ignorance of the law is no excuse. But this rule is applicable only to the law of the land and, not to the foreign law.

Mistake of Fact

Mistake of fact may be either bilateral mistake or unilateral mistake.

Bilateral Mistake

Here both the parties of the contract make a mistake, which may be either common mistake or mutual mistake. Common mistake or identical bilateral mistake, occurs where both parties have made the same mistake. Mutual mistake or not identical bilateral mistake occurs where the parties make different mistakes. Section 20 lays down that "where both the parties to an agreement are under a mistake as to a matter of fact, essential to the agreement, the agreement is void".

The cases falling under bilateral mistake are as follows:

1. **Mistake as to the Subject Matter:** Here both the parties to an agreement are working under a mistake relating to the subject matter. It falls under six heads, viz., (a) existence, (b) identity, (c) title, (d) price, (e) quantity, (f) quality.

   (a) *Mistake as to Existence of the Subject matter:* It relates to a maxim "Res extincta", i.e., thing extinct. If both the parties to a contract believe the subject matter to be in existence, which in fact at the time of the contract is non-existent, the contract is void.

In *Couturier* v. *Hastie* (1856) 5 H.L. C. 673, A agreed to sell a cargo of corn supposed to be on its way from Salonica to the United Kingdom. At the time of the contract, however, the cargo having fermented had been sold by the Master of the ship at Tunis. It was held that the contemplated subject-matter being non-existent, no contract could emerge and the contract was held to be void.

(b) *Mistake as to the Identity of the Subject matter:* If a mutual mistake relates to the identity of the subject matter, the contract is void.

In *Raffles* v. *Wichelhaus* (1864) 159 E.R. 375, the plaintiff sued for breach of a contract to deliver 125 bales of Surat Cotton to arrive "Ex peerless" from Bombay. There were two ships of that name sailing from Bombay, one sailing in October and the other in December. The plaintiff took the reference in the contract to "ex peerless" as meaning the ship sailing in December whereas the defendant thought that it meant the ship sailing in October. Held, there was a mutual mistake and there was no contract.

(c) *Mistake as to the Title of the Subject matter:* If the vendor is selling the goods which he is not entitled to sell both the parties are acting under a mistake, the contract is void.

In *Cooper* v. *Phibbs* (1867) L.R. 2 H.L. 149, A agreed to take a lease of fishery from B. But A was a tenant for life of the fishery and B had no title at all. It was held that the lease was void.

(d) *Mistake as to the Price of the Subject matter:* The contract is void if there is a mutual mistake as to the price of the subject matter.

Example: Where a seller of certain plots mentioned in his letter the price as Rs.5,500, when he really intended to write ₹7,500 the agreement is void.

(e) *Mistake as to the Quantity of the Subject matter:* The agreement is void and there is no contract if both parties are under a mistake as to the quantity of the subject matter.

Example: Where the broker gave the invoices under a contract to a seller and buyer, and if the two invoices differed as to the quantity sold and purchased, there was no enforceable contract.

(f) *Mistake as to the Quality of the Subject matter:* There is no contract, if the subject matter is something essentially different from what the parties thought it to be.

Example: A contract for the sale of a horse believed to be a race horse would be void if it turned out to be a cart horse.

2. **Mistake as to the Possibility of Performing the Contract:** Where the agreement is impossible to perform but the fact of impossibilities is unknown to both the parties, the agreement is void. This mistake may be classified into: (a) physical impossibility, and (b) legal impossibility.

(a) *Physical Impossibility:* The performance of an agreement becomes impossible when the purpose for which it is made has been defeated.

Example: A hired a room from B for watching the coronation procession of King Edward VII. Unknown to both the parties, the procession has already been cancelled. This agreement was held to be void as both the parties were mistaken about the fact of the impossibility of performance. [*Griffith* v. *Brymer* (1903) 19 TLR 434].

(b) *Legal Impossibility:* A contract is void where it provides that something should be done which cannot legally be done.

Example: A person cannot take lease of his own land.

Unilateral Mistake

In this case of mistake, only one of the parties is mistaken, but the other is aware or ought to be reasonably aware of the mistake. Section 22 of the Act says "A contract is not voidable merely because it was caused by one of the parties to it being under a mistake as to a matter of fact".

A party's ignorance as to the meaning of a trade description, his offering a price higher than the good's real value, or his mistake as to his ability to perform the contract, are not grounds for avoiding the contract. But to this rule there are certain exceptions,

(a) *Unilateral Mistake as to the Nature of the Contract:* Where a person is made to enter into a contract through the inducement of another, but not through the fault of his own, there is a mistake as to the nature of the contract, and the contract is void.

In *Foster* v. *Mackinnon*, an illiterate old man signed a bill of exchange believing that it was a guarantee. This was held to be void. In the case of negotiable instruments the person pleading a mistake should not only prove the mistake but should also prove that there was no negligence on his part. In this case the jury found that the old man was misled by false representation and he was not negligent.

(b) *Mistake as to the Identity of the Party Contracted with:* The mistake about identity occurs when one of the parties represents himself to be some person other than he really is or where a party enters into an agreement with some person believing him to be some other person.

Example: If A intends to enter into an agreement only with B but enters into an agreement with C believing him to be B. In such a case the contract is void.

In *Boulton* v. *Jones* (1887) 2H & N.564, it was held that the contract was vitiated by a mistake. Where W intended to contract only with X but entered into a contract with Y, believing him to be X.

In *Philips* v. *Brooks* (1919) 2KB.234, a fraudulent person X entered a jewellers shop and selected certain jewels and signed a cheque in payment pretending that he was Y, a respectable gentleman. X was allowed to take away the jewels in exchange for the cheque. Here, as the jeweller was dealing with a casual customer there was no mistake as to the identity of the person and the contract was not void as being vitiated by mistake but only voidable because of the fraud.

(c) *Mistake as to the Quality of Promise:* If a party to an agreement is under a mistake as to the quality of the promise which the seller is making, the agreement is void.

Where X accepted an offer from Y but if Y knows that X really does not so assent, there will be no genuine agreement. The misapprehension on the part of X, if known to Y invalidates the contract.

The mistake as to the quality of promise should not be confused with the mistake as to the quality of the subject matter. Here, the maxim is "Caveat emptor", let the buyer beware.

REVIEW QUESTIONS

1. Define the term 'consent'. When is consent said to be free? What is the effect of flaw in consent on the formation of the contract?

2. Define the term 'coercion'. What is the effect of coercion on the validity of the contract?

3. Define the term 'undue influence'. What is the effect of undue influence on the validity of a contract?

4. Define the term 'fraud'. What is its effect on the validity of a contract?

5. Define 'misrepresentation'. Distinguish it from fraud.

6. Define the term 'mistake'. Explain the law relating to the effect of mistake on contracts.

PRACTICAL PROBLEMS

Attempt the following problems, giving reasons.

1. X, an old man of feeble sight endorsed a bill of exchange of ₹5,000 thinking that it was a guarantee. Is X liable?

   Hint: No. [*Foster* v. *Mackinnon*]

2. A, a T.B. patient is induced by B his medical attendant to agree to pay B an unreasonable fee for his professional services. Can A avoid the contract? Give reasons.

   Hint: Yes. A can avoid the contract on the plea of undue influence.

3. P advanced money to his son Q during his minority. Upon Q coming of age P gets a bond from Q for a larger amount than the sum due in respect of the advances. Is Q bound by the bond?

   Hint: The contract is voidable at the option of Q as it is induced by undue influence.

4. A woman fraudulently represented to a firm of jewellers that she was the wife of a certain baron and thus obtained two pearl necklaces on credit on some pretext to buy them. She sold those necklaces to P, a third person. Can the jewellers recover the necklace from P?

   Hint: Yes.

5. A agreed to sell B a cargo of corn supposed to be on its way from Salonica to the U.K. At the time of the contract, however, the cargo having fermented had been sold by the Master of Ship. Discuss the rights of A and B.

   Hint: The agreement is void [*Couturier* v. *Hastie*].

7

Legality of Consideration and Object

Every agreement of which the object or consideration is unlawful is void.

—Sec. 23

INTRODUCTION

In agreements, the terms 'object' and 'consideration' are not synonymous. The object indicates purpose or design of an agreement. It implies the manifestation of intention. The consideration is some act or abstinence or reciprocal promises. In all agreements, both the object and the consideration should be lawful, otherwise the agreement is void. In certain cases consideration for an agreement may be lawful but the object for which the agreement was entered into may be unlawful. In these cases the agreement would also be void.

> **Example:** X executes a promissory note for ₹5,000 in favour of Y. Y has paid ₹5,000 to X. This payment by Y is the consideration. X wants to utilise the money for the marriage of his son who is a minor. This is the object and this object is forbidden by the Child Marriage Restraint Act as it is unlawful.

UNLAWFUL CONSIDERATION

The consideration of an agreement is unlawful when it is:

1. **Forbidden by Law:** The agreement is forbidden by law if the legislature penalises it or prohibits it.

   Example: X promises to pay Y ₹500 in consideration of Y setting fire to the house of Z. The consideration is forbidden by law.

2. **Fraudulent:** An agreement to defraud creditors in order to defeat their rights is void.

Example: X promises to pay ₹2,000 to Y in consideration of Y taking an ostensible transfer of the entire property of X to defeat and delay creditors of A.

3. **Implied or Involved Injury to the Person or Property of Another:** The word injury means criminal or wrongful harm. The consideration of an agreement is said to be unlawful if it tends to injure, the person or property of another.

> **UNLAWFUL CONSIDERATION**
> - Forbidden by law
> - Fraudulent
> - Implied or involved injury to the person or property of another
> - Calculated to defeat provisions of any law
> - Immoral
> - Opposed to public policy

Example: X agrees to pay ₹2,000 to Y in consideration of Y causing hurt to Z.

4. **Calculated to Defeat Provisions of any Law:** If the consideration of an agreement is of such a nature that, if permitted it would defeat the provisions of any law, the agreement is void.

Example: An agreement to extend the period of limitation as laid down by the Limitation Act.

5. **Immoral:** The term immoral means inconsistent with what is right. Where the consideration of an agreement is such that the Court regards it as immoral, the consideration is void.

Example: An agreement for illicit cohabitation, or for separation between husband and wife.

6. **Opposed to Public Policy:** Public policy is that principle of law which holds that no citizen can lawfully do that which has a tendency to be injurious to the public. A contract which is opposed to the public policy cannot be enforced by either of the parties thereto.

Example: An agreement which tends to promote corruptions or injustice or is against the interest of the public.

UNLAWFUL OBJECTS

1. Agreement in restraint of marriage of a major. 2. Agreement in restraint of trade. 3. Agreement in restraint of legal proceedings. 4. Wagering agreements.

UNLAWFUL AND ILLEGAL AGREEMENTS

An agreement is said to be unlawful when the object for which it is made is forbidden by law. An unlawful agreement renders the transaction between the immediate parties void, but has no effect on collateral transactions. In other words an unlawful agreement affects only the immediate parties and has no further consequences. The term illegal agreement is defined as the agreement which is expressly or impliedly prohibited by law.

> **Example:** An agreement to commit a murder or to publish a libel.

An illegal agreement is not only void as between the immediate parties, but has further effect that the collateral transactions to it also become tainted with illegality.

> **Example:** X borrows ₹500 from Y to purchase some prohibited goods from Z, an alien enemy. If X enters into an agreement with Z, it is illegal and the agreement between X and Y also becomes illegal, being collateral to the main transaction which is illegal. So Y cannot recover the amount. He can recover the amount only if he did not know the object of the loan.

Every illegal agreement is unlawful, but every unlawful agreement is not necessary illegal. It is, therefore, to be decided whether an act is illegal or unlawful.

Illegal acts are those which involve the commission of crime or contain element of obvious moral turpitude.

> **Example:** Acts opposed to public policy, illicit cohabitation, and act to defraud the revenue or commit a crime.

Unlawful acts are those which are less rigorous in effect and involve non-criminal breach of law.

> **Example:** Acts in restraint of trade, marriage or legal proceeding, etc.

AGREEMENTS OPPOSED TO PUBLIC POLICY

An agreement which is harmful to the public welfare is said to be an agreement opposed to public policy.

In *Egerton* v. *Brownlow* (1853) 4 H.L. Cas.1, Lord Truro observed that "public policy is the principle of law which holds that no subject can lawfully do that which has a tendency to be injurious to the public or against public good".

The term is vague and elastic. It is not defined with precision anywhere. A judge can, therefore, invalidate with an excuse any contract which he violently disliked.

In *Richardson* v. *Mellish* (1824) 2 Bind.229, 252, Burlough J. pointed out that "public policy is a very unruly horse and when once you get astride it, you may never know where it will carry you". It will lead you from the sound law. No doubt, public policy, which is variously described as a very unruly horse, should be keenly handled, otherwise it will take the Courts to difficult and unexpected heights and regions.

Although the law relating to public policy cannot remain immutable, it is the policy of the Courts in the interest of the stability not to discover new heads of public policy.

The following agreements are void as being against public policy but they are not illegal:

(a) **Agreement in Restraint of Marriage:** An agreement not to marry at all or not to marry any particular person or class of person, other than minor, is void as it is restraint of marriage.

(b) **Agreement in Restraint of Parental Rights:** An agreement by which a party deprives himself of the custody of his child is void.

(c) **Agreements which Interfere with Administration of Justice:**

   (i) *Interference with the Court of Justice:* An agreement for using improper influence of any kind with the judges or officers of justice is void.

   (ii) *Stifling Prosecutions:* An agreement not to prosecute an offender is an agreement for stifling prosecution and is void.

   (iii) *Maintenance and Champerty:* Maintenance means an officious meddling in a suit in which the meddler has no interest, especially by providing funds to aid the prosecution or defence. Here the desire on the part of the person is simply to stir up litigation.

AGREEMENT OPPOSED TO PUBLIC POLICY
• Agreement in restraint of marriage
• Agreement in restraint of parental right
• Agreements which interfere with administration of justice
• Agreement in restraint of personal freedom
• Marriage brokerage agreement
• Agreement in restraint of trade

Champerty means the sharing of the proceeds of litigation by a person who promotes it or carries it on, illegal in many jurisdictions. Here the desire is to share the proceeds of litigation.

In England, both maintenance and champerty are illegal and unenforceable. In India, however, maintenance and champerty are not regarded as unlawful.

(d) **Agreements in Restraint of Personal Freedom are Void:** Where a man agreed with his moneylender not to change his residence or his employment or to part with any of his property or to incur any obligation on credit without the consent of the moneylender, it was held that the agreement was void [*Horwood* v. *Millar's Timber & Trading Co.* (1917) 1 K.B. 305].

(e) **Marriage Brokerage Agreement:** An agreement to procure marriage for reward is void.

(f) **Agreement in Restraint of Trade:** An agreement in restraint of trade is one which seeks to restrict a person from freely exercising his trade or profession.

Section 27 of the Contract Act provides that "every agreement by which any one is restrained from exercising a lawful profession, trade or business of any kind, is to that extent void".

From the above wordings it is clear that every kind of restraint, whether partial or total falls within the prohibition of this Section.

In England, Courts have held that if a restraint is reasonable, it is valid. A celebrated case on this point is *Nordenfelt* v. *Maxim Nordenfelt Guns Co.* (1894) A.C. 535.

In the above case Nordenfelt was an inventor and a manufacturer of guns and ammunition. He sold his worldwide business to Maxim, with a promise that he would not make guns anywhere in the world for 25 years.

The House of Lords held that the agreement was reasonable and enforceable as it was not injurious to the public. In this regard, unlike the English Law, the Indian Law has certain statutory exceptions.

EXCEPTIONS

Where a partial and reasonable restraint falls under any of the following exceptions, the agreement will, be enforceable.

(a) *Sale of Goodwill.* If the seller of the goodwill of a business undertakes not to carry on similar business within the specified local limits for a specified period with the buyer of the goodwill the contract is enforceable.

(b) *Partner's Agreement.* Agreements between partners to provide that a partner shall not carry on any business other than that of the firm so long as he remains a partner [Sec. 11(2) of the Partnership Act, 1932].

(g) A partner may make an agreement with his partners that on ceasing to be a partner he will not carry on any business similar to that of the firm within a specified period or within specified local limits [Sec. 36(2) and 54 of the Partnership Act, 1932].

REVIEW QUESTIONS

1. Under what circumstances are the object and consideration of an agreement deemed to be unlawful? Explain with examples.
2. Distinguish between unlawful and illegal agreements. What are the effects of illegal agreements on main transaction and on collateral transaction?
3. Explain the doctrine of public policy. Give examples of agreements contrary to public policy.
4. Write short notes on:

    (a) Agreement in restraint of trade
    (b) Agreements which interfere with administration of justice
    (c) Unlawful objects
    (d) Agreement in restraint of marriage

PRACTICAL PROBLEMS

Attempt the following problems, giving reasons.

1. P promises to drop prosecution which he had instituted against Q for a dacoity and Q promises to restore the value of the things taken. Is this agreement enforceable?

    Hint: No, as it is an agreement for stifling prosecution.
2. X sells the goodwill of his business to Y, and agrees with him to refrain from carrying on a similar business within the specified local limits. Is this agreement valid?

    Hint: Yes.

3. X promises to pay ₹1,000 to Y who is an intended witness in a suit against X in consideration of Y's absconding at the trial. Y absconds but fails to obtain the money. Can Y recover the money?

   Hint: No. Y cannot recover the money as the agreement is void, being opposed to public policy.

8

Contingent Contracts and Wagering Contracts

A contingent contract is a contract to do or not to do something if some event collateral to such a contract does or does not happen.

—Sec. 31

CONTINGENT CONTRACT

A contract may be either, an absolute contract or a contingent contract. An absolute contract is one in which the promise is to be performed independently of any contingency or condition. A contingent contract is a contract which is dependent on the happening or non-happening of some event. The performance of a contingent contract becomes due only on the happening or non-happening of some future uncertain event. A contracts to pay ₹5,000 if the house of X is harm. This is an instance of contingent contract. Contracts of insurance, indemnity and guarantee, etc., are further examples.

The essential features of the contingent contract are the following:

(a) There must be a valid contract.

(b) The performance of the contract must be conditional.

(c) The condition must relate to a future event which may or may not happen.

(d) The event should be collateral to the contract.

The rules relating to the contingent contracts are dealt with in Secs. 32 to 36 of the Contract Act. Contingent contracts cannot be enforced until the occurrence of contingency. If the circumstances have rendered the occurrence or the non-occurrence of that contingency impossible, the contract becomes void. Where the contingency is the non-happening of some event, the contract can be enforced when the happening becomes impossible. Where a time is stipulated for the happening or non-happening of a specified uncertain event and such a stipulation expires without the happening or non-happening of the event, as the case may be, the contract can be enforced. Where the

59

events contingent are inherently impossible, the contract is void. As for instance, X promises to pay Y ₹2,000 if Y touches the sky with his finger, the contract is void.

WAGERING CONTRACT (SEC. 30)

A wager is an agreement to pay money or money's worth on the happening of a specified uncertain event.

A wagering contract is one in which reciprocal promises are made to give money or something of value upon the result of a future uncertain event with regard to which the parties hold opposite views.

Wager means a bet. It is a game of chance, i.e., the chance of either winning or losing is wholly dependent upon an uncertain event. Each party stands equally to win or lose the bet. One of the essential ingredients of wagering contract is that neither of the parties should have any interest in the contract other than the sum which will win or lose.

> **Example:** Suppose X and Y take a bet that if it rains tomorrow Y will pay X ₹500 and if it does not rain tomorrow X will pay Y ₹500. This is a Wagering contract.

In India except the Bombay Presidency, wagering contracts are void. In Bombay, wagering contracts have been declared illegal by the Avoiding Wagers (Amendment) Act, 1865. So in the Bombay Presidency, a wagering contract being illegal is void, but it also taints and renders void a collateral agreement to it.

> **Example:** Suppose, X bets with Y and loses, applies to Z for a loan who, pays Y in settlement of the loss of X. Z cannot recover the amount from X because this is money paid 'under' or 'in respect of' a wagering transaction which is illegal in Bombay. But in the other parts of India such a transaction only being void, Z could recover the amount from X. But if X refuses to pay Y, the amount of the bet that he has lost, Y could not sue X anywhere.

Sometimes, commercial transactions assume the form of wagering contracts. The simple test is to know whether a particular transaction is a wager or a genuine commercial transaction. Where delivery of the goods sold is intended to be given and taken it is a valid contract, but where only the differences are intended to be paid, it will be a wagering contract and unenforceable.

A lottery is a wagering transaction and hence it is illegal and punishable under Sec. 294A of Indian Penal Code. But the

Government may give sanction for conducting lotteries. The only effect of such a sanction is that no prosecution can be had under the penal law.

Difference between a Wager and a Contingent Contract

(a) Under Sec. 30, wagering contracts are void, but contingent contracts are good if they are not declared by law to be bad.

(b) In a wagering contract neither of the parties should have any interest in the contract except for the stake. But in a contingent contract the parties should have interest on the happening or non-happening of the event.

(c) In a wagering contract, there must be mutual promises, but in a contingent contract mutual promises are not necessary.

(d) In the case of a wagering contract, the parties have no intention to perform the contract itself. But in a contingent contract the parties have an intention to perform their respective obligation.

REVIEW QUESTIONS

1. Define 'contingent contract'. What are the rules relating to contingent contract?

2. Distinguish between a wagering agreement and a contingent contract.

PRACTICAL PROBLEMS

Attempt the following problems, giving reasons.

1. X agrees to pay a sum of ₹1,000 to Y when Y marries Z. Z marries W. Is the agreement enforceable?

   Hint: No. When Z marries M, the marriage of Y to Z becomes impossible, although it is possible that M may die and Z may afterwards marry Y. The contract, till this contingency happens, stands discharged and Y cannot recover the amount from X.

2. X promises to pay Y a sum of ₹5,000 if a certain yacht does not return. The yacht is sunk. X refuses to pay. Advice Y.

   Hint: Y can enforce the agreement when the yacht sinks.

3. P lends a sum of ₹1,000 to Q in Bombay in order to enable him to bet with R as to the result of a horse race. Can P recover the amount from Q?

   Hint: Yes.

9

Quasi Contracts

"Law as well as justice should try to prevent unjust enrichment." The term *unjust enrichment means the enrichment of one person at the cost of another.*

—Lord Mansfield

INTRODUCTION

Quasi means 'as if'. In a Quasi contract there is no real contract, arising from the meeting of the minds, but the law attributes to a particular situation and the consequences which are similar to those of a contract. Under English law, quasi contract is an obligation, which the law creates in the absence of any agreement. However the Indian Contract Act does not use the term 'quasi contract' for such an obligation. It describes the quasi contracts as "Certain relations resembling those created by contract."

A quasi contract rests on the equitable principle that a person shall not be allowed to enrich himself unjustly at the expense of another. The maxim is "Nemo debet Locuplatari ex lina justua". No man must grow rich out of another person's loss.

Definition

Winfield defines quasi contract as a "liability, not exclusively referable to any other head of law, imposed on a particular person to pay money to another, on the ground of unjust benefit".

Jenks defines quasi contract as "a situation in which law imposes upon one person on grounds of natural justice, an obligation similar to that which arises from a true contract, although no contract, express or implied, has in fact been entered into by them".

INSTANCES OF QUASI CONTRACTS

Sections 68 to 72 deal with the following types of quasi contracts:

(a) Necessaries supplied (Sec. 68).

(b) Suit for the recovery of money (Secs. 69 and 72).

(c) Quantum Meruit.

(d) Obligation of finder of lost goods (Sec. 71).

(e) Obligation of person enjoying benefit of a non-gratuitous act (Sec. 70).

(a) Necessaries Supplied (Sec. 68): A person who supplies the necessaries to an incompetent person, is entitled to be reimbursed from the property of such incompetent person even if there is no contract between them.

Example: A supplied to B, a lunatic, the necessaries suitable to his conditions in life. In this case, A is entitled to be reimbursed from the property of B.

(b) Suit for the Recovery of Money (Secs. 69 and 72): The right to file a suit for the recovery of money may occur under the following conditions:

1. *Where the plaintiff paid money to the defendant:* (i) under a mistake; (ii) in pursuance of a contract the consideration for which has failed; (iii) under coercion, oppression, extortion or other such means.

   Example: A pays ₹1,000 to B by mistake. It is really due to C. B must refund the money to A. C, however, cannot recover the amount as there is no privity of contract between B and C.

   A debtor may recover from a creditor any excess payment made to him by mistake. The mistake may be one of facts or of laws:

   Example: An insurance company paid the amount on a policy under the mistake that the goods had been destroyed by a peril insured against. The goods in fact had been sold. Held, the money could be recovered by the insurance company [*Norwhich etc., Society Ltd.* v. *Price (W.H.) Ltd*].

2. *Payment of money to a third party which another is bound to pay:* It should be remembered that, in order to be able to recover, the plaintiff must have been compelled by the law to pay, or the plaintiff himself has an interest in the payment.

   Example: Where A's goods are wrongfully attached in order to realise arrears of Government revenue from B, and A pays the amount to save his goods from being sold, he is entitled to recover the amount from B.

3. *Money obtained by the defendant from third parties on the plaintiff's account*

Example: Where an agent has got a secret commission or a fraudulent payment from a third party, the principal can recover the amount from the agent.

(c) **Quantum Meruit:** Quantum Meruit means "as much as he deserves". A claim for the recovery of reasonable remuneration may be enforced even if there is no express agreement provided the services are not intended to be gratuitous.

Example: A renders services to B without intending them to be gratuitous. B has to pay quantum meruit.

Actual quasi contractual claims arise in situations where the obligation of payment is imposed irrespective of any contract between the parties. Such claims arise in the following cases: (i) Necessaries supplied to persons under disability. (ii) When a contract is frustrated, the person who has received the benefit has to refund it. (iii) When a party to a contract commits a breach of it.

(d) **Obligation of Finder of Lost Goods (Sec. 71):** A person who finds goods belonging to another and takes them into his custody is bound to account for the goods to the owner. The liability of a finder of goods is that of a bailee and hence he must not appropriate the goods to his own use. If the owner is traced, he must return the goods to him. The finder is entitled to get any reward that may have been offered by the owner, and also any expenses he may have incurred in protecting the property.

Example: F found a diamond on the floor of the shop of H and handed it over to H to keep it till the true owner is found. In spite of the best efforts, the true owner could not be traced. After some time F tendered to H the expenses incurred by him for tracing the true owner and requested him to return the diamond. H refused to return the diamond to F. Held, H must return the diamond to F as he alone was entitled to retain it as against every other person except the true owner. [*Hollins* v. *Fowler* LR. 7 H.L. 757].

(e) **Obligations of Person Enjoying Benefit of Non-Gratuitous Act (Sec. 70):** Where a person lawfully does anything for another, or delivers anything to him not intending to do so gratuitously, and when such another person enjoys the benefit thereof the latter is bound to make compensation to the former in respect of or to restore, the thing so done or delivered.

Example: X, a merchant leaves some goods at the house of Y by mistake. Y treats the goods as his own. He is bound to pay X for them.

REVIEW QUESTIONS

1. Define 'Quasi contracts'. State and discuss their nature and kind.

2. Write short notes on:

   (a) Quantum meruit

   (b) Obligation of finder of lost goods

   (c) Nemo debet Locuplatari ex lina justua

PRACTICAL PROBLEMS

Attempt the following problems, giving reasons.

1. Certain furniture belonging to X are wrongfully attached in order to realise arrears of Government revenue due by Y. X pays the amount to save the furniture from sale. Is X entitled to recover the amount from Y?

   Hint: Yes.

2. X, a merchant leaves some goods at the house of Y by mistake. Y treats the goods as his own. What are the rights of the X?

   Hint: Y is bound to pay for them to X.

3. P saves the property of Q from fire, intending to do so gratuitously. Subsequently he claims compensation from Q on the ground that Q enjoyed the benefit of the act of P. Will P succeed?

   Hint: No.

10

Performance of Contract

Performance of contract consists in doing or causing to be done what the promisor has promised to do.

INTRODUCTION

Performance of contract takes place when the parties to a contract fulfil their respective obligations. Performance may be actual or attempted. Actual performance occurs when a party has done what he undertook to do. A contract need not be actually performed. The party who is bound to perform his obligation under the contract may make an offer to the other party to perform his obligation. An offer to perform obligation is called 'attempted performance' or 'tender of performance'.

Performance of obligations undertaken by the parties of the contract is called the discharge by performance. But the performance must be in conformity with the terms of the contract. Section 37 of the Act lays down that "the parties to a contract must either perform, or offer to perform their respective promises, unless such performance is dispensed with or excused under the provisions of this Act, or any other law".

In case the promisor dies before the performance of a contract, his promises are binding to his representatives, unless a contrary intention appears from the contract. In the case of contracts involving special personal qualifications of the promisor, the promisor himself must perform the contract.

> **Example:** X promises to paint a wall for Y on a certain day at a certain price. X dies before the day, the contract cannot be enforced either by representatives of X or by Y.

OFFER OF PERFORMANCE OR TENDER

Tender is an offer of performance. Where the promisor has made an offer of performance and the offer has been refused, the promisor is not responsible for non-performance.

> **Example:** A party who has entered into a contract to deliver goods or to pay money to another is deemed to have performed it if he has offered the goods or money to the party to whom the delivery or payment was to be made.

An offer of performance is also known as 'attempted performance'. It falls short of actual performance solely because of the wrongful refusal by the promisee. The effect of the tender is to discharge the promisor from responsibility for non-performance and at the same time to preserve his right intact, under the contract.

Section 38 reads, thus, "where a promisor had made an offer of performance to the promise, and the offer has not been accepted, the promisor is not responsible for non-performance, nor does he thereby lose his rights under the contract".

Conditions of a Valid Tender

To be valid a tender has to fulfil the following conditions:
  (a) It should be unconditional.
  (b) It must be made at a proper time and place.
  (c) Opportunity should be given to inspect the goods; and the goods offered must be identical with the sample.
  (d) The person tendering should have the ability to perform the promise.
  (e) Tender to one of several joint promisees is tender to all of them.

CONTRACTS WHICH NEED NOT BE PERFORMED

A contract need not be performed:
  (a) If the parties to a contract agree to substitute a new contract for it or to rescind or alter it (Sec. 62).
  (b) When the promisee dispenses with or remits, wholly or in part, the performance of the promise or extends the time for such performance or accepts any satisfaction in lieu thereof (Sec. 63).

(c) When a voidable contract is set aside, the other party need not perform his promise (Sec. 64).

(d) Where the promisee neglects or refuses to afford the promisor reasonable opportunities for the performance of his promise (Sec. 67).

(e) When it is illegal.

WHO CAN DEMAND PERFORMANCE?

It is only the promisee or his agent who can demand performance of the promise, even if the promise is not made for the benefit of the promisee. When the promisee dies, his legal representative can demand performance.

PERSONS WHO SHOULD PERFORM THE CONTRACT

(a) If the contract is personal by the promisor himself.

(b) If the contract is non-personal:

  (i) by the promisor himself, or

  (ii) by the agent of the promisor, or

  (iii) by the legal representatives in the event of the promisor's death.

(c) If the contract is made by joint promisors—by the promisors jointly or the third person on behalf of the promisors or their legal representatives.

MODE OF PERFORMANCE

Unlike the English Law, the Indian Law requires demand for performance unless dispensed with (Sec. 48). With regard to the time and place of performance, it should be performed within the time and at the place fixed in the contract. Unless the time is fixed, the performance should be made within a reasonable time according to the circumstances of the case (Sec. 50). Unless the place is mentioned in the contract, the place of performance should be in the place implied in the contract, or the promisor must ask the promisee where the place of performance is to be (Sec. 49). It is a general rule that it is the duty of the promisor to seek out the promisee and perform the contract.

JOINT PROMISORS AND JOINT PROMISEES

A promise made by two or more persons may be either a joint promise or a joint and several promise. In India, all joint promises are joint and several in the absence of a contract to the contrary. But in England, every joint promise is not a joint and several promise.

JOINT PROMISES

When two or more individuals are bound to perform the promises together and one of them is sued alone, he has a right to insist on the other being joined as co-defendants.

JOINT AND SEVERAL PROMISES

In the case of joint and several promises, each promisor will be bound along with the other promisors and also individually to perform the whole of the promise.

DEVOLUTION OF JOINT LIABILITIES

When two or more persons have made a joint promise, all such persons should fulfil the promise in the absence of a contract to the contrary. If any one of them dies, his legal representative along with the survivors must perform the promise. After the death of the last survivor, the legal representatives of all are jointly liable to carry out the promise (Sec. 42).

In the case of joint promises any one of the joint promisors may be compelled to perform the whole promise in the absence of express agreement to the contrary. In such cases, each promisor may compel every other joint promisor to contribute equally to the discharge of the promise, unless otherwise provided. In case any one of the joint promisors makes a default in such a contribution, the remaining joint promisors should equally bear the loss arising from such a default (Sec. 43).

> **Examples:** (a) X, Y and Z jointly promise to pay a sum of ₹5,000 to W. W may compel either X, or Y or Z, to pay him ₹5,000. (b) X, Y and Z jointly promise to pay a sum of ₹3,000 to W. Z is compelled to pay the whole. X is insolvent but his assets are sufficient to pay one half of his debts. Z is entitled to receive ₹500 from the estate of X and ₹1,250 from Y.

DEVOLUTION OF JOINT RIGHT

When a person has made a promise to two or more persons jointly, the right to demand the performance of the promise rests with the joint promisees during their joint lives unless otherwise provided. In case any one of them dies, the legal representatives of the deceased along with the survivors have the right to claim the performance. After the death of the last survivor, the legal representatives of all jointly have the right to claim performance (Sec. 45).

> **Example:** X and Y jointly lend ₹3,000 to Z who promises X and Y jointly to repay them that sum with interest on a day specified. Y dies. The right to claim performance rests with the representatives of Y jointly with X during the life of X and after the death of X with representatives of X.

APPROPRIATION OF PAYMENTS

Where a debtor owes several distinct debts to his creditor and pays him a sum of money which is insufficient to discharge the entire debt, the debtor has a right to appropriate it either expressly or by implication towards any debt due to his creditor (Sec. 59).

> **Example:** X owes Y among other debts a sum of ₹367. Y writes to X and demands the payment of this sum. X sends a sum of ₹367 to Y. This payment is to be applied to the discharge of the debt of which Y had demanded payment.

Where the mode of payment is not expressed or implied from circumstances, the right of appropriation of payment to various debts devolves upon the creditor and it is open to him to apply the payment to any debt lawfully due from the debtor even to the one barred by limitation (Sec. 60).

> **Example:** X owes several debts to Y and one of them of ₹6,000 is time barred. X sends ₹11,000 to Y, without indicating to which debt the amount is to be appropriated. Y may appropriate ₹6,000 against the time barred debt if he so chooses.

If the creditor or the debtor has not made any appropriation then it has to be applied in the discharge of the debts in order of time. If there are more than one debt on the same day, the payment shall be applied in the discharge of each proportionately (Sec. 61).

Example: X owes two debts of ₹4,000 each, which are time barred and another debt of ₹8,000 to Y. X sends ₹4,000. Neither party makes any appropriation. A sum of ₹4,000 would be appropriated ratably against the two debts of ₹4,000 each, which are time barred, i.e., ₹2,000 would be appropriated against each debt.

ASSIGNMENT OF CONTRACTS

Assignment of a contract means transfer of contractual rights and liabilities under the contract to a third party.

Assignment is possible by operation of law or by act of parties in certain cases. An assignment by operation of law arises on the death, insolvency, or marriage of one of the parties. An assignment by act of the parties is subject to the following rules.

(a) Contracts involving personal skill or ability or other personal qualifications cannot be assigned.

(b) A promisor cannot assign his liabilities or obligations under a contract.

(c) The rights and benefits under a contract may be assigned if the obligation under a contract is not of a personal nature.

(d) An actionable claim can always be assigned but the assignment to be complete and effectual must be effected by an instrument in writing.

Examples of actionable claim are: A money debt, shares in a company and a right of action arising out of contract.

REVIEW QUESTIONS

1. What do you understand by performance of a contract? Explain the rules of law relating to time and place of performance of a contract.

2. Explain the term 'tender'. What are the conditions of a valid tender?

3. Write short notes on:
   (a) Joint promises   (b) Devolution of joint liabilities
   (c) Assignment of contracts

4. What do you understand by appropriation of payment? State the rules relating to appropriation of payments made by a debtor to his creditor.

PRACTICAL PROBLEMS

Attempt the following problems, giving reasons.

1. P, Q and R jointly promise to pay W a sum of ₹10,000. Can W compel P or Q or R to pay him ₹10,000?

   Hint: Yes.

2. X, Y and Z jointly promise to pay W ₹5,000. X and Y are untraceable. Can W compel Z to pay him in full?

   Hint: Yes.

3. P lends three sums to Q of Rs. 200, ₹400 and ₹1,000. Q sends a cheque of ₹200 asking P to appropriate this money towards the third debt of ₹1,000. P wants to appropriate this money to the first loan. Can he do so?

   Hint: No.

11

Discharge of Contract

Discharge of contract means the termination of the contractual relationship between the parties thereto.

A contract is said to be discharged when the rights and liabilities created by it come to an end. A contract may be terminated or discharged by any one of the following ways:

1. By performance (Secs. 37 and 38)
2. By agreement or consent (Secs. 62 and 63)
3. By impossibility (Sec. 56)
4. By lapse of time
5. By operation of law
6. By breach of contract (Sec. 39)

DISCHARGE BY PERFORMANCE

Performance of contract is one of the obvious methods of discharging a contract. It takes place when the parties to a contract fulfil their respective obligations (Refer to previous chapter too).

DISCHARGE BY AGREEMENT OR CONSENT

The rule of law in this regard is based on the maxim "Eodem modoe quo quid constitutur, eodem modo destruitur". It means that a thing may be destroyed in the same manner in which it is constituted. The discharge by consent may be expressed or implied. Sections 62 and 63 deal with provisions of discharge by mutual agreement.

Section 62 provides that if the parties to a contract agree to substitute a new contract for it, or to rescind or alter it, the original contract need not be performed.

73

Section 63 embodies that "every promisee may dispense with or remit, wholly or in part, the performance of the promise made to him, or may extend the time of such performance, or may accept instead of any satisfaction which he thinks fit".

The various modes of discharge of a contract by mutual agreement under Secs. 62 and 63 are:

1. **Novation:** Novation is the super-session of one contract by a new contract. The new contract may be between one of them and a third party.

   Example: X owes Y ₹5,000. He enters into an agreement with Y and gives Y a mortgage of his (X's) estate for ₹2,500 in place of the debt of ₹5,000.

   > **METHODS OF DISCHARGE OF CONTRACT BY MUTUAL AGREEMENT**
   > - Novation
   > - Rescission
   > - Alteration
   > - Remission
   > - Waiver
   > - Accord and satisfaction
   > - Merger

   This is a new contract which extinguishes the old one. Novation should take place before the breach of the contract occurs. If for any reason, the new contract proves to be invalid, the old contract which is superseded stands revived.

2. **Recission:** Recission is the cancellation of the agreement. If the parties to an agreement agree to rescind it, the original agreement need not be carried out.

   Example: X promises to deliver certain goods to Y on a certain date. Before the date of performance, X and Y mutually agree that the contract will not be performed. The contract is said to be rescinded.

3. **Alteration:** Alteration of a contract occurs when the terms of the contract are varied by mutual consent of the parties to a contract.

   Example: X enters into a contract with Y for the supply of 200 bales of cotton by the 10th of the next month. X and Y may vary the terms of the contract by mutual consent.

4. **Remission:** Remission of a contract indicates the acceptance of a lesser sum than what was contracted for.

   Example: X owed ₹4,000 to Y. X paid ₹3,000 to Y and Y accepted it in full satisfaction. In this case X is discharged from his liability of ₹4,000.

5. **Waiver:** Waiver is the intentional relinquishment of a claim which a person is entitled to. Neither an agreement nor a consideration is required to constitute a waiver.

Example: X promises to paint a picture for Y. Y later on forbids him to do so. X is no longer bound to perform the promise.

6. **Accord and Satisfaction:** Accord and satisfaction is the acceptance of any other satisfaction than the performance originally agreed. In other words, accord is the agreement by which the obligation is discharged and satisfaction is the consideration which makes the agreement operative.

   Example: A owes B ₹2,000. B agrees to accept ₹1,500 in full satisfaction. The agreement to pay ₹1,500 is an accord and the actual payment is the satisfaction.

7. **Merger:** Merger occurs when a superior right and an inferior right concur and meet in one and the same person, the inferior right vanishes into the superior right.

   Example: A holds a property under a lease. He later buys the property. His right as a lessee merges into his right as an owner.

DISCHARGE BY IMPOSSIBILITY OF PERFORMANCE

Discharge by impossibility of performance is based on the maxims:

(a) "lex non cogit ad impossibilia", i.e., the law does not recognise what is impossible, and

(b) "impossibilium nulla obligatio est", i.e., what is impossible does not create an obligation.

Impossibility of the performance of a contract may appear on the face of it, or may exist unknown to the parties at the time of making the contract or may arise after the contract is made. In the first case the contract is void ab initio. In the second case the contract is void and it is known as the doctrine of 'supervening impossibility' or 'supervening illegality'.

A contract is discharged by supervening impossibility in the following circumstances:

(a) Destruction of subject matter of the contract, (b) Death or disablement of parties, (c) Contract becoming subsequently illegal, (d) Declaration of war, (e) Non-existence of particular state of things, (f) Frustration.

(a) **Destruction of Subject matter of the Contract:** When the subject matter of the contract is destroyed without any fault of the parties, the contract is said to be discharged.

   In *Taylor* v. *Caldwell* (1863) 122 E.R. 299, a music hall was agreed to be let out on certain dates, but before those dates it was destroyed by fire. Held, the contract was void.

(b) **Death or Disablement of Parties:**   When the death or illness of a particular person prevents him from fulfilling the promise, he should be absolved from performance. This is because of the fact that the death or disablement is an act of God over which he has no control.

In *Robinson* v. *Davison* (1871) L.R. 6 Ex. 269, a pianist fell ill, and could not play at a concert as promised by him. Held, the contract was discharged and the pianist's illness excused him from performance.

(c) **Subsequent Illegality:**   Whereby subsequent to the formation of contract the law changes and thereby the performance of a contract is forbidden, the parties are exonerated from liability to perform it.

In *Baily* v. *De Crespigny* (1868) L.R. 4 Q.B. 180, D leased some land to B and agreed to erect some ornamental building on the adjoining land. A railway company under statutory powers, acquired this adjoining land and built a railway station on it. Held, D was excused from performance of the contract.

(d) **Declaration of War:**   A contract entered into with an alien enemy during the war is void 'ab initio'. A contract entered into prior to the outbreak of war is suspended during the war and may be revived after the war.

(e) **Non-existence or Non-occurrence of Particular State of Thing:**   If there is any change in the state of the things which formed the basis of the contract, or if the state of the things which ought to have occurred does not occur, the contract is discharged.

In *Krell* v. *Henry* (1903) 2 K.B. 740, the contract was to hire a flat for viewing the coronation procession of the King in 1902. Owing to the king's illness, the procession was given up. A suit was filed for the recovery of the rent. Held, the hirer need not pay the rent, as the existence of the procession was the basis of the contract, and its cancellation discharged the contract.

(f) **Frustration:**   Frustration means the discharge of a contract rendered impossible of performance by external causes beyond the contemplation of the parties. The effect of frustration is that the contract becomes void.

Example: X and Y contract to marry each other. Before the time fixed for the marriage, X goes mad. The contract becomes void.

The basis of the doctrine of frustration is rested upon an implied term of the contract. In England the doctrine of frustration is the parallel concept of supervening impossibility under Sec. 56 of the Contract Act. This doctrine is invoked in two classes of cases:

(i) Where a supervening event makes the performance of the obligation impossible [*Taylor* v. *Caldwell*].

(ii) Where there is a fundamental change in the situation, even though performance may not have become physically impossible.

When a contract is frustrated, future obligations are at an end.

DISCHARGE BY LAPSE OF TIME

The Limitation Act, in some circumstances, affords a good defence to suit for breach of contract, and in fact terminates the contract by depriving the party of his remedy at law.

> **Example:** Where a debtor has failed to repay the loan on the stipulated date, the creditor must file the suit against him within three years of the default. If he fails to take action before the expiration of three years he will be barred from his remedy and the other party is discharged of his liability to perform.

DISCHARGE BY OPERATION OF LAW

Discharge by operation of law may be taken place as follows:

(a) By merger. When the parties embody the inferior contract in a superior contract.

(b) By insolvency. When a person is adjudged insolvent, he is discharged from all the liabilities incurred before the adjudication.

(c) By the unauthorised alteration of terms of a written document.

Where a party to a written agreement makes any material change without the knowledge of the other, the agreement can be avoided by the other party.

DISCHARGE BY BREACH OF CONTRACT

Where the promisor neither performs his contract nor does he tender performance, or where the performance is defective, there is a breach of contract. It may be:

(a) Actual Breach of Contract; or

(b) Anticipatory or Constructive Breach of Contract.

(a) Actual Breach of Contract: The actual breach may occur either at the time the performance is due, or when actually performing the contract.

(b) Anticipatory Breach of Contract: It indicates a breach before the performance is due. This may occur either by the promisor doing an act which makes the performance of his promise impossible or by the promisor in some other way showing his intention not to perform it.

Section 39 provides that where a party to a contract refuses to perform his part of the contract, prior to the date of performance the promisee has certain rights. He can either:

(i) treat the contract as discharged so that he is exonerated of the performance of his part of the promise, or

(ii) immediately take a legal action for breach of contract or wait till the due date of the performance.

Anticipatory breach does not necessarily discharge the contract, unless the aggrieved party so chooses.

In *Hochster* v. *De La Tour* (1853) 2 E&B. 678, A entered into a contract with B for B's services for three months on a foreign tour commencing from a particular date. Even before that date A wrote to B dispensing with his services. Held, B was immediately entitled to sue, without waiting till the date of performance.

Where the promisee refuses to accept the repudiation of the promisor and treats the agreement as alive, the Consequences are:

(i) The promisor may carry out his promise on the due date and the promisee should be bound to accept the performance.

(ii) If, while the agreement is alive, an event occurs which discharges the agreement legally, the promisor may take the benefit of such a discharge. In such a case, the promisee loses his right to sue for damages.

In *Avery* v. *Bowden* (1856) 116 E.R. 1122, A hired the ship of B to carry a cargo from Russia. Later B repudiated the contract. A delayed taking action hoping B would change his mind before the performance date. War broke out between Russia and Britain before the performance date, frustrating the contract held, A lost his right to sue B for damages by his delay.

REVIEW QUESTIONS

1. What do you mean by discharge of contract? State the various ways in which a contract may be said to be discharged.
2. "The law does not compel the impossible". Comment.
3. Explain the effect of supervening impossibility on the performance of contract.
4. Discuss with illustrations the doctrine of frustration.
5. What do you understand by breach of contract? Discuss in detail giving suitable examples.
6. Write short notes on:

    (a) Accord and satisfaction

    (b) Novation

    (c) Anticipatory breach of contract

    (d) Discharge of contract by 'remission'

PRACTICAL PROBLEMS

Attempt the following problems, giving reasons.

1. An artist undertook to paint a picture for certain price, but before he could do so, he met with an accident and lost his eye sight. Is the artist absolved from performing the contract?

    Hint: Yes. [*Robinson* v. *Davision*]

2. A agreed to let his hall to B for some public entertainment, on 1st October, 1991. On 20th September, 1991 the hall was destroyed by fire. Discuss the right of A and B.

    Hint: Yes. [*Taylor* v. *Caldwell*]

3. P owned a room in a hotel which was hired to Q for watching the coronation procession of King Edward II at £141 payable at the time of contract. £100 were paid in cash. But before the balance was paid, the procession was cancelled. Q instituted a suit for the recovery of the amount he had paid. Decide.

    Hint: Q can recover £100 paid in cash and is not bound to pay the balance.

12

Remedies for Breach of Contract

Remedy is the means given by law for the enforcement of the right.

The process of enforcing rights is known as the remedies for breach of contract. Where there is a breach of contract, the injured party has one or more of the following rights:

1. Rescission of the contract.
2. Suit for damages.
3. Suit upon quantum meruit.
4. Suit for specific performance of the contract.
5. Suit for injunction.

RESCISSION

If one party has broken his contract, the other party may treat the contract as rescinded and refuse further performance. He may also successfully defend an action of non-performance, or an action brought for specific performance.

Section 64 provides that "the party treats the contract as rescinded, if he has received any benefits thereunder from another party to such a contract and has restored such benefits to the person from whom it was received".

Section 75 provides that "a person who rightfully rescinds a contract is entitled to compensation for any damage which he has sustained through the non-fulfilment of the contract".

DAMAGES

The common law remedy for breach of contract is damages. Damages are a monetary compensation adjudged to be paid to the injured party for the loss or injury suffered by him. The principle of awarding damages is to put the injured party in the same financial position as if the contract had been performed.

Kinds of Damages

Damages are of various kinds. They are as follows:

    (a) General or ordinary or substantial damages.

    (b) Special damages.

    (c) Exemplary, or Punitive or Vindictive damages.

    (d) Nominal damages.

(a) Ordinary Damages: Damages arising from the breach of contract which are necessary to compensate the injured party for the loss sustained by such a breach.

Ordinary or general damages are usually assessed on the basis of the actual loss suffered. In the case of a breach of contract for delivery of goods, the measure of damages is the difference between the contract price and the market price.

(b) Special Damages: Special damages are granted to compensate the plaintiff for the losses resulting from special circumstances which are known to both the parties at the time of making the contract.

Example: X delivered goods to the Railway Administration to be carried to a place where an exhibition was being held and told the goods clerk that if the goods did not reach the destination on the specified date he (X) would suffer a special loss. The goods reached late. He was entitled to claim the special damages.

(c) Exemplary Damages: Exemplary damages are awarded to the plaintiff not on the basis of the actual loss caused to him but of the injury to the feelings of the aggrieved party; in order to deter other similar minded persons from doing similar wrongs.

Generally vindictive damages are not awarded for breach of contracts but are as a rule awarded in actions on tort. But there are two exceptions to this rule, viz:

    (i) breach of contract to marry,

    (ii) breach of contract by a banker possessing the funds of the customer, to honour his cheque.

Example: A libel was committed by an author and its publisher against a renowned naval officer. The officer sued for damages. He was awarded £15,000 as compensatory and £25,000 exemplary damages against both defendants. [*Broome* v. *Cassell & Co.* (1971)].

(d) Nominal Damages: Nominal damages are awarded in the case of breach of contract when there is only a technical violation of legal right, but no substantial loss is incurred. Nominal damages are only nominal in value and it is also known as contemptuous damages.

Example: A contracted to buy a Bajaj Scooter from a dealer. But he failed to buy the scooter. However, the demand for Bajaj Scooters far exceeded the supply and the scooter dealer could sell the scooter agreed to be bought without loss or profit. The dealer is entitled only to nominal damages.

MEASURE OF DAMAGES

Provisions regarding the measure of damages, both in India and England are to be found in the judgement in the leading case of *Hadley* v. *Baxendale* (1854) 9 EX 341. The facts of the case were:

The plaintiff (Hadley), the owner of the mill entrusted a broken crank shaft to the defendant (Baxendale) who was a carrier for conveying it to the repairer at Greenwich. There was a delay on the part of the carrier in sending the broken part to the repairer. The defendant was not made known that for want of the crank shaft the whole mill would remain idle. The suit was brought for damages under two heads:

1. for failure to deliver the broken part in the specified time.

2. for the loss of profit caused by the mill remaining idle.

The House of Lords allowed damages under the first head but disallowed damages under the second head as the defendant was not told of the existence of the special circumstances.

The rules based on the judgement of *Hadley* v. *Baxendale* are dealt with in Sec. 73 of the Indian Contract Act. They are:

(a) The injured party is placed in the same position as if the contract had been carried out.

(b) Damages which naturally arise in the usual course of things from such breach can be recovered.

(c) Special damages are not recoverable, unless the special circumstances are brought to the notice of the other party before the contract is made.

(d) Such a compensation is not to be given for any remote and indirect loss or damage sustained by reason of the breach.

(e) Compensation for quasi contract as damages is the same as for a contract.

LIQUIDATED DAMAGES AND PENALTY (SEC. 74)

Where the contracting parties fix at the time of the contract the amount of the damages that would be payable in the case of breach, the question may arise in the English Law whether the term amounts to a 'penalty' or liquidated damages. The Courts in England usually give effect to liquidated damages, but relieve a party against penalty.

The essential ingredient of a penalty is a payment of the money stipulated as "in terrorem" of the faulty person. But the essence of liquidated damages is a genuine covenanted pre-estimate of damages.

Thus, the liquidated damages are the fair assessment of the amount which will compensate the aggrieved party for the loss suffered due to breach of contract. Stipulation in the nature of liquidated damages is enforceable. But, the penalty is not the fair assessment of the loss for breach. The sum fixed by way of penalty is unreasonable and is used to compel the other party to perform the contract. Penalty is not recoverable.

> **Examples:** (a) A borrowed ₹200 from B and agreed to repay the same on a specified date. The contract further provided that if A failed to make the payment on the specified date, he would pay ₹400 to B as damages. In this case, the amount fixed as damages is to be considered as penalty and is not recoverable.
>
> (b) Where a building contractor contracts to build a building and deliver it to a firm to enable it to start a mill, and in the event of his failure to do so, agrees to pay ₹50 for everyday's default, the stipulation amounts only to liquidated damages and it is recoverable.

In India, there is no such difference between liquidated damages and penalty. According to Sec. 74 "Where the sum is fixed in a contract as the amount to be paid in the case of breach the party suffering from breach is entitled to receive 'reasonable compensation' up to the stipulated amount whether it is by way of liquidated damages or penalty". The court cannot increase the amount of damages beyond the amount specified in the contract itself.

Example: X borrows ₹1,000 from Y and promises to pay ₹2,000 in case he fails to repay ₹1,000 on the specified date. On the failure of X to repay on the stipulated date, Y is entitled to recover from X such a compensation, not exceeding ₹2,000 as the Court may consider reasonable.

QUANTUM MERUIT

The term quantum meruit indicates "as much as earned or in proportion to the work done". A right to sue on a quantum meruit arises where a contract partly performed by one party, has become discharged by the breach of the contract by the other party. In such cases the plaintiff is entitled to the value of the services rendered or the goods delivered till the moment of discharge not on the basis of the original contract but on the basis of the quasi contract.

SPECIFIC PERFORMANCE

Specific performance means the actual carrying out of the contract by the parties thereto. Where a party fails to carry out the contract, the Court may at its discretion, direct the defendant to perform his undertaking as per the terms of the contract. Provisions regarding the granting of this relief are dealt with in Specific Relief Act, 1877. Some of the cases in which specific performance of an agreement may be enforced are:

(a) Where compensation in money is not an adequate remedy for the breach of a contract.

(b) When there exists an impossibility for ascertaining actual damages due to non-performance.

(c) When it is probable that monetary consideration on non-performance of the act cannot be obtained.

Specific performance is not usually ordered under the following circumstances:

(a) When the compensation in money is an adequate remedy.

(b) Where the Court cannot supervise the execution of the contract, e.g., a building contract.

(c) In case the contract is for personal service.

(d) If one of the parties of a contract is a minor.

INJUNCTION

An injunction is a mode of securing the specific performance of a negative term of the contract. Where a party in a contract is in breach of a negative term of a contract (i.e., where he is doing something which he promised not to do), the Court may in its discretion issue an order to the defendant restraining him from doing what he promised not to do. Such an order of the Court is called an injunction.

In *Lumley* v. *Wagner* (1852) 90 R.R. 125, W agreed to sing at the theatre of L and nowhere else. W, in breach of contract with L entered into a contract to sing for Z. Held, W could be restrained by injunction from singing for Z.

REVIEW QUESTIONS

1. What remedies are available to an aggrieved party for the breach of a contract?
2. Examine the rule in *Hadley* v. *Baxendale*.
3. Explain briefly the principles on which damages are awarded on the breach of a contract.
4. Write short notes on:

   (a) Injunction

   (b) Special Damages

   (c) Exemplary Damages

   (d) Nominal Damages

5. Distinguish between liquidated damages and penalty.
6. When does a claim on quantum meruit arise?
7. When will a court refuse specific performance of a contract?

PRACTICAL PROBLEMS

Attempt the following problems, giving reasons.

1. P enters into a contract with Q for singing at a theatre for four nights for a fee of ₹200 for every night. She sings for three nights and falls ill. Can Q ask for damages for loss of profit from P?

   Hint: No.

2. P promised to sell to Q certain shares to be delivered on 1st January, 2006. On that date the price of shares had gone down and Q refused to take shares. P subsequently sold the

shares at a higher price than that agreed to be paid for them by Q (a) Is P entitled to sue Q for breach of contract? (b) If so, what would be the measure of damages?

Hint: (a) Yes. (b) The damages should be equivalent to the difference between the market price and the contract price on 1st January.

3. A promised to work as a personal manager for the P company for a period of 2 years at a monthly salary of ₹2,000. A worked for 3 months and then left and joined another company at a higher price. What are the rights of P company?

Hint: P company may not only treat the agreement as rescinded but also bring suit against A to recover any monetary loss suffered by it as a result of the breach.

13

Indemnity and Guarantee

The term 'indemnity' means an act to compensate or protect against loss. 'Guarantee' is a promise to pay a debt owing by a third person in case the latter does not pay.

Contracts of indemnity and guarantee, being a species of contract, are subject to all the rules of contract. Chapter VIII of the Indian Contract Act (Secs. 124 to 147) deals with the special principles relating to indemnity and guarantee.

CONTRACT OF INDEMNITY

To indemnify means to compensate or make good the loss. The object of a contract of indemnity is essentially to protect the promise against the anticipated loss. Sec. 124 of the Indian Contract Act defines a contract of Indemnity as "a contract by which one party promises to save the other from loss caused to him by the conduct of the promisor himself, or by the conduct of any other person". The person who undertakes to indemnify the loss is known as the indemnifier or promisor and the person whose loss is to be made good is called the indemnified or promisee.

> **Examples:** (1) X contracts to indemnify Y against the consequences of any proceedings which Z may take against Y in respect of a sum of ₹6,000. This is a contract of indemnity.
>
> (2) X and Y enter a shop. Y says to the owner of the shop. "Let him X have the goods, I will see you are paid". It is a contract of indemnity.

A contract of indemnity may be express or implied. An implied contract of indemnity can be inferred from the circumstances of a particular case.

CONTRACT OF GUARANTEE

Section 126 of the Indian Contract Act defines a contract of guarantee as "a contract to perform the promise, or discharge the liability of a third person in the case of his default". The person who gives the guarantee is known as the 'Surety' or 'Guarantor'; the person in respect of whose default the guarantee is given is known as the 'Principal Debtor'; and the person to whom the guarantee is given is known as the 'Creditor'.

> **Examples:** (1) X and Y enter a shop. Y says to the trader, "supply the goods required to X and if he does not pay I will". It is a contract of guarantee, the primary liability being with X, and secondary liability with Y.
>
> (2) X requests Y to lend ₹1,000 to Z and guarantee that Z will repay the amount within a specified time and on Z's failing to pay he will himself pay to Y. It is a contract of guarantee.

A contract of guarantee may be express or implied. It may be either oral or written (Sec. 126). But in England a guarantee must be in writing and signed by the party to be charged.

Distinction between indemnity and guarantee

Contract of Indemnity	*Contract of Guarantee*
1. There are two parties to it, viz., the indemnifier (promisor) and the indemnified (promisee).	There are three parties to it, viz., the creditor, the principal debtor, and the surety.
2. There is only one contract, i.e., between the indemnifier and the indemnified.	There are three contracts, i.e., one between the principal debtor and the creditor, the second between the creditor and the surety, and the third between the surety and the principal debtor.
3. The liability of the indemnifier is primary and independent.	The surety's liability is secondary or collateral arising only on the default of the principal debtor.
4. The liability of the indemnifier arises only on the happening of a contingency.	The liability of the surety is not contingent but subsisting.
5. It is made for the reimbursement of loss.	It is made to provide necessary security to the creditor against his advance.
6. It is not necessary for the indemnifier to act at the request of the indemnified.	It is necessary that the surety should give the guarantee at the request of the debtor.

RIGHTS OF INDEMNITY HOLDER OR INDEMNIFIED

Section 125 states the rights of indemnified. An indemnified is entitled to recover from the indemnifier:

(a) all damages which he may be forced to pay under the contract in any suit,

(b) all costs he may be forced to pay in any such suit. But the indemnified can recover such costs only if he had acted prudently,

(c) all sums which he may have paid under the terms of any compromise of any such suit. The compromise must not be opposed to the orders of the indemnifier and must be prudent or authorised by the indemnifier.

KINDS OF GUARANTEE

1. **Retrospective Guarantee:** A guarantee which is given for an existing debt or obligation is called retrospective guarantee.

2. **Prospective Guarantee:** A guarantee which is given for a future debt or obligation is called prospective guarantee.

KINDS OF GUARANTEE
• Retrospective guarantee
• Prospective guarantee
• Fidelity guarantee
• Specific guarantee
• Continuing guarantee

3. **Fidelity Guarantee:** A guarantee which is given for the good conduct or honesty of a person employed in a particular office is called fidelity guarantee.

4. **Specific Guarantee:** A specific or simple guarantee is one which extends to a single transaction or debt.

5. **Continuing Guarantee:** A continuing guarantee is one which extends to a series of transactions (Sec. 129).

   A continuing guarantee may be revoked or terminated as to the future transactions, by notice to the creditor (Sec. 130) or on the death of surety (Sec. 131).

NATURE OF SURETY'S LIABILITY

Section 128 of the Indian Contract Act enumerates the nature and extent of surety's liability. The liability of surety is secondary or contingent. It means that surety's liability arises only on the default of the principal debtor. So before the default of the principal debtor, if the surety becomes insolvent, the creditor cannot proceed against the surety's assignee in insolvency. But once the liability arises it is co-extensive with that of the principal debtor. It indicates that the creditor can proceed against the surety or the principal debtor at his option. The surety is liable as if he were the principal debtor. Notice of default of the principal debtor is not at all a condition precedent for proceeding against a surety. It is the duty of the surety to see the prompt payment of debt.

The quantum of obligation of a surety is the same as that of the principal debtor unless otherwise provided. The liability of surety can neither be more nor less than that of the principal debtor, though by a special agreement, it may be made less than that of the principal debtor, but never greater.

> **Example:** P gives a loan of ₹4,000 to Q. R agrees to stand as a surety for repayment to the extent of ₹2,500. Q fails to pay the whole amount. R is liable only to the extent of ₹2,500.

Further, a creditor is not bound to proceed first against the principal debtor before suing the surety, unless otherwise provided. He can sue the surety without suing the principal debtor.

A SURETY IS VERY OFTEN CALLED A 'FAVOURED DEBTOR'

This is due to the fact that, it is not open to the creditor to call upon the surety to pay upon the contract of guarantee if the creditor has not carried out his part of the contract. In the words of Lord Selborne "a surety is undoubtedly and not unjustly an object of some favour, both at law and in equity". A contract of guarantee should thus be strictly construed in favour of surety.

In *Whicher* v. *Hall*, a surety guaranteed the milking of 30 cows leased to the principal debtor. The evidence was that the lessor let the lessee 32 cows for a certain period, and 28 for another period. This variation of supply did not actually affect the profit. Held, the surety was not liable as the contract was for 30 cows and neither more nor less.

RIGHTS OF SURETY

A surety has certain rights against:

1. the creditor, 2. the principal debtor, 3. the co-sureties.

1. **Rights against the Creditor**

   (a) *Rights before Payment:* Before payment, the surety has the right to file an action for a declaration that the principal debtor is the person bound to pay the amount. In the case of fidelity guarantee, the surety can call upon the employer to dismiss the employee in the event of his proved dishonesty.

(b) *Rights when Paying:* At the time of payment, a surety is subrogated all the rights of the creditor. A surety is entitled to the benefit of every security which the creditor has (Sec. 141).

(c) *Rights of Set off:* The surety is entitled to the benefit of the principal debtor's set off against the creditor if it occurs out of the same transaction.

2. Rights against the Principal Debtor

(a) *Rights to Subrogation* (Sec. 140): After payment, the surety steps into the shoes of the creditor. He can exercise against the principal debtor all those rights and remedies which were available to the creditor.

(b) *Rights to be Indemnified* (Sec. 145): Under Sec. 145 the surety is entitled to recover from the principal debtor whatever sum he has rightfully paid under the guarantee.

(c) *Rights against Securities* (Sec. 141): As per Sec. 141 a surety is entitled to all securities which existed at the time of the contract of suretyship.

3. Rights against Co-Sureties

(a) *Rights to Contribution:* Section 146 provides, when a surety has paid more than his shares of the debt to the creditor, he has a right of contribution from the co-sureties who are equally bound to pay with him.

(b) *Liabilities of Co-sureties Bound in Different Sums* Section 147 provides, when co-sureties have agreed to contribute different sums, they are bound to contribute equally as far as the limits of their respective obligations permit.

DISCHARGE OF SURETY

A surety is said to be discharged when his liability comes to an end. A contract of suretyship may be discharged: (a) by the revocation of the contract of suretyship (b) by the contract of suretyship being invalid (c) by the contract of the creditor.

REVIEW QUESTIONS

1. Define a contract of indemnity. Explain the legal rules for a valid contract of indemnity.
2. What is a contract of guarantee? Explain the distinction between a contract of indemnity and a contract of guarantee.
3. "A surety is very often called a favoured debtor". Discuss.
4. Briefly discuss the rights of a surety against

   (a) Creditor   (b) Principal debtor

   (c) Co-sureties
5. Write short notes on:

   (a) Continuing guarantee   (b) Fidelity guarantee

   (c) Discharge of surety

PRACTICAL PROBLEMS

Attempt the following problems, giving reasons.

1. R contracts to lend Q ₹2,000 on 1st January, 2006. P guarantees repayment. R pays ₹1,000 on 1st December, 2006. Is P liable if Q makes a default?

   Hint: No.
2. X advances Y, a minor ₹10,000 on the guarantee of Z. On demand for the repayment Y refuses to pay on the ground of his minority. Can X recover the amount from Z.

   Hint: Yes.

14

Bailment and Pledge

'Bailment' means a delivery of goods on condition to redeliver them when the condition is satisfied.
'Pledge' is a transfer of goods as security for the payment of a debt or performance of a promise.

Chapter IX (Secs. 148 to 186) of the Indian Contract Act, 1872, deals with the provisions relating to bailment and pledge. They are also a special class of contracts.

BAILMENT

The term bailment originated from a French word 'bailor' which means to 'deliver'. It is a delivery of goods on condition to redeliver them when the condition is satisfied.

Section 148 of the Contract Act defines bailment as "the delivery of goods by one person to another for some purpose, upon a contract that they shall, when the purpose is accomplished, be returned or otherwise disposed of according to the direction of the person delivering them". The person who delivers the goods is called the 'bailor' and the person to whom they are delivered is called the 'bailee'.

> **Examples:** (1) X lends a book to Y to be returned after the examination. It is a contract of bailment between X and Y.
>
> (2) X deposited goods in a cloak room at railway station. The railway is liable for the goods as a bailee.

THE ESSENTIALS OF BAILMENT

1. **Delivery of Possession:** The first unique feature of bailment is that the bailor must transfer his possession of goods to the bailee. Mere custody of goods does not create the relationship of bailor and bailee.

2. **Delivery of Goods must be for a Specific Purpose:** Section 148 provides, the delivery of goods from bailor to bailee must be for some purpose. Where goods are delivered by mistake to a person, there is no bailment.

ESSENTIALS OF BAILMENT
• Delivery of possession • Delivery of goods must be for a specific purpose • Contracts • Return of goods

3. **Contract:** Bailment is based on a contract between the bailor and the bailee. Bailment also implies that there is an indirect contract between the finder of goods and the real owner.

4. **Return of Goods:** In a contract of bailment, goods must be delivered on condition that the goods should be returned to the bailor or disposed of according to his direction either in their original or in an altered form, when the purpose of bailment is over.

KINDS OF BAILMENT

Bailment may be gratuitous and non-gratuitous. Gratuitous bailment is one where the bailee keeps the goods of the bailor without reward. Non-gratuitous bailment, on the contrary is one where some consideration passes between the parties.

Bailment may also be divided in accordance with the benefits derived by the parties. They are:

(a) Bailment for the exclusive benefit of the bailor.

Example: Delivery of some valuables to a neighbour for safe custody, without charge.

(b) Bailment for the exclusive benefit of the bailee.

Example: Lending of a car to a relative for his use, without charge.

(c) Bailment for mutual benefit.

Example: Giving a watch for repair.

CONSIDERATION IN A CONTRACT OF BAILMENT

In a contract of bailment, the consideration is usually in the form of money payment by the bailor or the bailee.

Examples: (a) Giving a watch for repair.

(b) Hiring of furniture.

But consideration in the form of money is not essential to support the promise of the bailee to return the goods. The detriment suffered by the bailor, in parting with the possession of the goods, is a sufficient consideration to support a contract of bailment.

BAILEE'S LIEN

Lien is the right to retain the goods by a person in possession of the goods of another until his claims in respect of the goods are satisfied. This right is sometimes known as "possessory lien".

Possessory liens are of two types. They are: (i) Particular lien or Special lien, and (ii) General lien

(i) *Particular Lien (Sec. 170)*: A particular lien is one which is available only against that property in respect of which the skill and labour are used.

Example: Charges for the services rendered for the goods bailed.

(ii) *General Lien (Sec. 171):* A general lien is a right to detain any property belonging to the other and in the possession of the person trying to exercise the lien in respect of any payment lawfully due to him. General lien is available only to bankers, factories, wharfingers, attorneys and policy brokers.

FINDER OF LOST GOODS

Section 71 provides that "a person who finds goods belonging to another and takes them into his custody, is subject to the same responsibility as a bailee, on the basis of quasi contract."

Sections 168 and 169 deal with the rights of finder of goods. They are as follows:

1. **Right of Lien:** The finder has a right of particular lien over the property and as such he can detain the goods until he receives compensation for the troubles and expenses incurred in preserving the property and finding out the real owner. But the finder cannot file a suit for the recovery of the compensation (Sec. 168).

2. **Right to Sue for Reward:** The finder can sue the owner for any reward that might have been offered, and may retain the goods until he receives the reward (Sec. 168).

3. **Right for Sale:** The finder has a right to sell the property:

(a) Where the owner cannot be found after reasonable search, or

(b) When found, he refuses to pay the lawful charges of the finder, or

(c) If the things are in danger of perishing or losing greater parts of its value, or

(d) When the lawful charges of the finder amounts to two-thirds of the value of the things (Sec. 169).

RIGHTS OF BAILER AND BAILEE AGAINST THIRD PARTY (SECS. 180 AND 181)

When the goods are claimed by a third party, the bailee may apply to the Court to stop the delivery of the goods to the bailor until the title of the goods is finalised. If a third person wrongfully causes any injury to the goods bailed, the bailee also is entitled to file a suit against the third person as the bailor himself might have done.

TERMINATION OF BAILMENT

A contract of bailment terminates under the following circumstances:

(a) As soon as the period of bailment expires or the object of the bailment has been accomplished (Sec. 160).

(b) Where the bailee wrongfully uses or disposes of the goods bailed (Sec. 153).

(c) If the bailment is gratuitous, it can be terminated at any time (Sec. 159).

(d) A gratuitous bailment terminates by the death of either the bailor or the bailee (Sec. 162).

DUTIES OF BAILEE

(a) **To Take Care of the Goods:** The bailee is bound by the contract of bailment to return the goods when the purpose of bailment is fulfilled. He has to take care of the goods while they are in his possession. He is also responsible for any loss or damage caused by virtue of his negligence.

In accordance with the English Law, there are three degrees of negligence and three degrees of diligence which may be exercised by a bailee, as per the circumstances of each case. But in the Indian Law, there is only one degree of diligence or care, i.e., the care of a reasonable and prudent man. The degree of care required from the bailee is the same whether the bailment is for reward or gratuitous.

Section 151 provides, "the bailee must take as much care of the goods bailed to him as a man of ordinary prudence would, under similar circumstances, take of his own goods of the same bulk, quality and value as the goods bailed".

Section 152 states, "If the bailee has taken as much care as described in Sec. 151, he is not responsible for the loss, destruction, or deterioration of the goods bailed.

The bailee may take special care of the goods by special contracts, for instance, he may agree to keep the property safe from all perils, and answer for accidents or thefts. But even such a bailee should not be liable for loss occurring by an act of God, or by public enemies.

(b) **Duty Not to Mix with his Own Goods:** Sections 155 to 157 of the Indian Contract Act deal with the provisions governing the rights of bailor and bailee when there is an inter-mixing of their goods. The bailee has an obligation to keep the goods of the bailor separate from his own. But where the goods of the bailor and bailee become mixed, such mixing may be:

1. with the consent of the bailor, or
2. it may be the result of an accident, mistake or inadvertence, or
3. it may be the result of wilful or intentional act without the consent of the bailor.
   - If the bailee, with the consent of the bailor mixes the goods of the bailor with his own goods then the bailor and the bailee will have an interest in the mixture in proportion to their respective shares in the mixture thus produced (Sec. 155).
   - If the goods of the bailor got mixed up with the like goods of the bailee by an accident or inadvertence or by an act of God then it belongs to the bailor and the bailee as tenants in common; but the cost of separation will have to be borne by the bailee.
   - In the case of inter-mixture without the consent of the bailor if the goods are separable, each party can claim his proportionate share and the cost of separation will have to be borne by the bailee (Sec. 156); but when the mixture is inseparable, the bailor is entitled to be compensated by the bailee for the loss of the goods (Sec. 157).

(c) **Duty not to Set up Adverse Title:** As a rule the bailee is estopped from challenging the right of the bailor to receive the goods back. A bailee is not authorised to set up the plea of jus tertii, i.e., to say that the goods belong to a third person.

(d) **Duty to Return the Goods Bailed:** It is the duty of the bailee to return the goods without demand, on the expiration of the time specified or when the purpose is accomplished (Sec. 160). If the bailee fails to return the goods, he shall be liable for any loss, destruction or deterioration of the goods, even without negligence on his part (Sec. 161).

(e) **Duty not to Use Bailed Goods in an Unauthorised Manner:** The bailee has an obligation not to use the goods in an unauthorised manner or for an unauthorised purpose (Sec. 153). If he does so, the bailor can terminate the bailment, and claim damages for any loss or damage caused by the unauthorised use (Sec. 154).

(f) **Duty to Return any Accretion of the Goods:** The bailee must return to the bailor any increase or profits which have accrued from the goods bailed. Section 163 states that the bailor is entitled to the profits accruing from the goods bailed, unless there is a contract to the contrary.

DUTIES OF BAILOR

(a) **Duty of Disclosure:** The bailor must disclose all the known faults to the bailee in the case of gratuitous bailment, and in that case he is liable only if he knows the faults. But in the case of bailment for reward the bailor is responsible irrespective of the knowledge of the faults in the goods bailed (Sec. 150).

(b) **Duty to Bear Expenses:** In the case of gratuitous bailment, it is the duty of the bailor to bear the expenses of the bailment. But in the case of the bailment for reward, even though the bailee is to bear the ordinary and resonable expenses of bailment (e.g., feeding a horse lent), the bailor is bound to pay any extra ordinary expenses incurred by the bailee (e.g., treating a hired horse if it is sick) (Sec. 158).

(c) **Duty to Indemnify the Bailee:** The bailor should indemnify the bailee for any cost or costs which the bailee may incur because of the defective title of the bailor to the goods bailed (Sec. 164).

PAWN OR PLEDGE

Section 172 of the Indian Contract Act provides that pledge is "the bailment of goods as security for the payment of a debt or the performance of a promise". The bailor or depositor is called the pledger or pawnor and the bailee or depositee is called the pledgee or pawnee.

Pledge is a special kind of bailment for a specific purpose, i.e., by way of security. But bailment may be for any purpose, e.g., repairs, safe custody, etc.

As pledge is a species of bailment, delivery is the essence in this case, and this distinguishes a pledge from a mortgage.

RIGHTS AND DUTIES OF PAWNOR AND PAWNEE

The rights and duties of pawnor and pawnee are almost similar to those of bailor and bailee. But the rights of the pawnee and pawnor are required to be specially mentioned.

Rights of Pawnee

(a) **Right of Retainer:** The pawnee has a right to retain the goods bailed till the debt is paid with interest thereon and with all incidental expenses incurred by the pawnee for the possession and preservation of the goods pledged (Sec. 173).

(b) **Right to Extraordinary Expenses:** Section 175 provides, the pawnee is entitled to recover from the pawnor extraordinary expenses incurred by him for the preservation of the goods pledged. But he cannot retain the goods pledged for extraordinary expenses incurred.

(c) **Right of Retainer for Subsequent Advances:** A pawnee cannot retain the goods for any debt other than that for which the pledge was made. But in the absence of anything to the contrary, there is a presumption that he can retain the security for the subsequent advances too (Sec. 174).

(d) **Right in the Case of Default of the Pawnor:** Where the pawnor fails to redeem his pledge, as per Sec. 176, the pawnee can exercise the following rights:

1. He can file a suit for the amount due to him, keeping the goods pledged as a collateral security.

2. He may have the right to sue for the sale of the goods in his possession and realise the money due to him.

3. He can sell the goods in his possession after giving reasonable notice.

   In case the sale proceeds are more than the amount due, the surplus shall be given to the pawnor. Of course, he can sue for deficiency, if there is any.

Rights of Pawnor

Before the actual sale of goods pledged, the defaulted pawnor can redeem the goods by paying the amount due with the expenses arising out of such default (Sec. 177).

PLEDGE BY NON-OWNERS

The general rule is that only the owner of goods can make a valid pledge. This rule is based on the well known rule in contract of sale "nemo dat quod non habet", i.e., no man can pass a better title than he himself has. But Secs. 178, 178A and 179 deal with cases where a pledge made by a non-owner is valid and binding.

1. **Pledge by a Mercantile Agent:** A mercantile agent, who is with the consent of the owner, in possession of the goods or document of title to the goods may, in the ordinary course of his business as a mercantile agent, pledge the goods. Such a pledge will be bound by the owner (Sec. 178).

2. **Pledge by Seller or Buyer in Possession after Sale:** A seller left in possession of the goods after the sale and the buyer to whom possession has been delivered before payment of the price may make a valid pledge of them provided that the pawnee has acted in good faith and has no notice of prior sale.

3. **Pledge by Co-owner:** One of the joint owners in sole possession of the goods, with the consent of the others, can make a valid pledge.

4. **Pledge by a Person in Possession under Voidable Title:** Where the pawnor has obtained the possession of goods under a contract which is voidable and the contract has not been rescinded at the time of the pledge, the pawnee acquires good title to the goods provided he acts in good faith and without the notice of the pawnor's defect in title.

REVIEW QUESTIONS

1. Define 'bailment'. Discuss its essentials.
2. Explain the rights and duties of a bailee.
3. "The position of a finder of goods is exactly that of a bailee". Comment.
4. Write short notes on:

   (a) Gratuitous bailment   (b) Bailee's lien
   (c) Termination of bailment   (d) Pledge by non-owners

5. Define 'pledge'. What are the respective rights and duties of pawnor and pawnee?

PRACTICAL PROBLEMS

Attempt the following problems, giving reasons.

1. P entered a restaurant to dine. His coat was taken by a waiter and hung on a hook behind P. The coat was stolen. Is the restaurant proprietor liable for the loss?

   Hint: Yes.

2. P gives a cloth to Q, a tailor to make a coat, Q promises P to deliver the coat as soon as it is made and to give P two months credit for the charges. Is Q entitled to retain the coat until the charges are paid?

   Hint: No.

3. P asked Q, a driver to drive his car in order to show for sale. Q drove it unskilfully and collided with a house. Is Q liable for the loss?

   Hint: Yes.

4. A who wanted to attend a cinema left his car in the grounds of B after having paid ₹2 and got a 'car park ticket'. Later he found that the car had been stolen by someone. A sues B as Bailee for negligence. Decide.

   Hint: B is liable to make good A's loss.

15

Agency

'Agency' is a relation between two parties created by agreement.

INTRODUCTION

The law of agency is based on the maxim. "Qui facit per alium facit per se", i.e., he who does an act through another does it by himself. The provisions relating to agency are dealt with in Chapter 10 (Secs. 182–238) of the Contract Act.

Owing to the complexity of the modem business, it is not possible for an individual to carry on the business singly. He must delegate some of his powers to another. Then the former is called the 'principal' and the latter is called an 'agent'. The contract which creates the relationship of principal and agent is called an 'agency'.

DEFINITION

In the English Law, a contract of agency is defined as the employment of one person by another, in order to bring the latter into legal relation with a third person.

Section 182 provides:

"An agent is a person employed to do any act for another or to represent another in dealing with third persons. The person for whom such an act is done, or who is so represented, is called the principal".

The definition indicates that an agent is a mere connecting 'link between the principal and third parties. But during the period in which an agent is acting. for his principal, he is endowed with the capacity of his principal'.

102

WHO CAN EMPLOY AN AGENT?

Section 183 says that "any person who is of the age of majority according to the law to which he is subject, and who is of sound mind, may employ an agent". Thus, a lunatic or a minor or a drunken person cannot employ an agent.

WHO MAY BE AN AGENT?

Section 184 lays down that "as between the principal and third person any person may become an agent, but no person who is not of the age of majority and of sound mind can become an agent so as to be responsible to his principal".

Thus, a minor or a lunatic or a drunken person may be an agent. But if a person who is not competent to contract is appointed as an agent, the principal is liable to the third party for the acts of the agent.

ELEMENT OF CONSIDERATION

Section 185 provides that "no consideration is necessary to create an agency". This is due to the fact that the principal has consented to be represented by the agent is a sufficient 'detriment' and consideration to support the promise by the agent to act in that capacity. When X employs Y as his agent, much of the affairs of X are placed in the hands of Y. X suffers a detriment, and so no further consideration in the form of remuneration is to be present. In other words, a gratuitous contract of agency is fully valid, and an agent under it will be as much bound by his contract as a paid agent.

AGENT AND SERVANT

The difference between a servant and an agent, is that a servant is completely under the control of the master, and he has no discretion. But an agent is responsible only for the final results of the transaction and is not controlled by the principal. In other words, a principal has the right to direct the agent what work is to be done, while a master has the further right to direct the servant how the work is to be done.

An agent as such is not a servant, but a servant is generally his master's implied agent, the extent of agency banking upon the obligation and position of the servant. This is why an agent is known as a 'superior servant'.

AGENT AND INDEPENDENT CONTRACTOR

The difference between an agent and an independent contractor is that an agent is bound to exercise his authority according to the lawful instructions and control of the principal, while an independent contractor merely undertakes to carry out certain specified work without the employer's control or interference.

CREATION OF AGENCY

An agency may be constituted:

(1) by express agreement, or (2) by implication of law, or (3) by ratification, or (4) by operation of law.

1. **Agency by Express Agreement:** An express agency is created when a principal appoints an agent either by word of mouth or by an agreement in writing (Sec. 187). The usual mode of a written contract of agency is the power of an attorney on a stamped paper.

2. **Agency by Implication:** Agency by implication of law may arise by conduct, situation of parties, or necessity of the case (Sec. 187). Implied agency consists of: (a) Agency by estoppel; (b) Agency by holding out; (c) Agency by necessity.

   (a) *Agency by Estoppel:* In the words of Lord Halsbury, "Estoppel arises when you are precluded from denying the truth of anything which you have represented as a fact, although it is not a fact". Thus, where A allows third parties to believe that B is acting as his authorised agent, he will be estopped from denying the agency if such third parties relying on it make a contract with B, even when B has no authority at all.

   Section 237 of the Contract Act lays down, "When an agent has, without authority, done acts or incurred obligations to third persons on behalf of his principal, the principal is bound by such acts or obligations, if he has by his words or conduct induced such third persons to believe that such acts and obligations were within the scope of the agents authority".

   (b) *Agency by Holding Out:* Agency by holding out is also a part of the law of estoppel and resembles it. In this case, a prior positive or affirmative act on the part of the principal is necessary to establish an agency subsequently. The common examples of this type of agency are a servant, wife, etc.

Example: A allows his servant, X to habitually buy articles for him on credit from B and pays for them. On one occasion, A pays X cash to buy the articles. X misappropriates the money and buys articles on credit from B. B can recover the price from A as he had held out his servant X as his agent on a prior occasion.

(c) *Agency by Necessity (Secs. 188 and 189):* Generally an agent has to conduct the principal's business in accordance with the latter's instructions. However, in certain cases a person who has been entrusted with another's property, may have to incur unauthorised expenses to protect or preserve it. Such an agency is known as an agency by necessity. This doctrine applies only when there is a real emergency, and when the agent is not in a position to get instructions from the principal and acts bona fide in the best interests of the principal.

Example: A deserted wife forced to live apart from the husband can pledge her husband's credit to buy all necessaries of life in accordance with the position of the husband even against his wishes.

3. **Agency by Ratification (Secs. 196–200):** Section 196 provides that "where acts done by one person on behalf of another but without his knowledge or authority, he may elect to ratify or to disown such acts. If he ratifies them, the same effect will follow as if they had been carried out by his knowledge or authority". This kind of agency is called ex post facto agency or agency arising after the event.

Such an agency will be taken to have come into existence from the time the agent first acted, and not from the date of the principal's ratification. It is said that the ratification is tantamount to prior authority or ratification relates back to the date of the act ratified.

Essentials

(i) Ratification may be express or implied in the conduct of the person on whose behalf the acts are done (Sec. 197).

(ii) No valid ratification is possible by a person whose knowledge of the facts of the case is materially defective (Sec. 198).

(iii) A person ratifying any unauthorised act done on his behalf ratifies the whole of the transaction of which such an act forms a part (Sec. 199).

(iv) Ratification cannot be made so as to subject third persons to damage or terminate any right or interest of a third person (Sec. 200).

(v) Ratification should be made within a reasonable time after the contract was entered into by the agent.

(vi) A ratification must be by a person existing at the date of the act ratified, e.g., A company not incorporated at the time of the act but incorporated subsequently cannot ratify that act.

(vii) It cannot be made valid for criminal acts, e.g., Ratification of forged signature.

(viii) Ratification should be only of those acts in which the person ratifying it has the power to do so, e.g., acts of directors which are ultra vires to the powers of the company cannot be made binding on the company even by the ratification of all the shareholders.

4. **Agency by Operation of Law:** When a company is first established, the promoters are its agents. A partner is the agent of the firm for the purpose of the business of the firm. In all these cases, agency is implied by the operation of law.

CLASSIFICATION OF AGENTS

The most important classification of agents, is the classification into mercantile or commercial agents and non-mercantile agents. Non-mercantile agents may be commission agents, house agents, law agents, election agents, etc.

Another classification of agents is 'general agent' and 'special agent'. A general agent is one who is appointed to perform anything within the authority given to him relating to a particular trade, business or employment, e.g., Managing Directors of a company. Special agent, on the contrary, is one who has authority to do some special act, or enter into some particular contract. In both these cases, a principal will not be liable to the acts done in excess of the agent's authority, unless they are subsequently ratified.

The mercantile agents may be of different kinds. They are:

1. **Factors:** A factor is a mercantile agent to whom goods or bills of lading or other documents of title are consigned for sale by a merchant. He is entrusted with the possession of goods. He is the apparent owner of the goods in his custody and can sell them in his own name. He has an insurable interest in the goods. He has also a lien in respect of any claim he may have, arising out of the agency.

2. **Brokers:** A broker is a mercantile agent who is employed to buy or sell articles on behalf of another. He usually brings contractual relations between the principal and the third parties. The acts are in the name of the principal. He has no lien over the goods as he is not in possession of them.

> **DIFFERENT KINDS OF MERCANTILE AGENTS**
> - Factors
> - Brokers
> - Auctioneers
> - Bankers
> - Partners
> - Del credere agents

3. **Auctioneers:** An auctioneer is an agent appointed by a seller to sell his goods by auction, i.e., to the highest bidder in a public competition. He acts for a reward generally in the form of commission. He has no authority to warrant his principal's title to the goods. He is an agent for the seller, but after the goods have been knocked down he is an agent for the buyer.

4. **Bankers:** The relationship between a banker and his customer is that of debtor and creditor. In addition, a banker is an agent of his customer when he purchases or disposes of securities, collects cheques, dividends, bills or promissory notes on behalf of his customer.

5. **Partners:** In a partnership, every partner is an agent of the firm and his co-partners for the purposes of the business of the firm.

6. **Del Credere Agents:** A del credere agent is one who in consideration of extra remuneration called the del credere commission, guarantees to his principal that third persons with whom he enters into contract shall perform their obligation. In the event of a third party failing to pay, the del credere agent is bound to pay his principal the sum owed by the third party.

EXTENT OF AGENTS AUTHORITY

The authority of an agent may be brought under three heads. They are: (a) actual or real authority (b) ostensible authority (c) authority in an emergency.

(a) **Actual or Real Authority:** An actual authority of an agent may be express or implied (Sec. 186). An authority is said to be express when it is given by words, spoken or written. An authority is said to be implied when it is to be inferred from the circumstances of the case. (Sec. 187).

(b) Ostensible Authority: Section 188 provides that "an agent having an authority to do an act has authority to do everything lawful which is necessary for the purpose or usually done in the course of conducting business". Such an authority is called Ostensible authority.

(c) Authority in an Emergency: Section 189 states that an agent has authority, in an emergency to do all such acts for the purpose of protecting his principal from loss as would be done by a person of ordinary prudence, in his own case, under similar circumstances.

DELEGATION OF AUTHORITY

The contract of agency is fiduciary in nature. It is based on a confidence, reposed by the principal in the agent. The rule of law, therefore, is that an agent cannot delegate his powers or duties to another without the consent of the principal. This principle is expressed by the Latin maxim "delegatus non potest delegare" a delegate cannot further delegate. An agent being himself a delegate of his principal, cannot pass on that delegated authority to someone else. The basic reason behind this doctrine is that the authority given to an agent is personal and cannot be exercised through another.

Section 190 of the Contract Act lays down that "an agent cannot lawfully appoint a sub-agent to do acts which he has undertaken to do personally". To this rule there are certain exceptions:

(a) Where the custom of the trade permits the appointment of a sub-agent.

(b) Where the nature of work is such that further delegation is essential. Apart from these, there are some more exceptions recognised by the English Law and which are accepted in India. They are:

(c) Where the act to be done is purely ministerial and not involving any skill or confidence;

(d) Where an unforeseen emergency arises;

(e) Where the principal knows that the agent intends to delegate his authority and does not forbid delegation.

SUB-AGENT

Section 191 defines "a sub-agent is a person employed by, and acting under the control of the original agent in the business of the agency".

A sub-agent may be a properly appointed one or an improperly appointed one. Where an agent having authority to do so appoints a sub-agent, he is known as a sub-agent property appointed (Sec. 192). Where an agent without authority appoints a sub-agent, he is called a sub-agent improperly appointed (Sec. 193).

When the sub-agent is properly appointed, he can represent the principal as regards third parties. There is no privity of contract between the sub-agent and the principal. The agent would be responsible to the principal for the acts of the sub-agent. In the case of fraud or wilful wrong, the sub-agent is also directly responsible to the principal.

When the sub-agent is improperly appointed the principal is not bound by the acts of the sub-agent. The agent would be responsible to the principal as well as to the third parties.

SUBSTITUTED AGENT

A co-agent or a substituted agent is a person who is appointed by the agent to act for the principal in the business of the agency with the consent of the principal.

Section 194 enacts, "where an agent holding an express or implied authority to name another person to act for his principal, names another person accordingly, he is not a sub-agent but a substituted agent for the principal.

> **Example:** X directs Y, his solicitor to sell his estate by auction, and to employ an auctioneer for the purpose. Y names Z an auctioneer, to conduct the sale. Z is not a sub-agent, but is the agent of X for the conduct of the sale.

DIFFERENCE BETWEEN A SUB-AGENT AND A SUBSTITUTED AGENT

(a) A sub-agent is under the control of the agent, but a substituted agent acts under the directions of the principal.

(b) There is no privity of contract between the principal and the sub-agent, but there is privity of contract between the principal and a substituted agent.

(c) In the case of a substituted agent, an agent's duty ends once he has named him, but in the case of sub-agent, the agent remains responsible to the principal for the acts of the sub-agent.

(d) The agent not only appoints a sub-agent but delegates to him a part of his own duties as well. The agent does not delegate any part of his task to a substituted agent.

TERMINATION OF AGENCY

A contract of agency may come to an end by the operation of law or by the act of the parties. Provisions on this point are dealt with in Section 201 of the Contract Act, but it is incomplete. They are:

1. By agreement between the principal and the agent.
2. By the performance of the contract of agency.
3. By the death of the principal or the agent.
4. By the insanity of either the principal or the agent.
5. By the expiration of the period fixed for the contract of agency.
6. By the renunciation of his authority by the agent.
7. By the revocation of authority by the principal.
8. By the destruction of the subject-matter (Sec. 56).

WHEN AGENCY IS IRREVOCABLE

Revocation of agency is impossible in the following circumstances.

(1) *Agency Coupled with Interest (Sec. 202).* An agency is said to be coupled with interest where authority is given for securing some advantage to the agent or effecting any security or protecting any interest of the agent. Even the death or insanity of the principal does not terminate the authority in this case.

(2) *Where the agent has incurred personal liability.*

(3) Where the agent has partly exercised the authority, it is irrevocable, in particular with regard to the obligations which arise from the acts already done (Sec. 204).

WHEN TERMINATION OF AGENCY TAKES EFFECT

The termination of agency is complete, as regards the agent, when it comes to the knowledge of the agent. As regards the third persons, it takes effect when it becomes known to them (Sec. 208).

If an agent whose authority has been terminated, knowingly enters into a contract with a third person who deals with him bona fide the agent will bind the principal by his act.

The termination of agent's authority, terminates the authority of the sub-agent too (Sec. 210).

DUTIES OF AN AGENT

1. *Duty to Follow Instructions (Sec. 211):* An agent should act within the extent of authority conferred upon him and follow strictly the instructions of the principal.

2. *Duty to Follow Customs in the Absence of Instructions (Sec. 211):* In the absence of express instructions, an agent must act as per the custom prevailing in the same kind of business at the place where he conducts such business.

3. *Duty to Exercise Skill and Diligence (Sec. 212):* An agent is bound to exercise reasonable skill and diligence in the business of agency.

4. *Duty to Render Accounts (Sec. 213):* An agent is bound to render proper accounts to his principal on demand.

5. *Duty to Communicate (Sec. 214):* If there is difficulty, the agent must communicate with the principal and get his instructions.

6. *Duty not to Deal with his Own Account (Secs. 215 and 216):* An agent must not deal on his own account without the consent of the principal. If the agent has been acting privately in the business of agency, the principal has the right, on discovering this fact, either to claim the profit in case the particular transaction has been profitable or to disown the losses in case it has ended in loss.

7. *Duty to Pay over All Money (Sec. 218):* An agent must pay to his principal all sums received on his account.

8. *Duty not to make secret profit.*

9. Duty to protect and preserve the interests of the principal in the case of his death or insolvency (Sec. 209).

10. *Duty not to set up an adverse title.*

11. *Duty not to delegate authority.* This is subject to certain exceptions as per Sec. 190.

RIGHTS OF THE AGENT

Sections 217 to 223 deal with the rights of the agent. They are:

1. *Right of Retainer (Sec. 217):* The agent has a right to retain his principal's money until his claims in conducting the business of agency are paid.

2. *Right to Remuneration (Secs. 219 and 220):* Where the services rendered by the agent are not gratuitous, he is entitled to receive the agreed remuneration or if nothing has been agreed, a reasonable remuneration. Payment for the performance of any work is not due until the completion of such a work unless otherwise provided (Sec. 219).

   An agent who is guilty of misconduct in the business of agency is not entitled to any remuneration in respect of that part of the business which he has misconducted (Sec. 220).

3. *Right of Lien (Sec. 221):* An agent is entitled to retain goods until the amount due to him has been paid or accounted for.

4. *Right of Indemnification (Secs. 222 and 223):* As the agent represents the principal, the agent has a right to be indemnified by the principal against all charges, expenses and liabilities properly incurred him in the business of agency.

5. *Right to Compensation (Sec. 225):* An agent has a right to claim compensation for the injury caused to him by the principal's neglect or want of skill.

RIGHTS AND DUTIES OF THE PRINCIPAL

The rights of an agent are the duties of a principal and the duties of an agent are the rights of a principal.

LIABILITIES OF AN AGENT TO THIRD PARTIES

An agent is personally liable in the following cases:

(a) Where the contracts expressly provide;

(b) Where according to trade usage an agent is personally liable in that kind of business;

(c) Where the agent signs a negotiable instrument in his own name without making it clear that he is signing it only as an agent;

(d) Where an agent acts for a foreign principal;

(e) Where an agent acts for a principal who cannot be sued (e.g., minor);

(f) Where an agency is coupled with interest;

(g) When there is breach of warranty of authority. Where an agent enters into a contract purporting to do so on behalf of the principal, if it is found that the agent has no authority to do so and the principal refuses to ratify the act, the party has a right to proceed against the agent and claim damages;

(h) Where an agent receives money by mistake or by fraud from the third parties;

(i) Where an agent acts for an undisclosed principal;

(j) An agent is also liable to his torts committed in the course of agency.

LIABILITY OF PRINCIPAL TO THIRD PARTIES

1. The principal must be liable to third parties by all acts of the agent within the extent of actual, ostensible or emergency authority (Sec. 226).

2. The principal must be liable to misrepresentation or fraud of the agent committed in the course of employment in matters falling within the authority of the agent even though it is for the agent's benefit (Sec. 238).

3. The principal is liable to any notice given or information obtained by the agent in the course of business as per the principle of constructive notice (Sec. 229).

4. In the case of undisclosed principal third parties can, on discovering the name of the undisclosed principal, proceed against him for the contract entered into by the agent.

5. The principal is liable where he has by words or conduct induced the third party to believe that the act of agent was within the scope of his authority. The liability of principal in this case is not based on any real authority, but is by estoppel (Sec. 237).

6. Where an agent exceeds his authority and it is separable, the principal is liable to that part which is within his authority (Sec. 227).

Where an agent exceeds his authority and it is inseparable from that which is within his authority, the principal is not liable. He is in such a case entitled to repudiate the whole transaction.

REVIEW QUESTIONS

1. "Delegatus non protest delegare". Comment.

2. Define agent and principal. How is an agent appointed? Can a minor (i) appoint an agent (ii) be appointed an agent?

3. How is an agency created? Distinguish between an agent and a sub-agent.

4. Define ratification. State the conditions that should be fulfilled before the doctrine of ratification can apply to an act of an agent.

5. Explain the nature and extent of the authority of an agent?

6. Distinguish between a sub-agent and a substituted agent.

7. Discuss briefly the different modes in which the agency can be terminated. When is an agency irrevocable? When does the termination take effect?

8. What are the rights and duties of an agent towards his principal?

9. Write short notes on:

   (a) Agency coupled with interest

   (b) Substituted agent

   (c) Agency by holding out

PRACTICAL PROBLEMS

Attempt the following problems, giving reasons.

1. P, a businessman entrusts Q, his agent certain goods and instructs Q not to sell the goods for less than a certain price. Q sells the goods for less than that price. Advice P.

   Hint: P is bound by the sale. He can, however, recover damages from Q for any loss he may sustain.

2. A, a carrier discovers a consignment of tomatoes owned by B, has deteriorated badly before the destination has been reached. He therefore, sells the consignment for what he can get: this is about a third of the market price for good tomatoes. B sues A for damages. A claims he was an agent of necessity. Advice.

   Hint: A as an agent of necessity is not liable.

16

Sale of Goods Act, 1930

Contract of sale is "a contract by which the ownership of movable goods is transferred from the seller to the buyer".

The law relating to sale of goods is primarily found in the Sale of Goods Act, 1930. Prior to the enactment of the Sale of Goods Act, 1930, the law relating to the sale of goods was related in Chapter VII of the Indian Contract Act, 1872,

CONTRACT OF SALE

A contract of sale of goods is a contract whereby the seller transfers or agrees to transfer the property in goods to the buyer for a price (Sec. 4). It is a generic term and includes both a 'sale' and an 'agreement to sell'.

SALE

Section 4(3) provides "Where under a contract of sale the property in the goods is transferred from seller to the buyer, the contract is called a sale".

In other words, where the property in the goods (i.e., legal ownership of the goods) is immediately transferred to the buyer, the contract of sale is called a sale. Thus, the sale has the immediate effect of transferring the ownership of the goods.

AGREEMENT TO SELL

The agreement to sell is also defined in Sec. 4(3) of the Sale of Goods Act which reads as under:

"Where under a contract of sale the transfer of property in the goods is to take place a future time or subject to some condition thereafter to be fulfilled, the contract is called an agreement to sell". In other words, where the property in the goods is to be transferred to the buyer at some future date or on the fulfillment of a certain condition, the contract of sale is called an agreement to sell. Thus, in agreement to sell, ownership of goods is not immediately transferred from a seller to a buyer.

Section 4(4) lays down, an agreement to sell becomes a sale, when the time elapses or the conditions are fulfilled subject to which the property in the goods is to be transferred.

Sale and agreement to sell—Distinction

Agreement to Sell	*Sale*
1. It gives rise to jus in personam, i.e., a right available against an ascertained person.	It creates a jus in rem, i.e., a right available against the world at large.
2. It is an executory contract, i.e., transferring of ownership at a later date.	It is an executed contract, i.e., the ownership having been already transferred to the buyer.
3. If the goods are destroyed, the loss falls on the seller, even if the goods are in the possession of the buyer.	If the goods are destroyed, the loss falls on the buyer, even if the goods are in the possession of the seller.
4. In the case of breach by the buyer, the seller is entitled only to damages.	Seller can sue for the price of the goods.
5. The seller can sell the goods to third parties.	The seller cannot sell to third parties.
6. The buyer can claim only ratable dividend if the seller become insolvent.	The buyer is entitled to recover the specific property from the assignee if the seller becomes insolvent.
7. The seller may refuse to sell the goods to the buyer without payment if the buyer becomes insolvent.	The seller is only entitled to the ratable dividend of the price due if the buyer becomes insolvent.
8. Ownership of the goods does not pass to the buyer but remains with the seller.	Ownership passes to the buyer.

SALE AND HIRE–PURCHASE AGREEMENT

A transaction of hire is a type of bailment which is distinguished from a contract of sale in that, even if the hirer pays money on consideration of the use of goods, the ownership remains with the seller.

In the hire–purchase agreement, if the hirer pays the specified instalment promptly he gets the option of purchasing the goods on making a nominal payment. Until this option is exercised, the ownership of the goods remains with the seller. If the hirer sells the goods, in the meantime, he is guilty of conversion. The bona fide third parties purchasing the goods from the hirer get no title unlike in a sale.

The terms of contract determine whether a particular transaction is contract of sale or contract of hire–purchase.

SALE AND BAILMENT

In the case of sale, ownership of goods is transferred from seller to buyer, but in the case of bailment no ownership is transferred to bailee.

SALE AND CONTRACT FOR WORK OR LABOUR

Sale contemplates the delivery of goods but the contract for work is the exercise of skill, or labour, and the delivery of goods is only subsidiary.

SALE AND CONTRACT OF AGENCY

In a contract of sale, the title in the goods is transferred for a price paid or promised to be paid. The transferee in such a case is liable to the transferor as a debtor for the price to be paid. In a contract of agency, goods are transferred to a person who is to sell them not as his own property, but as the property of the principal, and the agent is bound to account for the sale proceeds.

SALE AND GIFT

Sale is always made for a consideration, but in the case of gift, goods are transferred by one person to another without any price or consideration.

SALE AND BARTER

In a sale, property in goods is transferred from seller to buyer for a price, but in a barter, goods are exchanged for goods.

ESSENTIALS OF A CONTRACT OF SALE

The following essential elements are to be present to constitute a valid contract of sale:

(a) *Contract:* All the vital elements of a valid contract are to be present in a contract of sale.

(b) *Two Parties:* To constitute a contract of sale, there must be two parties, the seller and the buyer.

(c) *Transfer of General Property:* There should be the transfer of general or absolute property in goods from the seller to the buyer.

(d) *Price:* The consideration for the contract of sale must be money paid or promised, called price.

SUBJECT MATTER OF CONTRACT OF SALE

Goods form the subject-matter of a contract of sale (Sec. 6).

Goods mean every kind of movable property, other than actionable claims and money; and includes stock and shares, growing crops, grass and things attached to, or forming part of the land which are agreed to be severed before sale or under the contract of sale (Sec. 2(7)).

Actionable claims and money are not goods. An actionable claim is something which is enforceable only by action in a Court of law, e.g., a debt due.

Goods may be grouped under three heads. They are: 1. Existing goods 2. Future goods 3. Contingent goods.

1. **Existing Goods:** Goods which are owned and possessed by the seller at the time of sale are called existing goods. Only existing goods can be the subject-matter of sale. Existing goods are again brought under three heads. They are: (a) specific goods, (b) ascertained goods, and (c) unascertained goods.

   (a) *Specific Goods:* It means goods identified and agreed upon at the time when a contract of sale is made (Sec. 2(14)).

   (b) *Ascertained Goods:* Ascertained goods are those goods which are identified in accordance with the agreement after the contract of sale is made.

   (c) *Unascertained Goods:* It means goods which are not identified at the time of the contract of sale. They are defined only by description.

2. **Future Goods:** It means goods which are to be manufactured or produced or acquired by the seller after the
contract of sale is made [Sec. 2(6)].

3. **Contingent Goods:** It means a type of future goods, the
acquisition of which by the seller depends upon a contingency
which may or may not happen [Sec. 6(2)].

GOODS PERISHING BEFORE SALES BUT AFTER AGREEMENT TO SELL

Where the contract does not amount to sale, but is only agreement
to sell and the goods without any fault of either the seller or the
buyer perish or become so damaged subsequent to the agreement,
but before the risk-passes to the buyer becomes void (Sec. 8).

Document of Title to Goods

It is a proof of possession and control of goods. Document of title
authorizes, either by endorsement or by delivery its possessor to
transfer or receive goods represented by it [Sec. 2(4)].

The term document of title consists of a bill of lading, dock
warrant, warehouse keeper's certificate, delivery order, railway
receipt, etc.

Price

In a contract of sale, no sale can take place without a price. It
means the money consideration for sale of goods [Sec. 2(10)]. It is
not necessary that the price should be fixed at the time of sale. It
must, however, be payable.

CONDITIONS AND WARRANTIES

A stipulation in a contract of sale with reference to goods which are
the subject thereof may be a condition or a warranty [Sec. 12(1)].

A condition is a stipulation essential to the main purpose of
the contract, the breach of which gives rise to a right to treat the
contract as repudiated [Sec. 12(2)].

A warranty is a stipulation collateral to the main purpose of the
contract, the breach of which gives rise to a claim for damages but
not a right to reject the goods and treat the contract as repudiated
[Sec. 12(3)].

Whether a stipulation in a contract of sale is a condition or a warranty depends in each case on the structure of the contract. A stipulation may be a condition, though called warranty in the contract [Sec. 12(4)].

When Condition Sinks to the Level of Warranty?

In some cases a condition is to be treated as a warranty. They are:

(a) A condition becomes a warranty where the buyer waives the condition; or

(b) A condition is to be treated as a warranty when the buyer elects to treat the breach of condition as a breach of warranty; or

(c) When the contract is not divisible and the buyer has accepted the goods or part thereof, the breach of any condition to be fulfilled by the seller can be treated as breach of warranty, unless otherwise provided.

The first two cases depend upon the will of the buyer [Sec. 13(1)], but the third is compulsory and acts as estoppel against him [Sec. 13(2)].

Distinction between Conditions and Warranties

1. *Difference as to Value:*   Where stipulation in a contract is essential to the main purpose of the contract, it is a condition. But if the stipulation is only a collateral to the main purpose of the contract, it is only a warranty.

2. *Difference as to Breach:*   When there is a breach of condition the aggrieved party can repudiate the contract, but in the case of breach of warranty, he has the right to claim only damages.

3. *Difference as to Treatment:*   A breach of condition may be treated as a breach of warranty, but in the case of breach of warranty, it cannot be treated as a breach of condition.

Implied Conditions and Warranties (Secs. 14 to 17)

Implied conditions or warranties are those which are attached to the contract by operation of law or custom. Like express conditions, implied conditions may also sink to the level of a warranty.

Implied Conditions

1. *Conditions as to Title* [Sec. 14(a)]: In a contract of sale, it is implied that the seller has a right to sell the goods as agreed to be sold. If the title of the seller turns out to be defective, the buyer is entitled to reject the goods and can recover the whole amount.

   In *Rawland* v. *Daivall* (1923)s, 2K. B. 500, X had purchased a car from Y. After X had used it for six months, he was deprived of it as Y had no title to it.

   It was held that X could recover the whole amount paid from Y even if he had used the car for six months, as the consideration had totally failed.

2. *Sale by Description:* In a sale by description there are the following implied conditions:

(a) *Goods must Correspond to Description (Sec. 15):* Where the goods do not correspond to the description in the contract, the buyer may at his option accept it or claim damages.

   Example: A contract of sale of an Ambassador Motor Car 2005, Model is a contract for sale by description.

   In *Beale* v. *Taylor* (1967) 1W.L.R.1193, it was held that even if the buyer has seen the goods it is no excuse for the goods not being as per the description.

(b) *Conditions as to Merchandability [Sec. 16(2)]:* Even if the goods may be sold by description and the goods answer to the description yet they must be merchandable. It means goods should be such as are commercially saleable. The condition as to merchandability cannot be applied when the defect is patent and the buyer has examined it.

   In *Jackson* v. *Rolex Motor and Cycle Co. Ltd.* (1910) 2K. B. 937, a manufacturer supplied 6000 horns under a contract. The horns were found to be dented, scratched and otherwise a faulty manufacture. It was held that the buyer was entitled to reject the whole consignment.

(c) *Condition as to Wholesomeness:* The condition as to merchantability must be deemed to include suitability for consumption in the case of eatables and provisions.

   In *Frost* v. *Aylesbury Dairy Co. Ltd.* (1905) 1 K.B. 608, F purchased milk from A, and the milk contained typhoid germs. The wife of F became infected and died. It was held that F could recover damages.

(d) *Condition as to Fitness for a Particular Purpose (Sec. 16):*
Ordinarily in a contract of sale there is no implied condition
or a warranty as to the quality of fitness of the goods supplied
for any specific purpose. But there is an implied condition
that the goods sold are reasonably fit for the purpose for
which they are purchased if:

(i) the buyer makes known to the seller the specific purpose;

(ii) the buyer relies on the judgement or skill of the seller;
and

(iii) the seller happens to be a person whose course of
business is to sell the goods to that description.

There is no such implied condition when the goods are sold
or bought under a patent or other trade name.

In *Pries* v. *Last* (1903) 2 K.B. 148, a hot bottle was
purchased from the defendant, a retail chemist, on the
understanding that the bottle stands boiling water. The
bottle burst when used and injured the plaintiff's wife. Held,
the seller was responsible to damages.

3. *Sale by Sample (Sec. 17):* In a sale by sample, there are
the following implied conditions:

(a) The bulk of the goods corresponds to the sample;

(b) The buyer shall have a reasonable opportunity of
comparing the goods delivered with the sample;

(c) The goods shall be free from any latent defect rendering
them unmarketable.

4. *Sale by Sample as well as by Description [Sec. 15]:* When the
sale is by sample as well as by description, the goods must
correspond to the sample and the description.

In *Nichol* v. *Godts* (1854) 10 Ex. 191, there was a sale of
"Foreign refined rape oil" warranted only equal to sample.
The oil tendered was the same as the sample, but contained
an admixture of hemp oil. It was held that the buyer could
refuse to accept the goods.

Implied Warranties

Implied warranties in a contract of sale are given below:

1. *Warranty of Quiet Possession [Sec. 14(6)]:* In a contract of
sale, there is an implied warranty that the buyer shall have
and enjoy quiet possession of the goods, unless otherwise
provided. In case the buyer is in any way disturbed he has
a right to sue the seller for damages.

2. *Warranty against Encumbrances [Sec. 14(c)]*: There is also an implied warranty that the goods purchased are not subject to any charge or right in favour of a third party.

Caveat Emptor

It means—"let the buyer beware", i.e., the seller is under no duty to reveal the defects in the goods he is selling. But the buyer has to make sure that he is buying the right quality of goods. If he depends upon his own skill and judgement and the goods turn out to be defective, he cannot blame anybody but himself.

The maxim 'caveat emptor' does not apply and the contract will be subject to the implied conditions under the following circumstances.

(a) Sale under fitness for buyer's purpose [Sec. 16(1)].

(b) Sale under merchandable quality [Sec. 16(2)].

(c) Sale under a patent or trade name [Sec. 16(1)].

(d) Sale under usage of trade [Sec. 16(3)].

(e) Consent by fraud.

PASSING OF PROPERTY OF TRANSFER OF OWNERSHIP

Property signifies control over an object, together with the right to the possession of the same.

The paramount object of sale is the passing of ownership of the property from the seller to the buyer. The delivery of property has nothing to do with the passing of property. It is always open to the parties concerned to mention the precise moment of time at which the property in goods passes to the buyer. Unless such intention has been expressed by the parties to the contract, Secs. 18–26 of the S.O.G. Act provide as to when the property or ownership will ordinarily pass.

For determining the time passing the ownership, the goods are brought under two heads. They are:

1. Specific or ascertained goods.

2. Generic or unascertained goods.

Ascertained goods may again be brought under goods in a deliverable state or in a non-delivarable state.

Goods are said to be in a deliverable state when they are in such a state that the buyer would under the contract be bound to take delivery of them.

Goods are said to be in a non-deliverable state when they are in such a state that there still remains something to be done in respect of the goods to put them into a deliverable state.

In the case of 'specific goods in a deliverable state', the property in them passes to the buyer immediately the contract is entered into (Sec. 20).

In the case of 'specific goods in a non-deliverable state', the property in them passes only when they are put in a deliverable state and the buyer has notice thereof (Sec. 21).

In the case of sale of 'unascertained goods', the property in them passes only when the goods in a deliverable state are unconditionally appropriated or ascertained. The ascertainment of unascertained goods can be made by putting them in appropriate containers. When the seller delivers the goods to a common carrier for transmission, without reserving himself the right of disposal it amounts to unconditional appropriation or ascertainment (Sec. 23).

In the case of goods which are delivered to the buyer "on sale or return", the property in them passes to the buyer when he signifies his approval or acceptance to the seller. The buyer is also deemed to have approved the sale if he returns the goods without giving notice of rejection within the specified time or within a reasonable time when no time limit is specified (Sec. 24).

Goods delivered on sale or return indicates that they are sent to the buyer on approval. It is not considered to be a contract of sale but only an agreement to sell. That is why the risk of loss would be that of the seller.

PASSING OF RISK IN THE GOODS

The rule in this context is based on a maxim-rest perit domino, i.e., the loss falls on the owner. It signifies that immediately the property in the goods passes to the buyer, the buyer will bear the loss and before that of the seller. This rule is subject to two exceptions:

1. When the parties agree to contrary provision.
2. When delivery is delayed through the fault of either the buyer or the seller, the goods are at the risk of the party at fault.

SHIPPING DOCUMENTS

It consists of (a) the invoice showing the cost of the goods (b) the bill of lading containing the freight and (c) the insurance policy.

C.I.F. Contracts

The three letters C.I.F. stand for cost, insurance and freight. These types of contract arise when the seller and buyer happen to live at distant places. Here, the contract price consists of the cost of the goods, the cost of insurance and the freight.

F.O.B. and F.O.R. Contracts

F.O.B. stands for Free on Board and F.O.R. stands for Free on Rail. In F.O.B. contract, the seller puts the goods on board a ship and in F.O.R. contract, on rail at his own expenses. Afterwards the buyer takes the risk of the goods.

Ex-ship Contracts

In contracts where the delivery has to be made "Ex-ship", the ownership in the goods will not pass until actual delivery. Here, the goods will be at the seller's risk during voyage.

Sale or Transfer of Title by Non-owners

In the case of transfer of ownership of goods, where the seller is not an absolute owner of the goods, the buyer cannot acquire a better title than what the seller has. The general rule is expressed in the Latin maxim "Nemo dat quod non-habet", i.e., no one can pass a better title than he himself has.

> **Example:** If X steals a watch and sells it to Y, Y does not become the owner of the watch.

Where goods are sold by a person who is not the owner thereof and who does not sell them under the authority or with the consent of the owner, the buyer gets no better title to the goods than the seller has (Sec. 27). This rule is subject to certain exceptions.

EXCEPTIONS UNDER THE SALE OF GOODS ACT

1. *Sale by a Mercantile Agent (Sec. 27):* A buyer will acquire a good title if he purchases in good faith from a mercantile agent who is in possession of the goods or documents of title to goods with the consent of the owner, and who sells the goods in the ordinary course of his business.

2. *Sale under Estoppel (Sec. 27):* If goods are sold by a person other than the true owner, but the real owner is prevented by his conduct to deny the seller's authority to sell the goods, the buyer acquires a good title to the goods.

3. *Sale by Co-owner (Sec. 28):* When a co-owner having possession of the goods with the permission of the other co-owners, sells the goods, the buyer in good faith of those goods acquires a good title to the goods.

4. *Sale by a Person with Voidable Title (Sec. 29):* A person in possession of goods under a voidable contract can transfer a good title to the buyer who buys the goods in good faith and without notice of the seller's defect of title provided the sale takes place before the voidable contract is rescinded.

5. *Sale by Seller in Possession of Goods after Sale [Sec. 30(1)]:* Where a seller who having once sold the goods continues to be in possession of the goods or of the document of title to the goods, sells them either himself or through a mercantile agent to a person who purchases them in good faith and without notice of the previous sale, the buyer acquires a good title.

6. *Sale by Buyer in Possession after Sale [Sec. 30(2)]:* Where a buyer in possession of the goods with the consent of the seller, sells them, the new buyer who acts in good faith and without notice of the lien or any other right of the first seller will acquire a good title.

7. *Sale by an Unpaid Seller [Sec. 54(3)]:* Where an unpaid seller who has a right of lien or stoppage in-transit resells the goods, the buyer gets a good title to the goods as against the original buyer.

8. *Sale in Market Overt:* In England, if sales are made at prescribed places and time, the purchaser gets good title to the goods irrespective of the sellers not having a saleable interest in the goods sold. This exception is not recognised in India.

EXCEPTIONS UNDER OTHER ACTS

1. Sale by a finder of lost goods (Under Sec. 169 of the Indian Contract Act, 1872).

2. Sale by a pawnee or pledgee under certain circumstances (Sec. 176 of the Indian Contract Act, 1872).

3. Sale by an Official Receiver or Official Assignee or Liquidator of Companies.

4. A holder in due course (Under the Negotiable Instrument Act, 1881). In all the above cases, the buyer acquires a better title.

PERFORMANCE OF CONTRACT

Performance of a contract of sale means as regards the seller, delivery of the goods to the buyer, and as regards the buyer, acceptance of the delivery of the goods and payment for them, as per the terms of the contract of sale (Sec. 31).

Delivery of goods means 'Voluntary transfer of possession of goods from one person to another' [Sec. 2(2)]. Delivery may be actual, constructive or symbolic.

Actual or physical delivery arises when the goods are handed over by the seller to the buyer or his duly authorised agent.

Constructive delivery arises when a third person who is in possession of the goods acknowledges that he holds the goods on behalf of the buyer.

> **Example:** X sells to Y 20 bags of rice lying in Z's warehouse. X gives an order to Z, asking him to transfer the goods to Y. Z assents to such an order and transfers the goods in his books to Y. This is a constructive delivery. Symbolic delivery is made by indicating or giving as symbol:

> **Example:** Handing over the key of a godown to the buyer.

RULES AS TO DELIVERY

1. *Mode of Delivery (Sec. 33):* Delivery should have the effect of putting the buyer in possession.

2. *Delivery and Payment (Sec. 32):* Delivery and payment of price must be as per the terms of the contract.

3. *Effect of Part Delivery (Sec. 34):* A delivery of the part of the goods has the same effect as a delivery of the whole, provided such a part delivery is made in progress of the delivery of the whole.

4. *Buyer to Apply for Delivery (Sec. 35):* The seller is to deliver the goods when the buyer applies for delivery. The buyer is bound to claim delivery.

5. *Place of Delivery (Sec. 36):* Where the place of delivery is stated in the contract, the goods must be delivered at the specified place during working hours on a working day. Where no place is mentioned, the goods sold are to be delivered at the place at which they are at the time of sale.

6. *Goods in Possession of a Third Party [Sec. 36(3)]:* Where at the time of the sale the goods are with a third person, there will be delivery only when that person acknowledges to the buyer that he holds the goods on his behalf.

7. *Time of Delivery [Sec. 36(2) and (4)]:* In a contract of sale, the delivery of goods should be made within a reasonable time unless, a time is fixed in the contract. No demand of delivery can be made before the expiration of a reasonable time. What is a reasonable time is a question of fact. Tender or demand of delivery is also to be made at a reasonable time.

8. *Expenses of Delivery [Sec. 36(5)]:* The seller has to bear the cost of delivery unless otherwise provided.

9. *Instalment Delivery (Sec. 38):* Unless otherwise agreed the buyer is not bound to accept the delivery in instalments.

10. *Delivery to a Carrier or Wharfinger (Sec. 39):* Delivery of goods to a carrier for transmission to the buyer or delivery of goods to a wharfinger for safe custody, is a prima facie deemed to be a delivery of goods to the buyer.

RIGHTS OF AN UNPAID SELLER OR VENDOR

An unpaid seller is a seller who has not been paid the whole of the price or who has received any negotiable instruments which is subsequently dishonoured.

Who is an Unpaid Seller?

Section 45(1) provides that a seller is deemed to be an unpaid seller when:

(a) the whole of the price has not been paid or tendered;

(b) a bill of exchange or other negotiable instrument has been received as a conditional payment, and the condition on which it was received has not been fulfilled by reason of dishonour of the instrument, or otherwise.

In other words, an unpaid seller is a seller who has not been paid the whole of the price or one who has received any negotiable instrument which is subsequently dishonoured.

1. **Rights of an Unpaid Seller against the Goods:** Although the property in the goods has passed to the buyer, an unpaid seller has four important rights for realisation of the price of the goods. They are: (a) Right of lien. (b) Right of stoppage in-transit. (c) Right of resale. (d) Right to withhold delivery.

(a) *Right of Lien (Secs. 47 to 49):* An unpaid seller who is in possession of the goods sold, may exercise his lien on the goods, i.e., is entitled to retain such possession, until the full payment or tender of the price of the goods in the cases where:

(i) The goods are not sold on credit.

(ii) The goods have been sold on credit, but the period of credit has expired.

(iii) The buyer becomes insolvent.

The seller's lien is a possessory lien and as such it can only be exercised for the non-payment of the price and not for any other charges.

(b) *Right of Stoppage in-transit (Secs. 50 to 52):* The right of stoppage in-transit is a right preventing the goods from being delivered to the buyer, and resuming their possession while in-transit and retaining them until the price is paid.

The right of stoppage in-transit comes into existence only when the lien is not available (i.e., when the unpaid seller has parted with the possession of the goods) but it arises either on the insolvency of the buyer or when the goods are in-transit.

The buyer is said to be insolvent if he has ceased to pay his debts in the ordinary courses of business, or cannot pay his debts when they become due.

The goods are in-transit from the time they are delivered to a carrier or other bailee for giving it to the buyer and until the buyer takes delivery of them.

The transit is at the end in the following cases:

(i) If the buyer obtains the possession of the goods before its arrival at the destination.

(ii) If, after the arrival at his destination, the carrier acknowledges to the buyer that he holds the goods on his behalf, even though further destination of it is mentioned by the buyer.

(iii) If the carrier wrongfully refuses to deliver the goods to the buyer.

The right of stoppage in-transit may be effected either by making actual possession of the goods or by giving notice of claim to the carrier or other person having control of the goods.

Distinction between Lien and Stoppage in-transit

(i) An unpaid seller can exercise lien only when the goods are in his possession. But the right of stoppage in-transit can be exercised only after the seller has parted with the possession of goods.

(ii) Right of stoppage in-transit is available only when the buyer becomes insolvent, but right of lien is available, even when the buyer is not insolvent, in case the period of credit has expired and the price has not been paid.

(iii) The right of lien is to retain possession of goods, but the right to stoppage in-transit is to regain or resume possession of the goods.

Effect of Sub-sale or Pledge by Buyer (Sec. 53)

The unpaid seller's right of lien or stoppage in-transit is not affected by the buyer's selling or pledging of the goods unless the seller has assented to it. This is based on the principle that the sub-buyer cannot acquire a better position than his seller has. But this right is not available if he has transferred a document of title to goods to the buyer, and the buyer transfers it by way of sale to a person who takes it in good faith and for consideration.

(c) *Right of Re-sale (Sec. 54):* An unpaid seller exercising the right of lien or stoppage in-transit can re-sell the goods and sue the buyer for damages, if any, under the following circumstances, provided he has given notice of his intention to re-sell to the buyer and asked him to pay the price within a reasonable time:

(a) where the goods are of a perishable nature, or

(b) when the buyer does not pay or tender the price.

An unpaid seller may also re-sell the goods if he has expressly reserved the right of re-sale in the contract. On re-sale if there is a surplus, the re-seller can keep it. If there is a deficiency, he is entitled to recover it from the buyer.

(d) *Right to Withhold Delivery [Sec. 46(2)]:* Where the property in goods has not passed to the buyer, the unpaid seller has a right of withholding delivery similar to and co-extensive with his right of lien and stoppage in-transit.

Auction Sale (Sec. 64)

A sale by auction is a public sale in which goods are offered to the highest bidder.

Where goods are put up for sale in lots, each lot is a prima facie deemed to be the subject of a separate contract of sale. The sale is complete when the auctioneer announces its completion by the fall of the hammer or in some other customary manner. Until such an announcement is made, any bidder may retract his bid.

Where the goods are destroyed or damaged before the completion of sale, the loss will be borne by the seller.

A right to bid may be reserved expressly or on behalf of the seller [Sec. 64(3)].

The sale may be notified to be subject to a reserved or upset price [Sec. 64(5)].

If the seller makes use of pretended bidding to raise the price, the sale is voidable at the option of the buyer [Sec. 64(6)].

2. **Rights of an Unpaid Seller against the Buyer Personally:** The rights of the unpaid seller against the buyer personally are known as rights 'in perosnam'. This right is available to the seller apart from his right against the goods. They are as follows:

(i) *Suit for Price (Sec. 55):* Where under a contract of sale, the property in the goods has passed to the buyer and the buyer wrongfully neglects or refuses to pay the price, the seller may institute a suit for the recovery of the price [Sec. 55(1)].

Where under a contract of sale, the price is payable on a certain day irrespective of delivery and the buyer wrongfully neglects or refuses to pay the price, the seller may file a suit for the realisation of the price even if the property in the goods may not have passed [Sec. 55(2)].

(ii) *Suit for Damages for Non-acceptance (Sec. 56):* Where the buyer wrongfully neglects or refuses to accept and pay for the goods, the seller may file a suit for damages for non-acceptance.

(iii) *Suit for Damages for Breach of Contract (Sec. 60):* If the seller elects to treat the buyer's refusal to pay as breach of contract, the seller may institute a suit for damagers for breach of contract.

(iv) *Suit for Interest (Sec. 61):* The court may award interest on the price from the date of the tender of the goods or from the date when the price is payable, unless otherwise provided in the contract. In this case, the seller can only recover interest when he is in a position to recover the price.

REVIEW QUESTIONS

1. Define the term 'contract of sale'. Distinguish between sale and agreement to sell.

2. Define the term goods. What are the different types of goods?

3. Define the terms conditions and warranties. What are the implied conditions and warranties in a contract of sale?

4. Write short notes on:

   (a) Caveat emptor

   (b) Sale and hire–purchase agreement

   (c) Sale and bailment

   (d) Sale by sample and description

5. What do you mean by property in the goods? State the legal provisions relating to passing of property in the case of (a) sale of specific goods, (b) sale of unascertained goods and (c) sale on approval.

6. Nemo dat quod non habet—Comment. Are there any exceptions to this rule?

7. What do you mean by the term delivery of goods in a contract of sale? State the legal provisions relating to the delivery of goods.

8. Who is an unpaid seller? What are his rights against the buyer personally, and against the goods?

9. Write short notes on:

   (a) Right of Lien   (b) Right of Stoppage in-transit

   (c) Auction Sale   (d) Ex-ship contracts

PRACTICAL PROBLEMS

Attempt the following problems, giving reasons.

1. P, a dentist makes a set of false teeth for his patient with materials wholly found by the dentist and Q, the buyer agrees to pay ₹500 when they are properly fitted into his mouth. Is it a contract for the sale of goods?

   Hint: Yes.

2. P contracts to sell to Q a piece of cotton. P thinks that it is an Indian cotton. P knows that Q thinks so, but knows that it is not an Indian cotton, P does not correct the impression of Q. Q afterwards discovers that is not an Indian cotton. Can he repudiate the contract?

Hint: No, as the rule Caveat Emptor will apply.

3. P finds a costly ring and after making reasonable efforts to discover the owner, sells to Q, who buys without the knowledge that P was merely a finder. Can the true owner recover the ring from Q?

   Hint: Yes, as sale does not come under the exceptions when the finder has the right to sell.

4. P of Bombay ordered certain specified goods from Q of Madras. Q sends the goods, not ordered, along with them. What can P do?

   Hint: P may either reject the whole or accept the goods ordered by him and reject the rest.

17

Negotiable Instruments Act, 1881

A negotiable instrument is one, the property in which, acquired by any one who takes it bonafide and for value, notwithstanding any defect of title in the person from whom he took it.
—Justice Willis, The Law of Negotiable Securities, 5th ed., p. 5

INTRODUCTION

By virtue of convenience, modern businessmen prefer credit instruments to 'money' as a medium of exchange. Credit instruments used in business consist of either negotiable instruments or non-negotiable instruments.

The word negotiable means "transferable from one person to another in return for consideration" and instrument means "written document by which a right is created in favour of some person". Thus, a negotiable instrument is a document which can be used to secure the payment of money. It is transferable by mere delivery or by endorsement and delivery. Delivery means to hand over the document. Endorsement means to sign the document for the purpose of negotiation. Instances of negotiable instruments are bill of exchange, promissory notes, cheques, etc.

In the case of non-negotiable instruments, negotiability is restricted. The ownership of these instruments can be transferred only after fulfilling certain legal conditions. Instances of non-negotiable instruments are share warrants, postal orders, letters of credit, bill of lading, etc.

HISTORY OF THE LAW

The law of negotiable instruments in India is based almost entirely on the principle of Mercantile Law of England. In India, the law relating to negotiable instruments is contained in the Negotiable

Instruments Act, XXVI of 1881. It mainly deals with only three types of negotiable instruments, viz., promissory note, bills of exchange and cheque. Besides these, the Act also applies to Native Bills of Exchange called Hundis, unless a contrary local usage is proved. Again the Act does not affect Sec. 25 of the Paper Currency Act of 1882 which has been repealed and replaced by Sec. 31 of the Reserve Bank of India Act of 1934, which prohibits the making of the negotiable instruments payable to order or demand with the exception of a cheque.

MEANING AND DEFINITION OF NEGOTIABLE INSTRUMENTS

According to Sec. 13 of the Negotiable Instrument Act "a negotiable instrument means a promissory note, bill of exchange, or cheque, payable either to order or to bearer". This is not a satisfactory definition and it does not explain the characteristics of a negotiable instrument.

According to Justice Willis "a negotiable instrument is one, the property in which is acquired by anyone who takes it bona fide and for value notwithstanding any defect of title in the person from whom he took it". To put it in simple words, a negotiable instrument is a 'chose-in action' with characteristic of negotiability attached to it.

A chose means a thing, and therefore a chose-in action means a thing in action. A 'chose-in action' or a thing in action may be defined therefore, as a thing which can be recovered only through a Court of law by resorting to a legal action.

The term negotiability is not mere assignability. It is something, more than assignability. 'Assignability or transferability' of a thing is simple delivery without any other formality like writing, stamping, etc. When a bona fide transferee for value without notice of the defect in title of the thing gets a title better than the transferor's, it is called negotiability.

> **Example:** A bought some goods from a shop and paid a stolen cheque. If the shopkeeper accepted the cheque in good faith, (without knowing that the cheque is a stolen one) the real owner cannot get back the cheque from the shopkeeper. This is due to the fact that the shopkeeper (transferee) has a better title to the cheque than A (transferor).

CHARACTERISTICS OF A NEGOTIABLE INSTRUMENT

The following are the main characteristics of a negotiable instrument:

1. It is a contract to pay money.
2. It is freely transferable either by delivery or by endorsement and delivery.
3. It can be transferred ad infinitum till maturity.
4. The transferor need not give any notice of transfer to the person liable to pay the instrument.
5. It possesses the quality of negotiability. That is the holder in due course of such an instrument has a good title even if the title of the transferor is defective.
6. Transferee can use it in his own name.
7. It is as good as cash because cash can be obtained at any time paying a small commission.
8. It enables the holder to expect prompt payment because a dishonour or non-payment of an instrument means the ruin of the credit of all persons who are party to it.
9. It is capable of proof as it has got special rules of evidence.

NEGOTIATION

Negotiation is the transfer of an instrument from one person to another in such a manner so as to convey the title and constitute the transferee the holder thereof. According to Sec. 14 of the Act "When a promissory note, bill of exchange or cheque is transferred to any person, so as to constitute that person the holder thereof, the instrument is said to be negotiated".

Negotiation is effected by mere delivery of a bearer instrument and by endorsement and delivery of an order instrument. It shows that 'delivery' is a must in negotiable instruments. Until the instrument is actually delivered, the contract on negotiable instrument is incomplete. Delivery must also be voluntary with the intention of passing property in the instrument to the person to whom it is given.

Negotiable by Mere Delivery

A bill or cheque payable to the bearer is negotiated by mere delivery of the instrument. In such a case no endorsement is necessary.

Example: X, the holder of a negotiable instrument payable to bearer delivers it to the agent of Y to keep it for Y. The instrument has been negotiated.

An instrument is payable to bearer:

(i) Where it is made so payable, or

(ii) Where it is originally made payable to order but the only or the last endorsement is in blank.

(iii) Where the payee is a fictitious or a non-existing person.

Negotiable by Endorsement and Delivery (Sec. 48)

An instrument payable to order can be negotiated only by endorsement and delivery. Unless the holder signs his endorsement on the instrument, the transferee does not become a holder. The effects of negotiation by endorsement and delivery are:

(i) to transfer property in the instrument from the endorser to the endorsee;

(ii) to vest in the endorsee the right of further negotiation; and

(iii) a right to endorsee to sue, on the instrument all other parties.

HOLDER (Sec. 8)

A holder is the person who is entitled to hold a negotiable instrument. He need not be in possession of the instrument but is considered to be the lawful owner in the event of loss or destruction of the instrument. As per the Indian Law, every person who is in possession of the instrument cannot be called a holder. To be a holder, the person must be named in the instrument as the payee, or the endorsee, or he must be the bearer thereof. A person who has obtained possession of an instrument by theft, or under a forged endorsement, is not a holder, as he is not entitled to recover the amount of the instrument.

HOLDER IN DUE COURSE (Sec. 9)

A holder in due course is the person who actually possesses the instrument. He should obtain the possession of the instrument in good faith, that too in payment of value before the maturity of the instrument.

A holder in due course is in a privileged position. He is not only himself protected against all defects of the person from whom he received the instrument as current coins, but also serves as a channel to protect all subsequent holders. A holder in due course can recover the amount of the instrument from all previous parties, although no consideration was paid by some of the previous parties to the instrument or there was defect of title in the parties from whom he took it. Once an instrument passed through the hands of a holder in due course, it is purged of all defects. It is like current coins. Whoever takes it can recover the amount from all the parties previous to such a holder.

ENDORSEMENT (Secs. 15 and 16)

The literal meaning of the word endorsement is writing on the back of an instrument. But under the Negotiable Instruments Act, it means, writing of the name of the endorsee on the back of the instrument by the endorser under his signature with the object of transferring the rights therein. It is customary to endorse a negotiable instrument on the back. If an instrument is fully covered with endorsements, and no space is left, further endorsement can be made on a slip of paper (called allonge) annexed thereto. The person who effects an endorsement is called the 'endorser'. The person to whom the instrument is endorsed is called the 'endorsee'.

Kinds of Endorsement

An endorsement may be of the following kinds:

1. **Blank or General Endorsement (Secs. 16 and 54):** An endorsement is said to be in blank when an endorser puts his signature on the instrument without mentioning the name of the endorsee.

KINDS OF ENDORSEMENT
• Blank or general endorsement
• Special or full endorsement
• Restrictive endorsement
• Conditional or qualified endorsement
• Partial endorsement

   By blank endorsement, an order instrument becomes a bearer instrument. An instrument endorsed in blank can be negotiated further by mere delivery even though it was an order instrument originally.

   Example:

   Sd./-

   D. Mohan

2. **Special or Full Endorsement (Sec. 16):** An endorsement is said to be full when the endorsement contains not only the

signature of the endorser but also the name of the endorsee. Further negotiation of such an instrument requires further endorsement by the holder.

Example: Pay to Ghosh or order.

Sd./

D. Mohan

An endorsement in blank can be converted into an endorsement in full. The holder of a negotiable instrument endorsed in blank may, by writing above the endorser's signature a direction to pay any person as endorsee convert the endorsement in blank into endorsement in full. In such a case the person is not liable as an endorser on the bill (Sec. 49).

3. **Restrictive Endorsement (Sec. 50):**   An endorsement is said to be restrictive when it prohibits or restricts the further negotiation of the instrument. In this case, the subsequent endorsees acquire only the title of the first endorser. Hence the quality of negotiability is lost by such endorsement.

Example: Pay to Ghosh only–

Sd./-

D. Mohan

4. **Conditional or Qualified Endorsement:** An endorsement is conditional or qualified if it limits or negates the liability of the endorser.

Example: Pay to Ghosh on signing a receipt.

Sd./-

D. Mohan

An endorser may limit his liability on any of the following ways:

(a)   *'Sans Recourse' Endorsement:* In the case of sans recourse endorsement, the endorser makes it clear that he will not be liable in the event of dishonour of the instrument. So the subsequent holders cannot hold such an endorser liable in the case of non-payment.

Example: Pay to Ghosh without resource to me.

Sd./-

D. Mohan

If an endorser excludes or limits his liability by using the word sans recourse and afterwards becomes the holder of the same instrument, all intermediate endorsers continue to be liable to him (Sec. 52).

Example: A, the holder of a bill endorses it 'sans recourse' to B, B endorses it to C, C to D, D to E and E endorses it again to A. A can recover the amount of the bill from B, C, D and E or any of them.

(d) *Liability Dependent upon a Contingency:* An endorser may endorse an instrument in such a way that his liability depends upon the happening of a specified event which may or may not happen.

Example: Pay Ghosh or order on his marrying Sita.

Sd./

D. Mohan

(d) *Facultative Endorsement:* In a facultative endorsement, the endorser waives some of his rights, like the right to receive notice of dishonour.

Example: 'Pay to Ghosh. Notice of dishonour waived'.

Sd./

D. Mohan

(d) *'Sans Frais' Endorsement:* An endorsement is said to be sans frais if the endorser does not want the endorsee or any subsequent holder to incur any expense on his account on the instrument.

Example: 'Pay to Ghosh or order, Sans frais'.

Sd./

D. Mohan

5. **Partial Endorsement (Sec. 56):** An endorsement is said to be partial when an endorser endorses only a part of the amount mentioned in the instrument. A partial endorsement is irregular and does not operate as a negotiation of the instrument.

Example: X was the holder of a bill for ₹2,000. He endorsed it as pay to Y or order ₹1,000. This is a partial endorsement and is irregular for the purpose of negotiation.

Effect of Endorsement (Sec. 50)

An endorsement is said to be completed only when the endorser signs his name on the document and delivers it to the endorsee. A completed endorsement has the following effects:

(a) The property together with the rights of further negotiation is transferred from the endorser to the endorsee.

(b) The endorsee obtains the rights to bring an action for recovery against all the parties whose names appear on the instrument.

Who May Endorse?

The payees of an instrument is the rightful person to make the first endorsement. Thereafter, the instrument may be endorsed by any person who has become the holder of the instrument. The maker or drawer of the negotiable instrument may endorse the same only if he has become the holder thereof (Sec. 51).

Cancellation of Endorsement (Sec. 40)

When the holder of a negotiable instrument without the consent of the endorser destroys or impairs the endorser's remedy against prior party, the endorser is discharged from liability to the holder to the same extent as if the instrument had been paid at maturity.

NEGOTIATION BACK

When an endorser negotiates an instrument and again becomes its holder before its maturity the instrument is said to be negotiated back to that endorser. In such a case none of the intermediate holders is liable to him.

> **Example:** A, the holder of a bill of exchange, endorsed it to B, B endorsed it to C, C to D, D to E and E endorsed it again to A. In this case, the endorsement by E to A is a 'negotiation back'. And B, C, D and E are not liable to A.

When an instrument is negotiated back to a prior party, the holder can enforce payment against all intermediate parties if the prior endorsement was 'without resource'.

> **Example:** In the above example, A at the time of the first endorsement expressly excludes his liability. He is not liable to B, C, D or E and if the bill is negotiated back to him, B, C, D and E are all liable to him and he can recover the amount from all or any of them.

INSTRUMENTS OBTAINED BY UNLAWFUL MEANS OR FOR UNLAWFUL CONSIDERATION

Stolen and Lost Instruments

A person who steals or finds a lost negotiable instrument does not acquire a title to the instrument as against the real owner. He cannot enforce payment on it against any party thereto. If he gets payment on it, he is liable to the real owner.

If he negotiates a bill or note payable to bearer by mere delivery to a bona fide transferee for value, the latter acquires a good title to it. But if the thief or finder of a bill or note payable to order forges the endorsement of the real owner and negotiates it to a bona fide transferee for value, the latter acquires no title to it.

Instrument Obtained by Coercion or Fraud

If a negotiable instrument is obtained by coercion or fraud, the person who defrauds is not entitled to recover anything. But if such an instrument passes into the hands of holder in due course, the plea of fraud will not be available against him.

Instrument Obtained for An Unlawful Consideration

A negotiable instrument given for a consideration which is illegal, or opposed to public policy, or immoral is void and creates no obligation between the parties thereto.

> **Example:** A bill of exchange given in consideration of future illicit cohabitation is void. But if such an instrument passes into the hands of a holder in due course, he obtains a good and complete title to it.

Forged Instruments

Forgery is the fraudulent making or alternation of a negotiable instrument to the prejudice of another man's right. A forged instrument is treated a nullity. A title which never came into cannot be improved even if it passes into the hands of a holder in due course.

> **Example:** X forges the signature of Y on a promissory note and transfers the same to Z who takes it bona fide for value. Z gets no title for the note even though he is holder in due course.

Forged Endorsement

If an instrument is endorsed in full, it cannot be negotiated except by endorsement signed by the person to whom or to whose order the instrument is payable. If an endorsement is forged, the endorsee acquires no title to the instrument even though he is a bona fide purchaser.

> **Example:** A bill is payable to 'Ghosh or order'. It is stolen from Ghosh and the thief forges the endorsement of Ghosh and endorses it to Gopal who takes it bona fide and for value. Gopal acquires no title to the bill.

Where an instrument is endorsed in blank, it becomes payable to the bearer. The endorsee of such an instrument derives title by delivery and not by forged endorsement. He can negotiate it further by simple delivery. The transferee can sue any of the parties to the bill without taking the slightest notice of the forgery.

> **Example:** A bill is endorsed 'Pay Ghosh or order'.

Ghosh endorses the bill in blank. It comes into the hands of X. X passes it on to Y by simple delivery. Y forges the endorsement of X and transfers it to Z. As Z the holder, does not derive his title through the forged endorsement of X, but through the endorsement of Ghosh which is genuine, he can sue any of the parties to the bill without taking notice of the forged endorsement of X.

PROMISSORY NOTE

The term promissory note may be defined as a promise in writing, by a person to pay a certain sum of money to a specified person. Section 4 of the Negotiable instruments Act, 1981 defines a promissory note as—

"An instrument in writing containing an unconditional undertaking signed by the maker to pay a certain sum of money only, to or to the order of a certain person".

The following negotiable instruments signed by X are valid promissory notes on the basis of the above definition.

(i) I promise to pay Y or order ₹1,000

(ii) I acknowledge myself to be indebted to Y for ₹2,000 to be paid on demand, for value received.

Parties to a Promissory Note

There are only two parties to a promissory note viz., the maker and the payee.

Maker. The person who makes the promissory note and promises to pay is called the maker.

Payee. The person to whom the payment is to be made is called the payee.

Specimen of a Promissory Note

₹ 500.00	Bombay March 31, 2006

Three months after date, I promise to pay Ghosh or order the sum of rupees five hundred for value received.

Sd/-Krishnan

STAMP

To
Ghosh,
Gandhi Nagar,
Bomaby

In this promissory note Krishnan is the maker and Ghosh is the payee.

Essentials of a Valid Promissory Note

1. It must be in writing.
2. It must contain an undertaking to pay money. A mere acknowledgement of debt is not a promissory note.
3. The promise to pay should be unconditional. If any condition is included in the promise, the instrument will not be a promissory note.

    Example: I promise to pay B ₹1,000 when he delivers the goods.
4. It should be signed by the maker.
5. The maker must be certain. If the maker cannot be identified with certainty from the instrument itself, the instrument, even if it contains an unconditional promise to pay, is not a promissory note.
6. The sum payable must be certain and must not be capable of contingent additions or subtractions. The following instruments signed by X are not promissory notes (as the sum payable is not certain):

   (i) "I promise to pay Y ₹ 2,000 and the fine as per the rules".

   (ii) "I promise to pay Y ₹ 2,000, and all the other sums due to him".

7. The payee must be certain.

BILL OF EXCHANGE

The term Bill of Exchange is an order, in writing requiring a certain person to pay a certain sum of money to a specified person. Section 5 of the Negotiable Instruments Act, 1881 defines a bill of exchanges as "an instrument in writing containing an unconditional order, signed by the maker, directing a certain person to pay a certain sum of money only to or to the order of a certain person or to the bearer of the instrument".

Generally, a bill of exchange is drawn by the creditor, who directs his debtor to pay the money to the person specified in the instrument.

> **Example:** X wrote and signed an instrument ordering Y to pay ₹1,000 to Z. This is a Bill of Exchange. In this instrument Y has been ordered to pay ₹1,000 to Z.

Parties to a Bill

Usually there are three parties to a bill of exchange, viz. drawer, drawee and payee.

Drawer. The person who makes the bill is known as the drawer.

Drawee. The person who is directed to pay the amount of the bill is called the drawee. When the bill is accepted by the drawee, he becomes the acceptor of the bill.

Payee. The person to whom the payment of the bill is to be made is known as the payee.

The drawer or the payee who is in possession of the bill is known as the 'holder'. The holder must present the bill of the drawee for his acceptance.

When the holder endorses the bill to another, he is known as the 'endorser'. The person to whom the bill is endorsed is known as the 'endorsee'.

When in the bill or any endorsement thereon the name of another drawee is mentioned in addition to the original drawee, such a drawee is known as a drawee in case of need. Where a drawee in case of need is named in the bill of exchange, the bill is not dishonoured still such a drawee refuses to accept or pay the bill.

Specimen of a Bill of Exchange

₹ 1,000	Madras, March 31, 2006

Two months after date pay to Krishnan or order the sum of One thousand rupees, for value received.

Sd/-Gopal

Accepted
Ghosh

STAMP

To
Ghosh,
Gandhi Nagar,
Calcutta

Ghosh of Calcutta purchases goods on credit from Gopal of Madras for ₹1,000 to be paid 2 months after date. Gopal purchases goods from Krishnan of Bombay for ₹1,000 on the terms. Now Gopal may order Ghosh to pay the sum of ₹1,000 to Krishnan. This order is a bill of exchange.

Essentials of Bill of Exchange

The essential elements of a bill are as follows:

(a) The bill of exchange must be in writing.

(b) It should contain an order to pay.

(c) The order must be unconditional. If the order contains any condition, e.g., pay to A if he gets a first class for M.A., the bill is invalid.

(d) It must be signed by the drawer.

(e) It requires three parties, i.e., drawer, drawee and payee.

(f) The sum payable must be certain.

(g) It must contain an order to pay money.

(h) It should be stamped according to the provisions of the Indian Stamp Act, 1889.

(i) It should be accepted by the drawee by putting his signature on the face of the instrument with or without the word accepted.

TENOR OF THE BILL

The time fixed for the payment of the bill is known as the tenor of the bill. On the basis of the payment, the bills are brought under two categories. They are: (i) Demand Bills, and (ii) Time Bills.

(i) **Demand Bills:** These are bills which are made payable on demand or at sight. No time is fixed for the payment of such bills.

(ii) **Time Bills:** These are bills which are made payable only on the expiry of a fixed period say, 2 or 3 months. Time bills are drawn payable 'after date' or 'after sight'. In the case of after date bill, the date of payment is ascertained from the date on which the bill is drawn. But in the case of 'after sight bill', the date of payment is calculated from the date of the acceptance.

MATURITY DATE AND DAYS OF GRACE

Maturity date or due date is the date on which the payment of an instrument falls due (Sec. 22). Every instrument payable otherwise than 'on demand' is entitled to three days of grace originally allowed as a gratuitous favour to the debtor.

> **Example:** A bill drawn on 1st January, 2006 and payable after three months becomes due on 4th April, 2006 (1st April plus three days of grace).

Calculation of Maturity Date (Secs. 23 to 25)

(i) If the bill is worded as 'pay three months after date, the maturity date is to be ascertained' from the date of the bill. But if the bill is worded as pay 3 months after sight, the maturity date is to be ascertained from the date of acceptance.

> **Example:** If a bill is drawn on 20th January, 2006 and accepted on 25th January which, is payable three months 'after sight', becomes due only on 28th April 2006. Here the date of acceptance, i.e., 25th January is to be considered for calculating the due date.

(ii) If the day on which the bill becomes mature is a public holiday, it is deemed to be due on the next preceding business day. The expression 'public holiday' includes Sundays and any other day declared by the Central Government, by notification in the Official Gazette, to be a public holiday.

> **Example:** A bill dated 12th May, 2006 and payable after three months falls due on 15th August, 2006. But 15th

August is a public holiday and hence, the bill is payable on 14th August.

(iii) If the month in which the period of a bill terminates has no corresponding day, the period shall be deemed to terminate on the last day of such a month.

Example: A bill dated 31st August, 2006 is made payable 3 months after date. The bill becomes mature on 3rd December.

(iv) If the bill is drawn payable after a certain number of days, the due date is calculated by excluding the date of the bill.

Example: A bill drawn on 1st January, 2006 and made payable after 20 days becomes due on 24th January, 2006, (i.e., the period of 20 days is counted from 2nd January and 3 days of grace is added to it).

PAYMENT IN DUE COURSE (Sec. 10)

'Payment in due course' means payment made in accordance with the apparent tenor of the instrument. A payment would not be a payment in due course if it is made to a person not entitled to receive it or if it is made before the date of maturity.

Payment in due course, which results in the discharge of a negotiable instrument should fulfil the following conditions:

1. The payment should be in accordance with the apparent tenor of the instrument.

2. The payment must be made by or on behalf of the drawee or acceptor.

3. The payment must be made in good faith and without negligence.

4. The person to whom the payment is made should be in possession of the instrument.

5. The payment should be made in money only unless agreed to by the parties to receive payment by cheque or another bill.

6. There must not exist any ground for believing that the possessor is not entitled to receive payment.

ACCEPTANCE OF A BILL

Acceptance is the act of putting the signature of the drawee on the bill of exchange. The bill is said to be accepted when the drawee writes the word 'accepted' on the bill and signs his name below it.

The liability of the drawee arises only when the bill of exchange has been validly accepted by him. The following are the essentials of a valid acceptance.

1. It must be in writing;
2. It should be signed by the drawee or his duly authorized agent;
3. It must appear on the bill itself;
4. It will be completed only when the drawee hands over the bill accepted to the holder.

Modes of Acceptance

There are two types of acceptance, viz., (a) General Acceptance and (b) Qualified or Conditional Acceptance.

(a) *General Acceptance:* An acceptance is said to be general when the assent to the order of the drawee is given without any condition. It is also called the 'qualified acceptance'. It is a type of acceptance where the drawee signs his name on the bill with or without the word acceptance. He agrees to pay the amount on the due date as per the terms and conditions of the bill.

(b) *Qualified Acceptance:* An acceptance is said to be qualified if some condition or qualification is added to the assent of the drawee. Acceptance is qualified when the acceptance makes the payment of the money dependent upon the happening of an event. Qualified acceptance can be of different types.

1. **Conditional:** Conditional acceptance is one where the drawee accepts the bill adding some conditions.

   Example: Accepted, payable when goods are sold.

   Sd/-

   Drawee.

2. **Partial:** Partial acceptance is one where the drawee undertakes to pay only a part of the amount due on the bill.

   Example: A bill drawn for ₹1,500 and accepted in words reading as "accepted for ₹1,000"

   Sd/-

   Drawee.

KINDS OF QUALIFIED ACCEPTANCE
• Conditional
• Partial
• Qualified as to time
• Qualified as to place
• Acceptance by some of the drawee

3. **Qualified as to Time:**   If the drawee accepts the bill with a maturity date other than the date specified in the bill, the acceptance is qualified as to time:

   Example: A bill drawn payable 50 days after date and accepted in words reading as 'accepted payable 90 days, 'after date'.

   Sd/-

   Drawee.

4. **Qualified as to place:**   Acceptance is said to be qualified as to place when a drawee accepts a bill with a condition that it is payable at a specified place only.

   Example: Accepted payable on Punjab National Bank, Bombay.

   Sd/-

   Drawee.

5. **Acceptance by some of the Drawee:**   If a bill is drawn on several drawees, it should be accepted by all of them. But if one of the several drawees undertakes to pay the amount due on the bill, the acceptance is said to be the acceptance by some of the drawee only. It is a valid acceptance.

Presentment for Payment

When a bill is presented to the drawee on the due date for payment, it is known as 'Presentment of a bill for payment'. The holder of the bill must present it to the drawee for payment. The purpose of presentment is to give the party concerned an opportunity to pay. Valid presentment for payment means presentment: (a) on the proper day, (b) at the proper hour, (c) by the proper person, and (d) in the proper manner.

   If the bill is not presented, all the parties except the maker and acceptor are discharged from liability to the holder. There is a distinction between the liability of the maker and the acceptor and that of the drawer and the endorser. The liability of the maker and the acceptor is absolute, but that of the endorser and the drawer is conditional. There will be no cause of action without presentment.

DISHONOURING OF BILLS

A bill of exchange may be dishonoured due to non-acceptance or non-payment. According to Sec. 91, a bill of exchange is treated as dishonoured due to its non-acceptance in any of the following cases:

(i) When the drawee does not accept the bill within 48 hours from the time of presentment for acceptance, or refuses to accept it.

(ii) When the drawee accepts the bill but he seeks to qualify his acceptance, the holder is not bound to take a qualified acceptance.

(iii) Where presentment for acceptance is excused and the bill remains, unaccepted.

Under the following circumstance the presentment for acceptance is excused:

(a) Where the drawee cannot be found after a reasonable search.

(b) If the drawee is incompetent to contract.

(c) If the drawee is a fictitious person.

(d) If drawee becomes bankrupt.

(e) If drawee is dead.

Dishonour by Non-payment

As per Sec. 92, when the acceptor refuses to pay the amount of the bill on due date, the bill is said to be dishonoured by non-payment.

When a bill is dishonoured by non-payment, the holder should give notice of dishonour to the drawer and all previous endorsers. If he commits default to it, they will be discharged from their liability. In such a case, the holder can recover the amount only from the acceptor. The notice of dishonour must be given within a reasonable time after dishonour.

Noting and Protesting

The term 'noting' may be defined as the recording of the fact of dishonour of an instrument by a 'Notary public'. Notary public is government official who is appointed under the Notaries Act to attest certain documents.

When a bill is dishonoured, the holder can, after giving due notice of dishonour, sue the liable parties to realise the amount due on bill. However, before suing, the holder may also get the fact of dishonour, authenticated by 'noting' by a Notary Public. When a dishonoured bill is given to a Notary Public for noting, he will present it again to the acceptor to confirm the dishonour. Then he notes the fact of dishonour on the document and puts his signature with date.

The noting should be made within a reasonable time after the dishonour of the bill. As per Sec. 99, the noting should specify the following particulars:

(a) The fact of dishonour, (b) The date of dishonour, (c) The reason, if any, for dishonour, and (d) The charges of the Notary Public.

After the bill is 'noted' the holder may get a 'protest' from the Notary Public.

The term 'Protest' may be defined as the formal certificate of dishonour issued by the Notary Public to the holder of a bill. As per Sec. 100 this certificate should contain the details of the bill, the fact of dishonour, the date and place of dishonour and the signature of the Notary Public.

Noting and protesting are not compulsory in the case of inland bills. But noting and protesting are compulsory in the case of foreign bills.

DISCOUNTING OF BILLS

A holder of bill of exchange who requires money urgently can discount it with the commercial bank without waiting till the maturity of the bill. The bank on endorsing the bill to it, pays the money after deducting a small amount called discount. This practice of transferring the bill to the bank and obtaining the amount before the maturity date is known as discounting.

Through discounting, the holder is not discharged from his liability. He will continue to be liable as an endorser. If the discounted bill is dishonoured the bank can get the amount from him.

RETIREMENT OF A BILL AND REBATE

An acceptor of a bill may make payment before maturity, and the bill is then said to be retired. If a bill is paid off before maturity, the drawer may permit a certain deduction from the amount of the bill considering the element of interest involved. This deduction permitted by the drawer to the acceptor is called 'Rebate'.

ACCOMMODATION BILLS

Accommodation bill is one which is made only to provide financial help to some party by discounting the bill. It does not involve any valuable consideration and hence is not a genuine trade bill. Such, bills are also known as 'fictitious bills' or 'kites'.

Example: A is in need of money and approaches his friend B who instead of lending the money directly proposes to draw an "Accommodation Bill". Thus, A draws a bill on B who in turn accepts the same. The bill is then discounted with a bank by A and he gets the amount. On the maturity date, A pays the amount of the bill to B to enable him to meet the bill. Here A and B merely act as drawer and acceptor without any business transaction. The purpose of drawing the bill is to assist A.

DOCUMENTARY AND CLEAN BILLS

If a bill of exchange is attached with document such as bill of lading, railway receipt, invoice, etc., it is known as 'documentary bill'. Such documents are delivered to the buyer only on the acceptance of payment of the bill.

When no documents of title are attached to a bill of exchange, it is called a 'Clean bill'.

Bill in Sets

Foreign bills are usually drawn in sets to avoid the danger of loss. They are drawn in sets of three, each of which is called 'via' and as soon as any one of them is paid, the others become in-operative.

Where a bill is drawn in set each part contains a reference to the other part and all the parts constitute one bill. In such cases only one part of the bill needs to be accepted. A person who acquires the title first to a part of the bill is entitled to the whole bill.

Foreign Bills

'It is one which is drawn in India and made payable in a foreign country or drawn on one who is a resident of a foreign country'.

CHEQUES

A cheque is a means by which a person who has funds in the hands of a bank withdraws the same or part of it. Section 6 of the Negotiable Instruments Act defines a cheque as:

"A bill of exchange drawn on a specified banker payable on demand". A cheque is a species of a bill of exchange but it has two additional qualifications, viz., (a) it is always drawn on a specified banker, and (b) it is always payable on demand.

Parties to a Cheque

There are three parties to a cheque viz.,

(a) *Drawer (Depositor):* The drawer is the person who makes or draws the cheque.

(b) *Drawee (Banker):* The drawee is the person on whom the cheque is drawn.

(c) *Payee:* The payee is the person to whom the cheque is made payable.

Specimen of a Cheque with Counterfoil

CENTRAL BANK OF INDIA Fort, Bombay 400001. ___200___	CENTRAL BANK OF INDIA Fort, Bombay 400001.
Issued To:_____	Ch. No. [ ] ____200___
Particulars:_____	PAY _____ _____ OR BEARER
Amount:_____	RUPEES _____ ₹ [ ]
₹:_____	A/c No. [ ] L.F. [ ] Intl. [ ]

Dating of a Cheque

Before issuing a cheque, the drawer should put the date on the cheque. The banker may return the cheque unpaid unless it is dated. The drawer can put any date on the cheque including a holiday. The date shown on the cheque is considered as the date of issue of the cheque.

Ante-dated Cheque

When a cheque bears a date earlier than the date of issue, it is known as an ante-dated cheque. This cheque is valid up to three months from the date of issue.

Post-dated Cheque

When a cheque bears a date subsequent to the date of issue, it is known as a post-dated cheque. This cheque is payable only on or after the date specified in the cheque.

Stale Cheque

A cheque which has been in circulation for more than three months from the date of issue, is known as a stale cheque. It is an outdated cheque and the bankers need not honour such cheques.

MARKING OF CHEQUES

Marking is "the writing on a cheque by the drawee banker that it would be honoured when duly presented for payment". The marking of a cheque is made by the drawee bankers at the instance of the drawer, or the holder or the collecting banker. A cheque may be marked in a variety of ways. It may be marked with the words 'approved' or 'good'. Sometimes the drawee banker simply initials the cheque. Such cheques are also called certified cheque. The effect of marking is that the payee is certain to get the payment. Therefore, the drawee banker (paying banker) sets side the required amount for the payment of such cheques from the accounts of the drawer.

CROSSING OF CHEQUES

Cheques are either open cheques or crossed cheques. Open cheque is one which is paid over the counter of the bank. When such a cheque is in circulation, there is every possibility that it may be stolen or lost. The finder or thief can, therefore, get it encashed at the bank unless the drawer has in the meantime stopped the payment. To avoid such possibilities cheques are crossed.

A cheque is said to be crossed when two parallel transverse lines are drawn across the face of it. Usually, the parallel lines are drawn on the left hand top corner of the cheque. The payment of such a cheque can be obtained only by opening an account with a bank. The unique object of the crossing of a cheque is to assure that only the real holder obtains the payment of the cheque.

Types of Crossing of the Cheque

There are two modes of crossing, namely, General crossing and Special crossing.

General Crossing (Sec. 123)

A cheque is said to be crossed generally where it bears across its face an addition of: (i) the words and company or any abbreviation thereof, between two parallel transverse lines, either with or without the words 'not negotiable', or (ii) two parallel transverse lines simply, either with or without the words 'not negotiable'.

The payment of a cheque containing general crossing is always collected by the payee through some banker.

Specimen of General Crossing

(1) | (2) and Company | (3) & Co., | (4) Not Negotiable | (5) Not Negotiable & Co.

Special Crossing (Sec. 124)

When a cheque bears across its face an addition of the name of a banker either with or without the words 'not negotiable' the cheque is deemed to be crossed specially.

Transverse lines are not necessary for a special crossing. Special crossing is safer than general crossing. When a cheque is crossed specially, the drawee banker will pay the amount only to the bank specified in the crossing.

Specimen of Special Crossing

(1) State Bank of India | (2) State Bank of India | (3) Account Payee State Bank of India | (4) Not Negotiable State Bank of India

The words 'A/c Payee' on a cheque are a direction to the collecting banker to credit the proceeds of the cheque only to the account of the drawee or to the specified person.

The effect of the addition of the words 'not negotiable' on a crossed cheque is that when such a cheque is endorsed, the endorsee cannot get a better title than that of the endorser (Sec. 130). In other words, 'not negotiable crossing' materially reduces the negotiable value of the cheque, in the sense that the person taking it shall get only the rights of the transferor, but no better rights.

Who may Cross a Cheque? (Sec. 126)

A cheque may be crossed by:

1. The drawer.

2. The holder. In the case of an open cheque, a holder can cross it generally or specially. If it is crossed generally, he can cross it specially. He can also add words like 'A/c Payee' 'not negotiable' in a crossed cheque.

3. The Banker. If a specially crossed cheque is sent to a banker for collection, he can cross it again specially.

Paying and Collecting Banks of a Crossed Cheque

A banker who honours his customers' cheque is known as the 'paying banker'. A banker who collects payment on behalf of its customer is known as the 'collecting banker'.

If a banker has paid a crossed cheque in accordance with the direction in the cheque, the banker is discharged from liability as if the cheque has been paid to and received by the rightful owner thereof. But the banker is liable to the rightful owner if the crossed cheque is paid contrary to the direction given by the crossing.

A banker receiving payment (i.e., collecting bank) in good faith and without negligence for a customer of a crossed cheque is not liable to the rightful owner in case the title of the cheque is defective. A bank will be guilty of negligence when it ignores a direction on the cheque like 'account payee' or if it fails to note the difference between the name of the payee as given in the cheque and in the endorsement.

Comparative study of promissory note, bill of exchange and cheque

Promissory Note	Bill of Exchange	Cheque
1. Two parties.	Three parties.	Three parties.
2. Unconditional undertaking.	Unconditional order.	Unconditional order.
3. Irrevocable.	Irrevocable.	Revocable.
4. Not payable on demand.	Not payable on demand.	Payable on demand.
5. Drawee may be any person.	Drawee may be any person.	Drawee always a banker.
6. Presentment for acceptance, protest, notice of dishonour, etc., not applicable.	Presentment for acceptance, protest, notice of dishonour, etc., applicable.	Presentment for acceptance, protest, notice of dishonour, etc., applicable.
7. Maker is the principal debtor.	In an accepted bill, acceptor is the principal debtor. In an unaccepted bill drawer is the principal debtor.	Drawer is the principal debtor. There is a presumption of drawer's having funds in the bank.

CAPACITY OF PARTIES TO A NEGOTIABLE INSTRUMENT

Capacity of parties here means competency of parties to enter into a valid contract. Every person is competent to contract who is of the age of majority, and is of sound mind and is not disqualified from contracting by any law which he is subject to (Sec. 11 of the Contract Act, 1872). The capacity of a person to incur liability as a party to a bill of exchange, promissory note or cheque is co-extensive with his capacity to contract. The following are the provisions regarding the incapacity of certain persons in connection with the negotiable instruments.

Minor

A contract with a minor is void and he is not liable under contracts on negotiable instruments. However, a minor may draw, endorse, deliver and negotiate a negotiable instrument so as to bind all other parties except himself (Sec. 26).

> **Example:** X, Y and Z executed a promissory note in favour of A. Z is the minor. In this case, Z is not liable under the note. But X and Y shall remain liable to pay the money to A.

However, the minor's rights under the negotiable instrument are not affected. He can enforce payment if he is the payee or endorsee or holder.

> **Example:** X draws a cheque in favour of Y, a minor. In this case Y can recover the money due on the cheque.

Persons of Unsound Mind

Contracts of lunatics, idiots and drunken persons are void. Bills and notes drawn or made by persons of unsound mind are void as against them. But the other parties remain liable.

Corporation

A corporation or a company is an artificial person created by law. A trading company has implied power, and a non-trading company must take express power, to draw, make, endorse and accept negotiable instruments.

Agent

An agent is a person who acts on behalf of his principal. An agent who signs a negotiable instrument on behalf of his principal may bind his principal if he:

(a) signs the principal's name or states on the face of the instrument that he signs as agent, and

(b) acts within the scope of his authority.

Partners

In a trading firm, each partner has implied authority to bind other partners by drawing, endorsing, accepting or negotiating negotiable instruments.

LIABILITY OF PARTIES TO A NEGOTIABLE INSTRUMENT

1. **Liability of Drawer (Sec. 30):** The drawer of a bill of exchange or cheque is bound to compensate the holder if the instruments have been dishonoured by non-acceptance or by non-payment. Such a liability arises only if due notice has been given to the drawer.

2. **Liability of Drawee of Cheque (Sec. 31):** If a banker (a drawee) without justification, fails to honour his customer's cheque, he is liable to compensate the drawer (the depositor) for any loss or damage suffered by him.

3. **Liability of Maker of Note and Acceptor of Bill (Sec. 32):** The maker of a promissory note and the acceptor of a bill of exchange are 'primarily' liable to pay the amount due on the instrument. In default, they become liable to compensate to any subsequent party for the loss caused to him by the dishonour.

4. **Liability of Endorser (Sec. 35):** The liability of an endorser to all subsequent holders arises only in the case of dishonour of the instrument provided:

   (a) there is no contract to the contrary;
   (b) the endorser has not limited or qualified his liability by using appropriate words; and
   (c) due notice has been given to him or received by him.

5. **Liability of Prior Parties to a Holder in Due Course (Sec. 36):** Every prior party to a negotiable instrument is liable thereon to a holder in due course until the instrument is duly discharged.

Basic Principles of Liability of Parties

The liability of parties of an instrument is based on the principle of suretyship, i.e., certain parties are liable as principal debtors, and certain are liable as sureties (guarantors) (Sec. 37). The following parties are liable as principal debtors, i.e., their liability is primary:

(a) The maker of a promissory note.

(b) The drawer of a cheque.

(c) The drawer of a bill until acceptance.

(d) The acceptor of a bill.

All the other parties are liable as sureties. Their liability arises only on default by a party who is primarily liable. Among the parties who are liable as sureties, each prior party is liable as principal debtor in respect of each subsequent party unless otherwise provided (Sec. 38).

DISCHARGE OF A PARTY OR PARTIES FROM LIABILITY

When any particular party or parties are discharged, the instrument continues to be negotiable and the undischarged parties remain liable on it.

> **Example:** The non-presentment of a bill on the due date discharges the endorsers from their liability, but the acceptor remains liable on it.

A party may be discharged on the following modes:

(a) *By Cancellation:* When the holder of a negotiable instrument or his agent cancels the name of a party on the instrument with the intention of discharging him.

(b) *By Release:* When the holder releases any party to the instrument.

(c) Discharge of secondary parties, i.e., endorsers.

(d) By operation of law, e.g., by insolvency of the debtor.

(e) By allowing drawee more than 48 hours to accept the bill, all previous parties are discharged.

(f) By non-presentment of cheque promptly the drawer is discharged.

(g) By material alteration.

WHAT IS MATERIAL ALTERATION? (SEC. 87)

An alteration is material which in any way alters the operation of the instrument and the liabilities of the parties thereto. A material alteration renders the instrument void, but it affects only those persons who have already become parties at the date of the alteration. Examples of material alteration are:

Alteration (i) of the date of the instrument, (ii) of the sum payable, (iii) in the time of payment, (iv) of the place of payment, (v) of the rate of interest, (vi) by addition of a new party, (vii) by tearing the instrument in a material part.

SOME IMPORTANT TERMS

1. *Bank Draft or Demand Draft:* A bank draft is a bill of exchange drawn by one bank on another bank, or by its own branch. It is a negotiable instrument.

2. *Traveller's Cheque:* A traveller's cheque is a cheque drawn by a specified banker upon self. It is payable on demand and the payee may get the money from any branch of the banker. The object of such cheques is to avoid risk.

   A traveller's cheque contains two spaces for payee's signature usually one at the top and the other at the bottom. He has to sign at the top at the time of getting the cheque from the banker and at the bottom at the time of taking payment of cheque.

3. *Gift Cheque:* A gift cheque is an order by a banker directing itself (i.e., branches) to pay a specified amount to a specified person on demand. It has a special form which is particularly meant for sending money by way of gift.

4. *Escrow:* A bill may be delivered conditionally or for a specific purpose only and not for the purpose of transferring the property absolutely. The effect of the delivery of the bill is thus limited by the condition attached to the delivery. A bill thus delivered conditionally is called an 'escrow'.

5. *Inchoate Instrument (Incomplete Bills):* If an instrument is wanting in any material particulars, it is known as an inchoate instrument. An instrument may be blank as to the drawer, as to the payee, or in any other particulars. The person in possession thereof has prima facie authority to complete such a bill by filling up the blanks in the bill. Until such blanks are filled up, the instrument is invalid and no action is maintainable on it.

HUNDIS

The term 'hundi' is derived from a sanskrit word 'hund' which means to collect. Hundis are indigenous bills of exchange drawn in a vernacular language. It is governed by local usages and customs. Although, the provisions of the Negotiable Instruments Act are not applicable to hundis, it also recognises, them as such.

Kinds of Hundis

The following are the important types of hundis.

1. **Darshani Hundis:** It is a hundi payable at sight. It is just like a demand bill.

2. **Muddate Hundis:** It is a hundi payable after a specific period.

3. **Shah Jog Hundis:** 'Shah' means respectable person. Shah jog hundi means a hundi which is payable only to a shah. It is freely transferable by mere delivery.

4. **Nam Jog Hundis:** These hundis are payable to or to the order of a specified person.

5. **Firman Jog Hundis:** Firman means order. A firman jog hundi is one which is payable to order. It is transferable only by endorsement and delivery.

KINDS OF HUNDIS
• Darshani Hundis
• Muddate Hundis
• Shah Jog Hundis
• Nam Jog Hundis
• Firman Jog Hundis
• Dhani Jog Hundis
• Jokhmi Hundis

6. **Dhani Jog Hundis:** Dhani means a 'holder'. A dhani jog hundi is like a bearer bill, which is payable to the holder or bearer. It is also freely transferable by mere delivery.

7. **Jokhmi Hundis:** A jokhmi hundi is one which implies a condition that the money shall be payable by the drawee who is the purchaser of goods, only in the event of the safe arrival of the goods against which the hundi is drawn. It is a sort of insurance.

PENALTIES IN THE CASE OF DISHONOUR OF CERTAIN CHEQUES FOR INSUFFICIENCY OF FUNDS IN THE ACCOUNTS

The Amendment Act of 1988 has inserted a new chapter XVII in the Negotiable Instruments Act, 1881. It comprises Secs. 138 to 142.

Dishonour of Cheque for Insufficiency, etc., of Funds in the Account (Sec. 138)

A drawer of a dishonoured cheque shall be deemed to have committed an offence and shall, without prejudice to any other provisions of the Negotiable Instrument Act, 1881, be punished with imprisonment for a term which may extend to one year or with fine which may extend to twice the amount of the cheque or with both provided:

(i) the cheque has been dishonoured due to insufficiency of funds in the account maintained by him with a banker for the payment of any amount of money to another person from out of that account.

(ii) the payment for which the cheque was issued, should have been in discharge of a legally enforceable debt or liability in whole or part of it.

(iii) the cheque should have been presented by the payee or the holder in due course within a period of six months from the date of which it is drawn or within the period of its validity, whichever is earlier.

(iv) the payee or the holder in due course of the cheque should have given a notice demanding payment within 15 days to the drawer on receipt of the information of dishonour of cheque from the bank.

(v) the drawer is liable only if he fails to make the payment within 15 days of such a notice period; and

(vi) the payee or holder in due course of the cheque dishonoured should have made a complaint within one month of the cause of action arising under Sec. 138.

Presumption in Favour of Holder (Sec. 139)

It shall be presumed, unless contrary is proved that the holder of a cheque received the cheque of the nature referred to in Sec. 138 for discharge, in whole or in part of any debt or other liability.

Defence which may not be Allowed in any Prosecution under Sec. 138 (Sec. 140)

It shall not be a defence in a prosecution for an offence under Sec. 138 that the drawer has no reason to believe that when he issued the cheque that the cheque may be dishonoured for the reasons mentioned in Sec. 138.

Offences by Companies (Sec. 141)

If the person committing an offence is a company, the company as well the person who was in charge of the company for the conduct of the business of the company, shall be deemed to be guilty of offence and shall be punished accordingly. Further a director, manager, secretary or other officer shall be deemed to be guilty of that offence unless:

(i) such a person proves that the offence was committed without his knowledge, or

(ii) he had exercised all due diligence to prevent the commission of such an offence.

Cognisance of Offences (Sec. 142)

Notwithstanding anything contained in the Code of Criminal Procedure, 1973:

(a) no Court shall take cognisance of any offence punishable under Sec. 138 except under a complaint, in writing, made by the payee or, as the case may be, the holder in due course of the cheque.

(b) such a complaint is made within one month of the date on which the cause of action arises under Sec. 138.

(c) no Court inferior to that of a Metropolitan Magistrate or a Judicial Magistrate of the First Class shall try any offence punishable under Sec. 138.

REVIEW QUESTIONS

1. What is a negotiable instrument? Explain its characteristics.

2. Define the term promissory note. What are its essential elements?

3. State the comparison between a promissory note, bill of exchange and a cheque.

4. What is meant by the term crossing a cheque? What are the various types of crossing?

5. Write short notes on:

   (a) Bill in sets   (b) Inchoate instruments

   (c) Escrow   (d) Accommodation bill

   (e) Bearer and order instruments

6. Define the term 'Holder'. Distinguish between holder and holder in due course.

7. Write notes on:

   (a) Gift cheque

   (b) Traveller's cheque

   (c) Documentary and clean bill

   (d) Marking of cheques

8. Define the term 'negotiation'. What are the different modes of negotiation?

9. What do you mean by endorsement? Explain the various kinds of endorsement.

10. What is meant by acceptance of a bill of exchange? Explain the various kinds of acceptance.

11. What is meant by dishonour by non-acceptance and dishonour by non-payment.

12. Write notes on:

   (a) Presentment for sight

   (b) Conditional or qualified acceptance

   (c) Noting and protest

   (d) Forged instruments

   (e) Allonge

13. Explain the rules regarding negotiation of a lost instrument, a forged instrument, an instrument obtained by fraud, or for unlawful consideration.

14. What are the various methods of discharge from liability of parties to a negotiable instrument?

15. What is material alteration? What are its effects?

16. State the circumstances under which a banker would be justified in dishonouring a cheque.

17. Write notes on:

   (a) Payment in due course

   (b) Maturity date and days of grace

   (c) Assignment

   (d) Hundis

18. Examine to what extent a minor can be a party to a negotiable instrument.

19. Define the term hundi. What are its various kinds?

PRACTICAL PROBLEMS

Attempt the following problems, giving reasons.

1. A company issued a cheque to its bankers. A receipt was appended to the cheque and it ordered the banker to make the payment "provided the receipt form at foot hereof is duly signed, stamped and dated". Is the cheque valid?

   Hint: The cheque is not valid because its payment is made conditional upon signing of the receipt.

2. P draws on Q a bill payable 2 months after sight. It passes through several hands before R becomes its holder. On presentation by R, Q refuses to accept it. Discuss the right of R on the bill.

   Hint: All parties prior to R continue to be liable to R for the payment of the bill.

3. P sells a TV to Q, a minor who pays for it by his cheque P endorses the cheque to R, who takes it in good faith and for value. The cheque is dishonoured on presentation. Can R enforce the payment of the cheque against P or Q?

   Hint: R can enforce the payment against P and not against Q.

4. P makes a pronote payable to Q who endorses it to R, who takes it as a holder in due course. R sues P on the note and P proves that he made it for an illegal consideration. Can R recover the amount?

   Hint: Yes.

5. A bill is payable to P or order. It is stolen from P and the thief forges the signature of P and endorses it to Q who takes it as a holder in due course. Can Q recover upon the bill?

   Hint: No.

6. A bill is endorsed to Gopal or order. Another person of the same name gets the bill and presents it. The acceptor pays him. Is the acceptor liable to the real Gopal?

   Hint: Yes.

18

Partnership

Partnership as "the relation which subsists between persons who have agreed to share the profits of a business carried on by all or any of them on behalf of all of them".
—Sir F. Pollock

The formation of partnership is governed by the provisions of the Indian Partnership Act of 1932, which came into force on 1st October, 1932. Prior to the enactment of this Act, the law relating to partnership was contained in Chapter XI of the Indian Contract Act, 1872.

DEFINITION

Section 4 of the Act defines partnership as "the relation between persons who have agreed to share the profits of a business carried on by all or any of them acting for all". The following characteristics of partnership emerge from this definition:

1. *Association of Two or More Persons:* At least two persons must join together for business. One person cannot enter into partnership himself. Only persons recognised by law can enter into an agreement of partnership. Any person who is not a minor and who is of sound mind can be a partner. The minimum number of persons required to form a partnership is two.

> **CHARACTERISTICS OF PARTNERSHIP**
> - Association of two or more persons
> - Agreement
> - Business
> - Sharing of profits
> - Mutual agency

The Partnership Act does not mention anything about the maximum number of partners, but under the Companies Act, 1956, a partnership consisting of more than 20 persons for a general business and 10 persons for a banking business would be illegal. Hence, these should be regarded as the maximum limits to the number of persons in a partnership firm.

2. *Agreement:* It relates to the voluntary contractual nature of partnership. The business is set up by a contract between persons concerned called partners. The agreement which forms the basis of this contract may be in writing or formed verbally, or by conduct.

3. *Business:* An association of person will become a partnership only when it is meant to do some kind of business. 'Business' here includes any trade, occupation or profession. It means any activity which if successful would result in profit.

4. *Sharing of Profits:* The object of partnership should be to earn profits and there must be an agreement to share them. Profit means net profit, i.e., excess of returns over outlays.

5. *Mutual Agency:* The business of partnership must be carried on by all the partners or some of them acting for all. Thus, every partner is an agent of the other members of the firm.

TEST OF PARTNERSHIP

With a view to determining the existence of partnership between a group of persons, the definition in Sec. 4 is used as a test, i.e., one must look into the agreement between them. If the agreement is to share the profits of a business, and the business is carried on by all or any of them acting for all, there is a partnership, otherwise not.

It is often difficult to determine in the absence of a definite partnership agreement, whether a group of persons working together is a partnership or not. In such a case one must refer to Sec. 6 which embodies the rule laid down in the case of *Cox* v. *Hickman*, (1860) H.L.C. 268.

Section 6 of the Act states that "in determining whether a group of persons is or is not a partner in a firm, regard shall be had to the real relation between the parties, as shown by all relevant facts taken together", and not merely on their expressed intention. The real relation between the parties is to be determined from all the facts, i.e., the written or verbal agreement, surrounding circumstances at the time when the contract was entered into, conduct of the parties, and their relevant facts, e.g., books of account, correspondence, evidence of employees, etc. These facts are not considered individually to determine the existence of partnership, but are taken collectively.

Explanations I and II of Sec. 6 further enumerate cases where partnership relation does not exist. These cases are:

1. *Joint Owners Sharing Gross Returns (Explanation I):* Joint owners of some property sharing profits or gross returns arising from the property do not become partners.

   Example: If two joint owners of a house let it and divide the rent equally between themselves, they are not partners.

2. *Sharing of Profits (Explanation II):* The receipts by a person of a share of the profits of a business or of a payment contingent upon the earning of profits or varying with the profits earned by a business does not by itself make him a partner with the persons carrying on the business. The following categories of persons would not be regarded as partners on receipt of such share of profits or payments:

   (a) by a lender of money to persons engaged or about to engage in any business;

   (b) by a servant or agent as remuneration;

   (c) by a widow or child of a deceased partner as annuity;

   (d) by a previous owner of the business as consideration for the sale of goodwill or its share thereof.

   In short, there can be no partnership without the sharing of profits but at the same time a sharing of profits is not a conclusive test that a partnership exists. Agency is an essential element of partnership. The true test of partnership is, therefore, the existence of a relationship of principal and agent between the members.

PARTNERSHIP DISTINGUISHED FROM OTHER RELATIONSHIP

Partnership and Co-ownership

Co-ownership means joint ownership of some property which does not necessarily result in partnership. In partnership, the partners are necessarily co-owners of property of the firm, but in co-ownership the co-owners are not necessarily partners. The main points of difference between a partnership and co-ownership are:

Difference between partnership and co-ownership

Partnership	Co-ownership
1. It arises from contract.	It need not necessarily arise from contract.

2. It involves a community of interest.	It does not involve a community of interest.
3. A partner cannot assign his share to a stranger without the consent of the other partners.	A co-owner can alienate his share to strangers without the consent of other co-owners.
4. Each partner acts as an agent of the others.	One co-owner is not the agent of the others.
5. A partner has a lien on the partnership property for expenses incurred by him on such property on behalf of the firm.	A co-owner has no such lien.
6. The number of members cannot exceed the statutory limit.	There is no limit on maximum number.
7. A partner is entitled to claim a share in the surplus assets of the firm, but not a share in the properties of the firm in specie.	A co-owner can claim division of the joint property in specie.

Partnership and Joint Hindu Family Business

The 'Joint Hindu Family Business' represents a business organisation owned by co-owners or co-parceners of an estate belonging to a Hindu family which has not yet been partitioned. In Hindu Law, business descends like any other property upon members of the undivided family. The members of a Hindu undivided family carrying on family business as such are not partners in such business (Sec. 5).

The points of distinction between the two are as follows:

Partnership Firm	*Joint Hindu Family Firm*
1. It is the Result of an Agreement between the Members.	It is not the result of an agreement, but the result of status.
2. A member of either sex can be a partner in a firm.	A female does not become a member in a joint family firm by birth.
3. A new partner can be admitted only with the consent of all the partners.	A person becomes a member by his birth.
4. A minor can be admitted to the benefits of partnership with the consent of the other partners.	A male minor becomes a member by birth.
5. Every partner has a right to pledge the credit of the firm or the partnership business.	It is only the manager of the joint family firm who can contract a debt so as to bind the other members.

6. Every partner is personally liable for the debts of the firm.	The Karta is personally liable for the debts of the family whereas the other members are liable only to the extent of their interest in the joint family business. The other members are personally liable if they are also contracting parties.
7. Every partner can ask for dissolution and accounts of the firm.	The only right of a member is to ask for partition of the existing assets, and not to demand an account from the manager for his past dealings.
8. The number of partners should not exceed ten in the case of a firm carrying on banking business and twenty in the case of any other business.	In a joint family firm, there is no limit to the maximum number of members.

Partnership and Company

The points of differences between a company and a firm are as follows:

Firm	*Company*
1. A partnership firm has no separate legal existence apart from the members forming it.	A company is recognised by law as a person distinct from members composing it.
2. The liabilities of a firm can be enforced against each partner personally.	The liability of the shareholders is limited to the extent of their share capital, and the creditors of the company cannot proceed against the private properties of the shareholders.
3. A partner cannot assign his share to a stranger, without the consent of the other partners.	In the case of a public company shares are transferable without the consent of the other members.
4. Death, retirement, insolvency of a partner dissolves the partnership.	Death, retirement or insolvency of a shareholder does not affect the existence of a company.

PARTNERS, FIRM AND FIRM NAME

Persons who have entered into partnership with one another are called individually 'partners' and collectively 'a firm' and the name under which their business is carried on is called the 'firm name' (Sec. 4).

In law, 'firm' is only a convenient phrase for describing the partners, and the firm has no legal existence apart from the partners. As regards the 'firm name', partners have a right to carry on business under any name and style which they choose to adopt, provided they do not violate the rules relating to trade name or goodwill. A partnership firm cannot use the word 'limited' as a part of its name.

KINDS OF PARTNERSHIP

The following chart shows the various kinds of partnership:

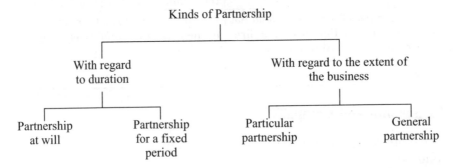

1. *Partnership at Will:*   A partnership formed without fixing the duration of its business is called a partnership at will. Such a partnership is expected to be continued for an indefinite period. However, a partnership at will may come to an end at any time, if any partner gives notice to other partners, expressing his desire to quit.

2. *Partnership for a Fixed Period:*   It is a partnership created for a particular period of time. Such a partnership comes to an end on the expiry of the fixed period. If the partners continue to carry on the business after the expiry of the fixed period, the partnership will be regarded as a partnership at will.

3. *Particular Partnership:* A particular partnership is one which is confined to a particular adventure or undertaking.

   Example: A partnership between an author and a publisher for a particular book.

   A partnership, constituted for a single adventure or undertaking is dissolved by the completion of that adventure or undertaking.

4. *General Partnership:* When a partnership is constituted with respect to the business in general, it is called a general partnership.

A general partnership differs from a particular partnership. In a particular partnership, the liability of the partners extends only to that particular adventure or undertaking, but it is not so in the case of general partnership.

LIMITED PARTNERSHIP

Limited partnership is not allowed in India. Such a partnership is allowed in several European countries and the USA. In England, the Limited Partnership Act of 1907 controls such a partnership.

A limited partnership is one where there are two types of partners. They are: (a) limited partners, and (b) general partners. The liability of a limited partner is limited to the extent of his capital contribution. But the liability of a general partner is unlimited.

Features

The chief features of limited partnership are:

1. In a limited partnership there must be at least one limited partner and one general partner.
2. A 'limited' or 'special' partner simply invests his money in the firm.
3. The general partners alone can take part in the business.
4. The bankruptcy, death or lunacy of a special partner does not dissolve the firm.
5. Registration is compulsory for a limited partnership.
6. A special partner cannot assign his share to an outsider without the consent of the general partners.

PARTNERSHIP DEED

A partnership is based on an agreement. This agreement may be either oral or written. However, it is in the interest of the partners that the agreement must be in writing. The document which contains this agreement is called the 'Partnership Deed'. The Deed has to be stamped in accordance with the Indian Stamps Act. Each partner should have a copy of the Deed.

The Partnership Deed usually contains provisions relating to the nature and the principal place of the business, the name of the firm, profit-sharing ratio, interest on capital and drawing, valuation of goodwill on the death or retirement of a partner, management, accounts, arbitration, etc.

REGISTRATION OF FIRMS

The Indian Partnership Act, 1932 contains provisions for the registration of a partnership firm. The Act does not make it compulsory for a firm to be registered, but there are certain disabilities which are attached to an unregistered firm. The registration can take place at any time. For this, a form containing the following particulars accompanied by a prescribed fee is to be sent to the Registrar of firms:

(a) The name of the firm.

(b) The principal place of business of the firm.

(c) The names of other places where the firm carries on business.

(d) The names in full, and addresses of the partners.

(e) The dates on which various partners joined the firm.

(f) The duration of the firm.

When the Registrar is satisfied that the provisions as laid down in the Act have been duly complied with, he records an entry of the statement in the Register of firms, and files the statement. He then issues a certificate of registration.

An unregistered firm cannot file a suit to enforce rights against third parties if such rights arise out of a contract. Similarly, a partner cannot file a suit to enforce his rights under the Partnership Deed. The rights of third parties against the firm are, however, not affected. Non-registration of a firm does not affect the following:

(a) The right of a partner to sue for dissolution of the firm or for accounts of, and his share in the dissolved firm.

(b) A suit not exceeding ₹100.

(c) The rights of a firm or its partners having no place of business in India.

(d) The power of the Official Assignee or Receiver to realise the property of an insolvent partner.

(e) Suits arising otherwise than under a contract.

TYPES OF PARTNERS

In a partnership organisation there can be different kinds of partners. They are as follows:

(a) *Sleeping Partner or Dormant Partner:* A sleeping partner is one who does not take an active part in the conduct of the business of the firm. He only contributes the capital and takes a share of the profit which is usually smaller than that of active partners. He is equally liable along with other partners for all the debts of the firm. His position is similar to that of an undisclosed principal.

(b) *Nominal Partner:* A partner who lends merely his name and reputation to a firm is called a nominal partner. He does not invest, does not get a share of interest, and is not entitled to take part in the management. But he is liable, like other partners, to third parties.

(c) *Active or Ostensible Partner:* A partner who takes active part in the day-to-day management of a partnership is called an active partner. He conducts the business on behalf of all the other partners.

(d) *Partner by Estoppel:* If a person behaves in such a fashion that he is mistaken to be a partner by third parties, he will be held liable to those third parties who extend credit to the firm on the reputation of his being a partner. Such a person is called as a partner by estoppel. He is not really a partner. As such, he is not entitled to a share in the profits of the firm.

(e) *Partner by Holding Out:* If a person is declared (by word or deed) to be a partner by another person, the person concerned should deny it immediately on coming to know of such a declaration. If he does not do so he is liable to those third parties who lend money or otherwise give credit to the firm on the basis of his being a partner. Such a partner is called a partner by holding out.

MINOR PARTNER (SEC. 30)

A person below the age of 18 is treated as a minor. Since a minor does not enjoy the capacity to enter into a contract in his own right, he cannot be a full-fledged partner in a partnership firm. But according to Sec. 30 of the Partnership Act, a minor can be admitted to the benefits of a partnership with the consent of all other partners.

The rights and liabilities of a minor partner are distinct from those of other partners. His liability in the firm is limited to the extent of his share in the firm. His estate cannot be called upon to contribute anything beyond what is already invested in the firm.

When a minor becomes a major, he can decide whether or not to continue as a partner. If he does not give a public notice of his choice within six months, he will be treated as having decided to continue as a partner. In case he chooses or is deemed to be a partner, his liability will become unlimited with effect from the date of his original admission to the benefits of the partnership.

INCOMING PARTNER (SEC. 31)

A firm can take a new partner in the business with the consent of all the existing partners. Such a new partner is known as an incoming partner.

An incoming partner is not liable for any act of the firm done prior to his admission. He may be held liable for such debts only if he agrees to it and the creditors are informed.

OUTGOING PARTNER (SEC. 32)

A partner who severs his connection with his firm is called as a retiring or outgoing partner. A partner may retire from the partnership either with the consent of all the other partners or in accordance with the provisions of the partnership deed. The retirement of a partner does not necessarily mean the dissolution of the firm. On retirement of a partner the firm continues to exist as such, which is not the case when a partnership is dissolved.

The outgoing partner is liable for all the acts of the firm done prior to his retirement to third parties. He may be freed from such liabilities by an agreement with the creditors and the remaining partners. An outgoing partner continues to be liable for all future acts of the firm until a public notice is given of the retirement.

An outgoing partner has the right to carry on business competing with that of the firm. But in the absence of a contract to the contrary he may not (a) use the firm name (b) canvass its customers (c) represent himself to be a partner of the old firm.

MUTUAL RIGHTS AND OBLIGATIONS

Partnership being the result of an agreement between the partners, their mutual rights and obligations are governed by the same. In the absence of a deed or if on any point the deed is silent, the mutual rights and obligations of the partners are determined by the various provisions of the Partnership Act.

Rights of a Partner

(a) Every partner has a right to take active part in the management of the firm [Sec. 12(a)].

(b) A partner is entitled to receive interest at 6 per cent on all loans given by him to the firm [Sec. 13(a)].

(c) A partner has the right to inspect and copy the accounts of the firm [Sec. 12(d)].

(d) A partner is entitled to have the property of the firm applied exclusively for the purpose of the firm (Sec. 15).

(e) Every partner has the right to share the profits of the firm equally, unless different proportions are stipulated [Sec. 13(b)].

(f) Every partner has the right to be consulted in all matters relating to the firm [Sec. 12(c)].

(g) A partner has the right to retire according to the terms of the deed or with the consent of the other partners. In the case of partnership at will, a partner can retire by giving notice on retirement [Sec. 32(1)(c)].

(h) A retiring partner has the right to get a share of the goodwill of the firm at the time of his retirement.

(i) On retirement, the partner is entitled to have a share in the profits of the firm earned with the help of the partner's share in the firm, or interest at 6 per cent per annum (as the partner may choose) until the amount due to him is paid off.

The same rule is applied in the case of the heirs of a deceased partner. Every partner has the right to prevent, the introduction of a new partner without his consent (Sec. 31).

Duties of a Partner

(a) Every partner is bound to carry on the business of the firm to the greatest common advantage (Sec. 9).

(b) Every partner must act in a just and faithful manner towards other partners (Sec. 9).

(c) A partner is bound to keep and render true, proper and correct accounts of the partnership (Sec. 9).

(d) Every partner is bound to indemnify the firm for any loss caused by his fraud in the conduct of the business (Sec. 10).

(e) Every partner is bound to attend diligently to the business of the firm and in the absence of any agreement to the contrary he is not entitled to receive any remuneration [Secs. 12(b) and 13(a)].

(f) In the absence of an agreement to the contrary, every

partner is bound to share the losses equally with the others [Sec. 13(b)].

(g) Every partner must hold and use the partnership property exclusively for the firm (Sec. 15).

(h) Every partner should account for any benefits derived from the partnership business without the consent of the other partners [Sec. 16(a)].

(i) A partner should not compete with the firm without the consent of the other partners. Any profits made by such an unauthorised competition can be claimed by the firm [Sec. 16(b)].

(j) No partner can assign or transfer his partnership interest to any other person, so as to make him a partner in the business (Sec. 29).

Liabilities of a Partner

(a) A partner is jointly and severally liable for all debts of the firm.

(b) A partner is liable to compensate the firm for any loss occurred by virtue of his wilful negligence or misconduct.

(c) A retiring partner is continued to be liable for all debts of the firm incurred before his retirement.

(d) An incoming partner is liable only for those debts of the firm which are incurred after his admission.

IMPLIED AUTHORITY OF A PARTNER

The authority of a partner means the capacity of a partner to bind the firm by his act. It may be either express or implied. An authority given to a partner by an agreement of all the partners is known as the express authority of the partner. But where there is no partnership agreement, an implied grant of power to each partner to do every act to carry on, in the usual way is a business of the kind carried on by the firm known as 'Implied Authority'. This authority is conferred on a partner by Sec. 19 of the Act. It is subject to the following conditions:

(a) The act done by the partner should relate to the normal business of the firm.

(b) The act should be such as is done within the scope of the business of the firm in the usual way.

(c) The act should be done in the name of the firm or in any other manner expressing or implying an intention to bind the firm (Sec. 22).

Acts within the Implied Authority of a Partner

1. Purchasing and selling goods on behalf of the firm.
2. Making payments to the firm's creditors.
3. Engaging servants of the partnership business.
4. Borrowing money on the credit of the firm.
5. Receiving money and issuing valid receipts on behalf of the firm.
6. Pledging any goods of the firm for the purpose of borrowing money.
7. Employing a solicitor to defend an action against the firm for goods supplied.

No Implied Authority

1. To purchase or sell immovable property.
2. To submit a dispute for arbitration.
3. To admit any liability in a suit.
4. To withdraw a legal proceeding.
5. To enter into partnership on behalf of the firm.

DISSOLUTION OF FIRM

The dissolution of partnership between all the partners of a firm is called the 'dissolution of the firm' (Sec. 39). It implies the complete, breakdown or extinction of the relationship between all the partners of a firm.

The Partnership Act makes a distinction between the 'dissolution of Partnership' and the 'dissolution of firm'. The dissolution of partnership involves an extinction of relationship between some of the partners only, whereas the dissolution of firm amounts to a complete closure of the business.

> **Example:** A, B and C are partners in a partnership firm. If C dies or retires or becomes insolvent, then the firm would come to an end. But if the partners had agreed that the death, retirement or insolvency of a partner would not dissolve the firm, then on the

happening of any of these events, the partnership would certainly come to an end, even though the firm may continue under the same name.

Thus, every dissolution of the firm implies dissolution of partnership but not vice versa, unless the firm consists of only two partners.

Dissolution of a firm may be either voluntary (without the order of the Court) or by the order of the Court.

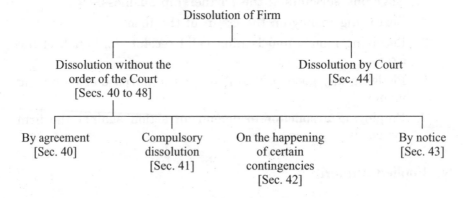

Dissolution of Firm

Dissolution without the Order of the Court

Dissolution without the intervention of the Court takes place in any of the following ways:

(a) *Dissolution by Agreement (Sec. 40):* Here the dissolution occurs with the consent of all the partners or in pursuance of a contract previously made.

(b) *Compulsory Dissolution (Sec. 41):* It implies that the firm ceases to exist in the eyes of law. A firm is compulsorily dissolved: (i) When all the partners but one are adjudged insolvent; (ii) When the business of the firm becomes unlawful.

(c) *Dissolution on the Happening of Certain Contingencies (Sec. 42):* Subject to the contract between the partners, a firm is dissolved by:

(i) the expiry of the term fixed.

(ii) the completion of the adventure of undertaking.

(iii) the death of a partner.

(iv) the insolvency of a partner.

(d) *Dissolution by Notice of Partnership at Will (Sec. 43):* Where the partnership is at will the firm may be dissolved at any time, by any partner giving notice in writing of his intention to dissolve, to all the other partners. The dissolution takes place from the date mentioned in the notice.

Dissolution by Court (Sec. 44)

Dissolution by the Court may take place on any of the following grounds:

(a) When a partner becomes of unsound mind;

(b) When a partner becomes permanently incapable of performing his duties as a partner;

(c) When a partner is guilty of misconduct affecting the business

(d) When a partner commits wilful or persistent breach of agreement;

(e) When the partner sells or transfers his interest;

(f) When the business cannot be carried on except at a loss;

(g) When the dissolution appears to the Court to be just and equitable.

The Court can order dissolution of a firm only on the filing of a suit by a partner for the same.

SETTLEMENT OF ACCOUNTS AFTER DISSOLUTION

Accounts between the partners after the dissolution of the firm are normally to be settled in the manner provided for by the partnership agreement. In the absence of specific agreement, the mode of settlement of accounts is based on the provisions of Sec. 48.

Losses [Sec. 48(a)]

Losses, including deficiencies of capital shall he paid first out of profits, next out of capital and lastly, if necessary, by the partners individually in the proportion in which they were entitled to share profits.

Application of Assets [Sec. 48(b)]

The assets of the firm, including the sums, if any, contributed by the partners to make up losses or deficiencies of capital, shall be applied in the following manners and orders:

(i) in paying outside creditors;

(ii) in repaying advances made by partners;

(iii) in repaying capital to partners;

(iv) the ultimate residue, if any, shall be divided among the partners in the profit sharing ratio.

REVIEW QUESTIONS

1. Define Partnership. What are the essential elements of partnership?

2. State the test of partnership. What are the legal rules for a valid partnership?

3. Distinguish between partnership and (a) Co-ownership; (b) Hindu Undivided family.

4. Write notes on:

   (a) Partnership deed

   (b) Partnership at will

   (c) Partners, firm and firm name

   (d) Partners by holding out

5. What is meant by registration of a firm? State the procedure of registration of a firm, and the effect of non-registration.

6. What do you understand by the implied authority of a partner? Discuss the cases in which a partner has no implied authority to bind the firm.

7. Write notes on:

   (a) Incoming and outgoing partners

   (b) Minor partner

   (c) Modes of settlement of accounts after the dissolution of the firm

8. Explain the rights and liabilities of a partner under the Indian Partnership Act.

9. Distinguish between 'dissolution of a firm' and 'dissolution of partnership'. Explain the grounds on which the partnership firm may be dissolved by the court.

PRACTICAL PROBLEMS

Attempt the following problems, giving reasons.

1. M, a publisher, agrees to publish at his own expense, a book written by N and to pay N 60 per cent of the net profits. Do M and N constitute a partnership?

   Hint: No.

2. P and Q carried on business in partnership. The deed prohibited a partner from borrowing money on behalf of the firm. Q borrowed money from R representing that it was required for partnership purposes. Can R recover the loan from the firm?

   Hint: No, as the firm is not a trading firm Q has no implied authority to borrow on behalf of the firm.

3. P, Q and R are partners, P is a dormant partner. He retired without giving a public notice. Is he liable for the subsequent debts incurred by Q and R?

   Hint: No.

4. P and Q carry on Business in partnership as bankers. R who owes the firm a sum of ₹2,000 pays it to P. P does not inform Q of such a receipt and afterwards P appropriates the money to his own use. Is R discharged of his debt to the firm?

   Hint: Yes.

5. A is indebted to P a sum of ₹20,000. Subsequently, P becomes liable a like sum to the firm of which A, B and C are partners. A and P agree that the debts should be set off against each other. Is P absolved from liability to the firm?

   Hint: No.

PART TWO

LAW OF INSURANCE

19

Insurance

Insurance is "a menas of shifting the risks to insurers in consideration of a nominal cost called the premium".

INTRODUCTION

Business is a hazardous road and hence the businessman has to drive with caution and proper planning to get at his destination of prosperity through profits. All along this road are innumerable risks. Some of which are averted by various means, some of which are borne by the businessman as a part of the game and some others are shifted by him to agencies or persons willing to share them. Insurance is a way of shifting the risks to insurers. It is thus a co-operative way of spreading risk.

CONTRACT OF INSURANCE

Insurance is "a contract either to indemnify against a loss which may arise upon the happening of some event, or to pay on the happening of some events, a sum of money to the person insured".

There are two parties in a contract of insurance. They are, insurer and insured. The person undertaking the risk is called the insurer, assurer or underwriter and the person whose risk is insured is called the insured or assured.

The instrument containing the contract of insurance is called the 'policy'. It is the evidence of the contract.

The consideration in return for which the insurer agrees to make good the loss is called the 'premium'.

The thing or property insured is called the 'subject matter' of insurance. The interest of the assured in the subject matter of insurance is called the 'insurable interest'.

Nature of Contract of Insurance

Since the very early stages, the contract of insurance had been recognized as a gaming or wagering contract. A wagering contract is one in which a person promises to pay money or transfer property upon the happening or non-happening of an uncertain event. Wagering contract cannot be enforced in a Court of law as it has no insurable interest.

With social evolution, the attitude that insurance was a contract on wagering changed, and the law came to recognise insurance as a system of spreading the risk over a large number of people. Now a contract of insurance is considered an absolutely valid contract because the assured has an insurable interest in the life or property sought to be insured.

Classification of Contracts of Insurance

Contracts of insurance are broadly classified as (i) Marine, and (ii) non-marine.

Non-marine insurance may be

(a) Personal insurance in which the person of the assured is affected.

Example: Life assurance, Personal accident insurance and Sickness insurance.

(b) Property insurance in which the property of the assured is affected.

Example: Fire insurance, Fidelity insurance, etc.

(c) Liability insurance in which the event results in liability.

Example: Motor vehicle insurance.

FUNCTIONS OF INSURANCE

The functions of insurance can be brought under two heads. They are primary functions and secondary functions.

Primary Functions

(i) **Insurance provides certainty:** Insurance provides certainty of payment at the uncertainty of loss. There are different types of uncertainty in a risk. Whether the risk will occur or not, the time and amount of risk are uncertain. Insurance removes all these uncertainties and the assured is given certainty of payment of loss. The insurer charges premium for providing the said certainty.

(ii) **Insurance provides protection:** Since the time and amount of loss are uncertain, a person will suffer loss in the absence of insurance. The insurance guarantees the payment of loss and thus protects the assured from sufferings. However, insurance cannot check the happening of risk but can provide for losses at the happening of the risk.

(iii) **Risk sharing:** Since the risk is uncertain, loss arising from the risk is also uncertain. When risk takes place, the loss is shared by all the persons who are exposed to the risk.

Secondary Functions

The following are the important secondary functions of the insurance.

(i) **Prevention of loss:** As the reduction in loss causes lesser payment to the assured, the insurance joins hands with those institutions which are engaged in preventing the losses of the society. In other words, insurance assists financially the health organisation, fire brigade, educational institutions and other organisations which are engaged in preventing the losses of the masses from death or damage.

(ii) **Providing capital:** Usually, the accumulated funds of the insurance are invested in productive channels. This helps in providing capital to the society. Thus, the industry, the business and individual are benefited by the investment and loans of the insurers.

(iii) **Improving efficiency:** Insurance eliminates worries and miseries of losses at death and destructions of property. Hence, the carefree insured person can devote his body and soul together for better achievement. It ultimately improves not only his efficiency, but the efficiencies of the masses also.

(iv) **Helping economic progress:** Insurance provides an initiative to work hard for the betterment of the masses by protecting the society from huge losses of damage, destruction and death. This immensely helps the masses in their economic progress.

PRINCIPLES OF INSURANCE

All insurance contracts are based on the following fundamental principles:

1. **Utmost Good Faith:** The contracts of insurance are brought under the category of the contracts uberrimae fidei,

i.e., those contracts which require absolute and utmost good faith on the part of the parties concerned. In this respect, insurance contracts are distinct from the ordinary business contracts, which are based on the rule of 'Caveat Emptor', i.e., let the buyer beware. In insurance contracts, every one of the parties has an obligation to disclose all material facts with a perfect degree of accuracy. This binding applies particularly to the insured party who is naturally in possession of all material facts relating to his life or property.

The non-disclosure or misrepresentation of any material fact gives the insurer an option to avoid the contract. The duty of disclosure, however comes to an end when the contract is complete, and the material facts which come to the knowledge of the assured subsequently need not be disclosed.

2. **Insurable Interest:**   Insurable interest is an interest in the preservation of a thing, or continuance of life, recognized by law. Whoever has such an interest in a thing or life may insure that thing or that life. It implies that no person can enter into a valid contract of insurance unless he has insurable interest in the object or the life insured.

Insurable interest is not a mere sentimental interest in the object insured. It is a pecuniary or financial interest and it follows that the loss caused by the risk insured against must be capable of estimation in terms of money. In life insurance, insurable interest must be present at the time when the insurance is effected. In fire insurance, it must be present both at the time of insurance and at the time of the loss of subject matter. In marine insurance, it must be present at the time of the loss of the subject mater.

The law recognizes an insurable interest in the following cases: (i) A person has insurable interest in his own life. (ii) A husband in the life of his wife and vice versa. (iii) Creditors in the lives of their debtors. (iv) A master in the life of his servants and vice versa. (v) One partner in the life of another partner.

PRINCIPLES OF INSURANCE
• Utmost good faith
• Insurable interest
• Indemnity
• Subrogation
• Contribution
• Mitigation of loss
• Causa proxima

3. **Indemnity:** All contracts of insurance (except life, personal accident and sickness insurances) are contracts of indemnity. It implies that the assured, in the case of loss against which the policy has been

issued, shall be paid the actual amount of loss not exceeding the amount of the policy. This is based on the principle that "the insured is not permitted to make a profit out of his loss". Moreover, in the absence of principle of indemnity, there might be a tendency in the direction of over insurance.

The principle of indemnity does not apply to the life insurance contracts. In life insurance contracts, a fixed sum is undertaken to be paid either on the death of a person or after the expiry of a fixed period. In this respect, life insurance contracts may be described as 'contingent contracts'.

4. **Subrogation:** The doctrine of subrogation is an extension and a corollary to the principle of indemnity and as such this principle does not apply to the life insurance contracts.

The term subrogation literally means substitution, i.e., substitution of the insurer in place of the insured in respect of the latter's right and remedies. In accordance with the principle of subrogation, the insurer steps into the shoes of the insured and becomes entitled to all rights of the insured regarding the subject matter of insurance after the claim of the insured has been fully and finally settled.

5. **Contribution:** Sometimes a person effects two or more insurances in respect of the same subject matter. This is referred to as 'double insurance'. But if there is a loss, the insured will have no right to recover more than the full amount of his actual loss. If he recovers the full amount of the actual loss from one insurer, he will have no right to get further payment from the other insurers. In such a case, the principle of contribution will apply. According to this principle, the insurer who has paid the insured the full amount of compensation, can recover the proportionate contribution from the other insurers.

6. **Mitigation of Loss:** When the event insured against occurs, it is the duty of the insured to take all necessary steps to mitigate or minimise the loss. He should act as an uninsured prudent person would act under similar circumstances in his own case. If he fails to do so, the insurer can avoid the payment of loss attributable to his negligence.

7. **Causa Promixa:** The assured can recover the loss only if it is proximately caused by any of the perils insured against. This is known as the rule of 'Causa proxima'. The maxim in this regard is causa proxima non-remote spectature, i.e.,

the nearest or the direct cause and not the remote cause is to be looked into.

8. **Example:** A ship was insured against a damage by enemy action. It was damaged by passing over a torpedoed ship. The Court held that no damages could be recovered as the loss in this case was due to the torpedoed ship and not because of direct enemy action.

   [*William & Co.* v. *North of England, etc., Assurance Co.*, (1917) 2K.B. 527].

ROLE AND IMPORTANCE OF INSURANCE

The role and importance of insurance can be studied under the following heads:

(a) Uses to individual (b) Uses to a special group of individuals, viz., business or industry and (c) Uses to the society

Uses to an Individual

(i) **Providing security and safety:** Insurance provides safety and security against the loss of earning at death or in old age, against the loss at fire, against the loss at damage, destruction or disappearance of property, goods, furniture and machines, etc.

(ii) **Affording peace of mind:** Security is the prime motivating factor of insurance. It prompts people to earn and save more. It also relieves them of tension, fear and uncertainty. Hence, insurance provides them with a peace of mind.

(iii) **Protecting mortgaged property:** On the death of the owner of the mortgaged property, the property is usually taken over by the lender of the money. Hence, the family will be deprived of the use of the property. In such a situation, insurance will provide adequate amount to the dependents (at early death of the property owner) to pay off the unpaid loans.

(iv) **Eliminating dependency:** On the death of the husband or father, the destruction of the family needs no elaboration. Similarly, on the destruction of property and goods, the family would suffer a lot. Insurance is here to assist them and provide adequate amount at the time of suffering.

(v) **Encouraging saving:** In the case of life insurance, the elements of both protection and saving are present whereas in property insurance, only the element of protection exists. But in most of the life policies, the element of saving dominates. Insurance facilitates saving because of the following facts:

(a) Regular premiums are required to be compulsorily paid.

(b) Deposited premium cannot be withdrawn easily before the expiry of the term of the policy.

(c) Insurance will pay the policy money irrespective of the premium deposited.

(vi) **Providing profitable investment:** Usually individuals find an outlet for their investment in life insurance policy as it provides certain additional returns. Endowment policies, multi-purpose policies and deferred annuities are certain better forms of investment for this purpose. In India, insurance policies carry a special exemption from income tax and wealth tax.

(vii) **Fulfilling the needs of a person:** Life insurance fulfils the needs of a person. Such needs are brought into the following categories.

(a) Family needs (b) Old-age needs (c) Readjustment needs (d) Special needs, and (e) Clean-up needs.

(a) **Family needs:** Death is certain, but the time is uncertain. Hence, there is uncertainty of the time when the sufferings and financial stringencies may befall on the family. Life insurance will adequately meet this financial requirement of the family. Whole life policies are the better means of meeting such requirements.

(b) **Old-age needs:** The provision for old age is an essential requirement in the modern life. The reduction of income during the old age creates serious problems to the persons and his family. Life insurance provides old age funds to the insured for the protection of his family under various schemes of policies.

(c) **Readjustment needs:** At the time of reduction in income, (whether by loss of unemployment, disability or death) adjustment in the standard of living of the family is required. In such a situation, life insurance helps to accumulate adequate funds. Endowment policy, anticipated endowment policy and guaranteed triple benefit policies are deemed to be a good substitute for old age needs.

(d) **Special needs:** Usually, every family has certain special requirements such as children's education, daughter's marriage and children's settlement. Such requirements are generally fulfilled by the earning member of the family. When the member becomes disabled to earn the income (due to old age or death) such requirements may remain unfulfilled and the family will suffer. In such a situation, there are certain policies and annuities which are useful for the education of children, marriage of daughters and settlement of children.

(e) **Clean-up needs:** After death, ritual ceremonies and payment of wealth taxes are certain requirements which decrease the amount of funds of the family member. Insurance comes as a help for meeting such requirements.

Uses to Business

Insurance is useful to the business society also. The following are some of the uses.

(i) **Reduction of uncertainty in business losses:** In the world of business, commerce and industry, a huge number of properties are employed. New construction and new establishment are possible only with the help of insurance. In the absence of it, the uncertainty will be to the maximum level and nobody would like to invest a huge amount in the business or industry.

(ii) **Increase of business efficiency with insurance:** The uncertainty of loss in business may affect the mind of the businessmen adversely. But the insurance removing such an uncertainty stimulates the businessmen to work hard. Hence, insurance helps businessmen to increase their efficiency.

(iii) **Key-man identification:** Key-man is that particular man whose experience and expertise makes him the most valuable asset in the business. The death or disability of such an employee will, in many instances, prove a more serious loss than that by fire or any other hazard. The potential loss to be suffered and the compensation to the dependents of such an employee require an adequate provision which is met by purchasing adequate life policies. The Term Insurance Policy or Convertible Term Insurance Policy is more suitable in this situation.

(iv) **Credit enhancement:** The business can obtain loan by pledging the policy as collateral for the loan. However, the amount of loan that can be obtained with the pledging of policy (with interest thereon) will not exceed the cash value of the policy. Hence, insurance properties are the best collateral and adequate loans are granted by the lenders.

(v) **Business continuation:** Any business, particularly partnership business may discontinue at the death of any partner although surviving partners can restart the business. But in both cases, the business and the partners will suffer economically. However, such sufferings can be alleviated with the help of insurance.

(vi) **Employees welfare:** The struggles and strife between employees and employer can be minimised easily with the help of various welfare schemes. Such schemes consist of provision for early death, provision for disability and provision for old age. While most of these requirements are met by the life insurance, accident and sickness benefit, pensions are provided by group insurance.

Uses to Society

The following are some of the uses of insurance to society.

(i) **Protecting the wealth of the society:** The loss of a particular wealth can be protected with the help of insurance. Life insurance provides the loss of human wealth. Similarly, the loss or damage of property at fire, accident, etc., can be well indemnified by the property insurance, cattle, crop, profit and machines are also protected against their accidental and economic losses. In short, insurance helps in observing happiness and prosperity everywhere.

(ii) **Providing the requirements for the economic growth of the country:** Insurance provides strong hand and mind for the economic growth of the country. It provides protection against loss of property and adequate capital to produce more wealth. Thus, insurance meets all the requirements of the economic growth of a country.

(iii) **Reduction in inflation:** Insurance reduces the inflationary pressure by extracting money in supply (to the amount of premium collected) and by providing sufficient funds for production (narrow down the inflationary gap). Thus, the main causes of inflation such as increased money in supply and decreased production are properly controlled by insurance business.

REINSURANCE

Reinsurance occurs when an insurer insures the risk undertaken by him with another insurer. It is done mainly to reduce the risk of the insurance company. It is the insurance of insurance. Reinsurance can be resorted to all kinds of insurance. The policy of reinsurance is co-extensive with the original policy. If the original policy for any person comes to an end or is avoided, the policy of reinsurance also comes to an end.

DOUBLE INSURANCE

Double insurance arises where the assured bona fide insures the same subject matter with two or more independent insurers and the total sum insured exceeds the actual value of the subject matter.

> **Example:** A insures his factory worth ₹60,000 with B for ₹50,000 and with C for ₹35,000. Here there is double insurance.

If he insures his factory with B and C for ₹30,000 each there is no double insurance.

If a loss occurs, the assured can claim payment from the insurers in such order as he thinks fit. But in no case can he recover more than the actual amount of loss. This is because a contract of insurance (other than life insurance) is a contract of indemnity.

REVIEW QUESTIONS

1. What is a contract of insurance? Explain and illustrate the fundamental principles of insurance.

2. Distinguish between a contract of insurance and a wagering agreement.

3. Write notes on:

   (a) Double insurance   (b) Premium

   (c) Reinsurance   (d) Insurable interest

   (e) Contract of uberrimae fidei

4. "Insurance is not to prevent risk, but to indemnify the losses arising from a certain risk." Comment.

5. Explain the various functions of insurance.

6. Describe in detail the importance of insurance. What are its uses to the business community and society as a whole.

7. "Insurance is able to curtail inflation, so it should be made compulsory". Comment.

PRACTICAL PROBLEMS

Attempt the following problems, giving reasons.

1. P contracted to construct a building for Q for which he was to be paid ₹50,000. All the materials were to be supplied by Q. Can P insure the material for the period during which the building is being built?

   Hint: Yes.

2. P contracted to build a house for Q for which he was to be paid ₹1,00,000. All the materials were to be supplied by Q. Can P insure the materials for the period during which the building is being constructed?

   Hint: Yes (Insurable Interest).

20

Life Insurance

Life insurance business means "the business of effecting contracts upon human life."
—Sec. 2(11) of the Insurance Act

INTRODUCTION

In India, insurance started with life insurance. The first Indian insurance company was the Bombay Mutual Assurance Society Ltd., formed in 1870. The contract of life insurance in India is governed by the Insurance Act, 1938 and Life Insurance Corporation Act, 1956. In 1956, life insurance business was nationalised and LIC of India came into being on 1st September, 1956. The government took over the business of 245 companies (including 75 provident fund societies) who were transacting the life insurance business at that time. Thereafter, LIC got the exclusive privilege to transact life insurance business in India.

It is a common belief that one of the most difficult products to sell is, 'life insurance' and one who sells life insurance can sell anything under the sun. This is due to the fact that selling life insurance is a difficult proposition primarily because what is sought to be marketed is an assurance, a belief and a faith.

DEFINITION OF LIFE INSURANCE

A life insurance contract may be defined as 'a contract whereby the insurer, in consideration of a premium, paid either in lump sum or in periodical instalments undertakes to pay an annuity or a certain sum of money either on the death of the insured or on the expiry of a certain number of years'. Thus, under a whole life assurance, the policy money is payable at the death of the assured and under an endowment policy, the money is payable on the policyholder's death or on his attaining a particular age, whichever is earlier.

MEANING OF LIFE INSURANCE

Life insurance business means "the business of effecting contracts upon human life". (Section 2(11) of the Insurance Act). It includes:

(i) Any contract whereby the payment of money is assured upon death or the happening of any contingency dependent on human life.

(ii) Any contract which is subject to the payment of premiums for a term dependent on human life.

(iii) Any contract which includes the granting of disability and double or triple indemnity, accident benefits, the granting or annuities upon human life, and the granting of superannuation allowances.

INSURANCE AND ASSURANCE

The terms 'insurance' and 'assurance' are not synonymous although they are interchangeably used to mean one and the same thing. Assurance refers to a contract in which the sum assured is bound to be payable sooner or later, e.g., life insurance. A contract of insurance is a contract for compensation for damages or loss, e.g., fire and marine insurance. In other words, the term assurance is used for life insurance and the human life is its subject matter. But the term insurance is applicable for non-life insurance and goods or property of any other kind is its subject matter.

FUNDAMENTAL PRINCIPLES OF LIFE INSURANCE

The following are the fundamental principles or essential features of a valid contract of life insurance. (i) Elements of valid contract (ii) Insurable interest (iii) Utmost good faith (iv) Warranties (v) Assignment and nomination (vi) Cause is certain (vii) Premium (viii) Terms of policy and (ix) Return of premium.

(i) **Elements of valid contract:** Since the life insurance contract is a contract as defined in the Indian Contract Act, it should have the essential elements of a general contract. A valid contract of life insurance comes into existence where the essential elements of agreement (offer and acceptance, competency of the parties, free consent of the parties, legal consideration and legal objective) are present.

(ii) **Insurable interest:** Insurable interest is the primary interest of a person in the object of insurance. In life insurance, it should exist at the time of the contract of insurance. A person cannot insure the life of another unless he has an insurable interest in it. A husband is presumed to have insurable interest in his wife's life and vice versa. A surety has insurable interest in the life of the principal debtor to the extent of his claim.

(iii) **Utmost good faith:** Insurance contracts are contracts of 'uberrimae fidei' (i.e., the contract of utmost good faith). As per this principle, the insured is bound to disclose, accurately and fully, all the material facts and figures known to him, whether asked for or not. Thus in life insurance, facts regarding age, height, weight, build, previous medical history, smoking/drinking habits, operations, hazardous occupation, etc. should be disclosed.

(iv) **Warranties:** Warranties are the basis of the contract between the proposer and insurer. In life insurance, if any statement (whether material or non-material facts and figures) is untrue, the contract shall be null and void and the premium paid may be forfeited by the insurer.

(v) **Assignment and nomination:** Another essential feature of life insurance policy is assignment and nomination. Assignment of a life policy means transferring the rights of the assured in respect of the policy to the assignee. But in the case of nomination, a person is merely named to collect the amount to be paid by the insurer on the death of the assured.

(vi) **Cause is certain:** In life insurance, since the death of the assured or his reaching a particular age is certain to occur, the insurer has to pay the assured amount one day or other.

(vii) **Premium:** The premium is the price for the risk of loss undertaken by the insurer. It is paid monthly or on annual instalments till the maturity of the policy. In life insurance, the premium is calculated on the average rate of mortality and the fixed periodical premium may continue either until death or for a specified number of years.

(viii) **Terms of policy:** A life insurance policy covers a specified number of years or balance of insured life. It also covers the nature of risk against which insurance is sought.

(ix) **Return of premium:** Premium is the consideration for the risk run by the insurers. In case the risk insured is not run (then the consideration fails), the premium paid can be recovered from the insurer.

POLICY CONDITIONS

This part covers the basic policy conditions which normally apply to all life insurance policies. The following are some of such conditions: (i) Age (ii) Days of grace (iii) Lapse and non-forfeiture (iv) Paid-up value (v) Keeping policy in force (vi) Extended term assurance (vii) Revival (viii) Assignment (ix) Nomination (x) Surrenders and loans (xi) Foreclosure (xii) Alterations (xiii) Indisputability of the policy (xiv) Married Women's Property Act Policies and (xv) Restrictions.

(i) **Age:** In life insurance, the age of the assured is important as premium calculation and underwriting of risk are based on age. It is particularly important in endowment policies wherein the money is payable to the assured on attaining a certain age. The insurer does not withhold the issue of the policy for want of proof of age. But any claim should not be admitted unless the age is proved to the satisfaction of the insurer.

The proof of age should be produced at the time of proposal or immediately after the proposal. It may be a horoscope or the birth certificate or any family record of document. However, if it is subsequently found that the age mentioned at the entry stage is less than the correct age, the assured sum is reduced to such an amount as would have been purchased at the true age. On the other hand, if the actual age comes out to be lower than the stated age, the difference is either refunded or adjusted towards future premium or policy amount.

(ii) **Days of grace:** Insurance company allows a certain number of days after the stipulated period of insurance during which the insured can pay the premium to renew or continue the policy. Such days are known as grace days or grace period. A grace period of one month but not less than 30 days is allowed for payment of yearly, half-yearly and quarterly premiums and 15 days for monthly premiums. Payment of premium within 'Days of Grace' is considered as payment on time. In such a case, premiums will be accepted without any interest.

(iii) **Lapse and non-forfeiture:** If the premium is not paid within the 'days of grace', it is a default on the part of the policyholder and the policy 'lapses'. No claim is entertained on a lapsed policy and all the premiums paid are forfeited. However, in practice, insurers do not forfeit all the premiums paid under a lapsed policy and the Insurance Act, 1938 does not permit it. In such a case various safeguards have been provided to the policyholders. These safeguards are known as non-forfeiture provisions.

(iv) **Paid-up value:** If a policyholder discontinues the payment of premium after two years the policy does not become void but continues as a paid-up policy.

$$\text{Paid-up value} = \frac{(\text{Number of Premiums Paid} \times \text{Sum Assured})}{\text{Number of Premiums Payable}} + \text{Bonus (if any)}$$

(v) **Keeping policy in force:** Under this option, if the premiums are in default, the policy is kept in force by advancing premiums out of the surrender value.

(vi) **Extended term assurance:** Under extended term assurance option, the insurer converts the policy into a single premium term assurance policy for original sum assured. The premium for term assurance will be 'for the age' at the time of lapse.

(vii) **Revival:** If a policy lapses, all (i.e., the insured, insurer and agent) are adversely affected. Hence, the revival of lapsed policies is permitted within a period of five years from the date of its lapsation. The normal requirements for effecting a revival are arrears of outstanding premiums with interest and evidence of continued good health. However, no evidence of good health will be required for revival:

- Within six months from the date of lapse.
- If the policy has been in force for at least five years (the period of six months is extended to 12 months).
- If the policy is due to mature within a year (except in the case of a money back policy).

The following are some revival schemes offered by insurers.

- Special revival scheme.
- Instalment revival scheme
- Loan-cum revival scheme

(a) **Special revival scheme:** Special revival scheme is allowed if:

- The policy had not acquired any surrender value as on the date of lapse.
- The period expired from the date of lapse is not less than six months and not more than three years.
- The policy had not been revived earlier under this scheme.

After revival, the policy will have the same plan and term as the original policy, but will have the following changes:

- Date of commencement will be advanced by a period equal to the duration of the lapse but not more than two years.
- Premium will be recalculated by considering the age on new date of commencements.

(b) **Instalment revival scheme:** Under instalment revival scheme, policyholder is required to pay monthly or quarterly or one half-yearly or yearly premium instead of full arrears of premium. The balance of premium arrears will be spread over the remaining due dates in the policy year current on the date of revival and two full policy years thereafter. However, this scheme is made available if:

- The policy cannot be revived under special revival scheme.
- The premiums are outstanding for more than one year.
- No loan is outstanding.

(c) **Loan-cum revival scheme:** Under this scheme, revival dues are advanced out of the surrender value of the policy as loan on policy. The policy is revived immediately and loan can be repaid as any other loan under the policy. If the loan permissible is more than what is required for revival, the excess amount may be paid to the policyholder, on request.

(viii) **Assignment:** It is a method of transferring rights of the assured in respect of life policy to another party.

Like any other property, life insurance policy can be sold, mortgaged, charged, gifted or bequeathed. Assignment transfers the right, title and interest of the assignor to the assignee. It can be made by an endorsement on the policy or through a separate deed of assignment.

(ix) **Nomination:** Nomination provides a simple way for payment of policy monies to a named person without any hassle in the case of death of the life assured. It can be made at the proposal stage or at any time thereafter during the currency of the policy. Section 39 of the Insurance Act, 1938 provides that the holder of the policy on his own life can nominate a person to whom the policy monies will be paid in the event of his death during the term of the policy. Thus, a person having policy on the life of another person cannot effect a nomination. The policyholder can change the nomination by making an endorsement.

Difference between assignment and nomination

Assignment	Nomination
1. All the rights pass to assignee.	It does not deprive the insured of his disposing power over the policy.
2. Consideration is essential of a valid contract.	Consideration is required for valid nomination.
3. It can be completed and effected either on the policy itself or by a separate deed.	It can be made by endorsement on the policy itself not by a separate deed or separate instruments.
4. It is irrevocable.	It can be changed or cancelled if the party holder is alive on the date of maturity or in the event of the death of the nominee if death occurs earlier.
5. The assignee is entitled to collect the amount under the policy.	It gives the nominee a bare right to collect the policy amount in the event of his death.
6. On valid assignment, the property in the policy passes to the assignee.	In nomination, the nominee gets a right to receive the insured amount but it does not provide for the title or the ownership of money.

(x) **Surrenders and loans:** Surrender involves voluntary termination of contract by the policyholder during the currency of the policy. The amount which he gets by surrendering the policy is called surrender value. It is calculated either as a percentage of premiums paid or as a percentage of paid-up value.

Loan facility is provided in most of the policies. Loans can be given up to 80 per cent or 90 per cent of the surrender value. It may be repaid in full or in part during the currency of the policy. Otherwise loan will remain as a debt on policy recoverable with interest from claim amount. Policy loan is interest bearing. Interest on loan is payable as per terms of sanction of loan by the insurer.

Loan facilities are not available on all policies. Policies like term assurance, annuity policies and money back policies are a few examples of such policies.

(xi) **Foreclosure:** Foreclosure means closure or writing off the policy before the date of maturity. Usually, foreclosure action is initiated in respect of policies whenever loan has been granted and interest on loan is not being received regularly. On foreclosure, nomination ceases to operate. If life assured dies before receiving balance of surrender value, this amount will go to the legal heirs of the deceased's life assured.

A foreclosed policy can be reinstated. Its procedure is the same as in the case of revival except that instead of premium arrears, interest arrears will have to be paid.

(xii) **Alterations:** Insurers allow certain types of alterations after the policy is issued. Usually, alterations relate to change of nomination, change of name, change of mode, increase or decrease in face value of the policy, addition or deletion of accident benefit, removal of critical illness cover, etc.

(xiii) **Indisputability of the policy:** If the proposer has made any untrue or incorrect statement or has not disclosed any material information in the proposal form or the personal statement, the policy contract becomes null and void. Hence, all benefits under the policy cease and premiums paid thereunder can be forfeited.

Section 45 of the Insurance Act, 1938 provides that after two years from the date of effecting of the policy it cannot be questioned on grounds of incorrect or false statement or any other concealment in the proposal form or other documents unless it is shown to be on a material matter and fraudulently and deliberately made.

(xiv) **Married Women's Property (MWP) Act Policies:** Section 6 of MWP Act, 1874 provides that:

- A policy of insurance effected by a married man on his own life and expressed on the face of it to be for the benefit of his wife, or his wife and children, or any of them.
- Shall ensure and be deemed to be a trust for the benefit of wife, or his wife and children, or any of them, according to the interests so expressed, and
- Shall not, so far as any object of the trust remains, be subject to the control of the husband, or of his creditors or form part of his estate.

The policy should be on his own life. But the beneficiaries can be

- Wife alone
- Any one or more children
- Wife or any one or more children

(xv) **Restrictions:** At the proposed stage, the underwriter takes note of the risks based on health, habits, occupation, etc. of the life assured. After acceptance of the risk, the changes in these factors do not affect the insurance contract unless there are specific exclusions.

CLASSIFICATION OF LIFE POLICIES

Life insurance can be divided on the basis of:

    I. Duration of policy   II. Premium payment

  III. Participation in profit   IV. Number of lives covered

    V. Method of payment of sum assured

From the above basis, the life insurance policies are further classified into

I. Policies According to Duration:

1. On the basis of Duration of Policies

  (a) Whole Life Policies

  (b) Limited Payment Whole Life Policies

  (c) Convertible Whole Life Policy

2. On the basis of Terms Insurance Policies

  (a) Temporary Assurance Policy

  (b) Renewable Term Policies

  (c) Convertible Term Policies

3. On the basis of Endowment Policies

  (a) Pure Endowment Policy

  (b) Ordinary Endowment Policy

  (c) Joint Endowment Policy

  (d) Double Endowment Policy

  (e) Fixed Term (Marriage) Endowment Policy

  (f) Educational Annuity Policy

  (g) Triple Benefit Policy

  (h) Anticipated Endowment Policy

  (i) Multi-purpose Policy

  (j) Children's Deferred Endowment Assurance

II. On the basis of Premium Payment

  (a) Single Premium Policy   (b) Level Premium Policy

III. On the basis of Participation in Profit

  (a) Without profit policies or non-participating policies

  (b) With profit policies or participating policies.

IV. On the basis of the Number of Persons Assured

(a) Single Life Policies   (b) Multiple Life Policies

(c) Joint Life Policies   (d) Last Survivorship Policy

V. On the basis of Method of Payment of Policy Amount

(a) Lump sum Policies   (b) Instalment or Annuity Policies

Life insurance policies can be classified as shown in the chart on next page.

Policies According to Duration

1. On the Basis of Duration of Policies

(a) **Whole Life Policy:** The policy where the premium is payable throughout the life of the assured is called the 'Whole Life Policy'. It is useful to the dependent of the assured against his/her death and to provide for payment of Estate Duty.

(b) **Limited Payment Whole Life Policy:** The policy where the premium payable is limited to a certain period is called 'Limited Payment Whole Life Policy'. This is a suitable form of life assurance for family provisions.

(c) **Convertible Whole Life Policy:** The policy which is designed to convert a Term Assurance Policy into Whole Life or Endowment Assurance Policy without having further medical examination of the assured is called the Convertible Whole Life Policy. This policy is issued on the basis of duration.

2. On the Basis of Term Insurance Policy

This policy provides the protection of death risk cover. Term assurance provides for payment only in the event of life dropping before a certain date or age.

(a) **Temporary Assurance Policy:** The policy which is designed to cover the risk against life assured for a period of less than two years is known as 'Temporary Assurance Policy'. A single premium is required to be paid at the outset.

(b) **Renewable Term Policy:** The policy which is renewable at the end of the selected term for an additional term period without having to undergo fresh medical examination is called 'Renewable Term Policy'. Under

Classification of Life Insurance Policies

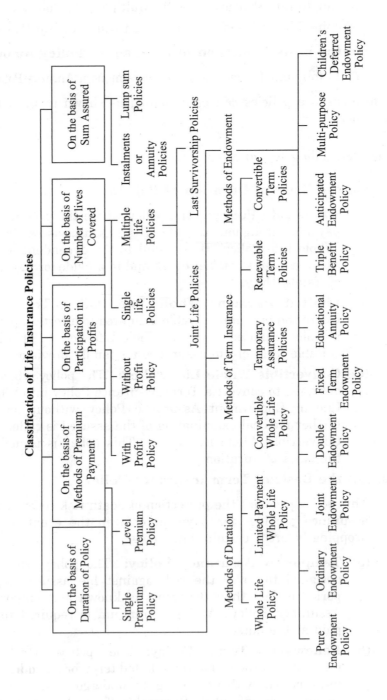

this policy, premiums are usually quoted according to the age attained at the time of renewal.

(c) **Convertible Term Policy:** The policy which is designed to meet the needs of those options to convert it into Whole Life or Endowment Assurance Policy is called 'Convertible Term Policy'. Under this policy, the assured is expected to exercise his choice of conversion before two years of the expiry term. If no option is exercised, the assurance comes to an end at the end of the selected term.

3. On the Basis of Endowment Policies

This is a popular policy issued by the Life Insurance Corporation of India. Under this policy the sum assured becomes matured on the policyholder's death or on his attaining a particular age, whichever is earlier.

There are various types of endowment policies. Such policies are as follows:

(a) **Pure Endowment Policy:** Under this policy the sum assured is payable on the policyholder surviving to the maturity date. The sum assured is payable in the event of death within the term of policy. Its main object is not only providing protection against risk of death but also encouraging investments.

(b) **Ordinary Endowment Policy:** The policy in which the sum assured is payable to the policyholder for a specific term of years (either on the assured's death or on his survival to the stipulated term, i.e., until the maturity date) is known as 'Ordinary Endowment Policy'. This policy provides a fund for family provision and investment.

(c) **Joint Endowment Policy:** The policy which is designed to cover the risk on two or more lives under a single policy is called Joint Endowment Policy. This policy is useful to partners of a firm and for husband and wife in a family.

(d) **Double Endowment Policy:** The policy in which the insurer agrees to pay the assured double the amount of the insured sum on the expiry of the term or on the death of the assured, whichever is earlier is called 'Double Endowment Policy'. Under this policy, premium is payable throughout the life term of the assured or for a selected term of years.

(e) **Fixed Term (Marriage) Endowment Policy:** The policy which is designed to meet the needs of the provision relating to marriage of any one of the family members of the policyholder is called 'Fixed Term (Marriage) Endowment Policy'. Here, the sum assured together with profit shall be payable at the end of the maturity or on the death of the life assured, which ever is earlier.

(f) **Educational Annuity Policy:** The policy which provides for a sum assured to be kept aside to meet the educational expenses of children is called 'Educational Annuity Policy'. Usually this policy is issued for a minimum term of 5 years and maximum term of 25 years subject to a maturity age of 70 years. The maximum sum assured under this plan is ₹10,000.

(g) **Triple Benefit Policy:** Under this policy, the benefits availing the policyholders on the death of the life assured during the term of the policy is thrice the basic sum payable or on survival to the date of maturity, only the basic sum assured is payable. This policy is most suitable for housing loan purpose.

(h) **Anticipated Endowment Policy:** Under this policy the sum assured will be payable on the basis of half of the sum assured paid before the death of the policyhoders and the balance of the sum assured is payable at the end of the maturity date. If the assured dies before the attainment of the term period, full lump sum assured amount is payable to the policyholder.

(i) **Multi-purpose Policy:** The policy in which several purposes are fulfilled under one policy is called 'Multi-purpose Policy'. It is useful to meet the expenses relating to the family of the assured and provision for education and marriage of his children.

(j) **Children's Deferred Endowment Assurance:** The policy which is designed to meet the expenses relating to children's education and marriage is called 'Children's Deferred Endowment Assurance'. This policy is usually issued on lives of both male and female children who have not completed 18 years. The main object of this policy is to cover the risk against the life of children on behalf of their parents and guardian.

Policies on the Basis of Premium Payment

On the basis of premium payment, the following important policies are issued.

(a) **Single Premium Policy:** This policy is useful to those who desire to provide the whole premium in one instalment at the time of taking the policy. This policy matures on the death of the assured or on his attainment of selected term, whichever occurs earlier.

(b) **Level Premium Policy:** The policy in which premiums are payable on a regular basis for a selected term or till prior death is called 'Level Premium Policy'. This policy is useful to those persons having regular earnings.

Policies on the Basis of Participation in Profits

The following are the important policies issued on the basis of participation in profits.

(a) **With Profit Policy/Participating Policy:** The policy in which the policyholders are entitled to get the share of profits or bonus or benefits or paid-up facilities as per the terms and conditions of the corporation is called participating policy. Under this scheme, the policyholders will get the sum assured with profits at the end of the maturity or in the event of death, whichever is earlier.

(b) **Without Profit Policy/Non-participating Policy:** The policy in which the sum assured will become payable without any paid-up facilities to the insured at the end of the term or on the death of assured (if earlier) is known as non-participating policy.

Policies on the Basis of the Number of Persons Assured

The following are the important policies on the basis of number of persons assured.

(a) **Single Life Policy:** The policy which covers the risk of one individual is called 'Single Life Policy'. This policy may be issued on one's own life or on an other's life.

(b) **Multiple Life Policy:** Multiple life policy may be joint life policy and last survivorship policy. Joint life policy covers the risk of more than two individuals. The sum assured is payable at the time of maturity or on the event of the death of the first assured, whichever is earlier. Under last survivorship policy, the sum assured is payable at the death of the last assured or on the attaining of a selected term, whichever is earlier.

Policies on the Basis of Methods of Payment of Policy Amount

The following are the policies to be issued on the basis of methods of payment of policy amount.

(a) **Lump sum Policy:** The policy in which the sum assured is payable in a lump sum to the policyholder at the end of the maturity date or on the assured's death (whichever is earlier) is known as 'Lump Sum Policy'.

(b) **Annuity Policy:** The policy in which the insured amount is payable to the assured by periodical instalments for a selected period of terms or till the death of the assured is known as 'Annuity Policy'.

Other Policies

(a) **Money Back Policy:** The policy which provides money back at regular intervals before the policy expires is known as 'Money Back Policy'. For instance, on a 15 years policy, one gets 20 per cent of the sum assured after five years, another 20 per cent on the expiry of another five years and the balance at the end of 15 years. If the assured dies within 2 years, the full sum assured is paid irrespective of the instalments already paid. Thus, this policy provides money in hand plus insurance cover.

(b) **Sinking Fund Policy:**   Sinking fund policy is usually taken in order to provide for the payment of liability or replacement of an asset.

(c) **Key-man Insurance:** It is an insurance taken by a company on the life of important employee—key-man of the company—against financial loss that may occur from the employee's premature death. The key-man (KM) can be an expert, a technocrat, a director, a shareholder or an executive.

CLAIMS

"Claim is the demand for performance of the promise made by the insurer at the time of making the contract."

Depending upon the plan of insurance, the following are the various forms of claims which may arise.

(a) Maturity claim

Claim on the completion of the policy term is known as maturity claim. If the policyholder dies during the currency of the policy term, it is a death claim.

(b) Survival benefit

Survival benefit arises on the survival of the life assured at the end of a specified interval.

(c) Rider claim

Accident benefit claim, critical illness claim, etc. are brought under the category of rider claims.

CLAIM INTIMATION

The claim intimation may be about the maturity; or the death of the life assured; or the life assured suffering a disability.

Maturity claim is intimated either to the life assured or to the assignee if the policy has been assigned. The intimation procedure of survival benefit is the same as in the case of maturity claims. Survival benefit becomes payable at the end of the specified periodical intervals during the policy term if the life assured is surviving. Death claim intimation is sent by the claimant who may be nominee, assignee, a relative or the agent. However, intimation has to be from the concerned person and should establish identity of the deceased life assured beyond doubt.

CLAIMS DOCUMENTS

Maturity claims: In the case of maturity claims, the insurer calls for the following documents:

(i) Policy Bond (Policy Document): If policy document is not available due to having been, lost/destroyed, 'indemnity bond' is required.

(ii) Age proof, if age is not already admitted.

(iii) Deed of Assignment, if any.

(iv) Discharge form duly signed by the life assured/assignee and witnessed.

Death claims: On receipt of the death intimation, the following documents are called for:

(i) Policy document

(ii) Deed of Assignment, if any

(iii) Proof of age, if age is not admitted earlier.

(iv) Certificate of death issued by Municipality or Local Board.

(v) Legal evidence of title, if there is no nomination or assignment.

(vi) Claimant's statement giving details like life assured's name, policy number, date and cause of death.

(vii) Certificate of identity and cremation/burial by an independent person who attended the same.

(viii) Form of discharge executed and properly witnessed.

The following additional requirements are called for if death occurs within three years from the date of issue of the First Premium Receipt or the date of last revival.

(i) Statement from the last medical attendant giving details of last illness and treatment.

(ii) Statement from the hospital if the deceased had been hospitalised.

(iii) Statement from the person who had seen the dead body and attended the funeral rites.

(iv) Statement from the employer showing details of leave, if the deceased was employed somewhere.

In the case of unnatural death such as accident/suicide/murder or unknown cause, FIR, PIR, chemical analysts report, post-mortem report, etc., will also be required.

ACCIDENT AND DISABILITY BENEFITS

The conditions applicable to accidental cases are:

(i) The accident should have been caused by outward and violent and visible means.

(ii) The accident should not have been caused by self-inflicted means.

(iii) The death (or disablement, as the case may be) should be a result of injuries caused by that accident.

(iv) The death should have occurred after the accident within the period as specified in the policy conditions (usually 120 days).

SETTLEMENT PROCEDURE

Maturity Claim

On the receipt of the required documents by the insurer the following procedures are to be adopted in the case of maturity claim.

  (i) Security of the documents.
 (ii) If such documents are found in order, the claim amount is sanctioned by the competent authority of the insurer.
(iii) The payment is made by an account payee cheque.
 (iv) Usually the claim amount is paid to the assured himself or the assignee in the case of an absolute assignment.
  (v) If the claim determines the policy finally, i.e., the contract comes to an end on claim payment, the policy document is cancelled.

Survival Benefits

  (i) The payment of survival benefit does not determine the policy finally, i.e., the contract does not come to an end. Hence, the policy document is not cancelled. After a suitable endorsement is made on the policy document, the same is returned along with the cheque.
 (ii) However, nowadays, some insurers do not call for policy document to make such an endorsement if survival benefit amount is less than certain amount (limit on such amounts or procedures in this regard vary from insurer to insurer).
(iii) In case the life assured dies after survival benefit becoming due but before its settlement, the survival benefit is not paid to the nominee. It is payable to the legal heirs of the life assured.

Unusual Situations

There may be certain unusual situations, such as:

  (i) The life assured (or the person to sign the discharge) is known to be mentally deranged. In such a case a certificate under Indian Lunacy Act, appointing a person to act as guardian to manage the properties of the lunatic is called for.
 (ii) The assured has been adjudged insolvent before the maturity of the policy and a notice to that effect was received. In such a case:

(a) The official assignee is intimated about the maturity;

(b) The payment of policy money is made to the official assignee under advice to the assured.

(c) If the policy has been sold in court auction, the purchaser will be entitled for the payment on production of the certificate.

(iii) The prohibitory order from a court of law or a Notice from Income Tax Authority u/s 226(3) subsists. In such a case:

(a) The life assured has to get withdrawal of such Order/ Notice,

(b) Otherwise payment is processed according to the Order/ Notice.

(iv) *Life assured missing*

If the life assured is reported to have disappeared and is not heard of for the last seven years, the person disappeared is presumed to be dead under the Indian Evidence Act. In such a case court order is required and the payment is made as per the status of the policy.

(v) *Miscellaneous*

(a) Under a policy financed through HUF funds, the policy moneys go to the Karta of HUF.

(b) The payment to non-resident Indians is governed by the Foreign Exchange Control Regulations.

Death Claim

(i) In the case of proper nomination or assignment, no further proof of title of the claimant is required.

(ii) If there is no nomination or assignment, legal evidence of title to the estimate of the deceased from a competent court is needed.

(iii) However, the evidence of the title may be dispensed with, up to a certain limit if:

(a) The claim amount involved is small.

(b) There is no other estate left by the deceased.

(c) There is no dispute amongst the claimants of the policy money.

(d) On the completion of the formalities as above, death claim is paid to the claimant.

Time-barred Death Claim

In case the intimation is received after three years from the date of death, the claim is time-barred. In such a case:

(a) If the claim is otherwise payable, ex gratia payment can be considered.

(b) If death had occurred within 3 years from the policy's commencement or the last revival, investigations are also conducted.

Early Death Claim

(i) In the case of death within two years from the issue of the first premium receipt or the last revival, investigation of the possibility of suppression of material information is required.

(ii) In the case of death within three years from the issue of first premium receipt or the last revival, the insurer would verify the possibility of intentional misrepresentation or concealment of material information at the time of proposal or revival, for which investigation may be conducted.

Claim Concession

In strict terms of the contract, if premium payment is in default, the policy lapses. If the policy is lapsed and the life assured dies, no claim is payable. Yet, insurers pay death claims in certain cases although the policy is in lapsed condition on the date of death. Such a settlement of death claim is known as 'claim concession'.

IRDA Regulations

The following are the IRDA regulations relevant to claim settlement.

(i) In the case of death claim, all the requirements should be asked for only once and not in piecemeal.

(ii) Insurer's decision to accept or repudiate a death claim should be made within 30 days from the date of receipt of claim papers.

(iii) If an investigation is required, it should be completed within six months.

(iv) In the case of delay in settlement of a death claim,

(a) If delay is on the part of insurer, interest at 2 per cent over the bank rate would be payable.

(b) If delay is due to claimant being not ready to collect the claim amount, interest at the savings bank rate is payable.

ANNUITIES

In annuity contract, the insurer undertakes to pay certain level sums periodically up to death or expiry of the term. Thus, an annuity is a periodical level payment made in exchange of the purchase money for the remainder of the lifetime of a person or for a specified period. The recipient of annuity is usually known as an annuitant.

The annuity is beneficial to those who do not want to leave the amount to others but want to use their money during their lifetime. Since the payment of annuity generally continues up to the life, the premium rate is determined in accordance with the longevity of an annuitant. The amount of premium is higher at younger age and lower at advanced age.

Annuity contracts vs. Life insurance policies

	Annuity Contract	*Life Insurance Policy*
1.	It liquidates gradually the accumulated funds.	It provides gradual accumulation of funds.
2.	It is taken for one's own benefit.	It is generally for benefits of the dependents.
3.	In annuity contract, the payment stops.	In life insurance, the payment is at death, usually given at death.
4.	The premium is calculated on the basis of longevity of the annuitant.	The premium is based on the mortality of the policyholder.
5.	It is a protection against living too long.	It is a protection against living too short.

CLASSIFICATION OF ANNUITIES

The annuities can be classified according to:
(i) commencement of income, (ii) number of lives covered, (iii) mode of payment of premium, (iv) disposition of proceeds, and (v) special combination of annuities.

Annuities According to Commencement of Income

1. **Immediate Annuity:** The immediate annuity commences immediately after the end of the first income period. The

annuity can be paid either yearly, half-yearly, quarterly or monthly. But the premium (or consideration) is paid in single amount. For instance, if the annuity is to be paid annually, then the first instalment will be paid at the expiry of one year. Similarly, in half-yearly annuity, the payment will begin at the end of six months. The immediate annuity contract is of special interest to persons without dependents.

2. **Annuity Due:** In annuity due, the payment of instalment commences from the time of contract. Thus, the first payment is made immediately on the finalisation of contract. The premium is generally paid in single amount. The annuity due contract is beneficial for acturial valuation.

   The difference between the immediate annuity and annuity due is that the payment of each period is paid at the end of the period in immediate annuity contract while in its beginning under the annuity due contract.

3. **Deferred Annuity:** Under deferred annuity contract, the payment of annuity commences after a deferred period or at the attainment by the annuitant of a specified age. The premium may be paid in single amount or in instalments. Generally, the deferred annuity is sold on level premium. But the payment of premium continues until the stated date for commencement of the instalments or until prior death of the annuitant. At the death, the premium may be returned without interest.

   The deferred annuity can be surrendered for a cash amount (or cash option) at the end of or before the deferment period. However, no surrender value is payable after a deferment period.

   Deferred annuity is beneficial to those who desire to provide a regular income for themselves and their dependants after the expiry of a specified period.

Classification of Annuity According to the Number of Lives

1. **Single Life Annuity:** Under this annuity, one single life is contracted. This annuity is the most beneficial to those who have no dependent and want to use all this saving during his lifetime.

2. **Multiple Life Annuity:** Under this annuity more than one life is contracted. This is brought into two types. They are

joint life annuity and last survivor annuity. While in joint life annuity, the payment of annuity stops at the first death, in survivor annuity the payment continues up to the death of the last person of the group.

Classification of Annuities According to Mode of Premium

1. **Level Premium Annuity:** In level premium annuity, the annuitant can deposit some amounts periodically for availing the sufficient amount of annuity in equal instalments at the end. Before the commencement of the payment of annuity, the annuitant is given option to get the surrender value in cash or to get the paid-up values reduced in proportion to the premium paid to the premium payable. At the death of the depositor, the beneficiary can get the surrender values or premiums paid, whichever is higher.

2. **Single Premium Annuities:** The annuity which is purchased by payment of a single premium is known as single premium annuity. Usually, the life insurance amount is utilised for purchasing this annuity.

Classification According to the Disposition of Proceeds

1. **Life Annuity:** The annuity which offers a regular income to the annuitant throughout the life is termed as life annuity. Under this annuity, no payment is made after the death of the annuitant. Thus, if the annuitant dies before receiving all the amounts of the purchase price, he suffers. But if he survives for a longer period than expected, he is benefited by this annuity.

2. **Guaranteed Minimum Annuity:** Under this annuity, the annuity payment up to a period is guaranteed by the insurer. In case the annuitant dies before the specified period, the annuity will continue up to the unexpired period.

   Guaranteed minimum annuity is of two types. They are (i) immediate annuity with guaranteed payment, and (ii) deferred annuity with guaranteed payment.

   (i) **Immediate Annuity with Guaranteed Payment:** Under this annuity, the payment for a fixed number of years is made irrespective of the death of the annuitant. Sometimes, instead of continuing the annuity payments after the death of the policyholder, the difference of the purchase money and annuity instalments already paid is returned in lump sum to the legal representative of the annuitant. This annuity is usually issued to safeguard the loss in the case of early death of the annuitant.

(ii) Deferred Annuity with Guaranteed Payments: This annuity and ordinary deferred annuity have no difference during the deferment period. But after the deferment period, the payment under this policy will continue for a fixed period and up to life, thereafter. This policy also guarantees refund of cash value of the balance of annuity where the insurer promises to pay a lump sum to the beneficiary (i.e., the difference, if any, between the total of annuities received before the annuitant's death and the purchase price).

REVIEW QUESTIONS

1. Explain briefly the fundamental principles of life insurance.

2. Define a contract of life insurance. What are the features of life insurance?

3. What is the difference between insurance and assurance?

4. When should insurable interest be present in the case of life insurance?

5. What do you understand by assignment of an insurance policy? How does an assignment differ from nomination?

6. Write notes on:
   (a) Days of grace   (b) Proof of death
   (c) Proof of age   (d) Paid-up value

7. Explain the terms
   (a) Key-man insurance   (b) Annuity policy
   (c) Money back policy   (d) Joint life policy.

8. Explain the various kinds of life policies.

9. What do you mean by endowment life policy? Explain various kinds of endowment life policies.

10. Write notes on:
    (a) Level premium policy
    (b) With profit and without profit policies
    (c) Group insurance policies

(d) Whole life policy

(e) Surrender value

11. What are the various conditions relating to continuation, alteration and foreclosure of policies?

12. Explain in detail the conditions of lapsation and claims.

13. Explain briefly the procedure for settlement of claim.

14. Define annuity. Distinguish between annuity contracts and life insurance policies.

15. Write notes on:

(a) Immediate annuity   (b) Deferred annuity

(b) Multiple life annuity   (d) Single premium annuities

16. "Life insurance is insurance against dying too soon and endowment insurance is insurance against living too long." Explain.

PRACTICAL PROBLEMS

Attempt the following problems, giving reasons.

1. P takes a policy on his wife's life and later divorces her. She dies. Discuss the liability of the insurer.

   Hint: The insurer is liable to pay the amount to P.

2. P owes of ₹10,000 to Q. Q insures the life of P for a like amount. P pays the debt to Q. P then dies. Q claims ₹10,000 from the insurers. Is the insurer liable to pay?

   Hint: Yes.

3. P insures his life with an insurer of ₹10,000. Subsequently, he became insane and committed suicide. Can the legal representative of P, subject to the terms of the policy, recover money from the insurer?

   Hint: Yes, provided one year has expired since the commencement of the policy.

4. M assigned his life insurance policy to N on 15th January, 1998 for valuable consideration by a separate deed of assignment. On 15th January, 1998 M transferred the same policy by endorsement thereon to P as a gift and gave a notice of transfer in favour of P to the Life Insurance Corporation of India in the prescribed manner and enclosing therewith the

original deed of assignment. Both N and P claim the policy money on maturity. Decide.

Hint: In this case, notice of assignment in favour of P has been given to the Life Insurance Corporation. Hence, P would be entitled to get the policy money.

5. Aravind is the holder of a life insurance policy on his life. Mrs. Aravind is mentioned in the policy as his nominee. Afterwards Aravind nominates by will his brother Joy in the place of his wife and sends a notice of change by post to Life Insurance Corporation. The letter is lost in-transit. The corporation pays the policy money to Mrs. Aravind upon the death of Mr. Aravind. Joy disputes the payments. Is the contention of Joy correct?

Hint: In this case, the notice of nomination in favour of Joy has not been delivered to the insurer and the insurer has made payment bona fide. Hence, Joy's contention is not correct and the insurer has no liability towards him.

6. Jain, the holder of a policy of life insurance on his own life, nominates Ajay as his nominee. Before the maturity of the policy Ajay dies. On the maturity of the policy Ajay's heirs claim the policy money. Will they succeed?

Hint: No, Ajay's heirs will not succeed because as per Sec. 39 of the Insurance Act where the nominee dies before the policy matures for payment, the policy money shall be payable to the policyholder or his heirs.

21

General Insurance

A contract of fire insurance is "a contract whereby the insurer undertakes, in consideration of the premium paid, to make good any loss or damages caused by fire during a specified period".

INTRODUCTION

In 1971, the Government nationalised the insurance business and passed a General Insurance Business (Nationalisation) Act in 1972. The Act empowered the Central Government to form the General Insurance Corporation of India. As such, General Insurance Corporation was formed with four subsidiaries viz., The New India Assurance Co. Ltd., United India Insurance Co. Ltd., The Oriental Insurance Co. Ltd. and National Insurance Co. Ltd. Now all general insurance businesses (such as fire, marine and miscellaneous) are transacted through these four subsidiaries. General Insurance Corporation (GIC) is the controlling body. Thus, all the insurance businesses are now under the ownership and control of the Central Government.

FIRE INSURANCE

Many provisions of the Insurance Act, 1938 and the General Insurance Business (Nationalisation) Act, 1972 relate to fire insurance business in India. From 1st January 1994, the fire insurance business is being transacted only by the General Insurance Corporation of India, and its four subsidiaries.

Meaning and Definition

A contract of fire insurance is "a contract whereby the insurer undertakes, in consideration of the premium paid, to make good any loss or damages caused by fire during a specified period". The document which contains the terms and conditions of the fire insurance contract is called the fire policy.

A claim for loss by fire must satisfy two conditions:

(a) There must be an actual fire.

(b) The fire must be accidental and not intentional, on the part of the insured.

Fire means the production of light and heat by combustion (burning). There is no fire unless there is actual ignition.

FUNDAMENTAL PRINCIPLES OF FIRE INSURANCE

The following are the fundamental principles for a valid contract of fire insurance.

(i) Contract of indemnity (ii) Insurable interest (iii) Utmost good faith (iv) Loss through fire (v) Contract from year to year (vi) Subrogation and contribution.

(i) **Contract of Indemnity:** As per the principle of indemnity, the insured can recover only the amount of actual loss subject to the sum assured. Its object is to place the insured, as far as possible in the same financial position after a loss as that occupied immediately before the loss.

(ii) **Insurable Interest:** Insurable interest is the interest in the preservation of a thing. In fire insurance, the insurable interest should exist not only at the time of effecting the insurance but at the time of loss also. Such an interest, however, may be legal or equitable or may arise under a contract of purchase or sale.

(iii) **Contract of Good Faith:** The contract of fire insurance is a contract of utmost good faith or uberrimae fidei. Hence, the insured should make full and detailed disclosure of all the material facts likely to affect the adjustment of fire officials in determining the rates of premium (or deciding whether the proposal should be accepted or not).

(iv) **Loss Through Fire:** Loss resulting from fire is the risk covered under a fire insurance. But the loss will not be covered if the fire is caused by the insured himself or with his connivance.

(v) **Contract from Year to Year:** A fire insurance policy is usually for one year. But it can be renewed every year.

(vi) **Principles of Subrogation and Contribution:** The term subrogation literally means substitution, i.e., substitution of the insurer in place of the insured in respect of the latter's right and remedies. As per the principle of subrogation, the insurer steps into the shoes of the insured and becomes entitled to all the rights of the insured regarding the subject matter of insurance after the claim of the insured has been fully and finally settled.

Where the subject matter has been insured with more than one insurer, each insurer has to meet the loss only rateably. If he has paid more than his share of loss, he is entitled to recover the excess paid from his co-insurers. Hence, the principle of contribution applies in the case of fire insurance.

Fire Policy: Fire policy is a document containing the written contract between the insurer and the assured. It contains the terms and conditions under which the insurance is issued, the particulars of the property insured, risks and hazards covered, the sum assured, the cost or the rate of premium and the period.

The Risk: The risk on the fire policy commences from the moment of time the cover note (or the deposit receipt) is given and continues for the term covered by the contract of insurance. It is the practice to allow a certain number of days as days of grace within which a fire policy may be renewed after the expiry of the term. In such a situation, if fire occurs within the period of days of grace, the insured would be entitled to recover damages. In this connection, it is noted that the days of grace apply only when the insured has the intention to renew the policy.

Payment of Claims: In the case of fire policy, if fire occurs, the insured should give notice to the insurance company. The claim to be made out should be for the exact value of the goods damaged, or destroyed on the date of the fire. In the case of partly destroyed or damaged goods, the details as to their value in good condition and in damaged condition ought to be made out and furnished to the insurance company. In the case of damaged building, the basis of claim should be the cost of repairs of the damage with due allowance for the greater value of the new premises over the old. This rule is applicable only if the full value of the property is insured. Where the property is partially insured, the claim to be made is to pay only a proportional loss (i.e., loss in proportion in which the amount insured stands to the full value of the property).

TYPES OF FIRE POLICIES

The main types of fire policies are as follows:

1. **Average Policy:** An average policy is that policy which contains the average clause. Average clause states that if the property is insured for a sum smaller than the actual value

of the property (under insured), the insurer shall bear only that proportion of the actual loss as his insurance bears to the actual value of the property at the time of loss.

Example: If a person insures his property worth ₹50,000 for ₹40,000 only, and the loss caused by fire is ₹30,000, then the amount of the claim to be paid by the insurer is:

$$\frac{40,000}{50,000} \times ₹30,000 = ₹24,000$$

The aim of this policy is to prevent 'under insurance'. Under insurance means insuring a property for an amount less than the actual value of it.

2. **Valued Policy:** It is a policy in which the value of the subject matter is agreed at the time of taking the insurance and is specified in the policy itself. In the event of loss, the agreed amount is payable irrespective of the actual amount of loss.

3. **Specific Policy:** It is a policy in which the value insured against is specified. In the case of any loss to the property insured under such a policy, the insurer will pay the whole loss of the insured if the loss falls within the specified sum.

4. **Floating Policy:** It is a policy which covers the property lying in different localities under one sum and for one premium. It is always subject to an average clause.

5. **Blanket Policy:** It is a policy which covers all assets (fixed as well as current) of the insured under one insurance.

6. **Comprehensive Policy:** It is a policy which is issued to cover such risks as fire, explosion, lightning, thunderbolt, riot, civil commotion, strikes, burglary, etc. This is also called 'All Insurance Policy' and is not common in our country.

7. **Consequential Loss Policy:** The object of this policy is to indemnify the insured against the loss of profit caused by any interruption of business by fire. It is also known as 'loss of profit policy'.

MARINE INSURANCE

Marine insurance is the oldest form of insurance. The law relating to it is codified in the Marine Insurance Act, 1963. This Act contains

92 Sections and a Schedule containing a form of marine insurance policy and the rules of construction.

Contract of Marine Insurance

A contract of marine insurance is "an agreement by which the insurance company agrees to indemnify the owner of a ship or cargo against risks which are incidental to marine adventure".

An instrument containing the contract of marine insurance entered into, between the insurer and the assured is called a marine policy or sea policy. The consideration for the policy is called the premium. The insurer in marine insurance is known as underwriter.

Marine risks generally relate to the ship or cargo. Accordingly, the cargo, the ship and the freight form the subject matter of insurance. On the basis of the subject matter, the marine insurance is classified into three heads: (i) cargo insurance (ii) hull insurance, and (iii) freight insurance.

- **(i) Cargo Insurance:** The cargo on the ship is exposed to risks arising from the act of God, or enemy, or fire, etc. The type of marine insurance that covers such risks is known as the 'cargo insurance'.

- **(ii) Hull Insurance:** If the subject matter of the insurance is the ship, the marine insurance is called the 'hull insurance'.

- **(iii) Freight Insurance:** When the subject matter of a marine insurance contract is the freight to be received, it is called the 'freight insurance'.

MARINE ADVENTURE [SEC. 2(D)]

Marine adventure includes, where (i) any insurable property is exposed to maritime perils; (ii) the earning or acquisition of any freight, passage money, commission, profit or other pecuniary benefit, or the security for any advances, loans or disbursements is endangered by the exposure of insurable property to maritime perils; (iii) any liability to a third party may be incurred by the owner of, or other person interested in, insurable property by reason of maritime perils.

Insurable property means any ship, goods or other movables which are exposed to maritime perils [Sec. 2(c)].

MARITIME PERILS [SEC. 2(E)]

'Maritime perils' mean the perils consequent on or incidental to, the navigation of the sea.

Perils of the Sea

It means all perils and misfortunes of a marine character or incidental to a ship.

FUNDAMENTAL PRINCIPLES OF MARINE INSURANCE

The following are the fundamental principles or essential features of marine insurance.

(i) Features of general contract (ii) Insurable interest (iii) Utmost good faith (iv) Contract of indemnity (v) Principles of subrogation and contribution (vi) Proximate cause (vii) Return of premium (viii) Assignment of policy (xi) Warranties.

(i) **Features of General Contract:** A marine policy should fulfil all the essentials of a valid contract such as offer, acceptance, agreement, competent parties, free consent, lawful consideration and legal object. Here, the proposal is made by a ship owner or a cargo owner or a freight receiver. When the insurer (known as underwriter) accepts the proposal, it becomes an agreement. The premium is determined on assessment of the proposal and is paid at the time of the contract. The premium is called consideration to the contract.

(ii) **Insurable Interest:** The insured should have an insurable interest in the subject matter insured at the time when the loss occurs. It is not essential that insurable interest should exist at the time of effecting the insurance. The Marine Insurance Act, 1963 states that "every person has an insurable interest who is interested in a marine adventure".

(iii) **Utmost Good Faith:** Marine insurance is a contract of uberrimae fidei or utmost good faith. Hence, the insured should disclose all those relevant facts to the insurer which are likely to affect his willingness to undertake the risk. Unless full facts are disclosed by either party, the contract can be avoided by the other party.

(iv) **Contract of Indemnity:** The principle of indemnity is the essence of a marine insurance contract. In such a contract, the underwriter agrees to indemnify the insured against losses by sea risks to the extent of the amount insured. As a result, the insured can recover only the actual loss suffered. In no case will he be allowed to make a profit out of his loss.

(v) **Principles of Subrogation and Contribution:** The principles of subrogation and contribution are applicable to the marine insurance contract. The aim of subrogation is that the insured should not get more than the actual loss or damage. After meeting the loss agreed, the insurer steps into the shoes of the insured. Hence, the insurer becomes entitled to all the rights and remedies available to the insured against third persons.

As per the principle of contribution, if the subject matter has been insured with more than one insurer, each insurer has to meet only the rateable proportion of loss. If an insurer has paid more than his share of loss, he is entitled to recover the excess paid from his co-insurers.

(vi) **Proximate Cause:** According to the Marine Insurance Act (subject to the provisions of the Act and unless the policy otherwise provides) the insurer is liable for any loss proximately caused by a peril insured against.

(vii) **Return of Premium:** Premium is the consideration for the risk run by the insurers. If the risk insured is not run, the consideration fails. Hence, the insured can recover the premium paid from the insurer.

(viii) **Assignment of Policy:** A marine insurance policy is assignable unless it contains terms expressly prohibiting assignment. It may be assigned either before or after loss by endorsement thereon or on other customary ways.

(ix) **Warranties:** Warranties are conditions which form part of a marine policy. These conditions should be adhered to and observed by the insured in a contract of marine insurance. There are two types of warranties or conditions viz., express and implied.

Express warranties are conditions which are specifically stated in the policy. Instances of express warranties are:

(a) The subject matter insured is safe at a particular time.

(b) The readiness of the ship to undertake the voyage on a particular day.

(c) The ship will proceed to the port of destination.

Implied warranties are those which are implied by law, in every contract of marine insurance. Instances of implied warranties are:

(a) The seaworthiness of the ship.

(b) The legality of the venture.

(c) The ship will follow the specified course.

TYPES OF MARINE POLICIES

The Marine Insurance Act generally deals with the following types of policies.

1. **Time Policy:** This is a policy whereby the subject matter is insured for a definite period of time. Time policy is suitable mainly for hull insurance.

2. **Voyage Policy:** It is a policy which covers a particular voyage. This policy is meant to insure the subject matter in transit from one place to another e.g., Bombay to London. The subject matter insured under such a policy is generally cargo which is exposed to marine risks in the course of transit.

3. **Mixed Policy:** Mixed policy is combination of 'voyage' and 'time' policies. It is a policy which covers the risk during a particular voyage for a specified period. Example from Bombay to London for six months.

4. **Valued Policy:** It is a policy which mentions the agreed value of the subject matter insured. In the absence of fraud or misrepresentation, this value is regarded as conclusive of the value of the subject matter, whether the loss is partial or total.

5. **Open or Unvalued Policy:** It is the policy which does not specify the value of the subject matter insured. The value of the subject matter is determined later when the loss occurs.

6. **Floating Policy:** It is a policy which describes the insurance in general terms and leaves the name or names of the ships and other particulars to be defined by subsequent declaration.

7. **Wagering Policy:** It is a policy which is issued when the assured has no insurable interest in the subject assured and has no expectation of acquiring such interest at the time of the contract.

CLAUSES IN A MARINE POLICY

1. **Lost or Not Lost Clause:** This clause covers any loss of goods that occurs between the shipment of goods and the issue of policy.

2. **Sue and Labour Clause:** It is also referred to as the S.L.T. (Sue Labour and Travel clause). As per this clause,

the insurer is to compensate the insured, all the expenses incurred by him for protecting the subject matter from the perils of the sea.

3. **Running Down or Collision Clause:** It is the clause which makes the insurer liable to contribute to a loss caused by a collision with other ships.

4. **Free of Particular Average Clause (F.P.A.):** This clause exempts the insurer from all liability for particular except in certain cases. In marine insurance, particular average means a partial loss of subject matter insured.

5. **Free of Capture and Seizure Clause (F.C. & S.):** This clause in a marine policy relieves the insurer from the liability of risks of losses due to destruction or capture of the ship and its cargo in war activities.

6. **Waiver Clause:** This clause declares that no act of an insurer or insured in saving, maintaining and preserving the goods to the hull will be considered as a 'waiver' or acceptance of abandonment.

7. **Inchmaree Clause:** It is a clause which covers, among other things, losses caused by the negligence of the master, crew, pilots, etc., or by explosive or any other latent defect in the machinery of the vessel.

8. **Jettison Clause:** It is a clause which gives the insurer the liability to compensate any loss caused by jettisoning of the goods. Jettison means the act of throwing the cargo over board to lighten the ship in emergencies.

9. **Barratry Clause:** 'Barratry' means the wrongful act done by the captain of a ship in destroying or stealing the vessel or cargo causing loss to the owner.

MARINE LOSSES

The insurer is liable for any loss proximately caused by the perils insured against unless otherwise provided. For the purpose of marine insurance, the losses are broadly divided into two categories: (i) Total Loss, and (ii) Partial Loss.

(i). **Total Loss:** A total loss means that the subject matter of insurance is totally lost and there is no question of regaining any part of the property. A total loss may be either an actual total loss or a constructive total loss.

A total loss is said to be actual when the subject matter is absolutely destroyed and is totally lost to the owner. An actual total loss may be presumed, if a ship is missing, and after a reasonable time no news of her has been received (Sec. 58).

A total loss is said to be constructive when the subject matter insured is reasonably abandoned on account of its actual total loss appearing to be unavoidable. In other words, the subject matter insured is not completely destroyed, but it is in such a condition that the cost of recovery or repair exceeds the value of the property.

Abandonment

When there is a constructive total loss, the assured may treat the loss as a partial loss or abandon the property insured to the insurer and treat the loss as if it were an actual loss (Sec. 61).

Abandonment means surrendering all proprietary rights in whatever remains of the subject matter (in case of its loss) to the insurer in order to claim the total loss from him. In the case of abandonment, a notice of abandonment should be given to the insurer. Otherwise the loss will be treated as a partial loss.

(ii) **Partial Loss:** A partial loss in marine insurance is called an 'average'. A loss is said to be partial when the damage of the subject matter insured is not complete. An average (partial loss) may be either 'General Average' or 'Particular Average'.

General average is incurred voluntarily for the common good of the voyage in an emergency.

Example: Expenses involved in loading and unloading of goods in order to refloat a ship, throwing cargo to lighten the ship in an emergency, etc.

The rule with regard to general average loss is that such a loss must be borne proportionately by all the parties interested in the voyage.

A particular average is a partial loss happening to a particular object due to the peril of the sea. It should be borne by the owner or the insurer.

Example: If some tins of egg powder are sent by sea and a few of them are damaged by sea water, the loss of this account will have to be borne by the owner of the ship or the insurer.

CLAIMS

When the policy under marine insurance has been insured, the risk for the peril insured against is covered. If loss occurs, the insured would make a claim on the insurer for indemnification of loss. Hence, a prompt notice of claim by the insured is essential. After the notice, the insured should take delivery of the damaged goods at once or otherwise deal with the damage because the insurer is not responsible for further and continued depreciation of the interest damaged.

Claims Documents: Claims under marine policies have to be supported by certain documents which vary in accordance with the type of loss as also the circumstances of the claim and the mode of carriage.

The following are the documents required for particular average claims:

(i) Original policy—certificate of insurance

(ii) Bill of lading—evidence that the goods were actually shipped

(iii) Invoice—evidence for the terms of sale

(iv) Survey report—shows the cause and extent of loss

(v) Debit note—claim bill

(vi) Copy of protest—protest on arrival at destination before a Notary Public

(vii) Letter of subrogation—legal document which transfers the right of claimant against third party to the insurer.

MISCELLANEOUS INSURANCE POLICIES

Besides the major forms of insurance mentioned above, insurance policies meant to cover a variety of other risks are also issued by the general insurance companies. The following are some of its major types.

1. **Motor Insurance:** For this purpose, motor vehicles are classified into three heads (i) Private Motors, (ii) Commercial Vehicles, and (iii) Motor Bicycles, including scooters. Commercial vehicles include all the vehicles which are used for commercial purposes, e.g., buses, taxis, trucks, tractors, road rollers, etc.

Generally, the owner of a vehicle is exposed to three types of risks. They are:

   (a) Risk arising from damage to the vehicle by fire or accident or loss due to theft of the vehicle.

   (b) Personal injury to the owner of the vehicle.

   (c) Injury to or death of some other party due to an accident in which the vehicle of the insured is involved.

     A policy converting all these three kinds of risks is known as a comprehensive policy.

2. **Third Party Insurance:** Under this policy, in addition to the risk of personal injury to a third party, the risk of damage to his property is also insured.

3. **Fidelity Insurance:** It is a policy which is taken by the owner of the business to cover the risks arising out of fraud and dishonesty on the part of his employees.

4. **Burglary Insurance:** It is a policy which covers the risks from burglary, theft and robbery.

5. **Credit Insurance:** It is a policy for shifting some of the trade losses arising out of bad debts from the merchant to the insurer.

REVIEW QUESTIONS

1. Define fire insurance contract. Explain the fundamental principles of fire insurance contract.

2. What is the meaning of 'fire' in a fire insurance policy?

3. How should a claim under a fire policy be made?

4. What is the effect of average clause in a fire policy?

5. A fire insurance is a contract of indemnity. Comment.

6. Explain the terms:

   (a) Floating policy   (b) Average clause

   (c) Valued policy   (d) Meaning of 'fire' in a fire policy

7. Define 'marine insurance'. What are the essential features of a marine insurance contract?

8. Distinguish total loss from partial loss in marine insurance. Discuss the rules regarding abandonment in the case of constructive total loss.

9. Discuss fully the express and implied warranties in a contract of marine insurance. What is the effect of breach of warranty?

10. Write notes on:
    (a) Inchmaree clause   (b) Lost or not lost clause
    (c) Constructive total loss   (d) Barratry
    (e) Claim documents in marine policy

PRACTICAL PROBLEMS

Attempt the following problems, giving reasons.

1. P, a bank manager of Delhi, insures his household goods against risks of fire. While smoking in his bed, 'P' falls asleep and the goods catch fire. P escapes with a few burns. Can 'P' recover under the policy?

   Hint: Yes, P can recover the loss under the policy.

2. A fire broke out on board a ship and caused damage to some cargo belonging to P. In puting out the fire by water some cargo of Q was damaged. Discuss either P or Q can claim general average contribution from the owners of the other interests in the ship and cargo.

   Hint: Q (and not P) can claim general average contribution from the owners of the other interests in the ship and cargo.

3. Mr. Ghosh got his goods insured against fire. Afterwards Mr. Ghosh and his wife quarrelled and she set fire to the goods. The goods were destroyed. Is Mr. Ghosh entitled to recover the loss from the insurer?

   Hint: Yes, Insurer may proceed against Mr. Ghosh's wife after paying compensation to Mr. Ghosh.

4. A ship is insured against loss due to enemy's action. The enemy had sunk a ship in the ocean and the insured ship suffered damage on account of the collision with the sunk ship. Is the insurer liable?

   Hint: Yes. Enemy's action is a proximate cause of the loss.

22

Insurance Regulatory and Development Authority (IRDA)

The "Redressal of Public Grievances Rules, 1998" is in respect of Ombudsman Scheme to resolve all complaints relating to the claims against insurers.

INTRODUCTION

In April 1993, the Government of India appointed a Committee of Reforms in insurance sector with Shri. R.N. Malhotra, a former governor of the Reserve Bank of India as its chairman. The committee submitted its report to the Government of India in January 1994. In accordance with the recommendations of the committee, the government set up a regulatory body known as "Insurance Regulatory Development Authority" and enacted the Act known as Insurance Regulatory and Development Act, 1999.

The Act seeks to open up the insurance sector for private companies with a foreign equity of 26 per cent. It is also aimed at ending the monopoly of the Life Insurance Corporation and General Insurance Corporation in the insurance sector of the country.

CONSTITUTION OF IRDA

Insurance Regulatory and Development Authority consists of:

(i) a chairman; (ii) not more than five whole-time members; and (iii) not more than four part-time members to be appointed by the Central Government.

The members should be persons of ability, integrity and standing. They should have experience in the fields of: (i) life insurance (ii) general insurance (iii) acturial science (iv) finance (v) economics (vi) law (vii) accountancy (viii) administration, and (ix) any other discipline, thought to be useful by the Central Government.

The chairperson, members, officers and other employees of the Authority shall be public servants.

OBJECTIVES OF IRDA

The following are the main objectives of the Insurance Regulatory and Development Authority.

(i) Take care of the policyholders' interest.

(ii) Open the insurance sector for private sector.

(iii) Ensure continued financial soundness and solvency.

(iv) Regulate insurance and reinsurance companies.

(v) Eliminate dishonesty and unhealthy competition.

(vi) Supervise the activities of intermediaries.

(vii) Amend the Insurance Act, 1938, the Life Insurance Corporation Act, 1956 and the General Business (Nationalisation) Act, 1972.

DUTIES AND POWERS OF IRDA

The duties and powers of the IRDA are:

(i) To regulate and ensure the orderly growth of the insurance business.

(ii) To exercise all powers and functions of the controller of insurance.

(iii) To protect the interest of policyholders in settlement of claims and terms and conditions of policies.

(iv) To promote and regulate professional organisations connected with insurance business.

(v) To control and regulate the rates and terms and conditions that may be offered by the insurers in respect of general insurance matters, not so controlled by the Tariff Advisory Committee under Section 64 (U) of the Insurance Act.

(vi) To prescribe the manner and form in which accounts will be maintained and submitted by insurers and intermediaries.

(vii) To regulate investment of funds.

(viii) To regulate margins of solvency.

(ix) To adjudicate disputes between insurers and intermediaries.

FUNCTIONS OF IRDA

The various functions of IRDA are:

(i) To issue certificate of registration, renew, withdraw, suspend or cancel such registrations.

(ii) To protect the interests of the policyholders/insured in the matter of insurance contract with the insurance company.

(iii) To specify requisite qualifications, code of conduct and training for insurance intermediaries and agents.

(iv) To specify code of conduct for Surveyors/Loss Assessors.

(v) To specify the form and manner for maintenance of books of accounts and the statement of accounts.

(vi) To promote efficiency in the conduct of insurance business.

(vii) To promote and regulate professional organisations connected with the insurance and reinsurance business.

(viii) To undertake inspection, conduct enquiries and investigations including audit of insurers and insurance intermediaries.

(ix) To control and regulate the rates, terms and conditions to be offered by the insurer regarding general insurance business not so controlled by Tariff Advisory Committee.

(x) To specify the percentage of Life Insurance business and General Insurance business to be undertaken in the rural or social sector.

(xi) To regulate investment of funds by the insurance companies.

(xii) To adjudicate disputes between insurers and intermediaries of insurance.

(xiii) To supervise the functioning of Tariff Advisory Committee.

INSURANCE OMBUDSMAN

The 'Redressal of Public Grievances Rules, 1998' is in respect of the Ombudsman Scheme to resolve all complaints relating to the claims against insurers. The Central Government have framed these rules in exercise of the powers vested in it under Sec. 114(1) of Insurance Act, 1938. The scheme was notified in the Gazette of India on 11-11-1998.

Complaints

The Ombudsman may receive and consider complaints relating to:

(i) Any partial or total repudiation of claim by an insurer;

(ii) Any dispute in regard to premium paid or payable in terms of the policy;

(iii) Any dispute in regard to the legal construction of the policies insofar as such disputes relate to the claims;

(iv) Delay in settlement of claims;

(v) Non-issue of an insurance document to the customers after receipt of the premium.

If request is made in writing jointly by the insured person and insurance company, the Ombudsman shall act as counsellor and mediator in matters, which are within his terms of reference. At any rate, the decision of the Ombudsman shall be final.

When can a Complaint be made to the Ombudsman?

In any of the following circumstances, a complaint can be made to the ombudsman.

(i) If the insurer has rejected a written representation of the complainant; or

(ii) The complainant had not received any reply within one month after the insurer received his representation; or

(iii) The complainant is not satisfied with the reply given to him by the insurer;

(iv) The complaint is made not later than one year after the insurer had rejected the representation or sent his final reply on the representation of the complainant;

(v) The complaint is not in the same subject matter, for which any proceeding before any court, or consumer forum, or arbitrator is pending or was so earlier.

Recommendations

When a complaint is settled through mediation of the ombudsman, he makes a 'recommendation' which he considers fair in the circumstances of the case. Such 'recommendation' shall be made not later than one month from the date of the receipt of the complaint and the copies of the same shall be sent to the complainant and the insurance company.

If a complainant accepts the recommendations of the ombudsman, he will communicate his acceptance within 15 days of receipt of the recommendation. However, the complainant should clearly state in the acceptance letter of the Ombudsman that the settlement reached is acceptable to him in totality (i.e., in full and final settlement of the claim). Thereafter, the Ombudsman will send a copy of the recommendation along with complainant's acceptance letter to the insurance company. The insurer shall comply with the terms of the recommendation immediately but not later than 15 days of the receipt of such recommendations. Finally, the insurer shall inform the ombudsman of its compliance.

Award

When a complaint is not settled through mediation, the ombudsman shall pass an award which he considers fair in the facts and circumstances of the case. The award shall be passed within a period of three months from the date of receipt of the complaint. It shall be in writing and shall contain the amount awarded to the complainant. However, the ombudsman shall not award any compensation in excess of the loss suffered by the complainant or ₹20 lakh, whichever is less.

Copies of the award shall be sent to the insurer and the complainant. The complainant, in turn, shall furnish to the insurer within one month, a letter of acceptance that the award is in full and final settlement of his claim. But the insurer, in turn, shall comply with the award within 15 days from the receipt of the acceptance letter and intimate compliance to the ombudsman.

Consequences of Non-acceptance of Award

If the complainant does not intimate acceptance within one month from the date of receipt of the award, the insurance company may not implement the award.

Ex gratia Payment

If the Ombudsman deems fit, he may award an ex gratia payment.

INSURANCE LEGISLATIONS IN INDIA

Up to the end of nineteenth century, the insurance was in its inceptional stage. Hence, no legislation was required till that time. Normally the Indian Companies Act, 1883 was applicable in business concerns, banking and insurance companies. Later it was asserted that the Indian Companies Act, 1883 was inadequate for the purpose. Therefore, two Acts were passed in 1912, namely

Provident Insurance Societies Act V of 1912 and Indian Life Insurance Companies Act VI of 1912. These two enactments were applicable only for life insurance and had numerous defects. Thus, in 1928, the Government of India passed a stopgap legislation with the main object of collecting statistics regarding insurance matters. This Act was not very comprehensive. Hence, the demand for another Act was made. The Government accepted the genuine demand and appointed one special officer for investigation of the special and required reform of legislation in 1935. His report was considered by the Advisory Committee appointed by the Government of India. The committee made several changes and the Government of India introduced the bill in the Legislative Assembly in 1937. After much debate and several changes, the bill emerged as the Insurance Act, 1938.

The following are the new legislations in insurance sector prevalent in India now.

(i) Insurance Act, 1938.

(ii) Life Insurance Act, 1956.

(iii) Marine Insurance Act, 1963.

(iv) General Insurance Business (Nationalisation) Act, 1972.

(v) The Insurance Regulatory and Development Authority Act, 1999.

(vi) Insurance Regulatory and Development Authority (Obligations of insurers to Rural or Social Sector).

(vii) Insurance Regulatory and Development Authority (Insurance Advertising and Disclosures) Regulations 2000.

(viii) Insurance Regulatory and Development Authority (Licensing of Insurance Agents) Regulations 2000.

(ix) Insurance Regulatory and Development Authority (Protection of Policyholders' Interest) Regulations 2002.

REVIEW QUESTIONS

1. Explain the functions of Insurance Regulatory and Development Authority.

2. Write a brief note on Insurance Regulatory and Development Authority.

3. State the duties and powers of IRDA.

4. Outline the recent development in the insurance sector in India.

PART THREE

COMPANY LAW

23

Introduction

*The Companies Act, 2013 has introduced new
concepts, supporting enhanced disclosure,
accountability, better board, governance, better
facilitation of business and so on.*

HISTORY

Companies Act in India is largely a copy of the English Law. The
earliest Act relating to the joint stock companies in England was
of the year 1844, succeeded by a number of Acts. These Acts were
repealed and replaced by the Companies Act, 1929. The said Act
was itself substantially amended by the Companies Act, 1947. The
amendments brought about by the Companies Act, 1947, were based
on the report of a committee under the chairmanship of Mr. Justice
Cohen, called the Cohen report. The Act of 1947 was soon after
repealed and replaced by the Companies Act, 1948 which is now in
force in England. It is divided into 13 parts comprising 462 Sections,
and 18 Schedules.

INDIAN LAW

The history of the Indian Company Law began with the Joint
Stock Companies Act of 1850. Since then the cumulative process
of amendment and consolidation has brought us to the most
comprehensive and complicated piece of legislation—the Companies
Act, 1956.

In 1913, the Indian Companies Act of 1913 was passed. This,
was mainly based on the English Act of 1908. One of the unique
features of this Act was the introduction of the institution of Private
Company. The Indian Companies Act of 1913, was amended in 1936
in conformity with the changes brought about in the English law by
the Act of 1929. The Indian Companies Act of 1956 has consolidated
the law. It has taken into account the changes brought about in
England by the Acts of 1947 and 1948.

THE COMPANIES ACT, 1956

The Indian Companies Act of 1956 which came into force on 1st April, 1956 extends to the whole of India and contains 658 Sections and 13 Schedules.

The Companies Act, 1956, is based on the recommendation of the Bhabha Committee which submitted its report in 1952, recommending wholesale amendments in the Indian Companies Act, 1913. The Act aimed at discouraging the concentration of economic wealth in a few hands and securing its more equitable distribution.

The Companies Act of 1956, has been amended from time to time to protect investors and to help in achieving the objectives of a socialistic pattern of society. In 1957, the Central Government appointed a committee known as the Sastri Committee to review the Companies Act, 1956. On the basis of the recommendations of the Sastri Committee, the Companies Act, 1956 was amended for the first time by the Companies (Amendment) Act, 1960. The Companies Act, 1956 was again amended in 1963, 1965, 1969, 1974, 1977, 1988, 1996, 1998, 1999, 2000, 2002 and 2006, respectively.

EVOLUTION OF THE COMPANIES ACT, 2013

The Companies Act, 1956 was enacted with the object to amend and consolidate the law relating to companies. This Act provided the legal framework for corporate entities in India and was a mammoth legislation. As the corporate sector grew in numbers and size of operations, the need for streamlining this Act was felt and as many as 24 Amendments had taken place since then. Major Amendments were made through the Companies (Amendment) Act, 1988 after considering the recommendations of the Sachar Committee, and then again in 1998, 2000 and in 2002 through the Companies (Second Amendment) Act, 2002. Unsuccessful attempts were made in 1993 and 1997 to replace the present Act with a new law. Companies (Amendment) Bill, 2003 containing important provisions relating to Corporate Governance and aimed at achieving competitive advantage was also introduced.

Till some time back, Companies Act, 1956 was the principal legislation governing the corporate sector in India. However, several changes had taken place in the national and international economic environment after the enactment of this Act during the last two to three decades. Thus, modernisation of company law governing, setting up and functioning of enterprises, structures for sharing risk and reward, governance and accountability to the investors and other stakeholders and structural changes in the law commensurate with global standards had become critical for governing and guiding a vibrant corporate sector and business environment.

To frame a law that enables companies to achieve global competitiveness in a fast changing economy, the Government had taken up a fresh exercise for a comprehensive revision of the Companies Act, 1956, albeit through a consultative process. A Committee was constituted on 2nd December, 2004 under the Chairmanship of Dr. J.J. Irani, Director, Tata Sons, with the task of advising the Government on the proposed revisions to the Companies Act, 1956 with the objective to have a simplified compact law. The Committee submitted its report to the Government on 31st May, 2005.

DR. J.J. IRANI COMMITTEE REPORT

Dr. J.J. Irani Expert Committee on Company Law had submitted its report charting out the road map for a flexible, dynamic and user-friendly new company law. The report of the Committee had also sought to bring in multifarious progressive and visionary concepts and endeavoured to recommend a significant shift from the "Government Approval Regime" to a "Shareholder Approval and Disclosure Regime."

The Expert Committee had recommended that private and small companies need to be given flexibilities and freedom of operations and compliance at a low cost. Companies with higher public interest which access capital from public need to be subjected to a stricter regime of Corporate Governance. Further, Government companies and public financial institutions should be subject to similar parameters with respect to disclosure and Corporate Governance as other companies are subjected to.

COMPANIES BILL, 2012

The Bill promised greater shareholder democracy, vesting the shareholders with greater powers, containing stricter corporate governance norms and requiring greater disclosures.
The objectives of the Bill were:

(i) Revising and modifying the Act in consonance with the changes in the National and International economy,

(ii) Bringing about compactness of company law by deleting the provisions that had become redundant and by re-grouping the scattered provisions,

(iii) Re-writing of various provisions of the Act to facilitate easy interpretation,

    (iv) Delinking the procedural aspects from the substantive law and provide greater flexibility in rule making to enable adoption to the changing economic and technical environment.

    (v) Enabling the corporate sector to operate in a regulatory environment of best international practices that fosters entrepreneurship, investment and growth.

The Companies Bill, 2009 after introduction in Parliament was referred to the Parliamentary Standing Committee on Finance for examination which submitted its report to Parliament on 31st August, 2010. Certain amendments were introduced in the Bill in the light of the report of the Committee and a revised Companies Bill, 2011 was introduced. This version was also referred to the Hon'ble Committee, which suggested certain further amendments. The amended Bill was passed by the Lok Sabha on 18th December, 2012 and by the Rajya Sabha on 8th August, 2013. The Bill was retitled as Companies Bill, 2012.

COMPANIES ACT, 2013

The Companies Bill, 2012 was assented to by the President of India on 29th August, 2013 and notified in the Gazette of India on 30th August, 2013. It finally became the Companies Act, 2013.

Highlights of the Companies Act, 2013

Passed in Lok Sabha	December 18, 2012
Passed in Rajya Sabha	August 08, 2013
President's assent	August 29, 2013
Total number of sections	470
Total number of chapters	29
Total number of schedules	7
Number of sections notified (282)	Section 1 on August 29, 2013 98 sections on September 12, 2013 183 sections on April 01, 2014
Total number of rules notified	Rules under 21 chapters notified

NEW CONCEPTS INTRODUCED

The Companies Act, 2013 has introduced new concepts supporting enhanced disclosure, accountability, better board, governance, better facilitation of business and so on. It includes the following aspects:

- Associate company
- One person company

- Small company
- Dormant company
- Independent director
- Women director
- Resident director
- Special court
- Secretarial standards
- Secretarial audit
- Class action
- Registered valuers
- Rotation of auditors
- Vigil mechanism
- Corporate social responsibility
- Cross border mergers
- Prohibition of insider trading
- Global depositories receipts

Certain important changes between the Companies Act, 1956 and 2013 have been tabulated as follow:

CHANGES WITH REGARD TO INCORPORATION PROCEDURE

S.No.	Particulars	Companies Act, 1956	Companies Act, 2013
1.	Types of companies.	Private company Public company	Private company Public company One person company
2.	Maximum number of members for private companies.	A private company can have a maximum of 50 members.	A private company can have a maximum of 200 members.
3.	Commencement of business.	Provision is applicable only to public limited companies.	Now it is applicable to all companies having share capital.
4.	Registered office.	Companies are required to furnish the details of the Registered office of the company by filing Form 18 at the time of incorporation.	A company from the 15th day of its incorporation shall have a registered office for receiving any communications and notices as may be addressed to it.
5.	Object clause of Memorandum of Association.	Object clause bifurcated into Main objects, Incidental or Ancillary objects and other objects.	Memorandum of Association is related to the objects for which company is proposed to be incorporated and such other matters considered necessary in furtherance thereof.

6.	Issue of shares at discount.	Section 79 permits issue of shares at discount subject to compliance with conditions.	Shares, other than sweat equity shares, cannot be issued at a discount.
7.	Issue of preference shares for more than 20 years.	Section 80 prohibits issue of irredeemable preference shares and preference shares redeemable after 20 years.	Preference shares have to be redeemed within 20 years of issue, except the shares issued for specified infrastructure project which can be redeemed every year in part as accepted by shareholders.
8.	Issue of shares on private placement, bonus shares and GDRs.	No specific provision for issue of shares on private placement, bonus shares, and GDRs exists in the Act.	Specific provision has been introduced for shares on private placement, bonus shares and GDRs in the Act.
9.	Notice of alteration of share capital.	Notice of redemption of preference shares is not required to be filed with ROC.	Company shall file a notice in the prescribed form with the Registrar within a period of thirty days of redemption of redeemable preference shares.
10.	Consolidation and division of shares.	Company permitted to consolidate or sub-divide its shares by passing resolution in general meeting.	Consolidation and division that changes the voting percentage of shareholders shall require approval of the Tribunal to be effective.

CHANGES WITH REGARD TO DIRECTORS AND THEIR POWERS

S.No.	Particulars	Companies Act, 1956	Companies Act, 2013
11.	Maximum number of Directors.	Twelve. Beyond this limit, Central Government approval is required.	Fifteen. More number of directors can be appointed by passing special resolution and no approval from Central Government is required.

12.	Maximum number of Directorship.	Fifteen [Excluding Private Companies, Unlimited Companies, Alternate Directorship, and Directorship in Non-profit Associations]	Twenty. Out of which not more than ten can be public companies. It includes Alternate Directorship also. No specific exclusions provided.
13.	Composition of the Board.	Minimum of two directors in the case of private companies and three in the case of public companies. Maximum twelve directors.	1. Prescribed class of companies are required to appoint at least one-woman director. 2. At least one director should be a person who has stayed in India for a period not less than 182 days in previous year. 3. Listed companies to have at least one third independent directors.
14.	Resignation of Directors.	No specific provision is available, except that any change in directors' composition is to be filed with ROC within thirty days.	Director has to send a copy of resignation letter and detailed reasons for resignation to the registrar within 30 days of resignation.
15.	Vacancy of office for not attending Board meetings.	In the absence of a director from three consecutive Board meetings or all the meetings of the Board [without obtaining leave of absence from the Board], his office shall become vacant.	The office of a director shall become vacant in case of his absence from all the meetings of the board of directors held during a period of twelve months with or without seeking leave of absence of the Board.
16.	Dislosure in Board's report.	Section 217 contains disclosure requirements of board's report.	Additional disclosures proposed by the Act, namely, Extract of Annual Return, Number of Board meetings, CSR initiatives and policy, particulars of loans, guarantees, etc.

CHANGES WITH REGARD TO BOARD MEETINGS

S.No.	Particulars	Companies Act, 1956	Companies Act, 2013
17.	First board meeting.	No specific time stipulated for holding first board meeting.	Every company shall hold the first meeting of the board of directors within thirty days of the date of its incorporation.
18.	Length of notice.	No specific length of notice specified.	Meeting of the Board shall be called by giving not less than seven days notice.
19.	Penalty.	Every officer of the company whose duty is to give notice as aforesaid and who fails to do so shall be punishable with fine up to one thousand rupees.	Every officer of the company whose duty is to give notice as aforesaid and who fails to do so shall be liable to a penalty of twenty-five thousand rupees.
20.	Time gap between two meetings.	At least one meeting to be held in every quarter.	Not more than one hundred and twenty days shall intervene between two consecutive meetings of the Board.

CHANGES WITH REGARD TO ANNUAL GENERAL MEETING

S.No.	Particulars	Companies Act, 1956	Companies Act, 2013
21.	Maximum time for holding first AGM.	18 months from incorporation or 9 months from closure of accounts, whichever is earlier.	9 months from closure of accounts.
22.	Time and Day	Every AGM shall be called during business hours, on a day that is not a public holiday.	Every AGM shall be called during business hours, that is, between 9 a.m. and 6 p.m. on any day that is not a National Holiday.
23.	Consent for shorter notice.	Consent shall be given by all members entitled to vote at the meeting.	Consent shall be given by not less than 95 per cent of the members entitled to vote at the meeting.

24.	Quorum	Private companies—2 members. Public companies—5 members.	Private companies—2 members. Public companies—5 members where total number of members do not exceed 1000. 15 members where total number of members exceeds 1000 but do not exceed 5000. 30 members where total number of members exceeds 5000.
25.	Penalty	Company, and every officer of the company who is in default, shall be punishable with fine up to fifty thousand rupees and in the case of a continuing default, with a further fine up to two thousand five hundred rupees everyday after the first during which such default continues.	Company, and every officer of the company who is in default, shall be punishable with fine up to one-lakh rupees and in the case of a continuing default, with a further fine up to five thousand rupees everyday after the first during which such default continues.

QUASI–JUDICIAL BODIES

National Company Law Tribunal (NCLT) and National Company Law Appellate Tribunal (NCLAT)

The Central Government shall, by notification, constitute, with effect from such date as may be specified therein, a Tribunal to be known as the National Company Law Tribunal consisting of a President and such number of Judicial and Technical members, as the Central Government may deem necessary, to be appointed by it by notification. There are wide powers granted under the Act to the NCLT. Most of the matters, earlier reserved for High Courts have now been shifted to the NCLT. In addition, new powers such as revival of sick companies, class action, freeze action, right to relax the condition of minimum holding for minority protection, etc., have been conferred on the NCLT.

The Law provides for appeal against orders of NCLT to the NCLAT. As per the provisions of the Companies Act, 1956, the decisions of the Company Law Board were appealable before the court. But, as per Section 421 of the Companies Act, 2013, the same has been vested with NCLAT. The new Act also provides that the appeal against decision of the NCLAT shall lie before the Supreme Court.

This book has been written purely based on the provisions of this new Act. The term 'Act' used in this book refers to the Companies Act, 2013 and the 'Sections' refer to the Sections of the Companies Act, 2013.

REVIEW QUESTIONS

1. Briefly trace the history of company legislation in India.
2. Briefly state the evolution of the Companies Act, 2013.
3. Write a brief note on J.J. Irani Committee Report.
4. State the objectives of Companies Bill, 2012.
5. Enumerate the new concepts introduced by the Companies Act, 2013.

24

Nature and Types of Company

A company is an incorporated association which is an artificial person created by law, having a separate entity, with a perpetual succession and a common seal". (Haney)

THE COMPANY (MEANING)

The term 'company' means a body of individuals associated for some common objects. Where a body of individuals joins together to form a company with a common capital comprising transferable shares or stock, it is known as a "Joint Stock Company". This body of individuals may be either incorporated or unincorporated. An incorporated company has a legal entity distinct from and independent of its members. An unincorporated company has no such legal entity, and is not distinguishable from its members. The law relating to companies in India is contained in the Companies Act, 2013 as amended up to date.

CORPORATION

The term 'corporation' is derived from the Latin word "Corpus" which means "body". Sometimes the term corporation is used for a company. Corporations are of two kinds. They are: (i) Corporation sole, and (ii) Corporations aggregate.

Corporation sole consists of one person who enjoys a corporate personality on account of his office, e.g., the President of India, King/Queen of England, Governors of State, Mayor of the City, etc. A corporation aggregate consists of a number of persons contemporaneously associated so that in the eye of the law they form a single person, e.g., A Limited Company, A Municipal Corporation.

DEFINITION

Under Sec. 2(20) of the Companies Act, 2013 a company means "a company formed and registered under this Act or under any previous company law."

This definition fails to give the distinctive features of a company. Thus, in general terms a company may be defined as "an artificial person created by law with a perpetual succession and a common seal". Thus, a company comes into existence by law. It is an artificial being as it is not made of blood and flesh. It does not die as a natural person dies, but it can be wound up.

Lord Justice Lindley defines a company as

> "an association of many persons who contribute money or money's worth to a common stock, and employ it in some common trade or business and who share the profit or loss arising therefrom. The common stock so contributed is denoted in money, and is the capital of the company. The persons who contribute it, or to whom it belongs, are members. The proportion of capital to which each member is entitled is his share. The shares are generally transferable although the right to transfer them is often more or less restricted".

CHARACTERISTICS OF A COMPANY

The principal characteristics of a company are as follows:

1. *Incorporated Association:* The registration or incorporation of a body corporate as a company marks the birth of a company. It comes into being from the date mentioned in the certificate of incorporation. Thus, registration is not optional unlike partnership.

2. *Artificial Legal Person:* A company is not a natural person as it is not born of parents. It exists in the eye of the law. But for many purposes a company can act like a natural person, i.e., it can acquire and dispose of the property, it can enter into contract with third parties in its own name, it can file suits against others and can be sued by others and so on.

CHARACTERISTICS OF A COMPANY

- Incorporated association
- Artificial legal person
- Separate legal entity
- Limited liability
- Perpetual succession
- Transferability of shares
- Separate property
- Common seal
- Capacity to sue and being sued

---

3. *Separate Legal Entity:* By incorporation under the Act, the company is vested with a corporate personality, which is distinct from the members who compose it. The enterprise acquires its own entity and becomes impersonalised. Thus, a company can own property and deal with it, as it likes. No one can claim any ownership rights in the assets of the company.

Even if a single shareholder virtually holds the whole shares, a company is to be separated from such a shareholder. This principle was pronounced in the well known decision of the House of Lords in *Salomon v. Salomon Co. Ltd.* (1879) A.C. 22.

4. *Limited Liability:* The liability of every shareholder of a company limited by shares or guarantee is limited to the extent of the face value of the shares or the amount of the guarantee given by him.

5. *Perpetual Succession:* An incorporated company never dies as it has an entity with perpetual succession. It means that in spite of a change in the membership of the company, its continuity is not affected. The death or insolvency, or exit of any shareholder does not, in any way, affect the existence of the company. "During the war all the members of one private company, while in general meeting, were killed by a bomb. But the company survived; not even a hydrogen bomb could destroy it". Members of the company may come and go, but the company can go on for ever.

6. *Transferability of Shares:* The shares or other interest of any members in a company shall be a movable property, transferable in the manner prescribed by the articles of the company. The articles of a public company may and those of a private company must restrict rights to transfer. This provides liquidity to the investor and stability to the company.

7. *Separate Property:* One of the distinguishing features of corporate personality is that the undertaking is something different from the totality of the shareholders. It means that the members have no direct proprietary rights to the company's property, but merely to their shares.

8. *Common Seal:* As a company is an artificial person, it is not bestowed with a body of a natural person. It, therefore, has to act through natural persons who are known as directors. But, no document issued by the company shall be binding on it unless it bears the common seal.

The common seal is the official signature of the company. The name of the company is engraved on it, as a substitute for its signature.

9. *Capacity to Sue and Being Sued:* A company, being a body corporate, can enforce its legal right. Similarly, it can be sued for breach of its legal duties.

LIFTING OR PIERCING THE CORPORATE VEIL

The unique feature of incorporation is, of course, the concept of separate and distinct entity of the company. The impact of this doctrine as laid down in *Salomon* v. *Salomon & Co.* (1897), is that there is a veil between the company and its members.

As the separate entity of the company is a statutory privilege, it cannot be pushed to unnatural limits. Where a fraudulent and dishonest use is made of the separate legal entity, the members concerned shall not be allowed to take shelter behind the corporate personality. The Court will break through the corporate shell and look at the persons behind. This principle is what is known as "lifting or piercing the corporate veil". Thus, it may be understood as the identification of a company with its members. When the corporate veil is lifted the individual members may be held liable for its acts. The corporate entity will be disregarded only in exceptional cases which are as follows:

1. *Protection of Revenue:* If the sole purpose for which the company was formed was to evade taxes, the Court will lift the veil and make the individuals liable to pay the taxes which they would have paid, but for the formation of the company.

   In Sir Dinshaw Manekjee Petit Re: A.I.R. (1927) Bom. 371, it was held that the company was formed by the assessee purely and simply as a means of avoiding super tax and the company was nothing more than the assessee himself.

2. *Prevention of Fraud:* The Court will disregard the corporate personality where the company has been formed for any fraudulent or unlawful purposes.

   In *Jones* v. *Lipman* (1962) 1 W.L.R., 832, the Court looked into the reality of the situation, ignored the transfer, and ordered that the company should transfer the land to Jones.

3. *Determination of the Character of the Company:* The Court may ignore the separate entity in public interest and examine the character of persons in real control of the corporate affairs [*Daimler Co. Ltd.* v. *Continental Tyre Co.* (1916) A.C. 307].

4. *Reduction of Number of Members Below Statutory Minimum:* Where the number of members falls below the statutory minimum (seven in the case of a public company and two in the case of a private company) and the company carries on business for more than six months after the number is so reduced, every person who is cognisant of the fact and is a

member during the time the company so carries on business after the six months, is severally liable for all the debts of the company contracted during that time, i.e., after six months.

5. *Company not Mentioned on Bill of Exchange:* Where an officer of a company signs on behalf of the company any bill of exchange, hundi, promissory note, cheque, or order for money and goods, such a person shall be personally liable to the holder unless the name of the company is mentioned.

6. *Holding and Subsidiary Companies:* A holding company is required to disclose to its members the account of its subsidiaries.

7. *Investigation of the Affairs of the Company:* Where an inspector is appointed to investigate the affairs of a company, he may look into the affairs of another related company in the same management or group.

8. *For Exchange Control:* The corporate personality may be disregarded in accordance with the law relating to the exchange control.

The cases stated above from 1 to 3 are under judicial interpretations and from 4 to 8 under express statutory provisions.

KINDS OF COMPANIES

The following chart gives the classification of companies into various categories:

Chart showing kinds of companies

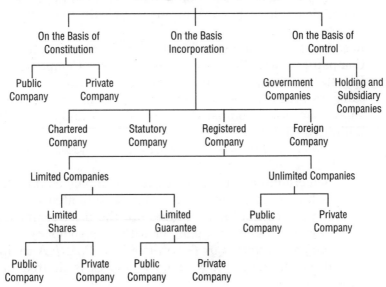

There are different kinds of companies. They are brought under different classes on the following points of view:

I. On the basis of incorporation.

II. On the basis of constitution.

III. On the basis of control.

ON THE BASIS OF INCORPORATION

On the basis of incorporation or formation, companies may be divided into the following four heads: (A) Chartered Companies; (B) Statutory Companies; (C) Registered Companies; and (D) Foreign Companies.

(A) *Chartered Companies:* These are incorporated under a Special Charter granted by the King or Queen of England. Examples of such companies are Bank of England and East India Company. These companies find no place in India after independence.

(B) *Statutory Companies:* A company established by a Special Act of the Central or State Legislature is called a Statutory Company. Such companies do not have any Memorandum or Articles of Association. They derive their powers from the Acts constituting them. Alterations in the powers of such companies can be brought about by legislative amendments. Reserve Bank of India, State Bank of India, Life Insurance Corporation, Unit Trust of India, etc., are some examples.

The provisions of the Companies Act shall apply to these companies unless they are inconsistent with those of Special Acts.

(C) *Registered Companies:* These are formed under the Companies Act, 2013 or some earlier Companies Act. Registered Companies may further be divided into three categories which may be either (i) a Company limited by shares, or (ii) a Company limited by guarantee, or (iii) an unlimited company.

(i) *Company Limited by Shares [Sec. 2(22)]:* When the liability of the members of a company is limited by the memorandum to the amount, if any, unpaid on the shares, such a company is called a company limited by shares. Companies limited by shares are the most common and may be a Public company or a Private company.

(ii) *Company Limited by Guarantee [Sec. 2(21)]:* A company in which the liability of its members is limited to the extent of the amount guaranteed is known as a company limited by guarantee. Every member of such a company undertakes to contribute to the assets of the company in the case of its winding up. A guarantee company may or may not have a share capital. If it has a share capital, it may be a Public company or Private company.

Guarantee companies are not formed for the purpose of profit. They are formed for the promotion of art, science, culture, charity, sport, commerce or for some similar purposes.

(iii) *Unlimited Companies [Sec. 2(92)]:* Companies incorporated with unlimited liability are known as unlimited companies. Every member of such a company is liable for its debts to an unlimited extent, as in an ordinary partnership.

(D) *Foreign Companies [Sec. 2(42)]:* "Foreign Company" means any company or body corporate incorporated outside India, which

(i) has an established place of business in India whether by itself or through an agent, physically or through electronic mode, and

(ii) conducts any business activity in India in any other means.

A company is said to have an established place of business in India if it has a specified place at which it carries on business such as an office store house or other premises with some visible indication of premises.

Sections 379 to 393 of Companies Act, 2013 contain provisions applicable to foreign companies functioning in India.

Foreign companies should file with Registrar certain documents relating to its principal office, directors and place of business. These companies are required to deliver copies of financial statements to the Registrar every calender year. Further, every foreign company shall exhibit its name followed with the country name in which it is being incorporated, on the outside of its all places of business in India. The name shall be written by using legible English character and in the language in general use in that particular locality. The same should also be used in its every official communication such as letters, notices, official publications, etc.

> Several significant concepts have been defined for the first time under the Companies Act, 2013 and two new concepts relating to types of companies are "One Person Company" and "Small Company". These are explained here.

ON THE BASIS OF CONSTITUTION

A registered company may be either Private or Public.

Private Company [Sec. 2(68)]

A private company means a company having a minimum paid-up share capital of one lakh rupees or such higher paid-up share capital as may be prescribed, and which by its articles:

    (a) restricts the right to transfer its shares, if any;

    (b) except in the case of one person company limits the number of its members to two hundred (excluding its employees);

    (c) prohibits any invitation to the public to subscribe for any shares in, or debentures of the company. Where two or more persons hold shares jointly, they are treated as a single member.

Public Company [Sec. 2(71)]

Public company means a company which is not a private company and has a minimum paid-up share capital of five lakh rupees or such higher paid-up capital, as may be prescribed. A company which is a subsidiary of another company, not being a private company, shall be deemed as public company.

Distinction between a Public and a Private Company

1. *Minimum Number:* The number of members in a Private Company is two while a Public Company must have at least seven.

2. *Maximum Number:* The maximum number of members in a Private Company cannot exceed two hundred (excluding its employees). In the case of a Public Company, there is no maximum limit on members.

3. *Number of Directors:* A Private Company shall have at least two directors, and a Public Company at least three. But the maximum number of directors of both these companies is fifteen.

4. *Transferability of Shares:* In a Private Company the right to transfer shares is restricted by the Articles. In a Public Company, the shares are freely transferable.

5. *Name of the Company:* A Private Limited Company's name should end with the words "Private Limited" or (P)

Ltd." A Public Limited Company's name should end with the word 'Limited' or Ltd.

6. *Restrictions on Directors:* In a Public Company, there are a number of restrictions on the 'Directors' relating to the number of directorship, retirement, remuneration, etc. There are no such restrictions on the directors of a Private Company.

7. *Restriction on Invitation to Subscribe for Shares:* A Private Company cannot invite the public to purchase its shares or debentures. A Public Company may do so by issuing a prospectus.

> **DISTINCTION BETWEEN A PUBLIC COMPANY AND A PRIVATE COMPANY**
>
> * Minimum number
> * Maximum number
> * Number of Directors
> * Transferability of shares
> * Name of the Company
> * Restriction of Directors
> * Restrictions on invitation to subscribe for shares
> * Prospectus
> * Commencement of Business
> * Statutory meeting
> * Minimum subscription
> * Managerial remuneration
> * Articles of association
> * Quorum
> * Share warrant

---

8. *Prospectus:* A Private Company need not issue a prospectus whereas a Public Company has to issue a prospectus.

9. *Commencement of Business:* A Private Company can commence business on getting the certificate of incorporation whereas a Public Company can commence business only after getting the certificate of commencement of business.

10. *Minimum Subscription:* A Private Company need not receive the minimum subscription to allot the shares whereas a Public Company can begin its first allotment of shares only on receiving the minimum subscription.

11. *Managerial Remuneration:* In a Public Company, the managerial remuneration shall not exceed eleven per cent of the net profits of the company. But in a Private Company there are no such limits.

12. *Articles of Association:* A Private Company should have its own articles and it cannot adopt the model articles. A Public Company can have its own articles or can adopt the model articles given in Table 'A' of the Act.

13. *Quorum:* For the general meeting of a Public Company the quorum required is five members where total number of members do not exceed 1,000, fifteen members where total number of members exceeds 1,000 but do not exceed 5,000 and thirty members where total number of members exceeds 5,000. But in the case of a Private Company it is two, unless otherwise provided in the articles.

14. *Share Warrant:* A Private Company cannot issue share warrants while a Public Company can.

Privileges or Advantages of a Private Company

Ordinary companies are like bees working in a glass hive. But Private Companies are able to keep their affairs to themselves. The Companies Act of 2013 applies both to public and private companies. However, Private Companies are expressly exempted from a number of its provisions. These exemptions are commonly known as the advantages of a Private Company. One of the main reasons behind a Private Company privileged with so many exemptions is that it is not permitted to employ public money. A Private Company has sometimes been described as an incorporated partnership as it combines the advantages of both elements—the privacy of partnership and the permanence and origin of the corporate constitution.

Some privileges and exemptions enjoyed by a private company or its advantages over a public company include the following.

(i) Financial assistance can be given to its employees for purchase of or subscribing to its own shares or shares in its holding company [Sec. 67(2)].

(ii) Need not prepare a report on the Annual General Meeting [Sec. 121(1)].

(iii) Need not prepare a statement indicating the manner in which formal annual evaluation has been made by the Board of its own performance and that of its committees and individual directors [Sec. 134(3) (P)].

(iv) Need not have more than two directors [Sec. 149(1)].

(v) Need not appoint independent directors on its Board [Sec. 149(4)].

(vi) A proportion of directors need not retire every year [Sec. 152(6)].

(vii) Additional grounds for disqualification for appointment as a director may be specified by the company in its Article [Sec. 164(3)].

(viii) Restrictive provisions regarding total number of directorships which a person may hold in a public company do not include directorship held in a private company which is neither a holding or subsidiary company of a public company [Sec. 165(1)].

(ix) Additional grounds for vacation of office of a director may be provided in the Article [Sec. 167(4)].

(x) The provisions relating to contract of employment with managing or whole-time directors do not apply to a private company [Sec. 190(4)].

(xi) Total managerial remuneration payable by a private company, to its directors, including, managing director and whole-time director, and its manager in respect of any financial year may exceed eleven per cent of the net profits [Sec. 197(1)].

Conversion of a Private Company into a Public Company

1. *Conversion by Default:* Where a default is made by a Private Company in complying with the provisions of Sec. 2(68), the company shall cease to be entitled to the privileges and exemptions conferred by or under the Act.

Then the whole Act apply to it as if it were a Public Company.

However, the Act provides for grant and relief to the company by the Company Law Tribunal on application on such terms and conditions as the Company Law Tribunal thinks to be just and equitable.

2. *Conversion by Choice:* A Private Company may of its own choice, become a Public Company. The procedures are as follows:

(i) A Private Company desiring to become a Public Company should pass a special resolution deleting from its articles the requirements of Sec. 2(68).

(ii) A prospectus or a statement in lieu of prospectus should be filed with the Registrar within thirty days of passing the resolution.

(iii) All other requirements of the Act should be complied with enhancing the number of members to seven and directors to three.

Conversion of a Public Company into a Private Company

With a view to converting a Public Company into a Private Company, the following procedures are necessary:

(i) Pass a special resolution by which the articles of the company shall be altered so as to incorporate the requirements of a Private Company as prescribed in Sec. 2(68).

(ii) Obtain the approval of the Tribunal (Not yet enforced)

(iii) Within fifteen days of the receipt of the order of approval, a copy of the special resolution and a printed copy of the altered articles shall be filed with the Registrar (Not yet enforced).

ON THE BASIS OF CONTROL

On the basis of control, companies are of two types. They are: (a) Government companies, (b) Holding and subsidiary companies.

(a) *Government Companies [Sec. 2(45)]:*   A Government Company is one in which not less than 51% of the paid-up capital is held by the Central Government, or by any State Government or Governments or partly by the Central Government and partly by one or more State Governments and includes a company which is the subsidiary of such a company. The share capital of a Government company may be wholly or partly owned by the Government, but it would not make it as the agent of the Government.

   The auditor of a Government company shall be appointed or reappointed by the Central Government on the advice of the Comptroller and Auditor General of India. The auditor of the company should submit a copy of his report to the C & A.G. who may comment upon, or supplement, the audit report.

   Apart from the general annual report on the working and the administration of the Companies Act, the Central Government must place before both Houses of Parliament an annual report on the working and affairs of each Government Company. Where a State Government is a participant in a Government Company, this report has likewise to be placed before the State

   Some of the examples of the Government companies are —State Trading Corporations Ltd., Bharat Heavy Electricals Ltd. and Hindustan Machine Tools Ltd.

(b) *Holding and Subsidiary Companies:*   Holding and subsidiary companies are relative terms. A company is a holding company of another if the other is a subsidiary [Sec. 2(46)].

   Where a company has control over another company it is known as the holding company and the company over which control is exercised is known as the Subsidiary company

[Sec. 2(87)]. A company is deemed to be under the control of another, if:

(i) the other company controls the composition of the Board of Directors, or

(ii) the other company holds more than half of the nominal value of the equity share capital.

ONE PERSON COMPANY [SEC. 2(62)]

One Person Company (OPC) is a one shareholder corporate entity. As per Sec. 2(62), "One Person Company" means a company which has only one person as a member. The Memorandum of a company shall state the last letters and word 'OPC Limited' in the case of a One Person limited company. Further, the Memorandum of a One Person Company shall indicate the name of the person who shall in the event of the subscriber's death, disability or otherwise, become the member of the company.

In the case of One Person Company, provisions pertaining to meetings including annual general meetings are exempted by law itself.

One Person Company can have only one director, in which case directors' meetings also become non-mandatory. The use of One Person Company has been kept limited to only very small business, as there are limits on paid-up capital and turnover, beyond which an OPC will have to convert itself into a regular company.

One Person Company to Convert itself into a Public Company or a Private Company in Certain cases

If the paid-up share capital of a One Person Company exceeds fifty lakh rupees or its average annual turnover during the relevant period exceeds two crore rupees, it shall cease to be entitled to continue as a One Person Company. Relevant period here means the period of immediately preceding three consecutive financial years.

Such One Person Company shall be required to convert itself, within six months of the date on which its paid-up share capital is increased beyond fifty lakh rupees or the last day of the relevant period during which its average annual turnover exceeds two crore rupees as the case may be, into either a private company with minimum of two members and two directors or a public company with at least of seven members and three directors.

The One Person Company shall alter its Memorandum and Articles by passing a resolution.

The One Person Company shall within a period of sixty days from the date of applicability of sub-rule (1), give a notice to the Registrar informing that it has ceased to be One Person Company. Thus, it is now required to convert itself into a private company or a public company by virtue of its paid-up share capital or average annual turnover, having exceeded the threshold limit laid down in sub-rule (1)

If One Person Company or any officer of the One Person Company contravenes the provisions of these rules, One Person Company or any officer of the One Person Company shall be punishable with a fine up to ten thousand rupees and with a further fine up to one thousand rupees for every day after the first day during which such contravention continues.

A One Person Company can get itself converted into a Private or Public Company after increasing the minimum number of members and directors to two or minimum of seven members and two or three directors as the case may be, and by maintaining the minimum paid-up capital as per the requirements of the Act.

Conversion of Private Company into One Person Company

A private company other than a company registered under Sec. 8 of the Act having paid-up share capital of fifty lakh rupees or less or average annual turnover during the relevant period is two crore rupees or less may convert itself into One Person Company by passing a special resolution in the general meeting.

Before passing such a resolution, the company shall obtain 'No Objection' in writing from members and creditors.

The One Person Company shall file a copy of the special resolution with the Registrar of Companies within thirty days from the date of passing such a resolution.

The company shall file an application in prescribed form for its convertion into One Person Company along with prescribed fees by attaching the following documents:

(i) Declaration of the directors of the company.
(ii) List of members and list of directors.
(iii) The latest Audited Balance Sheet and the Profit and Loss Account.
(iv) The copy of 'No Objection' letter of secured creditors.

On being satisfied and complied with requirements stated herein the Registrar shall issue the certificate.

SMALL COMPANY [SEC. 2(85)]

"Small Company" means a company, other than a public company Paid-up share capital of which does not exceed fifty lakh rupees or such higher amount as may be prescribed which shall not be more than five crore rupees; or

(e) Turnover of which as per its last profit and loss account does not exceed two crore rupees or such higher amount as may be prescribed which shall not be more than twenty crore rupees.

However, nothing in this clause shall apply to-

(i) a holding company or a subsidiary company;
(ii) a company registered under Section 8; or
(iii) a company or body corporate governed by any Special Act.

DORMANT COMPANY (SEC. 455)

Sec. 455 of the Companies Act, 2013 states that a company can be classified as dormant when it is formed and registered for a future project or to hold an asset or intellectual property and has no significant accounting transaction. Such a company or an inactive one may apply to the ROC in such a manner as may be prescribed for obtaining the status of a dormant company.

NON-GOVERNMENT COMPANIES

All other companies, except the Government companies, are called non-government companies. Such companies do not satisfy the characteristics of a Government company.

INDIAN COMPANIES

Companies which are registered in India under the Indian Companies Act and have registered office in India are known as Indian Companies. The nationality of the members in their case is immaterial.

LICENCED COMPANIES WITH CHARITABLE OBJECTS (SEC. 8)

A person or an association of persons desirous of incorporating a company with limited liability without the addition to its name of the word "Limited", or as the case may be, the words "Private Limited" shall make an application in the prescribed form along with the prescribed fee to the Registrar for a licence under Sub-section (1) of Sec. 8.

A limited company registered under this Act or under any previous company law and which is desirous of being registered under Sec. 8 without the addition to its name of the word "Limited" or as the case may be, the words "Private Limited" shall make an application in the prescribed form along with the prescribed fee to the Registrar for a licence under Sub-section (5) of Sec. 8.

ASSOCIATE COMPANY [SEC. 2(6)]

Associate company in relation to another company means a company in which other company has a significant influence. "Significant influence" means control of at least twenty per cent of total share capital, or of business decisions under an agreement.

INVESTMENT COMPANY (SEC. 186)

Investment company means a company whose principal business is the acquisition of shares, debentures or other securities.

PRODUCER COMPANY

Sec. 465(1) of the Companies Act, 2013 provides that the provisions of part IX A of the Companies Act, 1956 shall be applicable mutatis mutandis to a producer company in a manner as if the Companies Act, 1956 has not been repealed until a special Act is enacted for producer companies.

As per Sec. 581A(1) of the Companies Act, 1956, a producer company is a body corporate having objects or activities specified in Section 581(B) and which is registered as such under the provisions of the Act.

The membership of producer companies is open to such people who themselves are the primary producers engaged in some agricultural produce.

ILLEGAL ASSOCIATION [SEC. 464]

No association or partnership consisting of more than such number of persons as may be prescribed can be formed unless it is **registered under the Companies Act or is** formed in pursuance of some other Indian law. The number of persons which may be prescribed under this Section shall not exceed 100. If it is not so registered, it is deemed to be an illegal association. Effects of an illegal association are as follows:

(i) Every member is personally liable for all liabilities of the business.

(ii) It cannot enter into a contract.

(iii) It cannot sue or be sued for debts due to it or from it in carrying on its business.

(iv) It cannot be wound up under the Act.

REVIEW QUESTIONS

1. Define Joint Stock Company.
2. Define company.
3. What is common seal of a company?
4. What is corporation?
5. What do you mean by corporate veil?
6. What is Chartered Company?
7. What is Statutory Company?
8. Define Private Company.
9. What do you mean by perpetual existence?
10. What is Limited Liability?
11. What is a Small Company?
12. What is Associate Company?
13. What is Investment Company?
14. State two features of a company.
15. What is meant by Government Company?
16. Explain the company limited by guarantee.
17. Write a note on One Person company.
18. What is Dormant Company?
19. What is Foreign Company?
20. Enumerate the features of a Private Limited Company.
21. What do you mean by Illegal Association?
22. What is regarded as the official signature of the company?
23. What do you mean by lifting of corporate veil?
24. Enumerate the main features of a company.
25. Write a note on Holding and Subsidiary company.

26. Explain the procedures for converting a Private Company into a Public Limited Company.

27. Explain the law relating to the conversion of a Public Company into Private Company.

28. Explain the law relating to convert One Person Company into Public Company.

29. Explain the procedures of converting Private Company into One Person Company.

30. Explain the privileges and exemptions enjoyed by a private company.

31. "A company is a legal person and it has identity separate from members comprising it." Comment.

32. What is corporate veil? Under what circumstances is lifting of corporate veil possible?

33. Name the various kinds of companies that may be registered under the Companies Act, 2013.

34. Define Private Company. What privileges are enjoyed by a Private Company under the provisions of the Companies Act, 2013?

35. Distinguish between a Private Company and a Public Company.

PRACTICAL PROBLEMS

Attempt the following problems, giving reasons:

1. A husband and wife, who were the only two members of a private limited company, are shot dead by dacoits. Does the company also die with them?

   Hint: No, the company will continue as it has a perpetual succession.

2. During the war all the members of a private company, while in general meeting were killed by a bomb. Is the private company no longer in existence?

   Hint: No, it will continue.

3. An association of 13 members starts a banking business without being registered. Five members retire and thereafter a suit is instituted by one of continuing members for the partition of assets of business. Is this suit competent?

   Hint: No the suit is not valid as the association is illegal.

4. A Hindu undivided family consisting of a father and six major sons and another family consisting of a father, six major sons and one minor son carried on banking business, as owners thereof. Discuss if the organisation requires registration under the Companies Act, 2013.

   Hint: The organisation requires registration under the Companies Act, 2013 as it comprises 14 persons carrying on banking business.

25

Formation and Incorporation of Company

A company comes into existence when it is registered under the Companies Act.

The formation of a company involves four distinct stages: (i) Promotion (ii) Registration or incorporations (iii) Raising of capital, and (iv) Commencement of business.

A Private Company and a Public Company not having a share capital need to go through the first two stages only. But, a Public Company having a share capital, has to go through all the aforesaid four stages and only then it will be entitled to commence its business.

PROMOTION

Promotion is the first stage in the formation of a company. It is a process by which a company is incorporated or brought into being as a 'Corporate Body'. Gerstenberg in his book, "Financial Organization and Management" has defined "Promotion" as "the discovery of business opportunities and the subsequent organization of funds, property and managerial ability into a business concern for the purpose of making profits therefrom". Therefore, the preliminaries incidental to the formation of a company are as follows:

(a) The discovery of business opportunities.
(b) Detailed investigation of the feasibility of the idea.
(c) Organization of funds, property and managerial ability.
(d) Taking necessary steps to float a company.

PROMOTER

The word 'Promoter' is used to denote any individual, syndicate, association, partnership, or company, which takes all required steps to create and mould a company.

The term Promoter is a term not of law, but of business, usefully summing up, in a single word, a number of business operations familiar to the commercial world by which a company is brought into existence. According to Cockburn, a person, who undertakes to form a company with reference to a given project, and to set it going, and takes the necessary steps to accomplish that purpose, is a promoter.

LEGAL POSITION OF PROMOTERS

The 'Promoter' is neither an agent nor a trustee of the company before its formation. He is not an agent because there is no principal, and he is not a trustee, as there is no cestui que trust in existence. He stands in a fiduciary relation (relation of trust and confidence) towards the company. This relation of trust and confidence requires the promoter to make a full disclosure of all material facts relating to the formation of the company. He should act honestly, and should not make any secret profit at the expense of the company he promotes. Consequently, the promoter of a company is accountable to it for all the money secretly obtained by him from it as if the relationship of principal and agent or of trustee .... had really existed between him and the company when the money was so obtained. Moreover, his dealings with the proposed company should be open and fair.

The positions and powers of the promoter becomes clear from the following observations:

"The promoters stand undoubtedly in a fiduciary position. They have, in their hand, the creation and moulding of the company. They have the powers of defining how and when, and in what shape and under what supervision the company shall start into existence and begin to act as trading corporation."

DUTIES AND LIABILITIES OF PROMOTERS

The promoters stands in a fiduciary position towards the company. The following are the consequences arising from his fiduciary position.

(i) The promoters cannot make any profit unless the company consents. If they make any secret profit, they may be compelled to surrender the same.

(ii) The benefits of all transactions entered into by the promoters on behalf of the company must be given to the company itself. If the promoter appropriates any such benefits, the company is entitled to claim the same.

(iii) If the promoters enter into any contract with the company (directly or indirectly), any interest on the part of the promoters must be fully disclosed to the company.

(iv) The promoters should not cause any undue influence or fraud over any contracts with the company. In other words, the promoters should not make any unfair use of their position.

   When prospectus is issued, the promoters are vested with the following further duties:

(a) They should see that all the particulars in the Schedule II of the Companies Act are provided in the prospectus.

(b) They should ensure that any untrue statement has not been made in the prospectus.

REMUNERATION OF PROMOTERS

A promoter is entitled to a reasonable remuneration. The usual ways of receiving remuneration by the promoter are by:

1. selling his own property at an overvaluation.

2. taking a grant of some shares of the company.

3. taking a commission on the shares sold.

4. taking a grant of a lumpsum money from the company.

PRELIMINARY OR PRE-INCORPORATION CONTRACTS

A pre-incorporation contract is one which is entered into before the company is incorporated. For instance, before the registration of the company, the promoter acquires property, patent, etc., on behalf of an intended company from the vendors. A pre-incorporation contract never binds a company as the company was not in existence when the contract had been entered into. The promoters remain personally liable on the contract. A company cannot even ratify such a contract later on because the doctrine of ratification applies only if an agent contracts for a principal, who is in existence and who is competent to contract at the time of the contract by the agent.

Before the enactment of the Special Relief Act, 1963, the promoters found it very difficult to carry out the work of incorporation. But, Secs. 15 and 19 of the Specific Relief Act have considerably alleviated this difficulty. Secs. 15(h) and 19(a) of this Act provide that when the promoters of a company have, before its incorporation entered into a contract for the purposes of the company and such a contract is warranted by the terms of its incorporation, the contract may be specifically enforced by or against the company. However, for such a contract to be enforceable, acceptance of the contract by the company and its communication to the other party is essential.

INCORPORATION OR REGISTRATION

Procedure for Incorporation of Public Company having Share Capital

The procedures to be taken for the incorporation of a public company are as follows:

1. *Selecting name of the company and ascertaining its availability from Registrar of Companies:*
   (i) Promoters shall select at least six names for the proposed company. They secure the availability of names by making an application to the Registrar of Companies of the State in which they want to have the proposed company incorporated.
   (ii) The application shall be made in E-form INC-1 as prescribed in the Companies Act, 2013, for a purpose, along with the prescribed application fee of five hundred rupees.
   (iii) It is advisable to get a draft of Memorandum and Articles verified by the Registrar of companies concerned before printing in order to make changes, if required.
   (iv) In case, the proposed company has not been incorporated within such a period, the name shall be lapsed. Such a lapsed name will be made available for other applicants.
   (v) The Central Government has the power to direct the company to change the name even after its incorporation as per Sec.16 of the Companies Act, 2013.
   (vi) The Central Government may ask the company to change its name if it comes to Central Government's notice through an application that the name very nearly resembles that of another existing company or a registered trade mark.

2. *Drafting and Printing of Memorandum and Articles of Association:*
   (i) A public company limited by shares need not necessarily prepare and get its Articles of Association registered along with its Memorandum of Association. In such a case, Table "F" of Schedule 1 of the Companies Act, 2013 shall apply.

(ii) As a matter of practice, every company gets its articles prepared to suit its own requirements and register the same along with the Memorandum of Association.

(iii) It is advisable to get a draft of Memorandum and Articles verified by the Registrar of companies concerned before printing in order to make changes, if required.

(iv) It is advisable to send the draft of the Memorandum and Articles of Association to those stock exchanges for their scrutiny and suggestions, if the promoters plan to get the securities of the proposed company listed with one or more designated stock exchanges.

(v) To have certain Articles incorporated therein in compliance with the provisions of the Listing Agreements of the stock exchanges.

(vi) To get the Memorandum and Articles of Association for the proposed company drafted and printed.

3. *Stamping and Signing of Memorandum and Articles:*

(i) The Memorandum and Articles should be printed and stamped by the appropriate State Authority (Collector of Stamps) as per the Indian Stamp Act. Afterwards, the Memorandum and the Articles should be signed by at least seven subscribers.

(ii) Each subscriber to the Memorandum should write in his/her own hand his/her father's/husband's name, occupation, address and the number of shares subscribed for by him/her.

(iii) The signatures of all the subscribers should also be witnessed. The witness should also sign and write in his hand, his name, his father's name, occupation and address.

(iv) The Stamp Duty payable on the Memorandum and/or the Articles of Association should be determined as per the place of incorporation of the company.

4. *Dating of Memorandum and Articles of Association.*

The next step is the dating of Memorandum and Articles. The date should be on the date of stamping or a date later than the date of stamping and not a date prior to the date of their stamping.

5. *Filing of Documents and Forms for Registration.*

Forms to be Filed

A company having Memorandum and Articles of Association should file E-Form INC-7 as an application and declaration for incorporation. But, the details of subscribers should be filed as attachments.

Under the Companies Act, 2013 the following prescribed forms should be prepared, signed and filed with the Registrar of Companies concerned with a view to getting the company incorporated.

S.No.	E.-Form Companies Act, 2013	Purpose of Form as per Companies Act, 2013
1.	INC-1	Application for reservation of name.
2.	INC-2	Form for incorporation and nomination of One Person Company.
3.	INC-3	Form for consent of nominee of One Person Company.
4.	INC-4	Form for change in member/nominee of One Person Company.
5.	INC-5	Form of intimation of exceeding threshold of One Person Company.
6.	INC-6	Application for Conversion.
7.	INC-7	Application for Incorporation of Company (Other than One Person Company).
8.	INC-18	Application to Regional Director for conversion of company into any other kind of company (Sec. 8).
10.	INC-21	Declaration prior to the commencement of business.
11.	INC-22	Notice of situation or change of situation of registered office and verification.
12.	INC-23	Application to Regional director for approval to shift the registered office from one state to another state or from jurisdiction of one registrar to another within the state.
13.	INC-24	Application for approval of Central Government for change of name.
14.	INC-27	Conversion of public company into private company or private company into public company.
32.	URC-1	Application by company for registration under Sec. 366.
33.	FC-1	Information to be filed by foreign company.
34.	FC-2	Return of alteration in the documents filed for registration by foreign company.
35.	FC-3	List of all principal places of business in India established by foreign company.
37.	GNL-1	Form for filing an application with Registrar of Companies.

38.	GNL-2	Form for submission of documents with Registrar of Companies.
39.	GNL-3	Particulars of person(s) or director(s) or charged or specified for the purpose of Sec. 2(60).
40	ADJ	Memorandum of Appeal.
41	MSC-1	Application to ROC for obtaining the status of dormant company.
42.	MSC-3	Return of dormant companies.

Documents to be Submitted for Registration

(a) *Memorandum and Articles of Association:* A physical copy of the printed Memorandum and Articles of Association duly stamped, signed and dated should be submitted separately with the Registrar of Companies. Registration of Articles of Association with the Registrar is optional in the case of a public limited company. But, registration of Articles of Association with the Registrar is compulsory in the case of a private limited company.

(b) *Agreements:* Any agreement that the company on incorporation proposes to enter into with any person for appointment as its managing director or whole-time director or manager is to be submitted as an attachment (optional) with e-form 1.

(c) *Copy of Power of Attorney:* General power of attorney on a judicial stamp paper of the appropriate value as applicable in the State signed by all the subscribers, in favour of one of them or any other person, for making alteration, etc., on their behalf, in the Memorandum and Articles of Association and other documents/forms with the Registrar of companies suggested by the Registrar.

6. *Pre-Certification:* A company secretary or chartered accountant or cost accountant in a whole-time practice should pre-certify the form INC-22 and DIR-12.

7. *Registration and Filing Fee:* Promoters should make sure to remit to the Registrar, along with above forms/documents, the prescribed registration fee, and fee for filing of forms in accordance with the rates contained in the Companies (Registration of Offices and Fees) Rules 2014.

The fee for the same can be remitted either electronically or by cash/draft through challan generated electronically on submission of the e-form.

8. *Minimum Paid-up Capital:* The minimum paid-up capital is five lakh rupees or such higher paid-up capital as may be prescribed.

9. *Security of Documents and Forms by Registrar:* On receipt of the above documents, these will be scrutinised by the office of the Registrar of Companies. If everything is found complete in all respects, the Registrar will register the company and generate a CIN No. (Corporate Identity Number). On the other hand, if any defect or deficiency in any of the documents or forms is found, the attorney will be called to visit his office to remove the defect or make up the deficiency. Afterwards, the Registrar will register the company.

10. *Issue of Certificate of Incorporation by Registrar:* On registration of the company, the Registrar will issue (under the seal of his office) the Certificate of Incorporation in the name of the company and send it through post. The company may also take print out of the Certificate of Incorporation generated online.

The date given by the Registrar in the Certificate of Incorporation is the date of incorporation of the company. On such a date, the company is considered to have come into existence as a legal entity separate from its subscribers.

11. *Certificate of Commencement of Business:* A public company having share capital cannot commence its business on registration. But, it can commence its business only after getting the "Certificate of Commencement of Business."

PROCEDURE FOR INCORPORATION OF PRIVATE LIMITED COMPANY HAVING SHARE CAPITAL

The procedure for the incorporation of a private limited company is the same as that of a public limited company with the following exceptions:

(i) The company should have a minimum paid-up capital of one lakh rupees or such higher paid-up capital as may be prescribed.

(ii) There should be at least two subscribers to the Memorandum.

(iii) Registration of the Articles of Association is compulsory.

CAPITAL SUBSCRIPTION

Having completed the above stages, a private company and public company not having share capital can commence its business. But a public company having share capital has to pass through two more stages such as capital subscription and commencement of business. During the capital subscription stage the company takes the following steps:

(i) Completing the formalities to raise necessary capital.

(ii) Adhering strictly to the guidelines issued by SEBI in this regard.

(iii) Conforming to the "Guidelines for Disclosure and Investor Protection" issued by SEBI regarding public issues of capital and filing a copy of the Prospectus with the Registrar.

(iv) Appointing the company's banker for collecting the applications from the investors.

(v) Ensuring strict adherence to the conditions for valid allotment.

(vi) Passing a formal resolution for making allotment.

(vii) Sending allotment letters to the allottees.

(viii) Filing the return of allotment with the Registrar.

(ix) Issuing share certificates to the allottees in exchange of their allotment letters.

(x) The company cannot make any allotment unless minimum subscription is obtained.

COMMENCEMENT OF BUSINESS

In accordance with Sec. 11 of the Act, a company having share capital shall not commence business, or exercise any borrowing powers, unless a declaration is filed with the Registrar. It shall state that:

(i) Every subscriber of the Memorandum has paid the value of shares agreed to be taken by him;

(ii) Paid-up capital is not less than five lakh rupees in the case of a public company and one lakh rupees in the case of a private company.

The restrictions contained in Sec. 11 are applicable only to companies having share capital. A company not having a share capital may commence business and exercise borrowing powers immediately on incorporation.

When a private company is converted into a public company, it need not obtain a certificate of commencement of business on its conversion because the company had already commenced business on its incorporation as a private company.

Commencing business refers not only to business for which the company was incorporated, but also to any transaction including sale or purchase.

Procedure for Commencement of Business, where the Company has Issued Prospectus

(i) Issuing the Prospectus.

(ii) Obtaining the Minimum Subscription in cash.

(iii) In order that a transaction between a company and allottee of shares may amount to "payment in cash", each party should have an actual demand on the other for present payment.

(iv) To declare that directors who have applied or contracted to take up shares have paid in cash the application and allotment money on their shares in the same proportion as others.

(v) If the shares are to be quoted on the stock exchange, necessary application should be submitted to it and approval obtained within the prescribed time.

(vi) Shares issued for cash to the public should be allotted.

(vii) Declaration: File E-Form 19 of the Companies (Central Governments) General Rules and Forms, 1956 on the stamp paper of requisite value as required by the Stamp Act of the respective States with the Registrar. This form is in regard to a declaration of compliance with the provisions of Sec. 11 Clauses (a) and (b) of Sub-section (1). The form is to be filed electronically as well as physically.

(viii) To obtain the certificate for commencement of business from the Registrar.

The certificate is a conclusive evidence that the company is entitled to commence business.

REVIEW QUESTIONS

1. Define the term 'promotion'.
2. Who is a promoter?
3. What is certificate of incorporation?
4. What do you mean by commencement of business?
5. What is meant by incorporation?
6. Write down the minimum paid-up capital requirement of a public company and a private company.
7. What is CIN?

8. Enumerate the steps in drafting Memorandum and Articles of Association.

9. Enumerate the role of promoters.

10. What is a preliminary contract?

11. Enumerate the document to be submitted at the time of registration.

12. Explain the duties and liabilities of a promoter.

13. Enumerate the usual ways of receiving remuneration by a promoter.

14. Discuss in brief the procedure for incorporation of a private limited company.

15. What are the procedures to be adopted for commencement of a business?

16. Explain the provisions relating to stamping and signing of Memorandum and Articles of Association.

17. Explain the legal effects of pre-incorporation contracts.

18. Explain the steps in incorporation of a company.

19. What are the various forms to be submitted for incorporation?

20. "A certificate of incorporation is a conclusive evidence that all the requirements of the Companies Act have been complied with". Explain.

PRACTICAL PROBLEMS

Attempt the following problems, giving reasons:

1. The promoters of a company, before its incorporation, entered into an agreement with A to buy a building on behalf of the company. After incorporation, the company refuses to buy the said building. Has A any remedy either against the promoters or against the company?

   Hint: A has no remedy against the company. The promoters are personally liable on the contract.

2. Six of the seven signatories to the Memorandum of Association of a company were forged. The Memorandum was only presented, registered and a certificate of incorporation was issued. The existence of the company was subsequently attacked on the ground that the registration was void. Decide.

   Hint: The registration is valid.

26

Memorandum of Association

*Memorandum of Association is a document of great
importance in relation to the proposed company (Palmer).*

MEANING

The first step in the formation of a company is to prepare a document
called the Memorandum of Association. It defines the relationship
of the company with the outside world. It not only indicates the
purpose of the formation of the company, but also the boundaries
beyond which the action of the company cannot go.

According to Sec. 2(56) Memorandum means the Memorandum
of Association of a company as originally framed or as altered from
time to time in pursuance of any previous Company Law or of this
Act.

In *Ashbury Railway Carriage Co.* v. *Riche,* 1875, Lord Cairns
observed that "The Memorandum of Association of a company is its
charter and defines the limitations of the powers of a company".

In *Guinness* v. *Land Corporation of Ireland,* 1882 Bowen L.J.
observed that the Memorandum contains the fundamental conditions
upon which alone the company is allowed to be incorporated.

FORM OF MEMORANDUM [SEC. 4(6)]

The Memorandum of Association must be in one of the forms in
Table A, B, C, D and E in Schedule I of the Companies Act, 2013,
as may be applicable to the case of the company, or in a form as
near thereto as circumstances admit.

The Memorandum must be printed, divided into paragraphs
numbered consecutively and signed by each subscriber in the
presence of at least one witness who must attest the signature.

The Memorandum of a company shall be in respective forms as
given:

Sr. No.	Table	Form
1	Table A	MOA of a company limited by shares.
2	Table B	MOA of a company limited by guarantee and not having share capital.
3	Table C	MOA of a company limited by guarantee and having share capital.
4	Table D	MOA of an unlimited company and not having share capital.
5	Table E	MOA of an unlimited company and having share capital.

CONTENTS OF MEMORANDUM [SEC. 4]

The Memorandum of association contains the following fundamental clauses which have often been described as the conditions of the company's incorporation. (1) Name Clause, (2) Registered Office Clause, (3) Object Clause, (4) Liability Clause, (5) Capital Clause, (6) Association or Subscription Clause, (7) Successor Member Clause.

1. *Name Clause [Sec. 4(1)(a)]:* The company being a legal person, must have a name to establish its identity. It is the symbol of company's personal existence. A company may choose any name subject to the following restrictions:

   (a) The last word of the name must be "Limited" and in the case of a Private Company the last words must be "Private Limited". But, in the case of the One Person Company the last words must be OPC Limited.

   (b) The name must not be one which, in the opinion of the Central Government is undesirable.

   (c) The name should not resemble that of any other existing company.

   The Central Government may, by licence, allow a company to drop the word 'limited' from its name. This licence is granted on the basis of the following conditions:

   (a) The company should be formed for the promotion of commerce, art, science, religion, charity or any other useful object.

   (b) The company should apply its income in promoting its objects and must prohibit the payment of dividends to its members.

   Once the name is chosen and the company is registered in that name it must appear on the outside of every office or place of the company in a conspicuous manner in the language of general use in the locality [Sec.12].

2. *Registered Office Clause [Sec. 4(1)(b)]:* This clause states the name of the State in which the registered office of the company is to be situated. The registered office clause is very significant as it ascertains the domicile and nationality of a company.

   A company shall have a registered office within fifteen days of its incorporation or when it commences business, whichever is earlier and give notice to the Registrar of the Situation within thirty days of incorporation.

3. *Objects Clause [Sec. 4(1)(c)]:* This clause sets out the objects for which the company has been formed. It determines the capacity of the company whenever the doctrine of ultra-vires applies. It also shows the purpose for which the company had been set up and its contractual capacity. It cannot do anything beyond or outside the objects clause, and any act beyond it will be ultra-vires and void.

   The objects of the company should not be illegal or against the provisions of the Companies Act. For example, forming a company for dealing in lotteries or for trading, with the alien enemies.

4. *Liability Clause [Sec. 4(1)(d)]:* This clause contains the nature of liability that the members incur. If the company is to be incorporated with limited liability, the clause must state that "the liability of the members is limited by shares". The effect of this clause is that no member can be called upon to pay more than that remains unpaid.

   In a company limited by guarantee, the liability clause will state the amount on which each member undertakes to contribute to the assets of the company in the event of its liquidation. He cannot be called upon to pay anything before the company goes into liquidation.

5. *Capital Clause [Sec. 4(1)(e)]:* This clause contains the amount of the capital with which the company is registered and the number and value of the shares into which it is divided. The capital is variously described as "nominal", "authorised" or "registered".

6. *Association or Subscription Clause [Sec. 4(1)]:* The Memorandum concludes with the declaration of an association. The subscribers to the Memorandum declare, "we the several persons whose names and addresses are subscribed, are

desirous of being formed into a company in pursuance of this Memorandum of association, and we respectively agree to take the number of shares in the capital of the company set opposite our respective names". Then follow the names, addresses, occupations of the subscribers, and the number of shares each subscriber has taken and his signature attested by a witness.

There must be at least seven subscribers in the case of a Public Company and at least two in the case of a Private Company. A subscriber of Memorandum must take at least one share.

7. *Successor Member Clause [Sec. 4(1) (7)].* This clause is applicable to One Person Company only. This clause shall state the name of the successor member who will become the member of the company in the event of the death of the sole member.

IDENTICAL/UNDESIRABLE NAME

Sec. 4(2) and (3) further states that:

(i) The name stated in the Memorandum shall not be identical with or resemble to the name of an existing company registered under this Act or any previous company law.

(ii) The name stated shall not be such that, the use of which constitute an offence in any law.

(iii) The name stated shall not be an undesirable one in the opinion of the Central Government.

(iv) A company shall not be registered with a name which contains-

(a) any word or expression which is likely to give the impression that the company is in any way connected with, or having the patronage of the Central Government, any State Government, or any local authority, corporation or a body constituted by the Central Government or any State Government under any law for the time being in force; or

(b) such word or expression as prescribed in the Companies (Incorporation) Rules, 2014, unless the previous approval of the Central Government has been obtained for the use of any such word or expression

RESERVATION OF NAME [SEC. 4(4)]

A person may make an application in Form No. INC-1 along with the fee as provided in the Companies (Registration offices and fees) Rules, 2014 to the Registrar for the reservation of a name set out in the application as:

(a) The name of the proposed company; or

(b) The name to which the company proposes to change its name.

The Registrar may, on the basis of information and documents furnished along with the application, reserve the name for a period of sixty days from the date of application. If after the reservation of the name, it is found that the name was applied by furnishing wrong or incorrect information, then the following steps will be taken:

(i) The reserved name shall be cancelled and the person making application shall be liable to a penalty up to one lakh rupees.

(ii) If the company has been incorporated, the Registrar may give an opportunity to the company to make an explanation. Thereafter, the Registrar can take the following steps:

(a) Direct the company to change its name within a period of three months, after passing an ordinary resolution;

(b) Take action for striking off the name of the company from the register of companies.

(c) Make a petition for winding up of the company.

ALTERATION OF MEMORANDUM (SEC. 13)

Once the Memorandum is registered, the company cannot alter the conditions dealt with in it except as stated by the Act.

1. *Change of Name [Sec. 13(2)].* The name of the company can be altered at any time by a special resolution and with the written approval of the Central Government. But if a company has been registered with a name which subsequently appears to be undesirable or resembling the name of another company, it may change its name by passing an ordinary resolution and with the approval of the Central Government. In such a case the Central Government can also at any point of time after the registration of the company, direct the company to change its name. The company should alter its name within three months from the date of the direction unless the time is extended.

Where a company alters its name, the Registrar should enter the new name in the register and issue to the company a new certificate of incorporation with the necessary alterations. Alteration of name becomes effective only on the issue of such a certificate [Sec. 13(3)].

The change of name will not affect any rights or obligations of the company, or legal proceedings commenced under the old name.

2. *Change of Registered Office [Sec. 13(4)]:* A company can shift its registered office from one locality to another within the same town or city by giving notice to the Registrar within fifteen days of the change. If the office is to be shifted from one town, city or village to another within the same State, a special resolution to that effect must be passed. Within 30 days of the removal of the office, a notice to the Registrar should be given.

Sec. 13(4) of the Act deals with the change of place of registered office from one State to another State. In addition to the above, the following steps will be taken:

(i) A special resolution should be passed in a duly convened meeting [Sec. 13(b)(a)]. A copy of the same should be filed with the Registrar within thirty days.

(ii) An application in the prescribed form and prescribed manner shall be made to the Central Government for approval of such change in the place of registered office of the company [Sec. 13(6)(b)].

(iii) The alteration shall not take effect unless the resolution is confirmed by the Central Government (Sec. 13(5)). The Central Government, before confirming or refusing to confirm the change, will consider the interests of the company and its shareholders and whether the change is bonafide and not against the public interest. The Central Government may then issue the confirmation order on such terms and conditions as it may think fit.

(iv) After obtaining approval from the Central Government for change of registered office, a certified copy of the approval order shall be submitted to the Registrar of each of the States within the prescribed time. The Registrar of the State where the registered office is being shifted to, shall issue a fresh certificate of incorporation, indicating the alternation [Sec. 13(7)]

3. *Change of the Objects:* Section [13(8)] allows the change of the objects within certain defined limits. The company may,

by a special resolution change its objects if such an alteration is rendered necessary:

(a) to carry on its business more economically or more efficiently;

(b) to attain its main purpose by new or improved means;

(c) to enlarge or change the local area of operation;

(d) to carry on some business which under existing circumstances may conveniently or advantageously be combined with the business of the company.

(e) to restrict or abandon any of the objects specified in the Memorandum;

(f) to sell or dispose of the whole, or any part of the undertakings, or of any of the undertakings of the company;

(g) to amalgamate with any other company or body of persons.

The following are the formalities to be adopted for altering the objects of the company:

(i) The details in respect of such a special resolution should be published in the newspaper (one in English and one in vernacular language) which is in circulation at the place of its registered office.

(ii) The same can be placed on the website of the company indicating the reason for such a change.

(iii) The dissenting shareholders shall be given an opportunity to exit in accordance with the regulations to be specified by the SEBI.

(iv) The alteration of Memorandum with respect to the object clause shall be registered with the Registrar.

(v) (The Registrar will certify the registration within a period of thirty days from the date of filing of the special resolution.

ALTERATION IN THE CASE OF COMPANY LIMITED BY GUARANTEE [SEC. 13(11)]

Any provision in the Memorandum or Articles, in the case of a company limited by guarantee and not having a share capital, purporting to give any person a right to participate in the divisible profits of the company, otherwise than as a member, shall be void.

Effect of Non-registration with Registrar [Sec. 13(10)]

Any alteration, if not registered shall have no effect. If the documents required to be filed with the Registrar are not filed within one month of such an alteration and the order of the Central Government and all proceedings connected therewith shall at the expiry of such period become void and inoperative.

4. *Change of Capital [Sec.(61)]:* A company can change its capital only if it is so authorised by its articles of association. The capital of the company can be increased, consolidated, sub divided, converted into stock or reconverted into shares or cancelled simply by passing an ordinary resolution. But, a company can reduce its share capital only by passing a special resolution and obtaining the confirmation from the Court.

5. *Change in Liability Clause [13(1)]:* The liability of the members of a company limited by shares or guarantee can be increased through the alteration of the Memorandum only if all the members agree in writing to such a change either before or after the change.

   The other provisions in the Memorandum may be altered in the same manner as the alteration of the Articles of the company, i.e., by passing a special resolution.

DOCTRINE OF ULTRAVIRES

The term Ultra means beyond, and the term Vires means powers. Thus, 'Ultra Vires the Company' means 'beyond the powers of a Company'. The purpose of this doctrine is to protect the interest of the shareholders and creditors of the company.

The Memorandum of the company indicates its powers. Then it is the duty of the Court to check a company if it moves beyond its powers. Any activity of a company beyond its powers is, therefore, ultra vires the company. An ultra vires act is wholly void and inoperative. The company is not bound by such acts. It can never be subsequently ratified and validated, even if every shareholder consents to it. But if the act is ultra vires the directors only, the shareholders can ratify it. Or, if it is ultra vires the articles of association, the company can alter its articles in the proper way and if an act is within the powers of the company, any irregularity can be cured by the consent of all the shareholders.

The doctrine of ultra vires was first applied in a celebrated case of *Ashbury Railway Carriage Co., v. Riche*. In this case, a company had been established for the purpose of carrying on business as mechanical engineers and general contractors. The directors entered into an agreement for financing the construction of a railway in Belgium. The House of Lords held that the contract was ultra vires.

Effects of Ultra-Vires Transactions

1. *Injunction:* In case any ultra-vires act has been done or is about to be done, any member of the company can get an injunction from the Court restraining the company from proceeding with the ultra-vires act,

> **EFFECTS OF ULTRA VIRES TRANSACTIONS:**
> * Injunction.
> * Personal liability of directors.
> * Ultra vires contracts.
> * Ultra vires torts.

2. *Personal Liability of Directors:* The Directors of the company are personally liable to the company for the ultra vires acts. They are also personally liable to the third parties as they exceed their authority by doing ultra vires acts.

3. *Ultra Vires Contracts:* A contract which is ultra vires the company is absolutely void and of no legal effect. It cannot become intra vires even by subsequent ratification.

4. *Ultra Vires Torts:* A company is not liable for torts committed by its agents or servants during the course of ultra vires transactions.

EXCEPTIONS

In the following exceptional circumstances, the ultra vires acts are not absolutely inoperative:

(a) If the company takes an ultra vires loan and uses it to pay intra vires debts of its own, then the lender is placed in the position of the creditor and can recover his money.

(b) If the company acquires some property by ultra vires expenditure, the company's right over the property will be protected.

(c) If the company has expended cash upon an ultra vires transaction it can recover it provided that it can be traced in accordance with the rules of equity relating to the tracing of money.

> **Under the new Companies Act, 2013 this doctrine of ultra vires gives a ground to the members and depositor(s) of the company to file an application before the Tribunal on behalf of the members or depositor(s) for restraining the company from committing an act which is ultra vires the Articles or Memorandum of the company vide. Sec. 245(1)(a) of the Companies Act, 2013.**

REVIEW QUESTIONS

1. Define 'Memorandum of Association'.
2. What do you understand by doctrine of ultra vires?
3. What do you mean by reservation of name?
4. Write a note on name clause.
5. What is association clause?
6. What is the borrowing power of the company?
7. Explain the various types of ultra vires acts.
8. Write a note on alteration of capital clause.
9. Explain the significance of object clause of Memorandum of Association.
10. Enumerate the contents of Memorandum of Association.
11. Discuss the effects of ultra vires transaction.
12. Explain the provisions relating to change of registered office.
13. What are the exceptions to the doctrine of ultra vires?
14. Define Memorandum of Association. Discuss its contents.
15. Discuss how the different clauses of the Memorandum of Association of a company may be altered.
16. What do you mean by ultra vires transaction? Explain its various exceptions.

PRACTICAL PROBLEMS

Attempt the following problems, giving reasons:

1. A company has its registered office at Madras. Owing to some reasons favourable to the company, it wishes to shift its registered office to London. Can the company be permitted to shift its registered office?

   Hint: No.

2. A company put up telephone wires in a certain area. It had no powers to lay telephone wires there as per its Memorandum. The defendant, M cut them down. Can the company sue M for the damage done to the wires?

   Hint: Yes.

27

Articles of Association

The Articles define the duties, the rights and the powers of the governing body as between, themselves and the company at large and the mode and form in which the business of the company is to be carried on, and the mode and form in which changes in the internal regulations of the company may, from time to time, be made.

(Lord Cairns)

The 'Articles of Association' contain rules, regulations and bye-laws for the general administration of the company. They are like the partnership deed in a partnership. They are subordinate to and are controlled by the Memorandum.

According to Sec. 2(5) of the Companies Act, 2013, 'Articles' mean the Articles of Association of a company as originally framed or as altered from time to time or applied in pursuance of any previous company law or of this Act. Sec. 5 of the Companies Act, 2013 deals with Articles of Association.

Every type of company whether public or private and whether limited by shares or limited by guarantee having share capital or not having share capital or. an unlimited company, must register their Articles of Association.

A Public Company limited by shares may either register Articles of Association signed by the subscribers to the Memorandum or may adopt all or any of the regulations contained in Table F of First Schedule of the Act.

An unlimited company, or a company limited by guarantee, or a Private Company Limited by shares might adopt any of the appropriate regulations of Table G, H, I and J in Schedule I [Sec. 5(6)].

The Articles must be printed and divided into paragraphs, each consisting generally of regulations and numbered consecutively. Each subscriber of the Memorandum has to sign the document in the presence of at least one attesting witness, adding his address and occupation.

PROVISION FOR ENTRENCHMENT [SEC. 5(3)]

The Articles may contain provisions for entrenchment to the effect that specified provisions may be altered only if conditions or procedures that are more restrictive than those applicable in the case of special resolution, are met or complied with.

In accordance with Sec. 5(4), the provisions for entrenchment shall only be made by:

Public Company	Private Company
By a special resolution.	On formation of a company, or by an amendment in the Articles agreed to by all the members of the company.

NOTICE TO REGISTRAR

If the Articles contain the provisions for entrenchment, the company shall give notice to the Registrar of such provisions in Form No. INC-2 or Form No. INC-7, as the case may be along with the fee as provided in the Companies (Registration offices and fees) Rules, 2014 at the time of incorporation of the company or in the case of existing companies, the same shall be filed in Form No. MGT-14 within thirty days from the date of entrenchment of the Articles as the case may be along with the fee as provided in the Companies (Registration offices and fees) Rules, 2014.

MODEL FORM OF ARTICLES

Different model forms of Memorandum of Association and Articles of Association of various types of companies are specified in Schedule I of the Act. The Schedule is divided into following tables:

S.No.	Table	Form Applicable to
1.	Table F	Company Limited by Shares
2.	Table G	Company Limited by Guarantee and having share capital
3.	Table H	Company Limited by Guarantee and not having share capital
4.	Table I	Unlimited company and having share capital
5.	Table J	Unlimited company and not having share capital

A company may adopt all or any of the regulations contained in the model Articles applicable in such a company.

In framing Articles of Association, care should be taken to see that the regulations framed do not go beyond the powers of the company itself as contemplated by the Memorandum of Association nor should they be against any of the requirements of the Companies Act. All clauses in the Articles ultra vires the Memorandum or the Articles shall be null and void.

CONTENTS OF ARTICLES

The Articles may insert any stipulation as to the relations between the company and its members, and between members inter se. But, this document must not conflict with the provisions of the Act [Sec. 9]. In particular, the Articles provide for matters like:

1. the exclusion of whole or in part of Table F;
2. adoption or execution of pre-incorporation contracts;
3. share capital and the right of the shareholders;
4. allotment of shares;
5. forfeiture of shares;
6. alteration of share capital;
7. transfer and transmission of shares;
8. lien on shares;
9. share certificates and share warrants;
10. conversion of shares into stock;
11. dividend, reserves and capitalisation of profits;
12. appointment of managerial personnel;
13. remuneration of directors;
14. voting rights of members;
15. capitalisation of profits;
16. arbitration provision, if any;
17. general meeting, proxies and polls, rules as to resolutions;
18. proceedings of the Board of Directors;
19. winding up;
20. notice to members;
21. issue of share warrant;
22. fixing limits of number of directors; and
23. accounts and audit.

ALTERATION OF ARTICLES (SEC. 14)

As per Sec. 14, a company has the power to alter its Articles. The following are the provisions in this regard:

(i) Conversion of a private company into a public company or a public company into a private company is permitted.

(ii) Such a conversion shall comply with the provisions of the Act and conditions in its Memorandum.

(iii) A special resolution shall be passed for such a conversion.

(iv) The Act requires certain restrictions and limitations to be included in the Articles of a private company. Where a private company alters its Articles in such a manner, then the company shall cease to be a private company from the date of such an alteration.

(v) Approval shall be obtained from the Tribunal for converting public company into a private company.

(vi) Every alteration in the Articles and copy of the Tribunal's approval for conversion of a public company into a private company shall be filed with the Registrar, together with a printed copy of the altered Articles, within a period of fifteen days in such a manner as may be prescribed.

Limitations Regarding Alteration of Articles

(i) Alteration shall not be inconsistent with,

(a) Provisions of Companies Act or any other Statute.

(b) Conditions contained in Memorandum.

(ii) Approval of Central Government is to be obtained in certain cases.

(iii) Alteration should not deprive any person of his rights under a contract.

(iv) Alteration should not constitute a fraud on the minority.

(v) Alteration should be bona fide for the benefit of the company as a whole.

Articles in Relation to Memorandum

1. The Memorandum contains the fundamental conditions upon which alone the company is allowed to be incorporated. The Articles of Association are internal regulations of the company.

2. Memorandum being the charter of the company, is the supreme document. Articles are subordinate to the Memorandum. If there is any conflict between the Articles and the Memorandum, the latter prevails.

3. Some of the conditions in the Memorandum cannot be altered except in the manner and to the extent provided by the Act. Articles of association, on the contrary, can be altered simply by a special resolution.

4. An act done by a company, in contravention of its Memorandum, is ultra vires and is void and cannot be ratified even by the whole body of shareholders. But where the company does anything violating the Articles, it is considered to be only irregular and can be ratified by the shareholders.

EFFECTS OF MEMORANDUM AND ARTICLES

"The Memorandum and Articles, when registered, bind the company and its members to the same extent, as if they had been signed and sealed by each member to observe and be bound by all the provisions of the Memorandum and of the Articles".

Also, all monies payable by any member to the company under the Memorandum or Articles shall be a debt due from the company (Sec.10). The effect of Memorandum and Articles can be examined under the following propositions.

1. *Members to the Company:* The Memorandum and Articles constitute a binding contract as between the members and the company. Each member must, therefore, observe the provisions of the Memorandum and Articles.

   In *Borland's Trustee* v. *Steel Brothers & Co. Ltd.* (1901), Company's Articles provided that on the bankruptcy of a member his shares would be sold to a person at a price fixed by the directors. Boreland, a shareholder was adjudicated bankrupt. His trustee claimed that he was not bound by these provisions and was free to sell them at their true value".

   Held, the share having been purchased by Boreland on these conditions, he was bound by them, and must sell the shares as provided in the Articles.

2. *Company to the Members:* A company is bound to the members just as the members are bound to the company. "Each member is entitled to say that there shall be no breach of the Articles and he is entitled to an injunction to prevent the breach", e.g., an individual member can sue the company for an injunction restraining it from improper payment of dividend [*Hoole* v. *Great Western Railway* (1867) 3 ch. D 262].

3. *Members Inter Se:* As between the members inter se, each member is bound by the Articles to the other members [*Rayfield* v. *Hands* (1958) 2 W.L.R. 851]. The members are bound between themselves only on the basis of an implied contract. Thus, a member of a company has no right to bring a suit to enforce the Articles in his own name against any other member or members, It is the company alone which can sue the offenders so as to protect the aggrieved member.

4. *Company to the Outsiders:* No article can constitute a contract between the company and a third person. An outsider, therefore, cannot take advantage of the provisions contained in the company's Articles. This is based on the general rule of law that a stranger to a contract cannot acquire any rights and liabilities under the contract.

In *Browne* v. *La Trinidad*, it was held that no outsider can enforce Articles against the company even if they purport to give him certain rights.

CONSTRUCTIVE NOTICE OF MEMORANDUM AND ARTICLES OF ASSOCIATION

On registration, the Memorandum and Articles become Public documents. These documents are open and accessible to all [Sec. 610]. It is the duty of every person dealing with a company to inspect these documents and make sure that his contract is in conformity with their provisions. But, whether a person actually reads them or not, he is to be in the same position as if he had read them. Thus, a person who deals with the company is presumed not only to have read those documents, but to have understood them according to their proper meaning [*Oakbank Oil Co.* v. *Crum* (1882) 8 A.C. 65]. This kind of presumed notice is called constructive notice.

The doctrine of constructive notice is sometimes considered as unreal doctrine as it does not take notice of the realities of business life. A company is known by the people through its officers and not through its documents.

DOCTRINE OF "INDOOR MANAGEMENT"

The doctrine of indoor management is one limitation to the doctrine of constructive notice. The latter seeks to protect the company against the outsider, the former operates to protect outsiders against the company. The doctrine of indoor management had its Genesis in *Royal British Bank* v. *Turquand* (1856) 119 ER 886. According to this doctrine, the outsiders dealing with the company are entitled to assume that as far as the internal proceedings of the company are concerned, everything has been regularly done.

Royal British Bank v. *Turquand* (1856) 119 ER 886: The Directors of a company borrowed a sum of money from the plaintiff, Turquand and issued a bond to him. They had the power to issue such bonds, provided they were authorised by a resolution of the company. In fact, no such resolution had been passed. It was held that Turquand could sue the company on the bond, as he was entitled to assume that the necessary resolution had been passed. Lord Hatherley observed "Outsiders are bound to know the external position of the company, but are not bound to know its indoor management."

APPLICATION OF THE RULE OF INDOOR MANAGEMENT

The rule of indoor management may apply in the following cases:

1. Where there is an affirmative representation regarding the authority of the agent.
2. It may arise out of the act or conduct of the members.

Exceptions to the Doctrine of Indoor Management

(a) The rule does not protect any person who has actual or constructive notice of the want of authority of the person acting on behalf of the company.

(b) The rule does not apply to the transactions which are void or illegal *ab initio*, nor does it apply where requisite signatures are forged.

(c) The rule cannot be invoked in favour of a person who did not in fact consult the company's Memorandum and Articles and consequently did not act in reliance of those documents.

(d) The rule does not bind the company to its officers or other persons who should know whether the regulations in the articles have been observed.

(e) A person enters into a contract with the company through its officer who has no authority to act on behalf of the company. In such cases, he cannot take the benefit of this doctrine.

TABLE F

Table F consists of a series of regulations framed by the legislature for the conduct of the affairs of company. It forms part of the

Companies Act. If a public company limited by shares may not file its own Articles at the time of registration, the regulations contained in Table F (Schedule I) shall become its Articles. Even when such a company has its own Articles and it is silent on some points, the provisions of Table F will apply.

REVIEW QUESTIONS

1. Define Articles of Association.
2. What is the doctrine of constructive notice?
3. What is the doctrine of indoor management?
4. List down various model form of Articles of Association.
5. Enumerate limitations on power to alter Articles.
6. Explain the provisions for entrenchment.
7. Enumerate the application of the rule of Indoor Management.
8. Explain the provisions relating to the alteration of articles.
9. Bring out the difference between Memorandum and Articles of Association.
10. Mention any five items which are included in Articles.
11. Explain the effects of Memorandum and Articles.
12. What do you mean by Articles of association? Enumerate its contents.
13. Examine the doctrine of Indoor Management in the light of the decision in Turquand's case.

PRACTICAL PROBLEMS

Attempt the following problems giving reasons:

1. The articles of a company provided that in the event of a member becoming bankrupt, his shares would be offered for sale to other shareholders at a certain price. Is the provision binding on the shareholders?

   Hint: Yes, as the Articles constitute a contract between the members *inter se*.

2. A company issued a bond under its common seal signed by two directors. The articles provided that the directors might borrow on bond such sums as they should be authorised by an ordinary resolution of the company. No such a resolution was passed. Is the company liable on the bond?

   Hint: Yes, (*Royal British Bank* v. *Turquand*).

28

Prospectus

A Prospectus is "an invitation issued to the public to take shares or debentures of the company or to deposit money with the company".

INTRODUCTION

After the formation of a company, the next problem is to raise funds for its working. Every public company which intends to appeal to the public to take its shares or debentures has to issue a prospectus. A Private Company is prohibited from inviting public to subscribe to its share capital and, therefore, it is not required to issue a prospectus. When a Public Company can raise money from private source, it need not issue a prospectus. In such a case, it shall be required to file a statement in lieu of prospectus with the Registrar of companies.

Prospectus is a valuable document supporting the structure of the company. The facts and figures stated in a prospectus are meant to persuade the public to purchase shares or debentures of the company. It describes the prospectus as advantageous likely to accrue to the persons investing their savings in the share capital or debentures of the company. It appeals to the public to invest their savings in the company.

No application for shares or debentures of a company can be invited unless the appeal is accompanied with a prospectus.

DEFINITION [SEC. 2(70)]

"A prospectus means any document described or issued as a prospectus and includes a red herring prospectus referred to in Sec. 32 or shelf prospectus referred to in Sec. 31 or any notice, circular advertisement or other document inviting deposits from the public or inviting offers from the public for the subscription or purchase of any shares in or debentures of a body corporate". In essence, 'a prospectus' is an invitation issued to the public to take shares or debentures of the company or give deposits.

Meaning of the Phrase "Offer to the Public"

The provisions of the Act relating to the prospectus are not attracted unless the prospectus is issued to the public. The public here does not mean the whole public. A document will be deemed to be issued to the public, if the invitation is such as to be open to any one who brings his money and applies in due form whether the prospectus is addressed to him or not.

In *Re: South of England Gas Co. Ltd.* (1911), 1 ch. 573, a prospectus headed "For private circulation only" issued to the shareholders of certain gas companies, was held to be an offer to the public, even though only three thousand copies were distributed and there was no public advertisement.

An invitation is not, however, to be regarded as made to the public, if:

(a) it cannot be calculated to result directly or indirectly in the shares or debentures becoming available for subscription or purchase by persons other than those receiving the invitation,

(b) it is made to a few friends, relations or customers.

Issuing Houses and Deemed Prospectus [Sec. 25]

The onerous provisions relating to a prospectus are often evaded by companies through the allotment of the whole of the capital to an intermediary, called as an "Issuing House". The House then offers the shares to the public by way of an advertisement of its own. It is really not a prospectus and, thus, the requirements of the Act relating to prospectus are evaded. But, now all such advertisements sponsored by an "Issuing House" are known as "offer for sale" and are deemed to be a prospectus issued by the company.

CONTENTS OF A PROSPECTUS [SEC. 26]

Every prospectus is required to state the matters specified in Part I of Schedule II and set out the Reports specified in Part II of the Schedule. They are as follows:

1. The main objects of the company including the details about the signatories to the memorandum.

2. The number and classes of shares, and the nature and extent of the holders in the property and profits of the company.

3. The number of redeemable preference shares intended to be issued with the date of redemption.

4. The names, occupations and addresses of directors, managing director, managing agent, secretaries and treasurers and manager.

5. Qualification shares of directors, if any.

6. Subscribed capital of a body corporate which manages the company as managing agents or secretaries and treasurers.

7. The minimum subscription on which the directors may proceed to allot shares and the time of the opening of the subscription list.

8. The amount payable on application and allotment on each share. If any prospectus was previously issued within two years, the details of the shares subscribed for and allotted.

9. The particulars about any option or preferential right to be given to any person to subscribe for shares or debentures of the company.

10. The amount or estimated amount of preliminary expenses and the persons by whom any of these expenses have been paid or are payable.

11. The number of shares or debentures which within the two preceding years have been issued for a consideration other than cash.

12. The amount of premium, if any, paid or payable on each share issued within two years preceding the date of the prospectus.

13. Any amount or benefit paid or given within the two preceding years or intended to be paid or given to any promoter or officer, and the consideration for the payment or the giving of the benefit.

14. Particulars about vendors from whom any property has been or is to be acquired by the company and the price thereof is to be paid out of the proceeds of the issue.

15. The amount or rate of underwriting commission.

16. The names and addresses of the auditors, if any, of the company.

17. The voting rights of different classes of shares.

18. The names and addresses of creditors, if any, of the company.

19. Full particulars of the nature and extent of the interest if any, of every director or promoter (i) in the promotion of the company, or (ii) in any property acquired by the company within two years of the issue of the prospectus.

20. If the company has been carrying on business, the length of time of such a business.

21. If any reserves or profits of the company has been capitalised, the particulars of capitalisation and the particulars of the surplus arising from any revaluation of the assets of the company.

22. A reasonable time and place at which copies of all accounts on which the report of the auditors is based may be inspected.

STATEMENT IN LIEU OF PROSPECTUS

The Companies Act, 2013 has done away with the concept of Statement in lieu of prospectus. But, this concept has been described hereunder based on the provisions of the Companies Act, 1956.

If the promoters of a Public Company are confident of obtaining the required capital through private contracts, no prospectus need to be issued to the public. In such a case they are only required to prepare a draft prospectus containing the information required to be disclosed by Schedule II of the Act. This document is called as a statement in lieu of prospectus. A copy of it must be filed with the Registrar three days before any allotment of any shares or debentures can be made. Contravention of this provision renders the company and every director liable to a fine up to ₹ 1,000.

THE GOLDEN RULE AS TO THE FRAMING OF PROSPECTUS

It is the rule of conduct between the shareholders and directors. Since the purpose of issuing the prospectus is to induce persons to subscribe for or purchase corporate securities, it is required to give a full, accurate and fair picture of the state of affairs and prospect of the company. In other words, the prospectus shall not depict a picture of the company painted according to the fancies of those who frame it. It shall be an accurate photograph of the state of affairs of the company.

The golden rule as to the framing of a prospectus was laid down by *Kindersely V.C. in New Brunswick etc. Co.* v. *Muggeridge.* Briefly, the rule is that nothing should be stated as a fact which is not so and no fact should be omitted the existence of which might in any degree affect the nature or quality of the privileges and advantages which the prospectus holds out as an inducement to take shares.

WHAT IS AN UNTRUE STATEMENT?

A statement is said to be untrue if it is misleading in the form and context. However, the mis-statement must be of a fact and not of law.

In *Rex* v. *Kylsent* (1932) 1 K.B. 442, the prospectus stated that dividends of 5 to 8 per cent had been regularly paid over a long period. But, in fact, the company was suffering heavily during the seven years preceding the date of the prospectus. Dividends had been paid during this period only by using the reserve fund. Held, the prospectus was false and misleading.

A half truth, for instance, represented as a whole truth is tantamount to a false statement (*Aarsons Reefs* v. *Twissa* (1896) A.C. 273). Where a statement is true when it is made, but subsequently becomes untrue when allotment is made, the contract to take shares may be rescinded (*Rajagopal Iyer* v. *The South Indian Rubber Works* (1942) M.L.J. 228).

LIABILITIES IN THE CASE OF MIS-STATEMENT IN A PROSPECTUS

The Liabilities may be grouped under two heads: (I) Civil Liability and (II) Criminal Liability.

I. Civil Liability

An investor who is damnified by mis-representation in the prospectus may have claims against the following persons:

   (a) the company,

   (b) the directors, promoters and experts.

      (a) *Remedies Against the Company:* An investor has remedies against the company both under (1) the general law, and (2) the statute. But, in order to succeed he must prove that:

   (i) he is an allottee and not a purchaser on the market,

  (ii) he was in fact induced by the prospectus, and

 (iii) the prospectus was issued by the company or someone with the authority of the company.

1. Remedies under General Law

     (i) *Rescission:* An investor induced by a prospectus issued by or on behalf of a company and containing a mis-statement therein may rescind the contract. The effect of the rescission of the contract would be that the person would give up the shares and get back his money with interest. He must, however take action to rescind the contract within a reasonable time, and before does anything after notice of the mis-representation which is inconsistent with the right to repudiate, e.g., attempting to sell the shares.

(ii) *Damages of Deceit:* The liability of the company under this head can only be vicarious. In order to succeed, the plaintiff has to prove all the matters which he must prove in action for rescission. In addition, he must also prove here that the directors or other agents of the company who prepared the prospectus were fraudulent.

Prima facie, the damages that can be claimed by the allottee as a result of the deceitful prospectus is the difference between the price paid by him for the securities and the real value of them when he took them.

2. Statutory Remedies

In England, Sec. 2(1) of the Misrepresentation Act, 1967 has conferred a statutory right on a person who has induced to enter into a contract by a misrepresentation made by the other party. As per this Section an allottee is empowered to recover damages against the company for any loss sustained by him on account of the misrepresentation contained in a prospectus which induced him to subscribe for the securities. But the company can escape liability by showing that those who issued the prospectus had reasonable ground to believe and did believe up to the time of the allotment that the facts represented were true.

(b) *Remedies Against Directors, Promoters, Etc.:* A person induced to take shares on the faith of false prospectus may claim from the directors or promoters or from any one else who authorised the issue of false prospectus.

Their liability may be studied under the following heads:

(i) *Liability for Damages for Mis-statement in Prospectus* [Sec. 62]: Every director, promoter and every person who authorises to issue the prospectus is liable to pay compensation to the aggrieved party for loss or damage he may have incurred by reason of any untrue statement in the prospectus.

Defences Open to Directors, Promoters Etc. [Sec. 35(2)]

In a claim for compensation under Sec. 35, a director may prove in defence that:

1. he withdrew his consent to act as a director before the issue of the prospectus, and it was issued without his consent;

2. the issue was made without his knowledge or consent, and on becoming aware of the issue he gave a reasonable public notice of that fact;

3. he withdrew his consent after the issue of the prospectus, but before allotment and gave public notice;

4. he had reasonable ground to believe them to be true, and

5. the statement was a correct and fair representation or extract or copy of an official document.

(ii) *Liability for Damages for Non-compliance with Sec. 35:* Sec. 35(1) provides that a company's prospectus should contain certain particulars. Omission of any such particulars may give rise to an action for damages at the instance of the subscriber for shares or debentures who has suffered loss, thereby, even if the omission does not make the prospectus false or misleading.

(iii) *Liability under the General Law:* The persons responsible for the issue of false prospectus may also be held liable for the payment of damages under the general law. But, a person can only be liable in fraud if he makes a statement to be acted upon by others which is false and is made (a) knowingly, or (b) without belief in its truth; or (c) recklessly, not caring whether it was true or false.

II. Criminal Liability

Sec. 34 of the Companies Act, 2013 provides that, a person responsible for the issue of prospectus containing a false statement, may also be held criminally liable. He may be punished with imprisonment for a term not less than six months and not more than ten years with a fine not less than the amount involved in the fraud and not more than three times the amount involved in the fraud. However, if the fraud in question involves public interest, the term of imprisonment shall not be less than three years except when, in the opinion of the Court, (1) the statement in question was immaterial, or (2) that he had reasonable ground to believe and he did believe in the truth of the Statement till the issue of the prospectus.

ABRIDGED PROSPECTUS [SEC. 33]

Abridged prospectus is a memorandum containing the important features of a prospectus. Its purpose is to disclose all the relevant details about the company to the prospective investors.

Abridged prospectus should contain all the relevant details as laid down in the information memorandum. But if any person requests for the full prospectus before the closure of the subscription list, it should be given to him.

However in the following cases, a company need not issue abridged prospectus along with the application for shares and debentures.

  (i)   When shares or debentures are not offered to the public.

 (ii)   When the application form is issued to the existing members or debentureholders only (with or without the right of renunciation).

(iii)   When the application form is issued for issuing shares or debentures similar to the ones previously issued and dealt in on a recognised stock exchange.

(iv)   When an underwriter is invited on bona fide underwriting agreement to market the unsubscribed shares.

SHELF PROSPECTUS (SEC. 31)

Shelf prospectus means a prospectus issued by any financial institution or bank for one or more issues of the securities or class of securities specified in that document. It enables public financial institutions and banks to raise capital from the public more than once without the issue of fresh prospectus every time. Shelf prospectus is valid for a period of one year from the date of first issue of securities.

Within the validity period of the shelf prospectus, if the company wants subsequent issues, it is required to issue an 'information memorandum'. Such a memorandum indicates the changes that have occurred during the intervening period. Thus, the shelf prospectus together with the information memorandum can be treated as a prospectus.

RED HERRING PROSPECTUS (SEC. 32)

A public company may issue red herring prospectus along with an information memorandum before the actual opening of the subscription list. The information report is circulated to explore the demand for securities and the price at which securities can be offered to the public. Subsequently, a red herring prospectus should be filed at least three days prior to the opening of the offer. Red herring prospectus is a prospectus which does not have complete particulars on the price and the quantum of securities offered. If there is any variation between the information memorandum and the red herring prospectus, the same should be highlighted and individually communicated to the person invited to subscribe. However, the applicant has the right to withdraw within seven days of such a communication.

Finally, when the offer is closed, a final prospectus shall be filed with the Registrar of companies by an unlisted public company and with the SEBI by a listed company. This mode of issuing shares is also termed as 'book building mode' of issuing shares.

MINIMUM SUBSCRIPTION

No allotment should be made in respect of any shares offered to the public for subscription until the minimum subscription stated in the prospectus has been subscribed, and the amount payable on application has been received in cash by the company.

Minimum subscription is the minimum amount which should be raised by a company in the opinion of the directors by means of issue of shares to meet certain needs such as preliminary expenses, working capital, etc.

REVIEW QUESTIONS

1. What is prospectus?
2. What is deemed prospectus?
3. What is statement in lieu of prospectus?
4. What is misleading prospectus?
5. What is shelf prospectus?
6. What is an untrue statement?
7. Explain the meaning of the phrase "offer to the public".
8. What do you mean by "issuing house"?
9. What is minimum subscription?
10. Enumerate the objects of issuing a prospectus.
11. Explain the provisions contained in Sec. 26(1)(a) of the Companies Act, 2013.
12. Explain abridged prospectus.
13. Explain red-herring prospectus.
14. Explain the golden rule as to the framing of prospectus.
15. What is a prospectus? Enumerate its contents.
16. What are the remedies available in the case of a misstatement of prospectus?
17. Explain the legal provisions relating to issue and registration of prospectus.

PRACTICAL PROBLEMS

Attempt the following problems, giving reasons:

1. P applies for some shares on the basis of a prospectus which contains mis-statements and the shares are allotted to P, who thereafter transfers them to Q. Can Q bring an action for rescission on the ground of mis-statement?

   Hint: No, as the right to rescind the contract is available only to the original allottees.

2. A applied for 200 shares in the name of a fictitious person. Subsequently, shares were allotted to him in the fictitious name. Did A incur any liability under the Companies Act, 1956

   Hint: Yes.

29

Membership in a Company

The 'members' or 'shareholders' are "the persons who collectively constitute the company as a corporate entity".

MEMBERS AND SHAREHOLDERS

A member is a person whose name appears in the register of members of the company. A shareholder, on the contrary, is a person who holds shares from the company.

The two terms 'members' and 'shareholders' are used interchangeably. They are synonymous in the case of a company limited by shares, a company limited by guarantee and having a share capital and an unlimited company whose capital is held in definite shares. But, in the case of a guarantee and an unlimited company, a member is not necessarily a shareholder, for such a company may not have a share capital.

A shareholder may be distinguished from a member on the following points of view:

(a) A shareholder is a member but a member may not be a shareholder because the company may not have a share capital.

(b) A holder of a share warrant is a shareholder but not a member as his name is removed from the register of members.

(c) A legal representative of a deceased member is not a member until he applies for registration. He is, however, a shareholder although his name does not appear on the register of members.

MODE OF ACQUIRING MEMBERSHIP [SEC. 2(55)]

A person may become a member of a company in any of the following ways:

(i) *By Subscribing to the Memorandum:* A subscriber to the memorandum becomes a member the moment the company

313

is registered, even though his name is not entered in the register of members or allotment of shares is not made.

(ii) *By Application and Allotment:* A person who applies for a certain number of shares becomes a member when shares are allotted to him and a notice of allotment is given to him. And his name is entered in the register of members.

(iii) *By Taking a Transfer of Shares:* A person may buy shares from an existing member. He becomes a member when the transfer of shares is duly effected and his name is entered in the register of members.

(iv) *By Transmission of Shares:* A person may become a member by registration if he succeeds the estate of a deceased member. The Official Assignee is likewise entitled to be a member in place of a shareholder who is adjudicated insolvent. This method of acquiring membership is called transmission.

(v) *By Acquiescence or Estoppel:* A person is deemed to be a member if he allows his name, apart from any agreement to become a member, to be on the register of members or otherwise holds himself out or allows himself to be held out as a member.

(vi) *By Agreeing to Purchase Qualification Shares:* Before a person is appointed a director of a Public Company, he should sign and deliver to the Registrar a written undertaking to take and pay for qualification shares. He, thus becomes a member and is in the same position as a subscriber to the Memorandum of the company.

WHO CAN BE A MEMBER?

Subject to the memorandum and articles, any person who is competent to enter into a contract can become a member of a company. The membership rights of some categories of persons are noted below:

(i) *Minor:* A minor cannot become a member of a company as an agreement by a minor to take shares is void. If a person has been registered in ignorance of the fact of minority, the company can repudiate the allotment and remove his name from the register on coming to know the minority of the person. The minor can also repudiate the allotment at any time during his minority. In either case the company should pay back all the money received from him in respect of the allotted shares. According to the present position of the law as regards fully paid shares, a minor may be admitted to the membership through the name of his guardian.

(ii) *Insolvent:* An insolvent cannot become a member of the company but if a member has become an insolvent, he remains a member as long as his names appears in the register. He is entitled to vote even though his shares vest in the Official Assignee or Receiver.

(iii) *Partnership Firm:* A partnership firm, being not a person in the eyes of law, cannot be a member of a company except in company registered u/s 8 of the Companies Act, 2013. Partners may, however, be registered as joint holders in which case each of them becomes a member. In the case of a private company, joint holders are treated as a single member.

(iv) *Foreigner:* A foreigner may take shares in a company and become a member. But, when he becomes an alien enemy his right as a member of the company is suspended.

(v) *Company:* A company may become a member of another company if it is authorised by its memorandum or articles.

A company cannot buy shares in its own name [*Trevor* v. *Whitworth* (1887) 12APP, Cas. 409]. Also a subsidiary company cannot be a member of its holding company (Sec. 19).

TERMINATION OF MEMBERSHIP

A person ceases to be a member of a company in any of the following ways:

1. If he transfers his shares to another person. In such a case the transferor ceases to be a member as soon as the transferee is registered but not before.

2. If his shares are forfeited for the non-payment of calls.

3. If he makes a valid surrender of his shares.

4. If his shares are sold by the company to enforce a lien.

5. If his shares are purchased either by another member of the company or by the company by order of the Court.

6. If he rescinds the contract of membership on the ground of fraud or misrepresentation or mistake.

7. If the redeemable preference shares are redeemed.

8. If share warrants are issued to him in exchange or fully paid shares.

9. If he dies; his estate remains liable for calls.

10. If he is adjudicated insolvent, and the Official Assignee disclaims his shares.

11. If the company is wound up. But he remains liable as a contributory.

LIABILITY OF MEMBERS

The liability of members depends on the nature of the company.

 (i) *Company with Unlimited Liability:* Every member is liable in full for all the debts of the company contracted during the period of his membership.

 (ii) *Company Limited by Guarantee:* Each member is bound to contribute in the event of winding up, a sum of money specified in the liability clause of the memorandum.

 (iii) *Company Limited by Shares:* Each member is bound to contribute the full nominal value of his shares and his liability ends there.

RIGHTS OF MEMBERS

Rights of members or shareholders can be brought under two heads; namely, (1) Individual membership rights, (2) Corporate membership rights.

1. Individual Membership Rights

These rights are conferred on the members by the Companies Act. Some of these rights are:

 (a) To receive share certificate.
 (b) To transfer shares.
 (c) To attend meetings.
 (d) To appoint directors.
 (e) To receive notice of meetings.
 (f) To inspect the books of the company.
 (g) To have right issues.
 (h) To approach Court if there is an oppression and mismanagement.
 (i) To share the surplus assets on winding up.

2. Corporate Membership Rights

These rights can be exercised only by the majority and not by the single shareholder or minority shareholders. Thus, the shareholders in majority determine the policy of the company or exercise control over the management of the company.

REGISTER AND INDEX OF MEMBERS

Register of Members (Sec. 88). Every company should keep a register of its members and enter therein the following particulars:

1. Name, address and occupation of each member.
2. In the case of a company having a share capital a statement of shares held by each member, and the amount paid, or agreed to be paid, on those shares. Each share should be distinguished by its number.
3. The date on which each person was entered in the register as a member.
4. The date on which each person ceased to be a member.

If the company has converted any of its shares into stock and given notice of the conversion to the Registrar of Companies, the register should show the amount of stock held by each member instead of the shares.

If default is made in complying with the above provisions, the company and every officer of the company who is in default, shall be liable to a fine of not less than fifty thousand rupees and not more than three lakh rupees. If default is a continuing one with a further fine of one thousand rupees for every day after the first during which the default continues.

Power to Close Register (Sec. 91). A company may close the register of members for a total period of 45 days in a year and not exceeding 30 days at any one time. Before such a register is closed, the company shall give not less than 7 days previous notice by advertisement in some newspaper circulating in the district in which the registered office of the company is situated.

Rectification of Register (Sec. 59). Section 59 of the Companies Act, 2013 empowers the Tribunal to rectify the register of members.

ANNUAL RETURN (SEC. 92)

Every company has to file with the Registrar an annual return containing certain particulars.

Annual Return of a Company having a Share Capital

Every company having a share capital has, within sixty days from the date of the annual general meeting, to file every year with the Registrar a return known as the 'annual return'. The return shall contain the following particulars.

1. Its registered office.
2. The register of its members.
3. The register of its debentureholders.
4. Its shares and debentures.
5. Its indebtedness.
6. Its members and debentureholders—past and present.
7. Its directors, managing directors, managers and secretaries—past and present.

Annual Return of a Company not having a Share Capital

The return of a company not having a share capital shall state the following particulars:

1. the address of the registered office of the company.
2. the names of members and respective dates on which they became members and the names of persons who ceased to be members since the date of the last annual general meeting and the dates on which they ceased to be members.
3. all such particulars with respect to the persons who, at the date of return, were the directors of the company, its managers and its secretary.
4. a statement containing the particulars of the total amount of indebtedness of the company in respect of charges which are to be registered with the Registrar.

The return should be filed within 60 days from the date of the annual general meeting. It should be signed by a director and the company secretary. If there is no company secretary, by a company secretary in practice.

REVIEW QUESTIONS

1. Who can be a member of the company?
   Distinguish between a member and a shareholder. How is membership terminated?
2. "Every shareholder of a company is also known as a member, while every member may not be known as a shareholder" Comment.
3. Discuss the capacity of the following to become a member of the company. (a) Minor; (b) Insolvent; (c) Foreigner; (d) Partnership firm; (e) Company,

4. What are the several ways in which a person can become a member of a company?

5. Write notes on:
   (a) Rights and liabilities of the members of a company;
   (b) Register of members;
   (c) Annual return

PRACTICAL PROBLEMS

Attempt the following problems, giving reasons:

1. P agreed that he would place 2000 shares for the company in consideration of being appointed as the branch manager. The company registered P as a holder of 2000 shares but did not inform of the fact. Is P a shareholder?

   Hint: No, as he had not agreed to take the shares.

2. An application was made by a father as a guardian of his minor son, P, for certain shares. The company issued shares to and registered shares in the name of P. The company went into liquidation and the name of the father was placed on the list of contributories. Is he liable?

   Hint: No, as the transaction with P is void.

30

Share Capital

The different expressions of share capital found in the capital structure of a company are generally known as kinds of share capital.

MEANING

In relation to a company limited by shares, the word 'capital' means the share capital. It is that part of the capital of the company which is raised or to be raised by way of issuing shares. The different expressions of share capital found in the capital structure of a company are generally known as kinds of share capital.

KINDS OF SHARE CAPITAL

The share capital of the company may be classified under the following heads:

(a) *Authorised, Registered or Nominal Capital* [Sec. 2(8)]: This is the sum stated in the memorandum as the capital of the company with which the company is proposed to be registered and the division thereof into shares of a fixed amount. It is the maximum amount of capital which the company will have during its life time unless it is raised.

Example: Authorised Capital ₹ 5,00,000.

(b) *Issued Capital* [2(50)]: It is that part of the authorised capital which the company needs for the time being and has been offered to the public for subscription.

Example: Issued Capital ₹ 3,00,000.

(c) *Subscribed Capital* [2(86)]: It is that part of the issued capital which has been subscribed or taken up by the public.

Example: Subscribed Capital ₹ 2,00,000.

(d) *Called up Capital* [2(15)]: It is that part of the subscribed capital which is called up or demanded by the company.

Example: If ₹ 5 has been called up on each of 20,000 shares of a nominal value of ₹ 10, the called up capital is ₹ 1,00,000.

The remaining portion of the subscribed capital which is not yet demanded by the company is called 'uncalled capital'.

(e) *Paid-up Capital* [2(64)]: It is the actual amount received by the company from its shareholders.

Example: Paid-up Capital ₹ 80,000.

If some shareholders fail to pay the call money, then the amount due from the defaulting shareholders is known as the calls in arrears.

Example: Calls in arrears ₹ 20,000.

6. *Reserve Capital:* It is that part of the uncalled capital of a company which can be called up only in the event of winding up. Reserve capital can be created only in accordance with Section 99. It cannot be turned into ordinary capital without the leave of the Court nor can it be cancelled.

Example: Out of ₹ 5 per share, uncalled capital of ₹ 2 per share is to be a reserve capital, viz., ₹ 60,000.

CLASSES OF CAPITAL

The share capital of a company is of two classes; namely; preference share capital and equity share capital.

Preference Share Capital

It is that part of the capital of the company which (a) carries a preferential right as to the payment of dividend at a fixed rate; (b) carries, on winding up, a preferential right as to the repayment of the paid-up capital.

Equity Share Capital

It means all the share capital which is not the preference share capital.

ALTERATION OF CAPITAL [SEC. 64]

A company limited by shares may, if authorised by its articles, alter its share capital in the following ways:

1. It may increase its capital by creating and issuing new shares.

2. It may consolidate the whole or any part of its share capital into shares of larger amounts.

3. It may convert fully paid up shares into stock or vice versa.

4. It may subdivide the whole or any part of its share capital into shares of smaller amounts.

5. It may cancel shares which have not been taken up and reduce the amount of its capital by the amount of the shares so cancelled.

The power of alteration must be exercised by the company in a general meeting by passing an ordinary resolution. No sanction or confirmation of the Central Government or the Court is required for this alteration. Within '30' days of alteration, notice should be given to the Registrar.

REDUCTION OF CAPITAL [SEC. 66]

Subject to confirmation by the Tribunal on an application by the company, a company may, if authorised by its articles, by a special resolution, reduce its share capital by:

(a) reducing or extinguishing the liability of members in respect of the uncalled or unpaid capital;

(b) paying off or returning paid-up capital which is in excess of the wants of the company;

(c) writing off or cancelling capital which has been lost or is unrepresented by the available assets.

Procedure for Reduction of Share capital

[Secs. 66(1) to 66(5)] Yet to be notified

1. *Special Resolution* [Sec.66(1)]: A company shall first pass a special resolution for reduction of capital. The power to reduce capital should be given in the Articles, it is not sufficient if the Memorandum alone makes a provision thereof. If the Articles do not contain any provision for reduction of capital, the Articles must be altered so as to give such a power.

> It may be noted that reduction of capital shall not be made if the company is in arrears in the repayment of any deposits accepted by it either before or after the commencement of this Act, or the interest payable thereon.

2. *Notice by Tribunal* [Sec. 66(2)]: The Tribunal shall give notice of every application made to it under sub-section (1) to:

(a) the Central Government

(b) the Registrar

(c) the Securities and Exchange Board, in the case of listed companies, and

(d) the creditors of the company

3. *Confirmation of Reduction of Capital* [Sec. 66(3)]: If the Tribunal is satisfied that the debt or claim of every creditor of the company has been discharged or determined or has been secured or his consent is obtained, it may make an order conforming the reduction of share capital on such terms and conditions as it deems fit.

> No application for reduction of share capital shall be sanctioned by the Tribunal unless the accounting treatment proposed by the company for such reduction is in conformity with the accounting standards specified in Sec. 133 and a certificate to that effect by the company's auditor has been filed with the Tribunal.

4. *Publication of the order* [Sec. 66(4)]: The order of confirmation of the reduction of share capital shall be published by the company in such a manner as the Tribunal may direct.

5. *Deliver a copy of order to Registrar* [Sec. 66(5)]: The company shall deliver a certified copy of the order of the Tribunal and of a minute approved by the Tribunal to the Registrar within thirty days of the receipt of the copy of the order. The Registrar, in turn, shall Register the same and issue a certificate to that effect.

Diminution of Share Capital is not a Reduction of Capital [Sec. 61(1)]

Diminution of capital is the cancellation of the unsubscribed part of the issued capital. It can be effected by an ordinary resolution, provided Articles of the company authorises to do so. As per Sec. 61(2), cancellation of shares under Sec. 61(1) shall not be deemed to be reduction of share capital. It does not need any confirmation of the Tribunal as per Sec. 66.

In the following cases, the diminution of share capital is not to be treated as reduction of the capital.

(a) If the company cancels shares which have not been taken or agreed to be taken by any person.

(b) If redeemable preference shares are redeemed as per the provisions of Sec. 55.

(c) If any shares are forfeited for non-payment of calls and such forfeiture amounts to reduction of capital.

(d) If the company buys-back its own shares under Sec. 68 of the Act (Yet to be enforced).

(e) If the reduction of share capital is effected in pursuance of the order of the Tribunal sanctioning any compromise or arrangement as per Sec. 230 (Yet to be notified).

In all the above cases, the procedure for reduction of capital as per Sec. 66 is not attracted.

REDUCTION OF CAPITAL WITHOUT THE CONSENT OF THE TRIBUNAL

The capital of the company may be reduced without the consent of the Tribunal:

(i) by forfeiting shares.

(ii) by accepting a surrender of shares under circumstances where forfeiture is justified.

(iii) by reducing redeemable preference shares.

(iv) by cancelling unissued shares.

LIABILITY OF MEMBERS AFTER REDUCTION

A member of the company cannot be held liable for an amount exceeding the difference between the amount deemed to have been paid on his shares and the nominal value of the reduced shares. However, in certain cases the liability of the members shall not be reduced even if there has been a reduction of capital. This will happen when a creditor entitled to object to the reduction has been left out of the list of such creditors and subsequently the company has become unable to pay its debts.

VARIATION OF SHAREHOLDERS RIGHTS [SEC. 48)

The rights attached to the shares of any class may be varied, subject to the fulfilment of the following conditions:

(i) There should be provision in the memorandum or articles of the company with regard to such a variation.

(ii) The written consent of the holders of not less than 3/4 of the issued shares of that class must be obtained or a special resolution should be passed at the separate meeting of the shareholders of the class affected.

The shareholders who do not approve of the variation (holders of at least 10% of the issued shares of that class affected) may apply to the Tribunal to cancel the variation. The application should be made within 21 days after the giving of the consent or the passing of the resolution. On such application being made, the variation shall not take effect unless and until it is confirmed by the Court. Within 30 days of the Tribunal's order, the company should send a copy of it to the Registrar. If default is made in complying with this provision, the company shall be punishable with fine of not less than twenty five thousand rupees and not more than five lakh rupees. Further every officer of the company who is in default shall be punishable with imprisonment for a term up to six months or with fine of not less than twenty five thousand rupees and not more than five lakh rupees or with both.

RE-ORGANISATION OF SHARE CAPITAL

A company may reorganise its share capital by the consolidation of shares of different classes, or by division of shares into different classes, or by both of these methods [Sec. 230].

Where a re-organisation of share capital is proposed (i) between a company and its creditors, or (ii) between a company and its members, the Tribunal may on the application of the company or of any creditor or member of the company, order a meeting of the creditors, or of the members. A majority in number representing 3/4ths in value of the creditors or members, who are present and voting in person or proxy, must also agree to the re-organisation of share capital. The scheme should also be sanctioned by the Tribunal [Sec 230].

FURTHER ISSUE OF CAPITAL [SEC. 62]

Sec. 62 provides pre-emptive rights to the holders of equity shares in case of further issue of shares. It is required that such further issue must be offered to the existing equity shareholders in proportion to the capital paid-up on these shares. Such shares are called "right shares".

Sec. 62 applies whenever the directors wish to increase the subscribed capital within the limit of the authorised capital by allotment of further shares after one year of the first allotment of shares or after two years from the formation of the company, whichever is earlier.

The object of this section is to ensure an equitable distribution of shares.

The holding of shares by each shareholder is not affected by the issue of new shares. (*Nanalal Zaver* v. *The Bombay Life Insurance Co., Ltd,* A.I.R. (1950) S.C. 172).

Sec. 81 provides the following conditions with regard to further allotment of shares:

(a) Such shares shall be offered to the existing holders of equity shares of the company in proportion to the capital paid-up on those shares.

(b) The offer should be made by notice specifying the number of shares offered and the time within which it shall be accepted. Such a time should be not less than 15 days and not more than 30 days from the date of the offer. The notice should also furnish that unless the offer is accepted within the specified time, it shall be deemed to have been declined.

(c) Unless otherwise provided in the articles, the offer is deemed to include a right to renounce all or any of the shares in favour of any other person and the notice should contain a statement of this right.

(d) After the expiration of the time specified in the notice or on receipt of earlier notice from the person declining to accept the shares, the Board of directors shall dispose of them in such a manner as they think most beneficial to the company.

(e) Further shares may be offered to outsiders in any manner irrespective of the existing equity shareholders: (i) if a special resolution is passed by the company in general meeting, or (ii) if an ordinary resolution is passed to that effect and the approval of the Central Government is obtained.

(f) These provisions do not apply to (i) a Private Company, or (ii) to allotment of shares on conversion of debentures, or loans into debentures, or creditors subscribing for shares in terms of the loan raised.

REVIEW QUESTIONS

1. Explain the various kinds of share capital. How is preference share capital distinguished from equity share capital?

2. Discuss the procedure for increasing and re-organising share capital of a company.

3. How and in what circumstances can a company reduce its share capital?

4. "Issue of further share capital should first be made to the existing shareholders". Discuss.

PRACTICAL PROBLEM

Attempt the following problem, giving reasons:

1. The articles of company A provided that the new shares should first be issued to the existing shareholders. B company held so many shares in A company that it could control the voting power. A company proposed to issue new shares to all shareholders except B company. Advise B company.

    Hint: B company can file a suit for injunction.

31

Shares

A share is "the interest of a shareholder in a definite portion of the capital".

MEANING

The capital of a company is usually divided into certain indivisible units of a definite sum. These units are called shares. Section 2(46) of the Act defines a share as "a share in the share capital of a company, and includes stock except where a distinction between stock and shares is expressed or implied". Shares represent the interest of a shareholder in a company measured in terms of money. It carries with it certain rights and liabilities, while the company is a going concern or, while it is being wound up. The share or other interest of any member in a company is a movable property (Sec. 44).

CLASSES OF SHARES

The Companies Act provides different classes of shares with varying rights as to dividends and voting rights, etc.

The following chart gives a clear picture of the classification of different kinds of shares.

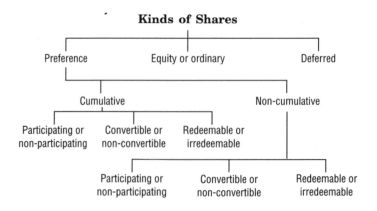

Kinds of Shares

A Private Company which is not a subsidiary of a Public Company may issue all or any of the above types of shares. But, a Public Company is allowed to issue only preference and equity shares.

Preference Shares

Preference shares are those shares which possess preferential rights in respect of dividend and repayment of capital in the event of the winding up of the company.

Equity or Ordinary Shares

Equity shares mean all shares which are not preference shares [Sec. 35(2)]. Thus, equity shares are those shares which do not satisfy the definition of the preference shares.

Equity shares carry the right to receive the whole of surplus profits after the preference shares, if any, have received their fixed dividend.

Deferred Shares or Founder's Shares

These are shares which are usually held by the promoters of the company. The holders of these shares are entitled to receive the entire profit remaining after the payment of dividends to other classes of shareholders. Deferred shares are not at all common nowadays. The Companies Act, 1956 prohibits the issue of such shares by Public Companies or deemed Public Companies or a Private Company which is a subsidiary of a Public Company. However, an independent Private Company is entitled to issue deferred shares. But, as per the provisions of the Companies Act, 2013 the private companies can issue only equity or preference shares.

KINDS OF PREFERENCE SHARES

A company may issue the following types of preference shares:

1. *Cumulative Preference Shares:* Cumulative preference shares are those shares which entitle the shareholders to demand the unpaid dividend in any year during the subsequent year or years when profits are ample and dividend is

KINDS OF PREFERENCE SHARES
1. Cumulative preference shares.
2. Non-cumulative preference shares.
3. Participating preference shares.
4. Non-participating preference shares.
5. Convertible preference shares.
6. Non-convertible preference shares.
7. Redeemable preference shares.
8. Irredeemable preference shares.

declared. All preference shares are considered cumulative unless otherwise mentioned. A fixed rate of dividend is guaranteed to such shares.

2. *Non-cumulative Preference Shares:*   Non-cumulative preference shares are those shares on which the dividend does not go on accumulating. In the case of such shares, a fixed rate of dividend is paid out of the profits of the company. If no profits are available in any year, the shareholders get nothing, nor can they claim unpaid fixed dividend in subsequent years.

3. *Participating Preference Shares:* Participating preference shares are shares which are not only entitled to a fixed preferential dividend but also to participate in the surplus profits alongwith equity shareholders. The right to participate may be given either in the memorandum or articles or in the terms of issue.

4. *Non-participating Preference Shares:*   Non-participating preference shares are shares which entitle the shareholder only the fixed preferential dividend and nothing more.

5. *Convertible Preference Shares:*   The holders of this type of shares have the option to convert them into equity shares within a certain period.

6. *Non-convertible Preference Shares:* These are the shares which cannot be converted into equity shares.

7. *Redeemable Preference Shares:*   These are the shares which are to be redeemed or refunded at the expiry of a determined period.

   A company can issue redeemable preference shares only if it is provided in the articles [Sec. 55]. Such shares are liable to be redeemed within a period not exceeding twenty years from the date of their issue. Furthermore, to redeem such shares, the proceeds of a fresh issue of shares or the Capital Redemption Reserve Fund must be used. The shares to be redeemed must be fully paid-up.

8. *Irredeemable Preference Shares:* Irredeemable preference shares are those shares which are repayable on winding up of the company only. Unless otherwise provided in the articles or in the terms of issue, all shares are irredeemable.

   Section 55 of the Companies Act, 2013 no company limited by shares shall, after the commencement of this Act, issue any preference shares which are irredeemable.

VOTING RIGHTS (SEC. 47)

An ordinary shareholder is entitled to vote on all matters affecting the company [Sec. 47(i) (a)]. His voting right on a poll shall be in proportion to his share of the paid-up equity capital [Sec. 47(i) (b)].

A preference shareholder has a right to vote on those resolutions which directly affect his rights, except when dividend has remained unpaid in which case he may vote on any resolution in respect of preference share capital [Sec. 47(2)]. The voting rights of the preference shareholders should be in the same proportions as the capital paid-up in respect of the preference shares that bears to the total equity capital of the company.

VARIATION OF SHAREHOLDERS RIGHTS (SEC. 48)

The rights of the holders of a class of shares may be varied with the written consent of the holders of not less than three fourths of the issued shares of that class. The variation of such rights can also be effected by a special resolution passed at a separate meeting if either the memorandum or the articles permit or the terms of issue of the shares or that class of shares do not prohibit.

SHARES NOT TO CARRY DISPROPORTIONATE RIGHTS (SEC. 47)

No company shall issue any equity shares carrying voting rights as to dividend, capital or otherwise which are disproportionate to the rights attaching to the holders of other shares (not being preference shares).

STOCK

Stock is really the shares of a company in a different form. It means "a bundle of fully-paid shares put together for convenience, so that it may be divided into any amount and transferred into any fractions without considering the original face value of the shares".

A company cannot issue stock originally. It is obtained only through conversion if shares are fully paid and the articles permit to do so. A company limited by shares can convert its fully paid-up shares into stock by passing an ordinary resolution. Stock may be converted into shares again by an ordinary resolution. Stockholders have the same right and privileges as the shareholders.

STOCK VS SHARE

1. Stock is always fully paid, while the share can be fully or partly paid-up.
2. Stock has no nominal value, whereas share has a nominal value.
3. Stock can be transferred in fractions, while the shares can be transferred only in multiples of one.
4. Stock does not possess a distinctive number, while each share possesses a distinctive number.
5. Stock cannot be issued directly to the public, whereas the shares can be issued directly.
6. Stock can be issued only by passing an ordinary resolution, while the shares can be issued without any resolution.

REVIEW QUESTIONS

1. Define 'share'. What are the different kinds of shares that a company may issue?
2. Define 'stock'. Distinguish between the stock and shares.
3. Write notes on:
   (a) Voting right;
   (b) Cumulative preference shares;
   (c) Deferred shares;
   (d) Variation of shareholders rights.

32

Application and Allotment of Shares

Application for share is "an offer by a prospective shareholder to take shares". Allotment is "an appropriation out of the previously unappropriated capital of a company".

Offer for shares are made on application forms supplied by the company. The allotment is the acceptance of that offer by the company. In other words, an allotment of shares is an appropriation by the Board of Directors of a company of a certain number of shares to a person in response to his application for shares.

Even though the allotment and its communication result in a contract between the company and the allottee; the allottee does not automatically become a member of the company. He will become a member when his name is placed on the register of members.

ALLOTMENT OF SHARES

Allotment is merely the act of allotting, distributing and appropriating shares of a company to particular persons. This is done either in response to applications or as per contracts already entered into with regard to them.

A valid allotment should be made as per the provisions of the Companies Act, 2013 and the Indian Contract Act, 1872.

General Principles Regarding Allotment

The following general principles should be observed with regard to allotment of shares:

    (i) *Allotment should be made by proper authority:* The authority for making allotment is specified in the Articles of the company. Usually, an allotment is made by a resolution of the Board of Directors.

    (ii) *Allotment should be made within a reasonable time:* Allotment should be made within the time specified in the application.

If no time is specified in the application, it should be made within a reasonable time. What is a reasonable time is a question of fact in each case. An applicant may refuse to take shares if the allotment is made after a long time.

(iii) *Allotment should be communicated:* Allotment should be properly communicated to the applicant in order to constitute a binding contract. The allotment may be communicated to the applicant either in writing or verbally. Generally, posting of allotment or allotment advice will be taken as a valid communication even though the letter is lost in transit.

(iv) *Allotment should be absolute and unconditional:* The allotment should be made on the same terms as stated in the application for shares. Further, allotment of shares subject to certain conditions is also not valid.

(v) *Allotment should be made against application only:* No valid allotment can be made on an oral request.

(vi) *Allotment should not be in contravention of any other law:* If shares are allotted on an application of a minor, the allotment will be void.

STATUTORY PROVISIONS REGARDING ALLOTMENT— COMPANIES ACT, 2013

A valid allotment has to comply with the requirements of the Act. These requirements are:

1. *Minimum Subscription:* No allotment must be made in respect of any shares offered to the public for subscription until the minimum subscription stated in the prospectus has been subscribed, and the amount payable on application has been received by cheque or other instrument by the company [Sec. 39(1)].

Minimum subscription is the minimum amount which must be raised by a company in the opinion of the directors by means of issue of shares to meet certain needs, namely, purchase price of any property to be defrayed partly or wholly out of the proceeds of the issue, preliminary expenses and working capital.

A company making any public issues of securities will allot the shares only if it has received a minimum of 90 per cent subscription against the entire issue.

Every listed public company, making initial public offer of any security for a sum of ₹ 10 crore or more, shall issue the same only in dematerialised form.

The provisions of Depositories Act, 1996 are to be complied with in the above case.

2. *Application Money:* The money payable on application for each share shall not be less than 5 per cent of the nominal value of the shares or amount as may be specfied by the SEBI [Sec. 39(2)].

All the money received from applicants for shares must be deposited and kept deposited in a scheduled bank until the certificate to commence business is obtained and if the certificate of commencement has been received until the entire amount payable on application for shares in respect of the minimum subscription has been received.

If the company does not receive the minimum subscription of 90 per cent of the issue amount and the sum payable on application is not received within a period of thirty days from the date of the issue of prospectus. The entire subscription will be refunded to the applicants within 15 days from the closure of the issue. If there is a delay in refund of such amount within such period the directors of the company who are officers in default shall jointly and severally liable to pay that money with interest at 15 per cent PA.

3. *Statement in Lieu of Prospectus:* Where prospectus has not been issued, no allotment shall be made unless at least three days before the first allotment of shares, a statement in lieu of prospectus has been filed with the Registrar.

4. *Effect of Irregular Allotment* [Sec. 71]: An allotment of shares is irregular when the company contravenes the provisions of Sec. 39. Such an allotment made by a company is voidable at the instance of the applicants of shares. This is so even if the company is being wound up.

The effects of irregular allotment are: (a) that it may be set aside within two months after the holding of the statutory meeting of the company; (b) that any director, who has the knowledge of the fact of the irregular allotment of shares is liable to compensate the company and the allottee for any loss or damage suffered thereby. Proceedings against the directors are to be commenced within two years of allotment.

5. *Opening of the Subscription List*: No allotment shall be made until the beginning of the 5th day from the date of the issue of the prospectus or on such later date as may be specified in the prospectus. This date is called "the opening of the subscription list".

6. *Shares to be Dealt in on Stock Exchange* [Sec. 40]: Every company issuing shares or debentures to the public by issue of

prospectus shall before such an issue make an application to one or more recognised stock exchanges for permission for enlistment of its shares or debentures. Thus, the Act has made an application to a stock exchange compulsory.

The Sub-section requires that the name of the stock exchange or exchanges to which an application for permission has been made to be specified in the prospectus itself. If any such stock exchange has not granted its permission, or has not disposed of the application within ten weeks, the allotment shall become void, even though some other exchanges have granted the permission. Where an appeal has been preferred under Sec. 22 of the Securities Contracts (Regulations) Act, 1956, against the refusal of a stock exchange, the allotment shall not be void until the dismissal of the appeal.

All monies received on application from the public for subscription to the securities shall be kept in a separate bank account in a scheduled bank. It shall not be utilised for any purpose other than specified in the Act.

Any condition purporting to require or bind any applicant for securities to waive compliance with any of the requirements of this Section shall be void.

If a default is made in complying with the provisions of this Section, the company shall be punishable with a fine of not less than five lakh rupees and not more than fifty lakh rupees. Further every officer of the company who is in default shall be punishable with imprisonment for a term of not more than one year or with fine of not less than fifty thousand rupees and not more than three lakh rupees, or with both.

A company may pay commission to any person in connection with the subscription to its securities subject to such conditions as may be prescribed.

OVER SUBSCRIBED PROSPECTUS

Where the permission of the stock exchange or exchanges for dealing in any shares or debentures has been obtained, and the sums received from the applicants are in excess of the aggregate of the application money relating to the shares or debentures in respect of which allotments have been made, the excess money received should be sent back to the applicants forthwith.

RETURN OF ALLOTMENT [SEC. 39]

A return of allotment in Form PAS-3 with specified fees must be filed with the Registrar within 30 days of the allotment whenever any

Limited company, public or private, allots shares. The return must contain: (a) particulars about the number and nominal amount of the shares allotted for cash, the names, addresses, and occupations of the allottees, and the amount paid on each share; (b) particulars about the shares (other than bonus shares) allotted as fully or partly paid up, for any consideration other than shares; (c) particulars about the number and nominal amount of bonus shares and their allottees;

REVIEW QUESTIONS

1. Define the term 'allotment of share'. What are the statutory provisions regarding the allotment of shares?
2. Write notes on:

   (a) Irregular allotment; (b) Return of allotment; (c) Minimum subscription; (d) Over subscribed prospectus
3. State general principles regarding allotment of shares.

33

Calls and Forfeiture of Shares

A call is "a demand by the company on its shareholders
to pay the whole or part of the balance remaining unpaid
on each share".
Forfeiture of shares means taking them away from the
member.

CALLS ON SHARES

A call is a demand made by the company on its shareholders to pay
the whole or part of the balance remaining unpaid on each share,
after the allotment of shares, at any time, during its life time. It is
usually made in pursuance of a resolution of the Board of Directors
and in accordance with the regulations of the articles. It may also
be made by the liquidator in the course of the winding up of the
company.

All the money payable by any member to the company under the
memorandum or articles is a debt due from him to the company.
But, he is not bound to pay until a valid call is made. Call is, thus,
an intimation to the shareholder to discharge his debt.

REQUISITES OF A VALID CALL

1. A call must be made in accordance with the provisions of
   the Companies Act and the articles of associations of the
   Company.

2. It must be made under a resolution of the Board of Directors
   [Sec. 179(3)(a)]. The calls resolution must specify the amount
   of the call, the date and place of the payment. The call is
   due on the date of the resolution, but its payment may not
   be legally enforceable until a proper notice has been given
   to the shareholders.

3. The power to make call is in the nature of a trust and to
   be exercised bona fide and for the benefit of the company.

4. The calls should be made on uniform basis on all shares falling under the same class [Sec. 49].

5. Calls may not be made until the company becomes entitled to commence business.

PAYMENT OF CALLS IN ADVANCE

The directors may, if authorised by the articles, allow shareholders to pay up the amount due on their shares before any call has been made [Sec. 50(1)]. The company may pay interest not exceeding the rate specified in the Articles without the sanction of the general meeting even out of capital in the case of insufficient profit. In winding up, the shareholder ranks after creditors in respect of the advance, but in priority to the other shareholders.

A member of the company limited by shares shall not be entitled to any voting rights in respect of the amount paid by him under Sub-section (1) until that amount has been called up.

LIEN ON SHARES

A lien is a form of security. It means right to retain possession of some property until some claim attaching to it is settled or discharged. Lien is not conferred on a company by the statute. The articles normally give the company a lien on the shares of a member for money owed by him to the company. This enables the company to secure and recover any debt due from a member. Where such power is given by the articles, the company may sell the shares on which it has lien for the recovery of a debt which is presently payable. By virtue of this lien, the company has a prior right over any creditor to whom they are given as security for loan.

FORFEITURE OF SHARES

Forfeiture of shares means confiscation of the shares of a shareholder by way of penalty in violation of the terms of contract. Shares cannot be forfeited unless authorised by the articles. It means that a company has no inherent power to forfeit shares.

RULES RELATING TO VALID FORFEITURE

1. Shares can be forfeited only against the non-payment of call due in respect of the shares.

2. Proper notice must be served on the defaulting shareholders requiring him to pay the money due on the call together with interest.

3. The notice must give at least 14 days time for payment from the date of its service and must also state that in the event of the non-payment within that date the shares will be liable for forfeiture.

4. If the member fails to comply with the notice, a formal resolution of forfeiture must be passed by the board of directors and a notice of the same is to be served on the defaulting shareholder (Article 30 of the Table F).

5. The power of forfeiture should be exercised bona fide and for the benefit of the company. Forfeited shares become the property of the company. To this extent forfeiture involves reduction of share capital, unless the shares are reissued. The company may sell the forfeited shares for any prices they fetch, i.e., the shares may be reissued at a discount.

A person, whose shares have been forfeited, ceases to be a member of the company. But, he continues to be liable for any money presently payable at the time of the forfeiture. The liability of such a person shall cease as and when the company receives payment in full in respect of the shares.

RE-ISSUE OF FORFEITED SHARES

Shares forfeited by a company may either be cancelled or re-issued to another person at the discretion of the Board. This is done by a Board resolution.

If the shares are re-issued at a price more than face value the excess of the proceeds of sale is not payable to the former owner, unless the Articles provide otherwise. The excess of the proceeds so retained shall constitute a premium and should, therefore, be transferred to the securities premium account.

SURRENDER OF SHARES

Surrender of shares, like forfeiture, is only lawful where the articles authorise it. It is a voluntary return of shares by the shareholder to the company for cancellation.

Surrender is lawful only in two cases: (a) As a short cut to forfeiture, to avoid the formalities for a valid forfeiture; and (b) where shares are surrendered in exchange for new shares of the same nominal value (but, with different rights).

Surrendered shares may be reissued in the same way as forfeited shares. If this is done no reduction in capital occurs.

The main distinction between the surrender and forfeiture is that the former is a voluntary act of the shareholder whereas, the latter is at the instance of the company. Moreover, the surrender of shares is not recognised by the Companies Act, whereas the forfeiture of shares is recognised by the Act. However, the final effect of both surrender and forfeiture is the termination of membership of a shareholder.

REVIEW QUESTIONS

1. What is meant by a 'call'. State the essentials of a valid call.
2. Write notes on:
   (a) Forfeiture of shares;
   (b) Surrender of shares;
   (c) Payment of calls in advance;
   (d) Lien on shares.
   (e) Re-issue of forfeited shares.

34

Share Certificate and Share Warrant

A share certificate is "a document certifying that the allottee is the holder of the specified number of shares in the company".
A share warrant is "a document issued under the common seal of the company stating that the bearer is entitled to the specified number of shares".

SHARE CERTIFICATE [SEC. 56]

Every person whose name is entered in the register of members is entitled to have from the company a document, called share certificate without payment, certifying that he is the holder of the specified number of shares in the company.

As per Sec. 56(4) of the Act, every company, (unless prohibited by any provision of law or any order of any Court, Tribunal or other authority) should deliver the certificates of all securities allotted, transferred or transmitted.

(a) Within a period of two months from the date of incorporation, in the case of subscribers to the Memorandum.

(b) Within a period of two months from the date of allotment, in the case of- any allotment of any of its shares;

(c) Within a period of one month from the date of receipt by the company of the instrument of transfer or, as the case may be, of the intimation of transmission, in the case of a transfer or transmission of securities;

(d) Within a period of six months from the date of allotment in the case of any allotment of debenture.

However, if the securities are dealt with in a depository, the company shall intimate the details of allotment of securities to depository immediately on allotment of such securities.

If any default is made in complying with the above provisions, the company shall be punishable with fine of not less than ₹25,000 and not more than ₹5 lakh. Further, every officer of the company who is in default shall be punishable with fine of not less than ₹10,000 and not more than ₹1 lakh [Sec. 56(6)].

Every certificate of share or shares shall be in Form No. SH.1 or as near thereto as possible.

A share certificate must be under the seal of the company. It must specify the shares to which it relates and the amount paid-up thereon. It should also state the name, address and occupation of the holder of the shares [Sec. 44].

EFFECT OF SHARE CERTIFICATE

A share certificate under the common seal of the company, specifying any shares held by any member shall be prima facie evidence of the title of the member to such shares [Sec. 46(1)]. It enables the shareholder to sell his shares by showing at once a marketable title. The company may, therefore, be estopped from disputing the title of the registered holder, or alleging that the amount stated as being paid on the share had not been paid.

DUPLICATE CERTIFICATE [SEC. 46(2)]

A share certificate should be kept in safe custody. A shareholder is not entitled to a duplicate certificate unless he proves that the original has been lost or destroyed or having been defaced or mutilated or torn, is surrendered to the company.

The particulars of every share certificate issued shall be entered forthwith in a Register of Renewed and Duplicate Share Certificate maintained in Form No. SH.2.

SPLIT CERTIFICATE

A split certificate is a separate certificate claimed by a shareholder for a portion of his holding.

The following are the advantages of a split certificate:

(a) The shareholder may benefit in the case of transfer by way of sale or mortgage in small lots.

(b) The right to multiply the certificates into as many shares held by the shareholder.

SHARE WARRANTS

A share warrant is a document issued by a public limited company under its common seal stating that the bearer is entitled to the shares specified therein. It is a negotiable instrument. As it is a bearer instrument it is transferable by mere delivery.

Share warrants should state the number of shares in respect of which they have been issued. When it is issued, the name of the shareholder is removed from the Register of members. So the warrant holder is not a member of the company. Usually, dividend coupons are attached to the share warrants to facilitate the warrant holders to collect dividends.

The conditions for the issue of share warrants are as follows:

(a) The shares must be fully paid up;

(b) Only public limited company can issue share warrants;

(c) The articles must authorise the issue;

(d) Approval of the Central Government should be obtained.

DISTINCTION BETWEEN SHARE WARRANTS AND SHARE CERTIFICATES

1. A share warrant is a negotiable instrument, but a share certificate is not.

2. A share warrant can be issued only in respect of fully paid-up shares, while a share certificate can be issued in respect of the partly or fully paid-up shares.

3. Holders of the share warrant are not members of the company, whereas the holders of the share certificate are members of the company.

4. A share warrant is issued only by a public company, while a share certificate can be issued both by a public and a private company.

5. Share warrant holders do not enjoy voting rights but share certificate holders enjoy voting rights.

6. Prior sanction of the Central Government is required to issue share warrants but no Government sanction is required to issue a share certificate.

REVIEW QUESTIONS

1. What is share certificate? What is the object and effect of the share certificate?

2. Define 'share warrant'. Distinguish between a share certificate and a share warrant.

3. Write notes on:
   (a) Duplicate certificate
   (b) Split certificate
   (c) Share warrant

35

Transfer and Transmission of Shares

Transfer of shares means "the voluntary conveyance of the right and duties of a member from a person who holds the shares but wishes to cease to be a member to a person who wishes to become a member".

Transmission of shares means "transfer of party (ownership) in shares by operation of law".

A TRANSFER OF SHARES

The shares of a company are movable property and can be transferred by the shareholders in the manner prescribed by the Articles (Sec. 44). It does not mean that the shares can be transferred by mere delivery as in the case of movable property, e.g., furniture. But, members of a company have an inherent right to transfer shares in the manner prescribed in the Act and the Articles which may impose fetters upon the right of transfer. A transfer of shares in the present context, takes place where the registered shareholder transfers, by sale or otherwise his shares to another person voluntarily.

PROVISIONS OF THE ACT RELATING TO TRANSFER

1. *Instrument of Transfer* [Sec. 56(1)]: A share is transferable by executing a duly stamped instrument of transfer both by the transferor and the transferee. The instrument of transfer should specify the name, address and occupation, if any, of the transferee. It should be delivered to the company along with the certificate relating to the shares transferred, or in case no such certificate is in existence, along with the letter of allotment of shares. No instrument of transfer is required in the case of transmission of shares [Sec. 56(2)].

The instrument of transfer should be in a prescribed form (Form No. SH.4). It should be submitted to the prescribed authority (viz., the Registrar) before it is signed by or on behalf of the transferor and before any entry is made in it. The prescribed authority shall stamp or otherwise endorse on the instrument the date on which it is so presented. The instrument of transfer duly completed in all respects should then be presented to the company for registration. Presentment to the company should be made within a period of sixty days from date of execution along with the certificate relating to the securities if no such certificate is in existence, then along with the related letter of allotment of securities. In any other case the presentment should be made within two months from the date of presentation to the prescribed authority. Any instrument of transfer which contravenes these provisions shall not be accepted.

2. *Transfer by Legal Representatives* [Sec. 56(5)]: Although, the legal representative of a deceased member is not himself a member, a transfer executed by him is as valid as the one executed by the member himself.

3. *Application for Transfer:* An application for registration of transfer may be made either by transferor or by the transferee. Where the application has been made by the transferor and relates to partly paid shares, the transfer shall not be registered unless the company gives notice of the application to the transferee and the latter raises no objection to the transfer within two weeks from the receipt of the notice. But, no such notice is to be served when the application for transfer has been made by the transferee himself. The transferee becomes a member of the company only when the transfer is registered by the company. When this is done, a new share certificate or the old certificate duly endorsed in the name of the transferee is issued to the transferee.

4. *Refusal by the Company to Register Transfer* (Sec. 58): The right of the holder of securities to transfer his securities in a company is absolute as it is inherent in the ownership of the securities.

If a private company limited by shares refuses to register the transfer or transmission, the transferee may appeal to the Tribunal against the refusal within 30 days from the date of receipt of the notice. If no notice has been sent by the company, such an appeal may be preferred within 60 days from the date on which the instrument of transfer or the intimation of transmission (as the case may be) was delivered to the company [Sec. 58(3)].

If a public company without sufficient cause refuses to register the transfer or transmission, the transferee may appeal to the Tribunal against the refusal within 60 days from the date of receipt of the notice. If no notice has been sent by the company, such an appeal may be preferred within 90 days from the date on which the instrument of transfer or the intimation of transmission (as the case may be) was delivered to the company [Sec. 58(4)].

The Tribunal, while dealing with an appeal made as stated above, after hearing the parties, either dismiss the appeal, or by order:

(a)   direct that the transfer or transmission shall be registered by the company and the company shall comply with such order within 10 days of the receipt of the order, or

(b)   direct rectification of the register and also direct the company to pay damages, if any, sustained by any party aggrieved [Sec. 58(5)].

If a person contravenes the order of the Tribunal, he shall be punishable with imprisonment for a term of not less than one year and not more than three years and with fine of not less than one lakh rupees and not more than five lakh rupees [Sec. 58(6)].

POWER OF DIRECTORS TO REJECT TRANSFER

The power of directors to refuse transfer may be brought under two heads:

(a)   Where the Articles contain no clause allowing the directors to reject the transfer:

In this case, shares may freely be transferred by a shareholder. He may also compel the directors to register the transfer.

(b)   Where the Articles contain a clause allowing the directors to reject the transfer:

The Articles usually provide a clause empowering the directors to refuse transfer of shares without assigning reasons. But, even in such a case, the rejection must be in the interest of the company and subject to Sec. 22A(33) of the Securities Contracts (Regulation) Act, 1956.

In the following circumstances, however, the Company Law Board may rescind the decision of the directors in refusing to register the transfer:

(i)   *Mala Fide:*   Where it is proved that the directors have not acted bona fide and in the interest of the company.

(ii)   *Inadequacy of Reasons:*   Where it is found that the reasons given by the directors for refusing the transfer are insufficient.

(iii)   *Irrelevant Considerations:*   A refusal based on extraneous consideration will be wrong.

PROVISIONS OF SEC. 22A OF SECURITIES CONTRACTS (REGULATION) ACT, 1956

Sec. 22A has been inserted in the Securities Contracts (Regulation) Act, 1956 by the Securities Contracts (Regulation) Amendment Act, 1985 which came into force on January 17, 1986.

As per Sec. 22A(3) a company may refuse to register the transfer of shares on any one or more of the following grounds and on no other grounds:

   (i) If there are defects and deficiencies in the transfer deed.

  (ii) The transfer of shares is in contravention of any law.

 (iii) The transfer of shares is likely to result in such a change in the composition of the Board of Directors as would be prejudicial to the interests of the company or to the public interest.

 (iv) The transfer of shares is prohibited by any order of any Court, Tribunal or other authority under any law for the time being in force.

CERTIFICATION OF TRANSFER

Certification of transfer is required when there is a part disposal of shares or there are multiple purchasers. It is "an act of endorsement on the instrument of transfer by an officer of the company that the share certificate relating to the shares to be transferred has been pledged with the company".

After certification, the company will register the transferee as the holder of shares sold to him, cancel the old certificate and prepare two certificates, one for the shares sold which will be given the transferee and the other for the unsold shares which will be handed over to the transferor.

FORGED TRANSFER

When an instrument of transfer bears a forged signature of the transferor, it is called forged transfer. A forged transfer is nullity, even if it may have been registered by the company.

BLANK TRANSFER

Blank transfer is a transfer whereby the transferor hands over to the transferee the share certificate and a blank transfer deed. In a blank transfer, the transfer deed contains neither the transferee's name and signature nor the date of sale.

The advantage in giving a blank deed is that the buyer will be at liberty to sell it again without filling his name and signature to a subsequent buyer. It is used to avoid taxes and to conceal the identity of the real owner. The process of buying and selling can be repeated any number of times with blank deed and ultimately when it reaches in the hands of one who wants to retain the shares, he can fill in his name and date and get it registered in the company's books.

TRANSMISSION OF SHARES

Transmission of shares means the transfer of property or title in the shares by operation of law. It takes place on the death or bankruptcy of a member or if the member is a limited company, on its going into liquidation.

The legal representatives of the deceased member can transfer the shares to another person, without getting themselves registered as members. No instrument of transfer is required in the case of transmission of shares. The person to whom the shares are transmitted should make an application to the company for the transmission of shares in his name.

DISTINCTION BETWEEN TRANSFER AND TRANSMISSION OF SHARES

1. Transfer of shares is effected by the act of the parties whereas transmission of shares occurs by operation of law.
2. In the case of transfer of shares, an instrument of transfer is necessary whereas no instrument of transfer is required in the case of transmission of shares.
3. Shares are generally transferred for consideration. But, in the case of transmission there is no such consideration.
4. If there is a lien on shares, it will subsist even if the transmission of shares has occurred. But, the company loses the right of lien when there is a transfer of shares.

ISSUES OF SHARES AT A PREMIUM [SEC. 52]

A company can issue its shares at a premium, i.e., for a value higher than the face value of the shares, in accordance with the provisions of the articles. But, the Act clearly provides that the premium so received shall have to be transferred by the company to the 'share premium account'. The Share Premium Account may be applied by the company only for any of the following purposes:

(a) to issue to the members fully paid-up bonus shares;

(b) to write-off preliminary expenses;

(c) to provide for the premium payable on the redemption of preference shares or debentures of the company;

(d) to write-off expenses, commission or discount on the issue of shares or debentures of the company.

PROHIBITION ON ISSUE OF SHARES AT DISCOUNT (SEC. 53)

1. A company shall not issue shares at a discount except as provided in Sec. 54.

2. Any share issued by a company at a discount price shall be void.

3. If a company contravenes the provisions of this Section the company shall be punishable with fine of not less than one lakh rupees and not more than five lakh rupees. Further every officer who is in default shall be punishable with imprisonment for a term up to six months or with fine of not less than one lakh rupees and not more than five lakh rupees or with both.

SWEAT EQUITY SHARES

Sweat equity shares mean equity shares issued by a company to its directors or employees at a discount or for consideration, other than cash for providing know-how or value additions [Sec. 2(88)].

1. As per Sec. 54, a company may issue sweat equity shares of a class of shares already issued, if the following conditions are fulfilled:

   (a) The issue is authorised by a special resolution passed by the company.

   (b) The resolution specifies the number of shares, the current market price, consideration, if any, and the class or classes of directors or employees to whom such equity shares are to be issued.

   (c) Not less than one year has at the date of such issue, elapsed since the date on which the company has commenced business.

(d) If the equity shares of the company are listed on a recognised stock exchange, sweat equity shares are issued as per the regulations made by the SEBI in this behalf. On the other hand, if they are not listed, the sweat equity shares are issued as per such rules as may be prescribed.

2. The rights, limitations, restrictions and provisions as are for the time being applicable to equity shares shall be applicable to the sweat equity shares issued under this Section.

The holders of such shares shall rank pari passu with equity shareholders.

EMPLOYEE STOCK OPTION (ESOP)

'Employees Stock Option' means the option given to the directors, officers or employees of a company or of its holding company or subsidiary company or companies, if any, which gives such directors, officers, or employees, the benefit or right to purchase, or to subscribe for, the shares of the company at a future date at a pre-determined price.

Rule 12 of Companies (Share Capital and Debentures) Rules, 2014

1. Rule 12(1) states that the issue of Employees Stock Option Scheme, has been approved by the shareholders of the company by passing a special resolution.

2. Rule 12(2) states that the company shall make the following disclosures in the explanatory statement annexed to the notice for passing of the resolution:

   (a) total number of stock options to be granted;

   (b) identification of classes of employees entitled to participate in the Employees Stock Option Scheme;

   (c) the appraisal process for determining the eligibility of employees to the Employees Stock Option Scheme;

   (d) the requirements of vesting and period of vesting;

   (e) the maximum period within which the options shall be vested;

   (f) the exercise price or the formula for arriving at the same;

   (g) the exercise period and process of exercise;

   (h) the Lock-in period, if any;

    (i) the maximum number of options to be granted per employee and in aggregate;

    (j) the method at which the company shall use to value its options;

    (k) the conditions under which option vested in employees may lapse, e.g. in the case of termination of employment for misconduct;

    (l) the specified time period within which the employee shall exercise the vested options in the event of a proposed termination of employment or resignation of employee; and

    (m) a statement to the effect that the company shall comply with the applicable accounting standards.

Rule 12(3) states that the companies granting option to its employees pursuant to Employees Stock Option Scheme will have the freedom to determine the exercise price in conformity with the applicable accounting policies, if any.

Rule 12(4) states that the approval of shareholders by way of separate resolution shall be obtained by the company in the case of:

    (a) grant of option to employees of subsidiary or holding company; or

    (b) grant of option to identified employees; during any one year, equal to or exceeding one per cent of the issued capital of the company at the time of grant of option.

Rule 12(5)(a) states that the company may by special resolution, vary the terms of Employees Stock Option Scheme not yet exercised by the employees provided such variation is not prejudicial to the interests of the option holders.

Rule 12(6)(a) states that there shall be a minimum period of one year between the grant of option and vesting of option.

Rule 12(6)(b) states that the company shall have the freedom to specify the lock-in period for the shares issued pursuant to exercise of option.

Rule 12(6)(c) states that the Employees shall not have right to receive any dividend or to vote or in any manner enjoy the benefits of a shareholder in respect of option granted to them, till shares are issued on exercise of option.

Rule 12(7) states that the amount, if any payable by the employees, at the time of grant of option:

    (a) may be forfeited by the company if the option is not exercised by the employees within the exercise period; or

(b) the amount may be refunded to the employees if the options are not vested due to non-fulfilment of conditions relating to vesting of option as per the Employees Stock Option Scheme.

Rule 12(8) states the following conditions:

(a) The option granted to employees shall not be transferable to any other person.

(b) The option granted to the employees shall not be pledged, hypothecated, mortgaged or otherwise encumbered or alienated in any other manner.

(c) No person other than the employees to whom the option is granted shall be entitled to exercise the option.

Rule 12(8) states that in the event of the death of employee while in employment, all the options granted to him till such date shall vest in the legal heirs or nominees of the deceased employee.

Rule 12(9) states that the Board of Directors, shall, inter alia, disclose in the Directors Report for the year all the details of the Employees Stock Option Scheme.

Rule 12(10) states that the company shall maintain a Register of Employee Stock Options in Form No. SH.6.

PURCHASE BY THE COMPANY OF ITS OWN SHARES [SEC. 67]

Sec. 67 provides that no company having a share capital can buy or subscribe its own shares unless the consequent reduction of capital is effected and sanctioned in pursuance of the provisions of the Companies Act. Further no public company can be given any financial assistance in any shape towards the purchase of its own shares or of its holding company except in the following cases:

(a) Where a loan is made by a banking company in the ordinary course of its business.

(b) Where the provisions of money is made in accordance with a scheme, to enable the trustees to purchase fully paid shares in the company to be held for the benefit of the employees of the company.

(c) Where the company wants to redeem its own redeemable preference shares issued under this Act or under any previous company law.

(d) Where loans are made by a company to the employees to enable them to subscribe or purchase the company's share to be held as beneficial owners. The amount of loans cannot exceed the amount of wages or salaries of an employee for six months.

REVIEW QUESTIONS

1. Define the term transfer of shares. Outline the procedure of transfer of shares.

2. Under what circumstances can a company refuse to register a transfer of share? What is the remedy of an aggrieved party when the transfer of shares is wrongly refused by the company?

3. Define "transmission of shares". Distinguish between transfer and transmission of shares.

4. Write notes on:

   (a) Certification of transfer; (b) Blank transfer; (c) Forged transfer; (d) Issue of shares at a premium; (e) Purchase by the company of its own shares.

5. Mention rules relating to Employees Stock Option Scheme.

6. State the provisions under the Companies Act, 2013 relating to the issue of sweat equity shares.

PRACTICAL PROBLEMS

Attempt the following problems, giving reasons:

1. P purchases 5000 shares from Q in a company on the faith of a share certificate issued by the company. P tenders to the company a transfer form from Q to himself duly executed together with the share certificate of Q. The company finds that the certificate in the name of Q has been fraudulently obtained and refused to register the transfer. Is P entitled to get registration of the transfer?

   Hint: No. P can however, claim compensation from the company at the market price of shares,

2. A company was authorised by its articles to purchase its own shares. P sold his shares to the company and before the price was paid, the company went into liquidation. Is P entitled to prove in the liquidation for the price of the shares?

   Hint: No. Sec. 67.

36

Borrowing Powers

Every corporation, unless restricted by its Act of incorporation, has the same power as an individual to enter into contracts, including that of borrowing money. [The Queen v. Charles Reed (1880) 3 Q.B.D. 483].

POWER OF COMPANY TO BORROW

The Companies Act does not contain any provision empowering companies to borrow money. The power of a company to borrow money for carrying on its business is implied in the case of all trading companies. Non-trading companies require express power to borrow. This power, in the case of such a company, should be taken in the memorandum or the articles. A power to borrow, whether express or implied includes the power to charge the assets of the company by way of security to the lender.

A public company can exercise its borrowing powers only after obtaining the certificate of commencement of business. But a private company can exercise its borrowing powers immediately after obtaining the certificate of incorporation.

The power of a company to borrow is exercised by the directors. But, this power is subject to the following limitations:

1. The directors of a Public Company or a Private Company being a subsidiary of a Public Company shall not borrow money exceeding the aggregate of the paid-up capital of the company and its free reserves, except with the consent of the company in general meeting [Sec. 180(1)(c)].
2. Limitations as stated in the memorandum or articles.

ULTRA VIRES BORROWING

Borrowing by a company may be borrowing which is: (1) ultra vires the company, or (2) ultra vires the directors.

1. Ultra Vires the Company

If a company borrows without or in excess of the powers conferred on it by the memorandum, the borrowing is ultra vires the company. Any act which is ultra vires the company is void and as such, any borrowings which are ultra vires the company are also void.

Lender's Right: If the borrowing is ultra vires the company, the lender cannot sue the company for the return of the loan. The securities given for such ultra vires borrowing are also void and inoperative.

In *Sinclair* v. *Broughman* (1914) A.C. 398, it was held that even subsequent power to borrow and subsequent issue of securities shall not make ultra vires loans binding on the company.

The lender has, however, in equity, the following rights:

(a) *Injunction:* If a lender intervenes before the money has been spent, he may obtain an injunction to restrain the company from parting with the money.

(b) *Subrogation:* If the money borrowed has been used by the company in paying off its lawful debts, then the second creditor (lender) steps into the shoes of the creditor paid off, and to that extent shall have the right to recover its loan from the company

Example: A building society borrowed money, ultra vires, to pay off principal and interest due or, mortgage. It was held that the lenders were subrogated to the rights of the creditors paid off. [*Neath Building Society* v. *Luce* (1889) 43 ch. D. 158].

(c) *Identification and Tracing:* If the lender can identify his money or other property purchased with it, he can obtain a tracing order and follow the property. But, when the lenders money and that of the company have become mixed up, his only remedy is to stand pari passu amongst other depositors and shareholders, proportionately.

(d) *Recovery of Damages:* The directors shall be liable for damages to the lender for the breach of the implied warranty of authority, unless the fact that the borrowing was ultra vires could have been discovered from the memorandum and articles.

2. Ultra Vires the Directors

Any borrowing which is ultra vires the company, but beyond the authority of the directors, is ultra vires the directors.

Borrowings which are beyond the authority of directors, but intra vires the company, are irregular and securities given by the directors are inoperative. However, the company may elect to ratify the directors act and in this case the loan shall be binding on the company. If the company refuses to ratify the director's act, the lender can rely on the rule in *Royal British Bank* v. *Turquand* and recover the amount of loan from the company. The company may, in turn proceed against the directors and claim indemnity.

FIXED AND FLOATING CHARGES

The power of a company to borrow includes the power to create a charge on its assets. The charge on the assets of the company may be a fixed charge or a floating charge.

Fixed Charge

A fixed or specific charge is a charge on definite or specific property of a permanent nature, e.g., land or heavy machinery. It prevents the company from dealing in that property without the consent of the holder of the charge. In the winding up of a company, a debentureholder secured by a specific charge is in the highest ranking class of creditors, namely, in that of secured creditors.

Floating Charge

A floating charge is one which is not attached to a definite property, but covers property of a fluctuating type, e.g., stock-in-trade. In other words, it is an equitable charge on the assets for the time being of a going concern. In a floating charge the property can be dealt with by the company without consulting the holders of the charge. The company is left free to deal with the property so charged as if no charge has been created.

Characteristics of a Floating Charge

1. It is a charge on a class of assets, present and future.
2. The class is one which in the ordinary course of business, is changing from time to time.
3. Until some steps are taken to enforce the charge, the company may carry on its business in the usual way.

CRYSTALLISATION OF A FLOATING CHARGE

Crystallisation is the conversion of a floating charge into a fixed charge. A floating charge crystallises and becomes fixed in the following cases:

1. When the company goes into liquidation, or
2. When the company ceases to carry on business, or
3. When the debentureholders take steps to enforce their security, e.g., by appointing a receiver.

EFFECT OF WINDING UP ON FLOATING CHARGE [SEC. 332]

A floating charge on the undertaking or property of the company created within 12 months immediately preceding the commencement of the winding up is void unless:

(i) the company was solvent immediately after the charge was created; and

(ii) the amount was paid to the company in cash at the time of or subsequently to the creation of, and in consideration for, the charge together with interest at 5 per cent per annum or the rate prescribed by the Central Government.

The purpose of this Section is to prevent the insolvent companies from creating any floating charge on their assets in order to secure past debts to the prejudice of the unsecured creditors.

REGISTRATION OF CHARGES [SEC. 77]

When a company creates a charge over its property, Sec. 77 requires that charge to be registered with the Registrar of Companies. The charges, which must be registered, are:

(a) A charge for the purpose of securing any issue of debentures;

(b) A charge on uncalled share capital of the company;

(c) A charge on any immovable property, wherever situated, or any interest therein;

(d) A charge on any book debts of the company;

(e) A charge, not being a pledge, on any movable property of the company;

(f) A floating charge on the undertaking or any property of the company including stock-in-trade;

(g) A charge on calls made, but not paid;

(h) A charge on a ship or any share in a ship; and

(i) A charge on goodwill, on a patent or a licence under a patent, on a trade mark, or on a copyright or a licence under a copyright.

Effects of Non-registration of a Charge

Where a charge which requires registration is not registered within 30 days from its creation, the consequences are as follows:

1. The charge is void against the liquidator and any creditor of the company [Sec. 77(1)].
2. The debt in respect of which the charge was created remains valid an unsecured debt and the charge holder becomes an unsecured creditor [Sec. 77(2)].
3. All the money secured by charge becomes immediately payable [Sec. 77(3)].

DATE OF NOTICE OF CHARGE [SEC. 80]

If a charge is registered, any person acquiring such a property is deemed to have acquired the same with notice of the charge. Such a notice is from the date of registration of the charge with the Registrar.

Acquisition of Property Subject to a Charge [Sec. 79]

If a company acquires any property which is subject to a charge, registrable in accordance with Sec. 177, the company has to file with the Registrar particulars of such a charge within 30 days of its acquisition.

CERTIFICATE OF REGISTRATION [SEC. 77]

The Registrar shall give a certificate of registration furnishing the amount secured by the charge. The certificate is a conclusive evidence that the legal requirements have been complied with [Sec. 77]. The certificate is also a conclusive even if some particulars of the property charged as entered in the register are discovered to be incorrect.

COMPANY'S REGISTER OF CHARGES [SEC. 85]

Every company shall keep at its registered office a register of charges. It shall enter therein all charges specifically affecting property of the company and all floating charges of the undertaking of any other property of the company, giving in each case:

(a) a short description of the property charged;

(b) the amount of the charge; and

(c) the names of the persons entitled to the charge.

PUNISHMENT FOR CONTRAVENTION [SEC. 86]

If any company contravenes any provision of this chapter, the company shall be punishable with fine of not less than one lakh rupees and not more than ten lakh rupees. Further, every officer of the company who is in default shall be punishable with imprisonment for a term up to six months or with fine of not less than twenty five thousand rupees and not more than one lakh rupees, or with both.

DEBENTURES

The word 'debenture' signifies any instrument under seal evidencing a deed, the essence of it being the admission of indebtedness. (Palmer).

Meaning

Debenture is a certificate issued by a company under its seal acknowledging a debt by it to its holders. Sec. 2(30) of the Companies Act defines "debenture as including debenture stock, bonds and any other securities of a company, whether constituting a charge on the assets of the company or not".

Kinds of Debentures

Debentures are classified into the following categories:

1. *Registered Debentures:* The names of such debentureholders are found in the register of debentureholders of the company. These debentures are not negotiable instruments.

2. *Bearer or Unregistered Debentures:* Bearer debentures are those debentures which are payable to bearer. Such debentures are negotiable instruments, transferable by mere delivery free from equities.

3. *Secured Debentures:* Secured debentures are those which are secured by some charge on the property of the company. The charge may be fixed or floating.

4. *Unsecured or Naked Debentures:* These are debentures which are not secured by any charge on the assets of the company. These are like unsecured creditors.

5. *Redeemable Debentures:* These are debentures which are usually issued on the condition that they shall be redeemed on a specified date or on demand.

6. *Irredeemable Debentures:* Irredeemable or perpetual debenture is one which contains no clause as to the payment or which contains a clause that it shall not be paid back.

7. *Convertible Debentures:* These are debentures which give an option to the debenturebolders to convert them into preference or equity shares at a stated rate of exchange.

Debenture and Debenture Stock

A debenture is a document acknowledging a particular debt but a debenture stock is a borrowed money consolidated into one mass for the sake of convenience. The distinction between debentures and debenture stock is the same as the distinction between shares and stock.

Debentures with Pari Passu Clause

The term Pari Passu means equal as regards charge and repayment. Debentures are usually issued in a series with Pari Passu clause. In such a case, they are to be discharged ratably, though issued at different and varying times.

In the absence of a Pari Passu clause, the debentures would be payable in accordance with the date of issue and if they are issued on the same date, according to the consecutive numbers.

REVIEW QUESTIONS

1. Discuss the borrowing powers of a company.

2. What do you understand by ultra vires borrowing? What remedies are available to a lender if the borrowing is ultra vires the company?

3. Distinguish a 'floating charge from a fixed charge'. In what events does it crystallise?

4. Mention the 'charges' which require registration under the Companies Act. Explain the effects of non-registration of such charges.

5. What are the different kinds of debentures? What is the effect of pari passu clause in the repayment of debentures?

PRACTICAL PROBLEMS

Attempt the following problems, giving reasons:

1. The articles of a company provide that the managing director may with the previous permission of the Board borrow money up to rupees five lakh. The managing director with the permission of a board borrows six lakh and misappropriates it. Can the creditor sue the company for the recovery of the loan?

   Hint: No, as the borrowing is ultra vires the company.

2. A company charged all its machinery, stock-in-trades and movable goods. Discuss the nature of the charge.

   Hint: Floating charge.

37

Directors

The Board of Directors are the brain and the only brain of the company which is the body and the company can and does act only through them.   *(Nevile J.)*

INTRODUCTION

Having no physical shape and form, a company should act through some human agency. The persons, through whom a company acts are known as directors, collectively termed as the Board of Directors or the Board. Between the two organs of the company, namely the board of directors and the members in general meeting, the former occupies pre-eminently a higher position.

LEGAL POSITION OF THE DIRECTORS

The Companies Act does not make any effort to define the position of directors. According to Sec. 2(34) of the Companies Act, 2013, 'director' means a director appointed to the Board of a company. The articles of a company may therefore designate its directors as governors, council, managing committees, etc.

In the words of Bowen, L.J. (*Imperial Hydropathic Co.* v. *Hamson* (1882), 23 Ch. 1).

"Directors are described sometimes as agents, sometimes as trustees and sometimes as managing partners. But each of these expressions is used not as exhaustive of their powers and responsibilities, but as indicating useful points of view from which they may for the moment and for the particular purpose, be considered".

Directors as Agents

The directors in the eyes of law are agent of the company, and the ordinary rules of agency are applicable to them. "Whenever an agent is liable those directors would be liable; where the liability would attach to the principal and the principal only, the liability is the liability of the company". Hence, in respect of the transactions entered into by the directors in the name of the company, or on its behalf, it is the company as the principal which is liable and not the directors.

Directors as Employees

Directors, as such are not employees of the company, but there is no legal bar for a director to hold a salaried office or employment in the company. Mc Cardie points out that "a director is in fact a director or controller of the company's affairs. He is not a servant".

Director as Trustees

In *York and North Midland Railway* v. *Hudson, Romilly M.R.* points out that the directors are trustees of the company's properties. They are persons selected to manage the affairs of the company for the benefit of the shareholders. It is an office of trust, which if they undertake, it is their duty to perform fully and entirely.

Directors are not trustees in the true sense of the term. A trustee is the legal owner of the property which he holds in trust for a beneficiary, a director does not hold any property in trust for the company; the company itself is the legal owner. Further, a trustee contracts in his own name; but a director contracts in the name of the company.

Jessel, M.R. in *Re: Forest of Dean Coal Mining Co.* (1878), observes that "directors are commercial men managing a trading concern for the benefit of themselves and of all the shareholders in it. They stand in a fiduciary position towards the company in respect of their powers and capital under their control".

NUMBER OF DIRECTORS (SEC.149)

Every Public Company shall have at least three directors and every Private Company shall have at least two directors and One Person Company shall have one director.

The maximum number of directors that a company can have shall not exceed fifteen. Based on this Statutory limit, the Articles may specify minimum and maximum number of directors for its board of directors. Section 149 permits that the number of directors may be increased to more than fifteen, by passing a special resolution in an annual general meeting. This Section also insists that such class or classes of companies (as may be prescribed) shall have at least one woman director.

APPOINTMENT OF DIRECTORS

1. First Directors (Sec. 152)

The first directors of the company are appointed usually by the Articles.

If no such directors are appointed by the Articles, the subscribers to the Memorandum who are individuals, shall be deemed to be the first directors of the company. They hold office until directors are duly appointed in the annual general meeting.

2. Subsequent Appointment of Directors by Members (Sec. 152)

Section 152 lays down that directors should be appointed in annual general meeting. The following are the statutory provisions relating to the appointment of directors:

(i) A person to be appointed as a director of a company shall have the Director Identification Number allotted by the Central Government.

(ii) Every person, proposed to be appointed as a director shall furnish his Director Identification Number and a declaration that he is not disqualified to become a director under this Act.

(iii) A person appointed as a director shall provide his consent to hold the office as a director. Further this consent should be filed with the Registrar within thirty days of his appointment.

(iv) Every company shall have at least one director who has stayed in India for a total period of not less than one hundred and eighty two days in the previous calendar year.

(v) Every listed Public Company shall have at least One-third of the Board strength as independent directors.

(vi) In the case of appointment of independent director in the general meeting, an explanatory statement for such appointment should be annexed to the notice of the general meeting.

Unless otherwise provided in the Articles, at least two-thirds of directors of a public company or a private company which is subsidiary of a public company shall be rotational directors. This means that at least two-thirds of total number of directors shall be liable to retire by rotation at every annual general meeting. Thus, they are called 'Rotational Directors'.

The Articles may provide for the retirement of all directors at every annual general meeting. But in the case of a private company, all directors can be permanent if the Articles so provide.

The provision for rotation of directors does not apply to independent directors.

Retirement of Directors by Rotation

At every subsequent annual general meeting, one-third (or the number nearest to one-third) of such directors who are liable to retire by rotation, shall retire from office.

Directors who retire by rotation at every annual general meeting shall be those who have been serving in the company for a longer duration than others.

If the date of appointment of two directors' is the same, the director who has to retire first can be decided based on the agreement among them or shall be determined by lot. Section 152(6) (2) paves way for the same.

Re-appointment of Retiring Directors

The following procedures are to be adopted for the reappointment of retiring directors:

(i) At the annual general meeting at which a director retires by rotation, the company may fill up the vacancy by appointing the retiring directors or someone else.

(ii) If such a place is not filled up in that meeting, the same shall be adjourned to the same day in the next week.

(iii) If, in such an adjourned meeting also, the place of retired director is not filled up, nor is there a resolution not to fill the vacancy, the retiring director is deemed to have been reappointed at the adjourned meeting subject to the following exceptions:

(a) If the resolution for re-appointment of retiring director is lost;

(b) If retiring director is not willing to be re-appointed and the same has been communicated to the Board of writing;

(c) If he is disqualified for appointment; and

(d) If a special or ordinary resolution is required for his appointment or re-appointment;

It shall also be resolved in annual general meeting that the vacancy shall not be filled up.

Appointment of New Directors other than Retiring Directors

The following procedures are adopted in this regard:

   (i)   If a person is to be appointed as a director, he should be an eligible person to hold the office as the director.

  (ii)   Such an intention of the person shall be made known to the company by serving a notice at least fourteen days before the meeting.

 (iii)   A notice shall be served along with a deposit of one lakh rupees or such higher amount as may be prescribed which shall be refunded, is to be made by such a person or by the person who proposes him to be elected as the director.

  (iv)   Company in turn shall inform all the members at least seven days before the meeting about this candidature.

   (v)   It shall be informed to all the members individually by sending a notice or by giving advertisement in at least two newspapers circulated in the place where the registered office of the company is located.

  (vi)   In case such a person who served to become the director (is elected as director) the amount deposited by him will be refunded to him.

 (vii)   In case he is not elected as director, then the amount deposited by him will be forfeited by the company.

(viii)   Every person whose name is proposed as a candidate for the office of a director shall sign and file with the company his consent in writing to act as a director, if appointed.

  (ix)   Similarly a person who for the first time has been appointed as a director has also to file such consent in writing to the Registrar within thirty days from the date of his appointment (Sec. 152).

   (x)   Directors shall be appointed individually by a separate ordinary resolution.

  (xi)   E-Form No. 32 shall be submitted by the director so appointed for giving his consent with the Registrar within thirty days of appointment.

 (xii)   The company shall also file E-Form No. 32 with the Registrar of Companies within thirty days giving particulars of appointment of directors.

3. Appointment of Independent Directors (Sec. 149)

Every listed public company shall have at least one-third of the total number of directors as independent directors. However the Central Government may prescribe the minimum number of independent directors in the case of any class or classes of public companies.

An independent director in relation to a company means a director other than a managing director or a whole-time director or a nominee director:

(i) who in the opinion of the Board, is a person of integrity and possesses relevant expertise and experience;

(ii) who is not a promoter of the company or its holding, subsidiary or associate company;

(iii) who is not related to the promoters or directors in the company, its holding, subsidiary or associate company;

(iv) who has or had no pecuniary relationship or transaction with the company, its holding, subsidiary or associate company, or their promoters, or directors during the two immediately preceding financial years or during the current financial year.

(v) where neither himself nor any of his relatives:

(a) holds the position of a key managerial personnel or employee of the company or its holding, subsidiary or associate company in any of the three financial years immediately preceding the financial year in which he is proposed to be appointed;

(b) holds together with his relatives two per cent, or more of the total voting power of the company; or

(c) is a Chief Executive or director, by whatever name called of any non-profit organisation that receives twenty-five per cent or more of its receipts from the company or from any of its promoters or directors;

(d) who possesses such other qualifications as may be prescribed.

An independent director may be appointed for a fixed term of up to five consecutive years. However, he is eligible for re-appointment on passing of a special resolution by the company and the disclosure of such an appointment in the Board's report.

The independent directors can hold office only for a maximum of two consecutive terms. Thereafter, there is a minimum cooling off period of three years after which the person becomes eligible for reappointment as independent director.

Code of Conduct for Independent Directors

A detailed code for the independent directors is laid down in Schedule IV of the Act. In accordance with this Schedule:

(i) Selection of an independent director should be done by the Board.

(ii) The selection shall be approved at the meeting of the shareholders.

(iii) An independent director can be selected from a data bank of independent directors, maintained by an institution as notified by the Central Government.

(iv) The appointment so made shall be formalised through a letter of appointment.

(v) The Central Government may prescribe the manner and the procedure of selection of independent directors who fulfil the requirements specified under Section 149.

(vi) An independent director shall not be entitled to any stock option and may receive remuneration by way of fee provided under Section 197(5).

(vii) The provisions of retirement of directors by rotation shall not be applicable to appointment of independent directors.

(viii) A separate meeting of independent directors shall be conducted at least once a year and shall review the performance of non-independent directors too.

4. Appointment by Board of Directors

The Board of Directors may appoint a director: (a) as an additional director; (b) to fill in a casual vacancy; or (c) as an alternate director.

(a) *Additional Directors [Sec. 161]*: Such directors shall hold office only up to the date of the next annual general meeting of the company. In no case shall the total number of the directors and additional directors together exceed the maximum strength fixed for the Board by the Articles.

(b) *Casual Vacancies [Sec. 161(4)]*: A casual vacancy means a vacancy which arises due to death, resignation, disqualification or failure of an elected director to accept the office. In the case of a Public Company or a Private Company being a subsidiary of a Public Company, if the office of any director appointed by the company in general meeting is vacated before his term of office will expire in the normal course, the resulting casual vacancy may be filled by the Board of Directors at a meeting of the Board. This is subject to any regulations in the articles of the company. Any person so appointed shall hold office only up to the date up to which the director in whose place he is appointed would have held office.

(c) *Alternate Directors [Sec. 161(2)]:* The Board of Directors of a company may, if so authorised by its Articles or by a resolution passed by the company in general meeting appoint an alternate director in place of the "Original Director" who may have to be absent for a period of not less than 3 months from India.

An alternate director shall not hold office as such for a period longer than that permissible to the original director. He shall vacate office as and when the original director returns to the State in which meetings of the Board are ordinarily held.

5. Appointment by Proportional Representation [Sec.163]

Notwithstanding anything contained in this Act, the Articles of a company may provide for the appointment of not less than two third of the total number of the directors of a Public Company or of a Private Company being a subsidiary of a Public Company according to the principle of proportional representation. The proportional representation may be by the voting procedure of single transferable vote or by cumulative voting or otherwise. The directors appointed under proportional representation will hold office for three years. They cannot be removed by the company in a general meeting.

6. Appointment by Third Parties

The articles may empower debentureholders or other creditors to appoint their nominee or nominees to the Board. However, the number of directors so appointed cannot exceed one-third of the total strength of the Board.

7. Appointment of Directors by Small Shareholders

A listed company may have one director elected by such small shareholders (holders of shares of nominal value of not more than twenty thousand rupees or such other sum as may be prescribed) in such a manner and with such terms and conditions as may be prescribed.

NUMBER OF DIRECTORSHIPS (SEC. 165)

The following are the provisions regarding the number of directorships:

(i) No person shall hold the office as director, including any alternate directorship, in more than twenty companies at the same time.

(ii) The maximum number of public companies or private companies (which are either holding or subsidiary of a public company) in which a person can be appointed as director shall not exceed ten.

(iii) Any person holding office as director in companies more than this specified limit, immediately before the commencement of this Act shall, within a period of one year from such commencement:

    (a) choose the companies, within this specified limit, in which he wishes to continue his directorship;

    (b) resign his office as director in the other remaining companies; and

    (c) intimate the choice made by him to each of the companies and also to the Registrar of the Companies.

(iv) His appointment shall become void if the director fails to vacate the office of other company as the director within this specified time limit.

(v) Any person who holds office or acts as a director of more than twenty companies at the same time shall be punishable with a fine of not less than five thousand rupees and not more than twenty-five thousand rupees for every day after the first day during which this contravention continues.

DIRECTOR IDENTIFICATION NUMBER

Every individual intending to be appointed as director of a company shall make an application for allotment of Director Identification Number to the Central Government in a prescribed form along with prescribed fee. The Central Government shall in turn, within one month from the receipt of the application allot a Director Identification Number to the applicant.

Every existing director shall, within one month of the receipt of Director Identification Number from the Central Government, intimate his Director Identification Number to the company in which he is a director. The company, in turn shall furnish the same to the Registrar or any other officer (as may be prescribed) within fifteen days of receipt of intimation from the director.

DISQUALIFICATION [SEC. 164]

Sec. 164 states that a person shall not be capable of being appointed director of a company, if:

(a) he has been found to be of unsound mind by a competent Court;

(b) he is an undischarged insolvent;

(c) he has applied to be declared as an insolvent and his application is pending;

(d) he has been convicted of any offence involving moral turpitude and sentenced to imprisonment for not less than six months, and a period of five years has not elapsed from the date of expiry of the sentence;

(e) he has not paid any call in respect of shares of the company held by him and six months have elapsed from the last day fixed for the payment of the call;

(f) a person who has been convicted of the offence dealing with related party transactions under Sec. 188 at any time during the last preceding five years.

(g) a person who has not been allotted Director Identification Number under Sec. 154.

(h) a person who is already a director of a public company, which has not filed the annual accounts and returns for any continuous three financial years; or has failed to repay its deposits or interest thereon on due date and such failure continues for one year or more. In such a case, he shall not be eligible to be appointed as director for five years from the date of such failure to submit the returns and accounts or payment of dividend, etc. as the case may be.

However, the Central Government is empowered to remove the disqualification in the case of (d) and (e) by notification in the Official Gazette.

VACATIO1N OF OFFICE OF DIRECTOR (SEC. 167)

As per Section 167, the office of a director becomes vacant on the following grounds:

(i) He incurs any of the disqualifications specified in Section 164.

(ii) He absents himself from all the meetings of the Board of Directors held during a period of twelve months with or without seeking leave of absence of the Board.

(iii) He acts in contravention of the provisions of Section 184 relating to entering into contracts or arrangements in which he is directly or indirectly interested.

(iv) He fails to disclose his interest in any contract or arrangement in which he is directly or indirectly interested.

(v) He becomes disqualified by an order of a court or the Tribunal.

(vi) He is convicted by a court of any offence, whether involving moral turpitude or otherwise and sentenced in respect thereof to imprisonment for not less than six months.

(vii) He is removed in pursuance of the provisions of this Act.

A private company may, by its Articles, provide any other ground for the vacation of the office of a director in addition to those specified above.

If a person functions as a director when he knows that the office of director held by him has become vacant on account of the above disqualifications, he shall be punishable with imprisonment for a term of not more than one year or with a fine of not less than one lakh rupees and not more than five lakh rupees or with both.

RESIGNATION OF DIRECTOR (SEC. 168)

A director may resign from his office by giving notice in writing. The Board shall, on receipt of such notice within thirty days intimate the Registrar in such a manner as may be prescribed for this purpose. The same is to be specified in the report of directors laid in the immediately following general meeting by the company.

A director shall also forward a copy of his resignation along with detailed reasons for the resignation to the Registrar within thirty days of resignation. The resignation of a director shall take effect from the date on which the notice is received by the company or the date, if any specified by the director in the notice, whichever as latter. The director who has resigned shall be liable even after his resignation for the offences which occurred during his tenure.

REMOVAL OF DIRECTORS (SEC. 169)

Removal of directors by shareholders. Sec.169 empowers the company to remove a director by ordinary resolution before the expiration of his period of office. A special notice of a resolution is also required for this purpose so as to enable the company to inform the members beforehand.

The vacancy 'thus' created may be filled at the same meeting. The person so appointed will hold office for the residue of the period of the removed director. Such an appointment can, however, be made only if special notice thereof has also been given. If the vacancy is not filled at the meeting, it may be filled by the Board of Directors as a casual vacancy, but the Board cannot appoint the removed director.

RIGHTS OF DIRECTOR TO MAKE A REPRESENTATION

The following provisions are laid down in this regard:

(i) The director concerned has a right to make representations.

(ii) The director may require the company to circulate representation among the members.

(iii) The company shall state the fact of representation having been received in the notice of the resolution given to its members.

(iv) If for any reason, a copy of representation has not been sent, the director may require that the representation to be read out at the meeting.

MANAGERIAL REMUNERATION

Basically, the directors have no right to claim any remuneration for their services. However, the Articles of the company generally provide for the payment of remuneration to directors. Once the Articles provide for such payment, it operates as an authority to the directors to pay remuneration from the funds of the company.

Part II of Schedule V of the Companies Act, 2013 acts as the standing guide for fixing remuneration to managerial personnel. The term 'managerial personnel' in relation to a company indicates the managing director/whole-time director or manager. However, it excludes executives who are not members of the Board of Directors of the company.

Remuneration—Meaning

According to Sec. 2(78) the term "remuneration means any money or its equivalent given or passed to any person for services rendered by him and includes perquisites as defined under the Income Tax Act, 1961."

Remuneration of Directors [Secs. 197 and 198]

The remuneration payable to the directors shall be subject to the provisions of Secs. 197 and 198.

The remuneration payable to the directors shall be determined either by the articles of the company or by a resolution of the company in general meeting. Sec. 197 provides the overall maximum of managerial remuneration which can be paid by a Public Company or a subsidiary of a Public Company. The net profits for this purpose shall be computed in the manner referred to in Sec. 198.

Overall Maximum Managerial Remuneration

The total remuneration payable to the directors, managing directors and whole time director shall not exceed eleven per cent of the net profits of the company for that financial year excluding the sitting fees payable to directors for attending the board and committee meetings.

If in any financial year, a company has no profits or its profits are inadequate, the company shall not pay to its managerial personnel by way of remuneration any sum (exclusive of any fees payable to directors for attending the Board or Committee meeting) under sub-section (5) . Provisions given in Schedule V in this regard are to be strictly followed.

Rules Regarding Directors Remuneration

1. A director may receive remuneration by way of a fee for each meeting of the Board or a Committee of the Board attended by him.

2. A managing or whole time director may be paid either on a monthly basis or a specified percentage of the net profits of the company or partly by one way and partly by the other. But the amount must not exceed five per cent of the net profits in favour of one such director or, if there are more than one, ten per cent of all of them put together.

3. A director who is neither a whole time nor a managing director, remuneration may be paid to him by way of monthly, quarterly or annual payment with the approval of the Central Government or by way of commission if the company by a special resolution authorises such a payment.

The remuneration payable to all the directors of this category must not exceed one per cent of the net profits of the company if the company has managing or whole time directors, or a manager, and three per cent in other cases.

4. If any director receives any sum in excess of the above limits, he should hold the excess amount in trust for the company and shall be bound to refund it. The company cannot waive the recovery of any such sum.

5. The net profits of the company for managerial remuneration are to be computed in the prescribed manner without deducting the directors remuneration from the gross profit.

6. A whole time director or managing director who receives a commission from the company shall not be disqualified to receive a commission or remuneration from any subsidiary of the company. But this fact is to be disclosed by the company in the Board's report.

7. A company should not pay to any officer or employee the remuneration free of tax [Sec. 200].

8. An independent director may receive remuneration by way of fees, reimbursement of expenses for participation in the Board and other meetings and profit related commission as may be approved by the members.

9. The above restrictions do not apply to a Private Company not being a subsidiary of a Public Company.

POWERS OF DIRECTORS

For the successful management of the company, powers have been given to the Board of Directors. The directors have to exercise these powers as a Board. Secs. 179 to 183 provide the powers of the Board and the restrictions thereon. The powers of the directors can be broadly discussed under the following heads:

General Powers

The Board is empowered to exercise all such powers and do all such acts and things, as the company is authorised to exercise and do. The effect of this power is that subject to the restrictions contained in the Act, and in the Memorandum and Articles, the powers of the directors are co-extensive with those of the company itself.

Powers to be Exercised by the Board only at Meeting

Sec. 179 states that the following powers can be exercised only by means of resolution passed at the meetings of the Board. The power (a) to make calls; (b) to issue debentures; (c) to borrow money; (d) to invest the funds of the company; and (e) to make loans.

The powers specified in clauses (c), (d) and (e) can be delegated by the Board at a meeting by a resolution to any committee of directors, the managing director, the manager or any other principal officer of the company.

Restrictions on Powers [Sec. 180]

The Board of Directors of a Public Company or of a Private Company which is a subsidiary of a Public Company can exercise the following powers only with the consent of the company in general meeting:

(a) Power to sell or lease of the company's undertakings.

(b) Power to remit or extend the time for payment of a debt due by director.

(c) Power to invest the amount of compensation received on compulsory acquisition in securities other than the trust securities.

(d) Power to borrow money beyond the paid-up capital of the company. "Borrowing" does not include temporary loan obtained from the company's bankers in the ordinary course of business.

(e) Power to contribute to any charitable or other funds beyond fifty thousand rupees in one financial year or 5% of the average net profits during the preceding three financial years, whichever is higher (Sec. 181).

(f) To contribute to any political party the amount which exceeds 7.5 per cent of its average net profits during the three years immediately preceeding the financial year (Sec. 182). However, the government company and a company which has been in existence for less than three years cannot make any such a contribution.

Power of Board to make Contributions to National Defence Fund, Etc. (Sec. 183)

The Board is authorised to contribute such an amount as it thinks fit to the National Defence Fund or any other fund approved by the Government for the purpose of national defence.

The company is required to disclose in its profit and loss account the total amount or amounts contributed by it during the financial year.

Powers of the Board to be Exercised by a Unanimous Vote

Any decision to be taken in the Board meeting shall be decided by the simple majority, subject to the provision given in the Articles. Each director has one vote for each resolution put to vote at the meeting. If there is no majority of votes in favour or against a resolution, i.e., in case of equality in votes, the chairman shall have a second or casting vote.

DUTIES OF DIRECTORS (SEC. 166)

For the first time, duties of directors have been defined in the Act. As per Section 166, a director of a company shall:

   (i) act in accordance with the Articles of the company;

   (ii) act in good faith;

  (iii) exercise his duties with due and reasonable care, skill and diligence and shall exercise independent judgement;

  (iv) not involve in a situation in which he may have a direct or indirect interest that conflicts, or possibly may conflict, with interest of the company;

   (v) not involve in a situation in which he may have a direct or indirect interest that conflicts, or possibly may conflict, with the interest of the company;

  (vi) not achieve or attempt to achieve any undue gain or advantage either to himself or to his relatives, partners or associates. If such a director is found guilty of making any undue gain, he shall be liable to pay an amount equal to that gain to the company;

 (vii) not assign his office and an assignment so made shall be void.

    If a director of the company contravenes the provisions of this Section such a director shall be punishable with a fine of not less than one lakh rupees and not more than five lakh rupees.

LIABILITIES OF DIRECTORS

The various liabilities which directors of a company may incur can be considered under the following heads:

  1. *Liability to Outsiders:* The directors are personally liable to third parties of contracts in the following cases:

    (a) They contract with outsiders in their personal capacity.

   (b) They enter into a contract on behalf of a prospective company.

   (c) They contract as agents of an undisclosed principal.

   (d) When the contract is ultra vires the company.

   (e) Where the prospectus contains any untrue statement.

   (f) Where the allotment of shares is irregular.

   (g) They fail to repay the application money if minimum subscription is not subscribed.

   (h) They fail to repay application money if the allotment of shares or debentures is not dealt with in stock exchange as provided in the prospectus.

2. *Liability to Company:* In certain circumstances, the directors are liable to the company.

These are:

   (a) Where the acts of the directors are ultra-vires the company.

   (b) Where the directors are negligent in performing their duties.

   (c) Where there is a breach of trust.

   (d) Where the directors are guilty of misfeasance.

3. *Criminal Liabilities of Directors:* For acts of fraud, default in discharging their duties and mis demeanour, the Act provides penalties by way of fine or imprisonment.

REVIEW QUESTIONS

1. Define director.
2. Who is an additional director?
3. Who is a casual director?
4. Who are rotational directors?
5. Mention two grounds when a director shall vacate his office.
6. Name two disqualifications of a person to become a director.
7. Who is an alternate director?
8. What do you mean by an independent director?
9. State provisions relating to the appointment of directors by small shareholders.
10. Mention two code of conduct of independent directors as per Schedule IV of the Act.

11. Explain how a company can increase the number of directors.

12. What do you mean by director identification number.

13. State provisions relating to resignation of director as per Sec. 168 of the Act.

14. Enumerate the rights of a director to make representation when he is removed from office.

15. State the power of the Board to make contribution to National Defence Fund, etc. as per Sec. 183 of the Act.

16. Enumerate the duties of directors.

17. Explain the legal position of directors.

18. Explain the provisions relating to number of directorships as per Sec. 165 of the Act.

19. State provisions regarding retirement of directors by rotation.

20. Explain provisions regarding overall maximum managerial remuneration.

21. State the powers to be exercised by the Board only at meeting.

22. Define 'director'. Explain the powers and duties of directors.

23. Enumerate and explain the different modes of appointment of directors of a public limited company.

24. State the liabilities of the directors of the company.

25. Explain the provisions for removal of company directors.

26. Explain the provisions relating to the re-appointment of retiring directors.

27. Explain provisions relating to the appointment of independent directors as per Sec. 149 of the Companies Act, 2013.

28. State provisions relating to the remuneration of directors as per the Act.

PRACTICAL PROBLEMS

Attempt the following problems, giving reasons:

1. A Private Company having two directors has just become a Public Company by choice. Is it obligatory for the company to appoint a third director?

   Hint: Yes.

2. Mr. X is a director in 19 companies. He is offered the directorship of the AB Private Limited.

State with reasons whether he can accept the above mentioned directorship.

Hint: Yes, he can accept the directorships of AB Private Limited.

3. A public limited company has fifteen directors, four of whom are not subject to retire by rotation. Is it a validly constituted Board?

Hint: Yes.

38

Board Meetings and Committees

Quorum for Board Meeting means the specified minimum number of directors to be present at the meeting for transacting a legally binding business.

Meetings of the directors provide a means to discuss the business and take formal decisions. The directors can only act at a meeting of the Board of Directors through resolutions passed at such a meeting. However, the Board may take decisions by resolutions passed by circulation, in lieu of assembling at a Board meeting.

FREQUENCY OF BOARD MEETINGS

As per Sec. 173 every company shall hold the first meeting of the Board of Directors within thirty days of the date of its incorporation. Thereafter, the company shall hold a minimum of four meetings of its Board of Directors every year. However, the time gap between two Board meetings shall not be more than one hundred and twenty days.

In the case of One Person Company (OPC), small company and dormant company, at least one Board meeting should be conducted in each half of the calendar year and the gap between two meetings should not be less than ninety days.

NOTICE OF THE MEETING

Provisions relating to notice of meeting are laid down in Sec. 173. The following are such provisions:

  (i) Not less than seven days notice in writing shall be given to every director at the registered address as available with the company. The notice can be given by hand delivery or by post or by electronic means.

(ii) If the Board meeting is called at shorter notice, at least one independent director shall be present at the meeting. If he is not present, then decision of the meeting shall be circulated to all directors and it shall be final only after ratification of decision by at least one independent director.

Other provisions laid down in this Section are as follows:

(a) The participation of directors in a meeting of the Board may be either in person or through video conferencing or other audio-visual means.

(b) Audio-visual media chosen shall be capable of recording and recognising the participation of the directors and of recording and sorting of proceedings of such meetings along with date and time.

(c) The Central Government may notify the matters which cannot be discussed through video conferencing.

QUORUM FOR BOARD MEETING (SEC. 174)

The term quorum means the specified minimum number of directors to be present at the meeting for transacting a legally binding business. The quorum should be present throughout the Board meeting. If quorum is not present the business transacted is void. According to Sec. 174, the quorum for meeting of the Board of Directors of a company shall be one-third of its total strength (any fraction contained in that one-third being rounded off as one), or two directors, whichever is higher.

'Total strength' means the total strength of the Board of Directors of a company as determined in pursuance of this Act, after deducting therefrom the number of the directors, if any, whose places may be vacant at the time.

The participation by a director through video conferencing or other audio–visual means shall also be counted for the purpose of determining quorum.

If at any time, the number of interested directors exceeds or is equal to two-thirds of the total strength of the Board of Directors, the number of directors who are not interested and present at the meeting (being not less than two) shall be the quorum during such time.

If the meeting of the Board cannot be held for want of quorum, it automatically stands adjourned till the same day in the next week, at the same time and place unless the Articles provide otherwise. In case the day in the next week happens to be a national holiday, the adjourned meeting should be held on the next working day.

AUTHORITY FOR CONVENING BOARD MEETING

The Companies Act does not prescribe the competent authority for convening a Board meeting. A director and the manager or secretary on the requisition of a director shall, at any time, summon a meeting of the Board.

Generally, it is the practice of the companies that the directors (at a meeting already convened and held) determine tentatively on a date convenient for the purpose of holding the next Board meeting. As such the secretary is authorised to issue notice of the meeting at the appropriate time.

CHAIRMAN OF BOARD MEETING

A Chairman shall preside over a Board meeting. The person who has to act as the Chairman may be specified in the Articles. But, if no such information is available in the Articles, the directors may elect a chairman of their meetings and determine the period of his office.

A committee of the Board may have its separate Chairman appointed as per the Articles. The Chairman of a Board meeting and of a committee should have a 'second' or casting vote in the case of an equality of votes.

Duties of the Chairman of the Meeting

The following are the duties of the Chairman of the Board meeting:

   (i) To see that the meeting is properly convened.
  (ii) To ascertain that the required quorum is present.
 (iii) To find that the requirements of the Act and the Articles are complied with.
  (iv) To preserve the order at the meeting.
   (v) To see that the proceedings are conducted in a proper way.
  (vi) To act in good faith and to be impartial in the performance of his duties.
 (vii) To find that the proper minutes of proceedings are kept.
(viii) To adjourn the meeting, if necessary.
  (ix) To declare the meeting closed.

RESOLUTION BY CIRCULATION

Usually, directors take decisions by passing resolution on matters presented at the meeting. But, if meeting is unable to be convened at any cause, the Board may pass a resolution by circulation. In accordance with Sec. 175, if the following two conditions are satisfied the resolution passed by circulation shall be deemed to have been passed at Board meeting.

(i) The resolution is to be circulated in draft together with the necessary papers among all directors present in India and the number of directors among whom it is circulated should not be less than the quorum fixed for the Board meeting, and

(ii) It is approved by a majority of them who are entitled to vote on the resolution.

GENERAL POWERS OF BOARD (SEC.179)

As per Sec. 179, the Board of Directors is entitled to exercise all such powers and do all such acts which the company is authorised to do. This is subject to a condition that certain powers can be exercised only at annual general meeting. However, the directors should act for the benefit of the company only.

In the following exceptional cases the shareholders can intervene with the power of Board:

(i) When directors are acting mala fide.

(ii) When there is deadlock in management.

(iii) When Board is becoming incompetent to act.

Powers to be Exercised by the Board at Meetings

The Board of Directors of a company can exercise the following powers at the Board meetings by means of passing of resolutions:

(i) Power to make calls on shareholders in respect of money unpaid on their shares.

(ii) The power to authorise buy-back of securities under Sec. 68.

(iii) The power to issue debentures.

(iv) The power to borrow money otherwise than on debentures.

(v) The power to invest the company's funds.

(vi) The power to make loan.

(vii) The power to invest the funds of the company and to make loans.

(viii) The power to diversify the business of the company.

(ix) Power to delegate to any committee of directors, the managing director, the manager, or any other principal officer.

(x) The power to approve amalgamation, merger or reconstruction.

(xi) The power to approve financial statement and Board's report.

PROCEDURE FOR HOLDING FIRST MEETING OF THE BOARD OF DIRECTORS

The following are the procedural steps for first Board meeting:

(i) The authorised person has to issue notice for convening a Board meeting and follow the procedure as laid down by Articles in this regard.

(ii) Not less than seven days notice in writing should be issued to every director of the company for the time being in India and at his usual address in India in the case of every other director [Sec. 173(3)].

(iii) The notice should also contain that it is the first Board meeting.

(iv) The day of the meeting should not be a national holiday.

(v) The first meeting should be convened and held within thirty days from the date of incorporation (Sec. 173).

(vi) It is not obligatory to enclose an Agenda for the meeting in the notice, but it is a good secretarial practice to do so.

(vii) At least half an hour before the meeting, the persons responsible for conducting meeting should place the folders containing agenda, business plan, etc., for ready reference of all directors. This enables them to deliberate and discuss each item of the agenda in detail.

(viii) The signature of the directors' should be obtained in the Register before holding the meeting.

(ix) If quorum (as per Sec. 174) is present, declare the meeting in order and inform the names of the directors who sought leave of absence from attending the meeting.

(x) The directors who are present at the meeting may elect one of them as the Chairman of the meeting. Then he should be requested to take the chair.

(xi) Provide all assistance to the Chairman to conduct the meeting in accordance with the agenda.

(xii) If any director wants to place any other item for the discussion at the meeting, then such an item shall be taken up with the permission of the Chairman.

(xiii) The date, time and place of the next Board meeting should be decided.

(xiv) When meeting is over, the draft minutes of the meeting should be prepared and got it reviewed by the Chairman.

(xv) The copy of draft minutes of the meeting should be sent to each of the directors of the company for information and comments.

(xvi) The copy of the draft minutes should be collected from the directors with their comments. Thereafter, the minutes should be finalised in consultation with the Chairman/ Managing Director and the same should be entered in the Minutes Book.

(xvii) The final minutes shall be signed and dated by the Chairman of the meeting or by the Chairman of the succeeding meeting. All pages of the minutes should consecutively numbered and initialled. But, the last page of the minutes should be signed and dated by the Chairman.

PROCEDURE FOR HOLDING SUBSEQUENT BOARD MEETINGS

The procedure for all subsequent meetings of the Board of Directors shall be the same as detailed for the first Board meeting. But in the notice of the subsequent Board meetings, the following matters are required to be specifically mentioned:

(i) Appointment of Managing Director who is already a Managing Director or Manager of another company (Sec. 203).

(ii) Appointment of Manager who is already a Manager or Managing Director of another company (Sec. 203)

(iii) Making loan or investment or giving of guarantee or security (Sec.186).

BOARD COMMITTEES

Committees are usually formed as a means of improving Board effectiveness and efficiency in areas where specialised and technical discussions are required. These committees prepare the ground work for decision-making and report at the subsequent Board meeting. Thus, establishment of committees is one way of managing the work of the Board and strengthening the Board's governance role.

Corporate Boards usually comprise the following minimal standing committees:

(i) Audit (ii) Compensation (iii) Executive, and (iv) Governance and nominating.

Sometimes, committee names might differ slightly (i.e., the compensation committee may be known as the compensation and benefits committee or the governance and nominating committee may be referred to as the nominating committee).

Audit Committee (Sec. 177)

Audit Committee is now the gatekeeper of financial information that shareholders and the investing public rely upon. Thus, the Companies Act of 2013 has enlarged the responsibilities of auditors. Such responsibilities relate to:

(a) monitoring of auditors' independence,

(b) evaluation of their performance,

(c) approval of modification of related-party transactions,

(d) scrutiny of loans and investments,

(e) valuation of assets, and

(f) evaluation of internal controls and risk management.

1. Constitution of Audit Committee

The requirement of constitution of Audit Committee has been limited to:

(a) Every listed company; or

(b) The following class of companies:

    (i) all public companies with a paid-up capital of ten crore rupees or more;

    (ii) all public companies having turnover of one hundred crore rupees or more;

    (iii) all public companies having in aggregate, outstanding loans or borrowing or debentures or deposits exceeding fifty crore rupees or more.

Explanation

The paid-up share capital or turnover or outstanding loans, or borrowings or debentures or deposits, as the case may be, as existing on the date of last audited Financial Statements shall be taken into account for the purpose of this rule.

2. Qualified and Independent Audit Committee

The norms provided for the audit committee are as follows:

(a) The audit committee shall have minimum three directors as its members. But two-thirds of the members of such a committee shall be independent directors.

(b) All members of audit committee shall be financially literate*.**But at least one member shall have accounting or related financial management expertise.

(c) The chairman of the audit committee shall be an independent director. He shall be present at the annual general meeting to answer shareholders queries.

(d) The audit committee may invite the executives, as it considers appropriate to be present at the meetings of the committee.

(e) The company secretary shall act as the secretary to the committee.

3. Meeting of Audit Committee

The audit committee should meet at least four times in a year. But not more than four months shall elapse between two meetings. The quorum shall be either two members or one-third of the members of the audit committee whichever is higher. However, there should be a minimum of two independent members present.

4. Powers of Audit Committee

The following are the powers of the audit committee:

(a) It has the power to seek information from any employee.

(b) It can investigate any activity within the terms of reference.

(c) It has the power to obtain outside legal or other professional advice.

(d) It can secure attendance of outsiders with relevant experts, if any.

5. Role of Audit Committee

The important functions of audit committee are:

(a) to ensure the accuracy of financial statement;

(b) to recommend to the Board the appointment, re-appointment and replacement or removal of the statutory auditor;

---

* Ability to read and understand basic financial statement.

(c) to approve payment to statutory auditors for any other services rendered by them;

(d) to review (with the management) the annual financial statements before submission to the Board for approval;

(e) to review (with the management) the performance of statutory and internal auditors and adequacy of the internal control system;

(f) to discuss with the internal auditor regarding any significant findings and follow-up thereon;

(g) to review the findings of any internal investigations by the internal auditors if there is a suspected fraud or irregularity in reporting the matter to the Board;

(h) to discuss with statutory auditors before the audit commences, about the nature and scope of audit (including post-audit) for ascertaining any area of concern;

(i) to look into the reasons for substantial defaults in the payment to stakeholders;

(j) to review the functioning of the Whistle Blower mechanism, if the same is existing; and

(k) to perform any other function as is mentioned in the terms of reference of the audit committee.

Nomination and Remuneration Committee (Sec. 178)

Nomination and remuneration committee helps the Board of Directors: (i) in the preparations relating to the election of members of the Board of Directors and (ii) in handling matters that relate to the conditions of employment and remuneration of senior management.

Constitution of the Committee

The Board of Directors of the following companies shall constitute Nomination and Remuneration Committee of the Board:

(a) Every listed company; or

(b) the following class of companies:

    (i) all public companies with a paid-up capital of ten crore rupees or more;

    (ii) all public companies having turnover of one hundred crore rupees or more;

    (iii) all public companies, having in aggregate, outstanding loans or borrowings or debentures or deposits exceeding fifty crore rupees or more.

The committee shall consist of three or more non-executive directors out of which not less than one-half shall be independent directors.

The chairperson of the company may be appointed as member, but shall chair such a committee.

The Chairman of the Nomination and Remuneration committee could be present at the Annual General Meeting to answer the shareholders' queries. However, it would be up to the Chairman to decide who should answer the queries.

Duties of the Committee

The following are the duties of the Nomination and Remuneration Committee:

(a) To identify persons who are qualified to become directors and who may be appointed in senior management as per the criteria laid down.

(b) To recommend to the Board their appointment and removal.

(c) To carry out evaluation of every director's performance.

(d) To formulate the criteria for determining qualifications, positive attributes and independence of a director.

(e) To recommend to the Board a policy relating to the remuneration for the directors, KMP and other employees.

Role of the Committee

The role of the committee shall consist of the following:

(i) Formulation of the criteria for determining qualifications, positive attributes and independence of a director.

(ii) Formulation of criteria for evaluation of independent directors and the Board.

(iii) Devising a policy on Board diversity.

(iv) Identifying persons who are qualified to become directors.

Stakeholders Relationship Committee [Sec. 178(5)]

As per Sec. 178(5) the Board of Directors of a company that has more than one thousand shareholders, debentureholders, depositholders and any other securityholders at any time during a financial year is required to constitute a stakeholders relationship committee. The committee consists of a chairperson who shall be a non-executive director and such other members as may be determined by the Board.

The Stakeholders Relationship Committee shall consider and resolve the grievances of securityholders of the company.

The chairperson of each of the committee constituted under this Section or, in his absence, any other member of the committee authorised by him in this behalf shall attend the general meetings of the company.

Corporate Social Responsibility (CSR) Committee

The fundamentals of CSR rest on the fact that not only public policy but even corporates should be responsible enough to address social issues. The companies should deal with the challenges and issues looked after to a certain extent by the States.

CSR is not a new concept in India. Ever since its inception large corporate houses in India have been involved in serving the community. Through donations and charity events, many other organisations have been doing their part for the society. The basic objective of CSR in these days is to maximise the company's overall impact on the society and stakeholders.

Companies usually have specialised CSR teams that formulate policies, strategies and goals for their programmes and set aside budgets to fund them.

One of the key changes in the Companies Act, 2013 is the introduction of a Corporate Responsibility Section making India the first country to mandate CSR through a statutory provision.

Constitution of the Committee

The following companies shall constitute CSR Committee of the Board:

  (i) Companies having Net Worth of rupees five hundred crore or more.

 (ii) Companies having turnover of rupees one thousand crore or more.

(iii) Companies having Net Profit of rupees five crore or more.

The committee shall consist of three or more directors, out of which at least one director shall be an independent director.

Features of CSR Provision under the Companies Act

  (i) The Board shall approve the CSR policy for the company after considering the recommendation of the CSR Committee.

 (ii) The contents of the policy shall be disclosed in the Boards report.

(iii) It shall be placed on the company's website, if any, in a manner to be prescribed by the Central Government.

(iv) The Board shall ensure that the activities as are included in the CSR policy are undertaken by the company.

(v) While spending the amount earmarked for CSR activities the company shall give preference to the local area and areas around it where it operates.

(vi) If the company fails to spend the amount, the Board shall specify the reasons for not spending the amount in the Boards' Report.

(vii) The eligible companies are required to spend in every financial year, at least two per cent of the Average Net Profits of the company made during the three immediately preceding financial years in pursuance of its CSR policy. For this purpose average net profit shall be calculated as per the provisions of Sections 198 of the Companies Act, 2013.

Other Board Committees

Apart from the Committees of the Board mandated by the Companies Act, 2013 (viz, Audit Committee, Nomination and Remuneration Committee, Stakeholders Relationship Committee and the CSR Committee) Board of Directors may also constitute other committees to oversee a specific objective or project. A few examples of such Committees prevalent in the corporate sector in India and abroad are as follows:

(i) Corporate Governance Committee

(ii) Science, Technology and Sustainability Committee

(iii) Regulatory, Compliance and Government Affairs Committee

(iv) Risk Committee

REVIEW QUESTIONS

1. What is meant by resolution by circulation?
2. What is an agenda?
3. What do you mean by quorum?
4. What is disinterested quorum?
5. How frequently a Board meeting is to be held?
6. What is CSR?
7. What do you mean by audit committee?

8. What is board committee?
9. Write a note on board resolution.
10. Enumerate two duties of the chairman of the board meeting.
11. Enumerate the powers to be exercised by a Board at the Meeting.
12. What do you mean by stakeholders relationship committee?
13. Enumerate the duties of nomination and remuneration committee.
14. Write a note on meeting of audit committee.
15. Write about the meeting of committee of directors.
16. What are the powers to be exercised by a board at the meeting?
17. List the powers of audit committee.
18. Write about the constitution of the audit committee.
19. Enumerate the duties of the chairman of the board meeting.
20. What are the general powers of the board?
21. Explain the procedure of holding subsequent board meeting.
22. Explain provisions relating to companies board meeting as per Sec. 173 of the Companies Act, 2013.
23. Describe the procedure for holding first meeting of the Board of Directors.
24. Explain the role of audit committee as per Section 177 of the Act, 2013.
25. What is CSR Committee? Explain the features of CSR Committee.

39

General Body Meetings

A 'meeting' is "a gathering or assembly of a number of persons with certain objects in view or for certain purposes."

MEANING

Meetings play a solemn role in the administrative work of the company. It is defined in Black's Law Dictionary as a 'coming together of persons, an assembly'. A meeting is, therefore, a gathering or assembly of a number of persons with certain objects in view or for certain purposes.

The meetings of a company are of different kinds. They are as follows:

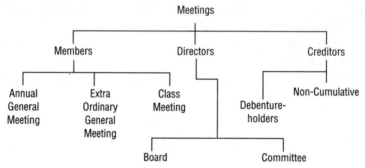

In this chapter the discussion is confined to the meetings of the shareholders.

ANNUAL GENERAL MEETING [SEC. 96]

Every company shall in each year hold a general meeting as its annual general meeting in addition to any other meetings in that year, and shall specify the meeting as such in the notices. A period of not more than 15 months shall elapse between the two annual general meetings.

Section 96 of the Companies Act, 2013 states that every company other than One Person Company shall hold annual general meeting in addition to any other meeting.

A company may hold its first annual general meeting within a period of nine months from the date of closing of the first financial year of the company and in any other case, within a period of six months, from the date of closing of the financial year.

In case a company holds its first annual general meeting as aforesaid, it need not hold any annual general meeting in the year of its incorporation.

The Registrar may, for any special reason, extend the time within which annual general meeting shall be held by a period not exceeding three months. However, this provision is not applicable to first annual general meeting.

Every annual general meeting shall be called during the business hours on a day that is not a public holiday and shall be held either at the registered office of the company or at some other place within the city, town or village in which the registered office of the company is situated. The Central Government may, however, exempt any class of companies from this provision.

A general meeting of a company may be called by giving to every member not less than 21 days notice in writing. An annual general meeting may be called by giving a shorter notice, if it is consented to by all the members entitled to vote at the meeting.

Annual general meeting is a unique institution for the protection of the shareholders of a company. They get an opportunity to discuss the affairs and review the working of the company. It is at this meeting that some of the directors will retire and come up for re-election. Appointment of auditors is also made at this meeting. Directors have to present annual accounts for the consideration of the shareholders and the dividends are declared.

The business to be transacted at the meeting is known as the ordinary business. The meeting may take up any other business also that is known as the special business.

Power of Tribunal to Call Annual General Meeting (Sec. 97)

If the company defaults in holding an annual general meeting as per Section 96, any member of the company can make an application to the Tribunal. On receiving such an application, the Tribunal may call or direct the calling of a general meeting of the company. It may also give such ancillary or consequential directions as it thinks fit in relation to the calling, holding and conducting of the meeting. A general meeting so held shall, subject to any directions of the Tribunal, be deemed an annual general meeting of the company.

Default in Holding the Meetings

If default is made in holding this meeting, either under Sec. 96, or under Sec. 97, the company and every officer who is in default is punishable with a fine up to ₹ 1,00,000 and in the case of continuing default, with a further fine which may extend to ₹ 5,000 per day during the default (Sec. 99).

EXTRAORDINARY GENERAL MEETING [SEC. 100]

Every general meeting other than the annual general meeting is known as the extraordinary general meetings. It is usually called by the board of directors. It can be called at any time to transact business which cannot conveniently be postponed until the next annual general meeting. All the businesses at an extraordinary meeting are deemed to be the special businesses.

Who Can Convene Extraordinary General Meetings?

(i) The Board of Directors [Sec. 100(1)

(ii) The Board of Directors on the requisition of members [Sec. 100(2)]

(iii) The requisitionists themselves [Sec. 100(4)], and

(iv) The Tribunal [Sec. 98 (not yet enforced)]

The directors may, whenever they think for convene an extraordinary general meeting by passing a resolution to that effect in the Board's meeting. The Article empowers the Board to call an extraordinary general meeting and the Board has to abide by the provision given in Secs. 101 to 109 of the Companies Act, 2013 relating to the holding of general meeting.

An extraordinary general meeting also becomes necessary on requisition. The directors should convene an extraordinary general meeting on the requisition of members holding not less than one tenth of the paid-up capital carrying the right to vote, or if the company has no share capital, members representing not less than one-tenth of the total voting rights. When a requisition is deposited at the registered office of the company the directors should within 21 days, move to call a meeting and the meeting should actually be held within 45 days from the date of the requisition. In case the directors fail to do so, the requisitionists may themselves proceed to call the meeting not later than 3 months after the date of the deposit of the requisition at the registered office of the company. They can also claim necessary expenses from the company.

Power of the National Company Law Tribunal to Call Meeting [Sec. 98]

Where the holding of an extraordinary general meeting has for any reason become impracticable, the proper course is to apply to the National Company Law Tribunal. In such circumstances the National Company Law Tribunal on its own motion or on the application of the director or a member, order a meeting to be called and held as per its directions.

Notice of the Meeting (Sec. 101)

All businesses transacted at an extraordinary general meeting shall be deemed to be of special businesses. Thus, the notice of the meeting should specify the special businesses to be transacted and should be accompanied by an explanatory statement. The notice for an extraordinary general meeting is 21 clear days.

Explanatory Statement

The notice conventing an extraordinary general meeting should be accompanied by an 'Explanatory Statement'. The purpose behind it is to explain to the members the reasons of passing a resolution to ensure its smooth adoption.

Explanatory statement is essential for each item of special business. In the case of annual general meetings, all businesses other than the ordinary businesses shall be considered as special businesses. But, in the case of extraordinary general meetings, all businesses to be transacted there shall be treated as special businesses.

Where any item of businesses to be transacted at the meeting is deemed to be special, the same should be annexed to the notice of the meeting. Such an annexure shall contain all material facts concerning the item of business, including the nature and extent of the interest of every director, and the manager, if any.

The explanatory statement should be approved by the Chairman before it is actually issued.

Procedures for Holding the Meeting

   (i) The Board meeting is to be convened to determine the date, time and place of the meeting.

  (ii) The directors have to decide about the resolutions to be passed at the meeting.

(iii) Drafting and issuing notice of the meeting along with explanatory statement to the shareholders at least twenty-one days before the meeting.

(iv) Arrangements shall be made to publish the notice in newspapers.

(v) The Secretary is to prepare a detailed agenda in consultation with the directors.

(vi) If the meeting is convened on the requisition of members, then the statutory norms must be strictly adhered with.

(vii) The chairman of the Board is to act as chairman of the meeting.

(viii) The quorum should be ascertained.

CLASS MEETINGS

Class meetings of the holders of different classes of shares are to be held in order to obtain the consent of a particular class of shareholders for altering their rights and privileges or for the conversion of one class into another.

Requisites of a Valid Meeting

A general meeting of shareholders is said to be valid when it is properly convened and legally constituted. Secs. 171 to 186 of the Act provide provisions relating to the holding of a valid general meeting. The following are the essential requisites of a valid meeting: (1) Proper authority;. (2) Notice; (3) Quorum; (4) Chairman; and (5) Minutes.

1. *Proper Authority:* The first important requisite of a valid meeting is that it must be called by the right person. Normally, the Board of Directors is the convening authority for every general meeting. They should pass a resolution to call a meeting, at a duly convened Board meeting. If they fail to call the meeting, the members or the National Company Law Tribunal or the Central Government may call the meeting.

2. *Notice* [Sec. 101]: The second requisite of a valid meeting is that a proper notice of the meeting should be given to every shareholder, auditors of the company, each director of the company and to every such a person who is entitled to attend the meeting [Sec. 101(3)]. Deliberate omission to give notice to a single member may invalidate the meeting. The accidental omission to give notice to or non-receipt of the notice by any member will not be fatal.

Notice of the meeting must be in writing and should specify the date, place and hour of the meeting. It should also contain a statement of the nature of business to be transacted. An explanatory statement is to be annexed to notices in respect of any item of special business. Any resolution not covered by the terms of notice cannot validly be passed by a meeting.

Every notice of the meeting must be given at least 21 days before the date of the meeting unless a shorter notice is agreed to by all the members in the case of Annual General Meeting and by members holding not less than 95 per cent of the voting power in the case of other general meetings. In computing 21 days, 48 hours from the date of posting should be excluded. Further, in the celebrated case Re: Railway Sleepers Supply (1885) Ch.D.204, it was held that 'days' means 'clear days', i.e., the date of posting and the date of meeting should be excluded. Thus, a valid notice should be sent at least 25 days prior to the date of the meeting.

No fresh notice is required to be sent in the case of an adjourned meeting since it is considered in law as a continuance of the original meeting [*Seadding* v. *Lorant* (1851) 3 H.L.C. 418]. But a fresh notice of the adjourned meeting should be served in case the original meeting is adjourned 'sine die' (i.e., without fixing a day for the holding of adjourned meeting) or if fresh business is to be discussed.

Notice through Electronic Mode [Rule 18 of Companies (Management and Administration) Rules, 2014]

A company may give notice through electronic mode. Electronic mode means any communication sent by a company through its authorised and secured computer programme. This programme is capable of producing confirmation and keeping record of such communication addressed to the person entitled to receive such communication at the last electronic mail address provided by the member.

3. *Quorum:* Quorum means the minimum number of members required to be present for transacting a legally binding business at the meeting. The quorum is generally fixed by the Articles. Unless the articles provide for a larger number, two members personally present in the case of a Private Company shall be the quorum for a meeting. But in the case of Public Company, the quorum will be decided based on the number of members on the date of the meeting which are as follows:

No. of Members	Quorum
Below 1000	5
1000–5000	15
Above 5000	30

The Articles cannot provide for a quorum smaller than the statutory minimum. Only members present in person, and not proxies, can be counted for the purpose of quorum. Joint holders of shares are treated as one member for the purpose of quorum. A nominee of the President of India or the Governor of a State where the latter holds shares in a company, shall be counted for the purpose of quorum. A company present by its representative is treated as a member present in person and is counted in the quorum. If the total number of members of a company is reduced below the quorum fixed by the Articles, the rules as to quorum will be satisfied if all the members are present.

Any resolution passed without a quorum is invalid. However, third parties without notice are not affected by reason of any irregularity in the quorum [*County of Gloucester Bank* v. *Rudry Morthyr* (1895) 1ch. 629].

In accordance with the rule in *Sharp* v. *Dawes*, one shareholder cannot constitute a meeting. But this rule has the following exceptions:

(a) where one person holds all the shares of a particular class.

(b) quorum is required to be present at the beginning of the meeting. It need not be present throughout or at the time of taking votes on any resolution. If quorum is not present within half an hour of the meeting, the meeting shall stand adjourned to the same day in the next week at the same time and place. If at the adjourned meeting also a quorum is not present within half an hour of the time of the meeting the members present shall be a quorum. In such a case even one member may constitute the meeting.

Disinterested Quorum: It means quorum of those directors who are not interested, directly or indirectly, in the motion under discussion, i.e., for the purpose of finding a quorum.

4. *Chairman* [Sec. 104]: Another necessary element of a valid meeting is that there must be a leader called chairman to preside over the proceedings of the meeting. He must be a member of the company. Usually the Chairman is appointed by the Articles of Association of a company. If the articles do not designate any person as chairman, then the members personally present at the meeting must elect one of them to be the Chairman thereof on a show of hands. If a poll is demanded in the election of the Chairman, it has to be taken forthwith under the chairmanship of the person elected by the show of hands.

It is the function of the Chairman to keep order and see that the meeting is properly conducted. He must ascertain the sense of the meeting properly with regard to any question before it. He must decide incidental questions arising for decision during the meeting, exercise his casting voting bona fide in the interests of the company, and exercise correctly his powers of adjournment and of demanding a poll. He must see to it that the majority does not refuse to hear the minority.

The Chairman has no power to stop or adjourn a meeting without the consent of the shareholders if all the proceedings at the meeting are in order. If he wrongly adjourns or stops the meeting, the meeting may appoint another chairman and continue the proceedings [*Narayanan Chettiar* v. *Kaleshawar Mills Ltd.* (1952) A.I.R. 515].

5. *Minutes of the Meeting* [Secs. 118]: Minutes are the official records of the proceedings of a meeting. They are the permanent records of the decisions and resolutions arrived at the meeting. Every company must keep minutes containing a fair and correct summary of all proceedings of general meetings and Boards meetings in books kept for that purpose. The pages of the minute book must be consecutively numbered and minutes must be recorded within 30 days of the conclusion of the meeting. The minutes have to be written by hand on the numbered pages. Each page of a minutes book which records the proceedings shall be initialled or signed by the Chairman of the same meeting or the next succeeding meeting, adding the date on the last page of the record.

All the appointments of officers at any of the meeting must be included in the minutes of the meeting. In the case of a meeting of the Board of Directors or of a Committee of the Board, the minutes shall also contain the names of directors present at the meeting and the names of directors dissenting from, or not concurring in a resolution passed at the meeting. The Chairman may exclude from the minutes any matter which he reasonably regards defamatory of any person or irrelevant or immaterial to the proceedings.

Where the minutes of a meeting are duly kept as per the above provisions, they are presumptive evidence that the meeting is duly called and held and all the proceedings are duly taken.

The minute books are to be maintained at the registered office of the company and open, during the business hours, to the inspection of any member without charge for at least two hours a day. Members are also entitled to obtain copies on payment of such a sum as may be prescribed, for every one hundred words, or fractional part thereof. But minutes book of the Board meetings are not open to inspection. The company and every officer of the company who is in default shall be punishable with a fine which may extend to ₹500 for each offence.

Alteration of Minutes

Minutes once written cannot be materially altered. However, if there is a clerical error it can be rectified and must be initialled by the Chairman. If the error is a material one, it must be neatly ruled out and initialled by the Chairman. Where it is desired to change a decision taken at an earlier meeting, a fresh resolution rescinding or altering the previous resolution should be passed.

VOTING

The term vote means an expression of a wish or opinion in an authorised formal way for or against any proposal. Every holder of equity shares possesses normal voting rights. It means that they have the right to vote on every resolution placed before the company at a general meeting. The preference shareholders do not possess normal voting rights. A preference shareholder has the right to vote only on resolutions which directly affect the rights attached to his preference shares.

In the case of joint shareholders, the vote of the person whose name appears first in the register of members shall be accepted.

Methods of Voting

Voting may be by show of hands or by taking a poll. Voting by secret ballot is not allowed by the Companies Act.

1. *Voting by Show of Hands (Sec. 107):* In the first instance, resolutions put to vote are decided by a show of hands, unless a poll is demanded. Under this method of voting, one member has one vote only and proxy has no right to vote unless otherwise provided in the articles. A declaration by the Chairman of the result of voting by show of hands is a conclusive evidence.

2. *Voting through Electronic Means (Sec. 108):* Every listed company having five hundred or more shareholders may provide to its members facility to exercise their right to vote at general meetings by electronic means. A member may exercise his right to vote at any general meetings by electronic means and company may pass any resolution by electronic voting system.

It may be noted that 'voting by electronic means' or electronic voting system' means a 'secured system' with adequate 'cyber security'.

'Secured system' means computer hardware, software and procedure that:

(a) are reasonably secure from unauthorised access and misuse;

(b) provide a reasonable level of reliability and correct operation;

(c) are reasonably suited to performing the intended functions; and

(d) adhere to generally accepted security procedures.

'Cyber security' means protecting information, equipment devices, computer, computer resource, communication device and information stored therein from unauthorised access, use, discloures, disruption, modification or destruction.

3. *Voting by Poll (Sec. 109):* Poll means counting of heads. Taking a poll indicates recording the number of votes cast for or against a resolution. A poll is to be taken if the Chairman or a prescribed number of members are dissatisfied with the result of voting by show of hands. A poll may also be demanded even before the declaration of results on a show of hands.

A poll may be ordered to be taken by the Chairman of the meeting on his own motion. A poll shall also be ordered to be taken By him on a demand made in that behalf by the following person(s):

(a) in the case of a company having a share capital: by the members present in person or by proxy, where allowed and having not less than one-tenth of the total voting power or holding shares on which an aggregate sum of not less than five lakh rupees or such higher amount as may be prescribed, has been paid-up; and

(b) in the case of any other company: By any member or members present in person or by proxy, where allowed, and having not less than one-tenth of the total voting power.

The demand for a poll may be withdrawn at any time by the persons who made it. When a poll is demanded upon the question of adjournment and also on the election of the Chairman it must be taken forthwith. A poll on any other questions may be taken out at any time within 48 hours as the Chairman may direct.

On poll each member is entitled to record the number of votes, in proportion to equity shares held by him on a vote card for and against a resolution. Voting by proxy is also allowed. In the case of a company not having a share capital every member is entitled to only one vote and voting by proxy is not allowed. A member is free to split his votes for and against the same resolution.

The manner of taking poll is to be decided by the Chairman. He appoints two scrutinisers, one of whom must be a member of the company to scrutinise the votes given on the poll. The result of the poll is deemed to be the decision of the meeting.

POSTAL BALLOT (SEC. 110)

As per Sec. 2(65) 'Postal ballot' means voting by post or through any electronic mode.

The Act provides that a company in respect of such items of business (as the Central Government by notification declares) shall be transacted only by postal ballot.

The following items of business shall be transacted only by means of voting through a postal ballot. (Rule 22 of the Company Rules, 2014):

(a) Alteration of the objects clause of the Memorandum and in the case of the company in existence immediately before the commencement of the Act, alteration of the main objects of the Memorandum.

(b) Alteration of Articles of Association in relation to insertion or removal of provisions which, consider Sub-section (68) of Section 2 are required to be included in the Articles of a company in order to constitute it as a private company.

(c) Change in place of registered office outside the local limits of any city, town or village as specified in Sub-section (5) of Section 12.

(d) Change in objects for which a company has raised money from public through Prospectus and still has any unutilised amount out of the money so raised under Sub-section (8) of Section 13.

(e) Issue of shares with differential rights as to voting or dividend or otherwise under Sub-clause (ii) of Clause (a) of Section 43.

(f) Variation in the rights attached to a class of shares or debentures or other securities as specified under Section 48.

(g) Buy-back of shares by a company under Sub-section (1) of Section 68.

(h) Election of a director under Section 151 of the Act.

(i) Sale of the whole or substantially the whole of an undertaking of a company as specified.

(j) Giving loans or extending guarantee or providing security in excess of the limit prescribed under Sub-section (3) of Section 186.

Section 110(1)(b) further provides that a company may pass any item of business, other than ordinary business and any business in respect of which directors or auditors have a right to be heard.

PROXIES [SEC. 105]

Proxy is an instrument appointing another person to vote for the appointer. The person so appointed is known as proxy. A proxy need not be a member of the company. A member may vote either in person or by proxy. A proxy is not entitled to vote except on a poll unless otherwise provided in the articles. The proxy shall not have a right to speak at the meeting, but he can demand a poll. As it is the relationship of principal and agent a proxy is not entitled to act against the instructions of the shareholder in the matter.

The instrument of proxy shall be in writing and signed by the appointer or his duly authorised attorney, and must be deposited with the company forty eight hours before the meeting. Proxy forms are to be supplied to the members alongwith the notice for the meeting. Proxies can be inspected by every member entitled to vote at a meeting of the company during the 24 hours preceding the meeting till the conclusion of the meeting.

A proxy can be revoked subject to the provisions of the articles. Revocation should, however be made before the proxy has voted. Death of a member revokes the proxy but if the company has no notice of such a death, then the vote casted by the proxy shall be valid. Further, a member can prevent the proxy from exercising the right to vote by himself attending and voting at the meeting.

AGENDA

Literally, the term agenda means "things to be done". It is the programme of business to be transacted at a meeting. It is prepared for all kinds of meetings in order that the meeting may be conducted systematically. It is normally typed on a foolscap paper leaving a margin on the right hand side for making remarks. The Chairman of the meeting usually takes up the items on the agenda in the same order but the order may be changed with the wishes of the members who are present.

It is the duty of the secretary to draw up the agenda in consultation with the Chairman or Managing Director of the company. The Secretary prepares two types of agenda one for the guidance of the chairman and the other to be sent to the members alongwith the notice of the meeting. Sometimes, companies maintain an agenda book which becomes a permanent record for future.

The items of agenda are supplied in advance with the notice convening the meeting to every person entitled to receive the notice. In the case of Board meetings it is a common practice to supply a copy of the detailed agenda to every director.

The following guiding principles may be kept in view while drafting the agenda:

(a) It should be clear and explicit.

(b) It should be prepared in summary manner.

(c) All items of routine matters should be put down first and the other matters later, and

(d) All items of similar or allied nature should be placed in a continuous order.

ADJOURNMENT AND POSTPONEMENT OF MEETING

Adjournment of a meeting is discontinuing a meeting with the object of resuming it on a future date. It is done when the meeting becomes disorderly or the quorum is not present or the business is not completed within a scheduled time. Adjournment of a properly convened meeting is governed by the articles of the companies. An adjourned meeting is regarded in law as a continuation of the original meeting and the resolutions passed at an adjourned meeting are to be treated as passed on the date on which they were in fact passed.

Postponement of a meeting indicates that the commencement of the meeting itself is deferred. It shall be done when the meeting is not properly convened. There can be no postponement of a meeting by subsequent notice unless the articles specifically permit. But under certain unforeseen circumstances, when a meeting is required to be postponed, the proper procedure would be to hold the meeting without transacting any business and adjourn it.

PROCEEDINGS OF THE DEBATE

(a) *Motions:* The term motion refers to a proposition which is formally made at a meeting for the discussion and ultimate decision. A motion is liable to alteration or amendment before it is adopted by the meeting. Thus, a motion when passed with or without amendment is called a resolution. Generally, a motion requires a prior notice, but formal motions like motion for condolence, motion for adjournment of the meeting, and motion for appointment of Chairman may be moved without prior notice. A motion should also be seconded. However, a motion initiated by the chairman needs no seconding.

Requisites of a Valid Motion: A motion to be valid should satisfy the following conditions:

(a) It must be within the scope of the meeting.

(b) It must be moved only by the members.

(c) It must be in writing and signed by the mover.

(d) It should be clear and not ambiguous.

(e) It must be introduced with a prior notice.

(f) It should be in a positive or affirmative form and begin with the word 'That' so that when passed it reads 'Resolved that'.

(g) It should be formally proposed by one at the meeting and seconded by another.

If the Chairman has approved the motion, it is put before the house. Members who like to speak for and against the motion shall be allowed to speak only once. But the proposer is entitled to speak twice on his motion once when he makes the proposal and once when he wishes to make a reply to the debate. In the course of discussion, the proposer may be allowed to withdraw his motion if the seconder agrees to it and the meeting gives its assent. After the discussion, the Chairman puts it to vote unless the meeting adopts it unanimously. In case the majority votes are casted in favour of the motion, the chairman declares "The motion is carried" and hence the motion becomes a 'Resolution'.

Owing to technical flaws if a motion is not acceptable, it is said to "fall to the ground".

Interruptions of Debate: When the Chairman invites a debate on a motion, the debate on the original motion is diverted by a number of ways. Such interruptions of stopping the flow of the discussion are: (a) Amendment; (b) Formal or dilatory motions; and (c) Points of order.

Amendments: An amendment is a proposed alteration or modification in the wording of or in terms of the motion which is yet to be considered at the meeting.

With regard to an amendment to a motion the following rules are to be followed:

(i) The amendment should be restricted to addition, deletion, substitution or changing the order of the word.

(ii) The amendment should be in affirmative.

(iii) The amendment must be in writing.

(iv) The amendment must be seconded.

(v) The amendment should not be a counter proposal.

(vi) If the amendment is carried out it is incorporated in the original motion.

(vii) The altered motion becomes a substantive motion and when passed, becomes a resolution.

(viii) The amendment cannot be withdrawn without the permission of the meeting.

No amendment is permissible to a special resolution and to a resolution requiring a special notice.

(b) *Formal Motions:* Formal motions are also known as procedural or dilatory motion as they are concerned with the procedure at a meeting. They are meant for the purpose of interrupting the proceedings. They need not be in writing and do not require any previous notice. A member may move such motions during the proceedings of the meeting. They should also be seconded. The main formal motions are:

(i) *The Closure:* If a member feels that the debate on the question before the meeting has been dragged on for a long time, he may propose that 'the question be now put'. Such motion is called 'The closure' or 'The Gag'. It can be proposed even to an amendment. If a majority of the members favours it, the chairman will apply 'Gag' and close the debate for putting the question to vote; or else the discussion may be resumed.

(ii) *The Previous Questions:* The purpose, of the Previous Question Motion is to set aside the discussion on the motion before the house. When a main motion (but not the amendment to it) is under discussion, a member (other than the proposer or the seconder of the original motion) thinks that no useful purpose will be served to discuss it any more at the meeting. He may, therefore, move the 'previous question' or propose that "the question be not now put". If the Previous Question Motion is carried, the main motion is shelved so far as the meeting at least is concerned. If it is lost, the original motion is put to vote immediatᵒly without further discussion.

(iii) *Proceed to the Next Business:* Like the previous question, it is also aimed at the dropping of the motion immediately before the meeting. It is put in the form that the meetings do proceed to the next business. The motion is put to vote and if it is carried, the subject under discussion is dropped. In case it is lost, the discussion on the main motion is resumed.

(iv) *Adjournment Motion:* A member (other than the proposer or seconder of the original motion) of the motion before the meeting may move that the debate on the motion be adjourned or postponed to some other time and/or day. If the motion is carried, the dabate is postponed to an agreed date. In case it is lost, the debate is resumed.

(c) *Points of Order:* A point of order is a sort of corrective device in the hands of the members. It is raised only to seek some clarification or to remind the speaker that he is not speaking to the point. Any member can raise points of order if he finds that the meeting is not properly convened and constituted. The Chairman's ruling on this point is final and binding on the members whether it be right or wrong. When a 'point' of order is settled, the discussion is resumed.

PRIVILEGED OCCASION

An occasion is said to be a 'Privileged Occasion' when no legal action for defamation can be taken against the person who makes certain written or oral statement on that occasion though the statement is defamatory.

Meetings of directors and shareholders are considered privileged occasions. The privilege extended to the members attending these meetings is qualified privilege. A qualified privilege enjoys legal protection only if a defamatory statement is based on truth, good faith, without malice and in the common interest.

Members of Parliament delivering speeches inside the House enjoy 'Absolute Privilege'. In the case of absolute privilege no legal action will lie at all with regard to defamatory statements, irrespective of their truth or falsity.

RESOLUTIONS

A resolution may be defined as the formal decision of a meeting on any proposal before it. Three kinds of resolutions are approved by the Companies Act. The Companies Act and the Articles of Association provide the type of resolution required for any particular business. Sec. 114 provides provisions with regard to Ordinary and Special Resolutions.

Kinds of Resolutions

1. *Ordinary Resolutions:* A resolution passed by a simple majority of shareholders is known as an ordinary resolution. Simple majority means that the votes cast in favour of a particular proposal including the casting vote of the Chairman are more than the votes against it. The votes may be cast on a show of hands or on a poll in general meeting of which 21 days notice is given.

    An ordinary resolution is normally used for transacting the so called ordinary business in the Annual General Meeting. Unless in the Companies Act or the Articles of the company expressly provided otherwise an ordinary resolution is sufficient to carry out any business.

2. *Special Resolution:* A resolution which is passed by three-fourth majority of the members voting by a show of hands or on a poll either in person or by proxy is known as a special resolution. The intention to propose the resolution as special resolution must be specifically stated in the notice calling the general meeting. The special resolution must be passed in the matters specifically provided by law. All special resolutions must be filed with the Registrar within 30 days of passing the same.

    A special resolution is necessary in the following cases:
    (a) Change in the name of the company.
    (b) Change of registered office from one State to another State.
    (c) Change in the objects clause of the company.
    (d) Alteration of Articles of Association.
    (e) Reduction of share capital.
    (f) Payment of interest out of capital.
    (g) Determination of remuneration payable to any director.
    (h) Determination to create reserve capital.

    (i) Making of loans to another company under the same management.

    (j) Declaration of investigation of the affairs of the company.

    (k) Voluntary winding up.

3. *Resolutions Requiring Special Notice [Sec.115]:* It is a kind of ordinary resolution, with the difference that here the mover of the proposed resolution should give to the company not less than 14 days notice before moving the resolution (Exclusive of the day on which the notice is served and the day of the meeting). The company in turn must give notice of any such a resolution to its members in the same manner as it gives notice of any general meeting (i.e., 21 days notice). If however, it is not practicable to give 21 days notice, the company must give notice either by advertisement in a newspaper having an appropriate circulation or in any other mode allowed by the articles not less than 7 days before the meeting.

    Special notice is required by the Act in the following matters:

    (a) Appointment of an auditor other than the retiring auditor.

    (b) Provision that a retiring auditor shall not be reappointed.

    (c) Removal of director before the expiration of his term.

    (d) Appointment of another person as a director in place of the director removed.

SPECIMEN NOTICE OF AN ANNUAL GENERAL MEETING

ARUN Co. Ltd. Ernakulam

NOTICE

Notice is hereby given that the 12th Annual General Meeting of the Company will be held on Monday, the 12th June 2012, at 3 p.m. at the Company's Registered office, T.C. 50/91, Cochin, Ernakulam to transact the business as per agenda annexed hereto.

Dated: 10th May, 2014   By Order of the Board

Secretary

Encl: 1. Agenda

     2. Copies of audited accounts together with the Director's Annual Report

     3. An explanatory statement

     4. Proxy form.

N.B.: 1. A member entitled to attend and vote at the meeting is entitled to appoint a proxy to attend and vote instead of himself and a proxy need not be a member.

2. The Transfer books and register of members will be closed from 15th May to 12th June, 2014 both days inclusive.

3. Members are requested to notify change of address, if any

SPECIMEN OF RESOLUTIONS

(i) RESOLVED: That 100 equity shares of ₹50 each bearing numbers from 1001 to 1100 inclusive, whereon ₹25 per share have been paid, and which at the date of his resolution were registered in the name of Shri. P.K. Bose of Dwaraka, Ernakulam be and hereby forfeited for non-payment of the first call of ₹10 per share made on the 1st day of March 2007 and for non-payment of interest thereon and that the said shares be disposed of as the Directors shall think fit.

(ii) RESOLVED: That the 1000 number of shares entered in the Allotment List against the names of each respectively, bearing numbers 1 to 1000 each of ₹100 be and are hereby allotted to the parties and in the proportions set out in the list, and that notice of such allotment be given to the respective parties, and secretary is hereby instructed to prepare and send the letters of allotment to the parties concerned forthwith.

SPECIMEN OF MINUTES OF A BOARD MEETING

Minutes of the Sixteenth meeting of the Board of Directors held at the Registered Office of the company on the 10th May, 2014, at 3.00 p.m.

Present: 1. Mr. A.L. Jayan in the chair
2. Mr. A.K. Babu Director
3. Mr. C.S. Manu ,,
4. Mr. T.K. Abu ,,

In Attendance

Mr. T.R. Das Secretary
Mr. S. Sabu Accountant
Mr. K. Vinayan Manager

Sl. No.	Subject	Details of Minutes
10	Minutes of last meeting	The minutes of the last meeting held on 8th March, 2014 were read, approved as correct and signed.

11	Cash statements and payments	The secretary produced the bank pass book and a statement of cash receipts and payments during the month ending on 30 April. The statement was checked and approved.
12	Trading returns	The monthly trading returns were submitted which showed a turnover of ₹ 2,00,000. The returns were duly approved.
13	Report of Transfer Committee	The report of the Transfer Committee was next considered. It showed that applications were received for transfer of 100 shares from 5 shareholders, all of which were accepted and the transfers were given due effect to. It was unanimously resolved that the said report be adopted in full.
14	Next meeting	The next meeting was fixed to be held on 8th November, 2014 at the company's office. Date: 10-5-2014
		Sd/- Chairman

SPECIMEN OF MINUTES OF AN ANNUAL GENERAL MEETING

Minutes of the 10th Annual General meeting of the ABC Co. held at the Registered Office of the company on Wednesday the 3rd May 2014 at 3 p.m.

Present: Shri. A.L. Jayan   in the chair
  ,, A.K. Babu   Director
  ,, C.R. Manu   ,,
  ,, T.K. Abu   ,,
and 60 other members whose names appear in a separate sheet attached.

In Attendance

Shri. T.R. Das   Secretary
  ,,   G. Saji   Solicitor
  ,,   S. Sam   Auditor

Sl. No.	Subject	Details of Minutes
59	Notice	The Secretary read out the notice convening the meeting.
60	Minutes of last Annual General Meeting	The minutes of last Annual General meeting were read, approved and signed by the chairman.

61	Director's report and auditor's report	At the request of the Chairman, the Director's report, profit and loss account for the year ended 31st March, 2013 and the balance sheet as on that date and the auditor's report thereon previously circulated were taken as read.
62	Chairman's report	The chairman delivered a speech outlining in brief the achievements of the company since the last meeting and the present position and future prospects of the company. He invited questions from members on the report and accounts and answered them satisfactorily.
63	Adoption of report and account	On the motion of the chairman and the same being seconded by Suku, it was resolved unanimously that the director's report and the audited profit and loss account for the year ended 31st March, 2013 and the balance sheet as at the date be and are hereby approved and adopted."
64	Declaration of dividend	On the motion of the chairman and the same being seconded by Shri Roshan it was resolved "That a dividend ₹10 per share on 20,000, 5 per cent preference shares and on 1,00,000 equity shares, as recommended by the directors, be declared for the year 2012–2013 and that dividend be paid to those shareholders whose names appear in the companies register of members as on 1st May, 2014."
65	Election of	On the motion of the chairman and the same being seconded by Shri. Ram and the motion being carried by a majority of 52 to 8 votes it was resolved "That Shri C.S. Manu, a Director, who retires by rotation but is eligible for re-election be and is hereby re-elected a Director of the company."
66	Appointment of auditors	On the motion of Shri. Suku and the same being seconded by Shri. Roshan it was resolved "That M/s Ram and Co. Chartered Accountants, auditors of the company, be and are hereby re-appointed as auditors of the company for the current year on the remuneration of ₹10,000."
67	Vote of thanks	There being no other business before the meeting, on the motion of Shri. Muthu and the same being seconded by Shri. Ajayan the meeting terminated with a vote of thanks to the chairman, and the secretary and the staff for their services rendered, for the development and prosperity of the company. Date: 03-05-2014 A.L. Jayan Chairman

REVIEW QUESTIONS

1. What is meeting?
2. What is annual general meeting?
3. What do you mean by proper notice?
4. What is quorum?
5. What is agenda?
6. Define 'minutes'.
7. What is resolution?
8. What is class meeting?
9. What is disinterested quorum?
10. Who is called a proxy?
11. What is an amendment?
12. What is an ordinary resolution?
13. What is special resolution?
14. What is meant by adjournment of a meeting?
15. What is substantive motion?
16. What is meant by e-voting?
17. What do you mean by voting through postal ballet?
18. What do you mean by voting through show of hands?
19. Distinguish between adjournment and postponement of the meeting.
20. What are the requisites of an agenda?
21. What are the essentials of a valid motion?
22. What are the requisites of valid amendment?
23. Distinguish between motion and resolution.
24. What is the quorum for general meeting?
25. What is the closure motion?
26. Write a note on resolutions requiring special notice.
27. Distinguish between motion and resolution.
28. Distinguish between ordinary resolution and special resolution.
29. Explain the statutory provisions regarding recording of minutes of company meetings.
30. Enumerate the different kinds of company meetings.
31. Enumerate the purposes of special resolution.
32. Explain the law relating to the contents of notice.
33. Describe briefly the passing of resolution by postal ballot.

34. Enumerate and explain the requisites of a valid meeting.

35. Explain the statutory provisions relating to annual general meeting.

36. What is extraordinary general meeting? Explain its statutory provisions.

37. Explain the statutory provisions relating to proxy.

38. What is a 'poll'? When and by whom can a demand for poll be made? How is poll conducted?

39. Explain the two different modes of voting.

PRACTICAL PROBLEMS

Attempt the following problems, giving reasons:

1. A company having its registered office in Madras wants to hold its general meeting in Patna. Can it do so?

   Hint: Yes, with the permission of the Central Government.

2. At a meeting of a company, 15 shareholders were present, 9 voted for a special resolution and 2 against, the four did not vote at all. No poll demanded and the chairman declared the resolution to be carried. Is this a valid resolution?

   Hint: Yes.

3. Accounting year of a public limited company closes on 30th June. It held its last annual general meeting on 31st August, 2004. Your advice is sought as to whether it can hold its next annual general meeting either on 31st December, 2005 or 31st January, 2006. Advise.

   Hint: The company can hold the annual general meeting on 31st December, 2005. with the permission of the Registrar.

4. W, a chairman at an annual general meeting, declares a motion carried after a show of hands and says "five in favour, twenty five against it, but sixty voting by proxy". Is he right in his judgement?

   Hint: No. Proxies are not to be counted in the case of voting by show of hands.

40

Disclosure and Transparency

Vigil Mechanism would enable a company to evolve a process to encourage ethical corporate behaviour.

ANNUAL RETURN (SEC. 92)

1. Every company shall prepare a return, known as annual return in the prescribed form containing the following particulars:

   (a) Its registered office, principal business activities particulars of its holding, subsidiary and associate companies;

   (b) Its shares, debentures and other securities and shareholding pattern;

   (c) Its indebtedness;

   (d) Its members and debentureholders along with changes therein since the close of the previous year;

   (e) Its promoters, directors, key managerial personnel along with changes therein since the close of the previous financial year;

   (f) Meetings of members or a class thereof, Board and its various committees along with attendance details;

   (g) Remuneration of directors and key managerial personnel;

   (h) Penalty or punishment imposed on the company, its directors or officers and details of compounding of offences and appeals made against such penalty or punishment.;

   (i) Matters relating to certification of compliances, disclosures as may be prescribed;

   (j) Details (as may be prescribed) in respect of shares held by or on behalf of the Foreign Institutional Investors indicating their names, addresses, countries of incorporation, registration and percentage of shareholding held by them; and

(k) Such other matters as may be prescribed.

It shall be signed by a director and the company secretary, or where there is no company secretary, by a company secretary in practice.

But in respect of One Person Company and small company, the annual return shall be signed by the company secretary, or where there is no company secretary, by the director of the company.

2. The annual return filed by a listed company or, by a company having such paid-up capital or turnover as may be prescribed shall be certified by a company secretary in practice in the prescribed form.

3. An extract of the annual return in such form as may be prescribed shall form part of the Board's report.

4. Every company shall file with the Registrar a copy of the annual return, within sixty days from the date on which the annual general meeting is held or if no annual general meeting is held in any year, within sixty days from the date on which the annual general meeting should have been held together with the reasons of not holding the AGM with such fees or additional fees as may be prescribed within the time as specified under Sec. 403.

5. If a company fails to file its annual return as per Sub-section (4), before the expiry of the period specified under Sec. 403 with additional fees, the company shall be punishable with fine of not less than fifty thousand rupees and not more than five lakh rupees and every officer of the company who is in default shall be punishable with imprisonment for a term up to six months or with a fine of not less than fifty thousand rupees and not more than five lakh rupees or with both.

6. If a company secretary in practice certifies the annual return otherwise than in conformity with the requirements of this Section or the rules made thereunder, he shall be punishable with fine of not less than fifty thousand rupees and not more than five lakh rupees.

Return to be Filed with Registrar in Case Promoters' Stake Changes (Sec. 93)

Every listed company shall file a return in the prescribed form with the Registrar with respect to change in the number of shares held by promoters and top ten shareholders of such company, within fifteen days of such a change.

Place of Keeping and Inspection of Registers, Returns etc. (Sec. 94).

1. The registers required to be kept and maintained by a company as per Section 88 and copies of the annual return filed under Section 92 shall be kept at the registered office of the company.

2. The registers and their indices, except when they are closed under the provisions of this Act, and the copies of all the returns shall be open for inspection by any member, debentureholder, other security holder or beneficial owner during business hours without payment of any fees and by any other person on payment of such fees as may be prescribed.

3. Any such member, debentureholder, other security holder or beneficial owner or any other person may

   (a) take extracts from any register, or index or return without payment of any fee; or

   (b) require a copy of any such register or entries therein or return on payment of such fees as may be prescribed.

4. If any inspection or the making of any extract or copy required under this Section is refused, the company and every officer of the company who is in default shall be liable, for each such default, to a penalty of one thousand rupees for every day subject to a maximum of one lakh rupees during which refusal or default continues.

5. The Central Government may also, by order, direct an immediate inspection of the document, or direct that the extract required shall forthwith be allowed to be taken by the person requiring it.

BOARD'S REPORT

The Board's Report is an important means of communication by the Board of Directors. It serves to inform the stakeholders about the performance and prospects of the company, relevant changes in management, capital structure, major policies, recommendations as to the distribution of profits, future programmes of expansion, modernisation and diversification, capitalisation of reserves, further issue of capital, etc.

The various matters to be included in the Board's Report have been specified in Sec. 134(3) of the Companies Act, 2013. Besides, the Reserve Bank of India Act, 1934, the Securities and Exchange Board of India Act, 1992 and the regulations, rules, directions, guidelines, circulars, etc. issued thereunder, necessitate certain additional disclosures to be made in the Board's Report.

Disclosures under Sec.134 of the Companies Act, 2013

As per Sec. 134(3), the Board report shall include the following:

(a) The extract of the annual return as provided as per Sec. 92(3). It, in such form as may be prescribed, shall form part of the Board's report [prescribed under rule 12(1) and form MGT9, Companies (management and administration) Rule, 2014].

(b) Number of meetings of the Board.

(c) Directors' Responsibility Statement.

(d) A statement on declaration given by independent directors as per Sec. 149(6).

(e) In the case of a company covered as per Sub-section (1) of the Sec. 178, company's policy on directors' appointment and remuneration including criteria for determining qualifications, positive attributes, independence of a director and other matters as given as per Sub-section (3) of Sec. 178.

(f) Explanations or comments by the Board on every qualification, reservation or adverse remark or disclaimer made:

(i) by the auditor in his report; and

(ii) by the company secretary in practice in his secretarial audit report.

(g) Particulars of loans, guarantees or investments as per Sec. 186.

(h) Particulars of contracts or arrangements with related parties referred to in Sub-section (1) of Sec. 188 in the prescribed form.

(i) The state of the company's affairs.

(j) The amounts, if any, which it proposes should be carried to any reserves.

(k) The amount, if any, which it recommends should be paid by way of dividend.

(l) Material changes and commitments, if any, affecting the financial position of the company.

(m) The conservation of energy, technology absorption, foreign exchange earnings and outgo, in such manner as may be prescribed.

(n) A statement indicating development and implementation of a risk management policy for the company.

(o) The details about the policy developed and implemented by the company on corporate social responsibility initiatives taken during the year.

(p) In the case of a listed company and every other public company (having such paid-up share capital as may be prescribed) a statement showing the manner in which formal annual evaluation has been made by the Board of its own performance and that of its committees and individual directors.

(q) Such other matters as may be prescribed.

Directors Responsibility Statement

Section 134(5) referred to in Clause (c) Section 134(3) shall state that:

(a) in the preparation of the annual accounts, the applicable accounting standards had been followed along with proper explanation relating to material departures;

(b) the directors had selected such accounting policies and applied them consistently and made judgements and estimates that are reasonable and prudent;

(c) the directors had taken proper and sufficient care for the maintenance of adequate accounting records as per the provisions of this Act for safeguarding the assets of the company and detecting fraud;

(d) the directors had prepared the annual accounts on a going concern basis;

(e) the directors, in the case of a listed company, had laid down internal financial controls to be followed by the company and that such systems adequate and operating effectively; and

(f) the directors had devised proper systems to ensure compliance with the provisions of all applicable laws and that such systems were adequate and operating effectively.

Other Disclosures under the Companies Act, 2013

Independent Director

A director who is not related to the promoters or the other members of the company is known as an independent director.

An independent director shall hold office for a term up to five consecutive years on the Board of a company [Sec. 149(10)]. But he shall be eligible for reappointment on passing of a special resolution by the company. The disclosure of such appointments shall be made in the Board's report.

Audit Committee

The composition of audit committee under Sec. 177(8) shall be disclosed in the Board's report. The recommendation of the audit committee which is not accepted by the Board along with reason thereof should also be disclosed.

Sec. 177(10) states that the disclosure in Board's report includes the details of the establishment of vigil mechanism under Sec. 177(9). Vigil mechanism shall provide for adequate safeguards against victimisation of persons who use such mechanism. It shall also make provisions for direct access to the Chairperson of the Audit Committee in appropriate or exceptional cases.

> *VIGIL MECHANISM:* It is the whistle blowing provision which is a mandatory requirement under Sec. 177(9). This mechanism would enable a company to evolve a process to encourage ethical corporate behaviour. Every listed company shall establish a Vigil mechanism for their Directors and Employees to report their genuine concern or grievances.

Nomination and Remuneration Committee

All the listed companies and such other class or classes (as may be prescribed) should have a nomination and remuneration committee [Sec. 178(1)].

In accordance with Rule 6 of the Companies (Meeting of Board and its Powers) Rules, 2014, the following classes of companies shall constitute Nomination and Remuneration Committee:

(i) All public companies with a paid-up capital of ten crore rupees or more.

(ii) All public companies having turnover of one hundred crore rupees or more.

(iii) All public companies, having in aggregate, outstanding loans or borrowings or debentures or deposits exceeding fifty crore rupees or more.

> *EXPLANATION:* The paid-up share capital or turnover or outstanding loans or borrowings or debentures or deposits, as the case may be, as existing on the date of last audited Financial Statements shall be taken into account for the purpose of this rule.

As per Sec. 178(4), the Board's Report shall disclose such policy according to which the Nomination and Remuneration Committee ensure that:

(a) the level and composition of remuneration is reasonable and sufficient to attract, retain and motivate directors of the quality required to run the company successfully;

(b) relationship of remuneration to performance is clear and meets appropriate performance benchmarks; and

(c) remuneration to directors, key managerial personnel and senior management involves a balance between fixed and incentive pay reflecting short and long-term performance objectives appropriate to the working of the company and its goal.

Secretarial Audit for Bigger Companies

Every listed company and other prescribed companies in Rule 9, Companies (Appointment and Remuneration of Managerial Personnel) Rules, 2014 shall annex the secretarial audit report given by a Company Secretary in practice with Board's Report [Sec. 204(1)]. Board in its report shall explain any qualification or other remarks made by the Company Secretary in practice. Secretarial Audit Report given by a Company Secretary shall be in the Form No. MR-3.

Penal Provisions [Sec. 134(8)]

If a company contravenes the provisions of this Section the company shall be punishable with a fine of not less than fifty thousand rupees and not more than twenty five lakh rupees. Every officer of the company who is in default shall be punishable with imprisonment for a term up to three years or with a fine not less than fifty thousand rupees and not more than five lakh rupees, or with both.

REPORT ON ANNUAL GENERAL MEETING (SEC. 121)

Every listed public company is required to prepare a report on each annual general meeting [Sec. 121(1)].

A copy of the report shall be filed with the Registrar in Form No. MGT-15 within thirty days of the conclusion of annual general meeting along with the prescribed fee.

The report shall be prepared in the following manner (Rule 31)

(a) A report under this Section shall be prepared apart from the minutes of the general meeting.

(b) The report shall be signed and dated by the Chairman of the meeting. In the case of Chairman's inability to sign, the report shall be signed by any two directors of the company, one of whom shall be the Managing Director, if there is one.

(c) The following details shall be included in such report.

  (i) The day, date, hour and venue of the annual general meeting.

  (ii) Confirmation with respect to appointment of Chairman of the meeting.

  (iii) Number of members attending the meeting.

  (iv) Confirmation of quorum.

  (v) Confirmation with respect to compliance of the Act and the Rules, secretarial standards made there regarding calling, convening and conducting the meeting.

  (vi) Business transacted at the meeting and result thereof.

  (vii) Particulars regarding any adjournment, postponement of meeting and change in venue.

(d) Such report shall contain fair and correct summary of the proceedings of the meeting.

PROMOTERS HOLDING

Every listed company has to disclose to the ROC when there is any change in number of shares held by promoters or top ten shareholders (Sec. 93). Such a disclosure shall be made in Form, MGT-10 within fifteen days of such a change (Rule 13).

The word "change" means increase or decrease by two per cent or more in the shareholding of each of the promoters and each of the top ten shareholders of the company.

In the Case of Change in Volume

For the purpose of calculation of 2 per cent whether shareholder's holding or company's share capital is to be taken into account Logically, it should be in 2 per cent change of share capital of the company. For instance, If Mr. X holds 10 per cent share capital of ABC Limited then at the time of 2 per cent changes in upside or downside ABC Limited shall intimate to ROC.

The intimation should be on cumulative 2 per cent change of the shareholding. As and when change in holding reaches 2 per cent from the last intimation, fresh intimation will be mandatory.

In the Case of Change in Value

For the purpose of calculation of 2 per cent whether market value of the shares is to be taken into account or face value of shares is to be considered. As per wordings of the Rule, it should be on market value of shares.

Responsibility of Filing

Responsibility of filing under this provision is given to companies. The promoters and other top ten shareholders will not have to intimate to the company, but company has to keep track on their shareholdings.

INTERESTED DIRECTOR

A director who has interest in any company or companies or body corporate (including shareholding interest), firms or other association of individuals is known as an interested director.

Contracts in which a Director is Interested

When a director has to enter into a contract with the company for the sale, purchase or supply of goods, material, or services, such a contract should be approved by the Board by resolution passed at its meeting. A similar approval of the Board is essential when a contract of the aforesaid type is being made by a relative of the director or a firm in which the director or his relative is a partner or of any other partner in which a firm, or a private company in which the director is a member or director.

The approval of the Board shall be expressed either before the contract is made or within three months from the date of the contract. Unless the contract is approved, it becomes voidable at the option of the Board.

No approval of the Board is, however, necessary in the following cases:

(i) When the contract is made at the existing market price of the goods purchased or sold, or

(ii) When the contract relates to the goods or services in which the company or the other party regularly trades or does business. In this case it is necessary that the value of the contract or contracts, if there are more than one, does not exceed ₹5,000 in a year.

(iii) In the case of urgent necessity a contract shall be made beyond the above limit and without the approval of the Board, provided of course, the same is obtained within three months.

Disclosure of Interest by Director (Sec. 184)

Every director is required to disclose the nature of his concern or interest at the meeting of Board in which the contract or arrangement is discussed.

If a director is not concerned or interested at the time of the contract but, subsequently becomes concerned or interested is required to disclose his interest or concern at the first meeting of the Board.

In case a contract or arrangement entered into by the company without disclosure of interest by a director or with participation by a director who is concerned or interested in any way, directly or indirectly, in the contract or arrangement shall be voidable at the option of the company.

The contravention of the provisions leads to punishment for a term up to one year or with fine of not less than fifty thousand rupees and not more than one lakh rupees or both.

Any contract or arrangement entered into or to be entered into between two companies, where any director or any company hold more than two per cent of the paid-up capital in other company, the provisions of this Section shall not apply.

RELATED PARTY TRANSACTIONS (SEC. 188)

Related Party

With reference to the company, the term 'related party' includes the following.

(a) A director or his relative.

(b) KMP or their relative.

(c) A firm in which a director, manager or his relative is a partner.

(d) A private company in which a director or manager is a director or member.

(e) A public company in which a director or manager is a director or holds along with his relatives more than 2 per cent of its paid up share capital.

(f) A person on whose advice, directions or instruction (except given in professional capacity) a director or manager is accustomed to act.

(g) A holding/subsidiary or associate company, subsidiary's subsidiary, and such person as would be prescribed.

Nature of Transactions [Sec. 188(1)]

The following transactions shall be covered under the scope of this Section.

(a) Sale, purchase or supply of any goods or materials.

(b) Selling or otherwise disposing of, or buying, property of any kind.

(c) Leasing of property of any kind.

(d) Availing or rendering of any services.

(e) Appointment of any agent for purchase or sale of goods, materials, services or property.

(f) Such related party's appointment to any office or place of profit in the company, its subsidiary company or associate company.

(g) Underwriting the subscription of any securities or derivatives thereof, of the company.

The transactions done in ordinary course of business on arm length's basis shall be outside the scope of this Section.

The expression "arm's length transaction" means a transaction between two related parties that is conducted as if they were unrelated, so that there is no conflict of interest.

Entering into Contract or Arrangement with Related Party

[Rule 15 of the Companies (Meeting of Board and its Powers) Rules 2014]

Subject to the following conditions, a company shall enter into any contract or arrangement with a related party:

1. The agenda of the Board meeting at which the resolution is proposed to be moved shall disclose:

   (a) the name of the related party and nature of relationship;

(b) the nature, duration of the contract and particulars of the contract or arrangement;

(c) the material terms of the contract or arrangement including the value, if any;

(d) any advance paid or received for the contract or arrangement, if any,

(e) the manner of determining the pricing and other commercial terms, both included as part of contract and not considered as part of the contract;

(f) whether all factors relevant to the contract have been considered; and

(g) any other information relevant or important for the Board to take a decision on the proposed transaction.

2. If any director is interested in any contract or arrangement with a related party, such director shall not be present at the meeting during discussion on the subject matter of the resolution relating to such contract rearrangement.

3. In the case of wholly owned subsidiary, the special resolution passed by the holding company shall be sufficient for the purpose of entering into the transactions between wholly owned subsidiary and holding company.

4. The explanatory statement to be annexed to the notice of a general meeting (convened pursuant to Sec.101) shall contain the following particulars:

(a) Name of the related party;

(b) Name of the director or key managerial personnel who is related, if any;

(c) Nature of relationship;

(d) Nature, material terms, monetary value and particulars of the contract or arrangement; and

(e) Any other information relevant or important for the members to take a decision on the proposed resolution.

Disclosure in Board's Report

Every related party contract or arrangement shall be disclosed in the Board's report. It shall also be referred to shareholders alongwith the justification for entering into such type of transactions.

Other Disclosures

In relation to the transaction between the company and related parties the following disclosures are also required:

(i) Any arrangement between a company and its director in respect of acquisition of assets for consideration other than cash shall require prior approval by a resolution in general meeting. Further if the director or connected person is a director of its holding company, approval is required to be obtained by passing a resolution in general meeting of the holding company (Sec.192).

(ii) Where a One Person Company limited by shares or by guarantee enters into a contract with the sole member of the company who is also its director, the company shall (unless the contract is in writing) ensure that the terms of the contract or offer are contained in the Memorandum or are recorded in the Minutes of the first Board meeting held after entering into the contract. The company shall inform the Registrar about every contract entered into by the company are recorded in the Minutes.

(iii) As per the Companies Act, the Audit Committee is required to approve or modify transaction with related parties, scrutinise inter-corporate loans and investments and value undertaking or assets of the company, wherever it is necessary. Further, the Audit Committee has the authority to investigate into any matter falling under its domain. It has also the power to obtain professional advice from external sources.

Disclosures of Related Party Transactions under the Listing Agreement

The following disclosures are envisaged in terms of the listing agreement:

1. Details of all material transactions with related parties shall be disclosed quarterly along with the compliance report on corporate governance.

2. The company shall disclose the policy on dealing with Related Party Transactions on its website and also in the Annual Report.

Disclosure Requirements for Related Party Transactions under Accounting Standard (AS-18)

AS-18 is mandatory for accounting periods beginning on or after 1st April, 2001. It is to be complied with, for the preparation of financial statements of each reporting enterprise and consolidated financial statements of holding companies.

The objective of AS-18 is to establish requirements for disclosure of related party relationships and transactions between a reporting enterprise and its related parties.

The following are the disclosures which are required to be made under Accounting Standard:

1. The reporting enterprise should disclose:
   (a) the name of the transacting related party;
   (b) a description of the nature of transactions and relationship between the parties;
   (c) volume of the transactions either as an amount or as an appropriate proportion;
   (d) any other elements of the related party transactions necessary for an understanding of the financial statements;
   (e) Outstanding items and provisions pertaining to related parties at the balance sheet date; and
   (f) amounts written off in respect of debts due from or to related parties.
2. Items of a similar nature may be consolidated and disclosed by the related party.

ONLINE FILING OF DOCUMENTS

Terms Used in Online Filing

1. *E-Form:* An e-Form is the electronic equivalent of the paper form. The Ministry of Corporate Affairs (MCA) has recently launched a major e-governance initiative MCA-21. In the new system, it is envisaged that all company related documents would be filed electronically.
2. *Digital Signature Certificate (DSC):* Digital signature certificates are the digital equivalent (that is electronic format) a physical or paper certificates. Physical documents are signed manually. But electronic documents, for example e-forms are required to be signed digitally using a Digital Signature Certificate.

3. *Digital Signature:* A digital signature is the electronic signature duly issued by a certifying authority that shows the authority of the person signing the same. It is an electronic analogue of a written signature.

4. *Users of Digital Signature:* Under the MCA-21 system, the following four types of users are identified as users of Digital Signatures and are required to obtain digital signature certificate.

   (i) MCA (Government) Employees.

   (ii) Professionals (Company Secretaries Chartered Accountants, Cost Accountants and Lawyers) who interact with MCA and companies in the context of Companies Act.

   (iii) Authorised signatories of the company including Managing Director, Directors, Manager or Secretary.

   (iv) Representatives of Banks and Financial Institutions

Certified Filing Centre (CFC)

It is an extended arm of the Ministry which is manned by professionals from three core areas such as Company Secretaries, Chartered Accountants and Cost Accountants.

CFC is one of the various channels available to the stakeholders to do the statutory filing with ROC Offices across the country.

Infrastructure for e-filing

The following are the minimum system requirements for e-filing:

   (i) P-4 computer with printer.

   (ii) Windows 2000/Windows xp/Windows Vista/Windows 7.

   (iii) Internet Explorer 6.0 version and above.

   (iv) Above Acrobat Reader 9.4 and lower versions.

   (v) Scanner, and

   (vi) Java Runtime Environment (JRE) 1.6 updated version 30.

Corporate Identity Number (CIN)

Every company has been allocated a Corporate Identity Number (CIN). CIN can be traced from the MCA-21 ported through search based on:

- ROC Registration No.
- Existing Company Name
- Old Name of Company (In the case of change of name, the user is required to enter old name and the system displays corresponding current name)
- Inactive CIN (In the case of change of CIN, the user is required to enter previous inactive CIN Number)

Foreign Company Registration Number (FCRN)

Every foreign company has been allotted a Foreign Company Registration Number (FCRN).

Service Request Number (SRN)

Every transaction in e-filing is identified by a Service Request Number (SRN). On filing of an e-Form, the system will generate and provide a Service Request Number (SRN). The status of the document/transaction can be checked by a user by entering the SRN.

Pre-Certification of E-forms

Pre-certification means certification of correctness of any document by a professional before the same is filed with the Registrar.

Some e-Forms are required to be certified by practising professionals, namely, Company Secretaries, Chartered Accountants, Cost Accountants in whole-time practice.

Pre-fill

Pre-fill is a functionality in an e-Form that is used for filling automatically, the requisite data from the system without repeatedly entering the same.

For instance, by entering the CIN of the company, the name and registered office address of the company shall automatically be pre-filled by the system without any fresh entry.

Attachment

A document which is sent as an enclosure with an e-Form is known as attachment.

The object of attachment is to provide details relevant to the e-Form for processing. While some attachments are mandatory, some are optional in nature.

Check Form

By clicking 'Check Form' the user can find out whether the mandatory fields in an e-Form are duly filled in.

Modify

Once the user has done 'Check Form, the form gets locked and it cannot be edited. In case the user wants to bring any changes, the form can be overwritten by clicking "Modify" button.

Pre-Scrutiny

It is a functionality which is used for checking whether certain core aspects are properly filled in the e-Form. The user has to login on MCA portal to perform the pre-scrutiny of e-Form.

Addendum to e-Form

The user may have to submit some additional supporting documents which are not submitted during the e-Form filing. But, these are required for the processing of the e-Form.

The user can initiate this on their own by checking the track transaction status on My MCA portal or on being notified by MCA through e-mail. No fee is required for filing an addendum.

E-Stamp

Registrars of Companies are required to ensure that proper stamp duty is paid on the instruments registered with their office. Accordingly, physical submission of documents is necessary to ascertain that applicable stamp duty has been paid. Although, the e-Form is submitted instantly, the ROC office has to wait for receipt of physical stamp papers to initiate necessary processing.

The following are the list of e-Forms to which e-Stamping will be applicable.

INC-2 (including MOA, AOA)
INC-7 (including MOA, AOA)
FC-1
SH-7

Features of e-Form and e-Filing Process

The following are the features of e-Form and e-Filing process:

(i) The e-Form contains a number of mandatory fields which are required to be filled-in. Some other fields are non-mandatory which may be filled-in as may be relevant in any particular case.

(ii) For each e-Form, an instruction kit is available. It contains details of the instructions for properly filling the e-Form.

(iii) An e-Form can be filled in either online or offline. Online filling denotes that the e-Form is filled while being still connected to My MCA portal through the internet. But, the offline filling implies that the e-Form is downloaded into the user's computer and filled later without being connected to the internet.

(iv) Certain mandatory attachments are required to be filed along with e-Form. Certain optional attachments may also be filed with an e-Form. The list of such attachment is displayed in the e-Form.

(v) Next to attachment, there is a declaration that is sought from the person filing the e-Form to the effect that the information given in the e-Form and the attachments is correct and complete.

(vi) Most of the e-Forms require the digital signature of the Managing Director or Director, Manager or Secretary of the company for successful filing/submission.

(vii) In certain cases, the digital signature of a third party may also be required. In the case of e-Form for creation or modification of charges, such digital signature is also required from the Bank or Financial Institution.

(viii) In some cases, certification from the Chartered Accountant or Cost Accountant or Company Secretary in whole-time practice is also required to authenticate the particulars contained in the e-Form. For instance, this requirement is mandatory in respect of an e-Form for creation and modification of charges.

(ix) There are built-in facilities to check the filled-in e-Form for requisite validations.

(x) When the "Submitted" button is pressed, the e-Form gets uploaded into the MCA central document repository.

(xi) Afterwards, the requisite fees (as applicable for the e-Form) should be paid either on-line or off-line.

(xii) After the acceptance of the e-Form and acknowledgement of the payment of fees, a work item is created and assigned to the appropriate MCA employee.

(xiii) In the case of an e-Form, the authorised officer affixes his/her digital signature for registering/approving/rejecting the same.

(xiv) After the completion of the e-Form processing, an acknowledgement e-mail is sent to the user in respect of its approval/rejection.

Director Identification Number (DIN)

As per Sec. 153 and Rule 9 every individual intending to be appointed as director of a company shall make an application electronically in Form No. DIR-3 for allotment of Director Identification Number to the Central Government along with certain fee as may be prescribed. The Central Government shall, within one month from the receipt of the application, allot a Director Identification Number to an applicant (Sec. 154 and Rule 10).

The Director Identification Number so allotted under these rules is valid for the life time of the applicant and shall not be allotted to any other person.

All Director Identification Numbers allotted to individual(s) by the Central Government before the commencement of these rules shall be deemed to have been allotted to them under these rules.

General Provisions Regarding DIN

No individual shall apply for/obtain/possess another Director Identification Number who has already been allotted a Director Identification Number under Sec. 154 (Sec. 155).

Every existing director shall intimate his DIN to the company or all companies wherein he is a director within one month of the receipt of DIN from the Central Government (Sec. 156).

Every company shall, within fifteen days of the receipt of intimation, furnish the DIN of all its directors to the Registrar or any other officer as may be specified by the Central Government in this regard [Sec. 157(1)].

If a company fails to furnish Director Identification Number as per Sec. 157(1) before the expiry of the 270 days period from the date by which it should have been furnished with additional fee, the company shall be punishable with a fine of not less than ₹ 25,000 and not more than ₹ 1,00,000 and every officer of the company who is in default shall be punishable with a fine of not less than ₹ 25,000 and not more than ₹ 1,00,000.

Every person or company while furnishing any return, information or particulars as are required to be furnished under this Act, shall mention the Director Identification Number in such returns relating to the director (Sec. 158).

REVIEW QUESTIONS

1. What is annual return?
2. State the purposes of Board's Report.
3. What is 'vigil mechanism'?
4. What do you mean by 'secretarial audit'?
5. State the type of company which is required to prepare a report on each annual general meeting.
6. What do you mean by change in promoters holding?
7. What do you mean by an interested director?
8. What do you mean by disclosure of "related party transaction" under the listing agreement?
9. What is e-Form?
10. What do you mean by DSC?
11. What is CFC?
12. What is CIN?
13. What is FCRN?
14. What is SRN?
15. What do you mean by e-stamp?
16. What is DIN?
17. Enumerate the various matters to be included in the Board's Report.
18. What do you mean by Directors Responsibility Statement?
19. State provisions relating to Nomination and Remuneration Committee under Sec. 178(1).
20. State penal provisions under Sec. 134(8).
21. List provisions under the Companies Act in respect of contracts in which a director is interested.
22. State provisions regarding disclosure of related party transactions in Board's Report.
23. Enumerate the list of infrastructure for e-filing.
24. What do you mean by pre-certification of e-Forms?
25. What do you mean by addendum to e-Form?

26. State provisions under the Companies Act regarding the place of keeping and inspection of registers and returns.

27. State provisions regarding composition of Audit Committee under Sec. 177(8).

28. State the report on annual general meeting under Sec. 121.

29. Write a note on promoters holding.

30. State provisions under Sec. 184 in respect of disclosure of interest by a director.

31. Explain the nature of related party transactions under Sec. 188(1)

32. What are the disclosure requirements for related party transactions under AS-18

33. State general provisions regarding DIN.

34. State provisions under Sec. 92 in respect of Annual Return.

35. State disclosures under Sec. 134 of the Companies Act, 2013.

36. Explain the disclosure of interest by a director under Sec. 184.

37. What do you mean by related party? State the nature of related party transactions.

38. Explain the features of e-Form and e-Filing process.

41

Compliances, Governance and CSR

Secretarial audit is a part of total compliance management in an organisation.

INTRODUCTION

The executive management is responsible for the day-to-day affairs of a company. The Companies Act, 2013 has used the term 'key managerial personnel' to define the executive management. They are the point of first contact between the company and its stakeholders.

Chapter XIII of the Companies Act, 2013 read with companies (Appointment and Remuneration of Managerial Personnel) Rules, 2014 deals with the legal and procedural aspects of appointment of Key Managerial Personnel including Managing Director, Whole-time Director or Manager, managerial remuneration, secretarial audit, etc.

KEY MANAGERIAL PERSONNEL

The Companies Act, 2013 has recognised the concept of Key Managerial Personnel. In accordance with Sec. 2(51) "key managerial personnel", in relation to a company, means:

(a) the Chief Executive Officer or the managing director or the manager;

(b) the company secretary;

(c) the whole-time director;

(d) the Chief Financial Officer; and

(e) such other officer as may be prescribed.

Managing Director

A managing director, as defined in Sec. 2(54) of the Act, means a director who is entrusted with substantial powers of management which would not otherwise be exercised by him. The term includes a director occupying the position of a managing director or by whatever name he is called. The substantial powers of management may be conferred upon him by virtue of an agreement with the company, or of a resolution of the company or its Board, or by virtue of its Memorandum or Articles.

Whole-time Director

As per Sec. 2(94) of the Companies Act, 2013, whole-time director is a director in the whole-time employment of the company.

Manager

As per Sec. 2(53) of the Companies Act, 2013, Manager is an individual who, subject to the superintendence, control and direction of the Board of Directors, has the management of the whole or substantially the whole, of the affairs of a company, and includes a director or any other person occupying the position of a manager, by whatever name called, whether under a contract of service or not.

Chief Executive Officer and Chief Financial Officer

As per Sec. 2(18)/(19) of the Companies Act, 2013, Chief Executive Officer/Chief Financial Officer is an officer of a company who has been designated as such by it.

Company Secretary

As per Sec. 2(24) of the Companies Act, 2013, 'company secretary' or 'secretary means a company secretary (as defined in Clause (c) of Sub-section (1) of Sec. 2 of the Company Secretaries Act, 1980) who is appointed by a company to perform the functions of a company secretary under this Act.

Appointment of Managing Director, Whole-time Director or Manager

As per Sec. 196 of the Companies Act, 2013, no company shall appoint or employ at the same time a Managing Director and a Manager. Further, a company shall not appoint or reappoint any person as its Managing Director, Whole-time Director or Manager for a term not exceeding five years at a time and no re-appointment shall be made earlier than one year before the expiry of his term.

The terms and conditions of such appointments and remuneration payable be approved by the Board of Directors at a meeting which shall be subject to approval by a resolution at the next annual general meeting of the company and by the Central Government in case such appointments are at variance to the conditions specified in Schedule V. However, no approval of the Central Government is required if the appointments are made as per the conditions specified in Schedule V of the Act.

The appointment of a managing director or whole-time director or manager and the terms and conditions of such an appointment and remuneration payable thereon should be first approved by the Board of Directors at a meeting and then by an ordinary resolution passed at a general meeting of the company.

A notice convening Board or general meeting for considering such an appointment shall include the terms and conditions of such an appointment, remuneration payable and such other matters including interest of a director or directors in such appointments, if any.

As per Sec. 196(5), if an appointment of a managing director, whole-time director or manager is not approved by the company at a general meeting, any act done by him before such an approval shall not be deemed to be invalid.

In accordance with the Rule 3 of Companies Rules, 2014, a company shall file a return of appointment of a Managing Director, Whole-time Director or Manager, Chief Executive Officer (CEO), Company Secretary and Chief Financial Officer (CFO) within sixty days of the appointment, with the Registrar in Form No. MR-1 along with such fee as may be specified for this purpose.

Appointment with the Approval of Central Government

If the provisions of Schedule V of the Companies Act, 2013 are not fulfilled by company, an application seeking approval to the appointment of a managing director (whole-time director or manager) shall be made to the Central Government, in e-Form No. MR-2.

As per Sec. 200, the Central Government or a company while according its approval under Sec. 196, to any appointment of a managing director, whole-time director or manager, the Central Government or the company shall have regard to:

(a) the financial position of the company;

(b) the remuneration or commission drawn by the individual concerned in any other capacity;

(c) the remuneration or commission drawn by him from any other company;

(d) professional qualification and experience of the individual concerned;

(e) such other matters as may be prescribed.

In accordance with Rule 6 for the purpose of item (e) of Sec. 200, the Central Government or the company shall have regard to the following matters while granting approval to the appointment of managing director under Sec. 196:

   (i) Financial and operating performance of the company during the three preceding financial years.

  (ii) Relationship between remuneration and performance.

 (iii) The principle of proportionality of remuneration within the company, ideally by a rating methodology which compares the remuneration of directors to that of other executive directors on the Board and employees or executives of the company.

 (iv) Whether remuneration policy for directors differs from remuneration policy for other employees and if so, an explanation for the difference.

  (v) The securities held by the director, including options and details of the shares pledged as at the end of the preceding financial year.

Disqualifications

Sec. 196(3) states that no company shall appoint or continue the employment of any person as its managing director, whole-time director or manager who:

   (i) is below the age of twenty one years or has attained the age of seventy years.

     However, the appointment of a person who has attained the age of seventy years may be made by passing a special resolution. In such a case the explanatory statement annexed to the notice for such a motion shall indicate the justification for appointing such a person;

  (ii) is an undischarged insolvent or has at anytime been adjudged as an insolvent;

 (iii) has at any time suspended payment to his creditors, or makes, or has at any time made, a composition with them; or

 (iv) has at any time been convicted by a court of an offence and sentenced for a period of more than six months.

Reappointment of Managing Director

As per Secs.196 and 203 of the Companies Act, 2013, appointment includes re-appointment. Re-appointment of a managing director of a company should be considered before the expiry of his term of office. If the reappointment of the managing director is approved and if it is not in accordance with the conditions specified in Schedule V then the approval of the Central Government should be obtained for such re-appointment. Rest of the provisions for re-appointment of a managing director are same as in the case of appointment of a managing director.

Appointment of Key Managerial Personnel

Sec. 203 of the Companies Act, 2013 with Rule 8 mandates the appointment of key Managerial personnel. This Section makes it obligatory for a listed company and every other public company having a paid-up share capital of rupees ten crore or more, to appoint the following whole-time key managerial personnel:

(i) Managing Director, or Executive Officer or manager and in their absence, a whole-time director;

(ii) Company secretary; and

(iii) Chief Financial Officer.

Rule 8 and 8-A of Companies Rules, 2014

Rule 8. Appointment of Key Managerial Personnel:

Every listed company and every other public company having a paid-up share capital of ten crore rupees or more shall have whole-time key managerial personnel.

Rule 8-A Appointment of Company Secretaries in companies not covered under Rule 8-A company other than a company covered under Rule 8 which has a paid-up share capital of five crore rupees or more shall have a whole-time company secretary.

Every whole-time key managerial personnel of a company shall be appointed by means of a resolution of the Board containing the terms and conditions of the appointment including the remuneration.

An individual shall not be appointed or re-appointed as the chairperson of the company, as well the managing director, or Chief Executive Officer of the company at the same time unless the Articles of such a company provide otherwise, or the company does not carry multiple businesses. But, such a class of companies engaged in multiple businesses and which has appointed one or more Chief Executive Officers for each such business as may be notified by the Central Government are exempted from the above.

A whole-time key managerial personnel shall not hold office in more than one company except in its subsidiary company at the same time. But, he can hold such other directorship with the permission of the Board.

If a whole-time key managerial personnel holds office in more than one company at the same time, he shall choose one company within a period of six months from such a commencement.

A company may appoint or employ a person as its managing director, if he is the managing director or manager of one, and of not more than one, other company. Such an appointment or employment is made or approved by a resolution passed at a meeting of the Board with the consent of all the directors present at the meeting. In case the office of any whole-time key managerial personnel is vacated, the resulting vacancy shall be filled-up by the Board at a meeting of the Board within a period of six months from the date of such a vacancy.

Functions of Company Secretary (Sec. 205)

The following are the main functions of the company secretary:

(i) Reporting to the Board about compliance with the provisions of this Act, the rules made thereunder and other laws applicable to the company;

(ii) Ensuring that the company complies with the applicable secretarial standards;

(iii) Discharging such other duties as may be prescribed.

The expression "secretarial standards" means secretarial standards issued by the Institute of Company Secretaries of India constituted under Sec. 3 of the Company Secretaries Act, 1980 and approved by the Central Government.

Duties of Company Secretary (Clause C of Sub-section (1) of Sec. 205)

The following are the main duties of the Company Secretary:

(i) Providing to the directors of the company (collectively and individually) such guidances as they may require with regard to their duties, responsibilities and powers.

(ii) Facilitating the convening of meetings and attending Board, committee and general meetings, and maintaining the minutes of these meetings.

(iii) Obtaining approvals from the Board, general meetings, the Government and such other authorities as required under the provisions of the Act.

(iv) Representing before various regulators, Tribunals and other authorities under the Act in connection with discharge of various functions under the Act.

(v) Assisting the Board in the conduct of the affairs of the company.

(vi) Assisting and advising the Board to ensure good corporate governance and to comply with the corporate governance requirements and best practices.

(vii) Discharging such other duties as may be assigned by the Board from time to time.

(viii) Such other duties as have been prescribed under the Act and Rules.

Managerial Remuneration

Just as profits drive business, incentives drive the managers of business. Thus, it is important to incentivise the workforce performing the challenging role of managing companies.

Remuneration to Managerial Personnel

Overall managerial remuneration (Sec. 197): The overall managerial remuneration of a public company shall not exceed 11 per cent of the net profit of the company in that financial year computed as per Sec. 198 except that the remuneration of the directors shall not be deducted from the gross profits.

Further, the company in general meeting may, with the approval of the Central Government, authorise the payment of remuneration exceeding 11 per cent of the net profits of the company, subject to the provisions of Schedule V.

The net profits for the purpose of this Section shall be computed in the manner referred to in Sec. 198.

Remuneration to Managing Director/Whole-time Director/Manager: The remuneration payable to any one managing director or whole-time director shall not exceed 5 per cent of the net profits of the company. But, if there are more than one such director remuneration shall not exceed 10 per cent of the net profits to all such directors and manager taken together.

Remuneration by a Company having no Profit or Inadequate Profit: If in any financial year, a company has no profits or its profits are inadequate, the company shall not pay to its directors, including managing or whole-time director or manager, any remuneration exclusive of any fees payable to directors except in accordance with the provisions of Schedule V and if it is unable to comply with Schedule V, with the previous approval of the Central Government.

CORPORATE COMPLIANCES

Secretarial Audit

> Secretarial audit is an independent objective assurance intended to add value and improve an organisation's operations.

Secretarial audit is a compliance audit. It is a part of total compliance management in an organisation. It helps in detecting non-compliance and taking corrective measures.

Secretarial audit is a process to check compliance with the provisions of various laws by an independent professional. Its purpose is to ensure that the company has complied with the legal and procedural requirements and also followed the due process. In short, it is essentially a mechanism to monitor compliance with the requirements of stated laws. It helps to accomplish the organisation's objectives by bringing a systematic, disciplined approach to evaluate and improve effectiveness of risk management, control and governance processes.

Sec. 204 of the Companies Act, 2013 mandates every listed company and such other classes of prescribed companies to annex a Secretarial Audit Report, given by a company secretary in practice with its Board's report.

The Central Government through rules has prescribed such other class of companies as under:

(i) every public company having a paid-up capital of fifty crore rupees or more; or

(ii) every public company having a turnover of two hundred and fifty crore rupees or more.

It shall be the duty of the company to give all assistance and facilities to the company secretary in practice for auditing the secretarial and related records of the company.

The Board of Directors in their report, shall explain in full any qualification or observation or other remarks made in the Secretarial Audit Report.

CORPORATE GOVERNANCE

> Corporate governance is *"the conduct of business in accordance with shareholders' desires, which is to make as much money as possible, while conforming to the basic rules of the society embodied in law and local customs".*
> —Milton Friedman

The term 'governance' is derived from the Latin word 'gubernare' which means 'to steer'. Governance is, thus, about governing or steering. It is a degree of control to be exercised by key stakeholders' representatives.

The concept of corporate governance emerges as a result of an international effort to promote transparency, integrity and the rule of law. It is, therefore, a well recognised phenomenon in the competitive business environment. Good governance, however implies that the institution is run for the optimal benefit of the stakeholders in it. Business ethics, accountability to stakeholders, social responsibility, transparency and full disclosure are some of the ingredients of good governance. In short, maximisation of shareholders wealth is the cornerstone of good governance.

Corporate Governance—Meaning

Corporate governance is the way in which corporate bodies are governed or managed. In other words, it is a process or set of systems to ensure that a company is managed to suit the best interest of all stakeholders. It is an interplay between company's shareholders, creditors, capital markets, financial sectors, institutions and law.

Definition

A corporate governance is "a conscious, deliberate and sustained efforts on the part of corporate entity to strike a judicious balance between its own interest and the interest of various constituents on the environment in which it is operating".

Adrian Cadbury in U.K. emphasises "Corporate governance basically, has to do with power and accountability: who exercise power, on behalf of whom, and how the exercise of power is controlled."

In practice, Corporate Governance (CG) means the role of the board of directors of the company and its auditors, towards protecting the shareholders interest in every business decisions.

Thus, the following are the basic ingredients of CG:

(i) Accountability of board of directors to ultimate owners.

  (ii) Clarity in responsibilities of directors, chairman and managing director through empowerment to improve accountability.

 (iii) Transparency in timely disclosures of right information with integrity.

 (iv) Quality and competence of directors and their track record.

  (v) Conforming to laws, rules and spirit of codes.

Importance of Corporate Governance

The importance of corporate governance lies in its contribution to business world. In short, corporate governance is important on account of the following reasons:

  (i) *Framework for creating accountability:* Corporate governance ensures accountability. Its principles lay down the framework for creating accountability between companies and external investors.

 (ii) *Better direction and control:* The principles of corporate governance helps in providing better direction and control of corporate bodies.

 (iii) *Monitoring of risk:* Corporate governance helps in monitoring of risk that a firm faces globally through rationalised management.

 (iv) *Strategic thinking:* Corporate governance helps to improve strategic thinking at the top. This is done by inducting independent directors having experience and new ideas.

  (v) *Attracting local investors:* The principles of corporate governance helps in attracting local investors and broadening local markets.

 (vi) *Avoiding fraud:* Corporate governance avoids fraud and company failures. It, in turn helps in facilitating further progress of corporate economy.

 (vii) *Developing retail investors:* Good governance helps in developing retail investors, banks, mutual funds and other institutional investors.

(viii) *Limiting the liability:* Corporate governance helps in limiting the liability of top management and directors by articulating the decision-making process.

 (ix) *Foundation for future progress:* The corporate governance lays the foundation for future progress of business.

  (x) *Long-term reputation:* A firm which keeps proper rules and procedures in the governance process creates a reputation that other firms cannot acquire.

Background

The expression corporate governance is relatively new. It had its origin in United Kingdom. It subsequently spread to other countries. First, this expression appeared in 1983 as the title of an article 'Perspectives on Management'. However, the seeds of modern corporate governance are sown by the Watergate Scandal in the United States.

Although, the expression corporate governance evolved in eighties, it did not get the deserved attention from the corporate world. But, it caught the public attention only after the release of the Cadbury Report in 1992.

India has undergone the bitter experience of corporate frauds. These are the unethical stock market transactions of Harshad Mehta and the recent experience of the fraud by the CEO of Satyam Computers. Such events bring out the need for corporate governance.

Principles of Corporate Governance

Several principles have been identified as a result of the series of corporate collapses. The following are some of such principles.

(i) *Accountability:* Accountability of Board of Directors and their constituent responsibilities to the ultimate owners.

(ii) *Transparency:* A key element of good governance is transparency. It is a shared way of corporate functioning and not a set of rules. Transparency, in turn requires the right to information, timeliness and integrity of the information produced.

(iii) *System of check and balance:* There should be a system of checks and balances and greater simplicity in the process of governance.

(iv) *Resourceful Board:* The Board requires enough skills to deal with various business issues. It should have the ability to review and challenge management performance.

(v) *Clarity of responsibility:* There should be a clarity of responsibility to enhance accountability.

(vi) *Adherence to the rules:* Corporate actions should conform to letter and spirit to codes.

Corporate Governance—Recent Interest

The following are some reasons for recent awareness in corporate governance:

(i) *Directors position:* Directors should realise that their job is to represent the shareholders and other stakeholders.

(ii) *Safeguarding investors:* At present, there is a rise of institutional investors. Thus, an awareness of corporate governance is the need of the hour to safeguard the interest of institutional investors.

(iii) *Takeovers:* Another reason for the recent interest in corporate governance is the takeover moves in the world in the wake of globalisation.

(iv) Doing corporate governance with power and accountability.

(v) Activism of regulatory bodies such as SEBI.

Objectives of Corporate Governance

Good governance usually ensures company's commitment to higher growth and profit. It, in turn inspires and strengthens investors confidence. Thus, the following are the main objectives of corporate governance.

(i) *Accountability:* A properly structured Board capable of taking independent decision is in place at the helm of affairs. Such a Board is accountable for attaining the set goals of the company.

(ii) *Balanced Board:* The Board is balanced as regards the representation of adequate number of non-executive and independent directors. Such directors will take care of the interests and well-being of the stakeholders.

(iii) *Transparency:* In a company having good governance, the Board usually adopts transparent procedures and arrives at decisions on the strength of adequate information.

(iv) *Concerns of stakeholders:* The Board has an adequate machinery to sub-serve the concerns of stakeholders.

(v) *Informed shareholders:* The Board keeps the shareholders informed of relevant development while implementing the programmes.

(vi) *Monitoring:* The Board regularly monitors the functioning of the management team.

(vii) *Controlling:* The Board should control the affairs of the company at all times.

Statutory Measures

The corporate governance framework in India mainly comprises the following legislations and regulations:

(i) The Companies Act, 2013: The companies in India are mainly governed by the provisions of the Companies Act, 2013. The Act deals with the rules and procedures in respect of: (a) Incorporation of companies; (b)Prospectus and allotment of shares and debenture; (c) Management and administration of companies; (d) Maintenance of accounts; (e) Annual returns; (f) Shareholders' meetings and proceedings; (g) Board of Directors; (h) Prevention of oppression and mismanagement; and (i) Power of investigation into the affairs of company.

(ii) The Securities Contracts (Regulation Act), 1956: The Securities Contracts (Regulation Act), 1956 relates to the functioning of stock exchanges. It also pertains to the rules in respect of various types of tradeable securities such as shares, stocks, bonds and so on issued by the companies.

(iii) The Securities and Exchange Board of India Act, 1992: An independent capital market authority known as SEBI, has been set up under the Securities and Exchange Board of India Act. The purpose of SEBI is to regulate the securities market and protect the interest of investors.

(iv) The Depositories Act, 1996: This Act has created the legal framework for dematerialisation of securities and established share and securities depositories.

(v) Listing Agreement with Stock Exchanges: Clause 49 is the unique and key element of the listing agreement. This clause contains the corporate governance practices to be followed by the listed companies.

Apart from the above legislations, Competition Act, 2002, Foreign Exchange Management Act, 1999, Industries (Development and Regulation) Act, 1951 and so on also have a direct impact on company administration.

Constituents of Corporate Governance

The following are the three main elements of corporate governance:

(i) *Board of Directors:* The Board is the heart and soul of a company. It performs the pivotal role in the system of corporate governance. It is accountable to the stakeholders and directs the management. The Board sets strategic aims and leads the company in a transparent manner. It is the bounden duty of the Board to submit periodical report to the stakeholders regarding the activities and progress of the company.

(ii) *Shareholders:* The shareholders are the owners of the company. They are required to appoint the directors and auditors of the company. They have to hold the Board accountable for the proper governance of the company by requiring the Board to supply them requisite information periodically.

(iii) *Management:* The management is responsible to undertake the governance of the company in time with the directions given by the Board. It should provide adequate and timely information to the Board and put in place adequate control systems.

SEBI REGULATION—CLAUSE 49 OF LISTING AGREEMENT

The Security and Exchange Board of India (SEBI) was constituted through an Act known as SEBI Act which came into force on the 30th day of January, 1992. The objectives of this Act are:

(i) to protect the interest of the investors; (ii) to regulate the security market; (iii) to promote the development of the securities market; and (iv) to protect investors against unfair and fraudulent trade practices.

SEBI Regulations

In order to regulate the operations of the players of the capital market, SEBI has formulated various rules and regulations. All such rules and regulations help in corporate governance by:

(i) providing greater information to the investors; (ii) curbing insider trading and manipulations; (iii) ensuring transparency and fair play, integrity and confidence of the investors; (iv) ensuring equality of treatment and opportunities to minority shareholders; (v) providing investors with more effective means of redress in the case of abuse; (vi) preventing the actions which do not respect the interest of the shareholders; and (vii) ensuring greater transparency in the market for corporate control.

Guidelines Issued by SEBI

SEBI has issued various guidelines for strengthening corporate governance. In accordance with such guidelines, all corporate entities shall:

(i) strengthen the disclosure norms for initial public offers (IPOs); (ii) provide information in Directors Report for utilisation of funds; (iii) declare quarterly results; (iv) facilitate mandatory appointment of compliance officer for monitoring the share transfer process and ensuring compliance with various rules and regulations; (v) disclose all material and price sensitive information; (vi) dispatch one copy of abridged Balance Sheet to all shareholders, and complete Balance Sheet to every household; (vii) issue guidelines for preferential allotment at market-related prices; and (viii) issue regulations for takeovers and substantial acquisitions.

Clause 49

The major mechanism for regulating corporate governance is through Clause 49. When a company wants to list its shares in the stock exchange, it has to enter into an agreement with SEBI. This agreement contains certain specific clauses mentioned in Clause 49. This makes the principles of corporate governance complying on listed companies.

Mandatory Requirements

The corporate governance principles included in Clause 49 are a set of mandatory and non-mandatory requirements. Companies have no choice on mandatory requirements, but to comply with them. Such requirements are discussed under the following heads:

(1) Board of Directors; (2) Audit Committee; (3) Subsidiary Companies; (4) Disclosures; (5) CEO/CFO Certification; (6) Corporate Governance Report; and (7) Compliance.

1. *Board of Directors:* In accordance with the Clause 49 of the listing agreement, a company should comply with the following provisions in respect of its Board of Directors:

(i) *Composition of Board of Directors:* The Board of Directors of the company shall have an optimum combination of executive and non-executive directors. However, not less than fifty per cent of the Board of Directors should comprise non-executive directors. Further, it is stated that if the Chairman of the Board is a non-executive director, at least one-third of the Board should comprise independent directors. But, if the Chairman is an executive director, at least half of the Board should comprise independent directors.

The expression "independent director" means a non-executive director of the company who:

(a) does not have any material pecuniary relationships or transaction with the company (other than receiving director's remuneration);

(b) is not related to promoters or persons occupying management positions at the board level or at one level below the board;

(c) has not been an executive of the company in the immediately preceding three financial years;

(d) is/was not a partner or an executive during the preceding three years of any of the following:

(i) the statutory audit firm or the internal audit firm that is associated with the company, and

(ii) the legal firm and consulting firms that have a material association with the company.

(e) is not a material supplier, service provider or customer or a lessor or lessee of the company which may affect the independence of the director; and

(f) is not a substantial shareholder of the company (i.e., owning two per cent or more of the block of voting shares).

Further it is provided that nominee directors appointed by an institution which has invested in or lent to the company shall be deemed to be independent directors.

(ii) *Compensation to non-executive directors:* All fees/compensation paid to non-executive directors (including independent directors) shall be fixed by the Board of Directors. However, previous approval of shareholders is required for such a payment. But no such an approval is required to pay sitting fees to non-executive directors.

(iii) *Board procedure:* The Board shall meet at least four times a year. But the maximum time gap between two meetings shall be four months.

It is also stated that a director shall not be a member in more than ten Audit and/or Shareholders Grievance Committees across all companies in which he is a director.

Further, every director is required to inform the company (mandatory annual requirement) about the committee positions he occupies in other companies and notify the changes as and when the same takes place.

(iv) *Code of conduct:* A code of conduct for all Board members and senior management of the company shall be laid down by the Board. The same shall be posted on the website of the company.

All such members and personnel of the company shall affirm compliance with the code on an annual basis. Further, a declaration to this effect signed by the CEO shall be provided in the annual report of the company.

2. *Audit Committee:* For details see Module II.

3. *Subsidiary Companies:* The following are the important rules regarding subsidiary companies:

   (a) At least one independent director on the Board of Directors of the holding company shall be a director on the Board of Directors of a non-listed subsidiary company.

   (b) The audit committee of listed holding company shall also review the financial statements made by the subsidiary company.

   (c) The minutes of the board meeting of the unlisted subsidiary company shall be placed at the Board meeting of the listed holding company.

   (d) A statement of all important transactions entered into by the unlisted subsidiary company should be brought to the attention of the Board of Directors of the listed holding company.

4. *Disclosures:* The following are the provisions regarding disclosures.

   (i) *Basis of Related Party Transactions:* Following are the basis of related party transactions:

      (a) A statement in summary form of transactions with related parties shall be placed periodically before the audit committee.

      (b) Details of material individual transactions with related parties (which are not in the normal course of business) shall be placed before the audit committee.

   (ii) *Disclosure of Accounting Treatment:* If a different treatment (from that prescribed in an Accounting standard) in the preparation of financial statements has been followed, the fact shall be disclosed in the financial statements. Along with this disclosure, the management's explanation as to why it believes such an alternative treatment is more representative of the true and fair view of the underlying business transaction should be mentioned in the Corporate Governance Report.

(iii) *Board Disclosure Risk Management:* The company shall lay down various procedures to inform Board members about risk assessment and minimisation procedures.

(iv) *Proceeds from Issues:* When a company raises money through issue of shares, it shall be disclosed to the audit committee. The uses and applications of funds (by major category) shall also be disclosed on a quarterly and annual basis.

(v) *Remuneration of Directors:* It includes the following:

(a) All pecuniary relationship or transactions of the non-executive directors vis-a-vis the company shall be disclosed in the annual report.

(b) Further, certain disclosures such as remuneration package of individual directors, performance-linked incentives, service contracts and stock option plan shall also be made in the section on the corporate governance of the Annual Report.

(c) The company shall publish its criteria of making payments to non-executive directors in its annual report.

(d) The company shall disclose the number of shares and convertible instruments held by non-executive directors.

(e) Persons who are proposed to be appointed as non-executive directors in a listed company (prior to their appointment) shall disclose their shareholding. Such a disclosure shall also be made in the notice to the general meeting called for appointment of such directors.

(vi) *Management:* The management shall also place a report with the Director's report on the following matters.

(a) Industry structure and developments; (b) Opportunities and threats; (c) Segment-wise or product-wise performance; (d) Outlook; (e) Risks and concerns; (f) Internal control systems and their adequacy; (g) Discussion on financial performance; (h) Material developments in human resources/industrial relations front including number of people employed.

(vii) *Disclosures to Shareholders:* It includes the following:

1. In the case of appointment of a new director or re-appointment of a director, the following information should be provided to the shareholders:

   (a) A brief resume of the director.

   (b) Nature of his expertise in specific functional areas.

   (c) Names of companies in which the person also holds the directorship and the membership of committees of the Board.

   (d) Shareholding of non-executive directors.

2. A Board committee (under the chairmanship of a non-executive director) known as shareholders/investors' Grievance Committee, shall be formed to look into the redressal of shareholders and investors complaints.

3. The Board of the company shall delegate the power of share transfer to an officer or a committee or to the Registrar and share transfer agents. The purpose of such a delegation is to expedite the process of share transfer. However, the delegated authority shall attend to share transfer formalities at least once in a fortnight.

5. *CEO/CFO Certification.* The CEO is the managing director or manager appointed in terms of the Companies Act, 2013. But the CFO is the whole time finance director or any other person heading the finance function and discharging that function. The CEO/CFO shall certify to the Board that:

(a) They have reviewed financial statements and the cash flow statement for the year and that to the best of their knowledge and belief:

   (i) these statements do not contain any materially untrue statement or omit any material fact or contain statements that might be misleading.

   (ii) these statements together present a true and fair view of the company's affairs and are in compliance with existing accounting standards, applicable laws and regulations.

(b) They are to the best of their knowledge and belief, no transactions entered into by the company during the year which are fraudulent, illegal or violative of the company's code of conduct.

(c) They accept the responsibility for establishing and maintaining internal controls and that they have evaluated the effectiveness of the internal control system of the company. They should also certify that they have disclosed to the auditors and the audit committee, deficiencies in the design or operation of internal controls, if any of which they are aware and the steps they have taken or propose to take for rectifying such deficiencies.

(d) They have indicated to the auditors and the audit committee regarding:

   (i) significant changes in internal control during the year.

   (ii) significant changes in accounting policies during the year and that such changes have been disclosed in the notes to the financial statements; and

   (iii) instances of significant fraud of which they have become aware and the involvement therein, if any, of the management or an employee having a significant role in the company's internal control system.

6. *Corporate Governance Report:* A report on corporate governance should be given to the shareholders along with the annual reports. Similarly, stock exchanges should also be informed about the position of the company regarding corporate governance.

   (a) *Compliance report on corporate governance in the annual report:* There shall be a separate section on corporate governance in the annual report of the company. Non-compliance of any mandatory requirement of Clause 49 should be made with reasons for the failure. Similarly, the extent to which the non-mandatory requirements have been adopted should be specifically highlighted.

   (b) *Compliance report to stock exchanges:* The companies should submit a quarterly compliance report to the stock exchanges within fifteen days from the close of quarter. The report shall be signed either by the compliance officer or the chief executive officer of the company.

7. *Compliance:* It includes the following:

   (a) The company should get a certificate regarding compliance of corporate governance (as stipulated in Clause 49) from the auditors or practicing company secretary. Such a certificate shall be annexed to the director's report and also sent to the stock exchanges.

(b) The non-mandatory requirements may be implemented as per the discretion of the company.

Non-mandatory Requirements

A company may implement the non-mandatory requirements provided in the revised clause 49 at its own discretion. The following matters deal with the non mandatory requirements.

(i) *Chairman of Board.* The appointment of a non-executive chairman for the Board is the first non-mandatory requirement. The requirement also suggests that the chairman's office should be maintained at the company's expense.

The non-executive chairman may be permitted to reimburse the expenses incurred in performance of his duties.

(ii) *Remuneration Committee:* The Board of Directors of the company may set up a remuneration committee. The chairman of the committee shall be an independent director. The committee may comprise at least three directors all of whom shall be non-executive directors.

The remuneration committee would determine the remuneration packages of the executive directors. All the members of the remuneration committee shall be present at the meeting. But, the chairman of the committee shall be present at the Annual General Meeting to answer the shareholders' queries. However, it is up to the chairman to determine who should answer the queries.

(iii) *Shareholders Rights:* A half-yearly declaration of financial performance comprising summary of the important events in last six months may be sent to each household of shareholders.

(iv) *Audit Qualifications:* Company may move towards a regime of unqualified financial statements.

(v) *Training of Board Members.* A company may train its Board members in respect of the following:

(a) The business model of the company.

(b) The risk profile of the business parameters of the company.

(c) The responsibilities of the members as directors; and

(d) The best ways to discharge the responsibilities.

(vi) *Mechanism for Evaluating Non-executive Board Members:* A peer group comprising the entire Board of Directors (excluding the director being evaluated) shall do the performance evaluation of non-executive directors. The question of whether the terms of appointment of the non-executive directors shall extend/continue shall also be determined by the same method of Peer Group evaluation.

(vii) *Whistle Blower Policy:* 'Blowing the whistle' is an English expression. It is used in informal contexts to mean some act to make somebody stop doing something (illegal) usually by informing people in authority.

Whistle blowing is an act of disclosing information in the public interest. This term is used in a context where an employee makes a disclosure about any violation of laws, wastage of funds, mismanagement by the company. The employee who makes such a disclosure is at a great risk from the management of the company. Hence, there shall be specific provisions for the protection of whistle blowers.

In India, the Law Commission (in its 179th report in 2001) recommended for the necessity of law on whistle blowing. In spite of the Law Commission's recommendation for a comprehensive legislation, no such legislation has been made in India so far.

CORPORATE SOCIAL RESPONSIBILITY (CSR) (SEC. 135)

As per Sec. 135 of the Companies Act, 2013, companies having net worth of ₹500 crore or more or turnover of ₹1,000 crore or more or net profit of ₹5 crore or more during any financial year shall constitute a CSR Committee of Board. It comprises three or more directors, one of whom shall be an independent director.

CSR involves both internal as well as external stakeholders. Internal stakeholders include the employees of the company. But external stakeholders consist of community and environment, customers, vendors, shareholders, government, etc. To carry it out effectively, it is essentially that it has to be driven from top. So, leadership is very important in all CSR activities.

CSR—Meaning

CSR has many interpretations. But it can be understood to be a concept imposing a liability on the company to contribute to the society (whether towards environmental causes, educational promotion, social causes, etc.) along with the reinforced duty to conduct the business in an ethical manner.

Corporate Social Responsibility (CSR) is a form of self-regulation integrated into a business model. It is also known as corporate conscience, corporate citizenship, social performance or sustainable business/responsible business.

Composition of CSR Committee

The CSR committee shall consist of three or more directors. Out of them, one director shall be an independent director. The composition of such Corporate Social Responsibility Committee shall have to be disclosed in the Board's Report as required under Sec. 134(4).

An unlisted public company or a private company which is not required to appoint an independent director shall have its CSR Committee with independent director.

A private company having only two directors on its Board shall constitute its CSR Committee with two such directors.

In respect of foreign company, the CSR Committee shall comprise at least two persons of which one person is a resident in India and another person shall be nominated by the foreign company.

The CSR Committee shall institute a transparent monitoring mechanism for implementation of CSR projects or programmes or activities undertaken by the company.

CSR Policy

The CSR policy of the company shall include the following:

(a) A list of CSR projects or programmes which a company plans to undertake falling within the purview of the Schedule VII of the Act, specifying modalities of execution of such projects or programmes and the implementation schedule for the same; and

(b) Monitoring process of such projects or programmes.

But the activity should not be undertaken in pursuance of normal course of a company.

The Board shall ensure that the activities included by the company in its CSR policy are related to the activities mentioned in Schedule VII of the Act.

The CSR Policy of the company shall specify that the surplus arising out of the CSR projects or programmes or activities shall not form part of business profit of a company.

Functions of the CSR Committee

The committee shall formulate and recommend to the Board a Corporate Responsibility policy. Such a policy shall indicate the activities to be undertaken by the company as specified in Schedule VII of the Act.

The Committee shall also initiate a CSR policy, which shall stipulate how, where, and when they want to invest their funds with respect to this requirement.

The Committee shall recommend the amount of expenditure to be incurred on the activities referred to the above. Moreover, the CSR Committee is under an obligation to monitor the implementation of the CSR policy from time to time.

Benefits of CSR

The following are the main benefits of CSR:

(i) Strengthened brand positioning.

(ii) Enhanced corporate image and reputation.

(iii) Satisfaction of economic and social contribution to society.

(iv) Contribution to the surrounding society.

(v) Increased ability to attract, motivate and retain employees.

(vi) Enhanced sales and market share.

(vii) Increased appeals to investors and financial analysis.

(viii) Local economy gains in all dimensions.

CSR Activities

The Companies Act, 2013 does not prescribe the methodology by which CSR activities are to be undertaken. However, the CSR activities may be undertaken by way of the following methods:

(i) *By Charity:* Company can donate money to various charitable trusts, societies, NGOs, etc. who work for social economic welfare of society.

(ii) *By Contract:* Company can hire an NGO or any other agency which can carry out the projects on behalf of the company.

(iii) *By Itself:* Company can take up a project on its own trust and use its own staff for its proper working/monitoring or through other trusts/societies.

The companies may adopt any one, or all of the above ways for the purpose of CSR activities:

1. The CSR activities should be undertaken by the company as per its CSR policy.

2. The Board of a company may decide to undertake its CSR activities approved by the CSR Committee through a registered trust or a registered society or company established by the company or its holding or subsidiary or associate company.

3. Unless such a trust, society or company is established, it shall have an established track record of three years in undertaking similar programmes or projects.

4. A company may also collaborate with other companies for CSR activities.

5. The CSR activities should not be exclusively only for the benefit of employees of the company or their families.

6. Only those CSR activities would be taken into considerations which are undertaken within India.

7. Companies may build CSR capacity of their own personnel as well as those of their implementing agencies through institutions with established track records of at least three financial years. But, such an expenditure shall not exceed 5 per cent of total CSR expenditure of the company in one financial year.

8. Contribution of any amount directly or indirectly to any political party shall not be considered as CSR activity.

CSR Activities Under Schedule VII

The following activities are to be undertaken by the company in CSR activities as per Schedule VII:

 (i) Eradicating hunger, poverty and malnutrition providing preventive health care and sanitation and making available safe drinking water.

 (ii) Promoting education including employment enhancing vocation skills especially among children, women and elderly.

 (iii) Promoting gender equality, empowering women, setting up homes and hostels for women and orphans.

 (iv) Ensuring environment sustainability, ecological balance, protection of flora and fauna and maintaining quality of soil, air and water.

 (v) Protection of national heritage, art and culture.

 (vi) Measures for the benefits of armed forces veterans, war widows and their dependents.

(vii) Training to promote rural sports, nationally recognised sports, paralympic sports and olympic sports.

(viii) Contribution to the Prime Minister's National Relief Fund or any other fund set up by the Central Government or the State Governments for socio-economic development and relief and welfare of SC, ST, OBC, minorities and women.

(ix) Contributions or funds provided to technology incubates located within academic institutions which are approved by the Central Government.

(x) Rural development projects.

Role of the Board

In respect of CSR activities, the Board of every company has the following roles:

(i) The Board is required to constitute a Corporate Social Responsibility Committee.

(ii) After receiving recommendation and policy by the Corporate Social Responsibility Committee, disclose such policy-

(a) in the Board's Report.

(b) also place the contents of policy on its Company's website, if any.

(iii) Ensure that the activities which formulate by CSR Committee in the policy are duly undertaken by the company.

(iv) Ensure that the company spends in every financial year at least 2 per cent of the average net profits in pursuance of its Corporate Social Responsibility Policy.

(v) In case the company fails to spend such amount, the Board shall (in its report made under Sec. 134(3) (O)) specify the reasons for not spending the amount.

REVIEW QUESTIONS

1. Define the term 'managing director'.
2. Define secretary in whole-time practice.
3. Define the term 'manager'.
4. What do you mean by secretarial audit?
5. What do you mean by corporate governance?
6. What do you mean by key managerial personnel?
7. Explain the term 'chief executive officer.'

8. What is CSR?

9. Enumerate two benefits of CSR.

10. What do you mean by CSR Committee?

11. State "key managerial personnel" as per Sec. 2(51) of the Companies Act, 2013.

12. Explain the disqualifications with regard to appointment of managing director, whole-time director or manager.

13. State the provisions relating to the re-appointment of managing director.

14. State provisions relating to the overall managerial remuneration.

15. What do you mean by corporate compliance management?

16. Explain the term 'corporate governance report'.

17. Enumerate the constituents or corporate governance.

18. Explain the CSR policy of the company.

19. State provisions relating to the composition of CSR Committee.

20. State provisions under the Companies Act, 2013 regarding the appointment of Managing Director.

21. Explain the functions of company secretary.

22. State provisions relating to secretarial audit.

23. State the reason for recent awareness in corporate governance.

24. Enumerate the objective of corporate governance.

25. What is CSR? Explain its functions.

26. Explain the role of the Board in regard to CSR.

27. State the provisions of appointing a Key Managerial Personnel as per the Companies Act, 2013.

28. Enumerate the duties and liabilities of a Company Secretary.

29. Discuss the role of Company Secretary.

30. What is Corporate Governance? State its principles.

31. State the Statutory Measures in respect of corporate governance framework in India.

32. What is CSR? State various methods in which a company may undertake CSR activities.

33. State provisions of Schedule VII in regard to the CSR activities of a company.

42

Dividends

Dividend means "the share of profit that falls to each individual member of a company".

MEANING

The term 'dividend' is not defined under Sec. 2(35) of the Companies Act, 2013. The term "Dividend" includes any interim dividend. It is an inclusive and not an exhaustive definition. In common parlance it is used to describe that portion of a company's profit which has been declared to be distributed among the members. Since dividend is payable only out of the distributed profits, it follows that if no profits are made, or if none is distributed, no dividend will be declared.

The power to pay the dividends is inherent to a company, and is not derived from the Companies Act or the Memorandum, although the Articles generally regulate the manner in which the dividends are to be declared.

RULES REGARDING DIVIDENDS

1. Although, the Board of Directors has an absolute right to recommend the rate of dividend to be declared, the shareholders approval of the recommended rate of dividend in the annual general meeting is necessary before any dividend can be declared and distributed. The shareholders may reduce the rate recommended by the Board, but they cannot increase it.

2. The articles usually provide that the dividend shall be paid to the shareholders in proportion to the amount paid upon each share [Sec. 51]. If not, dividend has to be paid in proportion to the nominal amount of the shares.

3. The dividend can be declared and paid by a company only out of the current and previous year's profits or out of both or out

467

of the money provided by the Central or State Government for payment of the dividend in pursuance of a guarantee given by such Government [Sec. 123(1)].

4. No dividend can be declared and paid by a company unless:

   (a) depreciation has been provided as per Schedule II [Sec. 123(2)].

   (b) such percentage of the net profits for that financial year as it may consider appropriate has been transferred to the reserves of the company.

5. The dividend is payable only in cash. But this rule does not prohibit the payment of dividend through cheque or dividend warrant. However, if authorised by the articles, a company may pay dividends in the form of fully paid bonus shares.

6. In the event of inadequacy or absence of profits in any year if a company proposes to declare dividend out of the accumulated profits earned by it in previous years and transferred by the company reserves, such a declaration of dividend shall not be made except in accordance with such rules, as may be prescribed in this behalf [Sec. 123(1)].

7. The dividend should be paid only to the registered shareholder or to his order or to his bankers, or to the bearer of the share warrants [Sec. 123(5)].

8. A company which fails to comply with the provisions of Sections 73 (Prohibition of Acceptance of Deposits except in the manner provided) and 74 (Repayment of deposits etc. accepted before commencement of Companies Act, 2013) shall not, so long as such failure continues, declare any dividend on its equity shares [Sec. 123(6)].

9. All dividend should be paid or the warrant in respect thereof posted within thirty days from the date of the declaration (Sec. 127). Unless the dividends are so paid, every director of the company, who is knowingly a party to the default is punishable with imprisonment up to two years and with a fine of not less than ₹ 1,000 for every day during which such default continues. Further, the company shall be liable to pay simple interest at the rate of 18 per cent per annum during the period for which such default continues.

10. Once a dividend is duly declared, it becomes a debt payable by the company.

11. No dividend can be paid out of the capital. Such a payment is beyond the powers, even though sanctioned by the memorandum or the articles.

UNPAID DIVIDEND ACCOUNT

Where a company has declared a dividend but has not paid to any shareholder within 30 days from the date of the declaration, it shall, within seven days from the date of the expiry of the 30 days, transfer the total amount of unpaid dividend to a special account with any scheduled bank, to be called "Unpaid Dividend Account of—Company Limited/Company (Private) Limited [Sec. 124(1)]

Any amount transferred to the 'Unpaid Dividend Account' which remains unpaid or unclaimed for a period of seven years from the date of the transfer, shall be transferred by the company along with interest accrued if any, thereon to the Fund established under Sec. 125(1) known as Investor Education and Protection Fund (IEPF). The company shall send a statement, in the prescribed form of details of such transfer to the authority which administers the said Fund. The authority, in turn, shall issue a receipt to the company as evidence of such transfer.

INTERIM DIVIDEND [SEC. 123(3)]

Subject to the provisions of the articles, the directors of the company can pay interim dividend. An interim dividend is one which is paid on account of the full years dividend at any time between two annual general meetings. Before declaring an interim dividend, the directors should satisfy themselves that the payment of such a dividend is warranted by the financial position of the company. Interim dividend does not constitute a debt and hence the directors can rescind it by a resolution.

DECLARATION OF DIVIDEND OUT OF COMPANY'S RESERVES

Subject to the following conditions, a company may declare dividend out of its reserves in any year:

(i) The rate of dividend declared shall not exceed the average of the rates at which dividend was declared by it in the three years immediately preceding that year. However, this rule shall not apply to a company which has not declared any dividend in each of the three preceding financial years.

(ii) The total amount to be drawn from such accumulated profits shall not exceed 1/10 of the sum of its paid-up share capital and free reserves as appearing in the latest audited financial statement.

(iii) The amount so drawn shall first be utilised to set off the losses incurred in the financial year in which dividend is declared before any dividend in respect of equity shares is declared.

(iv) The balance of reserves after such withdrawal shall not fall below 15 per cent of its paid-up share capital as appearing in the latest audited financial statement.

(v) No company shall declare dividend unless carried over previous losses and depreciation not provided in the previous year are set off against profit of the company.

DIVIDEND WARRANT

A dividend warrant is a special kind of cheque or an order drawn by the company on its banker for the payment of the dividend to the members. The dividend warrants and counterfoils will be printed with consecutive numbers and the warrant may bear embossed cheque stamp.

Every warrant or cheque in payment of the dividend distributed by a company should show:

(a) the gross amount of dividend;

(b) the rate and amount of tax;

(c) the net amount actually paid; and

(d) the period to which it relates.

DIVIDEND MANDATE

Some shareholders may request the company to credit the dividends payable to them direct in their bank accounts. For this purpose they have to make a request to the company in a prescribed form known as dividend mandate. This mandate authorises the company to deposit dividends directly to the bank account of the shareholders. Bonus Shares (Sec. 63).

A company may (if its Articles provide) capitalise its profits by issuing fully paid bonus shares. When a company is prosperous and accumulates large distributable profits, it converts these accumulated profits into capital. Such a capital is divided among the existing members in proportion to their entitlements.

Sec. 63(1) states that a company may issue fully paid-up bonus shares to its members, out of:

(i) its free reserves;

(ii) the securities premium account; or

(iii) the capital redemption reserve account.

Sec. 63(2) states that no company shall capitalise its profits or reserves for the purpose of issuing fully paid-up bonus shares unless:

(a) it is authorised by its Articles;

(b) it has been authorised by in the general meeting of the company;

(c) it has not defaulted in payment of interest or principal in respect of fixed deposits or debt securities issued by it;

(d) it has not defaulted in respect of the payment of statutory dues of the employees;

(e) the partly paid-up shares, if any outstanding on the date of allotment are made fully paid-up; and

(f) it complies with such conditions as may be prescribed;

Sec. 63(3) states that the bonus shares shall not be issued instead of dividend.

REVIEW QUESTIONS

1. Define 'dividend'. Explain the law and procedure relating to the declaration and payment of dividend.

2. Explain the legal provisions relating to the capitalisation of profits by issue of bonus shares.

3. Write notes on:

   (a) Interim dividend; (b) Unpaid dividend account; (c) Dividend warran; (e) Dividend mandate; (f) Declaration of dividend out of Company's Reserves.

4. The shareholders in a duly convened annual general meeting passed a resolution for the payment of dividend at a rate higher than what was recommended by the Board. Discuss whether the resolution is void.

   Hint: No. The shareholders cannot enhance the rate of dividend as recommended by the Board of Directors.

43

Accounts and Audit

It is obligatory on all companies to keep proper books of account and to enter therein, full, true and complete accounts of the affairs and transaction of the company. (The Companies Act, 1956)

BOOKS OF ACCOUNT

Sec. 128 states that every company must keep proper books of account with respect to:

(a) all sums of money received and expended by the company and the matters in respect of which the receipt and expenditure take place;

(b) all sales and purchases of goods by the company;

(c) all assets and liabilities of the company; and

(d) in the case of a company engaged in production processing, manufacturing or mining activities, particulars relating to the utilisation of material or labour or other items of cost as may be prescribed by the Central Government.

The books of account may be kept either at the registered office of the company or at any other place if the Board of Directors so decides. Within seven days of any such a decision, the address of that place must be sent to the Registrar [Sec. 128(1)]. Where the company has a branch office, the books of account relating to the branch business must be kept at that office and at the intervals of '3' months the summarised accounts should be sent to the Registered office [Sec. 128(2)].

These books of account must contain a true and fair view of the state of affairs of the company. They should be kept on accrual basis and in accordance with the double entry system of accounting.

The books of accounts and other books and papers shall be open to inspection during the business hours by any director [Sec. 128 (3)], the Registrar, or any officer of Government authorised by the

Central Government in this behalf. Inspection under this Section can be made without giving previous notice to the company.

Every company shall preserve its books of account for a period of not less than 8 years immediately preceding the current year. The Registrar may direct a company to preserve any of these documents for a longer period.

STATUTORY BOOKS

Apart from the books of account to be maintained by a company under Sec. 128, a company should also maintain some other books, called the statutory books.

They are as follows:

1. Register of members
2. Index of members
3. Register of charges
4. Register of debentureholders with index
5. Register of director's shareholdings
6. Directors attendance book
7. Minute books—directors and of general meetings
8. Annual return to be made by a company having a share capital
9. Register of contracts in which directors are interested
10. Register of loans to companies under the same management
11. Register of investments in the shares of other companies
12. Register of directors and managers
13. Foreign register of members and debentureholders, if any.

ANNUAL ACCOUNTS AND BALANCE SHEET [SEC. 129]

The annual accounts of a company consist of the profit and loss account and the balance sheet. At every general meeting of a company, the Board of Directors must lay before the meeting the following documents:

(a) a report by the Company's Board of Directors,

(b) a balance sheet for the year, and

(c) a profit and loss account.

In the case of a company not carrying on business for profit, an income and expenditure account should be laid before the company at its annual general meeting in the place of a profit and loss account.

Board's Report [Sec. 134]

The report of the Board of Directors shall show the state of the company's affairs, the amount proposed to be carried to the reserve fund, the amount recommended to be paid as dividend, and material changes if any, affecting the financial position of the company. The report should also deal with any changes which have occurred during the financial year in the nature of the company's business, or in the business of its subsidiaries and the class of business, in which the company has interest.

The Board report shall also include a statement showing the names of employees of the company getting remuneration at a rate which is not less than such a sum per month as may be prescribed. The statement would state whether any such an employee is a relative of any director or manager of the company and if so, the name of such a director or manager.

The Board is also bound to give the fullest information and explanation in its report on every reservation, qualification or adverse remark contained in the auditor's report. The Board's report is to be signed by its chairman if he is authorised in that behalf. If he is not so authorised, it is to be signed by such a number of directors as are required to sign in the balance sheet and profit and loss account.

Balance Sheet and Profit and Loss Account

The period for which the profit and loss account should be made is as follows:

(a) In the case of a first annual general meeting, from the date of the incorporation of the company to a date not later than nine months previous to the date of the meeting.

(b) In the case of any subsequent annual general meeting, from the date immediately after the date of the last accounts to a date not later than six months previous to the date of the meeting.

The period to which the accounts aforesaid relate is referred to as 'financial year'. The financial year may be less or more than the calendar year, but it cannot exceed '15' months. It may be extended to '18' months with the special permission of the Registrar.

The balance sheet and profit and loss account must be in the form or forms as may be provided for different classes of companies in Schedule III. They are intended to give a true and fair view of the state of the company's affairs at the end of the financial year (Sec. 129).

Every balance sheet and profit and loss account must be signed by at least two directors. Out of them one shall be the managing director and the Chief Executive Officer, if he is a director in the company, the Chief Financial Officer and the company secretary of the company wherever they are appointed or in the case of a One Person Company, only by one director (Sec. 134).

The holding company shall annex to its balance sheet the following documents in respect of each of its subsidiaries:

(a) a copy of its balance sheet;

(b) a copy of its profit and loss account;

(c) a copy of the report of its directors;

(d) a copy of the report of its auditors;

(e) a statement about the extent of interest of the holding company in the subsidiary.

CIRCULATION OF ACCOUNTS (SEC. 136)

At least 21 days before the meeting, a copy of the balance sheet and profit and loss account together with the copies of all the documents annexed or attached thereto shall be sent to each member, each debentureholder, every trustee of debentureholders and every other person entitled to receive notice of such a meeting.

FILING OF ACCOUNTS WITH THE REGISTRAR (SEC. 137)

Sec. 137 requires that three copies of the balance sheet and profit and loss account must be filed with the Registrar within 30 days after the annual general meeting.

Where the annual general meeting of a company for any year has not been held, these documents shall be filed with the Registrar within 30 days from the latest day on or before which the meeting should have been held as per the provisions of the Companies Act, 2013.

In the case of non-compliance, the company shall be liable to a fine up to ₹ 1,000 for everyday during which the default continues, but which shall not be more than ten lakh rupees. Further, the managing director and the Chief Financial Officer of the company, if any, and in the absence of them, any other director who is charged by the Board with the responsibility of complying with this provision and in the absence of any such director, all the directors of the company, shall be punishable with imprisonment for a term of not less than six months or with fine of not less than one lakh rupees and not more than five lakh rupees or with both.

AUDIT

The audit of a joint stock company is intended to the protection of the shareholders and the auditor is expected to examine the accounts maintained by the directors with a view to informing the shareholders of the true financial position of the company. (*Institute of Chartered Accountants* v. *P.K. Mukherjee*, A.I.R. (1968) S.C.I. 104).

Meaning and Scope of Audit

An audit is "an examination of the books of accounts and vouchers of a business". It enables the auditor to satisfy himself that the balance sheet is properly drawn up, so as to give a true and fair view of the state of the affairs of the business, and whether the profit and loss account gives a true and fair view of the profit or loss for the financial period. Thus, the main object of an audit is the verification of accounts and statements prepared by a client or his staff. It is conducted to detect errors and fraud.

Appointment of Auditors (Secs. 139 and 140)

First Auditor

First Auditor of the company other than Government Company shall be appointed by the Board within thirty days of its date of registration. If the Board fails to do so, the members shall be informed and they shall appoint the same within 90 days from incorporation, who shall hold office till conclusion of first annual general meeting [Sec. 139(6)].

Subsequent Auditor

Every company shall at the first annual general meeting, appoint an individual or a firm as an auditor. Such an auditor shall hold office from the conclusion of that meeting till the conclusion of its sixth Annual General Meeting (AGM) and thereafter till the conclusion of every sixth meeting [Sec. 139(1) and Rule 3].

A written consent of the auditor should be taken before appointment [Sec. 139(1) and Rule 4]. Further, the company shall inform the auditor concerned of his or its appointment. It shall also file a notice of such an appointment with the Registrar in Form ADT-1 within 15 days of the meeting in which the auditor is appointed.

Appointment of Auditor in Government Company [Secs. 139(5), 139(7), 139(8), and 139(11)]

The appointment of auditor in Government company or government controlled (directly/indirectly) company shall be held in accordance with the following provisions:

The First auditor shall be appointed by the Comptroller and Auditor General within 60 days from the date of incorporation and in the case of failure to do so, the Board shall appoint auditor within next 30 days. If the Board fails to do so, the members shall be informed and they shall appoint the same within 60 days at an Extraordinary General Meeting (EGM). Such an auditor shall hold office till the conclusion of first annual general meeting.

In the case of subsequent auditor for existing Government companies, the Comptroller and Auditor General shall appoint the auditor within a period of 180 days from the commencement of the financial year. The auditor so appointed shall hold his position till the conclusion of the Annual General Meeting.

In the case of a company whose accounts are subject to audit by an auditor appointed by the Comptroller and Auditor General of India, be filled by the Comptroller and Auditor-General of India within thirty days. If the Comptroller and Auditor-General of India does not fill the vacancy within the said period, the Board of Directors shall fill the vacancy within next thirty days.

The Act also provides that if the company has an Audit Committee, then all appointments of Auditor including filling of casual vacancy, shall be made after taking into account the recommendations of the committee.

Automatic Re-appointment of Retiring Auditors: A retiring auditor shall be re-appointed unless:

(a) he is not disqualified for re-appointment;

(b) he has given the notice to the company in writing of his unwillingness to be re-appointed;

(c) a resolution has been passed at that meeting appointing somebody instead of him or expressly providing that he shall not be re-appointed;

(d) where notice has been given of an intended resolution to appoint some other person in the place of a retiring auditor, and by reason of death, incapacity or disqualification of the person nominated, the resolution cannot be proceeded with.

Casual Vacancy: Casual vacancies in the office of auditors may be filled up by the Board. But if such a vacancy has arisen due to the resignation of an auditor, it shall be filled by the company in a general meeting. Such an auditor shall hold office until the conclusion of the next annual general meeting.

Term of Auditor [Sec. 139(2) and Rule 5]

Listed company or all unlisted public companies having paid-up share capital of ₹ 10 crore or more, all private limited companies having paid-up share capital of ₹ 20 crore or more, all companies having public borrowings from financial institutions, banks or public deposits of ₹ 50 crore or more shall not appoint or re-appoint an individual as auditor for more than one term of 5 consecutive years; and an audit firm as auditor for more than two terms of 5 consecutive years. These auditors either (individual/auditor firm) can be re-appointed after cooling off period of 5 years. Three years transition period will be given to comply with this requirement.

No audit firm shall be appointed as auditor of the company for a period of five years, if same firm presently having a common partner(s) to the previous audit firm, whose tenure has expired in a company immediately preceding the financial year.

Rotation of Auditors [Sec. 139(3)]

By passing a special resolution, the members of a company can provide for the following.

(a) In the audit firm appointed by it, the auditing partner and his team shall be rotated at such intervals as may be resolved by members; or

(b) The audit shall be conducted by more than one auditor.

A transition period of 3 years from the commencement of the Act has been prescribed for the company existing on or before the commencement of the Act, to comply with the provisions of the rotations of auditor.

Resignation of Auditor [Secs. 140(2) and 140(3) and Rule 8]

The auditor who has resigned from the company shall file a

statement in Form ADT-3 indicating the reasons and other facts as may be relevant with regard to his as follows:

(i) In the case of other than Government Company, the auditor shall within 30 days from the date of resignation, file such statement to the company and the Registrar.

(ii) In the case of Government Company or Government controlled company, the auditor shall within 30 days from the resignation, file such a statement to the company and the Registrar and also file the statement with the Comptroller and Auditor General (C&AG) of India.

The onus to file such a statement containing relevant facts and reasons for resignation is on the resigning auditor. Any contravention of sub-clause (2) is punishable with a fine of not less than rupees fifty thousand and not more than rupees five lakh.

Removal of Auditors [Sec. 140(1)] and Rule 7

A company is empowered to remove an auditor before an expiry of his term through a resolution passed at a general meeting and with the previous approval of the Central Government. However the auditor concerned shall be given a reasonable opportunity of being heard.

Remuneration of Auditors (Sec. 142)

The remuneration of the auditors shall be fixed by the appointing body. If the auditors are appointed by the Board of Directors or the Central Government, their remuneration may be fixed by the Board or Central Government, as the case may be. If the auditors have been appointed by the shareholders in general meeting, their remuneration shall be fixed by the company in general meeting

Qualification of Auditors [Sec. 141(1) and (2)]

A person is not qualified for appointment as an auditor of a company unless he is a chartered accountant within the meaning of the Chartered Accountants Act, 1949. A firm may be appointed in its name provided all its partners are chartered accountants in actual practice.

DISQUALIFICATION [Sec. 141(3)] and Rule 10

None of the following persons can be appointed as an auditor of a company:

(i) A body corporate.

(ii) An officer or employee of the company.

(iii) A person who is a partner or who is in the employment of an officer or employee of the company.

(iv) A person who is indebted to the company for an amount, exceeding rupees five lakh or who has given a guarantee for the repayment of an amount exceeding rupees five lakh.

(v) A person who is disqualified for appointment as auditor of the company's subsidiary or holding company, or a subsidiary of its holding company.

If an auditor becomes disqualified in any of the above ways after his appointment as auditor, then he shall be deemed to have vacated his office as such.

Powers of an Auditor (Sec. 143)

Sec. 143 of the Companies Act confers the following powers on the auditors:

1. *Right of Access to the Books of Accounts:* Every auditor has a right to free and complete access, at all times, to the books of accounts, vouchers and other relevant records of the company wherever kept.

2. *Right to Call for Information and Explanation* [Sec. 143(1)]: An auditor is entitled to require from the officers of the company such information and explanations as he thinks necessary for the performance of his duties as auditor.

3. *Right to Inspect Branch Accounts* (Sec. 143): Where the accounts of any branch office are audited by a person other than the company's auditor, the company's auditor has a right to visit the branch office, if he deems it necessary to do so for the performance of his duties as auditor. He has also a right to access at all times to the books of accounts and vouchers of the company maintained at the branch office.

4. *Right to Attend General Meeting* (Sec. 146): An auditor has a right to receive notice of and to attend the general meeting of the company.

5. *Right to Remuneration* (Sec. 142): An auditor has the right to receive remuneration for auditing the accounts of the company.

Duties of an Auditor

1. *Acquaintance with Articles and Companies Act:* The auditor of a company is under the duty to make himself acquainted with his duties under the Articles and the Companies Act, 2013.

2. *Auditor's Report:* The auditor has to submit a report on the accounts of the company to its members. The report should state whether the accounts are kept as per the provisions of the Act and whether they give a true and fair view of the state of affairs of the company.

   Sec. 143(1) requires the auditor to enquire:

   (a) Whether the loans and advances made by the company on the basis of the security have been properly secured and whether the terms are not prejudicial to the interest of the company or its members;

   (b) Whether the transactions of the company which are represented by book entries are not prejudicial to the interests of the company;

   (c) Whether the loans and advances made by the company have been shown as deposits;

   (d) Whether the personal expenses have been charged to revenue account;

   (e) If the company is not an investment or banking company, whether any securities have been sold by the company at a price less than that at which they were purchased;

   (f) Whether cash has been received in respect of any shares allotted for cash. If no cash has been received, whether the position as stated in the books is correct, regular and not misleading.

3. *Duty of Care and Caution:* An auditor must be honest and must exercise reasonable skill and care in the performance of his duties, otherwise he may be sued for damages. But it is not his duty to give advice, and he has nothing to do with the way in which the business is carried on. He is not bound to be a detective, but he is justified in believing the paid servants of the company and in assuming they are honest, provided he takes reasonable care (*Kingston Colton Mills Co.* Re: (No. 2) (1896) 2 ch. 279).

4. *Duty to Certify Statutory Report:* An auditor is required to certify the correctness of the statutory report in respect of the number of shares allotted by the company and abstract of receipts and payments of the company.

COST AUDIT (SEC. 148)

The Central Government is empowered to issue necessary directions for conducting the cost audit of companies engaged in production, processing, manufacturing and mining activities. Such an audit will be conducted by a Cost Accountant within the meaning of Cost and Works Accountant Act, 1959. If the Central Government is of opinion that sufficient number of Cost Accountants are not available, the Government may by notification in the official Gazette, direct that for a specified period of time Chartered Accountants possessing the prescribed qualification may audit the cost accounts of the company.

The cost auditor shall be appointed by the Board of Directors of the company with the previous approval of the Central Government.

Cost auditor shall have the same powers and duties as an ordinary auditor of the company. He is to make a report to the Central Government and also to forward a copy of the report to the company. On receipt of the report of the cost auditor, the Central Government has powers to take necessary action.

DOUBLE AUDIT

The accounts of the Government company are to be audited by an auditor appointed by the Central Government as well as by the Comptroller and Auditor General of India.

REVIEW QUESTIONS

1. Name the books of accounts of a company registered under the Companies Act which is bound to maintain.
2. What are the provisions of the Companies Act relating to the maintenance, inspection, authentication and filing of accounts?
3. Discuss the provisions of the Companies Act regarding the qualifications, appointment, remuneration and removal of an auditor of the company.
4. State the rights and duties of a company auditor.
5. Write notes on:

   (a) Rotation of auditors; (b) Cost audit; (c) Statutory books; (d) Double audit; (e) Annual accounts.

44

Supremacy of Majority and Protection of Minority

A proper balance of the rights of majority and minority shareholders is essential for the smooth functioning of the company. (Palmer)

THE PRINCIPLES OF MAJORITY RULE

A company is run by a democratic process, and a majority of members acting in good faith in the interest of the company enjoys the supreme authority to exercise the powers of the company and generally to control its affairs. The Courts are prepared to uphold the claim of the majority shareholders that they should have the right to decide how the company's affairs are to be conducted. This principle, that the will of the majority shall prevail in respect of the internal affairs of the company, is generally known as the rule in *Foss* v. *Harbottle*.

Foss v. *Harbottle* (1843) 2 Hare, 461. The defendants who were the directors and promoters of a company sold property to the company at an undisclosed profit. The company was entitled to recover the secret profits from the directors. But at a general meeting the majority resolved that no action should be taken against the directors. Dissatisfied with the majority decision, two minority shareholders brought an action on behalf of themselves and all other shareholders for recovery of the undisclosed profits from the defendants.

The Court dismissed the action. It was held that as the actions were capable of confirmation by the majority it was for the majority to complain or to condone as they thought fit. It is, therefore, the company and not the individual members who should sue for a breach of the regulations of the company.

The principle of majority rule has since then been applied to a number of cases. In a recent case of *Rajahmundry Electric Supply Company* v. *A Nageswara Rao,* AIR. (1956) S.C. 213, the Supreme Court observed that "the Courts will not in general, intervene at the instance of the shareholders in the matter of internal administration, and will not interfere with the management of the company by its directors so long as they are acting within the powers conferred on them under the articles of the company. Moreover, if the directors are supported by the majority shareholders in what they do, the minority shareholders can, in general, do nothing about it".

ADVANTAGES OF RULE IN *FOSS* v. *HARBOTTLE*

1. The right of the majority to rule.
2. Recognition of the separate legal personality of company.
3. The prevention of a multiplicity of action.
4. Litigation at the suit of a minority futile if majority does not wish it.

EXCEPTIONS TO THE RULE IN *FOSS* v. *HARBOTTLE* (PROTECTION OF MINORITY)

The cases in which the majority rule does not prevail are commonly known as exceptions to the rule in *Foss* v. *Harbottle* and are available to the minority. These exceptions are based on the principles of natural justice and fair play. They are as follows:

1. *Where the Act Done is Illegal or Ultra Vires the Company*: Where the act is illegal or ultra vires the company any individual member may sue because the act cannot be confirmed by the majority.

2. *Where the Act Complained of Constitutes a Fraud on the Minority:* If a majority of the company's members uses their powers to defraud or oppress the minority, their conduct is liable to be impeached even by a single shareholder.

In *Menier* v. *Hooper's Telegraph Works Ltd.* (1874) 9 ch. App. 350, the majority of the members of company A were also members of company B. At a meeting of company A, they passed a resolution to compromise an action against company B, in a manner alleged to be favourable to company B but unfavourable to company A. Held, the minority of company A could bring an action to have the compromise set aside.

3. *Breach of Fiduciary Duty:* When a director is in breach of fiduciary duty, every shareholder shall be regarded as an authorised organ to bring the action.

4. *Where the Act Done is Supported by a Resolution Passed by an Insufficient Majority:* An action by minority is maintainable if it is brought to restrain the company from doing an act for which a special resolution is required, and such a resolution has not been properly passed or passed by means of a trick.

5. *Where the Personal Rights of an Individual Member have been Infringed:* Every shareholder has certain personal rights against the company.

If any such right is infringed, a single shareholder can, on principle, defy the majority.

6. *Oppression and Mismanagement:* The principle of majority rule does not apply to cases where Secs. 241 and 242 are applicable for prevention of oppression and mismanagement.

REVIEW QUESTIONS

1. What is the rule in *Foss* v. *Harbottle*? What are the exceptions to this rule?

2. "Majority must prevail" is the principle of company management. Are there any exceptions?

3. The minority shareholders in a company brought an action against the directors, alleging that they were responsible for losses which had been incurred. Will they succeed in their action?

   Hint: No. The company can itself take proceedings if it thinks fit to do so.

45

Prevention of Oppression and Mismanagement

The essence of the matter seems to be that the conduct complained of should at the lowest involve a visible departure from the standards of fair dealing, and a violation of the conditions of fair play on which every shareholder who entrusts his money to the company is entitled to rely.

[Lord Cooper in Elder v. Elder & Waston Ltd. (1952) S.C. 49]

MEANING OF 'OPPRESSION' (SEC. 241)

The term 'oppression' implies unjust or unfair conduct which is likely to result in some harsh or wrongful burden upon certain shareholders, e.g., depriving of certain members of their membership right.

MEANING OF MISMANAGEMENT (SEC. 242)

The term 'mismanagement' implies on any of the following grounds:

(a) Where the affairs of the company are being conducted in a manner prejudicial to the public interest or the interest of the company.

(b) Where a material change has taken place in the management or control, and that by reason of change, it is likely that the affairs of the company shall be conducted in a manner prejudicial to public interest or the interest of the company.

PREVENTION OF OPPRESSION OR MISMANAGEMENT

In the case of oppression or mismanagement of companies by majority, the minority shareholders can adopt the following measures:

1. Apply to the Tribunal for appropriate relief.
2. Apply to the Central Government for relief.

WHAT MAY APPLY TO THE TRIBUNAL FOR RELIEF? (SEC. 244)

The following members of a company have the right to apply under Sec. 241.

(i) In the case of a company having a share capital:

(a) At least 100 members of the company or one-tenth of the total number of its members, whichever is less, or

(b) Any number of members holding not less than one-tenth of the issued share capital of the company. The applicant or applicants should have paid all calls and other sums due on their shares.

(ii) In the case of a company not having a share capital:

At least one-fifth of the total number of members.

The Tribunal may, if in its opinion circumstances exist which make it just and equitable to do so, authorise any member or members (even if their number is less than the requisite number) to apply.

Once the consent of the requisite number has been obtained and the application made, the withdrawal of consent by some of them will not affect the right of the applicants to proceed with the application.

The Tribunal shall give notice of every application made to it under Sec. 241 or 242 to the Central Government and shall take into consideration the representations made to it by the Central Government before passing a final order.

POWERS OF THE TRIBUNAL (SEC. 242) NOT YET ENFORCED

To prevent oppression and mismanagement under Secs. 241 and 242, the Tribunal can pass any order which in its opinion is just and equitable. In particular it has the power to provide for:

(i) the regulation of the conduct of the company's affairs in future;

(ii) the purchase of the shares or interests of any member of the company by other members thereof or by the company;

(iii) in the case of purchase of shares by the company as aforesaid, the consequent reduction of its share capital;

(iv) the termination, setting aside or modification of any agreement between the company and its management upon such terms and conditions as may, in the opinion of the Tribunal, be just and equitable;

(v) the termination, setting aside or modification of any agreement between the company and any third person provided due notice to the person concerned and his consent obtained;

(vi) the setting aside of any fraudulent preference made within three months before the date of the application;

(vii) any other matter for which, in the opinion of the Tribunal it is just and equitable that provision should be made.

POWER TO PREVENT CHANGE IN BOARD OF DIRECTORS

When a complaint is made to the Tribunal by any director or manager of a company that as a result of a change the ownership of shares, a change in the Board of Directors is likely to take place which would prejudicially affect the affairs of the company, the Tribunal may, after making such inquiry as it thinks fit, order that no change in the Board of Directors can be made, without its prior confirmation. This does not apply to a private company, unless it is a subsidiary of a Public Company.

POWERS OF THE CENTRAL GOVERNMENT

1. *Power to Prevent Oppression or Mismanagement*: On one application by not less than 100 members of the company, or members holding not less than one-tenth of the voting power therein, the Central Government may appoint any number of persons to hold office as directors thereof to safeguard the interests of the company, or its shareholders of the public interest. Such directors can be appointed for any period, but not exceeding 3 years on any one occasion.

The directors so appointed shall not be required to hold qualification shares, nor shall they retire by rotation. The Central Government may require such directors to report to it from time to time with regard to the affairs of the company.

2. *Power to Remove Managerial Personal:* The Central Government is empowered to remove managerial personnel from office on the recommendation of the Tribunal.

REVIEW QUESTIONS

1. Define the terms 'oppression' and mismanagement'. State the provisions of Companies Act, 1956 for the prevention of oppression and mismanagement in a company.

2. Describe briefly the remedies available to minority shareholders against oppression or mismanagement.

3. A director of a public company apprehends that as a result of a change in the ownership of the shares held in the company, a change will occur in the Board of Directors which would affect prejudicially the company's affairs. Advise him.

   Hint: The director can make a written complaint to the Tribunal.

46

Compromises, Arrangements and Reconstructions

A compromise is an amicable settlement of a dispute or controversy by the method of making mutual concessions.

COMPROMISES AND ARRANGEMENTS

A compromise pre-supposes the existence of a dispute. Therefore, the term 'compromise' means "an amicable settlement of a dispute or controversy by the method of making mutual concessions". Thus, when a company has a dispute with a member or a class of members or with a creditor or a class of creditors, a scheme of compromise may be drawn up.

The term 'arrangement' is of very wide scope. It is not limited to compromise alone. It consists of all modes of reorganising the share capital, including variation of the special or preferential rights attached to shares. Sec. 3230 itself provides that the term 'arrangement' includes "a re-organisation of the share capital of a company by the consolidation of shares of different classes or by the division of shares of different classes or by both of these methods".

PROCEDURE FOR COMPROMISE AND ARRANGEMENT

The procedures of compromises and arrangements can be discussed under two heads: (1) Compromises when the company is a going concern; and (2) Compromises when the company is being wound up.

Compromise when the Company is a Going Concern (Sec. 230)

Where it is proposed to make a compromise or arrangement (a) between the company and its creditors or any class of them, or (b) between the company and its members or any class of them, an application to the Tribunal may be made by (i) the company, or (ii) any creditors, or (iii) any member. If the company is being wound up, the liquidator may also apply to the Tribunal.

Where an application is properly made, the Tribunal may order the calling of a separate meeting of each class of members or each class of creditors. The meeting should be held and conducted on such a manner as the Tribunal directs. Proper notice of meeting containing full particulars of the scheme should be given to all interested parties including the shareholders and the Central Government [Sec. 230(3)].

If at the meeting, the scheme is approved by a majority in number representing three-fourth in value of creditors or members, as the case may be, it may then be sanctioned by the Tribunal. Any scheme which is fair and reasonable and made in good faith shall be sanctioned by the Tribunal. The Tribunal may not sanction the compromise or arrangement unless it is satisfied that:

(i) the circumstances are such that the scheme should be sanctioned; and

(ii) the company or any other person by whom application has been made has disclosed to the Tribunal all material facts relating to the company.

The scheme when approved by the Tribunal shall be binding on all parties to it including the dissidents. However, an order may by the Tribunal shall have no effect until a certified copy of it has been filed with the Registrar. A copy of the Tribunal's order approving the scheme should also be annexed to every copy of the memorandum of the company issued after having filed it with the Registrar.

Where a Tribunal makes an order under Sec. 230, sanctioning a compromise or arrangement in respect of a company, it has the power to supervise the carrying out of the compromise or arrangement. It may also bring modification in the compromise or arrangement. Where the Tribunal is satisfied that the scheme cannot be worked satisfactorily it may make an order for the winding up of the company.

Compromise During the Winding up of a Company (Sec. 343)

When a company is being wound up by or subject to the supervision of the Tribunal, the liquidator can exercise the powers of compromise or arrangement with the permission of the Tribunal. In the case of a voluntary winding up, these powers can be exercised by the liquidator only with the sanction of a special resolution of the company. With the necessary sanction the liquidator may:

(i) pay any class of creditors in full;

(ii) make compromise with the debtors if such debts arise on account of calls or otherwise.

A compromise or arrangement can also be entered into between a company about to be, or in the course of being, wound up and its creditors. Such an arrangement is binding on the company and on the creditors only when it is sanctioned by a special resolution of the company acceded to by three-fourths in number and value of the creditors [Sec. 321].

RECONSTRUCTION AND AMALGAMATION (SEC. 232)

'Reconstruction' occurs "when a company transfers the whole of its undertaking and property to a new company consisting substantially of the same shareholders". Thus, reconstruction in this sense means the formation of a new company to take over the assets of an old company with an idea that substantially the same business shall be carried on by the same persons.

'Amalgamation' arises "when two or more companies join together to form a new company or where one company 'takes over' the control of two or more companies by acquiring its shares". Thus, amalgamation takes place when two or more companies are joined to form a third entity. This new company has all the property, rights and powers and is subject to all the duties and obligations of both the constituent companies.

If a compromise or arrangement is proposed with the object of reconstruction of a company or its amalgamation with another company, the scheme should be approved by the holders of three-fourths in value of the shares concerned and sanctioned by the Tribunal. The sanction of the Tribunal may provide for any of the following matters:

(i) Transfer of the whole or any part of the undertaking, property or liabilities of one company to another.

(ii) The allotment or appropriation by the transferee company of any shares, policies or other like interests.

(iii) The continuation of any legal proceedings pending by or against the transferee company.

(iv) The dissolution, without winding up, of any transferor company.

(v) The provision to be made for any persons who dissent from the scheme; and

(vi) Such other incidental matters as are necessary for carrying out reconstruction or amalgamation.

The Tribunal does not give sanction for the amalgamation of a company, which is being wound up, with any other company or companies if it has not received a report from the Registrar that the affairs of the company have not been conducted in a manner prejudicial to the interests of its members or to the public interest.

Within 30 days of the Tribunal's order, a certified copy thereof must be filed by the company with the Registrar.

DISSENTING SHAREHOLDERS (SEC. 235)

The term 'dissenting shareholders' includes (i) one who has not assented to the scheme or contract for transfer, and (ii) any shareholder who has failed or refused to transfer his shares to the transferee company in terms of the compromise or arrangement.

Where the scheme of reconstruction or amalgamation involves the acquisition of shares of one company by another company, the transferee company may do so by making an offer to the transferor company, so that the scheme may be placed before the shareholders in a general meeting of the company. The shareholders have the option to approve the offer within four months. Approval should be accorded by at least nine-tenths in value of the shares whose transfer is involved. The shares already held by the transferee company should be excluded while counting this number.

When the approval by the nine-tenths majority is accorded, the transferee company obtains the right to acquire the shares of the dissenting shareholders, if any. Within two months after the expiration or the above four months, the transferee company must give notice to the dissenting shareholders that it desires to acquire their shares. Within one month from the date of the notice, the dissenting shareholders may apply to the Tribunal. Where no application is made to the Tribunal or if the Tribunal refuses it, the transferee company is entitled to acquire such shares on the term on which the shares of the approving shareholders are to be taken.

Any sums received by the transferor company should be paid into a separate bank account and should be held by that company in trust for the several persons entitled to the shares in respect of which the said sums were received.

AMALGAMATION OF COMPANIES IN NATIONAL INTEREST (SEC. 237)

Where the Central Government is satisfied that the amalgamation of two or more companies is essential in the public interest, then the Government may, by order in the Official Gazette, provide for the amalgamation of those companies into a single company. The amalgamated company shall have such constitution, property, powers, rights, interests, authorities and privileges and shall be with such liabilities, duties and obligations as may be specified in the order.

Every member or creditor (including a debentureholder) of each of the companies shall have, as nearly as may be, the same rights and interests in the amalgamated company as he had in its constituent. If his rights in the new company are in any manner less, he is entitled to get compensation for the loss.

PRESERVATION OF BOOKS AND PAPERS OF AMALGAMATED COMPANY (SEC. 239)

The books and papers of the amalgamated company cannot be disposed of without the prior permission of the Central Government. Before granting the permission, the Central Government may appoint a person to examine the books and papers in order to find out whether they contain any evidence of the commission of any offence relating to the promotion, formation or the management of the affairs of the company.

REVIEW QUESTIONS

1. Define the terms 'compromise' and 'arrangements'. How can a company make a compromise or arrangement with its members and/or creditors without recourse to liquidation?

2. Define the terms 'reconstruction' and 'amalgamation'. What are the provisions of the Companies Act in respect of reconstruction and amalgamation of companies?

3. State the provisions of the Companies Act in respect of the powers of the Central Government to provide for amalgamation of companies in public interest.

47

Winding Up

Winding up of a company is "the process whereby its life is ended and its property administered for the benefit of its creditors and members".

MEANING

Winding up is the process of putting an end to the life of the company. In other words, it is a proceeding by which a company is dissolved. In the course of such a dissolution, the assets of the company are disposed of, the debts are paid off out of the realised assets and the surplus if any, is then paid off to the members in proportion to their holdings in the company.

The company is not dissolved immediately on the commencement of the winding up proceedings. Winding up of a company precedes its dissolution. Thus, in between the winding up and dissolution, the legal status of the company is in existence and it can be sued. On the dissolution, the existence of the company comes to an end and its name is struck off by the Registrar from the register of companies.

DISSOLUTION OF A COMPANY

The termination of the life of a company is termed as 'dissolution'. Thus, 'dissolution' is the end result of the process of winding up. The Tribunal shall make an order of dissolution when the affairs of a company have been completely wound up. The dissolution of the company shall take effect from the date of such an order by the Tribunal.

Winding up v. Dissolution

Winding up	Dissolution
1. First step in bringing about the end of a company.	1. Final step in bringing about the end of a company.
2. Involving the collection and realisation of the company's assets and the distribution of the proceeds among creditors and contributories.	2. Announcing that all such formalities are over at the date of the dissolution.

495

3. A company exists in the eye of law during the process of winding up.	3. The existence of the company comes to an end.
4. A company may carry on its business affairs during the process of winding up.	4. Business affairs cannot be carried out.
5. Since the company ceases, the liquidator can represent the company in winding up.	5. The liquidator cannot represent the company to exist.
6. Creditors can prove their debts.	6. Creditors cannot prove their debts.
7. It always precedes dissolution of the company.	7. It always succeeds winding up of the company.

WINDING UP AND BANKRUPTCY

Winding up and bankruptcy are entirely distinct and different. While in bankruptcy the property is divested from him and rests in the official receivers or the official assignee, in winding up the property of the company is not divested from it. A company cannot be declared insolvent although it is unable to pay its debts. It can only be wound up and the same can be done even when it is solvent.

Important changes which have been introduced in the Companies Act, 2013 are as follows:

  (i) The powers and functions of the High Court have been entrusted with NCLT now.

 (ii) Provisions relating to winding up under the supervision of the Court have been removed.

(iii) Winding up of smaller companies having assets not exceeding rupees one crore may be ordered by the Central Government.

 (iv) Compulsory winding up is applicable to insolvent companies only.

  (v) NCLT is empowered to direct for compulsory winding up under certain circumstances.

 (vi) Voluntary winding of healthy companies requires a declaration of solvency.

(vii) The secured creditors have been given greater participation in the Winding up Committee.

(viii) The line of distinction between members' voluntary winding up and the creditors' voluntary winding has been wiped out. These two have been clubbed under the Act.

(ix) Establishment of panel of professionals for selection of liquidators has been made mandatory.

(x) The stipulation of time frames at different stages of the procedure for winding up have been set up in this Act in order to curb delays in winding up inherently associated with the Companies Act, 1956.

Modes of Winding Up

The modes of winding up may be discussed under two heads. These are: (1) Winding by the Tribunal, and (2) Voluntary winding up. We will study about these two methods in the coming sections.

WINDING UP BY THE TRIBUNAL (SEC. 271)

The winding up of a company by the Tribunal is also called the compulsory winding up. Sec. 271 enumerates the grounds on which a company may be wound up by the Tribunal. These are:

(a) *Special Resolution by the Company:* In this case, the Tribunal may order the winding up of the company on a petition presented to it by the company or contributory.

(b) *Inability to Pay Debt:* It deals with the company's inability to pay its current liabilities. As per Sec. 271(2), a company is deemed unable to pay its debts in the following circumstances:

   (i) Failure of the company to pay its debts exceeding one lakh rupees within 21 days of the formal demand made by its creditors.

   (ii) Failure to satisfy a court decree in favour of a creditor either in whole or in part.

   (iii) If it is proved to the satisfaction of the Tribunal that the company is unable to pay its debts.

(c) *Under Chapter XIX:* The Tribunal can order for the winding up of the company under Chapter XIX.

   In the case of sick companies, if it is not possible to revive and rehabilitate them, the winding up order shall be made by the Tribunal.

(d) *Default in Filing Financial Statement:* In case the company has made a default in filing with the Registrar its financial statements or annual returns for immediately preceding five consecutive financial years, the Tribunal may order for its winding up.

(e) *Opinion of the Tribunal:*   In case the Tribunal is of the opinion that:

(i) the affairs of the company have been conducted in a fraudulent manner, or

(ii) the company was established for fraudulent and unlawful purpose; or

(iii) the persons concerned in the formation or management of its affairs have been guilty of fraud, misfeasance, or misconduct in connection therewith; it is proper that the company may be wound up.

(f) *Just and Equitable:*   The Tribunal may order for the winding up of a company if it is of opinion that it is just and equitable that the company should be wound up. What is just and equitable depends upon the facts of each particular case. The following are some of the instances in which the Tribunals have exercised their discretion under this head:

(i) When the substratum of the company has gone, i.e., its main purposes have failed or become impossible of achievement.

(ii) When there is a complete deadlock in the management.

(iii) Where the company was formed for fraudulent or illegal purposes.

(iv) Where the company is a bubble, i.e., it never had any real business.

(v) Where the business of the company cannot be carried on except at a loss.

(vi) Where a Private Company is in essence or substance a partnership.

(vii) Where the principal shareholders have adopted an aggressive or oppressive policy towards the minority.

Persons Entitled to Apply for Winding Up (Sec. 272)

The petition for winding up of a company may be presented to the Tribunal by any of the following persons:

(a) The company itself by the passing of a special resolution;

(b) Any creditor or creditors, including any contingent or prospective creditor or creditors;

(c) A contributory or contributories;

(d) Any combination of creditors or contributories acting jointly or separately;

(e) The Registrar;

(f) Any person authorised by the Central Government as per Sec. 243 on the basis of an Inspector's report;

(g) The Tribunal itself.

Commencement of Winding Up

The winding up of a company by the Tribunal is deemed to commence from the time of the presentation of the petition for the winding up. However, where before the presentation of a petition for the winding up of a company by the Tribunal, a resolution has been passed by the company for voluntary winding up, the winding up of the company is deemed to have commenced at the time of the passing of the resolution.

Power of Tribunal on Hearing Petition [Sec. 273(1)]

On hearing a winding up petition, the Tribunal may exercise any of the following powers:

(a) Dismiss it with or without costs;

(b) Adjourn the hearing;

(c) Make any interim order as it thinks fit;

(d) Make an order for winding up of the company with or without costs.

Consequences of Winding Up Order by the Tribunal

(a) Immediate intimation to the official liquidator and Registrar.

(b) A copy of winding up order to be filed with the Registrar within 30 days from the date of the making of the order.

(c) The order of winding up shall be deemed to be a notice of discharge to the officers and employees of the company, except when the business of the company is continued.

(d) Any suit or proceeding in any other Tribunal shall be transferred to the Tribunal in which the winding up of the company is proceeding.

(e) The order operates in favour of all the creditors and of all the contributories of the company as if it had been made on the joint petition of a creditor and contributory.

Procedure of Winding Up by the Tribunal

At any time after the presentation of a winding up petition and before the making of the winding up order, the Tribunal may appoint the official liquidator, to act as provisional liquidator.

On winding up order being made in respect of a company, the official liquidator, by virtue of his office becomes the liquidator of the company. An official liquidator is an officer who helps the Tribunal in conducting and completing the winding up proceedings.

Within 21 days of the date of the winding up order or the appointment of the official liquidator as provisional liquidator, a statement as to the affairs of the company should be made out and submitted to the official liquidator. On receiving the statement of affairs, the official liquidator shall submit a preliminary report to the Tribunal.

Official Liquidator

The Tribunal at the time of the passing of the order of winding up shall appoint an Official Liquidator or a Liquidator from the panel maintained under sub-section (2) as the Company Liquidator. The following persons shall be appointed as Official Liquidator.

A member from the panel maintained by the Central Government comprising the following names:

(a) Chartered Accountants

(b) Advocates

(c) Company Secretaries

(d) Cost Accountants

(e) Body Corporates having such other professionals as approved by Central Government.

Liquidator

As per the Act, only an Official Liquidator can act as Liquidator of the company. A Liquidator shall be described by the style of "The Official Liquidator" of the particular company in respect of which he acts as a Liquidator and not by his individual name.

Provisional Liquidator

The Tribunal may appoint the Official Liquidator as Provisional Liquidator (for the time being) at any time after receiving the winding up petition and before passing the winding up order. He shall have the same powers as Liquidator if the Tribunal does not restrict his powers by an order. If the Tribunal makes for an order for appointment of Provisional Liquidator, the same shall be informed to the Provisional Liquidator or the Company Liquidator (as the case may be) and to the Registrar within seven days from the date of passing of the order (Sec. 277). The Provisional Liquidator becomes the Liquidator of the company immediately on the winding up order.

Winding Up Committee

The Company Liquidator forms a committee known as winding up committee, to assist and monitor the progress of liquidation. This committee shall consist of the following persons:

   (i) Official Liquidator attached to the Tribunal;
  (ii) Nominee of secured creditors; and
 (iii) A professional nominated by the Tribunal.

The Company Liquidator shall summon the meetings of the winding up committee for the proceedings relating to:

   (i) Taking over assets;
  (ii) Scrutinising the statement of affairs;
 (iii) Recovery of property of the company;
  (iv) Review of audit reports and accounts of the company;
   (v) Sale of assets;
  (vi) Finalisation of list of creditors and contributories;
 (vii) Compromise, abandonment and settlement of claims;
(viii) Payment of dividends, if any and
  (ix) Any other function as the Tribunal may direct from time to time.

Duties of the Liquidator

  (a) To conduct equitably and impartially all the proceedings in the winding up.
  (b) To submit a preliminary report to the Tribunal.
  (c) To take over the company's assets.
  (d) To settle the list of contributories and make such a call as may be necessary.
  (e) To summon the meetings of creditors and contributories.

(f) To keep all sums received on behalf of the company into some Scheduled Banks.

(g) To submit the accounts of receipts and payments to the Tribunal.

(h) To appoint a committee of inspection.

(i) To make the payments into the public accounts of India.

Powers of Official Liquidator

The power of the liquidator can be brought into the following two classes: (a) Powers to be exercised with the sanction of the Tribunal, and (b) Powers to be exercised without the sanction of the Tribunal.

(a) *Powers to be Exercised with the Sanction of the Tribunal*

    (i) To institute or defend suits, prosecutions or other legal proceedings in the name and on behalf of the company.

    (ii) To carry on the business of the company so far as may be necessary for the beneficial winding up of the company.

    (iii) To sell the immovable and movable property and actionable claims of the company by public auction or private contract.

    (iv) To raise the required sum on the security of the assets of the company.

    (v) To do all such other things as may be necessary.

(b) *Powers to be Exercised without the Sanction of the Tribunal*

    (i) To do all acts and execute documents and deeds on behalf of the company under its seal.

    (ii) To inspect the records and returns of the company or the files of the Registrar without the payment of any fees.

    (iii) To prove, rank and claim in the insolvency of any contributory and to receive dividend of his estate.

    (iv) To draw, accept, make and endorse bill of exchange, pronote or hundi in the name and on behalf of the company.

    (v) To appoint agents, if necessary.

Contributory

Contributory means every person who is liable to contribute to the assets of the company in the event of its being wound up and includes the holders of fully paid-up shares.

A holder of fully paid-up shares is placed on the list of contributories for the purpose of distribution of assets, and for other procedural purposes even though his liability is nil. The other persons such as debtors or holders of the share warrants are not the contributories. On the commencement of the winding up, the shareholders are called the 'Contributories'. They are liable to pay the uncalled amount on their shares, which is realised by making the calls on them.

List of Contributories

List of contributories is brought into two parts, i.e., A and B. List A comprises the present members of the company. It is drawn up from the company's register of members. List B comprises the past members of the company. All the persons who were the members at any time during the 12 months before the commencement of winding up are included in this list.

Liability of the Contributories

The liability of the List 'A' contributories, is primary and absolute. However, their liability is limited to the extent of unpaid amount.

The liability of the List B contributories is secondary. The liability of these members arises only on the default of the present members.

Nature of Contributory's Liability

The liability of the contributory is ex lege, i.e., it arises by reasons of the fact that his name appears on the register of members of the company. His liability is not ex contractu, i.e., it does not arise by reasons of his contract to take shares.

General Powers of the Tribunal

The Companies Act has conferred the following powers to the Tribunal with a view to facilitating the winding up of the company:

(i) Power to order for the delivery of property to the liquidator (Sec. 283).

(ii) Power to settle the list of contributories (Sec. 285).

(iii) Power to stay winding up process (Sec. 289).

(iv) Power to make calls (Sec. 296).

(v) Power to adjust the rights of contributories (Sec. 297).

(vi) Power to order costs (Sec. 298).

(vii) Power to summon persons suspected of having property of the company, etc. (Sec. 299).

(viii) Power to arrest an absconding contributory (Sec. 301).

(ix) Power to order the dissolution of the company.

(x) Power to convene the meetings of creditors or contributories (Sec. 354).

(xi) Power to exclude creditors not proving in time.

VOLUNTARY WINDING UP

Voluntary winding up means winding up by the creditors or members without any intervention of the Tribunal. The purpose behind it is that the company, i.e., the members as well as the creditors are left free to settle their affairs without going to the Tribunal of Law. A company may be wound up voluntarily:

(a) If the company in general meeting passes an ordinary resolution for voluntary winding up when the period fixed by the Articles for the duration of the company has expired or the event has occurred on which under the Articles the company is to be dissolved.

(b) If the company resolves by special resolution that it shall be wound up voluntarily.

Compulsory winding up v. Voluntary winding up

Compulsory Winding up	Voluntary Winding up
1. Tribunal makes up order of winding up.	1. Company passes special resolution for winding up.
2. Declaration of solvency is not required.	2. Declaration of solvency is required.
3. Tribunal appoints the official liquidator.	3. The members or creditors in their meeting appoint liquidator.
4. There is no need of a Committee of Inspection	4. Committee of Inspection is appointed.
5. Tribunal directs and controls the winding up procedure.	5. The members and creditors control the winding up.

Declaration of Solvency (Sec. 305)

In case a company determines to wind up voluntarily, its directors have to make a declaration of solvency. The following are its related procedures:

(i) Convening of the Board meeting.

(ii) Making declaration by majority of its directors.

(iii) Verification of declaration by an affidavit.

(iv) The declaration has to state that, the company has no debts, or if it has any debts, it can be paid in full from the proceeds of the assets of the company.

(v) Making declaration within five weeks immediately preceding the date of passing of resolution to wind up.

(vi) Delivering the declaration to the Registrar for registration before that date.

(vii) The declaration shall state that it is not the intention of the company to defraud any person.

(viii) A copy of auditor's report and company's assets valuation report are to be attached with it.

Commencement of Voluntary Winding Up (Sec. 308)

A voluntary winding up shall be deemed to commence when the resolution for such winding up is passed.

Meeting of Creditors (Sec. 306)

The company shall arrange for meetings of its creditors either on the same day or on the next day of its company meeting. The resolution for voluntary winding up is made in such a meeting. This is because the distinction between members' voluntary winding up and the creditors' voluntary winding up has been wiped out. In fact both these types have been clubbed under the Act. Thus under the new Act, creditors' involvement has been largely increased. The various provisions relating to meeting of creditors are as follows:

(i) A notice of creditors' meeting is to be sent to the creditors by registered post.

(ii) The Board of Directors has to present a statement of affairs of the company together with a list of creditors of the company.

(iii) A copy of declaration of solvency with an estimated amount of claims should be presented in the meeting.

(iv) One of the directors shall be appointed to preside over the meeting.

(v) The company can be wound up voluntarily with the consent of two-thirds in value of creditors of the company.

(vi) In case the company is unable to pay off its debts in full from the proceeds of assets sold in voluntary winding up, a resolution can be passed that (at the interest of all parties) the company may be wound up by the Tribunal. In such a case the company can file an application before the Tribunal within fourteen days.

(vii) A notice of any resolution passed in the creditors' meeting shall be filed with the Registrar within ten days of passing of such resolution.

Consequences of Voluntary Winding up

The following are the main consequences of voluntary winding up:

(i) The company ceases to carry on its business from the commencement of the voluntary winding up.

(ii) The company will be permitted to carry on the business which may be required so far as for its beneficial winding up.

(iii) A company liquidator shall be appointed from the panel prepared by the Central Government at the company's general meeting.

(iv) The possession of the assets of the company vests in the liquidator.

(v) The liquidator should make all arrangements for realisation of such assets and distribute the realised amount to the creditors of the company.

(vi) The corporate status and corporate powers of the company shall continue till it is dissolved.

(vii) A resolution to wind up voluntarily operates as notice of discharges to the employees of the company, except when the business is continued by the liquidator for the beneficial winding up of the company.

(viii) All the powers of the Board of Directors, and of the managing or whole-time director shall cease on the appointment of a liquidator.

(ix) Any transfer of shares in the company or any alteration in the status of members of the company made after the commencement of the winding up shall be void. However, all these can be made with the permission of the liquidator.

Appointment of Committees

A committee can be apopointed at the meeting of creditors of the company (or if there are no creditors at its general meeting) to supervise the voluntary winding up and assist the Company Liquidator in discharging his or its functions.

Procedure for Voluntary Winding Up

The following are the procedures involved in the process of voluntary winding up:

(i) *Appointment of Liquidator* (Sec. 310): The company shall appoint one or more liquidators for winding up of the affairs of the company. The company in its general meeting shall fix the remuneration payable to a liquidator. However, this sum cannot be increased in the future. If the remuneration of the liquidator is not fixed in general meeting, he shall not take charge of his office.

(ii) *Board's Power to Cease:* On the appointment of the liquidator, all the powers of the Board come to an end [Sec. 313].

(iii) *Power to Fill Vacancy in the Office of Liquidator:* The company has the power to fill vacancy in the office of the liquidator (Sec. 311).

(iv) *Notice of Appointment of Liquidator:* Notice of appointment of liquidator is to be given to the Registrar within 10 days of such an appointment (Sec. 312).

(v) *Duty to Call Creditors Meeting:* Summoning of creditors meeting in the case of insolvency (Sec. 306).

(vi) *General Meeting at the End of the Year:* If winding up continues for more than one year, the liquidator must call a general meeting of the company at the end of the first year and at the end of each subsequent year [Sec. 314(3)].

(vii) *Final Meeting and Dissolution:* As soon as the affairs of the company are fully wound up, the liquidator must make an account of the winding up and call a final general meeting of the company. Within one week after the meeting, the liquidator shall send a copy of the account and of the return of the meeting to the Registrar, and to the official liquidator. The official liquidator shall make a scrutiny of the books and papers of the company and report to the Tribunal the result of his scrutiny. On the basis of this report, the Tribunal may order either further investigation of the affairs of the company or dissolution of the company with effect from the date specified in the order [Sec. 318].

Powers and Duties of Company Liquidator in Voluntary Winding Up

The following are the powers and duties of company liquidator in voluntary winding up:

(i) He shall carry out such functions and discharge such duties as specified by the company and its creditors.

(ii) He shall settle the list of contributories.

(iii) He shall maintain regular and proper books of accounts.

(iv) He shall call general meetings of the company.

(v) He shall prepare quarterly statements in such forms and manner as may be prescribed.

(vi) He shall pay the debts of the company and adjust the rights of the contributories among themselves.

(vii) He shall observe due care and diligence in discharging of his duties.

Winding Up on Insolvent Companies

The company which cannot pay all its debts is termed as insolvent company.

In the winding up of an insolvent company, the same rules shall prevail and be observed as are in force under the law of insolvency, with regard to (a) debts provable; (b) valuation of future and contingent liabilities; and (c) rights of secured and unsecured creditors.

All persons who would be entitled to prove for and receive dividends out of the assets of the company may come in under the winding up and make such claims against the company as they respectively are entitled to. But it is not required for a secured creditor to prove his debt in the winding up. He can, thus, stand wholly outside the winding up proceedings.

When a secured creditor (in lieu of abandoning his security and proving for his debt) proceeds to realise his security, he shall be liable to pay the expenses incurred by the liquidator for the preservation of the security before its realisation by the secured creditor.

Winding Up of Unregistered Company

Unregistered company comprises any partnership, association or company having more than seven members at the time when the petition for winding up is presented before the Tribunal.

An unregistered company may be wound up under this Act. In such a case, all the provisions of this Act regarding winding up shall apply to an unregistered company.

An unregistered company cannot be wound up voluntarily. But it can be wound up by the Tribunal. The Tribunal can wind up an unregistered company if:

(i) it is dissolved or has ceased business or is carrying on business only for the purpose of winding up its affairs; or

(ii) it is unable to pay its debts; or

(iii) the Tribunal is of opinion that it is just and equitable that the company should be wound up.

Effects of Winding Up on Various Parties

(i) *Members of the Company:* A member of a company is described as contributory at the time of winding up. His liability is limited to the amount remaining unpaid on shares held by him. This liability continues even after the company goes into liquidation. But a past contributory can only be called upon to pay when the present contributory is unable to pay.

(ii) *Secured Creditors:* A secured creditor on winding up:

(a) may rely on the security for the payment of all that may be due to him; or

(b) may value or realise the security and prove for the deficiency in the winding up; or

(c) may give up the security and prove for the whole amount.

While applying assets available with the liquidator for payment, the secured creditors will get first preference.

(iii) *Unsecured Creditors:* The unsecured creditors are considered at the time of winding, only after considering:

(a) secured creditors;

(b) cost of liquidation;

(c) preferential payments; and

(d) debentureholders secured by floating charge

(e) All debts due to unsecured creditors are to be created equally and paid 'pari passu'.

(iv) *Servants and Officers of the Company:* A winding up order by the Tribunal operates as a notice of discharge to the employees and officers of the company. But this provision is not applicable when the business of the company is continued.

The same principle will also apply in respect of discharge of employees in a voluntary winding up.

(v) *Company:* No suit or legal proceeding can be commenced and no pending suit or legal proceeding continued against the company (except with the leave of the Tribunal) when a winding up order is made or an official liquidator is appointed.

(vi) *Costs:* The Tribunal may make an order for payment (out of the assets) of expenses incurred in the winding up, when the assets of the company are insufficient to satisfy the liabilities.

(vii) *Documents:* Every document issued in the name of the company, after the commencement of winding up, should contain a statement that the company is being wound up.

(viii) *Books and Papers of the Company:* In the case of winding up by the Tribunal, the books and papers of the company and those of the liquidator may be disposed of in such a manner as the Tribunal directs.

In the case of members' voluntary winding up, the books and papers of the company may be disposed of by a special resolution. In the case of creditors' voluntary winding up, the books and papers of the company may be disposed of in the manner directed by Committee of Inspection or if there is no such a Committee, by the creditors.

DEFUNCT COMPANY

A company which no longer exists is known as a defunct company. A company is assumed to be defunct when:

(i) it has never commenced business, or

(ii) it is not carrying on business, or

(iii) it has either no assets or has such assets shall not be sufficient to meet the cost of liquidation.

Further, if a company (private or public) has failed to meet the paid-up capital norm, it shall be deemed to be defunct company and the Registrar of Companies shall strike off the name of the company.

However, a company is not considered defunct if the cessation of business is due to the conduct of winding up.

The Registrar has been given the power to remove the name of the defunct company from his register after completing the process under the Act.

REVIEW QUESTIONS

1. What is winding up of a company?
2. What is meant by dissolution of a company?
3. What do you mean by a contributory?
4. What do you mean by a provisional liquidator?
5. What do you mean by an official liquidator?
6. Who are called List A contributories?
7. What is meant by 'Declaration of solvency'?
8. What do you mean by committee of inspection?
9. What is voluntary winding up?
10. What do you mean by just and equitable ground?
11. Who are entitled to apply for compulsory winding up?
12. Explain defunct company.
13. Who can present petition for winding up by the Tribunal?
14. Enumerate the extent of the liability of a contributory.
15. Explain the List B contributories.
16. How does the winding up of a company differ from the dissolution of a company?
17. State the consequences of winding up by the Tribunal.
18. What are the consequences of voluntary winding up?
19. Explain the provisions relating to the winding up of an unregistered company.
20. What are the circumstances under which the company may opt for winding up by the Tribunal?
21. Explain how the liquidator is appointed under creditors' voluntary winding up.
22. Distinguish between compulsory winding up and voluntary winding up.
23. What do you mean by winding up of a company? Explain the different modes of winding up of a public limited company.
24. Discuss the procedures in compulsory winding up.
25. State the general powers of the Tribunal.
26. Explain the duties and powers of Official Liquidator.
27. Explain the provisions of the Companies Act regarding voluntary winding up.

PART FOUR

INDUSTRIAL LAW

48

The Factories Act, 1948

"Factories Act is a social enactment to achieve social reform". Supreme Court of India in Works Manager Central Railway Workshop".

—Jhansi v. Vishwanath, AIR, 1970

The law dealing with the factories in India is provided in the Factories Act, LXIII of 1948 which came into force on the 1st day of April, 1949. The Act was substantially amended in 1976 and in 1987. The Act was enacted mainly to protect workers employed in factories against industrial and occupational hazards and to regulate the conditions of work in manufacturing establishments.

DEFINITIONS

Adult [Sec. 2(a)]: An 'adult' means a person who has completed his eighteenth year of age.

Adolescent [Sec. 2(b)]: An 'adolescent' means a person who has completed his fifteenth but has not completed his eighteenth year.

Child [Sec. 2(c)]: A 'child' means a person who has not completed his fifteenth year of age.

Young Person [Sec. 2(d)]: A 'young person' means a person who is either a child or an adolescent.

Calendar Year [Sec. 2(dd)]: 'Calendar Year' means a period of twelve months beginning with the first day of January in any year.

Day [Sec. 2(e)]: 'Day' means a period of 24 hours beginning at midnight.

Week [Sec. 2(f)]: 'Week' means a period of seven days beginning at midnight on Saturday night or such other night as may be approved in writing for a particular area by the Chief Inspector of Factories.

Power [Sec. 2(g)]: 'Power' means electrical energy, and any other form of energy which is mechanically transmitted and is not generated by human and animal agency.

Prime Mover [Sec. 2(h)]: 'Prime Mover' means an appliance which generates or otherwise provides power.

Transmission Machinery [Sec. 2(i)]: It means any shaft, wheel, drum, pulley, system of pulleys, coupling, clutch, driving belt or other appliance or device by which the motion of a prime mover is transmitted to or received by any machinery or appliance.

Machinery [Sec. 2(j)]: Machinery includes prime movers, transmission machinery and all other appliances whereby power is generated, transformed, transmitted or applied.

Manufacturing Process [Sec. 2(k)]: It means any process for:

   (i) making, altering, repairing, ornamenting, finishing, packing, oiling, washing, cleaning, breaking up, demolishing, or otherwise treating or adapting any article or substance with a view to its use, sale, transport, delivery or disposal, or

  (ii) pumping oil, water, sewage, or any other substance, or

 (iii) generating, transforming, or transmitting power, or

 (iv) composing types for printing, printing by letter press, lithography, photogravure or other similar or book binding, or

  (v) constructing, reconstructing, repairing, refitting, finishing or breaking up ship or vessels, or

 (vi) preserving or storing any article in cold storage.

Worker [Sec. 2(1)]: A 'worker' means a person employed, directly or by or through any agency (including a contractor) with or without the knowledge of the principal employer, whether for wages or not, in any manufacturing process or in cleaning any part of the machinery or premises used for a manufacturing process, or in any other kind of work incidental to, or connected with the manufacturing process, or the subject of the manufacturing process, but does not include any member of the armed forces of the union.

Factory [Sec. 2(m)]: It means any premises including the precincts thereof:

  (i) Whereon 10 or more workers are working or were working on any day of the preceding twelve months, and in any part of which a manufacturing process is being carried on with the aid of power, or is ordinarily so carried on, or

 (ii) Whereon 20 or more workers are working on any day of the preceding twelve months, and in any part of which a manufacturing process is being carried on without the aid of power or is ordinarily so carried on.

In short, a factory is a premise where 10 or more persons are engaged if power is used or 20 or more persons are engaged if power is not used in a manufacturing process. The word premises including precincts is usually understood as enclosed by fencing or walls.

Occupier [Sec. 2(n)]: An occupier of a factory means the person who has ultimate control over the affairs of the factory and where the said affairs of the factory are entrusted to a managing agent, such agent shall be deemed to be the occupier of the factory.

In short, an occupier may be an owner, a lessee or a mere licensee, but he should have the right to occupy the property and dictate terms of management. A mere servant charged with specific duties is not an occupier.

If the premises are given to a partnership firm in return for periodic payment and owner of it has no control over the premises, he cannot be called an occupier, (*State of Maharashtra* v. *Jamanabar Asar,* AIR, 1968, S.C. 53)

APPROVAL, LICENSING AND REGISTRATION OF FACTORIES

The State Government may make rules and lay down the procedure to be followed for approval, licensing and registration of factories (Sec. 6). The effect of this Section is that a written permission of the State Government or of the Chief Inspector is to be sought before a site is used for a factory. But no licence shall be granted or renewed if the notice specified in Sec. 7 has not been given [Sec. 6(1)].

Section 7 enacts:

> "The occupier of a factory shall give full particulars as required by the rules of the factory, the nature of the manufacturing process, the number of workers, the nature and quantity of power used, etc., at least 15 days before he begins to occupy the factory".

If nothing is heard within three months from the date of the submission of application for permission it will be presumed that the permission is granted [Sec. 6(2)].

If the State Government refuses to issue such permission, an appeal can be preferred to the Central Government, within 30 days from the date of such a refusal [Sec. 6(3)]. In case such a refusal is made by any other authority, an appeal may be preferred to the State Government.

Where an occupier fails to apply for the registration of the factory and a licence under Sec. 6, he is liable for punishment under Sec. 92.

THE INSPECTING STAFF

The Act empowers the State Government, to appoint a Chief Inspector and Inspectors for the purpose of the administration of its provisions. Every District Magistrate is an ex officio Inspector for his district. According to Sec. 9 of the Act, an Inspector has the following powers:

   (i) He may enter any place which used to be a factory.

  (ii) He may make an examination of the premises and plant and the prescribed registers. He may also take statements of any person on the spot for carrying out the purpose of the Act.

 (iii) He may exercise other powers necessary for carrying out the purpose of the Act.

CERTIFYING SURGEONS

The State Government is empowered to appoint registered medical practitioners to be certifying surgeons for the purpose of this Act (Sec. 10).

The following are the powers of the certifying surgeons:

   (a) Examination and certification of young persons under this Act.

   (b) Medical supervision of all workmen working in the factory.

   (c) Medical supervision of young persons employed in any factory in such works which may cause injury to the workmen.

   (d) Any case of disease or illness which is believed to have occurred due to a manufacturing process carried on in the factory.

HEALTH

Sections 11 to 20 of the Factories Act, 1948 provide the provisions regarding the health of the workmen in connection with the working conditions of employment. They are as follows:

   1. *Cleanliness (Sec. 11):* Every factory should be kept clean free from effluvia arising from any drain, privy or other nuisance.

MEASURES IN REGARD TO HEALTH
• Cleanliness
• Disposal of Wastes
• Temperature and Ventilation
• Dust and Fume
• Artificial Humidification
• Overcrowding
• Lighting
• Drinking Water
• Urinal and Latrine
• Spittoons

2. *Disposal of Wastes (Sec. 12):* Arrangements shall be made in every factory for disposal of wastes and effluents due to the manufacturing process carried on.

3. *Temperature and Ventilation (Sec. 13):* There must be effective ventilation and suitable temperature in every work room.

4. *Dust and Fume (Sec. 14):* Effective measures should be taken for the prevention of accumulation of dust and fumes in workrooms, to avoid injury to the health of the workers.

5. *Artificial Humidification (Sec. 15):* Artificial humidification must be maintained within the prescribed standard. The State Government, may make rules about its standard and the method of increasing artificial humidity of air.

6. *Overcrowding (Sec. 16):* Overcrowding in factories is forbidden. There must be at least 320 cubic feet (for factories existing before April 1, 1949) or at least 500 cubic feet (for new factories) of space for every worker. In counting of the space, account shall not be taken of any space over 14 feet above the floor level.

7. *Lighting (Sec. 17):* Every part of the factory where workers are working, or passing, shall have adequate light, natural or artificial or both.

8. *Drinking Water (Sec. 18):* Effective and satisfactory arrangements must be made at such suitable points for wholesome drinking water. No such points shall be situated within 6 metres of any washing place, urinal, latrine, spittoon, open drain carrying sullage or effluent or any other source of contamination without the approval of the Chief Inspector (As per 1987 Amendment). Wherein more than 250 workers are working in any factory, provision may be made for cool drinking water during hot weather.

9. *Urinal and Latrine (Sec. 19):* Separate enclosed accommodation of urinals and latrines for male and female workers must be provided and maintained in sanitary conditions.

10. *Spittoons (Sec. 20):* Clean and hygienic spittoons must be provided at convenient places. No worker shall spit within the premises except in the spittoons.

SAFETY

Provisions relating to the safety of the workers are absolute in character and are dealt with in Secs. 21–41 of the Act. They are as follows:

1. *Fencing of Machinery (Sec. 21):* In every factory, a prime mover, and every moving part thereof, every part of transmission machinery and every dangerous part of any other machinery shall be securely fenced by safeguards of substantial construction.

2. *Work on or Near Machinery in Motion (Sec. 22):* Examination of any part of a machinery in motion may be performed only by a specially trained adult male worker, wearing light fitting clothing. The name of such a person shall be entered in the prescribed register and he shall be furnished with a certificate of his appointment [Sec. 22(1)]. No woman or young person shall be allowed to clean, lubricate or adjust any part of a machinery in motion if it would expose the woman or young person to a risk of any injury from any moving part [Sec. 22(2)].

3. *Employment of Young Persons on Dangerous Machines (Sec. 23):* Section 23 prohibits the employment of a young person to work at any machine unless he has been fully instructed as to the dangers arising in connection with the machine and he is given sufficient training to work at such machine or he is under adequate supervision by a person who has thorough knowledge and experience of the machine (As per 1987 Amendment).

4. *Striking Gear and Devices for Cutting of Power (Sec. 24):* In every factory suitable and efficient mechanical appliances such as striking gear shall be provided and maintained and always used to move driving belts.

MEASURES IN REGARD TO SAFETY

- Fencing of Machinery
- Work on or near machinery in motion
- Employment of young persons on dangerous machines
- Striking gear and devices for cutting of power
- Self-acting machines
- Casting of new machinery
- Prohibition of employment of women and children near cotton openers
- Hoists and lifts
- Lifting machines, chains, ropes and lifting tackles
- Revolving machinery
- Pressure plant
- Floors, stairs and means of access
- Pits, sumps, openings in floors, etc.
- Excessive weights
- Protection of eyes
- Protection against dangerous fumes
- Precaution against explosives
- Precaution in the case of fire
- Power to require specifications of defective parts or tests of stability
- Safety of building and machinery
- Maintenance of building
- Safety officer

Further, devices for cutting off power in emergencies from running machinery shall be provided and maintained in every work room.

The employer who does not comply with the safety rules shall be liable as it is a case of employment injury. (*Jayanthilal Dhanji & Co., Oil Mills V.E.S.T. Corporation 1968, H.P. 210*).

5. *Self Acting Machines (Sec. 25):* No traversing part of the self acting machine, and no material carried on it, must be allowed to run within a distance of 45 centimetres (as per 1987 Amendment Act), from any fixed structure which is not a part of the machine, in case the space over which it runs is one in which any person is likely to pass.

   Provided that the Chief Inspector may permit the continued use of a machine installed before the commencement of this Act.

6. *Casing of New Machinery (Sec. 26):* All machinery driven by power installed in the factory shall be encased to prevent accident or danger.

7. *Prohibition or Employment of Women and Children Near Cotton Openers (Sec. 27):* No woman or young person shall be employed for pressing cotton where a cotton opener is at work.

8. *Hoists and Lifts (Sec. 28):* Every hoist and lift shall be of good mechanical construction, sound material and adequate strength. It must be properly maintained and thoroughly examined once in every six months by a competent person. A register containing the prescribed particulars of every such examination shall be kept. It must be sufficiently protected by enclosures fitted with gates.

9. *Lifting Machines, Chains, Ropes and Lifting Tackles (Sec. 29):* Cranes and other lifting machinery shall be sound and well constructed, and free from defects. They shall be thoroughly examined at least once in every twelve months by a competent person.

10. *Revolving Machinery (Sec. 30):* In a factory where revolving machines are installed and operated upon, certain safety measures must be taken. For instance, the safe speed shall be stated on a notice to be kept near each machine where the process of grinding is carried on. The occupier must also ensure by necessary steps that the safe working peripheral speed of every revolving wheel, gauge, fly wheel, pulley, disc, etc., is not exceeded.

11. *Pressure Plant (Sec. 31):* If any plant or machinery or any part thereof is operated at a pressure above atmospheric pressure, effective measures must be taken to ensure that the safe working pressure is not exceeded. But, the State Government, can exempt any part of any plant from this provision.

12. *Floors, Stairs and Means of Access (Sec. 32):* The occupiers of the factories are obliged to take precaution in the construction and maintenance of all floors, space, stairs, passages and gangways so as to ensure safety to the life and limbs of the workers.

13. *Pits, Sumps, Openings in Floors, etc. (Sec. 33):* Pits, sumps fixed vessels, tanks, openings, etc., should be securely fenced. Securely fencing a pit means covering or fencing it in such a way that it ceases to be a source of danger to those who have occasion to go there (*State of Mysore* v. *Narayana Raghvendra* (1967) 2 L.L.J. 616].

14. *Excessive Weights (Sec. 34):* No person should be employed to lift, carry or move any load so heavy as to be likely to cause him injury.

15. *Protection of Eyes (Sec. 35):* In the case of manufacturing processes involving risk of injury to the eyes from particles of fragments thrown off in the course of the process, effective screens or suitable goggles should be provided for the protection of persons employed on that process.

16. *Precaution against Dangerous Fumes (Sec. 36):* No person should enter or be permitted to enter any chamber, tank, vat, pit, pipe, flue, or other confined space in which dangerous fumes are likely to be present unless it is provided with manhole of adequate size or other effective means of egress.

    No portable electric light exceeding 24 volts is permitted for use in any confined space as mentioned above (Sec. 36 A).

17. *Precaution against Explosive or Inflammable Dust, Gas, etc. (Sec. 37):* Effective enclosure of all possible source of ignition should be taken in order to prevent any explosion which might be the result of dust, gas, fume or vapour produced through any manufacturing process.

18. *Precaution in the Case of Fire (Sec. 38):* [Substituted by the 1987 Amendment]. All practicable measures shall be taken to prevent the outbreak of fire and its spread, both internally and externally.

All the doors shall be constructed to open outwards and all other means of escape in the case of fire shall be marked in red letters of adequate size in the language known to the majority of the workers.

19. *Power to Require Specifications of Defective Parts or Tests of Stability (Sec. 39).*

20. *Safety of Building and Machinery (Sec. 40).*

21. *Maintenance of Building (Sec. 40 A):* [As per 1976 Amendment Act]. If it appears to the Inspector that any building of a factory is detrimental to the health of the workers, he may ask the occupier or manager or both to carry out the suggested repairs.

22. *Safety Officers (Sec. 40 B):* [As per 1976 Amendment Act]. Where in a factory 1000 or more workers are ordinarily employed in manufacturing process which involves any bodily risk, poisoning or disease, the State Government may order for employment of such number of safety officers as specified in the notification.

The State Government may make rules requiring the provision in any factory for securing the safety of persons employed therein as it may deem necessary (Sec. 41).

WELFARE

Provisions regarding the welfare of workers are dealt with in Secs. 42–50 of the Act. The details of these provisions are:

> **MEASURES REGARDING WELFARE OF WORKERS**
> - Washing facilities
> - Storing and drying clothing
> - Facilities for sitting
> - First and appliances
> - Canteen
> - Rest rooms
> - Creches
> - Welfare officers

1. *Washing Facilities (Sec. 42):* In every factory, adequate and suitable facilities for washing shall be provided. It should be separate for male and female workers. Such facilities shall be conveniently placed and shall be kept clean.

2. *Storing and Drying Clothing (Sec. 43):* Provisions for a suitable place for keeping clothing not worn during working hours and for the drying of wet clothing shall be made.

3. *Facilities for Sitting (Sec. 44):* Suitable arrangements for sitting shall be provided and maintained for all workers who have to work in a standing position.

4. *First Aid Appliances (Sec. 45):* In every factory First Aid boxes or cupboard with the prescribed contents shall be kept and maintained by the occupier and there shall be one such box or cupboard for every 150 workers ordinarily employed at any one time.

   Where more than 500 workers are employed in a factory, an ambulance room of the prescribed size containing prescribed equipment shall be provided.

5. *Canteen (Sec. 46):* In every factory where more than 250 workers are employed a canteen shall be provided and maintained by the occupier of the factory for the use of the workers.

6. *Rest Rooms/Lunch rooms (Sec. 47):* In every factory in which more than 150 workers are ordinarily employed, there shall be a provision for shelters, rest rooms and suitable lunch rooms where workers can eat their meals. These rooms shall be adequately ventilated and lighted and provision for drinking water shall also be provided.

   If there is any canteen maintained as per the provision of Sec. 46, it shall be regarded as part of this requirement.

7. *Creches (Sec. 48):* Every factory with more than 30 women workers shall provide and maintain a suitable room for the use of children below six years. The State Government may also make rules for free distribution of milk and refreshment to children and facilities to mothers to feed their children which may not exceed 2 intervals of 15 minutes each.

8. *Welfare Officers (Sec. 49):* In every factory wherein 500 or more workers are working, the occupier shall engage such number of welfare officers as may be prescribed by the State Government.

The State Government may make rules for exempting factories from the compliance of the provisions of Secs. 42 to 49 (Sec. 50).

WORKING HOURS OF ADULTS

Weekly and Daily Hours of Work: No adult worker shall be required or allowed to work in a factory for more than 48 hours of week (Sec. 51). No adult worker shall he required or allowed to work in a factory for more than 9 hours in any day (Sec. 54). However, with the previous approval of the Chief Inspector the daily maximum specified in this Section may be exceeded in order to facilitate the change of shifts.

Weekly Holidays and Compensatory Holidays: No adult worker in a factory shall be required or allowed to work on the first day of the week, i.e., Sunday (Sec. 52). But the manager can substitute for Sunday any of the three days preceding or following it. He shall, however, display on the notice board a notice to this effect. A copy of such a notice shall also be delivered to the Inspector of the Factories. However, in no case to a worker be allowed to work for more than 10 days consecutively without a holiday.

Where a worker is asked to work on weekly holidays, he shall be allowed compensatory holidays of equal number to the holidays so lost either within the same month or within the next 2 months (Sec. 53).

Interval for Rest: No worker shall work for more than 5 hours before he has had an interval for rest of at least $\frac{1}{2}$ an hour (Sec. 55).

Spread Over: The periods of work of an adult worker shall be so arranged that including intervals for rest, the work shall not spread over for more than 10 hours in any day (Sec. 56). However, the Chief Inspector may extend this period upto 12 hours for specified reasons.

Night Shifts: If a worker is assigned night shift which goes beyond midnight, then the weekly or compensatory holiday to which he is entitled would mean holiday for 24 continuous hours beginning when his shift ends (Sec. 57).

Prohibition of Overlapping Shifts: The system of shifts shall not be so arranged that more than one relay of worker is engaged in work of the same type at the same time (Sec. 58).

Extra Wages for Overtime: Where a worker works for more than 9 hours a day and more than 48 hours in a week, he shall be paid overtime at the rate of double his ordinary rates of wages (Sec. 59).

Restriction on Double Employment: No adult worker shall be required or allowed to work in any factory on any day on which he has already worked in any other factory (Sec. 60).

Notice of Periods of Work for Adult Workers: A notice of periods of work for adult workers shall be displayed and perfectly maintained in every factory (Sec. 61). It shall show clearly for everyday the periods during which adult workers are required to work. Such periods should be fixed beforehand.

Register of Adult Workers: The manager of every factory shall maintain a register of adult workers which shall be available to the Inspector at all times during working hours (Sec. 62). It contains the following:

(a) The name of each adult worker.

(b) The nature of his work.

(c) The group, if any in which he is included.

(d) Where his group works in shifts, the relay to which he is allotted.

(e) Such other particulars as may be prescribed.

EMPLOYMENT OF WOMEN

The rules of the Factories Act are applicable both to the male and female workers except a few more special provisions which apply to adult female workers only. These provisions are:

1. *Work on or Near Machinery in Motion* (Sec. 22): No woman shall be allowed to work any part of the machinery while it is in motion.

2. *Prohibition of Employment of Women Near Cotton Openers* (Sec. 27).

3. *Creches* (Sec. 48): In every factory wherein more than 30 women are ordinarily employed there shall be provided a suitable room for the use of children below the age of six years.

4. *Restriction on Employment of Women* (Sec. 66):

   (a) No woman worker shall be required or allowed to work for more than 48 hours, in a week or 9 hours in a day.

   (b) No woman shall be required or allowed to work in any factory except between the hours of 6 a.m. and 7 p.m. But the State Government may vary this limit and no such variation shall authorise the employment of any woman between the hours of 10 p.m. and 5 a.m.

   (c) There shall be no change of shifts except after a weekly holiday or any other holiday.

5. *Dangerous Operation (Sec. 87):* The State Government may make rules prohibiting or restricting the employment of women in dangerous operation.

EMPLOYMENT OF YOUNG PERSONS

Chapter VII of the Factories Act deals with the employment of young persons. One of the main objects of these provisions is to discourage the exploitation of children by employing them in factories.

A young person indicates a person who is either a child or an adolescent. Section 67 prohibits the employment of children below the age of 14 in factories.

An adolescent who is above 15 but below 18 years of age, shall not be allowed to work in any factory unless he has been granted a certificate of fitness issued by the certifying surgeon and such a certificate is in the custody of the manager of the factory. The manager in such cases shall issue a token with reference to such a certificate to such a person. He has to carry it while at work (Sec. 68).

Effect of Certificate of Fitness: An adolescent who has obtained the certificate of fitness shall be deemed to be an adult for all the purposes of the Act (Sec. 70). But an adolescent who has not attained the age of 17 years shall not be employed or permitted to work during night. Night means a period of at least 12 continuous hours, which shall include an interval of at least 7 continuous hours falling between 10 p.m. and 7 a.m.

Working Hours (Sec. 71): No child shall be allowed to work in any factory for more than $4\frac{1}{2}$ hours a day. The period of work of all children in the factory shall be limited to two shifts. Such shifts shall not overlap. Spread over of such a person is limited to 5 hours each. Every child can be employed only in one relay which shall not be changed except once in 30 days. Further, no child shall be allowed to work in any other factory on the same day.

Notice of Work (Sec. 72): It is obligatory on the part of factory managers to display notices relating to the periods of work of children.

Register of Child Workers (Sec. 73): The factory manager shall maintain the register of child workers. No child shall be required to be employed in a factory for any such period which is not entered in the register of child workers.

ANNUAL LEAVE WITH WAGES

Chapter VIII (Secs. 78 to 84) of the Factories Act enumerates the number of holidays available to the workers employed in factories. The provisions of these sections are mandatory. Further, these provisions shall not operate to the prejudice of any right of a worker under any other law or under any award of agreement or contract of service (Sec. 78).

Annual Leave with Wages: Section 79 states that every worker who has worked for 240 days or more in a factory during a calendar year shall be allowed during the subsequent calendar years leave with wages on the following basis:

(i) in the case of an adult, one day for every 20 days of work performed by him during the previous calendar year;

(ii) in the case of a child, one day for every 15 days of work performed by him during the previous calendar year.

For computing the period of 240 days or more the following shall also be included:

(a) the days of lay off;

(b) the maternity leave to a female worker not exceeding 12 weeks; and

(c) the leave earned in the previous year.

The leave so admissible shall be exclusive of all holidays whether before or at the end of such holidays. A worker whose service commences after 1st day of January shall be entitled to leave with wages at the aforesaid rate if he has worked for 2/3 of the total number of days in the remainder of the calendar year. When a worker who is discharged or dismissed or who quits his employment or dies while in service, he or his heir or nominee shall be entitled to leave with wages even if he has not worked for 240 days (As per 1976 Amendment Act).

The unavailed portion of the due leave in any year shall be carried forward to the next year subject to a maximum of 30 days in the case of an adult and 40 days in the case of a child. The leave application shall be submitted at least 15 days (30 days in the case of public utility service) in advance. But in the case of illness, the advance application need not be given. The number of times in which leave can be taken in a year should not exceed three.

Section 80 provides the provisions for the calculation of wages during the leave period. For the leave allowed to a worker, he shall be paid at a rate equal to the daily average of his total full time earnings for the days on which he actually worked during the month immediately preceding his leave. The full time earnings shall be inclusive of dearness allowance and fringe benefits but exclusive of any overtime and bonus.

A worker shall be paid advance wages if the leave allowed is not less than four days in the case of an adult, and five days in the case of a child (Sec. 81).

REVIEW QUESTIONS

1. Define the following terms as used in the Factories Act, 1948.

   (a) Adult   (b) Young person

   (c) Occupier   (d) Manufacturing process

   (e) Factory

2. Explain the provisions regarding licensing and registration of a factory.

3. Who are certifying surgeons? What are their duties?

4. Discuss the provisions of the Factories Act, 1948 with regard to health, safety and welfare of the workers.

5. State the provisions of the Factories Act, 1948, relating to the regulation of hours of work.

6. Explain the restrictions imposed by the Factories Act, 1948 on the employment and work of women in a factory.

7. State the provisions of the Factories Act, 1948 regarding (a) Annual leave with wages (b) Weekly holidays (c) Extra wages for overtime work.

PRACTICAL PROBLEMS

Attempt the following problems, giving reasons.

1. A, an apprentice, was injured while cleaning a dangerous part of a machine which had been manufactured in the factory. The machine was unfenced while adjustments were made to it. Is the manager or occupier guilty of an offence?

   Hint: Yes, as the work done is incidental to, or connected with, the manufacturing process.

2. Wives of two workmen employed in a Jute factory work in place of their husbands for about an hour everyday after 7 p.m. while the latter takes meals brought by them. Is there a violation of any provision of the Factories Act, 1948?

   Hint: Yes, there is a violation of Sec. 66(a).

49

The Industrial Disputes
Act, 1947

*Strikes and lockouts are regarded as menaces to public
safety. They infringe upon property rights and become
malicious in their effects if not in their purpose and they
are regarded as war or at any rate a blockade.*

—Catlin, W.B. *The Labour Problems*. p. 416

INTRODUCTION

Industrial Disputes have adverse effects on industrial production,
efficiency, costs, quality, human satisfaction, discipline, technological
and economic progress and finally on the welfare of the society. A
discontent labour force, nursing in its heart mute grievances and
resentments, cannot be efficient and will not possess a high degree
of industrial morale. Hence, the Industrial Dispute Act of 1947, was
passed as a preventive and curative measure.

SCOPE AND OBJECT

The Industrial Dispute Act of 1947, came into force on the first day
of April, 1947. It was passed to remove certain limitations found in
the working of the Trade Disputes Act, 1929. Its aim is to protect
the workmen against victimization by the employers and to ensure
social justice to both employers and employees.

The unique object of the Act is to promote collective bargaining
and to maintain a peaceful atmosphere in industries by avoiding
illegal strikes and lock outs. The Act also provides for regulation of
lay off and retrenchment.

DEFINITIONS

The important terms and phrases which have a bearing on the
Industrial Disputes Act, 1947 are defined in clauses (a) to (s) of Sec. 2.

Appropriate Government [Sec. 2(a)]: Appropriate Government means the Central Government in relation to any industrial dispute concerning any industry carried on by or under the authority of the Central Government, any industry carried on by a Railway Company, any controlled industry specified by the Central Government, The Unit Trust of India, Corporations under the Central Statutes, Banking company, Insurance company, Mines, Oil field, Cantonment board, Major ports, etc.

In relation to any other industrial dispute, the appropriate Government is the State Government.

Average Pay [Sec. 2(aa)]: Average pay means the average of the wages payable to a workman in the case of:

    (a) monthly paid workman, in the three completed calendar months.

    (b) weekly paid workman, in the four completed weeks, and

    (c) daily paid workman, in the twelve full working days.

Award [Sec. 2(b)]: Award means an interim or final determination of any industrial dispute or any question relating thereto by any Labour Court, Industrial Tribunal or National Tribunal and includes an arbitration award made under Sec. 10A.

Controlled Industry [Sec. 2(ee)]: Controlled industry means any industry, the control of which by the Union has been declared by the Central Act to be expedient in the public interest.

Employer [Sec. 2(g)]: Employer means:

    (i) in relation to an industry carried on by or under the authority of any department of Central or State Government, the authority prescribed in this behalf, or where no authority is prescribed, the head of the department.

    (ii) in relation to an industry carried on by or on behalf of a local authority, the Chief Executive Officer of that authority.

Industry [Sec. 2(j)]: Industry means any business, trade, undertaking, manufacture or calling of employers and includes any calling, service, employment, handicraft or industrial occupation or avocation of workmen.

In *Bangalore Water Supply & Others* v. *A. Rajappa* (AIR 1978, S.C. 548), Krishna Iyer. J. laid down the principle of Triple Test to determine whether any activity is covered within the definition 'Industry'. It requires three ingredients to be fulfilled. They are:

    (a) Systematised activity.

    (b) Cooperation of labour and management.

    (c) Production of goods and services to satisfy human wants.

The memorable judgement delivered by Justice Krishna Iyer on 21st of July 1978 has brought clubs, research and charitable institutions, universities and other educational institutions within the ambit of the term 'Industry'. However, the 1982 amendment expressly excludes, hospitals, educational and research institutions, charitable and philanthropic services, activities of Government, Departments involving sovereign functions, etc., from the purview of industry.

Industrial Dispute [Sec. 2(k)]: Industrial dispute means any dispute or difference between employer and workman or between employer and employer or between workman and workman, which is connected with the employment or non-employment or the terms of employment or with the conditions of labour, of any person.

The word 'any person' may include a non-workman like a doctor as there is a community of interest.

Public Utility Service [Sec. 2(n)]: Public utility service means any railway service, any transport service for the carriage of passengers or goods by air, any postal, telegraph, telephone services, any industry which supplies power, light or water to the public, any system of public conservancy or sanitation, any section of an industrial establishment on the working of which the safety of the establishment or the workmen employed therein depends and any industry specified in the I Schedule.

Settlement [Sec. 2(p)]: Settlement means a settlement arrived at in the course of conciliation proceeding and includes a written agreement between an employer and a workman arrived at otherwise than in the course of conciliation proceeding where such agreement has been signed by the parties thereto in such manner as may be prescribed and a copy thereof has been sent to an officer authorised by the Appropriate Government and the Conciliation Officer.

Wages [Sec. 2(rr)]: Wages mean all remuneration capable of being expressed in terms of money, which would, if the terms of employment, express or implied were fulfilled, be payable to a workman in respect of his employment or of the work done in such an employment and includes:

(i) such allowances (including dearness allowance) as the workman is for the time being entitled to;

(ii) the value of any house accommodation, or of supply of light, water, medical attendance or other amenity or of any service or of any concessional supply of foodgrains or other articles;

(iii) any travelling concession. But the following are excluded:

(a) any bonus.

(b) any contribution paid or payable to any pension fund or provident fund, or for the benefit of the workman under any law for the time being in force.

(c) any gratuity payable on the termination of his service.

Workman [Sec. 2(s)]: 'Workman' means any person (including an apprentice) employed in any industry to do any skilled or unskilled, manual, operational supervisory, technical or clerical work for hire or reward, whether the terms of employment be expressed or implied.

The term workman also includes any such person who has been dismissed, discharged or retrenched in connection with or as a consequence of that dispute or whose dismissal, discharge or retrenchment has led to that dispute.

AUTHORITIES UNDER THE ACT

The I.D. Act provides an elaborate and effective machinery for the investigation and amicable settlement of industrial disputes by setting up the various authorities. These are:

1. Works Committee;
2. Conciliation Officer;
3. Conciliation Board;
4. Court of Enquiry;
5. Labour Court;
6. Industrial Tribunal;
7. National Tribunal;
8. Arbitrators;
9. Grievances Settlement Authority.

1. *Works Committee (Sec. 3):* In the case of an industrial establishment in which one hundred or more workmen are employed or have been employed on any day in the preceding twelve months, the appropriate Government may require the employer to constitute a 'Work Committee'. It consists of equal number of representatives of employers and workmen engaged in the establishment. The representatives of the workmen shall be chosen from amongst the workmen engaged in the establishment and in consultation with the registered trade union, if any.

It shall be the duty of the works committee to promote measures for securing and preserving amity and good relations between employers and workmen and to comment upon matters of common interest and endeavour to settle any material difference of opinion in respect of such matters.

2. *Conciliation Officer (Sec. 4):* The appropriate Government is empowered to appoint any number of persons, as it thinks fit, to be conciliation officers. They may be appointed for a specified area or for specified industries, and either permanently or for a limited period. Their task is to find a solution acceptable to both parties.

3. *Conciliation Board (Sec. 5):* The appropriate Government is also authorised to constitute a Board of Conciliation for promoting the settlement of an industrial dispute. It consists of a chairman who shall be an independent person, and two or four other members. The members appointed shall be in equal numbers to represent the parties to the dispute.

A Board, having the prescribed quorum, may act notwithstanding the absence of the Chairman or any of its members or any vacancy in its number.

4. *Court of Enquiry (Sec. 6):* The appropriate Government is authorised to constitute a Court of Enquiry for enquiring into any matter which appears to be connected with an industrial dispute. It consists of one or more independent persons as the Government may think fit. If a Court consists of two or more members, one of them shall be appointed as the chairman.

5. *Labour Court (Sec. 7):* The appropriate Government is empowered to constitute one or more Labour Courts. Its function is the adjudication of industrial disputes relating to any matter specified in the Second Schedule and for performing such other functions as may be assigned to them under this Act. The matters specified in the Second Schedule are as follows:

(a) The propriety or legality of any order passed by any employer under the standing orders.

(b) The application and interpretation of standing orders.

(c) Discharge or dismissal of workmen including reinstatement of or grant of relief to workmen wrongfully dismissed.

(d) Withdrawal of any customary concession or privilege.

(e) Illegality or otherwise of a strike or lockout.

(f) All matters other than those specified in the Third Schedule.

A Labour Court consists of one person only. A person is qualified to be appointed as presiding officer of a Labour Court, if:

(a) he is, or has been a judge of a High Court, or

(b) he has been a District judge or an Additional District judge for at least three years, or

(c) he has held the office of the chairman or any other member of the Labour Appellate Tribunal or of any Tribunal for at least two years, or

(d) he has held any judicial office in India for not less than seven years, or

(e) he has been the presiding officer of a Labour Court constituted under any Provincial Act or State Act for at least five years.

6. *Industrial Tribunal [Sec. 7(A)]:* The appropriate Government may, by notification in the Official Gazette, constitute one or more Industrial Tribunal. Its main function is the adjudication of industrial disputes relating to any matter which appears in the Second or Third Schedule.

A Tribunal consists of one person only. A person to be appointed a presiding officer of a Tribunal must be, or must have been, a judge of a High Court; or must have held the office of the chairman or any other member of the Labour Appellate Court, or of any Tribunal, for at least two years. The appropriate Government may appoint two persons as accessors to advise the Tribunal in the proceedings.

7. *National Tribunal [Sec. 7(B)]:* The Central Government may, by notification in the Official Gazette, constitute one or more National Industrial Tribunals. Its main function is the adjudication of industrial disputes which involve questions of national importance or affecting the interest of two or more States.

The Central Government shall appoint a National Tribunal consisting of one person only. A person to be appointed a presiding officer of a National Tribunal must be, or must have been, a judge of a High Court or must have held the office of the chairman or any other member of the Labour Appellate Tribunal for a period of not less than two years. The Central Government may appoint two persons as assessors to advise the National Tribunal.

8. *Arbitrators [Sec. 10(A)]:* An arbitrator is appointed by the Government for making reference of an industrial dispute.

If an industrial dispute exists or is apprehended and the employer and the workman agree to refer the dispute to an arbitration, they may refer the dispute to an arbitration. But such reference shall be made before the dispute has been referred under Sec. 19 to a Labour Court or Tribunal or National Tribunal by a written agreement.

The arbitrator may be appointed singly or more than one in number. The arbitrator or arbitrators shall investigate the dispute and submit to the appropriate Government the arbitration award signed by the arbitrator or all the arbitrators, as the case may be.

9. *Grievance Settlement Authority [Sec. 9(c)]:* This Section is incorporated as a new chapter II B of the Act. As per this Section, the employer in relation to every industrial establishment in which fifty or more workmen are employed or have been employed on any day in the preceding twelve months, shall provide for, in accordance with the rules made in that behalf under this Act, a Grievances Settlement Authority.

STRIKES AND LOCKOUTS

Strike [Sec. 2(q)]: Strike means "a cessation of work by a body of persons employed in any industry acting in combination or a concerted refusal under a common understanding of any number of persons who are or have been so employed, to continue to work or to accept employment".

Mere stoppage of work does not come within the meaning of strike unless it can be shown that such stoppage of work was a concerted action for the enforcement of an industrial demand *[Indian Iron and Steel Co., Ltd.* v. *Its Workmen (1967) I.L.L.J. 381* (part)].

Lockout [Sec. 2(1)]: Lockout means "the temporary closing of a place of employment, or the suspension of work, or the refusal by an employer to continue to employ any number of persons employed by him".

Lockout is the antithesis of strike. It is a weapon of the employer while strike is that of the workers. Just as a strike is a weapon in the hands of the workers for enforcing their industrial demands, lockout is a weapon available to the employer to force the employees to see his points of view and to accept his demands. The Industrial Dispute Act does not intend to take away these rights. However, the rights of strikes and lockouts have been restricted to achieve the purpose of the Act, namely peaceful investigation and settlement of the industrial disputes.

Prohibition of Strikes and Lockouts (Sec. 22): According to Sec. 22(1) no person employed in a public utility service shall go on strike, in breach of contract:

(a) without giving to the employer notice of strike, within six weeks before striking; or

(b) within 14 days of giving such notice; or

(c) before the expiry of the date of strike specified in any such notice; or

(d) during the pendency of any conciliation proceedings before a Conciliation Officer and seven days after the conclusion of such proceedings.

Under Sec. 22(2) no employer carrying on any public utility service shall lockout any of his workmen:

(a) without giving them notice of lockout, within six weeks before lockout; or

(b) within fourteen days of giving such notice; or

(c) before the expiry of the date of lockout specified in any such notice; or

(d) during the pendency of any conciliation proceedings before a Conciliation Officer and seven days after the conclusion of such proceedings.

The requisite notice of strike or lockout is not essential when a strike or lockout is already in existence in a public utility service [Sec. 22(3)]. But the employer shall send intimation of such strike or lockout to the specified authority on the day on which it is declared.

On receipt of notice for strike or on giving notice of lockout, the employer shall, within five days thereof report to the appropriate Government.

General Prohibition of Strike, and Lockouts (Sec. 23): Section 23 lays down for a general prohibition against strikes and lockouts in 'any industrial establishments' under the following circumstances:

(a) during the pendency of conciliation proceedings before a Board and seven days after the conclusion of such proceedings;

(b) during the pendency of proceedings before a Labour Court, Tribunal or National Tribunal and two months after the conclusion of such proceedings;

(c) during the period of operation of a Settlement or Award in respect of any of the matters covered by the Settlement or Award.

No notice of strike and lockout is necessary in industrial establishments except in public utility services.

ILLEGAL STRIKES AND LOCKOUTS (SEC. 24)

A strike or a lockout shall be illegal, if:

(a) it is commenced or declared in contravention of Sec. 22 or 23; or

(b) it is continued in contravention of the prohibitory order of the Government after the dispute has been referred to under Sec. 10.

According to Sec. 24(2) or (3) a strike or lockout shall not be regarded illegal, if:

(a) it is at its commencement in violation of the provisions of the Act; or

(b) its continuance has not been prohibited by the appropriate Government; or

(c) a strike is declared in consequence of an illegal lockout or a lockout is declared in consequence of an illegal strike.

No person shall knowingly expend or apply any money in direct furtherance or support of my illegal strike or lockout (Sec. 25).

LAY OFF AND RETRENCHMENT

Lay off [Sec. 2(kkk)]: Lay off means "the failure, refusal or inability of an employer on account of shortage of coal, power or raw materials or the accumulation of stocks or the breakdown of machinery or for any other reason to give employment to a workman whose name is borne on the muster rolls of his industrial establishment and who has not been retrenched".

Retrenchment [Sec. 2(oo)]: Retrenchment means the termination by the employer of the service of a workman for any reason whatsoever otherwise than as a punishment indicated by way of disciplinary action. It does not include:

(a) voluntary retirement of the workman; or

(b) retirement of the workman on reaching the age of superannuation; or

(c) termination of the service of a workman on the ground of continued ill-health.

The provisions of Chapter V A of the Act, relating to lay-off and retrenchment compensation do not apply to all industrial establishments. Section 25A embodies that the provisions of Secs. 25C to 25E shall not apply to industrial establishment:

(a) to which Chapter V B applies, or

(b) in which less than fifty workmen on an average per working day have been employed in the preceding calendar month; or

(c) which are of a seasonal character or in which work is performed only intermittently.

RIGHTS OF WORKMAN LAID OFF FOR COMPENSATION (SEC. 25C)

A workman who is laid off is entitled to compensation only if he complies with the following conditions:

(i) He must not be a badli or a casual workman.

(ii) His name must be borne on the muster rolls of the industrial establishment.

(iii) He must have completed at least one year of continuous service.

A worker is entitled to lay off compensation for the period of his lay off other than for weekly holidays which may intervene. The rate of compensation must be equal to 50 per cent of the total of the basic wage and dearness allowance that might have been payable to him, had he not been so laid off. No compensation can be claimed for more than forty-five days during the period of twelve months. Where the period of lay-off is more than forty-five days, the employer can either go on paying lay off compensation for such subsequent periods or retrench the workman. In case the employer adopts such a retrenchment, he can set off the amount of lay off compensation paid during the preceding twelve months against retrenchment compensation payable under Sec. 25F.

Under Sec. 25D the employer is required to maintain a muster roll and allow workmen to make entries thereon when they present themselves for work at the establishment, even if they have been laid off.

WORKMEN LAID OFF NOT ENTITLED TO COMPENSATION (SEC. 25E)

No compensation shall be paid to a workman who has been laid off:

(i) if he refuses to accept any alternative employment in the same or any other establishment belonging to the same employer situated in the same town or village or within a radius of five miles and it does not require any special skill or previous experience, provided the same wages are offered,

(ii) if he does not present himself for work at the appointed time during normal working hours at least once a day,

(iii) if lay off in the consequence of strike or slowing down of production by the workers in another part of the establishment.

CONDITIONS PRECEDENT TO RETRENCHMENT OF WORKMEN (SEC. 25F)

A workman employed in any industry who has been in continuous service for at least one year under an employer shall not be retrenched by that employer unless:

(a) the workman has been given one month's written notice mentioning the reasons for retrenchment and the period of notice has been expired or the workman has been paid, instead of such notice wages for the period of the notice. But no such notice is necessary where the retrenchment is under an agreement specifying a date for the termination of service;

(b) the workman has been paid at the time of retrenchment, compensation equivalent to fifteen days average pay for every completed year of continuous service or any part thereof, provided it exceeds six months; and

(c) notice in the prescribed manner served on the appropriate Government or on such an authority as specified.

PROCEDURE FOR RETRENCHMENT (SEC. 25G)

The procedure of retrenchment is based on the well-known doctrine of "first come, last go" or "last come first go". If an employer wants to go beyond this principle, he must record his reasons thereof.

REEMPLOYMENT OF RETRENCHED WORKMEN (SEC. 25H)

This section provides priority for a retrenched workman in the case of reemployment. In case the employer proposes to reemploy any person, he is under an obligation to offer first priority to the persons who have been retrenched.

REVIEW QUESTIONS

1. Define the following terms under the Industrial Disputes Act, 1947.

   (a) Workman   (b) Award
   (c) Wages   (d) Public utility service
   (e) Industry

2. Define the term 'Industrial dispute'. What are its essentials?

3. What are the various methods for the settlement of industrial disputes under the Industrial Disputes Act?

4. Explain the duties and powers of Conciliation Officers, Works Committee, and Boards of Conciliation in settlement of industrial disputes.

5. Define the terms 'Strike' and 'Lockout'. State the cases in which strikes and lockouts are prohibited and become illegal.

6. Define 'Award' and 'Settlement'. Who are the persons on whom settlements and awards are binding?

7. Define the terms 'Lay off' and 'Retrenchment'. Explain the circumstances when compensation is not payable to a workman who has been laid off.

50

The Trade Unions Act, 1926

Trade union is "a voluntary organization of workers formed to promote and protect their interest by collective action".

—V.V. Giri

Trade union is "a continuous association of wage earners for the purpose of maintaining or improving the conditions of their working lives".

—Sidney and Beatrice Webb

INTRODUCTION

The law relating to the registration and protection of the Trade Unions is contained in the Trade Unions Act, 1926 which came into force with effect from 1st June 1927. The Act extends to the whole of India except the State of Jammu and Kashmir.

In common parlance, trade union means an association of workers in one or more occupations. Its object is the protection and promotion of the interests of the working class. Trade Unions have a home grown philosophy based on workers' experience and psychology. It grows out of the workers' day-to-day experience.

DEFINITIONS

1. *Appropriate Government (Sec. 2):* In relation to Trade Unions whose objects are not confined to one state 'the appropriate Government' is the Central Government. In relation to other Trade Unions, the 'appropriate Government' is the State Government.

2. *Executive [Sec. 2(a)]:* Executive means the body of which the management of the affairs of a trade union is entrusted.

3. *Trade Dispute [Sec. 2(g)]:* A trade dispute means any dispute between the employers and workmen, the workmen and workmen and the employers and employers which is

connected with the employment or non-employment, or the terms of employment, or the conditions of labour of any person.

Workmen' mean all persons employed in trade or industry whether or not in the employment of the employer with whom the trade dispute arises.

4. *Trade Union [Sec. 2(h)]:* Trade union means any combination, whether temporary or permanent, formed primarily for the purpose of regulating the relations between workmen and employers or between workmen and workmen or between employers and employers for imposing restrictive conditions on the conduct of any trade or business and includes any federation of two or more trade unions.

5. *Registered Trade Union [Sec. 2(e)]:* A registered trade union means a 'Trade Union' registered under the Act.

CERTAIN ACTS DO NOT APPLY TO TRADE UNIONS

The registration of any Trade Union under the following Act is void:

(i) The Societies Registration Act, 1860.

(ii) The Cooperative Societies Act, 1912.

(iii) The Companies Act, 1956.

Trade Unions can be registered only under the Trade Union Act, 1926.

REGISTRATION OF TRADE UNIONS

The Act empowers the appropriate Government to appoint a person to be the Registrar of Trade Unions for each State (Sec. 3).

Sections 4–9 of the Act contain the provisions for the registration of Trade Unions.

'Section 4' states that any seven or more members of a Trade Union may, by subscribing their names to the rules of the trade union and by otherwise complying with the provisions of the Act with respect to registration, apply for registration of the Union under this Act. Every such application is to be made to the Registrar of Trade Unions (Sec. 5). It shall be accompanied by a copy of its rules and a statement of the following particulars:

(a) the names, occupations and addresses of the applicants;

(b) the name of the Trade Union and the address of its head office; and

(c) the names, titles, ages, addresses and occupations of the officers of the Trade Union.

Where a Trade Union has been in existence for more than a year before the making of an application for its registration, the applicants must also deliver to the Registrar a general statement of the assets and liabilities of the Trade Union.

MATTERS TO BE CONTAINED IN THE RULES OF A TRADE UNION (SEC. 6)

A trade union shall not be entitled to the registration unless its executive is constituted as per the provisions of this Act and its rules provide for the following matters:

1. the name of the Trade Union;
2. the whole of its objects;
3. the whole of the purpose for which the general funds of a Trade Union shall be applicable;
4. the maintenance of a list of its members and adequate facilities for the inspection thereof by the office bearers and members of the Trade Union;
5. the admission of ordinary members from the industry with which the Trade Union is connected and also the admission of a number of honorary or temporary office bearers to form the executive of the Trade Union;
6. the payment of a subscription by the members of the Trade Union which shall not be less than 25 paise per month per member;
7. the condition under which any member shall be entitled to any benefit assured by the rules and under which any fine or forfeiture may be imposed on the members;
8. the manner in which the members of the executive and other office bearers of the Trade Union shall be appointed and removed.
9. the manner in which the rules shall be amended, varied or rescinded;
10. the safe custody of the funds of the Trade Union, and annual audit of the accounts thereof, and adequate facilities for the inspection of the account books by the office bearers and members of the Trade Union; and
11. the manner in which the Trade Union may be dissolved.

The Registrar may require further particulars to satisfy himself that the Trade Union complies with the above provisions. Such particulars may be asked for only from the applicants and not from any other source *(Kondal Rao* v. *Registrar Trade Unions* (1952) NLJ). If the particulars are not furnished, 'the registration may be refused'. The Registrar may also refuse to register a Union if its name is identical with, or very nearly resembles, the name of another union, which is likely to deceive the public or the members of either union (Sec. 7).

The Registrar, on being satisfied that the Trade Union has complied with all the requirements of this Act in regard to registration, shall register the Trade Union by entering in a register (Sec. 8).

On registering the Union, the Registrar shall issue a certificate of registration in the prescribed form. It shall be a conclusive evidence that the Trade Union has been duly registered under the Act (Sec. 9).

CANCELLATION OF REGISTRATION (SEC. 10)

A certificate of registration of the Trade Union may be withdrawn or cancelled by the Registrar:

(a) on the application of the Trade Union, or

(b) if the certificate has been obtained by fraud or mistake, or

(c) if the Union has ceased to exist, or has wilfully, after notice contravened any provisions of this Act.

The Registrar has to give not less than two months previous notice in writing furnishing the grounds on which it is proposed to withdraw or cancel the certificate of registration. No such notice is required if such an application is made by the Trade Union itself.

Appeal (Sec. 11): An appeal can be preferred against an order of the Registrar refusing to register a Trade Union or withdrawing or cancelling registration. The proceedings by way of appeal should be commenced within 60 days of the date of which the Registrar passed the order against which the appeal is preferred.

Such an appeal shall be preferred to the High Court if the head office of the Trade Union is situated within the limits of the Presidency town. Where the head office of the Trade Union is situated in any other area the appeal shall be preferred to such a court which is not lower than the court of an Additional or Asstt: Judge or a Principal Civil Court of original jurisdiction as the appropriate Government may appoint.

The Appellate Court may dismiss the appeal, or order the Registrar to register the Union. The Registrar shall comply with such an order of the Court.

RIGHTS AND LIABILITIES OF REGISTERED TRADE UNIONS

A registered Trade Union has the right to maintain (a) a general fund, and (b) a separate fund for political purposes:

But the Unions are bound to utilize the funds only for the purposes specified in the Act.

OBJECTS ON WHICH GENERAL FUNDS MAY BE SPENT (SEC. 15)

The following are the purposes for which the general funds of the Union may be spent:

1. Payment of salaries, allowances, etc., to the office bearers of the Union.

2. Payment of expenses for the administration of the Union including other expenses spent on defending any legal proceedings by or against the Union.

3. Settlement of trade disputes.

> **OBJECTS ON WHICH GENERAL FUNDS MAY BE SPENT**
> - Payment of salaries etc., to office bearers
> - Payment of expenses for administration
> - Settlement of trade disputes
> - Special allowances to the members
> - Compensation of members
> - Providing educational benefits to the members
> - Undertaking of liability of assurance
> - Upkeep of periodicals
> - Any other object authorised by the appropriate Government

4. Special allowances to the members (including dependants) of the Trade Union on account of death, sickness or accidents, etc.

5. Compensation to members for loss arising out of trade disputes.

6. Providing educational, social and religious benefits to the members.

7. Issue of assurance policies on the lives of members and also against sickness, accidents, unemployment, insurance, etc.

8. Providing for publication of periodicals for the use of which is intended for the members benefit.

9. Any other object that may be notified by the appropriate Government in the Official Gazette.

If funds are spent for any purposes other than the above, such an expenditure is treated as unlawful and the Trade Union can be restrained by the Court for applying its funds in any other purposes.

CONSTRUCTION OF SEPARATE FUND FOR POLITICAL PURPOSES (SEC. 16)

Apart from the primary objects, a Trade Union may have certain other political objects which are not inconsistent with the primary objects. As per Sec. 16 a registered union may constitute a separate fund in addition to the general fund and the payment of such a fund shall be utilised for serving civic and political interest of its members. The fund can be utilised for the following purposes:

1. Holding of any meeting or distribution of any literature or document in support of any candidate for election as a member of legislative body constituted under the constitution or of any local authority.

2. For maintenance of any person who is a member of any legislative body constituted under the constitution.

3. For convening of political meeting of any kind or distribution of political literature or documents of any kind.

4. The registration of electors for selection of a candidate for legislative body.

The funds collected for political purposes shall not be clubbed with the general fund. No workman is compelled to contribute in this fund and the non-payment in this fund cannot be made a condition for admission to the Trade Union.

IMMUNITY FROM CRIMINAL AND CIVIL LIABILITY

Immunity from Punishment for Criminal Conspiracy (Sec. 17): No office bearer or member of a registered Trade Union shall be liable for punishment under Sec. 120B(2) of the Indian Penal Code in respect of any agreement made between the members unless the agreement is an agreement to commit an offence (Sec. 17). Immunity under Sec. 17 should not be made available unless the following conditions are fulfilled:

(a) The agreement between the members should have been made in furtherance of any object of the Trade Union on which general funds may be spent.

(b) Such an agreement must not be an agreement to commit an offence.

Further, this exemption is available for peaceful strikes only. For instance, a strike which is not accompanied by violence, assault, intimidation, threat, etc. [*Jay Engineering Works* v. *Workmen, A.I.R.* (1968) Col. 407].

Section 120B(2) of the Indian Penal Code deals with the punishment for criminal conspiracy. Criminal conspiracy is "an agreement of two or more persons to do an unlawful act or to do a lawful act by unlawful means".

IMMUNITY FROM CIVIL SUIT (Sec. 18)

No suit or legal proceedings shall be maintained in any Civil Court against any Trade Union or any office bearer or member thereof in respect of any act done in contemplation or furtherance of a trade dispute on any of the following grounds:

   (i) that such act induces some other person to break a contract of employment;

  (ii) that such act interferes with the trade, business or employment of some other person;

 (iii) that such act interferes with the right of some other person to dispose of his capital or his labour.

Section 18 further provides that a Trade Union is not liable in any legal proceedings in any Civil Court for any tortious act done in furtherance of a trade dispute even by an agent of a Trade Union unless it is proved that such a person acted without knowledge or express instructions given by the executive of the Union.

Acts of violence or vandalism or any act of deliberate trespass are not covered by Sec. 18 [*Dalmia Cement Ltd.* v. *Narain Das, A.I.R. (1939) Sind 256].*

PROVISIONS OF RIGHT OF MINORS TO THE MEMBERSHIP OF THE TRADE UNION (SEC. 21)

Any person who has attained the age of 15 years may become a member of a registered Trade Union. Such a member is competent to enjoy all the rights of a member. He can execute all instruments, and give all acquittances necessary to be executed under the rules of the Union. Although he may become a member of a registered Trade Union, he cannot be an office bearer of it until he has attained the age of 18 years as per Sec. 21(a).

DISQUALIFICATION OF OFFICE BEARERS OF A REGISTERED TRADE UNION (SEC. 21 A)

A person is disqualified for being chosen as a member of the executive or any other office bearer of a registered Trade Union if:

(a) he has not attained the age of 18 years,

(b) he has been convicted by an Indian Court for any offence involving moral turpitude and sentenced to imprisonment and a period of 5 years has not passed since the date of his release.

AMALGAMATION OF TRADE UNIONS (Secs. 24–26)

Any two or more registered Trade Unions may be amalgamated with or without any dissolution or division of funds of such Trade Unions. Such an amalgamation shall be effective only if votes of at least one half of the members of each Trade Union entitled to vote are recorded, and further at least sixty per cent of the votes recorded are in favour of such amalgamation (Sec. 24).

Notice in writing of every such amalgamation, signed by the secretary and seven members of each and every Trade Union that is a party to the amalgamation, shall be sent to the Registrar. Where the head office of the proposed amalgamated Union is situated in a different state, such a notice shall be sent to the Registrars of each state [Sec. 25(1)]. If the Registrar is satisfied that all necessary formalities have been complied with, he may order registration of the amalgamated Trade Union and it shall have effect from the date of such registration.

Any amalgamation of two or more Trade Unions shall not prejudice the right of any such Trade Union or any right of members against any such Trade Union [Sec. 26(2)].

DISSOLUTION OF TRADE UNION (Sec. 27)

The secretary and seven or more members of a Trade Union by signing a memorandum addressed to the Registrar may apply for dissolution. This application must be sent within '14' days of the date of dissolution. If the Registrar is satisfied that the dissolution has been effected in accordance with the rules of the Trade Union, he may register the dissolution and it shall have effect from the date of such registration. If the dissolution of a registered Trade Union has been registered and the rules of the Union do not provide for the distribution of funds of the Union on dissolution, the Registrar shall divide the funds amongst the members in such a manner as may be prescribed. This will apply to all properties, movable and immovable, provided such properties are acquired out of the general fund.

RETURNS TO THE REGISTRAR

Every registered Trade Union shall have to submit annually to the Registrar a general statement of all receipts and expenditures during the year ended the 31st day of December. Such a statement shall be accompanied by another statement containing assets and liabilities of Trade Union as existing on 31st December each year (Sec. 28).

REVIEW QUESTIONS

1. Define a 'Trade Union'. Discuss the provisions of the Trade Unions Act, 1926 relating to the registration of a union. What can be done if registration is refused to a union?

2. Define the following terms as used in the Trade Unions Act, 1926
   (a) Trade Dispute   (b) Appropriate Government
   (c) Registered Trade Union

3. What are the rights, duties and liabilities of a registered Trade Union?

4. State the objects on which general funds of a Trade Union may be spent.

5. Write notes on:
   (a) Amalgamation of Trade Unions
   (b) Dissolution of a Trade Union
   (c) Change of name of a Trade Union

51

The Minimum Wages Act, 1948

The Minimum Wages Act is "a piece of social legislation intended to do social justice to workers".

INTRODUCTION

The Minimum Wages Bill was introduced in the Central Legislative Assembly in April 1946 and the Act was enforced in March 1948. The whole philosophy underlying the enactment of this Act is to prevent the exploitation of labour through the payment of unduly low wages.

The passing of the Minimum Wages Act, 1948 is a landmark in the history of labour legislation in the country. It recognised that wages cannot be left to be determined entirely by market forces. Once a minimum wage is fixed in accordance with the provisions of the Minimum Wages Act, it is the obligation of the employer to pay the said wages irrespective of the capacity to pay.

The Act empowers the Central and State Governments to fix minimum rates of wages in respect of the Scheduled employments. Thirteen employments were originally included in the Schedule, but provisions were made enabling the State Governments to add to the list.

INTERPRETATION (SEC. 2)

1. *Appropriate Government [Sec. 2(b)]:* The appropriate Government in relation to any Scheduled employment carried on by or under the authority of the Central Government or a railway administration, or in relation to a mine, oilfield or major port or any corporation established by the Central Act, means the Central Government [Sec. 2(b)(i)].

   In regard to other employments specified in the Schedule, the appropriate Government means the State Government [Sec. 2(b)(ii)].

2. *Competent Authority [Sec. 2(c)]:* Competent authority means the authority appointed by the appropriate Government by notification in the Official Gazette to ascertain from time to time the cost of living index number applicable to the employees in the Scheduled employments specified in such a notification.

3. *Cost of Living Index Number [Sec. 2(d)]:* Cost of living index number means the index number ascertained and declared by the competent authority by notification in the Official Gazette to the cost of living index number applicable to employees in any Scheduled employment in respect of which minimum rates of wages have been fixed. \

4. *Employer [Sec. 2(e)]:* Employer in respect of any Scheduled employment has the meaning assigned to it in the Factories Act and the Industrial Disputes Act.

5. *Wages [Sec. 2(h)]:* 'Wages' mean all remuneration capable of being expressed in terms of money, which would, if the terms of contract of employment were fulfilled, be payable to a person employed in respect of his employment or of work done in such an employment. It includes house rent allowances but does not include:

    (i) the value of:

       (a) any house accommodation, supply of light, water, medical attendance, or

       (b) any other amenity or any service excluded by general or special order of the appropriate Government.

    (ii) any contribution paid by the employer to any Pension Fund or Provident Fund or under any Scheme of social insurance;

    (iii) any travelling allowance or the value of any travelling concession;

    (iv) any sum paid to the person employed to defray special expenses entailed on him by the nature of his employment; or

    (v) any gratuity payable on discharge.

6. *Employee [Sec. 2(i)]:* Employee means any person who is employed for hire or reward to do any work, skilled or unskilled, manual or clerical, in a Scheduled employment in respect of which minimum rates of wages have been fixed. The term includes:

(i) an outworker to whom any articles or materials are given out by another person to be made up cleaned, washed, altered, ornamented, finished, repaired, adapted, or otherwise processed for sale for the purpose of the trade or business of that other person; and

(ii) any person declared to be an employee by the appropriate Government.

It does not, however, include any member of the Armed forces of the Union.

Minimum Wages: Minimum wage represents the level below which the wage cannot be allowed to drop. It does not mean wage just sufficient for bare subsistence. The minimum wage should provide not merely for the bare subsistance of life, but for the preservation of the talents of the worker.

FIXING OF MINIMUM RATES OF WAGES (SEC. 3)

The appropriate Government is responsible for the fixation of minimum rates of wages. It shall fix the minimum rates of wages to employees employed in any Scheduled employment specified in Part I or Part II of the Schedule attached to this Act. The appropriate Government instead of fixing minimum rate of wages for the whole State may also fix such rate for a part of the State or for any class or classes of such an employment.

The appropriate Government shall review at such intervals not exceeding five years, the minimum rates of wages so fixed and revise the minimum rates, if necessary.

Section 3(1A) provides that the appropriate Government may abstain from fixing minimum rates of wages for any Scheduled employment in which less than one thousand employees are engaged in the whole State. But if at any time, the appropriate Government comes to know that the number of employees in such Scheduled employment has risen to one thousand or more, it shall fix for the minimum rates of wages.

The Act provides for the fixation of:

(a) a minimum time rate of wages;

(b) a minimum piece rate of wages;

(c) a guaranteed time rate of wages; and

(d) an overtime rate of wages, for different occupations, localities or classes of work and for adults, adolescents, children and apprentices.

MINIMUM RATE OF WAGES (SEC. 4)

The minimum rates of wages may consist of (a) Basic rate of wage and cost of living allowance; or (b) A basic rate of wage with or without the cost of living allowance and the cash value of the concession in respect of essential commodities supplied at concessional rate; or (c) An all inclusive rate: The competent authority appointed by the appropriate Government shall compute from time to time the cost of living allowance and the cash value of the concessions in respect of supplies of essential commodities at concessional rates.

The following considerations shall be taken into account in the fixation of minimum wages:

   (i) The cost of living in a place;

   (ii) The nature of the work to be performed;

   (iii) The prevailing economic conditions; and

   (iv) The condition in which the work is to be performed.

PROCEDURES FOR FIXING AND REVISING MINIMUM WAGES (SEC. 5)

For fixing and revising minimum rates of wages, the appropriate Government can adopt either of the following methods:

   (a) It appoints committees and subcommittees to hold enquiries, and advise the Government.

   (b) It publishes its proposal for the information of persons likely to be affected thereby and specifies a date, not less than two months from the date of the notification, on which the proposals shall be taken into consideration.

   After considering the advice of the committee or subcommittee under clause (a) or all representations received by it under clause (b) the appropriate Government shall fix or revise the minimum rates of wages by a notification in the Official Gazette. It shall come into effect on the expiry of three months from the date of the issue of notification unless otherwise provided. If the appropriate Government proposes to revise the minimum rate of wages under clause (b) it shall consult the Advisory Board also.

   The power of the Government to prescribe minimum rates of wages or to revise them does not include the power to vary other terms of the contract [*Bidi Leaves and Tobacco Merchants Association Gondia* v. *State of Bombay, A.I.R. 1962, S.C. (486)*].

COMMITTEES AND ADVISORY BOARDS (SECS. 7 TO 9)

Section 9 of the Act empowers the appropriate Government to appoint committees and subcommittees to advise them from time to time in connection with the fixation and revision of the minimum rates of wages for any Scheduled employment by holding enquiries, etc. The appropriate Government may also set up an Advisory Board for the purpose of the coordinating work of these committees (Sec. 7). To coordinate the working of the Advisory Boards in regard to the fixation and revision of the minimum wages and to advise the Central Government in the matter, the Act also provides for setting up a Central Advisory Board (Sec. 8).

The Advisory Boards have to consist of an equal number of employers, employees representatives and of independent persons not exceeding one third of its total strength. The appropriate Government may appoint one of these independent members as chairman. An 'independent person' means a person who is neither an employer nor an employee in the employment for which minimum wages are to be fixed. [*Dig Vijay Singhji Salt Works* v. *State of Gujarat, A.I.R. 1974, Gujarat 14*].

CORRECTION OF ERRORS (SEC. 10)

Section 10 empowers the appropriate Government to correct an order fixing or revising minimum rates of wages if such an order contains any clerical or arithmetical errors. Such an order may be corrected by a notification in the Official Gazette. Every such notification, after it is issued, shall be placed before the Advisory Board for information.

PAYMENT OF MINIMUM WAGES

Wages in Kind (Sec. 11): The Act lays down that wages shall be paid in cash, although the appropriate Government can authorise payments of minimum wages, wholly or partly in kind. The appropriate Government may also authorise the supply of essential commodities at concessional rates in the interest of the employees. All such authorisations should be made by a notification in the Official Gazette. The cash value of the wages in kind and of concession in respect of supplies of essential commodities shall be estimated by the appropriate Government in the manner prescribed under the rules.

Payment of Minimum Rates of Wages (Sec. 12): If minimum wages have been in force in respect of any Scheduled employment, the employer shall pay wages to every employee engaged in such an employment at a rate not less than the minimum rate of wages fixed under Sec. 5. Such wages shall be paid without any deductions except as may be authorised. This Section does not affect the provisions of Payment of Wages Act, 1936.

Fixing Hours for a Normal Working Day (Sec. 13): In respect of any Scheduled employment where minimum rates of wages have been fixed, the appropriate Government may:

(a) fix the number of hours for a normal working day, inclusive of one or more specified intervals;

(b) provide for a day of rest in every period of seven days for all the employees and for the payment of remuneration in respect of such a day of rest;

(c) provide for payment for work on a day of rest at a rate not less than the overtime rate.

The above provisions shall apply to the following classes of employees only to such an extent and subject to such conditions as may be prescribed:

(a) employees engaged on urgent or emergency work;

(b) employees engaged on preparatory or complementary work;

(c) employees whose employment is essentially intermittent;

(d) employees engaged in any work which for technical reasons has to be completed before the duty is over;

(e) employees engaged in a work dependent upon the irregular action of natural forces.

As per Sec. 13(3), the appropriate Government shall declare an employment as 'intermittent' on the ground that the daily hours of duty of the employee normally include periods of inaction during which the employee may be on duty but is not called upon to display either physical activity or sustained attention.

Overtime (Sec. 14): Where an employee whose minimum rates of wages have been fixed is required to work beyond the normal hours of his duty, he shall be paid an overtime allowance at the rate fixed either under this Act or in any law of the appropriate Government in force, whichever is higher.

Nothing in the Minimum Wages Act, 1948 shall prejudice the operation of the provisions of Sec. 59 of the Factories Act, 1948 in any case where those provisions are applicable.

Wages of a Worker who Works for Less than Normal Working Day (Sec. 15): Where an employee whose minimum rate of wages has been fixed by the day, works on any day for a shorter period than the required number of hours, he shall be entitled to receive wages for a full normal working day except:

(i) where his failure to work is caused by his unwillingness to work and not by the omission of the employer to provide him with work; and

(ii) in such other cases and circumstances as may be prescribed.

Wages for Two or More Classes of Work (Sec. 16): Where an employee works on two or more types of works and each of which is different and different minimum rate of wages are applicable, the employer shall pay in such cases in proportion to the time spent on each class of work. The wages in such cases should not be less than minimum rate of wages for each such a class.

Minimum Time Rate Wages for Piece Work (Sec. 17): Where an employee is employed on piece work for which minimum time rate and not a minimum piece rate has been fixed under this Act, the employer shall pay to such an employee wages not less than the minimum time rate.

MAINTENANCE OF REGISTERS AND RECORDS (SEC. 18)

Every employer is bound to maintain registers and records showing the following particulars of the persons employed by him:

1. the work performed by them;
2. the wages paid to them;
3. the receipts given by them; and
4. such other particulars in such term as may be prescribed.

Every employer shall also keep exhibited notices in the prescribed form containing prescribed particulars in the prescribed manner in the factory. In the case of out workers, he shall keep these notices exhibited in such a factory, workshop or place as may be used for giving out work to them.

THE SCHEDULE
PART I

1. Employment in any woollen carpet making or shawl weaving establishment.
2. Employment in any rice mill, flour mill or dal mill.

3. Employment in any tobacco (including bidi making manufactory).

4. Employment in any plantation.

5. Employment in any oil mill.

6. Employment under any local authority.

7. Employment in the construction or maintenance of roads or in building operations.

8. Employment in stone breaking or stone crushing.

9. Employment in any lac manufactory.

10. Employment in any public motor transport.

11. Employment in any mica works.

12. Employment in tanneries and leather manufactory.

13. Employment in gypsum mines.

14. Employment in barytes mines.

15. Employment in bauxite mines.

16. Employment in manganese mines.

17. Employment in the maintenance of buildings.

18. Employment in china clay mines.

19. Employment in kyanite mines.

20. Employment in copper mines.

21. Employment in clay mines.

22. Employment in magnesite mines.

23. Employment in fire clay mines.

24. Employment in quartzite mines.

25. Employment in quartz mines.

26. Employment in silica mines.

PART II

Employment in agriculture, that is to say, in any form of farming, dairy farming, the production, cultivation, growing and harvesting of any agriculture or horticultural commodity, the raising of livestock, bees or poultry.

REVIEW QUESTIONS

1. Define the following terms as used in the Minimum Wages Act, 1948.

   (a) Scheduled Employment (b) Wages

   (c) Employer (d) Employee

   (e) Competent authority (f) Cost of living index number.

2. Explain briefly the procedure for fixing and revising the minimum rates of wages. What is the composition of such a minimum rate of wages?

3. What are the functions of Advisory Board and Central Advisory Board respectively?

4. State how the inspectors are appointed under the Minimum Wages Act. What are their powers?

52

The Employees' State Insurance Act, 1948

The Act is a piece of social security legislation which aims at bringing about social and economic justice to the labour class of the country.

The Employees' State Insurance Act was passed in April 1948 as a means of extinction of the evils of the society, viz., want, disease, dirt, ignorance and indigence. It extends to the whole of India including the State of Jammu and Kashmir. The Act shall come into force on such date or dates as the Central Government may appoint and different dates may be appointed for different provisions of the Act and for different States or different parts thereof.

The Act is a landmark in the history of social security in India. It is designed to provide cash benefits in the case of sickness, maternity and employment injury, payment in the form of pension to dependants of workers who died of employment injury and medical benefits to workers.

DEFINITIONS

1. *Appropriate Government [Sec. 2(1)]:* It means the Central Government in respect of the establishments under its control or a railway administration or a major port or a mine or an oilfield. In all other cases, the expression means the State Government.

2. *Benefit Period [Sec. 2(2)]:* This Section has been omitted by the Amendment Act, 1989.

3. *Confinement [Sec. 2(3)]:* The expression means labour result-ing in the issue of a living child or labour after twenty-six weeks of pregnancy resulting in the issue of a child whether alive or not.

4. *Contribution [Sec. 2(4)]:* It means the sum of money payable to the Corporation by the principal employer in respect of an employee and includes any amount payable by or on behalf of the employee as per the provisions of this Act.

5. *Contribution Period [Sec. 2(5)]:* This Section has been omitted by the Amendment Act, 1989.

6. *Corporation [Sec. 2(6)]:* It means the Employees' State Insurance Corporation set up under Section 3 of the Act.

7. *Dependant [Sec. 2(6A)]:* Dependant means any of the following relatives of a deceased insured person, namely:

   (i) a widow, a minor legitimate or adopted son, an unmarried legitimate or adopted daughter;

   (ii) a widowed mother;

   (iii) if wholly dependant on the earning's of the insured person at the time of his death, a legitimate or adopted son or daughter who has attained the age of 18 years and is infirm;

   (iv) if wholly or in part dependant on the earnings of the insured person at the time of his death

   (a) a parent other than a widowed mother;

   (b) a minor illegitimate son, an unmarried illegitimate daughter or a daughter legitimate or adopted or illegitimate if married and a minor or if widowed and a minor;

   (c) a minor brother or an unmarried sister or a widowed sister if a minor;

   (d) a widowed daughter-in-law;

   (e) a minor child of a predeceased son;

   (f) a minor child of a predeceased daughter where no parent of the child is alive; or

   (g) a parental grandparent if no parent of the insured person is alive.

   The relatives in group (i) will be entitled to claim benefits under the Act by virtue of their relationship with the insured person, while the relatives in groups, (ii) and (iii) will have to prove their dependence on the insured workman in order to claim the benefit under the Act.

8. *Employment Injury [Sec. 2(8)]:* It means a personal injury to an employee caused by an accident or occupational disease

arising out of and in the course of his employment, being an insurable employment, whether the accident occurs or the occupational disease is contracted within or outside the territorial limits of India.

9. *Employment [Sec. 2(9)]:* The term employee means any person employed for wages in connection with the work of a factory or other establishment to which this Act applies and also includes any person who is directly employed by the principal employer on any work incidental to or connected with the work of any factory or establishment.

   The term employee also includes any person who is employed by or through an immediate employer in the premises of the factory or establishment whether under the supervision of the principal employer or his agent. Further, the term employee also includes those whose services are temporarily let on hire to the principal employer under a contract of service.

   But the term employee does not include:
   (a) any member of the Indian naval, military or air force; or
   (b) any person employed on a remuneration which exceeds the amount to be prescribed by the Central Government (Prior to the amendment in 1989, this limit was ₹1600).

10. *Exempted Employee [Sec. 2(10)]:* The expression means an employee who is not liable under the Act to pay the employees' contribution.

11. *Family [Sec. 2(11)] as Substituted by the Amendment Act, 1989]:* Family means all or any of the following relatives of an insured person; namely:
    (i) a spouse;
    (ii) a minor legitimate or adopted child dependent upon the insured person.
    (iii) a child who is wholly independent on the earnings of the insured person and who is:
       (a) receiving education, till he or she attains the age of '21' years,
       (b) an unmarried daughter;
    (iv) a child who is infirm by reason of any physical or mental abnormality or injury and is wholly dependent on the

earnings of the insured person, as long as the infirmity continues;

(v) dependant parents.

12. *Factory [Sec. 2(12) as Substituted by the Amendment Act, 1989]:* The meaning of 'factory' in the Employees' State Insurance Act has been brought in tune with the meaning in the Factories Act, 1948.

13. *Immediate Employer [Sec. 2(13)]:* The term immediate employer in connection with the employees employed by or through him, means my person who has undertaken the execution of work on the premises of a factory or any other establishment to which this Act applies. The work may be done also under the supervision of the principal employer or his agent either in part or in full. The term also includes a person by whom the services of an employee who has entered into a contract of service with him are temporarily lent or let on hire to the principal employer and includes a 'contractor'.

14. *Insurable Employment [Sec. 2 (13A)]:* It means an employment in a factory or establishment to which this Act applies.

15. *Insured Person [Sec. 2(14)]:* The expression means a person who is or was an employee in respect of whom contributions are or were payable under the Act and who is, by reason thereof, entitled to any of the benefits provided by the Act.

16. *Managing Agent [Sec. 2(14A)]:* 'Managing agent' means any person appointed or acting as the representative of another person for the purpose of carrying on such another person's trade or business. But the term does not include an individual manager subordinate to an employer.

17. *Miscarriage [Sec. 2(14B)]:* It means expulsion of the contents of a pregnant uterus at any period prior to or during the 26 weeks of pregnancy. But it does not include any miscarriage, the causing of which is punishable under the Indian Penal Code, 1860.

18. *Occupier [Sec. 2(15)3]:* It has the same meaning assigned to it as in the Factories Act, 1948.

19. *Disablement:* Disablement is either (1) Permanent disablement; or (2) Temporary disablement.

   1. *Permanent Disablement:* Permanent disablement may be (a) Permanent partial disablement; or (b) Permanent total disablement.

(a) *Permanent Partial Disablement [Sec. 2(15A)]:* Permanent partial disablement means such disablement of a permanent nature, as reduces the earning capacity of an employee in every employment which he was capable of undertaking at the time of the accident resulting in the disablement. Every injury specified in Part II of the Second Schedule shall be deemed to result in permanent partial disablement.

(b) *Permanent Total Disablement [Sec. 2(15B)]:* It means disablement of a permanent nature as incapacitates an employee for all work which he was capable of performing at the time of the accident resulting in such disablement.

Permanent total disablement shall be deemed to result from every injury specified in Part I of the Second Schedule or from any combination of injuries specified in Part II thereof, where the aggregate percentage of the loss of earning capacity against those injuries amount to one hundred per cent or more.

2. *Temporary Disablement [Sec. 2(21)]:* It means a condition resulting from an employment injury which requires medical treatment and renders an employee, as a result of such injury, temporarily incapable of doing the work which he was doing prior to or at the time of the injury.

20. *Principal Employer [Sec. 2(17)]:* In relation to a factory, 'principal employer' means the owner or occupier of the factory and includes:

(a) the managing agent of such owner or occupier, (b) the legal representative of deceased owner or occupier, and (c) where a person has been named as the manager of the factory under the Factories Act, 1948.

In relation to an establishment under the control of any department of the Government of India, the term 'principal employer' means

(a) the authority appointed by such Government in this behalf; or

(b) where no authority is so appointed, the head of the department.

21. *Sickness [Sec. 2(20)]:* The term sickness means a condition which requires medical treatment and attendance and necessitates abstention from work on medical grounds.

22. *Wages [Sec. 2(22)]:* The term 'wages' means all remuneration paid or payable in cash to an employee whether the terms of the contract are express or implied. It also includes other remunerations paid at intervals but it does not include the following:

   (i) Any contribution paid to any pension, provident fund.

   (ii) Any travelling allowances or value of any travel concession.

   (iii) Any sum paid to the employed person to defray special expenses as per the nature of employment.

   (iv) Gratuity paid on discharge.

23. *Wage Period [Sec. 2(23)]:* 'Wage period' in relation to an employee means the period in respect of which wages are ordinarily payable to him whether in terms of employment, express or implied or otherwise.

ADMINISTRATION OF THE SCHEME (SECS. 3 TO 25)

The administration of the Scheme is entrusted to the Employees' State Insurance Corporation (ESIC), an autonomous body set up by the Central Government (Sec. 3). It consists of representatives of the Central and State Government, the Parliament, employers, employees and the medical profession. Its Standing Committee acts as the executive body. The members of the Standing Committee are elected from among the members of the Corporation. A Medical Benefit Council has been set up to advise the Corporation on medical questions. The Chief Executive Officer of the Corporation is the Director General. Further, the corporation has set up Regional Boards, Regional Offices, Local Offices and Inspection Offices in various States.

EMPLOYEES' STATE INSURANCE CORPORATION

A statutory body known as the Employees' State Insurance Corporation has been set up with effect from 1st October, 1948 for the administration of the scheme of the Employees' State Insurance [Sec. 3(1)]. Such a Corporation is a body corporate having a perpetual succession and common seal [Sec. 3(2)].

Constitution of the Corporation (Sec. 4)

The Corporation consists of the following members:

1. A chairman, a vice chairman and not more than five members to be nominated by the Central Government;

2. One member is to be nominated by the Central Government for Union Territory;

3. One member representing each State wherein this Act is in force to be appointed by the State Government concerned;

4. Ten members (members raised from 5 to 10 by the Amendment Act, 1989) representing employers are to be nominated by the Central Government;

5. Ten members (members raised from 5 to 10 by the Amendment Act, 1989) representing employees are to be nominated by the Central Government;

6. Two members representing the medical profession are to be nominated by the Central Government;

7. Two members of the Lok Sabha who are to be elected by the members of that House;

8. One member of the Rajya Sabha is to be elected by the Members of that House;

9. The Director General of the Corporation, ex officio.

Term of Office of the Members of the Corporation (Sec. 5)

The term of office of the members of the Corporation, other than the members referred to in clauses (1), (2) and (3) above, and the ex officio member is four years from the date of their nomination or election. But they shall continue as members even after the expiry of the said period of four years, until the nomination or election or their successors is notified. The members referred to in clauses (1), (2) and (3) above shall hold office during the pleasure of the Government nominating them.

An outgoing member of the Corporation is eligible for renomination or re-election (Sec. 6).

Powers of the Corporation

1. Power to employ the necessary staff for the efficient transaction of its business (Sec. 17).

2. Power to promote measures for health, etc., of insured persons (Sec. 19).

3. Power to acquire, hold and sell or otherwise transfer any movable and immovable property [Sec. 29(1)].

4. Power to invest the money which are not immediately required [Sec. 29(2)].

5. Power to raise loans and take measures for discharging such loans with the previous permission of the Central Government [Sec. 29(3)].

6. Power to constitute provident or other fund for the benefit of its staff [Sec. 29(4)].

7. Power to appoint such persons as Inspectors for the purposes of the Act [Sec. 45(1)].

Duties of the Corporation

1. It shall, in each year make a budget showing the probable receipts and expenditures which it proposes to incur during the following year. A copy of the same is to be submitted to the Central Government prior to a specified date for its approval (Sec. 32).

2. It shall maintain correct accounts of its income and expenditure in such form and in such manner as may be prescribed by the Central Government (Sec. 33).

3. The accounts of the Corporation shall be duly audited by the auditors appointed by the Central Government (Sec. 34).

4. It shall submit to the Central Government an annual report of its activities (Sec. 35).

5. The annual report, the audited accounts together with the auditors report thereon and the budget as finally adopted by the Corporation shall be placed before the Parliament and published in the Official Gazette (Sec. 36).

STANDING COMMITTEE (SEC. 8)

The Standing Committee shall be constituted from the following office bearers and members of the Corporation:

(i) A chairman, nominated by the Central Government;

(ii) Three members of the Corporation nominated by the Central Government;

(iii) Three members of the Corporation representing such of the three States as the Central Government may notify;

(iv) The Director General of the Corporation, ex officio;

(v) Eight members elected by the Corporation in the following manner:

    (a) Three members representing employers;

    (b) Three members representing employees;

    (c) One member representing the medical profession;

    (d) One member from among the members of the Corporation elected by the Parliament.

Term of Office of the Members of the Standing Committee (Sec. 9)

The members referred to in clauses (i), (ii) and (iii) shall hold office during the pleasure of the Central Government. The term of office of the eight members referred to in clause (v) shall be two years. But they shall continue as members even after the expiry of the said term until the election of their successors is notified.

Further, any member of the Standing Committee shall cease to hold office when he ceases to be a member of the Corporation.

Powers and Duties of the Standing Committee (Sec. 18)

Subject to the general superintendence and control of the Corporation, the Standing Committee may exercise any of the powers and perform any of the functions of the Corporation. In addition to those stated above, the Standing Committee shall exercise the following powers:

(i) It shall submit for the consideration and decision of the Corporation all such cases and matters as may be specified.

(ii) It may in its discretion submit any other case or matter for the decision of the Corporation.

MEDICAL BENEFIT COUNCIL [SEC. 10]

A Medical Benefit Council has been constituted to advise the Corporation on the medical side of its operations. It consists of:

(i) The Director General, Health Services, ex officio, as Chairman;

(ii) A Deputy Director General, Health Services, to be nominated by the Central Government;

(iii) The Medical Commissioner of the Corporation, ex officio;

(iv) One representative from each State (Other than Union Territory) to be nominated by the State Government; where this Act is in force;

(v) Three members representing employers to be nominated by the Central Government;

(vi) Three members representing employees to be nominated by the Central Government;

(vii) Three members of whom not less than one shall be a woman, representing the medical profession, to be nominated by the Central Government.

A member referred to in clauses (ii) and (iv) shall hold office during the pleasure of the Government nominating him. The term of office of members referred to in clauses (v), (vi) and (vii) shall be four years from the date of the notification of their nomination. But they shall continue as members even after the expiry of the said term until the nomination of their successors is notified.

Powers and Duties of the Medical Benefit Council (Sec. 22)

1. It shall advise the Corporation and the Standing Committee on matters relating to the administration of medical benefit and other connected matters.

2. It shall have such powers and duties of investigation as may be prescribed in relation to complaints against the medical practitioners.

3. It shall perform such other duties as may be specified.

EMPLOYEES' STATE INSURANCE FUND (SEC. 26)

The Act provides for the creation of 'Fund' known as the Employees' State Insurance Fund. The purpose of the fund is to provide the payment of various benefits to the insured person under this Act. The fund is also utilized for meeting the cost of administration of the Corporation, and for making provisions for other authorized purposes.

The fund is mainly composed of contributions collected from the employees and employers. The Corporation may accept grants, donations and gifts from the Government, local authority or any individual or body for any of the purpose of this Act. All the money so received shall be paid into the Reserve Bank of India or any other

Bank as approved by the Central Government to the credit of the Employees' State Insurance Fund Account. Such account shall be operated on by such officers as may be authorised by the Standing Committee with the approval of the Corporation.

Purposes for which Fund may be Expended (Sec. 28)

The 'Fund' of the Corporation can be utilised only for the following purposes, namely:

1. Payment of benefit and provision of medical treatment and attendance to the insured persons.

2. Payment of fees and allowances to the members of the Corporation/Standing Committee/Medical Benefit Council/Regional Members/Regional Councils.

3. Provision of the medical benefit to the families of the insured person.

4. Establishment and maintenance of hospitals, dispensaries and other institutions for the benefit of the insured persons and their families.

5. Payment of salaries and all allowances, gratuity or pension or contribution to P.F. or other funds of the officers and servants of the Corporation.

6. Payment of contribution to State Government or local authorities towards the cost of medical treatment and attendance on the insured persons and their families including the cost of building and equipment.

7. Defraying the cost of maintenance of E.S.I. Court.

8. Defraying the cost of auditing the accounts of the Corporation and of the valuation of its assets and liabilities.

9. Payment of any sums in connection with any contract entered into by the Corporation.

10. Payment of sums under any decree, or award of any Court or Tribunal against the Corporation or its any officer or servant in the execution of his duty.

11. Defraying the costs and other charges to institute or defending of any civil or criminal proceedings under this Act.

12. Defraying the expenditure on measures taken for the improvement of the health and welfare services of the insured person.

13. All such other expenses as may be authorised by the Corporation with prior approval of the Central Government.

The welfare activities of the staff of the Corporation come within such categories. The construction of the staff quarters for the employees of the Corporation or Dispensaries is also a part of the welfare activity *[Bai Malimabu* v. *State of Gujarat, A.I.R. (1978), S.C. 515].*

CONTRIBUTIONS (Secs. 38 to 45B)

All the employees in factories and establishments to which the Act applies shall be insured in the manner provided in this Act (Sec. 38).

Rules as to Contribution

1. *Contributions (Sec. 39):* The contribution payable under the Act in respect of employees comprises employer's contribution and employee's contribution [Sec. 39(1)]. The contribution payable by the employer is called the employer's contribution and that by the employee is called the employee's contribution.

2. *Rate of Contribution:* The contribution shall be paid at the rates specified in the First Schedule of the Act [Sec. 39(2)]. The revised rates of employer's contribution shall be a sum equal to 5 per cent of the total wage bill of all employees rounded to the next higher multiple of 5 paise, while the employee's contribution will be a sum, equal to 2.25 per cent of his wages rounded to the next higher multiple of 5 paise.

3. *Unit of Payment:* The wage period in relation to an employee shall be the unit in respect of which all contributions shall be payable under the Act [Sec. 39(3)].

4. *Contributions when Payable:* The contributions payable shall ordinarily fall due on the last day of the wage period. Where an employee is employed for part of a wage period or is employed under two or more employers during the same wage period, the contribution shall fall due on the day as may be specified in the regulations [Sec. 39(4)].

5. *Principal Employer to Pay Contributions in the First Instance (Sec. 40):*

   (i) It is the primary duty of the principal employer to pay in respect of every employee whether directly employed by him or through an immediate employer, both the employer's contribution and the employee's contribution [Sec. 40(1)].

   (ii) The principal employer, in the case of an employee directly employed by him is entitled to recover the employee's contribution from the wages of the employee concerned. But no such deduction can be made from any wages other than such as relate to the period in respect of which the contribution is payable, or in excess of the sum representing the employee's contribution for the period [Sec. 40(2)].

   (iii) The principal employer or the immediate employer is not entitled to deduct the employer's contribution from the wages of the employee concerned. [Sec. 40(3)].

   (iv) Any sum deducted by the principal employer from the wages of an employee shall be deemed to have been entrusted to him by the employee in respect of his contribution [Sec. 40(4)].

   (v) The principal employer shall bear the expenses of remitting the contribution to the Corporation [Sec. 40(5)].

6. *Recovery of Contributions from Immediate Employer (Sec. 41):*

   (a) The principal employer is entitled to recover the employee's as well as the employer's contribution from the immediate employer in respect of an employee employed by or through an immediate employer. He may recover this amount either by deduction from any amount payable to the immediate employer or treat it as a debt payable by the immediate employer [Sec. 41(1)].

   The immediate employer shall maintain a register of employees employed by or through him as provided in the regulations and submit the same to the principal employer before the settlement of any amount payable under Sec. 41(1). [Sec. 41(1A) as inserted by the Amendment Act, 1989].

   (b) The immediate employer is entitled to recover the employee's contribution from the wages of the employee employed by or through him [Sec. 41(2)].

7. *General Provisions as to the Payment of Contributions (Sec. 42):* An employee whose average daily wage is less than such a wage as may be prescribed by the Central Government (such wage as may be prescribed is substituted in place of ₹6 by the Amendment Act, 1989) is not liable for the payment of contribution. But he is entitled to all the benefits under the Act [Sec. 42(1)].

   Contributions (both the employer's and employee's) are payable by the principal employer for each wage period in respect of the whole or part of which wages are payable to the employee and not otherwise [Sec. 42(2)].

8. *Method of Payment of Contribution (Sec. 43):* Subject to the provisions of the Act, the Corporation may frame regulations for:

   (i)   the manner and time of payment of contribution;

   (ii) the date by which evidence of contributions having been paid is to be received by the Corporation;

   (iii) the payment of contribution by means of stamps;

   (iv) the entry in books or cards of contribution paid and benefits distributed; and

   (v)   the issue, sale, custody, production, inspection and delivery of books or cards which have been lost, destroyed or defaced.

9. *Returns and Registers (Sec. 44):* Every principal and immediate employer shall maintain such registers or records in respect of his factory as may be required by regulations and shall submit to the Corporation such returns in such forms containing such particulars as may be specified in the regulations.

10. *Determination of Contributions in Certain Cases (Sec. 45A):* Where in respect of a factory or establishment, no returns, particulars or records are submitted, furnished or maintained or any inspector or other official of the Corporation is prevented in any manner by the principal or immediate employer or any other person, in exercising his functions or discharging his duties, the Corporation may, on the basis of information available to it, by order, determine the amount of contributions payable in respect of the employees of that factory or establishment [Sec. 45A(1)].

Recovery of Contributions

Any contribution payable under the Act may be recovered as an arrear of land revenue (Sec. 45B).

Liability of the Employer

If any contribution payable under this Act is not paid by the principal employer on the date on which such contribution becomes due, he is liable to pay simple interest at the rate of 12 per cent per annum or at such higher rates as may be specified in the regulations till the date of his actual payment. The higher interest specified in the regulations shall not be more than the lending rate of interest charged by the scheduled banks. The interest may be recovered as an arrear of land revenue [Sec. 39(5) as inserted by the Amendment Act, 1989].

Benefits

An insured person is entitled to get the following six types of benefits:

1. Sickness benefit
2. Maternity benefit
3. Disablement benefit
4. Dependant's benefit
5. Medical benefit
6. Funeral expenses

1. *Sickness Benefit [Secs. 46(1)(a), 48 and 49]:* Sickness benefit represents periodical payment to an insured person in case his sickness is certified by a duly appointed medical practitioner [Sec. 46(1)(a)].

   The qualification of a person to claim the sickness benefit, the condition subject to which such a benefit may be given, the rates and periods thereof shall be such as may be prescribed by the Central Government [Sec. 49 as substituted by the Amendment Act, 1989].

   The daily rate of the sickness benefit, in respect of the insured person during any benefit period, shall be the standard benefit rate corresponding to the average daily wages of that person during the corresponding contribution period (Clause 4 of Schedule 1).

   Example: An employee earns between ₹4 and ₹6 daily. The standard benefit rate in his case is ₹2.50 per day. The daily rate of the sickness benefit is ₹2.50.

Every insured person while claiming the sickness benefit shall furnish the evidence of sickness by means of a medical certificate given by the Insurance Medical Officer.

2. *Maternity Benefit [Secs. 46(1)(b) and 50]:* Maternity benefit implies periodical payments in use of confinement to an insured woman, certified to be eligible for such payments by a competent authority [Sec. 46(1)(b)].

   The qualification of an insured woman to claim maternity benefit, the conditions subject to which such benefit may be given, the rates and period thereof shall be such as may be prescribed by the Central Government (Sec. 50 as substituted by the Amendment Act, 1989).

   The rate of maternity benefit is equal to double the standard benefit rate, as is available in the sickness benefit.

   Example: An insured woman in the wage group of ₹4–6 will get ₹5 daily as maternity benefit.

   To obtain maternity benefit, the insured woman should get the certificates of pregnancy, of the expected date of confinement and of actual confinement and send them to the Local Office to which she is attached.

3. *Disablement Benefit [Secs. 46(1)(c), 51, 51A–51D, 52A, 53–54]:* This benefit is available to an insured person suffering from disablement, as a result of an employment injury if it is certified by an authority specified under the Act [Sec. 46(1)(c)]. The term 'employment injury' means "personal injury sustained by an employee as a result of an accident or occupational disease, arising out of and during the course of employment".

   For the purpose of this Act, an accident arising in the course of an insured person's employment shall be presumed, in the absence of evidence to the contrary, also to have arisen out of that employment [Sec. 51A].

   The accident happening while acting in breach of regulations shall also be deemed to have arisen out of and in the course of the employment under the following cases:

   (a) if at the time of accident the insured person was acting in breach of regulation, and

   (b) the act was being done by the insured person in connection with the employer's trade or profession (Sec. 51B).

   The accident would be deemed to have arisen out of and in the course of employment, if the insured person is travelling in the employer's transport in the following cases:

(a) at the time of the accident the vehicle is being operated by or on behalf of the employer, and

(b) the vehicle is not being operated in the ordinary course of public transport service (Sec. 51C).

The accident happening, while meeting emergency by an insured person in or about the premises at which he is employed for the time being for the purpose of the employer's trade or business. Such an accident shall be deemed to have arisen out of and in the course of employment (Sec. 51D).

Rate of Disablement Benefit: An insured person who sustains temporary disablement for not less than three days (excluding the day of accident) or permanent disablement, whether total or partial, shall be entitled to periodical payment at such rates and for such periods and subject to such conditions as may be prescribed by the Central Government (Sec. 51).

The daily rate of disablement benefit shall be the rate, 25 per cent more than the standard benefit rate rounded to the next higher multiple of 5 paise This rate is known as 'full rate'.

Example: ₹5 is the standard benefit rate for workers in the wage group of ₹8 to ₹12. Full rate of disablement benefit for this wage group is ₹6.25 (being 25 per cent more than the standard benefit rate).

The disablement benefit shall be payable as follows:

(a) for temporary/permanent total disablement at full rate;

(b) for permanent partial disablement resulting from an injury specified in Schedule II, at such percentage of the full rate according to the loss of earning capacity caused through the injury;

(c) for permanent partial disablement resulting from an injury not specified in the II Schedule, at such percentage of the full rate payable in the case of permanent total disablement as is proportionate to the loss of earning capacity permanently caused by the injury.

4. *Dependant's Benefit [Secs. 46(1)(d), 52 and 55A]:* Dependant's benefit is payable to the dependants of insured person who dies as a result of an employment injury [Secs. 46(1)(d)]. Whether or not he was in receipt of any periodical payment or temporary disablement in respect of the injury, dependant's benefit shall be payable to his dependants [Sec. 52(1)].

Dependant's benefit consists of periodical payment at the following rates to the dependants of the insured person:

(a) An amount equivalent to 3/5th of the full rate (i.e., half the average daily wage) to the widow during her life or until remarriage. If there are more widows, the amount payable is to be divided equally among them.

(b) An amount equivalent to 2/5th of the full rate to each legitimate or adopted son until he attains eighteen years of age and also to each legitimate unmarried daughter until she attains the age of eighteen years or until her marriage, whichever is earlier.

In the case of legitimate/adopted sons and daughters who are infirm and wholly dependent on the earnings of the insured person, the dependant benefit shall continue as long as they are infirm. The total amount to be distributed to the dependants is not to exceed the amount equal to the full rate.

In case none of the above dependants is left behind by the deceased persons, the dependant's benefit may be paid to a parent or grandparent for life or to certain other dependants for a limited period at such rate as may be determined by the Corporation.

5. *Medical Benefit [Secs. 46(1)(e), 46(2), and 56–59]:* Medical Benefit consists of treatment of an insured person and his family. This benefit is available to an insured person and his family for any week in which the contribution is payable in respect of the insured person.

Medical care to the insured person is comprehensive and includes outdoor treatment, domiciliary visits and provisions of drugs and dressings, specialists services, and indoor treatment.

The medical benefit, is provided either through the service system or the panel system. Under the former, State Insurance dispensaries are set up with full-time doctors or mobile dispensaries are provided. Under the latter, medical practitioners at whose clinics, treatment is available to the beneficiaries.

The administration of the medical benefit is the responsibility of the State Government under the Employees' State Insurance Act.

6. *Funeral Expenses [Sec. 46(1)(f)]:* This benefit is payable to the eldest member of the family or to any such other person who bears the expenses for this purpose. The amount of such payment shall not exceed the amount as may be prescribed by the Central Government. Any such claim can be preferred

within three months of the death of the insured person. However, this period of three months can be extended as may be allowed by the Corporation.

SCHEDULE I

The following table taken from the First Schedule of the Act is noted for the benefit of the readers.

Group of Employees whose Average Daily Wages	Corresponding Daily Standard Benefit Rate
(1)	(2)
	₹ Ps.
1. Below 6	250
2. ₹6 and above but below 8	350
3. ₹8 and above but below 12	500
4. ₹12 and above but below 16	700
5. ₹16 and above but below 24	1000
6. ₹24 and above but below 36	1500
7. ₹36 and above	2000

REVIEW QUESTIONS

1. Define the following terms under the Employees' State Insurance Act, 1948:

    (a) Appropriate Government

    (b) Employment injury

    (c) Principal and immediate employer

    (d) Temporary disablement

    (e) Contribution.

2. State briefly the powers and duties of the Employees' State Insurance Corporation, the Standing Committee and the Medical Benefit Council?

3. What is Employees' State Insurance Fund? State the purpose for which the fund may be expended.

4. Define the terms 'contribution' and 'contribution period'. State the rules regarding contribution of employees and employers under the Employees' State Insurance Act, 1948.

5. How are the Inspectors appointed under the Employees' State Insurance Act? State their functions and duties.

6. Discuss the conditions to be satisfied for the receipt of sickness of disablement benefit.

7. State the provisions regarding the constitution and powers of Employees' Insurance Court.

8. Explain the provisions of Employees' State Insurance Act relating to sickness and maternity benefit.

Part Five

GENERAL LAW

53

The Consumer Protection Act, 1986

This statute has been enacted to provide for better protection of the interests of consumers and for that purpose to make provisions for the establishment of consumer councils and other authorities for the settlement of consumer's disputes and for matters connected therewith.

The law relating to consumer protection is dealt with in the Consumer Protection Act, 1986. The Act extends to the whole of India except the State of Jammu and Kashmir [Sec. 1(2)]. The Act applies to all goods and services. However, the Central Government may, by notification, exempt any goods or services.

The moment one gets up in the morning till one goes to bed at night, one is a consumer in one way or the other. The Act, therefore, envisages a comprehensive coverage of any kind of grievance a consumer may face. The test is to go and file a complaint. The law shall see to the benefit of the general public. The proceedings under this Act are simple and fair. There is no need to fear any complexities or technicalities involved in the regular course of litigation. There is no court fee or stamp duty to be fixed, no matter whatever may be the amount involved in the complaint.

OBJECTS OF THE ACT

The following are the objects of the Act:

1. *Better protection of interests of consumers:* The Consumer Protection Act was enacted to provide for better protection of the interests of consumers. Thus, it makes provisions for the establishment of Consumer Councils and other authorities for the settlement of consumer disputes and for matters connected therewith.

2. *Protection of Right of Consumers:* The objects and reasons behind the Act are based on inherent rights. The Act shows how to exercise them as follows:

   (a) The right to be protected against marketing of goods and services which are hazardous to life and property.

   (b) The right to be informed about the quality, quantity, potency, purity, standards and price of goods and services to protect against unfair trade practices.

   (c) The right to be assured, whenever possible, access to an authority of goods and services at competitive prices.

   (d) The right to be heard and to be assured that the consumer's interests will receive due consideration at appropriate forums.

   (e) The right to seek redressal against unfair trade practices or restrictive trade practices or unscrupulous exploitation of consumers.

   (f) The right to consumer education.

3. *Consumer Protection Councils:* The above right of consumers are sought to be promoted and protected by the Consumer Protection Councils established at the Central and State levels.

4. *Quasi-judicial Machinery for Speedy Redressal of Consumer Disputes:* The Act seeks to provide speedy, inexpensive and simple redressal of consumer disputes. For this purpose, quasi-judicial bodies have been set up the District, State and National levels. The District Forum, the first court in the hierarchy has jurisdiction for claims not exceeding Rupees Five Lakhs (Sec. 11). Then, the State Consumer Disputed Redressal Commission, also known as the State Commission, has jurisdiction for claims exceeding Rupees Five Lakhs and up to Twenty Lakhs (Sec. 17). Finally, the National Consumer Disputes Redressal Commission has jurisdiction for claims exceeding Rupees Twenty Lakhs (Sec. 21). Apart from these, the Hon'ble Supreme Court of India is the final Court of appeal.

   The quasi-judicial bodies are required to observe the principle of natural justice. They are empowered:

   (a) to give relief of a specific nature, and

   (b) to award, wherever appropriate, compensation to consumers. Non-compliance of orders given by these bodies is subject to penalties.

DEFINITIONS (SEC. 2)

1. *Complainant [Sec. 2(1)(b)]:* 'Complainant' means:

   (i) a consumer; or

   (ii) any voluntary consumer association registered under the Companies Act, 1956 or under any other law for the time being in force; or

   (iii) the Central Government or any State Government, who or which makes a complaint; or

   (iv) one or more consumers, where there are numerous consumers having the same interest.

2. *Complaint [Sec. 2(1)(c)]:* It means any allegation in writing made by a complainant with a view to obtaining any relief provided by or under this Act. The allegation must be that:

   (i) an unfair trade practice or a restrictive trade practice has been adopted by any trader;

   (ii) the goods bought by him or agreed to be bought by him suffer from one or more defects;

   (iii) the services hired or availed of or agreed to be hired or availed of by him suffer from deficiency in any respect;

   (iv) a trader has charged for the goods mentioned in the complaint a price in excess of the price fixed by or under any law for the time being in force or displayed on the goods or any package containing such goods;

   (v) goods which will be hazardous to life and safety when used, are being offered for sale to the public in contravention of the provisions of any law for the time being in force requiring traders to display information in regard to the contents, manner and effect of use of such goods.

3. *Consumer [Sec. 2(1)(d)]:* Consumer means any person, who:

   1. buys any goods for a consideration: (a) which has been paid or promised or partly paid and partly promised, or (b) under any system of deferred payment.

      'Consumer' also includes any user of such goods other than the buyer himself. The use of such goods must be with the approval of the buyer for consideration paid or promised or partly paid or partly promised, or under any system of deferred payment. But consumer does not include a person who obtains goods for resale or for any commercial purpose.

Commercial purpose does not include use by a consumer of goods bought and used by him exclusively for the purpose of earning his livelihood, by means of self-employment.

2. hires or avails of any services for a consideration which has been paid or promised or partly paid and partly promised, or under any system of deferred payment. Consumer also includes any beneficiary of such services other than the person who hires or avails of such services. The beneficiary must acquire the use of such services with the approval of the hirer for consideration paid or promised, or partly paid and partly promised, or under any system of deferred payment, A patient hiring services of doctor for consideration has been held to be a consumer. [*B. Shekhar Hgde* v. *Dr. Sudhanshu Bhattcharya and another-II* (1992), CPJ 449].

4. *Consumer Disputes [Sec. 2(1)(e)]:* It means a dispute where the person against whom a complaint has been made, denies or disputes the allegations contained in the complaint.

5. *Defect [Sec. 2(1)(f)]:* It means any fault, imperfection, shortcoming or inadequacy in the quality, nature and manner or performance which is required to be maintained by or under any law for the time being in force under any contract, express or implied, or as is claimed by the trader in any manner whatsoever in relation to any goods.

6. *Deficiency [Sec. 2(1)(g)]:* It means any fault, imperfection, shortcoming or inadequacy in the quality, nature and manner or performance which (i) is required to be maintained by or under any law for the time being in force, or (ii) has been undertaken to be performed by a person in performance of a contract or otherwise in relation to any service.

7. *Goods [Sec. 2(1)(i)]:* It means goods as defined in the Sale of Goods Act, 1930.

8. *Manufacturer [Sec. 2(1)(j)]:* Manufacturer means a person who:

   (i) makes or manufactures any goods or parts thereof; or

   (ii) does not make or manufacture any goods but assembles parts thereof made or manufactured by others and claims the end product to be goods manufactured by himself; or

(iii) puts or causes to be put his own mark on any goods made or manufactured by any other manufacturer and claims such goods to be goods made or manufactured by himself.

9. *Person [Sec. 2(1)(m)]:* Person includes: (i) a firm whether registered or not, (ii) a Hindu undivided family, (iii) a cooperative society, and (iv) every other association of persons whether registered under the Societies Registration Act, 1960 or not.

10. *Restrictive Trade Practice [Sec. 2(1)(nn)]:* It means any trade practice which requires a consumer to buy, hire or avail of any goods, or as the case may be, services as a condition precedent for buying, hiring or availing of other goods or services.

11. *Trader [Sec. 2(1)(q)]:* Trader in relation to any goods means a person who sells or distributes any goods for sale and includes the manufacturer thereof, and where such goods are sold or distributed in package form includes the packer thereof.

12. *Unfair Trade Practice [Sec. 2(1)(r)]:* It means a trade practice in which a trader (for the purpose of promoting the sale, use or supply of any goods or for the provision of any service) adopts any unfair method or unfair or deceptive practice.

CONSUMER PROTECTION COUNCIL
Chapter II (Secs. 4–8)

The Central Consumer Protection Council (Secs. 4–6)

Establishment (Sec. 4): As per Sec. 4, the Central Government may, by notification establish a Council to be known as the Central Consumer Protection Council (referred to as the Central Council).

Memberships: The Central Council shall consist of:

(a) the Minister incharge of consumer affairs in the Central Government. He shall be its Chairman, and

(b) such number of other official or non-official members representing the prescribed interest. The Central Council shall consist of 150 members (Rule 3 of the Consumer Protection Rule, 1987).

The term of the Council shall be three years. Any member may, by writing to the Chairman, resign from the Central Council. The vacancies, so caused or otherwise, shall be filled from the same category by the Central Government. Such a person shall hold office so long as the member whose place he fills would have been entitled to hold office if the vacancy had not occurred.

Procedure for Meetings of the Central Council (Sec. 5)

1. The Central Council shall meet as and when necessary. But at least one meeting of the Council shall be held every year.

2. The Central Council shall meet at such time and place as the Chairman may think fit. It shall also observe the prescribed procedures in regard to the transaction of its business.

Objects of the Central Council (Sec. 6): The objects of the Council shall be to promote and protect the rights of the consumers. They are:

(a) the right to be protected against the marketing of hazardous goods and services;

(b) the right to be informed about the quality, quantity, potency, purity, standard and price of goods or services in order to protect against unfair trade practices;

(c) the rights to be assured, wherever possible, access to variety of goods and services at competitive prices;

(d) the right to be heard, and to be assured that consumers interests will receive due consideration at appropriate forms;

(e) the right to seek redressal against unfair trade practices or restrictive trade practices or unscrupulous exploitation of consumers; and

(f) the right to consumers' education.

The State Consumer Protection Councils (Secs. 7 and 8)

Establishment (Sec. 7): The State Government may, by notification establish with effect from the prescribed date a council to be known as the Consumer Protection Council for....(Referred to as the State Council)

Membership: The State Council shall consist of:

(a) the Minister incharge of consumer affairs in the State Government. He shall be its Chairman.

(b) such number of other official or non-official members representing the specified interests.

Procedure for Meetings of the State Council

1. The State Council shall meet as and when necessary. But it shall hold at least two meetings every year.

2. The State Council shall meet at such time and place as the Chairman may think fit. It shall also observe the prescribed procedures in regard to the transaction of its business.

Objects of the State Council (Sec. 8): The object of every State Council shall be to promote and protect within the State the rights of the consumers as laid down in Sec. 6.

CONSUMER DISPUTES REDRESSAL AGENCIES
Chapter III (Secs. 9 to 27)

Establishment of Consumer Disputes Redressal Agencies (Sec. 9)

The following agencies shall be established for the purpose of this Act:

(a) **A Consumer Disputes Redressal Forum:** It is to be known as the: "District Forum" established by the State Government in each district of the State by notification. The State Government may (if it deems fit) establish more than one District Forum in a district.

(b) **A Consumer Disputes Redressal Commission:** It is to be known as the 'State Commission' established by the State Government in the State by notification.

(c) **A National Consumer Disputes Redressal Commission:** It is established by the Central Government by notification.

CONSUMER DISPUTES REDRESSAL FORUM (THE DISTRICT FORUM—SECS. 10 TO 15)

Composition (Sec. 10): Each District Forum shall consist of:

(a) a person who is, or has been, or is qualified to be a District Judge. He shall be its President;

(b) two other members, who shall be persons of ability, integrity and standing. They should have adequate knowledge or experience of, or should have shown capacity in dealing with problems relating to economics, law, commerce, accountancy, industry, public affairs or administration. One of them shall be a woman.

Appointment on the Recommendation of Selection Committee

Every appointment in the District Forum shall be made by the State Government on the recommendation of a selection committee. The selection committee consists of:

(i) the President of the State Commission—Chairman

(ii) Secretary, Law department of the State—Member

(iii) Secretary-incharge of the Department dealing with consumer affairs in the state—Member

Term of Office: Every member of the District Forum shall hold office for a term of 5 years or up to the age of 65 years, whichever is earlier. He shall not be eligible for reappointment.

Resignation: A member may resign his office in writing to the State Government. If it is accepted, his office shall become vacant. The vacancy so caused may be filled by the appointment of a person possessing the qualifications mentioned above in relation to the category of the member who has resigned.

Salary and Terms of Condition of Service: The salary or honorarium and other allowance payable to, and the other terms and conditions of service of the members of the District Forum shall be such as may be prescribed by the State Government.

Jurisdiction (Sec. 11): The District Forum shall have the jurisdiction to entertain complaints where the value of the goods or services and the compensation, if any claimed does not exceed rupees five lakhs.

A complaint shall be filed in a District Forum within the local limits of whose jurisdiction:

(a) the opposite party (or each of the opposite parties, where there are more than one) at the time of the filing of the complaint, actually and voluntarily resides or carries on business or has a branch office or personally works for gain; or

(b) any of the opposite parties, at the time of the filing of the complaint, actually and voluntarily resides or carries on business or has a branch office or personally work for gain as the case may be, must acquiesce in such a filing; or

(c) the cause of action wholly or in part, arises.

Manner in which complaint shall be made (Sec. 12): A complaint (in relation to any goods sold or delivered or agreed to be sold or delivered or any service provided or agreed to be provided) may be instituted with a District Forum, by:

(a) the consumer to whom such goods are sold or delivered or agreed to be sold or delivered or such service provided or agreed to be provided;

(b) any recognised consumer association, if the consumer is a member of such an association or not;

(c) one or more consumers (where there are numerous consumers) having the same interest, with the permission of the District Forum, on behalf of, or for the benefit of all consumers so interested: or

(d) the Central or the State Government.

Procedure on Receipt of Complaint (Sec. 13)

Complaint Relating to Goods

Reference of complaint to opposite party

On receipt of a complaint, the District Forum shall refer a copy of the complaint to the opposite party mentioned in the complaint. It shall also direct the opposite party to give his version of the case within a period of thirty days or such an extended period not exceeding fifteen days as may be granted by the District Forum.

Denial of allegation, etc. by opposite party

Where the opposite party denies or disputes the allegation contained in the complaint (or omits or fails to take any action to represent his case) within the said period, the District Forum shall proceed to settle the consumer dispute in the following manner.

1. **Refer the sample to laboratory if the complaint alleges a defect in the goods which cannot be determined without proper analysis or test of the goods:** In such a case the District Forum shall obtain a sample of the goods from the complaint, seal it and authenticate it. Afterwards, it shall refer the sample so sealed to the appropriate laboratory along with required directions for an analysis or test whichever may be necessary. The laboratory shall report its findings to the District Forum within a period of forty-five days of the receipt of the reference or within such an extended period as may be granted by the District Forum.

2. **Deposit of fees:** The District Forum may require the complainant to deposit to the credit of the Forum the prescribed fees before any sample of the goods is referred to any appropriate laboratory for analysis or test. Such fees are required for payment to the appropriate laboratory for

conducting the necessary analysis or test in relation to the goods in question.

3. **Remission of fees to laboratory and forwarding of report to opposite party:** The District Forum shall remit the amount of fee deposited to its credit to the appropriate laboratory to enable it to conduct the analysis or test. On receipt of the report, a copy of it with such remarks shall be forwarded to the opposite party.

4. **Obligations by any of the parties:** If any of the parties disputes the correctness of the methods of analysis or test or the findings of the appropriate laboratory, the District Forum shall require the opposite party or the complainant to submit in writing his objections in regard to the report made by the appropriate laboratory.

5. **Reasonable opportunity to parties of being heard and issue of order:** The District Forum shall thereafter, give a reasonable opportunity to the complainant and the opposite party of being heard as to the correctness or otherwise of the report made by the appropriate laboratory and also to the objection thereto.

Complaint Relating to Services

Reference of claim to opposite party: Where the complaint received by the District Forum relates to any services, it shall refer a copy of such a complaint to the opposite party. The opposite party shall also be directed to give his version of the case within a period of 30 days or such an extended period not exceeding '15' days as may be granted by the District Forum.

Denial, etc., of allegation by the opposite party: On receipt of a copy of the complaint, the opposite party may deny or dispute the allegations contained in the complaint. He may also omit or fail to take any action to represent his case within the time given by the District Forum.

Settlement of dispute: If the opposite party denies, etc., of the allegations, the District Forum shall proceed to settle the consumer disputes:

1. on the basis of evidence brought to its notice by the complainant and the opposite party, if the opposite party denies or disputes the allegations made, or

2. on the basis of evidence brought to its notice by the complainant, if the opposite party omits or fails to take any action to represent his case within the given time.

The above proceedings of the District Forum cannot be called in question in any Court on the ground that the principles of natural justice have not been complied with.

Powers of the District Forum: The District Forum shall have the same powers as are vested in a civil court under the Civil Procedure Code, 1908, while trying a suit. They are:

(i) summoning and enforcing attendance of any defendant or witness and examining the witness on oath;

(ii) discovering and producing any document or other material object producible as evidence;

(iii) receiving of evidence on affidavit;

(iv) issuing of any commission for the examination of any witness; and

(v) any other matter which may be prescribed.

Every proceeding before the District Forum shall be deemed to be a judicial proceeding, and the District Forum shall be deemed to be a civil court.

Finding of the District Forum (Sec. 140): If the District Forum is satisfied with the proceedings, it shall issue an order to the opposite party directing him to take one or more of the following steps within the prescribed period. They are:

(a) to remove the defect pointed out by the appropriate laboratory from the goods in question;

(b) to replace the goods with new goods of similar description which shall be free from any defect;

(c) to return to the complainant the price, or as the case may be, the charges paid by the complainant;

(d) to pay compensation to the consumer for any loss or injury suffered due to the negligence of the opposite party;

(e) to remove the defects or deficiencies in the service in question;

(f) to discontinue the unfair trade practice or the restrictive trade practice or not to repeat them;

(g) not to offer the hazardous goods for sale;

(h) to withdraw the hazardous goods from being offered for sale;

(i) to provide for adequate costs to parties.

Every proceeding referred to above shall be conducted by the President of the District Forum and at least one member thereof sitting together. If the member, for any reason, is unable to conduct the proceeding till it is completed, the President and the other member shall conduct such a proceeding de novo.

Every order made by the District Forum shall be signed by its President and the member or members who conducted the proceeding. If the proceeding is conducted by the President and one member and they differ on any point or points, they shall state the point or points on which they differ. The same shall be referred to the other member for hearing on such point or points. Then, the opinion of the majority shall be the order of the District Forum.

The procedure relating to the conduct of the members of District Forum, its sittings and other matters shall be prescribed by the State Government.

Appeal (Sec. 15): Any person aggrieved by an order of the District Forum may prefer an appeal to the State Commission. This appeal may be preferred within a period of thirty days from the date of the order in the prescribed form and manner.

CONSUMER DISPUTES REDRESSAL COMMISSION (THE STATE COMMISSION—SECS. 16–19)

Composition (Sec. 16): Each State Commission shall consist of:

(a) a person who is or has been a Judge of a High Court, appointed by the State Government. He shall be its President. However, appointment under this clause shall be made only after consultation with Chief Justice of the High Court;

(b) two other members, who shall be persons of ability, integrity and standing. They should have adequate knowledge or experience of or should have shown capacity in dealing with, problems relating to economics, law, commerce, accountancy, industry, public affairs or administration. One of them shall be a woman. However, appointment under this clause shall be made by the State Government on the recommendation of a selection committee. It consists of:

   (i) President of the State Commission—Chairman

   (ii) Secretary of the Law Department of the State—Member

   (iii) Secretary-incharge of the Department dealing with consumer affairs in the state—Member.

The salary or honorarium and other allowance payable to, and the other terms and conditions of service of the members of the State Commission shall be prescribed by the State Government.

Every member of the State Commission shall hold office for a term of five years or up to the age of sixty-seven years, whichever is earlier. He shall not be eligible for reappointment.

Jurisdiction (Sec. 17): The State Commission shall have jurisdiction:

(a) to entertain: (i) complaints if the value of the goods or services and compensation, if any, claimed is more than rupees five lakhs but it is not more than rupees twenty lakhs; and (ii) appeals against the order of any District Forum within the state; and

(b) to call for the records and pass appropriate orders in any consumer dispute which is pending before or has been decided by any District Forum within the state where it appears to the State Commission that such District Forum (i) has exercised a jurisdiction not vested in it by law, or (ii) has failed to exercise a jurisdiction so vested, or (iii) has acted in exercise of its jurisdiction illegally or with material irregularity.

Procedure (Sec. 18): The provisions for the disposal of complaints by the District Forum shall, with necessary modifications be applicable to the disposal of disputes by the State Commission.

Appeals (Sec. 19): Any person aggrieved by an order made by the State Commission may prefer an appeal against such order to the National Commission. This appeal shall be preferred within a period of thirty days from the date of the order in the prescribed form and manner. However, the National Commission may entertain an appeal even after the expiry of the period of thirty days if it is satisfied with the cause of delay.

NATIONAL CONSUMER DISPUTES REDRESSAL COMMISSION (NATIONAL COMMISSION—SECS. 20–23)

Composition (Sec. 20): The National Commission shall consist of:

(a) a person who is or has been a Judge of the Supreme Court, to be appointed by the Central Government. He shall be its President. However, the appointment under this clause shall be made only after consultation with the Chief Justice of India;

(b) four other members who shall be persons of ability and integrity. They should have adequate knowledge or experience of, or should have shown capacity in dealing with problems relating to economics, law, commerce, accountancy, industry, public affairs or administration. One of them shall be a woman. However, every appointment under this clause shall be made by the Central Government on the recommendation of a selection committee. It consists of:

   (i) a person who is a Judge of the Supreme Court—Chairman.

   (ii) the Secretary in the Department of Legal Affairs in the Government of India—Member

   (iii) Secretary of the Department dealing with consumer affairs in the Government of India—Member

The salary or honorarium and other allowance payable to and the other terms and conditions of service of the members of National Commission shall be prescribed by the Central Government. Every member of the National Commission shall hold office for a term of five years or up to the age of seventy years, whichever is earlier. He shall not be eligible for reappointment.

Place of the National Commission: The office of the National Commission shall be located in the Union Territory of Delhi.

Jurisdiction (Sec. 21): The National Commission shall have jurisdiction: (a) to entertain (i) complaints of the value of the goods or services and compensation, if any claimed is more than ₹ 20 lakhs and (ii) appeal against the orders of any State Commission; and (b) to call for the records and pass appropriate orders in any consumer dispute which is pending before or has been decided by any State Commission when it appears to the National Commission that such State Commission:

   (i) has exercised a jurisdiction not vested in it by law, or

   (ii) has failed to exercise a jurisdiction so vested, or

   (iii) has acted in the exercise of its jurisdiction illegally or with material irregularity.

Procedure (Sec. 22): The National Commission shall (in the disposal of any complaints or any proceedings before it) have, (a) the powers of a civil court, (b) the power to issue an order to the opposite party. It shall follow the procedures prescribed by the Central Government.

Appeal (Sec. 23): Any person aggrieved by an order made by the National Commission in exercise of its powers, may prefer an appeal against such order to Supreme Court. This appeal shall be preferred within a period of '30' days from the date of the order. However, the Supreme Court may entertain an appeal even after the expiry of the period of '30' days if it is satisfied with the cause of delay.

Finality of Orders (Sec. 24): Every order of the District Forum, the State Commission or the National Commission shall be final unless an appeal has been preferred against such an order under the provisions of this Act.

Limitation Period (Sec. 24A): The District Forum, the State Commission or the National Commission shall not admit a complaint if it is not filed within two years from the date on which the cause of action has arisen. However, a complaint may be entertained even after the said period of two years if the District Forum, the State Commission or the National Commission as the case may be, is satisfied with the cause of delay.

Further, no such complaint shall be entertained, if the National Commission, the State Commission or the District Forum, as the case may be, does not record the reason for condoning such a delay. Administrative Control (Sec. 24B):

1. The National Commission shall have administrative control over all the State Commissions in respect of the following matters:

    (i) calling for periodical returns regarding the institution, disposal, pendency of cases;

    (ii) issuing instructions regarding adoption of uniform procedure in the hearing of matters, prior service of copies of documents produced by one party to the opposite parties, furnishing of English translation of judgements written in any language, speedy grant of copies of documents;

    (iii) generally, overseeing the functioning of the State Commission or the District Forum. This is required to ensure that the objects and purpose of the Act are best served, without in any way interfering with their quasi-judicial freedom.

2. The State Commission shall have administrative control over all the District Forums within its jurisdiction in all the matters mentioned above.

    Enforcement of orders by the Forum, the State Commission of the National Commission (Sec. 25): Every order made by the District Forum, the State Commission or the National Commission may be enforced in the same manner as if it were a decree or order made by a court in a suit ponding. In the case of its inability to execute such order, it shall be lawful to send it to the Court within the local limits of whose jurisdiction:

(a) in the case of an order against a company, the registered office of the company is situated, or

(b) in the case of an order against any other person, the place where the person concerned voluntarily resides or carries on business or personally works for gain, is situated. Thereupon, the court to which the order is so sent, shall execute the order as if it were a decree or order sent to it for execution.

Dismissal of Frivolous or Vexatious Complaints (Sec. 26): Where a complaint filed (before the District Forum, the State Commission or, as the case may be the National Commission) is found to be frivolous or vexatious, it shall dismiss the complaint after recording the reasons. It shall also make an order that the complainant shall pay to the opposite party such cost, not exceeding ten thousand rupees, as may be specified in the order.

Penalties (Sec. 27): Where a trader or a person against whom a complaint is made or the complainant fails or omits to comply with any order (made by the Forum, the State Commission or the National Commission, as the case may be), such trader or person, or complainant shall be punishable with imprisonment or fine, or both. The imprisonment may be up to three years, but it shall not be less than one month. The fine may be up to rupees ten thousand, but it shall not be less than rupees two thousand. However, the authority (the Forum, the State Commission or the National Commission, as the case may be) may impose a sentence of imprisonment or fine, or both, for a term less than the minimum term and the amount less than the minimum amounts specified in this Section.

Mode of Filing Complaint: There is no prescribed form of complaint. It should be preferably on a full scape paper, typed in double space wherein the aggrieved party should narrate his grievance. Consumers should always insist on receipts while purchasing anything as that will substantiate a transaction with a particular trader with respect to particular goods. Attach true copies of all the documents that the aggrieved party relies upon. The number of sets or copies of complaint to be filed should be as is the number of officers presiding over the Court plus the copies for the opposite party/parties.

One may also file an affidavit in support of the complaint or verify the complaint. In case there is some urgency, a separate application may be filed. Similarly, if one wants some kind of stay order it should be prayed for in a separate application. Here also one should attach Supportive Affidavits. The Affidavits are to be in plain paper attested by an Oath Commissioner, as are filed in the Courts.

It is pertinent to note that the National Commission has held that Consumer Forums have no powers for granting interim directions. [*New India Assurance Co.* v. *Dr. R. Venkateshwars Rao*, 1(1993) CPJ 61NC].

MODEL FORM FOR COMPLAINT BEFORE THE HON'BLE DISTRICT CONSUMER DISPUTES REDRESSAL FORUM AT (DISTRICT)

OR

BEFORE THE HON'BLE STATE CONSUMER DISPUTES REDRESSAL COMMISSION AT TRIVANDRUM

1. Particulars of complainant:

    (a) Full Name

    (b) Complete Address

    (c) Village, Taluk, District and State.

2. Particulars of the Opposite Party/Parties:

    (a) Full Name of dealer/shop/firm/manufacturer

    (b) Complete Address

    (c) Village, Taluk, District and State.

3. Particulars relating to goods/services complained of:

    (a) Details of goods/services

        (i) Item of goods with quantum/nature of service.

        (ii) Date when goods purchased/service obtained.

        (iii) Amount paid as consideration.

    (b) Whether the complaint relates to:

        (i) Loss of damage as a result of unfair trade practice adopted by the trader.

        (ii) One or more defects in the goods.

        (iii) Deficiency in services.

        (iv) Excess price charged by trader.

(c) If the complaints relates to (b) (i) above, indicate the nature of unfair trade practice adopted by the trader.

(d) If the complaint relates to (b) (ii), nature and extent of defects in goods.

(e) If the complaint relates to (b) (iii), nature and extent of deficiency in services.

(f) If the complaint relates to (b) (iv), details of price fixed and price charged.

(g) Any other details connected with the complaint.

4. Details of attempts made to get the matter complained of settled and result thereof.

5. Whether any other law/rules/regulations/procedure applicable.

6. Details of documents/witnesses relied upon to substantiate the complaint.

7. Reliefs clamed.

PRAYER

It is, therefore, most respectfully prayed that (give details of prayer). .... Through .... Authorised Representative/Advocate/ Voluntary Consumer Organisation (give here names and addresses)

Signature and name of
complainant

Date . . . .
Place. . . . .

VERIFICATION

I ....S/o................resident of................do solemnly declare and state that the particulars stated above are true to the best of my knowledge and belief and no part thereof is false and nothing has been concealed therefrom. The Enclosures are exact copies of the originals. I undertake to pay any sum required for the conducting of test in the laboratory as per the provisions of Sec. 13(1)(d) of the Consumer Protection Act, 1986.

Verified ....this................day of................Two thousand ....

Enclosures   Signature and name of deponent
1.
2.

54

Pollution Control Act

Trade effluent includes any liquid gaseous or solid substance which is discharged from any premises used for carrying on any trade or industry, other than domestic sewage.

—Sec. 2(k)

THE WATER (PREVENTION AND CONTROL OF POLLUTION) ACT, 1974

The law relating to water pollution control is contained in the Water (Prevention and Control of Pollution) Act, 1974. It applies in the first instance to most of the States and in the Union Territories. It shall apply to such other States which adopt this Act by resolution passed in that behalf under clause (i) of Article 252 of the Constitution.

OBJECTS OF THE ACT

The problem of pollution of rivers and streams has assumed considerable importance and urgency on account of the growth of industries and the increasing tendency to urbanisation. The discharge of the domestic and industrial effluents into the water courses would render the water unsuitable as source of drinking water and for use in irrigation. It also causes increasing damage to the country's economy. It is, therefore, essential to ensure that such discharges are not allowed into the water courses without adequate treatment.

A committee was set up in 1962 to draw enactment for the prevention of water pollution. Having considered the relevant local provisions existing in the country and recommendations of the committee, the Government came to the conclusion that the existing local provisions are neither adequate nor satisfactory. There is, therefore, an urgent need for introducing a comprehensive legislation for the prevention, abatement and control of pollution of rivers streams.

DEFINITIONS

Occupier [Sec. 2(d)]: Occupier in relation to any factory or premises means the person who has control over the affairs of the factory or the premises. Where the said affairs are entrusted to a managing agent, such agent shall be deemed to be the occupier of the factory or the premises.

Pollution [Sec. 2(e)]: Pollution means any of the following: (i) Contamination of water or (ii) Alteration of the physical, chemical or biological properties of water (iii) Discharge of any sewage or trade effluent or of any other liquid, gaseous or solid substance into water (whether directly or indirectly) as may, or is likely to, create a nuisance (iv) Render water harmful or injurious to public health or safety, or to domestic, commercial, industrial, agricultural or other legitimate uses, or to the life and health of animals or plants or of acquatic organisms.

Sewage effluent [Sec. 2(g)]: It means effluent from any sewage disposal works and includes sullage from open drains.

Stream [Sec. 2(j)]: It includes (i) river; (ii) water course (whether flowing or for the time being dry); (iii) inland water (whether natural or artificial); (iv) subterranean water; (v) sea or tidal waters to each extent or, as the case may be, to each point as the State Government may specify.

Trade effluent [Sec. 2(k)]: It includes any liquid, gaseous or solid substance which is discharged from any premises used for carrying on any trade or industry, other than domestic sewage.

PREVENTION AND CONTROL OF WATER POLLUTION (SECS. 19–33)

Power of the State Government to Restrict the Application of the Act to Certain Areas

1. The State Government after consultation with the State Board may (by notification in the Official Gazette) restrict the application of this Act to such area/areas.

2. Each water pollution, prevention and control area may be declared either by reference to a map or by reference to the line of any water-shed or the boundary of any district or partly by one method and partly by another.

3. The State Government may, by notification in the Official Gazette:

   (a) alter any water pollution, prevention and control area whether by way of extension or reduction; or

   (b) define a new water pollution prevention and control area in which may be merged one or more water pollution, prevention and control areas, or may part or parts thereof.

Power to Obtain Information (Sec. 20)

1. The State Board or any officer empowered by it in that behalf may take:

   (a) surveys of any area and gauge and keep records of the flow or volume and other characteristics of any stream or well in such area;

   (b) steps for the measurement and recording of the rainfall in such areas or any part thereof;

   (c) steps for the installation and maintenance for those purposes of gauges or other apparatus and works connected therewith and carry out stream surveys;

   (d) such other steps as may be necessary in order to obtain any information required for the above purposes.

2. A State Board may direct any person to give information as to the abstraction (water from any stream/well) or the discharge (sewage or trade effluent into any such stream/well) at such times and in such form as may be specified in the direction.

3. The State Board may give directions requiring any person-in-charge of any establishment to furnish it with information regarding:

   (a) the construction, installation or operation of such establishment, or

   (b) of any disposal system or of any extension or addition thereto in such establishment, and

   (c) such other particulars as may be prescribed.

Power to Take Samples of Effluents and Procedure to be Followed in Connection Therewith (Sec. 21)

1. A State Board or any officer empowered by it in this behalf shall have power to take for the purpose of analysis:

   (a) sample of water from any stream or well or

   (b) samples of any sewage or trade effluent which is passing from any plant/vessel or from/over any place into any such stream or well.

2. The results of any analysis of a sample of any sewage or trade effluent taken shall not be admissible in evidence in any legal proceeding if the provisions of the following subsections are not complied with.

3. The person taking the sample shall:

   (a) serve the occupier or any agent of such occupier, a notice, then and there in the prescribed form of his intention to have it so analysed;

   (b) divide the sample into two parts in the presence of the occupier or his agent;

   (c) cause each to be placed in a container. It shall be marked and sealed and shall also be signed both by the person taking the sample and the occupier or his agent;

   (d) send one container forthwith: (i) in a case where such sample is taken from any area situated in a Union Territory, to the laboratory established/recognised by the Central Board as per Sec. 16; and (ii) in any other case, to the laboratory established/recognised by the State Board under Sec. 17;

   (e) on the request of the occupier or his agent, send the second container (i) in a case where such sample is taken from any area situated in a Union Territory, to the laboratory established/specified under Subsection (1) of Sec. 51; and (ii) in any other case, to the laboratory established/specified under Subsection (1) of Sec. 52.

4. When a sample of any sewage or trade effluent is taken for analysis and the person taking the samples serves on the occupier or his agent a notice and the occupier of his agent wilfully absents himself, then:

   (a) the sample so taken shall be placed in a container. It shall be marked and sealed and shall also be signed by the person, taking the sample. The same shall be sent forthwith for analysis to the laboratory. He shall also inform the Government analyst in writing about the wilful absence of the occupier or his agent; and

(b) the cost incurred in getting such sample analysed shall be payable by the occupier or his agent. If any default is made in it, the same shall be recoverable as an arrear of land revenue or of public demand.

3. No such recovery shall be made unless the occupier or his agent as the case may be, has been given a reasonable opportunity of being heard in the matter.

4. When a sample of any sewage of trade effluent is taken for analysis and the person taking the sample serves on the occupier or his agent a notice and the occupier or his agent who is present at the time of taking the sample does not make a request for dividing the sample into two parts then:

(a) the sample so taken shall be placed in a container. It shall be marked sealed and also signed by the person taking the sample.

(b) the same shall be sent forthwith by such person for analysis to the laboratory.

Reports of the Analysis on Samples Taken Under Sec. 21 (Sec. 22)

1. Where a sample of any sewage or trade effluent has been sent for analysis, the concerned Board analyst shall analyse the sample. He shall submit its report in triplicate to the Central Board or the State Board, as the case may be.

2. On receipt of the report one copy of the same shall be sent to the occupier or his agent. Another copy shall be preserved for production before the court in case any legal proceedings are taken against him. The other copy shall be kept by the concerned Board.

3. Where a sample has been sent for analysis (as per clause (c)) of subsection (3) or subsection (4) of Sec. 21) to any laboratory mentioned therein, the Government analyst referred shall analyse the same. The report of it shall be submitted in triplicate to the Central Board or, the State Board as the case may be.

4. If there is any discrepancy or insistency between the analysis carried out by the laboratory established or recognised by the Central Board or, the State Board, and that of the laboratory established or specified under Sec. 51 or Sec. 52, the report of the latter shall prevail.

5. Any cost incurred in getting any sample analysed at the request of the occupier or his agent shall be payable by such occupier or his agent. In the case of default, the same shall be recoverable from him as arrears of land revenue or of public demand.

Power of Entry and Inspection (Sec. 23)

Any authorised person shall have a right at any time to enter any place with necessary assistance.

1. The purpose of entry is:

    (a) to perform any of the functions of the Board entrusted to him;

    (b) to determine (i) whether and if so in what manner, any such functions are to be performed or (ii) whether any provisions of this Act or the rules made thereunder or any notice, order, direction or authorisation served, made, given or granted under this Act is being or has been complied with.

    (c) to examine any plant, record, register, document or any other material object or to conduct a search of any place in which he has reason to believe that an offence has been/is being/is about to be committed and for seizing any such material object if it furnishes evidence of the commission of the offence punishable. The right to enter for the inspection of a well shall be exercised only at reasonable hours in a case where such well is situated in any premises used for residential purposes and the water thereof is used exclusively for domestic purposes.

2. The provisions of the Criminal Procedure Code, 1898 shall apply to any search or seizure as they apply to any search or seizure made under the authority of a warrant issued under Sec. 98 of the said Code.

Prohibition on Use of Stream or Well for Disposal of Polluting Matter, etc. (Sec. 24)

1. Subject to the provisions of this Section:

(a) no person shall knowingly cause or permit any poisonous, noxious or polluting matter determined as per such standards as may be laid down by the State Board to enter (whether directly or indirectly) into any stream or well; or

(b) no person shall knowingly cause or permit to enter into any stream any other matter which may tend to impede the proper flow of the water of the stream leading or likely to lead to a substantial aggravation of pollution due to other causes or of its consequences.

2. A person shall not be guilty of an offence by reason only of having done or caused to be done any of the following acts. They are:

(a) constructing, improving or maintaining (in/cross/on the bank/bed of any stream), any building, bridge, weir, dam, sluice, dock, pier, drain or sewer or other permanent works which he has a right to construct, improve or maintain.

(b) depositing any materials on the bank or in the bed of any stream for the purpose of reclaiming land or for supporting, repairing or protecting the bank of bed of such stream provided such materials are not capable of polluting such streams.

(c) putting into any stream any sand or gravel or other natural deposit which has flowed from or been deposited by the current of such stream.

(d) causing or permitting, with the consent of the State Board, the deposit accumulated in a well, pond or reservoir to enter into any stream.

3. The State Government may exempt, any person from its operation. This exemption is granted only after consultation with, or on the recommendation of, the State Board. It is also subject to conditions specified in the notification. Any condition so specified may by a like notification be altered, verified or amended.

Restrictions on New Outlets and New Discharge (Sec. 25)

1. No person shall without the previous consent of the State Board bring into use any new or altered outlet for the discharge of sewage or trade effluent into a stream or well or

begin to make any new discharge of sewage or trade effluent into a stream or well.

2. An application for consent of the State Board shall be made in the prescribed form.

3. The State Board may make necessary enquiry in respect of the application for consent.

4. The State Board grants its consent subject to the following conditions:

   (a) in the case of a new or altered outlet (i) conditions as to the point of discharge into the stream or well or (ii) the construction and usage of any outlet for sewage or trade effluent from the same kind or premises; and

   (b) in the case of a new discharge as to the nature and composition, temperature, volume or rate of discharge of the effluent from the land or premises from which the new discharge is to be made. Any such conditions imposed shall be binding on any person using the outlet, or discharging the effluent from the land or premises aforesaid.

3. If a new or altered outlet is brought into use without the consent of the State Board, it may serve a notice on the person concerned imposing any such conditions as it might have imposed on an application for its consent in respect of such outlet or discharge.

4. Every State Board shall maintain a register containing all particulars of the conditions imposed in relation to outlet. The register shall be open to inspection at all reasonable hours to any person interested in.

5. The consent shall (unless given or refused earlier) be deemed to have been given unconditionally on the expiry of a period of four months of the making of an application in this behalf complete in all respects to the State Board.

Provisions Regarding Existing Discharge of Sewage or Trade Effluent (Sec. 26)

Before the commencement of this Act, if any person was discharging any sewage or trade effluent into a stream or well, the provisions of Sec. 25 shall apply in relation to such person. This is subject to the modification that the application for consent shall be made within a period of three months of the constitution of the State Board.

Refusal or Withdrawal of Consent by State Board (Sec. 27)

1. A State Board shall not grant its consent if the concerned establishment fails to comply with any conditions imposed by the Board.

2. A State Board may from time to time review any condition imposed and serve, on the person concerned, a notice making any reasonable variation of or revoking any such condition.

3. Any condition imposed shall be subject to any variation made and it shall continue in force until revoked.

Appeals (Sec. 28)

1. Any person aggrieved by an order made by the State Board may prefer an appeal to the appellate authority. Such an appeal shall be preferred within thirty days from the date on which the order is communicated to him. However, the appellate authority may entertain the appeal after the expiry of said period of thirty days if such authority is satisfied with the cause of delay.

2. An appellate authority shall consist of three persons.

3. The form and manner in which an appeal may be preferred, the fees payable and the procedure to be followed by the appellate authority shall be as prescribed.

4. The appellate authority shall dispose of the appeal as expeditiously as possible after giving the appellant and the State Board an opportunity of being heard.

5. If the appellate authority determines that:

   (a) Any condition imposed is unreasonable, then such authority may direct either that the condition shall be treated as annulled or that there shall be substituted for it such condition as appears to it to be reasonable.

   (b) Any variation of condition is unreasonable, then such authority may direct either that the condition shall be treated as continuing in force unvaried or that it shall be varied in reasonable manner.

Revision (Sec. 29)

1. The State Government may call for the records of any case if an order has been made by the State Board under

Sec. 25, Sec. 26 or Sec. 27 for the purpose of satisfying itself as to the legality or propriety of any such order.

2. The State Government shall not revise any order made under Secs. 25, 26, 27 if an appeal against that order lies to the appellate authority.

Power of State Board to Carry out Certain Works (Sec. 30)

1. If any conditions have been imposed on any person while granting consent and such conditions require him to execute any work in connection therewith and such work has not been executed within the specified time, the State Board may serve on the person concerned a notice requiring him within the given time (not being less than thirty days) to execute the work specified therein.

2. If the person concerned fails to execute the work within the specified time, the State Board may itself execute or cause to be executed such works.

3. All expenses incurred by the State Board for the execution of the aforesaid work together with interest may be recovered by that Board from the person concerned as arrears of land revenue, or of public demand.

Furnishing of Information to State Board and Other Agencies in Certain Cases (Sec. 31)

This Section requires the person-in-charge of place or industry to furnish the information of the discharge of poisonous of polluting matter into a stream or well due to accident or other unforeseen act.

Emergency Measures in the Case of Pollution of Stream or Well (Sec. 32)

1. Where it appears to the State Board that any poisonous, noxious or polluting matter is present in any stream or well, it may carry out necessary operations for all or any of the following purposes:

   (a) removing that matter from the stream or well and disposing it of in the appropriate manner;

   (b) remedying or mitigating any pollution caused by its presence in the stream or well;

(c) issuing orders immediately restraining or prohibiting the person concerned from discharging any poisonous, noxious or polluting matter into the stream or well, or from making insanitary use of the stream or well.

2. The power conferred above is only for the works of a temporary character which are removed on or before the completion of the operations.

Power of Board to Make Application to Courts for Restraining Apprehended Pollution of Water in Streams or Wells (Sec. 33)

1. The Board may make an application to a court (not inferior to a Presidency Magistrate or a Magistrate of the First Class) for restraining a person who is likely to cause pollution of water in streams or wells.

2. On receipt of an application, the court may make necessary order.

3. If the Court makes an order restraining any person from polluting the water in any stream or well, it may in that order:

    (i) direct the person to desist from taking such action as is likely to cause pollution of the water in the stream or well.

    (ii) authorise the Board, if the above direction is not complied with by the person to whom such direction is issued, to undertake the removal and disposal of the matter in the specified manner.

4. All expenses incurred by the Board in removing any matter or in the disposal of any such matter may be defrayed out of any money obtained by the Board from such a disposal. Any balance outstanding shall be recoverable from the person concerned as arrears of land revenue or of public demand.

THE AIR (PREVENTION AND CONTROL OF POLLUTION) ACT, 1981

The Air (Prevention and Control of Pollution) Act, 1981, was enacted under Art. 253 of the Constitution with the object of implementing the decisions taken at the United Nations Conference on Human Environment held at Stockholm in June, 1972, in which India participated. It extends to the whole of India and shall come into force on such date as the Central Government may, by notification in the Official Gazette, appoint.

Objects and Reasons

The problem of air pollution has begun to be felt in the country with the ever increasing tendency of industrialisation. The problem is more acute in those heavily industrialised areas which are also densely populated. The presence in air, beyond certain limits, of various pollutants discharged, has a detrimental effect on the health of the people as also on animal life, vegetation and property. The decision taken at the United Nations Conference on Human Environment held at Stockholm in June, 1972, relate to the preservation of the quality of air and control of air pollution. That is why, the Government of India has decided to implement these decisions through an Act known as Air (Prevention and Control of Pollution) Act, 1981.

Definitions

Air pollutant [Sec. 2(a)]: It means any solid, liquid or gaseous substance present in the atmosphere in such concentration as may be or tend to be injurious to human beings, other living creatures or plant or property or environment.

Air pollution [Sec. 2(b)]: It means the presence in the atmosphere of any air pollutant.

Chimney [Sec. 2(h)]: It includes any structure with an opening or outlet from or through which any air pollution may be emitted.

Control equipment [Sec. 2(i)]: It means any apparatus, device, equipment or system to control the quality and manner of emission of any air pollutant. It also includes any device used for securing the efficient operations of any industrial plant.

Emission [Sec. 2(j)]: It means any solid or liquid or gaseous substance coming out of any chimney, duct or flue or any other outlet.

Industrial plant [Sec. 2(k)]: It means any plant used for any industrial or trade purposes and emitting any air pollutant into the atmosphere.

Occupier [Sec. 2(m)]: Occupier in relation to any factory or premises, means the person who has control over the affairs of the factory or the premises. If the said affairs are entrusted to a managing agent, such agent shall be deemed to be the occupier of the factory or the premises.

PREVENTION AND CONTROL OF AIR POLLUTION

Power to Declare Air Pollution Control Areas (Sec. 19)

1. The State Government may declare in the prescribed manner any area or areas within the State as air pollution control area or areas for the purpose of this Act.

2. The State Government may, after consultation with the State Board, by notification in the Official Gazette:

   (a) alter any air pollution control area whether by way of extension or reduction;

   (b) declare a new air pollution control area in which may be merged one or more existing air pollution areas or any part or parts thereof.

3. If the State Government, after consultation with State Board, is of opinion that the use of any fuel, other than an approved fuel, in any air pollution control area or part thereof may cause or is likely to cause air pollution, it may prohibit the use of such fuel in such an area or part thereof.

4. The State Government may direct that no appliance, other than an approved appliance shall be used in the premises situated in air pollution control area with effect from the specified date therein.

   However, different dates may be specified for different parts of an air pollution control area or for the use of different appliances.

5. If the State Government, after consultation with the State Board is of opinion that the burning of any material (not being fuel) in any air pollution control area or part thereof may cause or is likely to cause air pollution, it may prohibit the burning of the material in such areas or part thereof.

Power to Give Instructions for Ensuring Standards for Emission from Automobiles (Sec. 20)

With a view to ensuring the standards for emission of air pollution from automobiles are complied with, the State Government shall, in consultation with the State Board, give necessary instructions to the concerned authority. Such as authority shall be bound to comply with the instructions.

Restrictions on Use of Certain Industrial Plants (Sec. 21)

1. No person shall, without the previous consent of the State Board, operate any industrial plant for the purpose of any industry specified in an air pollution control area.

2. An application for consent shall be made in the prescribed form.

3. The State Board may make the necessary inquiry in respect of the application for consent.

4. Within a period of four months after the receipt of the application for consent, the State Board shall either grant or refuse the consent applied for. The order with the reason for it shall be in writing.

5. Every person to whom consent has been granted by the State Board shall comply with the following conditions. They are:

     (i) the control equipment of such specifications as the State Board may approve in this behalf shall be installed and operated in the premises if the industry is carried on or proposed to be carried on;

    (ii) the existing control equipment, if any shall be altered or replaced as per the directions of the State Board;

   (iii) the control equipment referred above shall be kept at all times in good running condition;

    (iv) chimney, wherever necessary, of such specification as the State Board may approve in this behalf shall be erected or re-erected in such premises;

     (v) such other conditions as the State Board may specify in this behalf; and,

    (vi) the conditions referred above shall be complied with within a specified period.

   In the case of a person operating any said industrial plant in an air pollution control area immediately before the date of declaration of such area as an air pollution control area, the period so specified shall not be less than six months.

   However, no control equipment or chimney shall be altered or replaced or as the case may be, erected or re-erected except with the previous approval of the State Board:

    (a) after the installation of any control equipment as per the specifications under clause (i), or

(b) after the alteration or replacement of any control equipment as per the directions of the State Board under clause (ii), or

(c) after the erection or re-erection of any chimney under clause (iv).

6. If the State Board desires to vary all or any of the conditions referred above on account of technological improvement or otherwise, it shall, after giving the person to whom consent has been granted an opportunity of being heard, vary all or any such conditions. Such a person shall thereupon be bound to comply with the conditions so varied.

7. Where a person to whom consent has been granted transfers his interest in the industry to any other person, such consent shall be deemed to have been granted to such other person. He shall, therefore, be bound to comply with all the conditions subject to which it was granted as if the consent was granted to him originally.

Person Carrying on Industry, etc. Not to Allow Emission of Air Pollutants in Excess of the Standards Laid Down by State Board (Sec. 22)

No person carrying on any industry specified in the schedule or operating any industrial plant, in any air pollution control area shall discharge or cause or permit to be discharged the discharge of any air pollutant in excess of the standards laid down by the State Board.

Furnishing of Information to State Board and Other Agencies in Certain Cases (Sec. 23)

1. Where in any air pollution control area, the emission of any air pollution into the atmosphere in excess of the standards occurs, the person-in-charge of the premises from where such emission occurs shall forthwith intimate it to State Board and to the prescribed authorities or agencies.

2. On receipt of the above information, the State Board and the authorities or agencies shall, as early as practicable, cause such remedial measures to be taken as are necessary to mitigate the emission of such air pollutants.

3. Expenses, if any, incurred together with interest (from the date when a demand for the expenses is made until it is paid)

may be recovered from the person concerned, as arrears of land revenue, or of public demand.

Power of Entry and Inspection (Sec. 24)

1. Any person empowered by a State Board in this behalf shall have a right to enter, at all reasonable times with necessary assistance, any place: (a) for the purpose of performing any of the functions of the State Board entrusted to him; (b) for the purpose of determining whether and if so in what manner, any such functions are to be performed; (c) for the purpose of examining and testing any control equipment, industrial plant, record, register, document or any other material object.

2. Every person carrying on any specified industry and every person operating any control equipment or any industrial plant, in any air pollution control area shall be bound to render all assistance to the person empowered by the State Board. If he fails to do so without any reasonable cause or excuse, he shall be guilty of an offence under this Act.

3. If any person wilfully obstructs an authority of the State Board in the discharge of his duties, he shall be guilty of an offence under this Act.

4. The provisions of Criminal Procedure Code shall apply to any search or seizure under this Section.

Power to Obtain Information (Sec. 25)

For the purpose of carrying out the functions entrusted to it, the State Board or any officer empowered by it in that behalf may call for any information from the occupier or any other person carrying on any industry or operating any control equipment or industrial plant.

Power to Take Samples of Air or Emission and Procedure to be Followed in Connection Therewith (Sec. 26)

1. A State Board or any other officer empowered by it in this behalf shall have power to take, for the purpose of analysis, samples of air or emission from any chimney, flue or duct or any other outlet in the prescribed manner.

2. The result of any such analysis shall not be admissible in evidence in any legal proceeding unless the following provisions are complied with.

3. When a sample of emission is taken for analysis, the person taking the sample shall: (a) serve on the occupier or his agent a notice, then and there, in the prescribed form, of his intention to have it so analysed, (b) in the presence of the occupier or his agent, collect a sample of emission for analysis, (c) cause the sample to be placed in a container or containers. It shall be marked, sealed and signed both by the person taking the sample and the occupier or his agent, (d) send, without delay, the container to the laboratory established or recognised by the State Board.

4. When a sample of emission is taken for analysis and the person taking the sample serves on the occupier or his agent, a notice, then:

   (a) in a case where the occupier or his agent wilfully absents himself, the person taking the sample shall collect the sample of emission for analysis to be placed in a container or containers. It shall be marked, sealed and signed by the person taking the sample, and

   (b) in a case where the occupier or his agent is present at the time of taking the sample but refuses to sign the marked and sealed container of the sample of omission as required, it shall be signed by the person taking the sample. Then, it shall be sent without delay by the person taking the sample for analysis to the laboratory established or specified. Such person shall inform the Government Analyst in writing about the wilful absence of the occupier or the agent, or as the case may be, his refusal to sign the container.

Reports of The Result of Analysis Taken Under Sec. 26 (Sec. 27)

1. Where a sample of emission has been sent for analysis to the laboratory established or recognised by the State Board, the Board analyst shall analyse the sample. A report of such analysis shall be submitted in the prescribed form in triplicate to the State Board.

2. On receipt of the report, one copy of the report shall be sent by the State Board to the occupier or his agent. Another copy shall be preserved for production before the court in case any legal proceedings are taken against him. The other copy shall be kept by the State Board.

3. Where a sample has been sent for analysis to any laboratory mentioned, the Government analyst shall analyse the sample. The result of the analysis shall be submitted to the State Board in the prescribed form in triplicate which shall comply with the provision of Subsection (2).

4. Any cost incurred in getting any sample analysed at the request of the occupier or his agent or when he wilfully absents himself or refuses to sign the marked and sealed container of sample of emission, shall be payable by such occupier or his agent. In the case of default the same shall be recoverable from him as arrears of land revenue or of public demand.

State Air Laboratory (Sec. 28)

1. The State Government may, by notification in the Official Gazette: (a) establish one or more State Air Laboratory; or (b) specify one or more laboratories or institutes as State Air Laboratories to carry out the functions entrusted to the State Air Laboratory.

2. The State Government may after consultation with the State Board, make rules prescribing:

   (a) the functions of the State Air Laboratory.

   (b) the procedure for the submission to the said laboratory of samples of air or emission for analysis or tests, the form of the Laboratory's report thereon and the fees payable in respect of such report.

   (c) such other matters as may be necessary or expedient to enable that Laboratory to carry out its functions.

Analysis (Sec. 29)

1. The State Government may by notification, appoint such persons as it thinks fit and having the prescribed qualifications to be Government Analysts for the purpose of analysis of samples of air or emission sent for analysis to any laboratory.

2. The State Board may appoint such persons as it thinks fit and having the prescribed qualifications to be Board analysts for the purpose of analysis of samples of air or emission sent for analysis to any laboratory. This appointment shall be by notification and with the approval of the State Government.

Reports of the Analysis (Sec. 30)

Any document purporting to be a report signed by a Government analyst or, as the case may be, a State Board analyst may be used as evidence of the facts stated therein in any proceeding under this Act.

Appeals (Sec. 31)

1. Any person aggrieved by an order made by the State Board may prefer and appeal to the appellate authority. This appeal shall be made within thirty days from the date on which the order is communicated to him. However, the appellate authority may entertain the appeal after the expiry of the said period of thirty days if such authority is satisfied with the cause of delay.

2. The appellate authority shall consist of a single person or three persons as the State Government may think fit.

3. The form and the manner in which an appeal may be preferred, the fees payable for such appeal and the procedure to be followed by the appellate authority shall be such as may be prescribed.

4. On receipt of an appeal preferred, the appellate authority shall, after giving the appellant and the State Board an opportunity of being heard, dispose of the appeal as expeditiously as possible.

SOUND POLLUTION

Sound pollution falls within the purview of the Air (Prevention and Control of Pollution) Act (14 of 1981).

Sound or noise is a nuisance and the same will pollute the environment. High frequency sound is a health hazard causing serious physical and mental ailments. It is an intolerable nuisance infringing the civil and constitutional right of the people as it endangers or impairs the fundamental right to have the enjoyment of quality of life and living guaranteed by our constitution. Therefore, the people are entitled to have a sound-free environment to lead a peaceful and decent life.

Where the sound produced from the functioning of an industrial undertaking, factories, machineries, equipment and any other devices including mikes and amplifiers are beyond the permissible or tolerable limits, it can be prevented by invoking the provisions of Pollution Control Act and the Municipal Laws. The District

Magistrate has the power to make appropriate action for ensuring noise-free atmosphere. However, the nature of restriction on sound will vary from place to place regarding the importance of the place, density of population, industries, social, educational, cultural and political background or people, policy of Government, and so on.

As per Sec. 440 of the Kerala Municipalities Act, 1994, the Local Administration has the power to take appropriate measures for abating the nuisance arising out of sound or noise.

Power of Secretary to Issue Directions to Abate Nuisances (Sec. 440)

1. Where the Secretary is satisfied that any act or omission, place or thing which causes or is likely to cause injury, danger, annoyance, disturbance or offence to sense of sight, smell or hearing or the rest or sleep which is or may be dangerous to life or injurious to health or property of any person or persons, he may issue such direction to such person at whose instance, he has reason to believe that such nuisance is caused or such act or omission is likely to be caused and take all steps as may be required to abate the said nuisance within such time as may be specified in the notice which shall not exceed forty-eight hours.

2. Any person to whom a direction has been issued under Subsection (1) shall be bound to comply with such direction within such time as may be specified there in and any person failing to comply with the direction shall be liable to prosecution.

   The corresponding Section in the Kerala Municipalities Act, 1960 (which is replaced by the above said new Act) is Sec. 286.

REVIEW QUESTIONS

1. Explain the objects of the Water (Prevention and Control of Pollution) Act, 1974.

2. Define the following terms as stated in the Water (Prevention and Control of Pollution) Act, 1974.

   Occupier, Pollution, Sewage effluent, Stream, Trade effluent, Central Board, State Board.

3. Discuss briefly the provisions under the Water (Prevention and Control of Pollution) Act, 1974 for the prevention and control of water pollution.

4. What are the powers of the State Board to take samples of effluents and the procedure to be followed in connection therewith under the Water (Prevention and Control of Pollution) Act, 1974?

5. What are the prohibitions on use of streams or well for disposal of polluting matter under the Water (Prevention and Control of Pollution) Act, 1974?

6. Discuss the objects and reasons of the Air (Prevention and Control of Pollution) Act, 1981.

7. Define the following terms as stated in the Air (Prevention and Control of Pollution) Act, 1981.

   (i) Air pollutant   (ii) Air pollution
   (iii) Emission   (iv) Occupier
   (v) Industrial plant   (vi) State Board
   (vii) Control equipment   (viii) Central Board

8. What are the powers of the State Government to declare air pollution control areas?

9. What are the powers of the State Board to take samples of air or emission and the procedure to be followed in connection therewith?

10. Explain briefly the provisions under the Air (Prevention and Control of Pollution) Act, 1981 for the prevention and control of air pollution.

11. Discuss the provisions under the Kerala Municipalities Act, 1994 for the prevention and control of sound pollution.

55

Corporate Governance

Corporate governance is "the conduct of business in accordance with shareholders' desires, which is to make as much money as possible, while conforming to the basic rules of the society embodied in law and local customs".
— *Milton Friedman*

INTRODUCTION

The term 'governance' is derived from the Latin word 'gubernare' which means 'to steer'. Governance is, thus, about governing or steering. It is a degree of control to be exercised by key stakeholders' representatives.

The concept of corporate governance emerges as a result of an international effort to promote transparency, integrity and the rule of law. It is, therefore, a well-recognised phenomenon in the competitive business environment. Good governance, however, implies that the institution is run for the optimal benefit of the stakeholders in it. Business ethics, accountability to stakeholders, social responsibility, transparency and full disclosure are some of the ingredients of good governance. In short, maximisation of shareholders wealth is the cornerstone of good governance.

CORPORATE GOVERNANCE—MEANING

Corporate governance is the way in which corporate bodies are governed or managed. In other words, it is a process or set of systems to ensure that a company is managed to suit the best interest of all stakeholders. It is an interplay between company's shareholders, creditors, capital markets, financial sectors, institutions and law.

Definition

A corporate governance is "a conscious, deliberate and sustained efforts on the part of corporate entity to strike a judicious balance between its own interest and the interest of various constituents on the environment in which it is operating".

624

Adrian Cadbury in U.K. emphasises "Corporate governance basically, has to do with power and accountability: who exercise power, on behalf of whom, and how the exercise of power is controlled."

In practice, Corporate Governance (CG) means the role of the board of directors of the company and its auditors, towards protecting the shareholders interest in every business decisions.

Thus, the following are the basic ingredients of CG:

(i) Accountability of Board of Directors to ultimate owners.

(ii) Clarity in responsibilities of directors, chairman and managing director through empowerment to improve accountability.

(iii) Transparency in timely disclosures of right information with integrity.

(iv) Quality and competence of directors and their track record.

(v) Conforming to laws, rules and spirit of codes.

Importance of Corporate Governance

The importance of corporate governance lies in its contribution to business world. In short, corporate governance is important on account of the following reasons:

(i) *Framework for creating accountability:* Corporate governance ensures accountability. Its principles lay down the framework for creating accountability between companies and external investors.

(ii) *Better direction and control:* The principles of corporate governance helps in providing better direction and control of corporate bodies.

(iii) *Monitoring of risk:* Corporate governance helps in monitoring of risk that a firm faces globally through rationalised management.

(iv) *Strategic thinking:* Corporate governance helps to improve strategic thinking at the top. This is done by inducting independent directors having experience and new ideas.

(v) *Attracting local investors:* The principles of corporate governance helps in attracting local investors and broadening local markets.

(vi) *Avoiding fraud:* Corporate governance avoids fraud and company failures. It, in turn helps in facilitating further progress of corporate economy.

(vii) *Developing retail investors:* Good governance helps in developing retail investors, banks, mutual funds and other institutional investors.

(viii) *Limiting the liability:* Corporate governance helps in limiting the liability of top management and directors by articulating the decision-making process.

(ix) *Foundation for future progress:* The corporate governance lays the foundation for future progress of business.

(x) *Long-term reputation:* A firm which keeps proper rules and procedures in the governance process creates a reputation that other firms cannot acquire.

Background

The expression corporate governance is relatively new. It had its origin in United Kingdom. It subsequently spreads to other countries. First, this expression appeared in 1983 as the title of an article 'Perspectives on Management'. However, the seeds of modern corporate governance are sown by the Watergate Scandal in the United States.

Although, the expression corporate governance evolved in eighties, it did not get the deserved attention from the corporate world. But it caught the public attention only after the release of the Cadbury Report in 1992.

Cadbury Committee

The Cadbury Committee on Financial Aspects of Corporate Governance was set up by the Financial Reporting Council of U.K. in 1992. It was chaired by Sir Adrian Cadbury. It issued its report in December, 1992. The report sought more transparency and accountability in company management with the following guidelines:

(i) Audit committee comprising a minimum three members, should have written terms of reference and authority to investigate.

(ii) Listed companies should publish full financial statements annually and half yearly reports interim.

The report had also attached a code of best practice with the following guidelines for corporate behaviour and disclosure.

(i) Board should present assessment of company's position.

(ii) Directors should report on effectiveness of internal control systems.

The report of the Cadbury Committee led to wide discussion across the globe. As a result of it, countries like France, Canada, Australia, South Africa and so on have appointed committees.

Greenbury Committee

Greenbury Committee of director's remuneration was set up under the Chairmanship of Sir Richard Greenbury in 1995. It submitted its report in July 1995 and amended the section within the Cadbury report concerning executive pay. The following are the main recommendations of the committee.

(i) Appointing of a remuneration committee to determine directors remuneration.

(ii) Appointing a nomination committee to oversee new appointments to the Board.

Organisation for Economic Co-operation and Development (OECD) Guidelines

Organisation for Economic Co-operation and Development (OECD) conducted a study on corporate governance in 1998. The study group had representation from U.S., Britain, France, Germany and Japan. As a result of the study, OECD proposed the development of global guidelines on corporate governance. Such guidelines ultimately helped to establish certain core principles of corporate governance.

Hampel Committee

The Hampel Committee on audit and accountability was set up in U.K. in 1998. The committee was named after Sir Ronald Hampel. It reviewed and consolidated the recommendations of the Cadbury and Greenbury Reports. It made recommendations on creating a 'Combined Code' and improving communication with shareholders. The committee, also recommended allowing companies to find their own ways of applying corporate governance principles.

Blue Ribbon Committee

Blue Ribbon Committee on improving the effectiveness of corporate audit committees was appointed in 1999. The committee provides the following guidelines:

(i) Members of Audit Committee should be independent.

(ii) Audit Committee should comprise independent directors only.

(iii) Audit Committee should have a minimum of three directors.

(iv) Audit Committee should have formal written charter approved by the Board.

(v) Charter should specify auditor's responsibility towards Board and Committee.

Apart from the above guidelines, the companies should attach with Annual Report a letter from Audit Committee as to whether or not:

(a) management reviewed the audited financial statement with the committee;

(b) outside auditors discussed with the committee, their judgements;

(c) the company's financial statements are fairly presented in conformity with Generally Accepted Accounting Practices (GAAP)

Comprehensive Code

Derek Higgs was appointed to draw a single comprehensive code on corporate governance in 2002. It issued its report in 2003 and passed the same to the Financial Reporting Council (FRC). The Financial Reporting Council drafted the code in 2003. This code with minor changes is still in force in U.K.

CORPORATE GOVERNANCE IN INDIA

India has undergone the bitter experiences of corporate frauds. These are the unethical stock market transactions of Harshad Mehta and the recent experience of the fraud by the CEO of Satyam Computers. Such events bring out the need for corporate governance.

The Confederation of Indian Industry (The first institution in Indian Industry) has made a special interest on corporate governance. Henceforth the Securities Exchange Board of India set up a committee under the Chairmanship of Kumar Mangalam Birla for promoting and raising standards of Corporate Governance.

The following are the significant developments in the area of corporate governance in India.

CII (Rahul Bajaj) Committee (1996)

The Confederation of Indian Industries (CII) is the torch bearers of corporate governance in India. CII, the largest industry and business organisation in India, set up a task force on corporate governance under the Chairmanship of Rahul Bajaj. The task force published its finding in April 1977 and placed the same for wider discussion. As a result of it, Desirable Corporate Governance Code for listed companies originated. However, as the companies followed the Code on a voluntary basis only, it was not binding on them.

Kumar Mangalam Birla Committee by SEBI (2000)

SEBI has constituted a committee under the Chairmanship of Kumar Managalam Birla. Its object is to promote and raise standards of corporate governance. The following are the main recommendations of the committee:

(i) It is the responsibility of the Board to set up qualified and independent audit committee.

(ii) A company is required to provide consolidated statements of its subsidiaries.

(iii) Shareholders should show greater interest in the appointment of directors and auditors.

However, Clause 49 of the 'Listing Agreement' contains many of its recommendations.

Companies (Amendment) Act, 2000

The main purpose of this Amendment is "to provide certain measures for better corporate governance and increased protection of the interests of smaller investors". With this end in view, provisions are made in the Amendment to set up Audit Committees, Secretarial Audit, Directors' Responsibility Statement in the Directors' Report, Postal Ballot and so on.

Naresh Chandra Committee (2002)

A committee on Corporate Governance has been set up under the Chairmanship of Naresh Chandra. Its object is to examine various corporate governance issues and suggest changes, if necessary. The following are the main recommendations of the committee:

(i) There is no requirement of the rotation of audit firm.

(ii) The rotation of audit partner should be made in every five years.

(iii) Audit Committee should be set up with independent directors.

(iv) Companies should have at least 50 per cent independent directors.

(v) Auditors should not undertake any professional assignments.

(vi) Some of such recommendations were incorporated into the Companies (Amendment) Bill, 2003.

N.R. Narayana Murthy Committee (2003)

SEBI has constituted a committee on Corporate Governance under the Chairmanship of N.R. Narayana Murthy. The committee consists of representatives from the stock exchanges, chamber of commerce and industry, investors associations and professionals. Several recommendations relating to audit, risk management, directorships, financial disclosures, independent directors and so on have been made by the committee.

On the basis of the above recommendations, SEBI has revised Clause 49 of the Listing Agreement. However, the revised guidelines are in force w.e.f. 29th October, 2004.

Listing Agreement

A company is required to enter into an agreement with the stock exchanges for permitting its shares to be listed in the stock exchanges. This agreement is termed as listing agreement. Such an agreement contains the principles of corporate governance. All listed companies with a paid-up capital of Rupees three crore and above or net worth of Rupees twenty five crore or more (at any time in the history of the company) are required to bind these principles.

Revised Clause of the Listing Agreement (2004)

A major step in the area of Corporate Governance in India is Clause 49 prepared by SEBI. The following are its detailed provisions:

Companies Bill, 2008

The Companies Bill, 2008 attempts to provide less government intervention. Thus, government control over internal corporate processes is likely to go down. The Bill also tries to protect the rights of minority shareholders and provide adequate provisions for disclosure.

SEBI Committee on Disclosures and Accounting Standards

On account of the recent events in Satyam Computers, it is found that the measures of corporate governance have not proved the desired impact in India so far. Thus, SEBI has immediately constituted a committee on Disclosures and Accounting Standards (SCODA). The committee has made a recommendation that a peer review of the working papers of auditors should be done on companies constituting the NSE and BSE Sensex. In this connection, SEBI is required to prepare a panel of auditors.

PRINCIPLES OF CORPORATE GOVERNANCE

Several principles have been identified as a result of the series of corporate collapses. The following are some of such principles:

(i) *Accountability:* Accountability of Board of Directors and their constituent responsibilities to the ultimate owners.

(ii) *Transparency:* A key element of good governance is transparency. It is a shared way of corporate functioning and not a set of rules. Transparency, in turn requires the right to information, timeliness and integrity of the information produced.

(iii) *System of check and balance:* There should be a system of checks and balances and greater simplicity in the process of governance.

(iv) *Resourceful Board:* The Board requires enough skills to deal with various business issues. It should have the ability to review and challenge management performance.

(v) *Clarity of responsibility:* There should be a clarity of responsibility to enhance accountability.

(vi) *Adherence to the rules:* Corporate actions should conform to letter and spirit to codes.

CORPORATE GOVERNANCE—RECENT INTEREST

The following are some reasons for recent awareness in corporate governance:

(i) *Directors position:* Directors should realise that their job is to represent the shareholders and other stakeholders.

(ii) *Safeguarding investors:* At present, there is a rise of institutional investors. Thus, an awareness of corporate governance is the need of the hour to safeguard the interest of institutional investors.

(iii) *Takeovers:*   Another reason for the recent interest in corporate governance is the takeover moves in world in the wake of globalisation.

(iv) *Accountability:*   Doing corporate governance with power and accountability.

(v) *Activism:*   Activism of regulatory bodies such as SEBI.

OBJECTIVES OF CORPORATE GOVERNANCE

Good governance usually ensures company's commitment to higher growth and profit. It, in turn inspires and strengthens investors confidence. Thus, the following are the main objectives of corporate governance:

(i) *Accountability:*   A properly structured Board capable of taking independent decision is in place at the helm of affairs. Such a Board is accountable for attaining the set goals of the company.

(ii) *Balanced Board:*   The Board is balanced as regards the representation of adequate number of non-executive and independent directors. Such directors will take care of the interests and well-being of the stakeholders.

(iii) *Transparency:*   In a company having good governance, the Board usually adopts transparent procedures and arrives at decisions on the strength of adequate information.

(iv) *Concerns of stakeholders:*   The Board has an adequate machinery to sub serve the concerns of stakeholders.

(v) *Informed shareholders:*   The Board keeps the shareholders informed of relevant development while implementing the programmes.

(vi) *Monitoring:*   The Board regularly monitors the functioning of the management team.

(vii) *Controlling:*   The Board should control the affairs of the company at all times.

STATUTORY MEASURES

The corporate governance framework in India mainly comprises the following legislations and regulations:

(i) *The Companies Act, 1956:*   The companies in India are mainly governed by the provisions of the Companies Act, 1956. The Act deals with the rules and procedures in respect of:

(a) Incorporation of companies; (b) Prospectus and allotment of shares and debenture; (c) Management and administration of companies; (d) Maintenance of accounts; (e) Annual returns; (f) Shareholders' meetings and proceedings; (g) Board of Directors; (h) Prevention of oppression and mismanagement; and (i) Power of investigation into the affairs of company.

(ii) *The Securities Contracts (Regulation Act), 1956:* The Securities Contracts (Regulation Act), 1956 relates to the functioning of stock exchanges. It also pertains to the rules in respect of various types of tradeable securities such as shares, stocks, bonds and so on issued by the companies.

(iii) *The Securities and Exchange Board of India Act, 1992:* An independent capital market authority known as SEBI, has been set up under the Securities and Exchange Board of India Act. The purpose of SEBI is to regulate the securities market and protect the interest of investors.

(iv) *The Depositories Act, 1996:* This Act has created the legal framework for dematerialisation of securities and established share and securities depositories.

(v) *Listing Agreement with Stock Exchanges:* Clause 49 is the unique and key element of the listing agreement. This clause contains the corporate governance practices to be followed by the listed companies.

Apart from the above legislations, Competition Act, 2002, Foreign Exchange Management Act, 1999, Industries (Development and Regulation) Act, 1951 and so on also have a direct impact on company administration.

CONSTITUENTS OF CORPORATE GOVERNANCE

The following are the three main elements of corporate governance:

(i) *Board of Directors:* The Board is the heart and soul of a company. It performs the pivotal role in the system of corporate governance. It is accountable to the stakeholders and directs the management. The Board sets strategic aims and leads the company in a transparent manner. It is the bounden duty of the Board to submit periodical report to the stakeholders regarding the activities and progress of the company.

(ii) *Shareholders:* The shareholders are the owners of the company. They are required to appoint the directors and auditors of the company. They have to hold the Board accountable for the proper governance of the company by requiring the Board to supply them requisite information periodically.

(iii) *Management:* The management is responsible to undertake the governance of the company in time with the directions given by the Board. It should provide adequate and timely information to the Board and put in place adequate control systems.

SEBI REGULATION—CLAUSE 49 OF LISTING AGREEMENT

The Security and Exchange Board of India (SEBI) was constituted through an Act known as SEBI Act which came into force on the 30th day of January, 1992. The objectives of this Act are:

(i) to protect the interest of the investors, (ii) to regulate the security market, (iii) to promote the development of the securities market, and (iv) to protect investors against unfair and fraudulent trade practices.

SEBI REGULATIONS

In order to regulate the operations of the players of the capital market, SEBI has formulated various rules and regulations. All such rules and regulations help in corporate governance by:

(i) providing greater information to the investors, (ii) curbing insider trading and manipulations, (iii) ensuring transparency and fair play, integrity and confidence of the investors, (iv) ensuring equality of treatment and opportunities to minority shareholders, (v) providing investors with more effective means of redress in the case of abuse, (vi) preventing the actions which do not respect the interest of the shareholders, and (vii) ensuring greater transparency in the market for corporate control.

Guidelines Issued by SEBI

SEBI has issued various guidelines for strengthening corporate governance. In accordance with such guidelines, all corporate entities shall:

(i) strengthen the disclosure norms for Initial Public Offers (IPOs), (ii) provide information in Directors Report for utilisation of funds, (iii) declare quarterly results, (iv) facilitate mandatory appointment of compliance officer for monitoring the share transfer process and ensuring compliance with various rules and regulations, (v) disclose all material and price sensitive information, (vi) dispatch one copy of abridged Balance Sheet to all shareholders, and complete Balance Sheet to every household, (vii) issue guidelines for preferential allotment at market related prices, and (viii) issue regulations for takeovers and substantial acquisitions.

CLAUSE 49

The major mechanism for regulating corporate governance is through Clause 49. When a company wants to list its shares in the stock exchange, it has to enter into an agreement with SEBI. This agreement contains certain specific clauses mentioned in Clause 49. This makes the principles of corporate governance complying on listed companies.

Mandatory Requirements

The corporate governance principles included in Clause 49 are a set of mandatory and non-mandatory requirements. Companies have no choice on mandatory requirements, but to comply with them. Such requirements are discussed under the following heads:

(1) Board of Directors; (2) Audit Committee; (3) Subsidiary Companies; (4) Disclosures; (5) CEO/CFO Certification; (6) Corporate Governance Report; and (7) Compliance.

1. *Board of Directors:* In accordance with the Clause 49 of the listing agreement, a company should comply with the following provisions in respect of its Board of Directors.

   (i) Composition of Board of Directors. The Board of Directors of the company shall have an optimum combination of executive and non-executive directors. However, not less than fifty per cent of the Board of Directors should comprise non-executive directors. Further, it is stated that if the Chairman of the Board is a non-executive director, at least one-third of the Board should comprise independent directors. But if the Chairman is an executive director, at least half of the Board should comprise independent directors.

      The expression "independent director" means a non-executive director of the company who:

      (a) does not have any material pecuniary relationships or transaction with the company (other than receiving director's remuneration);

(b) is not related to promoters or persons occupying management positions at the board level or at one level below the board;

(c) has not been an executive of the company in the immediately preceding three financial years;

(d) is/was not a partner or an executive during the preceding three years of any of the following:

(i) the statutory audit firm or the internal audit firm that is associated with the company, and

(ii) the legal firm and consulting firms that have a material association with the company.

(e) is not a material supplier, service provider or customer or a lessor or lessee of the company which may affect the independence of the director; and

(f) is not a substantial shareholder of the company (i.e., owning two per cent or more of the block of voting shares).

Further, it is provided that nominee directors appointed by an institution which has invested in or lent to the company shall be deemed to be independent directors.

(ii) *Compensation to non-executive directors:* All fees/compensation paid to non-executive directors (including independent directors) shall be fixed by the Board of Directors. However, previous approval of shareholders is required for such a payment. But no such an approval is required to pay sitting fees to non-executive directors.

(iii) *Board procedure:* The Board shall meet at least four times a year. But the maximum time gap between two meetings shall be four months.

It is also stated that a director shall not be a member in more than ten Audit and/or Shareholders Grievance Committees across all companies in which he is a director.

Further, every director is required to inform the company (mandatory annual requirement) about the committee positions he occupies in other companies and notify the changes as and when the same takes place.

(iv) *Code of conduct:* A code of conduct for all Board members and senior management of the company shall be laid down by the Board. The same shall be posted on the website of the company.

All such members and personnel of the company shall affirm compliance with the code on an annual basis. Further, a declaration to this effect signed by the CEO shall be provided in the annual report of the company.

2. *Audit Committee*

   (i) *Qualified and Independent Audit Committe:* The norms provided for the audit committee are as follows:

      (a) The audit committee shall have minimum three directors as its members. But two-thirds of the members of such a committee shall be independent directors.

      (b) All members of audit committee shall be financially literate.* But at least one member shall have accounting or related financial management expertise.

      (c) The chairman of the audit committee shall be an independent director. He shall be present at the annual general meeting to answer shareholders queries.

      (d) The audit committee may invite the executives, as it considers appropriate to be present at the meetings of the committee.

      (e) The company secretary shall act as the secretary to the committee.

   (ii) *Meeting of Audit Committee:* The audit committee should meet at least four times in a year. But not more than four months shall elapse between two meetings. The quorum shall be either two members or one-third of the members of the audit committee whichever is higher. However, there should be a minimum of two independent members present.

   (iii) *Powers of Audit Committee:* The following are the powers of the audit committee:

      (a) It has the power to seek information from any employee.

      (b) It can investigate any activity within the terms of reference.

      (c) It has the power to obtain outside legal or other professional advice.

      (d) It can secure attendance of outsiders with relevant experts, if any.

---

* Ability to read and understand basic financial statement.

(iv) *Role of Audit Committee.* The important functions of audit committee are:

(a) to ensure the accuracy of financial statement;

(b) to recommend to the Board the appointment, re-appointment and replacement or removal of the statutory auditor;

(c) to approve payment to statutory auditors for any other services rendered by them;

(d) to review (with the management) the annual financial statements before submission to the Board for approval;

(e) to review (with the management) the performance of statutory and internal auditors and adequacy of the internal control system;

(f) to discuss with the internal auditor regarding any significant findings and follow-up thereon;

(g) to review the findings of any internal investigations by the internal auditors if there is a suspected fraud or irregularity in reporting the matter to the Board;

(h) to discuss with statutory auditors before the audit commences, about the nature and scope of audit (including post-audit) for ascertaining any area of concern;

(i) to look into the reasons for substantial defaults in the payment to stakeholders;

(j) to review the functioning of the Whistle Blower mechanism, if the same is existing; and

(k) to perform any other function as is mentioned in the terms of reference of the audit committee.

3. *Subsidiary Companies:* The following are the important rules regarding subsidiary companies:

(a) At least one independent director on the Board of Directors of the holding company shall be a director on the Board of Directors of a non-listed subsidiary company.

(b) The audit committee of listed holding company shall also review the financial statements made by the subsidiary company.

(c) The minutes of the board meeting of the unlisted subsidiary company shall be placed at the Board meeting of the listed holding company.

(d) A statement of all important transactions entered into by the unlisted subsidiary company should be brought to the attention of the Board of Directors of the listed holding company.

4. *Disclosures:* The following are the provisions regarding disclosures.

(i) *Basis of Related Party Transactions:*

(a) A statement in summary form of transactions with related parties shall be placed periodically before the audit committee.

(b) Details of material individual transactions with related parties (which are not in the normal course of business) shall be placed before the audit committee.

(ii) *Disclosure of Accounting Treatment:* If a different treatment (from that prescribed in an Accounting standard) in the preparation of financial statements has been followed, the fact shall be disclosed in the financial statements. Along with this disclosure, the management's explanation as to why it believes such an alternative treatment is more representative of the true and fair view of the underlying business transaction should be mentioned in the Corporate Governance Report.

(iii) *Board Disclosure—Risk Management:* The company shall lay down various procedures to inform Board members about risk assessment and minimisation procedures.

(iv) *Proceeds from Issues:* When a company raises money through issue of shares, it shall be disclosed to the audit committee. The uses and applications of funds (by major category) shall also be disclosed on a quarterly and annual basis.

(v) *Remuneration of Directors:*

(a) All pecuniary relationship or transactions of the non-executive directors vis-a-vis the company shall be disclosed in the annual report.

(b) Further, certain disclosures such as remuneration package of individual directors, performance-linked incentives, service contracts and stock option plan shall also be made in the section on the corporate governance of the Annual Report.

(c) The company shall publish its criteria of making payments to non-executive directors in its annual report.

(d) The company shall disclose the number of shares and convertible instruments held by non-executive directors.

(e) Persons who are proposed to be appointed as non-executive directors in a listed company (prior to their appointment) shall disclose their shareholding. Such a disclosure shall also be made in the notice to the general meeting called for appointment of such directors.

(vi) *Management:* The management shall also place a report with the Director's report on the following matters:

(a) Industry structure and developments, (b) Opportunities and threats, (c) Segment-wise or product-wise performance, (d) Outlook, (e) Risks and concerns, (f) Internal control systems and their adequacy, (g) Discussion on financial performance, and (h) Material developments in human resources/industrial relations front including number of people employed.

(vii) *Disclosures to Shareholders:*

1. In the case of appointment of a new director or re-appointment of a director, the following information should be provided to the shareholders:

   (a) A brief resume of the director.

   (b) Nature of his expertise in specific functional areas.

   (c) Names of companies in which the person also holds the directorship and the membership of committees of the Board.

   (d) Shareholding of non-executive directors.

2. A Board committee (under the chairmanship of a non-executive director) known as shareholders/investors' Grievance Committee, shall be formed to look into the redressal of shareholders and investors complaints.

3. The Board of the company shall delegate the power of share transfer to an officer or a committee or to the Registrar and share transfer agents. The purpose of such a delegation is to expedite the process of share transfer. However, the delegated authority shall attend to share transfer formalities at least once in a fortnight.

5. *CEO/CFO Certification:* The CEO is the managing director or manager appointed in terms of the Companies Act, 1956. But the CFO is the whole time finance director or any other person heading the finance function and discharging that function. The CEO/CFO shall certify to the Board that:

(a) They have reviewed financial statements and the cash flow statement for the year and that to the best of their knowledge and belief:

   (i) these statements do not contain any materially untrue statement or omit any material fact or contain statements that might be misleading.

   (ii) these statements together present a true and fair view of the company's affairs and are in compliance with existing accounting standards, applicable laws and regulations.

(b) They are to the best of their knowledge and belief, no transactions entered into by the company during the year which are fraudulent, illegal or violative of the company's code of conduct.

(c) They accept the responsibility for establishing and maintaining internal controls and that they have evaluated the effectiveness of the internal control system of the company. They should also certify that they have disclosed to the auditors and the audit committee, deficiencies in the design or operation of internal controls, if any of which they are aware and the steps they have taken or propose to take for rectifying such deficiencies.

(d) They have indicated to the auditors and the audit committee regarding:

   (i) significant changes in internal control during the year.

   (ii) significant changes in accounting policies during the year and that such changes have been disclosed in the notes to the financial statements; and

   (iii) instances of significant fraud of which they have become aware and the involvement therein, if any, of the management or an employee having a significant role in the company's internal control system.

6. *Corporate Governance Report:* A report on corporate governance should be given to the shareholders along with the annual reports. Similarly stock exchanges should also

be informed about the position of the company regarding corporate governance.

(a) *Compliance report on corporate governance in the annual report:* There shall be a separate section on corporate governance in the annual report of the company. Non-compliance of any mandatory requirement of Clause 49 should be made with reasons for the failure. Similarly, the extent to which the non-mandatory requirements have been adopted should be specifically highlighted.

(b) *Compliance report to stock exchanges:* The companies should submit a quarterly compliance report to the stock exchanges within fifteen days from the close of quarter. The report shall be signed either by the compliance officer or the chief executive officer of the company.

7. *Compliance*

(a) The company should get a certificate regarding compliance of corporate governance (as stipulated in Clause 49) from the auditors or practicing company secretary. Such a certificate shall be annexed to the director's report and also sent to the stock exchanges.

(b) The non-mandatory requirements may be implemented as per the discretion of the company.

Non-mandatory Requirements

A company may implement the non-mandatory requirements provided in the revised Clause 49 at its own discretion. The following matters deal with the non-mandatory requirements.

(i) *Chairman of the Board:* The appointment of a non-executive chairman for the Board is the first non-mandatory requirement. The requirement also suggests that the chairman's office should be maintained at the company's expense.

The non-executive chairman may be permitted to reimburse the expenses incurred in performance of his duties. Further, independent directors may have a tenure not exceeding (in the aggregate) a period of nine years on the Board of the company.

(ii) *Remuneration Committee:* The Board of Directors of the company may set up a remuneration committee. The chairman of the committee shall be an independent director. The committee may comprise at least three directors all of whom shall be non-executive directors.

The remuneration committee would determine the remuneration packages of the executive directors. All the members of the remuneration committee shall be present at the meeting. But the chairman of the committee shall be present at the Annual General Meeting to answer the shareholders' queries. However, it is up to the chairman to determine who should answer the queries.

(iii) *Shareholders Rights:* A half-yearly declaration of financial performance comprising summary of the important events in last six months may be sent to each household of shareholders.

(iv) *Audit Qualifications:* Company may move towards a regime of unqualified financial statements.

(v) *Training of Board Members:* A company may train its Board members in respect of the following:

   (a) The business model of the company.

   (b) The risk profile of the business parameters of the company.

   (c) The responsibilities of the members as directors; and

   (d) The best ways to discharge the responsibilities.

(vi) *Mechanism for Evaluating Non-executive Board Members:* A peer group comprising the entire Board of Directors (excluding the director being evaluated) shall do the performance evaluation of non-executive directors. The question of whether the terms of appointment of the non-executive directors shall extend/continue shall also be determined by the same method of Peer Group evaluation.

(vii) *Whistle Blower Policy:* 'Blowing the whistle' is an English expression. It is used in informal contexts to mean some act to make somebody stop doing something (illegal) usually by informing people in authority.

Whistle blowing is an act of disclosing information in the public interest. This term is used in a context where an employee makes a disclosure about any violation of laws, wastage of funds, mismanagement by the company. The employee who makes such a disclosure is at a great risk from the management of the company. Hence, there shall be specific provisions for the protection of whistle blowers.

In India, the Law Commission (in its 179th report in 2001) recommended for the necessity of law on whistle blowing. In spite of the Law Commission's recommendation for a comprehensive legislation, no such a legislation has been made in India so far.

POSTAL BALLOT [SEC. 192(A)]

Sec. 192(A) of the Companies (Amendment) Act, 2000 has made a provision for postal ballots in the case of listed public limited companies. Such companies may pass resolutions by postal ballot (instead of transacting business in general meeting) relating to such matters as the Central Government may, by notification, declare to be conducted only by postal ballot. According to the Companies (Passing of Resolutions by Postal Ballot) Rules 2001, certain crucial matters like alteration of the object clause of memorandum, buy back of own shares by the company, etc., are expected to take decisions only by resolutions passed through postal ballot.

Where a company determines to pass any resolution by postal ballot, it shall send a notice to all the shareholders with a draft resolution explaining the reasons thereof. The company shall also request the shareholders to send their assent or dissent to the resolution in writing on a postal ballot within a period of thirty days from the date of posting of the letter.

The notice shall be sent by registered post acknowledgement due (or any other mode as may be prescribed by the Central Government in this behalf) and shall include with the notice, a postage pre-paid envelope to facilitate the assent or dissent of the shareholder.

Where a resolution is assented to by a requisite majority of the shareholders (by means of postal ballot), it shall be deemed to have been duly passed at a general meeting.

The Section also provides that 'postal ballot', includes voting by electronic mode. If anybody fraudulently defaces or destroys the ballot paper or declaration of identity of the shareholder, such a person shall be punishable with imprisonment up to six months or fine or both.

When a default is made in complying with this Section, the company and every officer of the company in default shall be punishable with a fine which may extend to Rupees fifty thousand in respect of each such default.

In the context of corporate governance, the provision for postal ballot is very much pertinent. In the case of postal ballot, any shareholder who is interested in an issue can cast his votes very easily from the comfort of his house.

AUDIT COMMITTEE (PROVISIONS UNDER SECTION 292(A) OF COMPANIES ACT)

Sec. 292(A) of the Companies (Amendment) Act, 2000 deals with the audit of public companies having a paid-up capital of not less than five crore. As per this Sec. such companies are required to constitute an 'Audit Committee' comprising Board of Directors. This committee shall comprise not less than three directors and such a number of other directors as the Board may decide. But two-thirds of the total number of members shall be directors other than managing or whole-time directors. The chairman of the committee can be selected from among the committee itself. However, the mode of the composition of the committee should be disclosed in the annual report of the company.

The auditors of the company, the internal auditor (if any) and the director in-charge of finance should attend and participate at the Audit Committee meeting, but such participants shall have no right to vote.

Powers and Duties of the Audit Committee

The following are the powers and duties of audit committee:

(i) It should act in accordance with the terms of reference specified in writing by the Board.

(ii) It should periodically discuss the following matters with the auditors.

(a) Internal control systems.

(b) The scope of audit including the observations of the auditors.

(c) Review of financial statements (half-yearly and annual) before submitting to the Board, and

(d) Ensuring the compliance of internal control systems.

(iii) It has the authority to investigate any matter specified in Sec. 292(A) or referred to it by the Board.

(iv) The recommendations of the Audit Committee shall be binding on the Board. In case the Board does not bind the Audit Committee's recommendations, it shall mention the reasons for the non-binding. Further, the Board shall also communicate such reasons to the shareholders.

(v) The chairman of Audit Committee should attend the annual general meetings of the company and provide clarifications on matters relating to audit.

Penalty

Every officer who does not comply with the provisions of Sec. 292(A) of the company shall be punishable with imprisonment up to one year or fine up to Rupees fifty thousand or both.

BENEFITS OF CORPORATE GOVERNANCE

"Corporate Governance" is an important concept of lasting value. It is unique in achieving corporate excellence. It contributes towards the efficiency of the company in particular and progress of a country's economy in general. Thus, the following are the main benefits of corporate governance:

(i) *Attracting long-term capital:* Usually, the confidence of investors depends on the ethical conduct of a corporation. Thus, a corporation having credibility offered by corporate governance creates confidence in investors. This in turn, will attract more long-term capital.

(ii) *Attracting talents:* A corporation which demonstrates good governance can attract and retain the best human capital from various parts of the world.

(iii) *Investor's preference:* Usually, well managed companies remain accountable to the shareholders. Such companies also provide sufficient freedom to the Board to make various decisions. Thus, investors prefer well managed companies to others.

(iv) *Co-operation of stakeholders:* The growth of a corporation mainly depends on the co-operation of its stakeholders like customers, employees, investors, government and society at large. When a corporation maintains fair policy in all its dealings, the co-operation of its stakeholders is best assured.

(v) *Building confidence:* Good corporate governance helps in building confidence among stakeholders as well as prospective stakeholders.

(vi) *Reducing risk:* Good governance generally reduces perceived risk. This will in turn, reduce cost of capital.

LIST OF ITEMS TO BE INCLUDED IN THE REPORT OF CORPORATE GOVERNANCE

1. A brief statement on company's philosophy on code of governance.

2. Board of Directors
   (i) Composition and category of directors, for instance, promoter, executive, non-executive, independent non-executive, nominee director, which the institution represented as lender or as equity investor.

(ii) Attendance of each director at the Board meetings and the last AGM.

(iii) Number of other Boards or Board Committees in which he/she is a member or chairperson.

(iv) Number of Board meetings held, dates on which held.

3. Audit Committee

   (i) Brief description of terms of reference.

   (ii) Composition, names of members and Chairperson.

   (iii) Meetings and attendance during the year.

4. Remuneration Committee

   (i) Brief description of terms of reference.

   (ii) Composition, names of members and Chairperson.

   (iii) Attendance during the year.

   (iv) Remuneration policy.

   (v) Details of remuneration to all the directors as per format in the main report.

5. Shareholders' Committee

   (i) Name of non-executive director heading the committee.

   (ii) Name and designation of compliance officer.

   (iii) Number of shareholders' complaints received so far.

   (iv) Number not solved to the satisfaction of shareholders.

   (v) Number of pending complaints.

6. General Body Meetings

   (i) Location and time, where last three AGMs held.

   (ii) Whether any special resolution passed in the previous three AGMs.

   (iii) Whether any special resolution passed last year through postal ballot details of voting pattern.

   (iv) Persons who conducted the postal ballot exercise.

   (v) Whether any special resolution is proposed to be conducted through postal ballot.

   (vi) Procedure for postal ballot.

7. Disclosures

   (i) Disclosures on materially related party transactions that may have potential conflict with the interests of company at large.

   (ii) Details of non-compliance by the company and penalties

imposed on the company by stock exchange or SEBI or any statutory authority, on any matter related to capital markets, during the last three years.

(iii) Whistle Blower policy and affirmation that no personnel has been denied access to the audit committee.

(iv) Details of compliance with mandatory requirements and adoption of the non-mandatory requirements of this clause.

8. Means of Communication

(i) Quarterly results.

(ii) Newspapers wherein results are normally published.

(iii) Any website, where displayed.

(iv) Whether it also displays official news releases.

(v) The presentations made to the institutional investors or to the analysts.

9. General Shareholder Information

(i) AGM: date, time and venue.

(ii) Financial year.

(iii) Date of book closure.

(iv) Dividend payment date.

(v) Listing on stock exchanges.

(vi) Stock code

(vii) Market price data; high, low during each month in last financial year.

(viii) Performance in comparison to broad-based indices such as BSE Sensex, CRISIL index, etc.

(ix) Registrar and transfer agents.

(x) Share transfer system.

(xi) Distribution of shareholding.

(xii) Dematerialisation of shares and liquidity.

(xiii) Outstanding GDRs/ADRs/Warrants or any convertible instruments, conversion date and likely impact on equity.

(xiv) Plant location.

(xv) Address of correspondence.

INFORMATION TO BE PLACED BEFORE BOARD OF DIRECTORS

(i) Annual operating plans and budgets and any updates.

(ii) Capital budgets and any updates.

(iii) Quarterly results for the company and its operating division or business segments.

(iv) Minutes of meetings of audit committee and other committees of the Board.

(v) The information on recruitment and remuneration of senior officers just below the board level, including appointment or removal of Chief Financial Officer and the Company Secretary.

(vi) Show cause, demand, prosecution notices and penalty notices which are materially important.

(vii) Fatal or serious accidents, dangerous occurrences any material effluent or pollution problems.

(viii) Any material default in financial obligations to and by the company, or substantial non-payment for goods sold by the company.

(ix) Any issue, which involves possible public or product liability claims of substantial nature, including any judgement or order which, may have passed strictures on the conduct of the company or taken an adverse view regarding another enterprise that can have negative implications on the company.

(x) Details of any joint venture or collaboration agreement.

(xi) Transactions that involve substantial payment towards goodwill, brand equity or intellectual property.

(xii) Significant labour problems and their proposed solutions. Any significant development in Human Resources/Industrial Relations front like signing of wage agreement, implementation of Voluntary Retirement Scheme, etc.

(xiii) Sale of material nature of investments, subsidiaries, assets, which is not in normal course of business.

(xiv) Quarterly details of foreign exchange exposures and the steps taken by the management to limit the risks of adverse exchange rate movement, if material.

(xv) Non-compliance of any regulatory, statutory or listing requirements and shareholders service such as non-payment of dividend, delay in share transfer, etc.

COMPANIES BILL, 2012

Companies Bill, 2012 contains certain clauses to promote corporate governance in alignment with global best practices. These include:

(i) Mandating listed companies to have at least a third of their directors to be 'independent' (meaning no family or pecuniary relationship with the promoters).

(ii) Not permittig perpetual re-appointment of the same auditor/firm (thereby mitigating the risks that could stem from a cosy auditor-client relationship).

(iii) Empowering shareholders and depositors to initiate 'class action' suits to claim damages against companies and their directors or auditors for wrongful conduct. The need for it became obvious after the Satyam Scandal, where the company's US shareholders got $125 million of compensation from filing a common suit alleging fraud ... and option denied to its 3,00,000 odd retail Indian investors.

REVIEW QUESTIONS

1. Define corporate governance.
2. Mention the various committees of the Board.
3. State the components of company management.
4. What do you mean by corporate governance?
5. Who is a non-executive director?
6. What do you mean by CFO certification?
7. What is the meaning of 'Whistle blowing'?
8. What is the relevance of Clause 49 of listing agreement?
9. What is audit committee?
10. What is CEO certification?
11. What are the new provisions incorporated in the revised Clause 49 of the listing agreement?
12. What is meant by 'whistle blower protection'?
13. Discuss the provisions relating to postal ballot.
14. Explain the principles of corporate governance.
15. List the basic ingredients of corporate governance.
16. What are the objectives of corporate governance?
17. Expláin the importance of corporate governance.
18. What is the role of SEBI in corporate governance?
19. What role is played by the Remuneration Committee in the good governance of a company?
20. State the need and importance of audit committee.

21. Explain briefly the historical developments that took place in corporate governance in India in the recent past.

22. Explain the various rules and regulations formulated by SEBI on corporate governance.

23. Explain the provisions of Sec. 292(A) of the Companies Act.

24. Write notes on report on corporate governance to be submitted by the company.

25. Explain the provisions included in Sec. 192(A) for postal ballot.

26. Explain the role of Board of Directors with regard to corporate governance.

27. Explain the mandatory and non-mandatory requirements of Clause 49 of the listing agreement.

28. Enumerate and explain various benefits of corporate governance.

56

Intellectual Property Right (IPR)

*"Intellectual property rights are the rights given to persons
over the creations of their minds."*
— *Ram Pratap Sinha*

MEANING AND CONCEPT OF INTELLECTUAL PROPERTY

The intellectual property is the product of human mind. Every
creation or performance takes its first shape in the mind of human
being and acquires a physical status on the execution of the ideal
so conceived. In other words, intellectual property relates to pieces
of information which can be incorporated in tangible objects at the
same time in an unlimited number of copies at different locations
anywhere in the world. However, the property right does not vest in
those copies, but in the information reflected in those copies. Like
property rights in movable and immovable property, intellectual
property is also characterised by certain rights and limitations such
as right to use and licence (limited duration in the case of copyrights and patents).

KINDS OF INTELLECTUAL PROPERTY

Generally, intellectual property is divided into two branches, namely,
industrial property and copyright. The Convention establishing
World Intellectual Property Organisation, 1967 provides that the
intellectual property shall include the rights relating to:

  (i)   literacy, artistic and scientific works;
 (ii)   performances of performing artists, phonograms and
        broadcasts;
(iii)   inventions in the field of human endeavour;
 (iv)   scientific discoveries;
  (v)   industrial designs;
 (vi)   trademarks, service marks, commercial names and designations;

(vii) protection against unfair competition; and all other rights resulting from intellectual activity in the industrial, scientific, literacy or artistic field.

Here, it is to be noted that the rights relating to (i) and (ii) above constitute copyright, while (iii), (v) and (vi) constitute industrial property. But the scientific discoveries, as mentioned under (iv) above, belongs to neither of the two branches of intellectual property as scientific discoveries and inventions are not the same.

WTO CLASSIFICATIONS OF IPRs

In accordance with the Trade Related Aspects of Intellectual Property Rights or TRIPs Agreement of the WTO, IPR are brought into the following two parts:

(i) *Copyrights and rights related to copyrights:* The rights of authors of literary and artistic works are protected for a minimum period of fifty years after the death of the author. Similarly, the copyrights and related rights are also protected. While the literary and artistic works consist of books and other writings, musical compositions, painting, sculpture, computer programmes and film, copyright and related rights include the rights of performers, (actors, singers, and musicians) and producers of phonograms (sound recording) and broadcasting organisations.

The main objective of all such protections is to encourage and reward creative work.

(ii) *Industrial property:* Industrial property is a kind of intellectual property and relates to creation of human mind, e.g., inventions and industrial designs. Inventions are new solutions to technological problems whereas industrial designs are aesthetic creations determining the appearance of industrial products. Industrial property also includes trademarks, service marks, commercial names and designations. However, the expression industrial property does not include movable and immovable property used for industrial production.

In the light of the above discussion, it is clear that industrial property right is a collective name for rights referring to the commercial or industrial activities of a person. Such activities may include the activities of industrial or commercial interests such as inventions, creations, process of manufacture, new designs or models, new products and a distinctive mark for goods, etc.

FEATURES OF TRIPS AGREEMENT

Following are the main features of the TRIPs agreement.

(i) *Standards:* The minimum standard of protection to be provided by each member is set out in the TRIPs agreement. Such a protection relates to each of the main areas of intellectual property covered by the TRIPs agreement. Moreover, each of the main elements of protection viz., (a) the subject-matter to be protected, (b) the right to be conferred, (c) permissible exceptions to those rights, and (d) minimum duration of protection is defined.

(ii) *Enforcement:* This provision deals with domestic procedures and remedies for the enforcement of intellectual property rights. The agreement lays down certain general principles applicable to all IPR enforcement procedures and provisions on civil and administrative procedures and remedies.

(iii) *Dispute settlement:* The TRIPs Agreement makes disputes between WTO members about the respect of the TRIPs obligations subject to the WTO's dispute settlement procedures. The Agreement provides for certain basic principles such as national and most favoured nation treatment and some general rules. Members are left free to decide the appropriate method of implementing the provisions of the Agreement within their own legal system and practice. However, the obligations under the Agreement will apply equally to all member countries, but developing countries will have a longer period to phase them in.

CLASSIFICATION OF IPRs

In accordance with the Trade Related Aspects of Intellectual Property Right of the World Trade Organisation, the IPRs (Intellectual Property Rights) may specifically be brought into the following seven categories:

Patent

Meaning and Concept

A patent is the exclusive right to own, use and dispose of an invention for a specified period. In other words, patent is a monopoly grant which enables the inventor to control the output and price of the patent products. It is granted by the Central Government to the first inventor or his legal representative. The main economic and commercial justification of the patent system is that it acts as stimulus to investment in the industrial innovation.

History of Patent

The grant of first patent can be traced as far back as 500 B.C. It was the city dominated by gaurmands, it was perhaps the first to grant what we nowadays call 'patent' right to promote culinary art. For it conferred exclusive rights of sale to any confectioner who first invented a delicious dish. As the practice was extended to other Greek cities and to other crafts and commodities, it acquired a name 'monopoly' a Greek Portmanteau word from 'mono' (alone) and 'polein' (sale). History shows that in 15th Century Venice there had been systematic use of monopoly privileges for inventors for the encouragement of inventions.

In England, during the 16th and 17th century, the inventor's patent of monopoly had become of great national importance. From the mid-seventeenth century through the mid-nineteenth century, the laws recognising the patent monopoly spread throughout Europe and North America.

In India, the law relating to Patents is contained in the Patent Act, 1970, which was last amended in the year 1999.

Trademark

Trademark is a legal term. When a brand is registered and legalised, it becomes a trademark. Hence, registered brands are trademarks. A brand is registered under the Trademark Name and Trademark Act. It is a brand enjoying legal protection. According to the American Marketing Association, "Brand or part of brand is that which is given legal protection because it is capable of exclusive appropriation."

A trademark is the exclusive property of the seller. Others cannot use it, otherwise legal action can be taken against them under the Trademark Act. In India, the law relating to trademark is contained in the Trade and Merchandise Marks Act, 1958, which has now been replaced by the Trademark Act, 1999.

Brand v. Trademark

	Brand		*Trademark*
(i)	It is used in broader sense. Hence, all trademarks are brands.	(i)	It is used in narrow sense. Hence, all brands are not trademarks.
(ii)	It denotes the qualities.	(ii)	It denotes the producer.
(iii)	It is a word, name, design, symbol, sign or a combination of them.	(iii)	When brand is registered, it becomes a trademark.
(iv)	It may be copied by the competitors and no legal action can be taken against them.	(iv)	It cannot be copied, otherwise legal action can be taken under the Trademark Act.
(v)	It can be used by all.	(v)	It can be used only by the person who got it registered in his firm's name.

Copyright

The right for literary works to be duplicated by mechanical processes instead of being copied by hand is called copyright. The idea of copyright emerged with the invention of printing. This led to the grant of privileges (by authorities and kings) entitling beneficiaries exclusive rights of reproduction and distribution, for limited period, with remedies in the form of fines, seizure, confiscation of infringing copies.

The copyright deals with the rights of intellectual creators in their creation. The copyright law deals with the particular forms of creativity, concerned primarily with mass communication. It is also concerned with virtually all forms and methods of public communication, not only printed publications, but also with such matters as sound, the television broadcasting, films for public exhibition, etc., and even computerised systems for the storage and retrieval of information. The creativity protected by copyright law is creativity in the choice and arrangement of words, musical notes, colours, shapes, and so on. In India, the law relating to copyright is contained in the Copyright Act, 1957, which was last amended in the year 1999.

Layout Designs of Integrated Circuits

The member countries are required to protect the layout designs of integrated circuits (Article 35 of the TRIPs Agreement).

A 'layout design (topography)' is the three-dimensional disposition of the elements. But an 'integrated circuits' means a product, in its final form or an intermediate form.

The obligation to protect layout designs applies to such layout, designs, which are original in the sense that they are the result of their creators own intellectual effort.

The exclusive rights consists of the right of reproduction and the right of importation, sale and other distribution for commercial purpose.

Breeders' Right

Breeders' right is a protection conferred on plant varieties which are new, stable, homogeneous and distinguishable. It permits the use of a protected variety as a basis for the development of a new variety and for the reuse by the partners of the seeds obtained from their own harvests.

Protection of Undisclosed Information or Trade Secrets

Trade secret is a confidential business information. It is the most valuable asset of business enterprises which is required to be protected. The protection to be provided is based on the secret nature of the information and its business value.

Civil and criminal actions are provided in most countries national legislation against the unauthorised disclosure or use of confidential information of technical and commercial nature.

'Know how' obtained by most developing countries to develop or establish their own industry is a form of trade secret. It has value so long as the information is secret, valuable and unpublished.

Industrial Design

The ornamental or aesthetic aspect of a useful article, (which must appeal to the sense of sight and may consist of the shape and/or pattern and/or colour of article) is known as an industrial design. Although, it belongs to the aesthetic field it is intended to serve as a pattern for the manufacture of products of industry or handicraft. An industrial design to be protectable, should be new and original. It is protected against unauthorised copying or imitation, for a period which usually lasts for five, ten or fifteen years.

The first designs legislations enacted in India was the Patterns and Designs Protection Act, 1872. The Act, however, left undefined the expression "new pattern or design". Thus, the (British) Patents and Designs Act, 1907, became the basis of the Indian Patents and Designs Act, 1911. This Act continues with some consequential amendments, with the title as the Designs Act, 1911. The new Designs Act, 2000 has been passed by the Parliament.

CONVENTIONS FOR PROTECTION OF IPRs

The most important conventions for protection of IPRs are as follows:

(i) The Paris Convention for the protection of industrial property.

(ii) The Berne Convention for the protection of literary and artistic works.

(iii) The Rome Convention to protect performers, phonograms and broadcasting organisations.

(iv) Washington Convention on intellectual property in respect of integrated circuits.

PATENT ACT, 1970

The law relating to patents is contained in the Patent Act, 1970. Later, it has been amended in 1999, 2002 and 2005. The Act extends to the whole of India.

The intellectual property laws are the laws of patents, trade -mark and copyright. These laws seek to protect the rights of an inventor, author, artists etc., and to provide remedies for unlawful misappropriation or infringement.

The patent office (under the Department of Industrial Policy and Promotion, Ministry of Commerce and Industry) carries out the duties in connection with the grant of patents for new inventions and registration of industrial designs.

Patent—Meaning

Patent is an exclusive right granted to a patent holder (for a limited period) as a reward of creative work based on his private initiative. It is a form of intellectual property. Sec. 2(m) states that a patent means a patent for an invention granted under the Patent Act, 1970.

Objectives of the Patent Act

The following are the main objectives of the Patent Act:

   (i) Protecting IPRs of a person to whom the patent has been granted.
  (ii) Encouraging scientific research, new technology and industrial progress.
 (iii) Permitting the owner of the patent to grant licence to others for exploiting the patent.

Requirements for Patentable Invention

An invention should satisfy the following tests to get 'patent':

   (i) Test of novelty: The subject-matter should be new.
  (ii) Test of utility: It should be useful.
 (iii) Test of vendibility: The subject-matter should be capable of being marketed for commercial purposes.

Patentable Inventions

Inventions to be patentable should be technical in nature and should meet the following criteria:

(i) *Novelty:* Before the date of filing of the patent application in India, the matter disclosed in the specification is not published in India.

(ii) *Inventive step:* Invention is not obvious to a person skilled in the art in the light of the prior publication/knowledge/document.

(iii) *Industrially applicable:* Invention should possess utility. Thus, it can be made or used in the industry.

Inventions in Respect of Atomic Energy (Sec. 4)

No patent shall be granted for invention in respect of atomic energy falling within Sub-section (1) of Section 20 of the Atomic Energy Act, 1962.

Persons Entitled to Apply for Patents (Sec. 6)

An application for patent can be submitted by:

(i) any person claiming to be the true and first inventor of the invention.

(ii) assignee of the person claiming to be the true and first inventor.

(iii) the legal representative of any person who immediately before his death was entitled to make such an application.

An application for patent may be made by any of the persons either alone or jointly with any other person.

Form of Application (Sec. 7)

An application for patent shall be made in the prescribed form and filed in the patent office. Every such an application shall be for one invention only and shall be accompanied by provisional or complete specification.

Provisional and Complete Specification (Sec. 9)

An application for patent shall be accompanied by a provisional or complete specification. If the application is accompanied by a provisional specification, a complete specification should be filed within twelve months from the date of filing the applications. The application shall be deemed to be abandoned, if such things are not done.

Contents of Specification (Sec. 10)

'Specification' is a description of the inventions.

The following description shall be made in every complete specification:

(i) Full and particular description of the invention.

(ii) The use and method of operation of invention.

(iii) Disclosure of the best method of performing the invention which is known to the applicant.

(iv) Defining the scope of the invention for which protection is claimed.

(v) An abstract providing technical information on the invention.

Examination of Application (Sec. 12)

If a complete specification is filed in respect of an application for a patent, then the controller shall refer the same to an examiner for making a report to him as regards:

(i) whether the application complies with the requirements of the Patent Act,

(ii) whether there exists any ground of objection to the patent,

(iii) whether the invention has already been published or claimed by any other person.

In case the report is adverse, the Controller is required to issue a notice to the applicant, giving particulars of objections.

Having heard the applicant, the Controller may refuse the application or may require the applicant to amend the same. In case the amendments are not made to his satisfaction, the Controller can refuse the application.

Opposition to Grant of Patents (Sec. 25)

If an application for a patent has been published but patent has not been granted, any person may (in writing) represent by way of opposition to the Controller against the grant of the patent. The representation with the statements and evidence, if any, and a request for hearing, if so desired shall be filed at the appropriate office.

The Controller shall constitute 'Opposition Board' comprising such officers, as may be determined. He will then refer the notice of opposition alongwith documents to the Board for examination and submission of its recommendations to him.

On receipt of the recommendation of the 'opposition board', the Controller shall make a hearing to the patentee and opponent. Then he can either maintain, amend or revoke the patent.

Grant of Patent (Secs. 43 to 53)

If an application for a patent is accepted with a decision in favour of the applicant, then the controller shall grant the patent on request being made by the applicant in the prescribed form. Hence, the patent shall be sealed with the seal of the patent office.

Every patent shall be dated as of the date on which the application for the patent was filed. It shall be in the prescribed form and shall have effect throughout India.

A patent shall be granted for one invention only and its term shall be twenty years from the date of filing application for the patent.

Patents of Addition (Secs. 54 to 56)

If an application is made for any improvement in or modification of main invention, the Controller may grant the patent for the improvement or modification as a patent of addition. However, a patent of addition shall not be granted prior to the grant of the patent for the main invention.

A patent of addition is granted for a term equal to that of the patent for the main invention. It shall run concurrently and terminate with the main patent. The patent of addition has no renewal fee so long as the main patent remains in force.

Right of Patentee (Sec. 48)

The following are the rights of the patentee:

(i) Exploiting the patent.

(ii) Granting patent licence to another person.

(iii) Assigning the patent in favour of another person.

(iv) Surrendering the patent.

Inventions for Purpose of Government (Sec. 100)

The Central Government is empowered to use any invention for Government purposes. The patentee is given royalty or fees as per terms agreed upon. In case the terms are not mutually agreed to, these can be determined by the High Court.

Acquisition of Patents by Central Government (Sec. 102)

By issue of notification for public interest, the Central Government can acquire the patent. But the patentee is given compensation as mutually agreed upon or as determined by the High Court.

Suits for Infringement of Patents (Sec. 106)

The court can grant relief, in the case of groundless threats of infringement, including an injunction and damages.

THE TRADEMARKS ACT, 1999

The Trademarks Act, 1999 is governed by the Trademarks Rules, 2002. Both the Act and Rules are effective from 15th September, 2003.

Trademark—Meaning

A trademark means a device, brand, heading, label, ticket, name, signature, word, letter or numeral. This work is capable of distinguishing goods or services of one person from those of the other.

Objectives of the Trademark Act

The following are the main objectives of the Act:

(i) Providing for the registration of the trademarks.

(ii) Providing for better protection of trademarks.

(iii) Preventing the use of fraudulent trademarks on merchandise.

Trademarks Registry

Under the Trademarks Act, 1999, a Trademarks Registry is established by the Central Government under the headship of the Registrar of Trademarks. A register of trademark is kept at the office of the Registry. The details of all the registered trademarks are contained in this register.

Procedure for Registration

The following are the steps of the procedure for registration:

(i) A person who wants to get a trademark registered is required to apply in the prescribed form.

(ii) When an application for registration of trademark is accepted, the Registrar shall give the conditions on which it has been accepted in the Trademark Journal. The purpose behind such an advertisement is to inform the trading public whose existing or future rights or interest might be adversely affected by such a registration.

(iii) Within three months from the date of such adverti-sement, any person may make a written opposition to the registration.

(iv) The registrar, in turn, shall serve a copy of the notice containing objections on the applicant for registration within two months.

(v) Within two months of receipts of notice, the applicant may send a counter statement.

(vi) In case the applicant sends such a counter statement, the Registrar shall serve a copy thereof on the person giving notice of opposition.

(vii) After hearing the parties and considering the evidence, the Registrar shall decide whether the registration is to be permitted.

(viii) In case the Registrar refuses the same, the applicant may go for an appeal to the High Court.

(ix) When the same is accepted, the Registrar shall register the said trademark. The date of making the applications shall be deemed to be the date of registration.

(x) The Registrar shall issue a certificate of registration under a seal of the Trademark Registry to the applicant.

(xi) The Act provides for registration of trademark for service apart from goods.

(xii) The Act provides for registration of collective marks owned by association of persons.

(xiii) The registration of trade mark shall be for a period of ten years, but it may be renewed from time to time as per the provisions of the Act.

Effects of Registration

Registration of trademark is a prima facie evidence of its validity. The proprietor of a registered trademark is conferred the exclusive use thereof in relation to the goods or services in respect of which the trademark is registered.

If the registered trademark is infringed in the manner provided by the Act, the proprietor can get relief under the law. A registered proprietor is empowered to assign a trade mark and provide receipts for any consideration for the assignment of the trademark. The assignee can get himself registered as a registered user of the trade mark as per the provisions of the Act.

Circumstances under which a Trademark is Deemed to be Infringed

A registered trademark is infringed which is used in the course of trade and is likely to cause confusion on the part of the public on account of the following facts:

(i) Its identity with the registered trademark and the identity or similarity of the goods or services covered by such registered trademark, or

(ii) Its similarity to the registered trademark and the identity or similarity of the goods or services covered by such registered trademark, or

(iii) Its identity with the registered trademark and the identity of the goods or services covered by such registered trademark.

Moreover, a registered trademark is infringed when the mark used:

(i) is identical with or similar to the registered trademark;

(ii) is used in relation to goods or services which are not similar to those for which the trade mark is registered and

(iii) the registered trademark has a reputation in India and the use of the mark without due cause takes unfair advantage of or is detrimental to the character or repute of the registered trademark.

Punishment for Infringement of the Trademark

When a registered trademark is infringed by a person, as regards enforcement of rights, the Act itself empowers the court to pass ex-parte injunction for:

(a) discovery of documents,

(b) preserving the infringed goods, documents or other evidence, and

(c) restraining the offender from disposing off or dealing with its assets in a manner which may adversely affect the plaintiff's ability to recover damages, cost and pecuniary remedies.

For trademark violations, minimum penalty prescribed is six months imprisonment with a fine of Rupees fifty thousand. But the maximum penalty prescribed for such violations is three years imprisonment with a fine of Rupees two lakh.

The trademark violation is a cognisable and non-bailable offence. A police officer, not below the rank of Deputy Superintendent of Police is now empowered to search and seize without warrant, the goods, blocks, machines, plates or other instruments or things involved in committing the offences.

Civil suits can be initiated by the trademark owners in any court having jurisdiction where they reside, work for gain or carry on business.

COPYRIGHT ACT, 1957

Artists, musicians and writers are considered to be the most precious treasures of a nation. In order to protect the skill of such persons, Copyright Act, 1957 has been framed. The Act came into effect on 21st January, 1958. It has been amended in 1983, 1984, 1991, 1992, 1994 and 1999.

By incorporating the major provisions of the TRIPs agreement, the Indian Copyright has been thoroughly revised in 1994. This Act extends to the whole of India.

Object of the Act

The following are the main objectives of the Copyright Act, 1957:

(i) To protect the hard work, genius, mediations and skills of the intellectuals.

(ii) To protect the original expression of thought or information in some concrete form rather than the original idea or concept, theme or plot.

(iii) To protect the intellectual property right of authors from unlawful reproduction, plagiarism, piracy, imitation and copying.

Work Subsisting Copyright (Sec. 13)

In the following classes of work, copyright shall subsist throughout India:

(i) Original literacy, dramatic, musical and artistic work,

(ii) Cinematograph films, and

(iii) Sound recording.

However, copyright shall not subsist in the following cases:

(i) In any cinematograph film if substantial part of the film is an infringement of the copyright of any other work.

(ii) In any sound recording made in respect of a literary, dramatic or musical work, if in marketing the sound recording, copyright in such work has been infringed.

COPYRIGHT—MEANING (SEC. 14)

As per the Act, copyright means an exclusive right to do or authorise the doing of any of the following acts in respect of a work or any substantial part thereof:

(a) In the case of a literary, dramatic or musical work, not being a computer programme:

(i) To produce the work in any material form including the storing of it in any medium by electronic means;

(ii) To issue copies of the work to the public not being copies already in circulation;

(iii) To perform the work in public, or communicate it to the public;

(iv) To make any cinematograph film or sound recording in respect of the work;

(v) To make any translation of the work;

(vi) To make any adaptation of the work;

(vii) To do, in relation to a translation or an adaptation of the work, any of the acts specified in relation to the work.

(b) In the case of a computer programme:

(i) To do any of the acts specified in clause (a);

(ii) To sell or give on commercial rental or offer for sale or for commercial rental any copy of the computer programme.

(c) In the case of an artistic work:

(i) To reproduce the work in any material form including depiction in three dimensions of a two-dimensional work or in two dimensions of a three-dimensional work;

(ii) To communicate the work to the public;

    (iii) To issue copies of the work to the public not being copies already in circulation;

    (iv) To include the work in any cinematograph film;

    (v) To make any adaptation of the work;

    (vi) To do in relation to an adaptation of the work any of the acts specified in relation to the work.

  (d) In the case of a cinematograph film:

    (i) To make a copy of the film including a photograph of any image forming part thereof;

    (ii) To sell or give on hire or offer for sale or hire, any copy of the film, regardless of whether such a copy has been sold or given on hire on earlier occasions;

    (iii) To communicate the film to the public.

  (e) In the case of a sound recording:

    (i) To make any other sound recording embodying it;

    (ii) to sell or give on hire, or offer for sale or hire, any copy of the sound recording, regardless of whether such a copy has been sold or given on hire on earlier occasions;

    (iii) To communicate the sound recording to the public.

Ownership of Copyright (Sec. 17)

The author of a work shall be the first owner of the copyright. The term 'author' means:

    (i) In relation to a musical work–the composer;

    (ii) In relation to artistic work other than a photograph–the artist;

    (iii) In relation to a photograph–the person taking the photograph;

    (iv) In relation to cinematograph film or sound recording–the producer;

    (v) In relation to any literary, dramatic, musical or artistic work which is computer-generated–the person who causes the work to be created.

Assignment of Copyright (Secs. 18 and 19)

The owner of the copyright may assign to any person the copyright wholly or partially. Such an assignment may be either generally or subject to limitations and either for the whole term of the copyright or any part thereof.

Copyrights in any future work can also be assigned. But such an assignment shall take effect only when the work comes into existence.

However, the assignment is valid only when it is in writing duly signed by the assignor or by his authorised agent.

Term of Copyright (Secs. 22 to 24)

The term of the copyright in any literary, dramatic, musical or artistic work (other than a photograph) published within the life time of the author is until sixty years from the beginning of the calender year next following the year in which the author dies.

In the case of joint authorship, the author who dies last will be considered.

In the case of anonymous or pseudonymous work, the term of copyright is until sixty years from the beginning of the calendar year next following the year in which work is first published. But in such a case, if the identity of the author is disclosed, it will be sixty years from the year following the year in which the author dies.

In the case of posthumous work, photography, cinematograph film, sound recording, government works, works of public undertaking and the works of an international organisation, the copyright shall subsist until sixty years from the beginning of the calendar year next following the year in which the work is first published.

Artistic Work

The term 'artistic work' means:

(a) a painting, a sculpture, a drawing, an engraving or a photograph, whether or not any such work possesses artistic quality;

(b) a work of architecture; and

(c) any other work of artistic craftsmanship.

Copyright Societies (Secs. 33 and 34)

A person or association of person cannot commence or carry on the business of issuing or granting licence relating to any work in which copyright subsists unless such a business (i.e., a copyright society) is registered by the Central Government.

A copyright society may accept from the owner of rights exclusive authorisation to administer any right in any work through the issue of licences or collection of licence fees or both. The collection of fees and distribution of the same among owners of rights are done by the society after making deductions for its own expenses.

A scheme for determining the quantum of remuneration payable to individual copyrights owners may be framed by the society having regard to the number of copies of work in circulation.

International Copyright (Secs. 40 to 42)

The Central Government may, by order, direct that all or any provisions of this Act shall apply to work published outside India or to unpublished work made out of India or work of foreign author who died.

Such a protection can be made only in respect of countries which grant similar protection to work made in India.

The Central Government can declare some international organisations as eligible to hold copyrights. However, the term of copyright in India to the foreign work, will not exceed that conferred by the foreign country.

According to the International Copyright Order, 1958, passed by the Government of India, any work first published in any country which is a member of Berne Convention or the Universal Copyright Convention will be accorded the same treatment as if it were first published in India.

Registration of Copyright (Secs. 44 and 45)

The registration of copyright is not compulsory. However, the copyright may be registered with the Registrar of copyrights. A register of copyrights which contains the names or title of works and names and addresses of authors, publishers and owners of copyrights shall be kept at the copyright office.

The author, or owner or publisher or any other person interested in the copyright in any work may make an application in the prescribed form accompanied by the prescribed fee to the registrar of copyrights for entering particulars of the work in the Register of copyrights.

Infringement of Copyrights (Sec. 51)

Copyright in a work shall be deemed infringed:

(i) When any person, without a licence granted by the owner of the copyrights or the Registrar of copyrights under this Act:

(a) does anything, the exclusive right to do which is by this Act conferred upon the owner of the copyright or

(b) permits for profit any place to be used for the communication of the work to the public where such communication constitutes an infringement of the copyrights in the work.

(ii) When any person:

(a) makes for sale or hire, or sells or lets for hire or by way of trade displays or offers for sale or hire, or

(b) distributes either for the purpose of trade or to such an extent as to affect prejudicially the owner of the copyright, or

(c) by way of trade exhibit in public, or

(d) import into India, any infringing copies of the work. But this shall not apply to the import of one copy of any work for the private and domestic use of the importer.

Civil Remedies for Infringement of Copyright (Secs. 55, 58 and 62)

If copyright in any work is infringed, the owner of the copyright is entitled to civil remedies through injunction, damages and accounts.

In case the defendent proves that on the date of infringement he was not aware and had no reasonable ground to believe of the existence of copyright, the plaintiff is entitled to a share of profit and injunction in respect of infringement.

The possession of all infringing copies and plates used or intended to be used for production of infringing copies can be taken over by the owner of the copyright.

The District Court having jurisdiction shall entertain all civil proceedings in respect of infringement of copyright in any work.

Punishment for Copyright Infringement (Secs. 63(A), 63(B), 65, 67 and 68)

Any person knowingly infringes or abets the infringement of copyrights in a work, shall be punishable for imprisonment of not less than six months and not more than three years with a fine not less than Rupees fifty thousand and not more than Rupees two lakh. However, if infringement has not been made for gain in the course of trade and business, the court may, impose a sentence of imprisonment for a term of less than six months or a fine of less than Rupees fifty thousand.

In a repeat offence, minimum imprisonment is one year, but which may extend to three years and the minimum fine is Rupees one lakh but which may extend to Rupees two lakh.

Any person who knowingly makes use of infringing copy of a computer programme shall be punishable for imprisonment of not less than seven days and not more than three years with a fine not less than Rupees fifty thousand and not more than Rupees two lakh.

Any person who knowingly copies or has in his possession, any plate for the purpose of making infringing copies of any work in which copyright subsists shall be punishable for imprisonment of not more than 2 years with a fine.

Penalty for making false statement with a view to deceiving or influencing any authority or officer under the Act, shall be punishable for imprisonment of one year or with fine or with both.

APPEALS (SECS. 71 AND 72)

In case any person is aggrieved by an order of the court, he can file an appeal within thirty days of the date of the order to the higher appellate authority.

Any person aggrieved by any final order of the Registrar of copyrights may within three months from the date of such an order, appeal to the Copyright Board.

Any person aggrieved by any final order of the Copyright Board may within a month from the date of such an order appeal to the High Court.

PLAGIARISM

The word plagiarism is derived from the Latin word plagiaries (literally kidnapper) which denotes someone stealing someone else's work. It is defined in dictionaries as "the wrongful appropriation, close imitation, and publication of another author's language thoughts, ideas or expressions, and the representations of them as one's own original work." In the sectors of academic and journalism, plagiarism is now considered academia dishonesty and a breach of journalistic ethics.

Within academia, plagiarism by students, professors, or researchers is considered academic dishonesty or academic fraud, and offenders are subject to academic censure, including expulsion. In journalism, plagiarism is considered a breach of journalistic ethics. Thus, reporters who are caught plagiarising typically face disciplinary measures ranging from suspension to termination of employment.

Cases of Plagiarism

The following are the cases of plagiarism:

  (i) Turning in someone else's work as one's own.

 (ii) Copying words or ideas from someone else without giving credit.

(iii) Failing to put a quotation marks.

 (iv) Giving incorrect information about the source of a quotation.

  (v) Changing words but copying the sentence structure of a source without giving credit.

 (vi) Copying so many words or ideas from a source that it makes up the majority of one's own work, whether give credit or not.

Plagiarism and Copyright Infringement

Plagiarism is not the same as copyright infringement. Although, both terms are applicable to a particular act, they are different concepts. While copyright infringement is a violation of the rights of a copyright holder, the moral concept of plagiarism is achieved through false claims of authorship.

Punishment for Plagiarism

The term 'plagiarism' is not mentioned even in civil statute or criminal statute. It may be brought up as a law suit on copyright infringement only if the copyright from the 'plagiarised' is substantial. Some cases may be treated as unfair competition or violation of the doctrine of moral rights.

Plagiarism is not the same as copyright infringement. Although both these terms may apply to a particular Act, these are different concepts. Copyright infringement is a violation of the rights of a copyright-holder, when material protected by copyright is used without consent. On the contrary, the moral concept of plagiarism is concerned with the concerned increment to the plagiarising author's 'reputation' that is achieved through false claims of authorship.

Plagiarism is not a crime. It may be a case for civil law, if it is sufficiently substantial to constitute copyright infringement.

Even a small part of a work is found to have been plagiarised, it is still considered a copyright violation. However, the amount that was copied probably will have bearing on the severity of the punishment. The work which is almost entirely plagiarised will almost certainly incur more penalties than a work that only includes a small amount of plagiarised.

In any wrong doing, the degree of intent and the nature of the offence determine its status. When plagiarism takes place in an academic setting, it is most often handled by the individual instructors and the academic institutions involved. In case the plagiarism involves money, prizes or job placement, it constitutes a crime punishment in court.

Most universities and colleges have zero tolerance for plagiarists. In fact, academic standards of intellectual honesty are often more demanding than Copyrights laws of the Government. Any form of plagiarism will not be tolerated by most corporations and institutions. There are a number of cases across the world where people have lost their jobs or been denied positions as a result of plagiarism.

In most cases, plagiarism are considered misdemeanours, shall be punishable for imprisonment of up to one year with a fine not less than Rupees five thousand and not more than Rupees two lakh fifty thousand.

REVIEW QUESTIONS

1. What is patent?
2. What is trademark?
3. What is meant by intellectual property right?
4. What is industrial property?
5. What is breeders' rights?
6. What is layout design?
7. What is copyright?
8. What is international copyright?
9. What is plagiarism?
10. What do you mean by patents of addition?
11. Enumerate two objectives of Patent Act, 1970.
12. What is patentable inventions under Patent Act, 1970?
13. When shall copyright in a work be deemed infringed?
14. Mention two features of TRIPs agreement.
15. Enumerate the conventions for protection of IPRs.
16. Explain provisions of inventions in respect of atomic energy.
17. Enumerate provisions relating to grant of patent.

18. Enumerate provisions relating to the assignment of copyright.

19. Explain the objectives of Patent Act, 1970.

20. What should be the contents of 'specification' under Patent Act, 1970?

21. What are the functions of copyright societies?

22. Explain the punishment for copyright infringement.

23. Explain 'artistic work' under the Copyright Act.

24. Explain the effects of registration of trademark.

25. Explain Trademark Registry.

26. Enumerate some cases of plagiarism.

27. Explain the procedure for registration of trademark under the Trade Mark Act, 1999.

28. Explain WTO classification of Intellectual Property Rights.

29. Explain the meaning of the term 'copyright' in regard to literary, dramatic, musical, sound recording and artistic work under Copyright Act, 1957.

30. Enumerate and explain the procedure to be followed to obtain the patent, under Patent Act, 1970.

31. Discuss the circumstances under which a trademark is deemed to be infringed. List the punishment for infringement of trademark.

32. Define 'plagiarism'. What acts are considered to be plagiarism? Mention the punishment for plagiarism.

57

Right to Information Act, 2005

Right to information means "the right to information accessible under this Act which is held by or under the control of any public authority
—*Sec. 3, RTI Act, 2005*

INTRODUCTION

The Government introduced the Right to Information Bill in the Parliament in order to ensure greater access to information. The bill was passed by both the Houses of Parliament and received the assent of the President on 15th June, 2005. It came on the Statute Book as The Right to Information Act, 2005 (22 of 2005). The Act extends to the whole of India except the State of Jammu and Kashmir and came into force on the 13th day of October 2005.

OBJECTS OF THE ACT

The objects of the Act are:

(i) to ensure smoother and greater access to information;

(ii) to secure access to information under the control of public authorities; and

(iii) to promote transparency and accountability in the working of every public authority.

DEFINITION

Appropriate Government [Sec. 2(a)]

Appropriate Government means in relation to public authority, which is established, constituted, owned, controlled or substantially financed by funds provided directly or indirectly

(i) by the Central Government or the union territory administration—the Central Government

(ii) by the State Government—the State Government.

Public Authority [Sec. 2(b)]

Public authority means any authority or body or institution of self-government established or constituted- (a) by or under the constitution, (b) by any other law made by parliament, (c) by any other law made by state legislature, and (d) by notification issued or order made by the appropriate government, and includes only-

(i) body owned, controlled or substantially financed;

(ii) non-government organisation substantially financed (directly or indirectly) by funds produced by the appropriate government.

Competent Authority [Sec. 2(e)]

Competent Authority means:

(i) The Speaker in the case of House of the People or the Legislative Assembly of a State.

(ii) The Chief Justice of India in the case of Supreme Court.

(iii) The Chief Justice of High Court in the case of a High Court.

(iv) The President or Governor, as the case may be, in the case of other authorities established or constituted by or under the Constitution.

(v) The Administrator appointed under Article 239 of the Constitution.

Information [Sec. 2(f)]

Information means any material in any form, including records, documents, memos, e-mails, opinion, advice, press releases, circulars, orders, log books, contracts, reports, papers, samples, models, and data material held in any electronic form and information relating to any private body which can be accessed by a public authority under any other law for the time being in force.

Right to Information (Sec. 3)

Right to information means the right to information accessible under this Act which is held by or under the control of any public authority. It includes the right to:

(i) inspection of works, documents, and records;

(ii) taking notes, extracts, or certified copies of documents or records;

(iii) taking certified samples of materials; and

(iv) obtaining information in the form of diskettes, floppies, tapes, video cassettes or in any other electronic mode or through printouts where such informations is stored in a computer or in any other device.

Information to be Disclosed by Public Authorities (Sec. 4)

A Public Authority should proactively disclose:

(a) Information like particulars of its organisation, its functions and duties;

(b) Information regarding its officers and employees;

(c) Rules and regulations of the organisation;

(d) Directory of officers and employees and their monthly salary;

(e) Details of electronically maintained information; and

(f) Particulars of Public Information Officers.

It shall be constant endeavour of every Public authority to take steps to provide as much information suo motu to the public at regular intervals through various means of communication internet.

Every information shall be disseminated widely and in such a manner which is easily accessible to the public. 'Dissemination' means making known or communicated the information to the public through notice boards, newspapers, public announcements, media broadcasts, the internet or any other means including inspection of offices of any public authority.

There are two methods in which the public authority can disseminate information. These methods are: (i) by proactively disclosing the routine information to the public, and (ii) by providing information upon the request of a citizen of India.

Exemption from Disclosure of Information (Sec. 8)

1. Notwithstanding anything contained in this Act, there shall be no obligation to give any citizen:

(a) information, disclosure of which would prejudicially affect the sovereignty and integrity of India.

(b) information which has been expressly forbidden to be published by any court of law or tribunal.

(c) information, the disclosure of which would cause a breach of privilege of Parliament or the State Legislature.

(d) information including commercial confidence, trade secrets or intellectual property, the disclosure of which would harm the competitive position of a third party.

(e) information available to a person in his fiduciary relationship.

(f) The exemption under (d) and (e) are allowed unless the concerned authority is satisfied that larger public interest warrants the disclosure of such information.

(g) information received in confidence from foreign government.

(h) information, the disclosure of which would endanger the life or physical safety of any person.

(i) information which would impede the process of investigation or apprehension or prosecution of offenders.

(j) cabinet papers including records of deliberations of the Council of Ministers, Secretaries and other officers.

(k) information which relates to personal information the disclosure of which has no relationship to any public activity or interest.

2. A public authority may allow access to information, if public interest in disclosure outweighs the harm to the protected interests. [Notwithstanding any of the exemptions under Sub-section (1)]

3. Any information relating to any event which has taken place twenty years before the date on which any request is made under Section 6 shall be provided to any person making a request under that Section.

(Subject to the provisions of Clauses (a) (c) and (i) of Sub-section (1))

From Whom Can Seek the Information

The information can be sought from Public Authorities comprising:

(i) All Central, State and Local bodies constituted under Indian Constitution or under Government notification.

(ii) Any body owned, controlled or financed by the Government.

(iii) A non-government organisation, substantially financed directly or indirectly by the Government.

Non-applicability of the Act

The Act does not apply to the following organisations:

The Central Intelligence and Security Organisations specified in the Second Schedule like RAW, IB, Directorate or Revenue Intelligence, B.S.F., Assam Rifles and Agencies by the State Government through notifications.

However, these organisations have an obligation to provide information pertaining to allegations of corruption and human rights violations, but only with the approval of the Central or State Information Commission, as the case may be.

Officers under the Act

The main officers designated under the Act are as follows:

(i) Central Assistant Public Information Officer.

(ii) State Assistant Public Information Officer.

(iii) Central Public Information Officer.

(iv) State Public Information Officer.

(v) Appellate Authority.

All Public Authorities under Central and State Government have designated Central or State Public Information Officers, as the case may be. Any citizen may submit an application for information before such officers.

Apart from such officers, the Act provides for Information Commission, both Central and State also.

REQUEST FOR OBTAINING INFORMATION (SEC. 6)

A person, who desires to obtain any information under this Act, shall make a request in writing or through electronic means in English or Hindi or in the official language of that area, accompanying such fees as may be prescribed, to:

(i) The Central or State Public Information Officer, as the case may be.

(ii) The Central or State Assistant Public Information Officer, as the case may be.

The application shall contain the name and address of the applicant.

However, an application making request for information shall not be required to provide any reason for requesting the information.

Time Limit

On receipt of the request, the Central or State Public Information Officer shall, as expeditiously as possible, and in any case within thirty days of the receipt of the request, either provide the information or reject the request.

Refusal of Request

The failure of the Central or State Public Information Officer to give decision on the request for information within the period specified shall be deemed to have refused the request.

Fees for Disclosure

Both Central and Kerala State Rules prescribe Rupees ten as application fees.

However no fees shall be charged from applicant below poverty line.

In addition to the application fees, the rules provide for additional fees for getting information. In case the Public Information Officer charges additional fees, he should inform the same to the applicant.

Procedure for Disclosure

After receiving prescribed fees, the Public Information Officer shall disclose information within the prescribed time. It should be provided, as far as possible in the format requested by the applicant. For instance, in writing or in CD.

The Central Information Commission (Sec. 12)

The Central Government shall, by notification in the official gazette, constitute a body to be known as the Central Information Commission. Such a commission is required to exercise the powers conferred on, and to perform the functions assigned to it under this Act.

The Central Information shall comprise:

(i) The Chief Central Information Commissioner.

(ii) Such number of Central Information Commissioners, not exceeding ten, as may be deemed necessary.

The Chief Central Information Commissioner and the Central Information Commissioner shall be appointed by the President of India on the recommendation of a committee comprising:

(i) The Prime Minister, who shall be the Chairperson of the committee.

(ii) The Leader of Opposition in the Lok Sabha.

(iii) A Union Cabinet Minister to be nominated by the Prime Minister.

Every Information Commissioner shall hold office for a term of five years or till he attains the age of sixty five years, which comes first.

The Chief Central Information Commissioner is not eligible for re-appointment, but a Central Information Officer may be re-appointed as Chief Central Information Commissioner.

The Chief Central Information Commissioner and Information Commissioner shall be persons of eminence in public life. They shall have wide knowledge and experience in law; science and technology, management, journalism and administration and social science.

The headquarters of Central Information Commission is at Delhi.

STATE INFORMATION COMMISSION (SEC. 15)

The State Information Commission is constituted by the State Government through a gazette notification. The State Information Commission comprises:

(i) The State Chief Information Commissioner, and

(ii) Such number of State Information Commissioner, not exceeding ten, as may be deemed necessary.

They shall be appointed by the Governor of the State on the recommendation of a committee comprising:

(i) The Chief Minister, who shall be the Chairperson of the committee.

(ii) The leader of the opposition in the Legislative Assembly.

(iii) A Cabinet Minister to be nominated by the Chief Minister.

The Kerala State Information Commission, at present, comprises one Chief State Information Commissioner and three State Information Commissioners. The Commissioners are appointed for a period of five years or till they attain the age of sixty five years, which comes first.

The Chief State Commissioner is not eligible for re-appointment, but a State Information Commissioner may be re-appointed as the Chief State Information Commissioner.

The State Chief Information Commissioner and the State Information Commissioner shall be persons of eminence in public life. They should have wide knowledge and experience in law, science and technology, social science, management, journalism, mass media or administration and governance.

The headquarters of State Information Commission is at Trivandrum.

POWERS AND FUNCTIONS OF INFORMATION COMMISSION

In accordance with the Right to Information Act, the Information Commission has the following powers:

(i) To receive complaint from any aggrieved citizen.

(ii) To issue order of enquiry into the complaint.

(iii) To impose penalties under this Act.

(iv) To reject the applications, if necessary.

(v) To issue order for compensation.

(vi) To issue orders directing the Public Authorities:

   (a) for appointing Public Information Officers;

   (b) for publishing information;

   (c) for enhancing the training facilities for officials;

   (d) for seeking annual report.

(vii) (To direct the Public Information Officer to compensate for any loss caused to the applicant.

The Central Information Commission or State Information Commission, as the case may be, shall (while enquiring into any matter) have the same powers as are vested in a Civil Court while trying a suit under the Code of Civil Procedure, 1908.

Both Central and State Information Commissions are required to send annual reports to the respective governments.

Appeals (Sec. 19)

The aggrieved party has the right to appeal before:

(i) Appellate Authority by way of first appeal.

(ii) Central Information Commission or State Information Commission:

   (a) by way of a complaint, or

   (b) by way of second appeal.

Every Public Authority shall designate an officer above the rank of Central/State Information Officers as an Appellate Authority.

Aggrieved Person

Any person who:

(a) does not receive a decision within the specified time;

(b) has been required to pay further fees which he thinks exorbitant;

(c) is aggrieved by the decision of the Central or State Public Information Officer.

The aggrieved party shall file this appeal within thirty days from the period specified for furnishing information or within thirty days from the receipt of any decision of the Public Information Officer.

However, the Appellate Authority should dispose of the appeal within a maximum period of forty five days.

The person aggrieved by the decision of the Appellate Authority may file a Second Appeal within ninety days from the date of decision of the Appellate Authority to Central or State Information Commission, or

An aggrieved person can file a complaint directly to Central or State Information Commission, as the case may be.

PENALTIES (SEC. 20)

The Central Information Commission or the State Information Commission (as the case may be) may impose penalty on Central Public Information Officer or State Public Information Officer (as the case may be) for any one of the following reasons:

(i) In case the information provided is incomplete or incorrect.

(ii) Application has been refused to receive without any reasonable cause.

(iii) The information has not been furnished within the stipulated period.

(iv) The application for information has been rejected unreasonably.

It shall impose a penalty of Rupees two hundred and fifty for each day till application is received or information is furnished. However, the aggregate amount of such a penalty should not go beyond Rupees twenty-five thousand.

The Central/State Information Commission:

(i) may recommend disciplinary action against the erred officers under service rules applicable to them, or

(ii) may order for compensation for the loss or injuries caused to the applicant for information.

RIGHTS TO ACCESS INFORMATION ON SPECIFIC ISSUES

Banking Transactions

The following procedures are usually adopted for obtaining information on banking transactions as per the Right to Information Act, 2005:

1. Any person who desires to obtain any information on banking transactions under this Act, shall make a request with prescribed fees to the public information officer specifying the particulars of the information sought. However, such a request shall be made in writing or through electronic means in English or Hindi or in the official language of the area in which the application is being made.

2. An applicant making request for information shall not be required to give any reason for the same or any other personal details.

3. Within thirty days of the receipt of a request, the public information officer shall either provide the information on payment of prescribed fee or reject the request for specified reasons.

4. When the information sought for concerns the life or liberty of a person, the same shall be provided within 48 hours of the receipt of the request.

5. If the public information officer fails to give decision on the request for information within the period specified it shall be deemed to have refused the request.

6. No fee shall be charged from the persons who are below the poverty line as per State Government.

7. The person making request for the information shall be provided the information free of cost if the bank fails to comply with the time limit specified above.

8. When a request has been rejected, the public information officer shall communicate the following to the person making the request:

(a) reasons for such rejection,

(b) the period within which an appeal against such rejection may be preferred, and

(c) the particulars of the appellate authority.

9. Any person who does not receive a decision within the time stipulated above, or is aggrieved by the decision, may within 30 days from the expiry of such a period, prefer an appeal to such an officer who is senior in rank.

Exemption from Disclosure

Notwithstanding the above, the bank may not disclose information about the affairs of the customer as it causes unwarranted invasion of privacy of the customer or such information has no relationship with any public activity or interest as envisaged by Section 8(i) of the Act.

Schedule of Fees/Charges

As per the Right to Information (Regulation of Fee and Cost) Rules, 2005, the following schedule of fees/charges has been prescribed.

(a) Application fee—₹ 10.

(b) Charges for each page (A4, A3 size paper)-created or copied —₹ 2 per page.

(c) In case of larger size paper-actual charges incurred.

(d) For information provided in diskettes or floppies — ₹ 50 per diskette or floppy.

(e) For information provided in printed form—at the price fixed for such a publication or ₹ 2 per page of photocopy for extracts from the publication.

(f) For inspection of records—no fee for the first 15 minutes and a fee of ₹ 5 for each 15 minutes or fraction thereof.

(g) The application fee/other charges should be paid by cheques/ DDs drawn on "Concerned Bank A/C-Public Information Officer" and they should be made payable at the centers where the office of the public information officer is located.

INSURANCE TRANSACTIONS

The Insurance Regulatory and Development Authority (IRDA) is a public authority as defined in the Right to Information Act, 2005.

As such, the Insurance Regulatory and Development Authority is obliged to provide information to members of public in accordance with the provisions of this Act.

Access to the Information Held by IRDA

The right to information includes access to the information which is held by or under the control of any public authority and includes the right to inspect the work, document, records, taking notes, extracts or certified copies of documents/records and certified samples of the materials and obtaining information which is also stored in electronic form.

Procedures for Obtaining Information

1. Any citizen of India who desires to obtain any information on insurance transactions under this Act shall make a request in writing, clearly specifying the information sought. The application for request should give the contact details (postal address, telephone number, fax number, e-mail address) so that the applicants can be contacted for clarifications or for further information.

2. A request for obtaining information under Section 6(1) of RIA needs to be accompanied by an application fee of ₹10 by way of cash against proper receipt or by DD or banker's cheque.

3. The fee can also be paid in cash along with the application. Applications can also be made over fax or e-mail. However, IRDA will take up the application for consideration, as required under the Act, only after the application fee has been received.

4. IRDA will, within thirty days of receipt of the application for information along with the fee communicate to the requester whether it can or cannot provide information.

Cost to get Information.   As per the Right to Information (Regulation of Fee and Cost) Rules, 2005, the public authority shall charge:

₹ 2 for each page (in A4 or A3 size paper) created or copied:
- actual charge or cost price of a copy in larger size paper;
- actual cost or price for samples or models; and
- for inspection of records, no fee for the first hour; and a fee of ₹ 5 per each 15 minutes (or fraction thereof thereafter)

Further, to provide information under Section 7(5) of the Right to Information Act, 2005, the public authority shall charge:

- ₹ 50 per diskette or floppy, and
- for information provided in printed form at the price fixed for such publication or ₹ 2 per page of photocopy for extracts from the publication.

If IRDA has the information and can provide it to the applicant, it will, within thirty days of its receiving the applications along with appropriate fees, communicate to him the cost of providing the information as prescribed under Section 7(1) of Rights to Information Act.

The applicant will get the information, once IRDA receives the payment towards providing the information.

Exemptions from Disclosure. The Right to Information Act, 2005 (under Secs. 8 and 9) exempts certain categories of information from disclosures. Such information have been given in the initial part of this chapter.

Right to Appeal. Under the Right to Information Act, 2005, the applicant has the right to appeal if he is not satisfied with the information provided by IRDA or its decisions not to provide the information requested.

If the applicant is not satisfied with the decision of the appellate authority within IRDA, he can appeal to the Central Information Commissioner appointed in terms of Chapter 3 of the Right to Information Act, 2005.

GOVERNMENT DEALINGS AND RELATED SERVICES

The Right to Information Act, 2005 specifies that citizens have the following rights of government dealings and related services:

(a) Request any information (as defined).

(b) Take copies of documents.

(c) Inspect documents, works and records.

(d) Take certified samples of materials of work.

(e) Obtain information in form of printouts, diskettes, floppies, tapes, video cassettes or any other electronic mode or through printouts.

Process. Under the Act, all authorities covered should appoint their Public Information Officer (PIO). Any person may submit a request to the PIO for information in writing. It is the PIO's obligation to provide information to the citizens of India who request information under the Act. If the request pertains to another public authority (in whole or part), it is the PIO's responsibility to transfer/forward the concerned portions of the request to a PIO of the other within 5 days.

In addition, every public authority is required to designate Assistant Public Information Officers (APIOs) to receive RTI requests and appeals for forwarding to the PIOs of their public authority. The citizen making the request is not obliged to disclose any information except his name and contract particulars.

Time limit of replying to the request. The request specifies the time limit for replying to the request.

1. If the request has been made to the PIO, the reply is to be given within 30 days of receipt of the same.

2. If the request has been made to an APIO, the reply is to be given within 35 days of receipt of the same.

3. If the PIO transfers the request to another public authority, the time allowed to reply is 30 days but computed from the day after it is received by the PIO of the transferee authority.

4. Information concerning Corruption and Human Rights Violations by scheduled security agencies (those listed in the second Schedule to the Act) is to be provided within 45 days, but with the prior approval of the Central Information Commission.

5. However, if life or liberty of any person is involved, the PIO is expected to reply within 48 hours.

6. Since the information is to be paid for, the reply of the PIO is necessarily limited to either denying the request in (whole or part) and/or providing a computation of "further fees". The time between the reply of the PIO and the time taken to deposit the further fees for information is excluded from time allowed.

7. If information is not provided within this period, it is treated as deemed refusal. Refusal with or without reasons may be a ground for appeal or complaint.

Further, information not provided in the times prescribed is to be provided free of charge.

Cost to get Information. For Central Departments as of 2006, there is a fee of ₹ 10 for filing the request, ₹ 2 per page of information and ₹ 5 for each hour of inspection after the first hour. If the applicant is a Below Poverty Cardholder, then no fee is applicable. Such BPL cardholders have to provide a copy of their BPL card alongwith their application to the Public Authority.

Exemption from Disclosure. The Rights to Information Act, 2005 (Under Secs. 8 and 9) exempts certain categories of information from disclosures. Such information have been mentioned in the initial part of this chapter.

Constitution of the Authorities and their Obligation. The Chief Information Commissioner (CIC) is the head of all the Information Officers. The State Information Commission will be selected by the State Government through a Gazette notification. It will have one State Chief Information Commissioner (SCIC) and not more than 10 State Information Commissioners (SIC) to be appointed by the Governor.

At the end of the year CIC is required to present a report which contains:

(a) the number of requests made to each public authority;

(b) the number of decisions where applicants were not given permission to access to the documents which they had requested, the provisions of the Act under which these decisions were made and the number of times such provisions were filed;

(c) details of disciplinary action taken against any officer in respect of the administration of the Act;

(d) the amount of charges collected by each public authority under the Act.

PIO shall deal with requests from persons seeking information. If the request cannot be made in writing the PIO shall render reasonable assistance to the person to reduce the same in writing.

REVIEW QUESTIONS

1. What is information?
2. Who is public authority?
3. What do you mean by right to information?
4. Enumerate two competent authorities.
5. Enumerate the organisations on which the Information Act does not apply.
6. Enumerate the officers designated under the Information Act.
7. List the qualification of the State Chief Information Commissioner and the State Information Commissioners.
8. Explain the composition of the Central Information Commission.
9. Explain the objectives of the Right to Information Act, 2005.
10. Who are the Public Authorities under the Right to Information Act, 2005?

11. Explain the powers and functions of Central and State Information Commission under the Right to Information Act.

12. Explain the schedule of fees to get information from Central departments under the Information Act.

13. Explain the information which are exempted from disclosure under the Provisions of the Rights to Information Act, 2005.

14. What is Information Commission? Explain the powers and functions of Information Commission.

15. Explain briefly the right to access information on banking and insurance transactions under the Right to Information Act, 2005.

16. Explain the right to access information on government dealings under the Right to Information Act, 2005.

58

Regulatory Authorities

Insurance is "a means of shifting the risks to insurers
in consideration of a nominal cost called the premium."

INSURANCE REGULATORY AND DEVELOPMENT AUTHORITY (IRDA)

In April 1993, the Government of India appointed a Committee of Reforms in insurance sector with Shri R.N. Malhotra, a former governor of the Reserve Bank of India as its chairman. The committee submitted its report to the Government of India in January 1994. In accordance with the recommendations of the committee, the government set up a regulatory body known as "Insurance Regulatory Development Authority" and enacted the Act known as Insurance Regulatory and Development Act, 1999.

The Act seeks to open up the insurance sector for private companies with a foreign equity of 26 per cent. It is also aimed at ending the monopoly of the Life Insurance Corporation and General Insurance Corporation in the insurance sector of the country.

Objectives of IRDA

The following are the main objectives of the Insurance Regulatory and Development Authority:

  (i) Take care of the policyholders' interest.
 (ii) Open the insurance sector for private sector.
(iii) Ensure continued financial soundness and solvency.
 (iv) Regulate insurance and reinsurance companies.
  (v) Eliminate dishonesty and unhealthy competition.
 (vi) Supervise the activities of intermediaries.
(vii) Amend the Insurance Act, 1938, the Life Insurance Corporation Act, 1956 and the General Business (Nationalisation) Act, 1972.

Features of IRDA

The following are the salient features of IRDA:

(i) It shall have the power to regulate and ensure the orderly growth of the insurance business.

(ii) It shall have to exercise all powers and functions of the controller of insurance.

(iii) It shall have to protect the interest of policyholders in settlement of claims and terms and conditions of policies.

(iv) It shall have to promote and regulate professional organisations connected with insurance business.

(v) It shall have to control and regulate the rates and terms and conditions that may be offered by the insurers in respect of general insurance matters, not so controlled by the Tariff Advisory Committee under Section 64(U) of the Insurance Act.

(vi) It shall have to prescribe the manner and form in which accounts will be maintained and submitted by insurers and intermediaries.

(vii) It shall have to regulate investment of funds.

(viii) It shall have to regulate margins of solvency.

(ix) It shall have to adjudicate disputes between insurers and intermediaries.

Constitution of IRDA (Sec. 4)

Insurance Regulatory and Development Authority consists of:
(i) a Chairman; (ii) not more than five whole-time members; and (iii) not more than four part-time members to be appointed by the Central Government.

The members should be persons of ability, integrity and standing. They should have experience in the fields of: (i) life insurance, (ii) general insurance, (iii) acturial science, (iv) finance, (v) economics, (vi) law, (vii) accountancy, (viii) administration, and (ix) any other discipline, thought to be useful by the Central Government.

The chairperson, members, officers and other employees of the Authority shall be public servants.

Tenure of Office of Chairperson and Other Members (Sec. 5)

(i) The Chairperson and every other whole-time member shall hold office for a term of five years. But they are eligible for re-appointment.

A Chairperson shall not hold office after he has attained the age of 65 years. Similarly, a whole-time member shall not hold office after he has attained the age of 62 years.

(ii) A part-time member shall hold office of a term not exceeding five years from the date of the assumption of the office.

Removal from Office (Sec. 6)

(i) The Central Government may remove from office any member who:

(a) is or at any time has been, adjudged as an insolvent; or

(b) has become physically or mentally incapable of acting as a member; or

(c) has been convicted by any offence which involves moral turpitude; or

(d) has acquired such a financial or other interest as is likely to affect prejudicially his functions as a member; and

(e) has so abused his position as to render his continuation in office detrimental to the public interest.

(ii) No such member shall be removed unless he has been given a reasonable opportunity of being heard in the matter.

Administrative Powers of the Chairperson (Sec. 9)

The chairman shall have the powers of general superintendence and direction in respect of all administrative matters of the Authority.

Meeting of the Authority (Sec. 10)

(i) The authority shall meet at such time and places and observe such rules and procedures in regard to transaction of business at its meeting, as may be determined by the regulations.

(ii) All questions which come up before any meeting of the authority shall be determined by a majority of votes by the members present and voting.

(iii) The authority may make regulations for the transaction of business at its meeting.

Functions of IRDA

The various functions of IRDA are:

(i) To issue certificate of registration, renew, withdraw, suspend or cancel such registrations.

(ii) To protect the interests of the policyholders/insured in the matter of insurance contract with the insurance company.

(iii) To specify requisite qualifications, code of conduct and training for insurance intermediaries and agents.

(iv) To specify code of conduct for Surveyors/Loss Assessors.

(v) To specify the form and manner for maintenance of books of accounts and the statement of accounts.

(vi) To promote efficiency in the conduct of insurance business.

(vii) To promote and regulate professional organisations connected with the insurance and reinsurance business.

(viii) To undertake inspection, conduct enquiries and investigations including audit of insurers and insurance intermediaries.

(ix) To control and regulate the rates, terms and conditions to be offered by the insurer regarding general insurance business not so controlled by Tariff Advisory Committee.

(x) To specify the percentage of Life Insurance business and General Insurance business to be undertaken in the rural or social sector.

(xi) To regulate investment of funds by the insurance companies.

(xii) To adjudicate disputes between insurers and intermediaries of insurance.

(xiii) To supervise the functioning of Tariff Advisory Committee.

FINANCE, ACCOUNTS AND AUDIT

Grants by Central Government (Sec. 15)

The Central Government may (after due appropriation made by the Parliament by law in this behalf) make to the authority grants of such sum of money as it may think fit for being utilised for the purpose of this Act.

Constitution of Fund (Sec. 16)

(i) A fund to be called the Insurance Regulatory and Development Authority Fund shall be constituted and there shall be credited to:

(a) all government grants, fees and charges received by the Authority.

(b) all sums received by the Authority from such other sources as may be determined by the Central Government.

      (c) the percentage of prescribed premium income received from the insurer.

  (ii) The fund shall be applied for meeting:

      (a) salaries, allowances and other remuneration of the members, officers and staff of the Authority.

      (b) other expenses of the Authority for discharging its function.

Accounts and Audit (Sec. 17)

   (i) The authority shall maintain proper accounts. It shall prepare an annual statement of account in such a form in consultation with the Comptroller and Auditor-General of India.

  (ii) The account of the Authority shall be audited by the Comptroller and Auditor General of India at such intervals as may be specified by him.

 (iii) The certified accounts of the authority together with the audit report shall be forwarded annually to the Central Government and the Government shall cause the same to be laid before each House of Parliament.

Power of Central Government to Issue Directions and Make Rules (Secs. 18 and 24)

The Authority shall be bound by such directions on questions of policy (other than those relating to technical and administrative matter) as the Central Government may give in writing to it from time to time.

    The Central Government may, by notification, make rules for carrying out the provisions of this Act.

Furnishing of Returns and Statements to Central Government (Sec. 20)

   (i) The Authority shall furnish to the Central Government such returns, statements and other particulars regarding any proposed and existing programmes. Such programmes should be for the promotion and development of the insurance industry as the Central Government may, from time to time require.

(ii) The authority shall within nine months after the close of each financial year, submit to the Central Government a report providing a true and full account of its activities. The activities for promotion and development of the insurance business during the previous financial year should also be included in such activities.

Establishment of Insurance Advisory Committee (Sec. 25)

(i) The Authority may, by notification, establish a committee to be known as the 'Insurance Advisory Committee.' This committee shall consist of not more than twenty-five members excluding ex-officio members.

(ii) The Chairperson and the Members of the Authority shall be the ex-officio Chairperson and ex-officio Members of the Insurance Advisory Committee.

(iii) The Advisory Committee shall advise the Authority on matters relating to the making of the regulations under Section 26.

Power of the Authority to Make Regulations (Sec. 26)

(i) The Authority may (in consultation with the Insurance Advisory Committee by notification) make regulations to carry out the purposes of this Act.

(ii) All rules and regulations made under this Act shall be laid (as soon as may be after it is made) before each House of Parliament (Sec. 27).

Procedure for Appointment of an Appointed Actuary

In accordance with the provisions of Insurance Regulatory and Development Authority (Regulations, 2000):

(i) An insurer registered to carry on insurance business in India shall appoint an Actuary, who shall be known as the 'Appointed Actuary' for the purpose of this Act.

(ii) A person shall be eligible to be appointed as an Appointed Actuary for an insurer, if he or she shall be:

    (a) ordinarily resident in India;

    (b) a fellow member of the Actuarial Society in India;

    (c) an employee of the life insurer, in the case of life insurance business;

(d) an employee of the insurer or a consulting Actuary, in the case of general insurance business;

(e) not an Appointed Actuary of another insurer;

(f) a person who possesses a Certificate of Practice issued by the Actuarial Society of India; and

(g) not over the age of seventy years.

Powers of Appointed Actuary

The following are the powers of an Appointed Actuary:

(i) The Appointed Authority shall have access to all information or documents in possession or under control.

(ii) The Appointed Actuary may seek any information from any officer or employee of the insurer.

(iii) The Appointed Actuary shall be entitled:

(a) to attend all metings of the management;

(b) to speak and discuss on any matter, at such meeting:

1. that relates to the actuarial advice given to the directors;

2. that may affect the solvency of the insurer;

3. that may affect the ability of the insurer to meet the reasonable expectations of policyholders; or

4. on which actuarial advice is essential.

(c) to attend:

1. any meeting of the shareholders or the policyholders of the insurer; or

2. any other meeting of members of the insurer at which the insurer's annual accounts or financial statements are to be considered.

Duties and Obligations of Actuary

The following are the duties and obligations of an Appointed Actuary:

(i) Rendering actuarial advice to the management of the insurer. Such an advice relates to the areas of product design and pricing, insurance contract wording, investment and reinsurance.

(ii) Ensuring the solvency of the insurer at all times.

(iii) Complying with the provisions of the Act in regard to the maintenance of required solvency margin in the manner required.

(iv) Complying with the provisions of the Act in regard to the certification of the assets and liabilities that have been valued in the manner required.

(v) Complying with the Authority's directions from time to time.

(vi) In the case of insurer carrying on life insurance business.

   (a) to certify the actuarial report and abstract and other returns as required;

   (b) to comply with the provisions of the Act regarding further information required by the Authority;

   (c) to comply with the provisions of the Act regarding the bases of premium;

   (d) to comply with the provisions of the Act regarding recommendation of interim bonus or bonuses payable by life insurer to policyholders whose policies mature for payment by reason of death or otherwise during the inter-valuation period;

   (e) to ensure that all the requisite records have been made available to him or her for conducting actuarial valuation of liabilities and assets of the insurer;

   (f) to ensure that the premium rates of the insurance products are fair;

   (g) to certify that the mathematical reserves have been determined by considering the guidance notes issued by the Actuarial Society of India and any directions given by the Authority;

   (h) to ensure that the policyholders reasonable expectations have been considered for valuation of liabilities and distribution of surplus to the participating policyholders who are entitled for a share of surplus;

   (i) to submit the actuarial advice in the interests of the insurance industry and the policyholder.

(vii) In the case of insurer carrying on general insurance business to ensure that the rates are fair in respect of those contracts which are governed by the insurer's in-house tariff.

(viii) Informing the Authority in writing of his or her opinion, within a reasonable time, whether:

   (a) the insurer has contravened the Act or any other Acts;

(b) the contravention is of such a nature that it may affect significantly the interests of the owners or beneficiaries of policies issued by the insurer;

(c) the directors of the insurer have failed to take such action as is reasonably necessary to enable him to exercise his or her duties and obligations under this regulation; or

(d) an officer or employee of the insurer has engaged (in conduct calculated) to prevent him or her exercising his or her duties and obligations under this regulation.

TELECOM REGULATORY AUTHORITY OF INDIA (TRAI)

The Telecom Regulatory Authority of India Bill was introduced in the parliament to regulate the telecommunication services by a statutory body. It was passed by both the Houses of Parliament and received the assent of the President on 28th March, 1997. It came on the Statute Book as the Telecom Regulatory Authority of India Act, 1997 (24 of 1997). The Act extends to the whole of India and the head office of the Authority shall be at New Delhi.

Objectives of the Act

The following are the objectives of this Act:

(i) Establishing the Telecom Regulatory Authority of India and Telecom Disputes Settlement and Appellate Tribunal to regulate the telecommunication services, adjudicate disputes, and dispose of appeals.

(ii) Protecting the interest of service providers and consumers of the telecom sector.

(iii) Bringing the quality of telecom services to world standard.

(iv) Promoting and ensuring orderly growth of telecom sector.

(v) Making arrangement for protection and promotion of consumer interest.

(vi) Participating the telecom companies registered in India in the area of basic and value-added telecom services.

(vii) Ensuring fair competition.

(viii) Providing wide range of services to meet the customers demand at reasonable price.

Features of TRAI

The following are the salient features of the Telecom Regulatory Authority of India:

(i) It shall have the power to regulate the telecommunication services to the whole of India.

(ii) It shall have an inbuilt dispute settlement mechanism.

(iii) It shall have to adjudicate disputes and dispose of appeals.

(iv) It will have to maintain transparency while exercising its powers and functions.

(v) It shall have to protect the interests of service providers and consumers of the telecom sector.

(vi) It shall have to vest the authority with a statutory status.

(vii) It shall have to function in a truly independent manner and discharge its assigned responsibilities effectively.

(viii) It shall have to promote and ensure orderly growth of the telecom sector.

Constitution of the Authority (Sec. 4)

The authority shall consist of a Chairperson, and not more than two whole-time members and not more than two part-time members. They are appointed by the Central Government from amongst persons who have special knowledge of, and professional experience in telecommunication, industry finance, accountancy, law, management or consumer affairs.

Term of Office (Sec. 5)

The chairperson and other members shall hold office for a term not exceeding three years from the date on which they enter upon their services or until they attain the age of sixty-five years, whichever is earlier.

Powers of Chairperson (Sec. 6)

The Chairperson shall preside over the meeting of the Authority. In addition to this, he shall have the powers of general superintendence and directions in the conduct of the affairs of the Authority. Further, he shall exercise and discharge such powers and functions of the Authority and discharge such other powers and functions as may be prescribed.

Removal and Suspension of Members from Office (Sec. 7)

The Central Government may remove from office any member of the authority, if he:

(i) has been adjudged an insolvent;

(ii) has been convicted of an offence which involves moral turpitude;

(iii) has become physically or mentally incapable of acting as a member.

(iv) has acquired such a financial or other interest as is likely to affect prejudicially his functions as a member.

Meeting of the Authority (Sec. 8)

The Authority shall meet at such times and places. It shall observe such rules of procedure relating to the transaction of business at its meeting.

If the chairperson is unable to attend a meeting of the Authority, the vice-chairperson shall preside at the meeting. In the absence of vice-chairperson, any other member (chosen by the members present from amongst themselves at the meeting) shall preside at the meeting.

All questions which come up before any meeting of the Authority shall be determined by a majority vote of members present and voting. In the case of equality of votes, the chairperson or in his absence, the person presiding shall have a second or casting vote.

Functions of the Authority (Sec. 11)

1. The functions of the authority shall be to:

   (a) make recommendations, either suo motu or on a request from the licensor on the matters relating to the:

      (i) need and timing for introduction of new service providers;

      (ii) terms and conditions of licence to a service provider;

      (iii) revocation of licence for non-compliance of terms and conditions of licence;

      (iv) measures to facilitate competition and promote efficiency in the operation of telecommunication services;

(v) technological improvement in the services provided by the service providers;

(vi) type of equipment to be used by the service providers after inspection of equipment used in the network;

(vii) measures for the development of telecommunication technology;

(viii) efficient management of available spectrum;

(b) discharge the functions in respect of:

(i) ensuring compliance of terms and conditions of licence;

(ii) fixing the terms and conditions of inter-connectivity between the service providers;

(iii) ensuring technical compatibility and effective inter-connection between different service providers;

(iv) regulating arrangement amongst service providers for sharing their revenue derived from providing telecommunication services;

(v) laying down the standards of quality of service to be provided by the service providers;

(vi) laying down and ensuring the time period for providing local and long distance circuits of telecommunication between different service providers;

(vii) maintaining register of interconnect agreements;

(viii) keeping register maintained under clause (vii) open for inspection to any member of public on payment of such fee.

(ix) ensuring effective compliance of universal service obligations.

(c) levy fees and other charges at such rates and in respect of such services as may be determined by regulations.

(d) perform such other functions as may be entrusted to it by the Central Government.

2. The authority may (from time to time, by order) notify in the official Gazette the rates at which the telecommunication services within India and outside India shall be provided.

3. While discharging its functions (under sub-section (1) or sub-section (2)), the authority shall not act against the interest of the sovereignty and integrity of India, friendly relations with foreign states, public order and decency or morality.

4. The authority shall ensure transparency while exercising its powers and discharging its functions.

The authority shall discharge the functions under sub-sections (1) and (2) notwithstanding anything contained in the Indian Telegraph Act, 1885 (13 of 1885).

Powers of the Authority

(i) Where the Central Government seeks recommendations of the Authority for new licences to be issued to a service provider, the Authority shall forward the same within a period of sixty days from the date of such a seeking.

(ii) Where the Authority requests the Central Government to furnish such information or documents for the purposes of making recommendations, the Government shall supply the same within a period of seven days from the receipt of such a request.

(iii) The Central Government may issue a licence to a service provider if no recommendations are received from the Authority within such a period as may be specified mutually agreed upon between the Central Government and the Authority.

The Authority may, from time to time, by order, notify in the Official Gazette the rate at which the telecommunication services within India and outside shall be provided under this Act including the rates at which messages shall be transmitted to any country outside India.

While discharging its functions, the Authority shall not act against the interest of the sovereignty and integrity of India, the security of the State, friendly relations with foreign states, public order, decency or morality.

The Authority shall ensure transparency while exercising its powers and discharging its functions.

Powers of Authority to Call for Information, Conduct Investigations, etc. (Sec. 12)

(i) Where the Authority considers it expedient to do, it may, by order in writing:

(a) call upon the service provider at any time to furnish in writing such information or explanation relating to its affairs as the Authority may require, or

(b) appoint one or more persons to make an enquiry in relation to the affairs of any service provider, and

(c) direct any of its officers to inspect the books of account or other documents of any service provider.

(ii) Where an enquiry in relation to the affairs of any service provider has been undertaken:

(a) every officer of the Government department, if the service provider is a department of the Government;

(b) every director, manager, secretary, if such a service provider is company;

(c) every partner, manager, secretary, if such a service provider is a firm; shall be bound to produce before the Authority making enquiry, all such books of account or other documents, within such time as may be specified.

(iii) Every service provider shall maintain such books of account or other documents as may be prescribed.

(iv) The Authority shall have the power to issue such directions to service providers, as it may consider necessary for proper functioning of service providers.

(v) The Authority may, for the discharge of its functions, issue such directions from time to time to the service providers, as it may consider necessary.

Appellate Tribunal (Sec. 14)

The Central Government shall, by notification, establish an Appellate Tribunal to be known as the Telecom Settlement and Appellate Tribunal to adjudicate any dispute:

(a) between a licensor and a licensee;

(b) between two or more service providers; and

(c) between a service provider and group of consumers.

Application of Settlement of Disputes and Appeal to Appellate Tribunal (Sec. 14A)

(i) The Central Government or a State Government or a Local Authority or any person may make an application to the Appellate Tribunal for adjudication of any dispute.

(ii) The Central Government or a State Government or a Local Authority or any person aggrieved by any direction, decision or order made by the Authority may prefer an appeal to the Appellate Tribunal.

(iii) On receipt of an application or an appeal, the Tribunal may, after giving the parties to the dispute or appeal on opportunity of being heard, pass such orders thereon as it thinks fit; within ninety days from the date of receipt of application or appeal.

(iv) The Appellate Tribunal shall send a copy of every order made by it to the parties to the dispute or appeal and to the Telecom Regulatory Authority.

Constitution of Appellate Tribunal (Sec. 14B)

The Appellate Tribunal shall comprise a Chairperson and not more than two members to be appointed, by notification, by the Central Government. All such persons shall be selected by the Central Government in consultation with the Chief Justice of Supreme Court.

Qualification of Chairperson and Members of the Appellate Tribunal (Sec. 14C)

A person shall not be qualified for appointment as the Chairperson or a Member of the Appellate Tribunal unless:

(i) he (in the case Chairperson) is or has been, a judge of Supreme Court or Chief Justice of a High Court.

(ii) he (in the case of a Member) has held the post of secretary to the Government of India or any equivalent post in the Central or State Government for a period of not less than two years or a person who is well-versed in the field of science and technology, telecommunication, industry, commerce or administration.

Term of Office of the Appellate Tribunal (Sec. 14D)

The Chairperson and every other member of the Appellate Tribunal shall hold office as such for a term not exceeding three years from the date of the assumption of their office. However, no Chairperson or other member shall hold office as such after he has attained:

(i) the age of seventy years (in the case of Chairperson).

(ii) the age of sixty-five years (in the case of any other member).

Transfer of Appeals (Sec. 14N)

All appeals before the High Court immediately before the commencement of the Telecom Regulatory Authority of India (Amendment) Act, 2000, shall stand transferred to the Appellate Tribunal.

Appeal to Supreme Court (Sec. 18)

An appeal shall lie against any order of the Appellate Tribunal to the Supreme Court on one or more of the grounds specified in Section 100 of the Civil Procedure Code.

Penalty for Wilful Failure to Comply with Orders of Appellate Tribunal (Sec. 20)

If any person wilfully fails to comply with the order of the Appellate Tribunal, he shall be punishable with a fine up to Rupee one lakh and in the case of second and subsequent offence with a fine up to Rupees two lakh and in the case of continuing contravention with additional fine up to Rupees two lakh for everyday during which such a default continues.

FINANCE, ACCOUNTS AND AUDIT

Grants by Central Government (Sec. 21)

The Central Government may grant such sums of money to the Authority for paying salaries and other allowances payable to the Chairperson and other members and the administrative expenses.

General Fund (Sec. 22)

(i) A fund to be called the Telecom Regulatory Authority of India General Fund shall be constituted and credited thereto:

    (a) all grants, fees, charges received by the Authority under this Act, and

    (b) all sums received by the Authority from such other sources as may be decided upon by the Central Government.

(ii) The fund shall be applied for meeting:

    (a) salaries and other allowance payable to the Chairperson and other members and administrative expenses.

    (b) expenses on objects and for purposes authorised by the Act.

Accounts and Audit (Sec. 23)

(i) The Authority shall maintain proper accounts and other relevant records and prepare an annual statement in such forms in consultation with the Comptroller and Auditor General of India.

(ii) The accounts of the Authority shall be audited by the Comptroller and Auditor General of India at such intervals as may be specified by him.

(iii) The accounts of the Authority as certified by the Comptroller and Auditor General of India together with the report thereon shall be forwarded annually to the Central Government and the Government shall cause the same to be laid before each House of Parliament.

Furnishing Annual Report to Central Government (Sec. 24)

The Authority shall prepare once in every year an annual report providing a summary of its activities during the previous year. The copies of the same shall be forwarded to the Central Government.

The Central Government shall cause the same to be laid before each House of Parliament.

Power of Central Government to Issue Directions (Sec. 25)

The Central Government may issue to the Authority such directions in the interest of the sovereignty and integrity of India, the security of the State, friendly relations with foreign States, public order, decency or morality.

Exemption from Tax on Wealth and Income (Sec. 32)

The Authority shall not be liable to pay wealth tax, income tax or any other tax in regard to its wealth, income, profits or gains derived.

Cognisance of Offences (Sec. 34)

No court shall take cognisance of any offence punishable under this Act. Further, no court inferior to that of Chief Metropolitan Magistrate or a Chief Judicial Magistrate shall try any offence punishable under this Act.

Power of the Central Government to Make Rules (Sec. 35)

The Central Government may, by notification, make rules for carrying out the purposes of this Act.

Power of the Authority to Make Regulations (Secs. 36 and 37)

The Authority may (by notification) make regulations consistent with this Act and the Rules made thereunder to carry out the purposes of this Act.

All rules and regulations made under this Act shall be laid before each house of parliament.

INSURANCE OMBUDSMAN

The Redressal of Public Grievances Rules, 1988 is in respect of the Ombudsman scheme. Such a scheme is provided to resolve all complaints relating to the claims against insurers.

The Ombudsman may receive and consider complaints relating to: (i) any partial or total repudiation of claim by an insurer, (ii) any dispute in regard to premium paid or payable in terms of the policy. (iii) delay in settlement of claims, and (iv) non-issue of an insurance document to the customers after the receipt of premium.

REVIEW QUESTIONS

1. What is IRDA?
2. How can IRDA be constituted?
3. What is TRAI?
4. Explain the constitution of the TRAI.
5. Mention two objectives of IRDA.
6. Enumerate two objectives of TRAI.
7. What are the administrative powers of the chairperson of the TRAI?
8. Enumerate the qualifications for appointment of chairperson of the TRAI.
9. Mention two features of TRAI.
10. Explain the provision of IRDA relating to the tenure of office of chairperson of the IRDA.
11. Explain the powers of IRDA to make rules and regulations.
12. What are the powers of chairperson of the TRAI?

13. Explain the powers of the Telecom Disputes Settlement and Appellate Tribunal.

14. Explain the qualification of the chairperson of TRAI.

15. What are the objectives of IRDA Act?

16. Explain the provisions of the IRDA Act regarding the constitution of the Insurance Regulatory and Development Authority Fund.

17. What are the qualifications of 'Appointed Actuary' in the insurance business?

18. Explain the provisions of the IRDA Act relating to the establishment of Insurance Advisory Committee.

19. What are the objectives of TRAI Act?

20. What is IRDA? State its functions.

21. Explain the provisions of the TRAI Act regarding the accounts and audit of TRAI.

22. Explain the functions of the TRAI.

23. Explain the provisions of the TRAI Act regarding the powers of the Authority to call for information and conduct investigation.

Index